W9-CJO-322

ENCYCLOPEDIA OF JUVENILE VIOLENCE

Andrew Carnegie Library
Livingstone College
701 W. Monroe St.
Salisbury, NC 28144

Andrew Carnegie Library
Livingstone College
701 W. Monroe St.
Salisbury, NC 28144

ENCYCLOPEDIA OF JUVENILE VIOLENCE

Edited by
LAURA L. FINLEY

GREENWOOD PRESS
Westport, Connecticut • London

Library of Congress Cataloging-in-Publication Data

Encyclopedia of juvenile violence / edited by Laura L. Finley.
  p. cm.
 Includes bibliographical references and index.
 ISBN 0-313-33682-2 (alk. paper)
 1. Juvenile delinquency—United States—Encyclopedias. 2. Violence in children—United
States—Encyclopedias. 3. Juvenile delinquency—Encyclopedias. 4. Violence in
children—Encyclopedias. I. Finley, Laura L.
 HV9104.E59 2007
 364.360973'03—dc22   2006029960

British Library Cataloguing in Publication Data is available.

Copyright © 2007 by Laura. L. Finley

All rights reserved. No portion of this book may be
reproduced, by any process or technique, without the
express written consent of the publisher.

Library of Congress Catalog Card Number: 2006029960
ISBN: 0-313-33682-2

First published in 2007

Greenwood Press, 88 Post Road West, Westport, CT 06881
An imprint of Greenwood Publishing Group, Inc.
www.greenwood.com

Printed in the United States of America

The paper used in this book complies with the
Permanent Paper Standard issued by the National
Information Standards Organization (Z39.48-1984).

10 9 8 7 6 5 4 3 2 1

CONTENTS

PREFACE

Crime and violence have long been topics of public concern. In particular, juvenile violence has drawn the attention of people from all facets of society, including citizens, educators, religious figures, and policymakers at all levels. Without a doubt, media has covered juvenile violence, perhaps ad nauseum. Too often, however, media focuses on juveniles as violent perpetrators, overlooking the ways juveniles are victimized.

The year 2005 marked the fifteenth anniversary of the United Nations Convention on the Rights of the Child. This watershed agreement, with 192 signatory nations, was intended to acknowledge the myriad ways children are victimized. Using a broader definition of violence, it recognizes that young people are victimized through unfair labor practices, by warfare, through social policies that do not meet their basic human needs, and through the application of unfair and even cruel juvenile justice policies. The United States has yet to sign this historic agreement, according to Human Rights Watch, because many policies and practices regularly used with youth would fall far short of the convention's goals. This volume is both important and timely, as it includes entries about juvenile-perpetrated violence, but also utilizes a broader definition of violence to include entries on the many ways juveniles are victims of violence.

While numerous texts examine the topic of juvenile violence, this volume provides readers with a more thorough and up-to-date reference about this critical topic. In addition to simply providing information about the frequency and types of juvenile violence, this text provides readers with historical information, an assessment of relevant theories, examination of issues regarding the media, information on the primary measures of juvenile violence, and background about a vast array of responses to juvenile violence. Further, since juvenile violence is a complex phenomenon, this text provides readers with the most current information about who is most likely to commit different types of violence, including drug, gang, sexual, and school-related offenses. Importantly, this text also includes attention to the victims of these forms of juvenile violence. Juveniles are not simply offenders; they are victims of violence, both from other juveniles as well as from adults. This, too, is covered in this important volume. Although the primary focus of the entries is on the United States, global juvenile violence is addressed in many places.

The entries in the encyclopedia are arranged alphabetically. Each entry provides a general overview of the topic, utilizing the most current and well-respected sources. Entries also include, where appropriate, discussion of controversial issues as well as evaluations of programs or theories. Many entries are cross-referenced so that readers can easily refer to other related entries. Also included in each entry is a list of further readings that will provide readers an important resource for research and education. Front matter sections that complement the encyclopedia include a chronology of key events, an alphabetical list of entries, and a guide to related topics.

Juvenile violence has been studied extensively by academics in fields such as criminal justice, sociology, psychology, education, and history. Because it is of such great concern to so many, a reference book that utilizes scholars from all these fields to describe the most current and important trends and issues in juvenile violence is an invaluable tool. The *Encyclopedia of Juvenile Violence* does this.

Historians have much to offer in regard to a greater understanding of juvenile violence. As this volume documents, approaches to juvenile justice have changed dramatically throughout the history of the United States. In colonial times there was no system of juvenile justice, so juvenile offenders, both violent and nonviolent, were treated with the same heavy hand as were adult offenders of the era. Over time, events in the United States as well as globally, changes in political administrations, and shifting public attitudes led to significant changes in juvenile justice, from policing to the courts and sentencing. This volume addresses those changes, looking at the colonial period, the civil war and reconstruction era, each decade of the twentieth century, and the present decade. Historians also help us to understand violence trends over time, including who is most likely to perpetrate and receive violence, the most common types of violence, and the responses to them.

Psychologists have contributed a great deal to our understanding of juvenile violence, primarily in offering and empirically testing theories to explain *why* adolescents become violent. This book includes a number of psychology-based theories, such as learning and psychodynamic theories. Psychologists can provide insight into the role of the family in juvenile violence, as well as the best ways to treat violent youth offenders and their families. In addition, psychologists have added much to the study of school violence and have also stressed the importance of victims of violence.

Sociologists have also contributed to our theory base regarding juvenile violence, from early theories about social disorganization to the conflict-based theories of the late 1960s and the more recent development of integrated theories, like age-graded theory. Sociology adds a broader view to the study of juvenile violence, emphasizing its social roots and the need for social policies for prevention and intervention. In addition, both psychologists and sociologists have addressed the important distinctions among juveniles who commit violent acts, emphasizing that boys and girls offend differently, at different rates, and are likely the recipient of different amounts and types of violence. Similarly, juvenile violence is different, albeit no less problematic, in urban, rural, and suburban areas. Sociologists have also been critical in adding to the knowledge base about gangs and gang-related violence, as well as addressing the media's role in representing and even perpetuating juvenile violence.

The fields of social work, policing, and education have been helpful in providing an understanding of juvenile violence from a practitioner's perspective. Social workers deal with juvenile offenders in a highly personal way and are thus able to offer predictions about an individual's behavior as well as important treatment ideas. Further, social workers have been important advocates for the rights of juveniles, both those involved in the juvenile justice system as well as the victims. Police officers are often the frontline in dealing with juvenile offenders, and their decisions impact not only the likelihood of an arrest for a specific incident but also overall policy changes in regard to juvenile offenders. Many of our statistics about juvenile violence are derived from police sources, such as the Uniform Crime Reports (UCR). Others contend that, aside from the family, educators have the most potential for influence with youth, as they are charged with the care of most juveniles in the United States during the daytime hours. As such, educators can inform us about all types of school violence, from shootings to systemic violence, as well as the ways educational access and success are tied to juvenile violence and, consequently, how education can be used as a form of treatment.

In sum, this book brings together work from a number of fields to provide readers a thorough examination of many facets of the problem of juvenile violence. While each entry includes the most important and up-to-date information, readers are provided still another great resource in the back matter of the book. References on many of the topics, including easy-to-use websites, are listed at the back of the book. It is my hope that readers will find the *Encyclopedia of Juvenile Violence* a well-written, informative tool in understanding the complex phenomenon of juvenile violence and that this greater understanding will contribute in some capacity to the end of violence by and against juveniles.

ACKNOWLEDGMENTS

Editing a volume, I have learned, is both rewarding and challenging. I have worked with many talented and wonderful people in the process of putting this work together, all of whom I owe tremendous gratitude. Most notably, I thank all the contributors for their efforts. Balancing a teaching schedule, other research, and a family myself, I understand how difficult it was for contributors to meet deadlines and to write quality entries. I believe all the contributors have succeeded in writing useful and engaging information and wish to acknowledge their sacrifices in doing so. In addition, thank you to the members of my advisory board—Shelby, Kristen, and Kristin. I also want to thank former Greenwood Acquisitions Editor Steven Vetrano, who not only allowed me the opportunity to do this work but also guided me through most of the process. I appreciate the helpful yet hands-off approach. Thanks also to Suzanne Staszak-Silva, who was helpful in the later stages of completing this project and got "stuck" with the tedious parts!

On a personal note, I thank my students, both at the University of Northern Colorado, where I was when I started this project, and Florida Atlantic University, where I was when I finished. You always inspire me. Most of all, thanks to my loving husband Peter, who suffered through my long work hours with little complaint. Your support is appreciated and your love needed. And to my daughter Anya—how hard it must be to be two-and-a-half-years old and have your mom want to write all the time! Your beautiful smile (and incessant talking) both helped and distracted!

CHRONOLOGY OF KEY EVENTS

1642	The first recorded state execution of a juvenile in Plymouth Colony, Massachusetts
1648	Massachusetts authorizes the death penalty for any child over sixteen who "shall curse or smite their natural father or mother"
1704	Pope Clement XI built the Hospice at San Michele in Rome, the first prison for youth
1721	English case of *Duke of Beaufort v. Berty* first to determine juveniles should be treated differently than adults
1763	*Rex v. Deleval* established the notion of individualized justice for youth
1817	Foundation of the Society for the Prevention of Pauperism, an early attempt to care for at-risk youth
	First "good time" law, a precursor to parole, established in New York
1825	First House of Refuge in New York City founded
1838	*Ex parte Crouse* affirms *parens patriae* philosophy
1841	First official probation officer begins work in Boston
1847	State institutions for juvenile delinquents open in Boston and New York
1849	First House of Refuge for Colored Delinquents opens in Philadelphia
1852	First compulsory school law in Massachusetts
1853	New York Children's Aid Society formed
1856	Massachusetts opens first reform school for girls
1862	Massachusetts adopts a law allowing for the incarceration of chronic truants at reform schools
1875	Society for the Prevention of Cruelty to Children (SPCC) formed in New York
1887	Formation of the Protective Agency for Women and Children to assist those who had been swindled, abused, or sexually assaulted
1890	Children's Aid Society, a foster home for delinquent youth, opens in Pennsylvania
1899	Illinois Juvenile Court Act establishes first juvenile court
1907	Establishment of the National Council on Crime and Delinquency
1909	First Juvenile Psychopathic Institute in Chicago
1912	Children's Bureau created
1913	First woman assistant judge assigned to hear cases regarding delinquent girls
1920	Child Welfare League of America created
1930	First Uniform Crime Reports (UCR) collected
1950	Publication of Sheldon and Eleanor Glueck's *Unraveling Juvenile Delinquency*
1954	*Brown v. Board of Education* establishes separate schools are inherently unequal

1962   *Gallegos v. Colorado* determines juveniles must receive due process during interrogations

1966   *Kent v. U.S.* mandates that juveniles being waived to adult courts receive full due process hearings

1967   *In re Gault* establishes that juveniles have the right to counsel, notice, and confrontation of witnesses

1968   The National Institute of Justice is born as part of the Omnibus Crime Control and Safe Streets Act

1969   *Tinker v. DesMoines* holds that juveniles have the right to free speech in schools

1971   First National Household Survey on Drug Abuse

        McKeiver v. Pennsylvania holds juveniles have no right to a jury by their peers

1972   Wolfgang, Figlio, and Sellin's *Delinquency in a Birth Cohort* originates the concept of the "chronic 6 percent"

        National Crime Victimization Survey (NCVS) is born

1973   Children's Defense Fund established

        Formation of the Drug Enforcement Agency

1974   Juvenile Justice and Delinquency Prevention Act requires deinstitutionalization of status offenders and housing juveniles apart from adults; also establishes the Office of Juvenile Justice and Delinquency Prevention (OJJDP)

        Child Abuse Prevention and Treatment Act (CAPTA)

1975   *Goss v. Lopez* determines that a student facing school suspension has the right to due process

        First Monitoring the Future survey

1976   First National Youth Survey

1977   Juvenile Justice Amendment Act

        First Court Appointed Special Advocate (CASA) program started in Seattle, Washington

1979   International Year of the Child

1984   *Schall v. Martin* establishes that states may use preventive detention with juveniles

1985   *New Jersey v. T.L.O* determines students have reduced privacy rights in schools

1988   Beginning of Rochester Youth Development study of high-risk youth and their families

        Publication of Sampson and Laub's reanalysis of the Gluecks' data

1989   Supreme Court upholds death penalty for children under sixteen

        Attack on Central Park Jogger draws attention to juvenile "wilding"

        Gang rape of a mentally retarded girl in Glen Ridge, New Jersey

        Start of successful mentoring initiative Quantum Opportunities Program (QOP)

1993   Establishment of the Center for the Prevention of School Violence (CPSV)

        Public attention to the sexual exploits of the Spur Posse

1994   Safe and Drug Free Schools Act (SDFSA) calls for the elimination of violence and drugs from schools

        First year of Operation Ceasefire in Boston, Massachusetts

1996   School shooting in Moses Lake, Washington

1997   School shooting in Pearl, Mississippi

1998   School shootings in Jonesboro, Arkansas and in Edinboro, Pennsylvania

1999   Columbine shooting leaves thirteen plus the two killers dead. One month later, school shooting in Georgia

2000   Sentence of twenty-five years to life for fourteen-year-old Nathaniel Brazil draws national attention

2001   SDFSA reauthorized as part of the No Child Left Behind Act

2005   Supreme Court strikes down death penalty for juveniles

Jeff Weise kills eight people and himself in Red Lake, Minnesota

LIST OF ENTRIES

GUIDE TO RELATED TOPICS

Drugs and Measuring Drug Use

Alcohol
Cocaine and Crack Cocaine
Drug Enforcement Agency (DEA)
Hallucinogens
Heroin
Marijuana
Methamphetamines
Monitoring the Future
National Household Survey on Drug Abuse
Prescription Drugs
Pride Surveys
Stimulants

Gangs and Gang Interventions

Boston Youth Strike Force
Detached Street Workers
Gang Involvement, Theories on
Gang Sweeps
Gang Types
Gang Units, Police
Gang Violence, against Bystanders
Gang-On-Gang Violence
Gangs, Female
GREAT

Gender and Juvenile Violence

Chivalry Hypothesis
Gender, Frequency of Perpetrating
   Violence by
Gender, Frequency of Receiving Violence by
Gender, Types of Juvenile Violence
Received by
Gender, Types of Violence Perpetrated by
Hormonal/Chemical Explanations for Gender
   Differences
Liberation Hypothesis

Power-Control Theory
Victims of Juvenile Violence, Treatment of

Juvenile Justice System

Boot Camps
Child Abuse Prevention and Treatment Act
   (CAPTA)
Child Savers
Children in Need of Services (CHINS)
Children's Aid Society
Community Treatment
Court Appointed Special Advocates (CTSA)
Death Penalty
Differences Between Juvenile Justice
   and Criminal Justice
Home Confinement/Electronic Monitoring
Illinois Juvenile Court
Intensive Aftercare
Intensive Supervised Probation (ISP)
Juvenile Detention Centers
Juvenile Justice and Delinquency Prevention
   Act, 1974 (JJDPA)
Juvenile Justice Reform Act, 1977
Juveniles in Adult Prisons
New York Houses of Refuge
Parens Patriae
Policing Juveniles
Probation
Waivers to Adult Court

Policies and Organizations

Children's Defense Fund
Curfews
National Center for Juvenile Justice
National Council on Crime and Delinquency
National Institute of Justice (NIJ)
Office of Juvenile Justice and Delinquency
   Prevention (OJJDP)

Situational Crime Prevention
United States Department of Justice (USDOJ)
Youthful Offender System (YOS)
Zero Tolerance Laws

Social Class and Juvenile Violence

Educational Opportunity and Juvenile
   Violence
Family Relations and Juvenile Violence
Homelessness and Youth Violence
Rural Juvenile Violence
Suburban Juvenile Violence
Urban Juvenile Violence

Time Periods

Juvenile Violence, 1600–1800 (Colonial Era)
Juvenile Violence, 1861–1865 (Civil War Era)
Juvenile Violence, 1865–1899 (Reconstruction
   and Late 1800s)
Juvenile Violence, 1900–1910
Juvenile Violence, 1910–1919
Juvenile Violence, 1920–1929
Juvenile Violence, 1930–1939
Juvenile Violence, 1940–1949
Juvenile Violence, 1950–1959
Juvenile Violence, 1960–1969
Juvenile Violence, 1970–1979
Juvenile Violence, 1980–1989
Juvenile Violence, 1990–1999
Juvenile Violence, 2000 to date

Measuring Juvenile Violence

Centers for Disease Control (CDC)
Chicago Area Project
Delinquency in a Birth Cohort
Glueck, Sheldon and Eleanor
National Crime Victimization Survey (NCVS)
National Youth Survey
Oregon Social Learning Center (OSLC)
Rochester Youth Development Study
Sampson and Laub's Analysis of Gluecks' Data
Uniform Crime Reports (UCR)

Minorities and Juvenile Violence

African Americans and Juvenile Violence
Asians and Juvenile Violence

Hispanics and Juvenile Violence
Native Americans and Juvenile Violence

Other Interventions

Diversion
Mentoring
Operation Ceasefire
Public Health Approach
Quantum Opportunities Program (QOP)
Restitution
Restorative Justice
Specialized Courts
Teen Courts
Youth Violence Strike Force

School Violence and Interventions

ADD/ADHD
Carneal, Michael
Center for the Prevention of School Violence
   (CPSV)
Conflict Resolution
Corporal Punishment
Golden, Andrew (and Mitchell Johnson)
Harris, Eric (and Dylan Klebold)
Hazing
In Loco Parentis
Kinkel, Kip
Loukaitis, Barry
National School Safety Center (NSSC)
Peaceable Schools
Rolland, Kayla, Shooting of
Safe and Drug Free Schools Act
School Crime Victimization Survey
School Police Officers
Solomon, T. J.
Surveillance in Schools
Systemic Violence in Schools
Weise, Jeff
Williams, Andy
Woodham, Luke
Wurst, Andy

Significant Cases

Brazil, Nathaniel
Central Park Jogger Case
Glen Ridge, New Jersey (1989)
Spur Posse

ABUSED/BATTERED CHILDREN

Types of Child Abuse

Child abuse takes in a host of actions that are harmful to children. Abuse or neglect can be defined as injury, sexual abuse, sexual exploitation, negligent treatment, or maltreatment of a child by any person under circumstances that indicate that the child's or adult's health, welfare, or safety is harmed. The degree of physical injury necessary for abuse is somewhat ambiguous, given the right of parents to utilize **corporal punishment**. What differentiates child abuse from appropriate parental discipline varies. Usually corporal punishment is limited in some manner, such as spanking that results in transient pain, but does not leave red marks or bruising. For abuse, injury must transcend common conceptions of appropriate parental discipline.

There are many definitions of child sexual abuse, but the central issue focuses on the use of the dominant position of the adult to force or coerce a child into sexual activity. Sexual abuse does not necessarily have to involve actual contact. It may involve sexual forms of exploitation. Sexual exploitation includes allowing, permitting, or encouraging a child to engage in prostitution by any person; or allowing, permitting, encouraging, or engaging in the obscene or pornographic photographing, filming, or depicting of a child by any person.

Negligent treatment can mean any act or omission that evidences a serious disregard of consequences of such magnitude as to constitute a clear and present danger to the child's health, welfare, or safety. Examples of negligent treatment would include failure to provide adequate nutrition, clothes, educational support, and medical care.

While the above definitions seem to focus upon the physical aspects of child abuse, there is also emotional abuse. Emotional abuse may include actions or omissions that cause or could cause serious behavioral, cognitive, emotional, or mental disorders. Examples of emotional abuse range from bizarre punishments, such as being locked up in a dark closet, to being used as a scapegoat or belittling name-calling.

Measuring Child Abuse

Accurate statistics on the prevalence of child and adolescent abuse are difficult to collect because of problems of underreporting and a lack of recognition of abuse. There is a general agreement among mental health and child protection professionals that child abuse is not uncommon and is a serious problem in the United States. The best national data on child abuse is collected by the National Child Abuse and Neglect Data System and began with federal legislation in 1974. The last report covered years 1986 to 1993. It concluded that a child's risk of experiencing harm-causing abuse or neglect was one and one-half times the child's risk in 1986. Physical abuse nearly doubled, sexual abuse more than doubled, and emotional abuse, physical neglect, and emotional neglect were all more than two and one-half times their 1986 levels. The total number of children seriously injured and the total number endangered both quadrupled during this time.

Risk Factors

Specific risk factors have been identified. Girls are sexually abused at a rate three times that of boys. However, boys have a greater risk of emotional neglect and of serious injury. Children of single parents are at greater risk of being harmed by physical abuse or physical neglect and at greater risk of suffering serious injury or harm from abuse. Children from large families have a greater risk of being physically neglected. Children from the poorest families were more likely to be sexually abused, educationally neglected, and more likely to be seriously injured from maltreatment.

A national study in 2002 estimated that there were 1,400 child fatalities resulting from abuse and neglect. This came to a rate of 1.98 children per 100,000 children in the general population. Very young children (ages 3 and younger) are the most vulnerable and most frequent victims of child abuse fatalities because they are dependent, of small size, and unable to defend themselves. The perpetrators of fatal abuse or neglect are usually the individuals responsible for the care and supervision of their victims. Males (in particular, fathers) cause most fatalities from physical abuse, and mothers are most often held responsible for deaths resulting from child neglect.

In 2003, child protective services agencies (CPS) found 45.9 per 1,000 children in the national population were abused or neglected. An estimated 906,000 children were found to be victims. Most of the victims experienced neglect, followed by physically abused, followed by sexual abuse. Girls were victimized more often than boys, and the youngest children had the highest rate of victimization. Pacific Islander children, American Indian or Alaska Native children, and African-American children had the highest rates of victimization. Children with a disability tended to be abused more often as well.

Impact of Child Abuse

In addition to the immediate deleterious effects of abuse, the long-term impact of abuse and neglect is significant. The long-term impact includes educational performance problems, substance dependence, and mental health risks, such as depression, suicidal behavior, promiscuity, anger/aggression, social isolation and anxiety, and post-traumatic stress disorder. Some of these issues follow victims into adulthood and adversely impact relationships such as marriage.

Historical Trends

The notion of child abuse is relatively new. Prior to the late 1800s, children were seen as the property of their parents. Child rearing was a private matter. Bolstered by religious teachings in the Old Testament, parents were free to severely whip their children. In 1875, the only applicable laws for prevention of abuse pertained to cruelty to animals. In 1976, the medical community began to recognize "battered child syndrome." Today, child abuse is recognized as a problem. A variety of approaches have been developed to detect and to protect children from child abuse. Many states now mandate that certain classes of adults must report suspected child abuse and neglect to the police or child protective services. Further, some states allow child protection services workers to interview children without notice to parents and to place them in foster care situations for protection. The rights of parents that abuse their children can be terminated. Lastly, shelters have been developed to house and maintain runaway youth from abusive homes.

See also Corporal Punishment

FURTHER READING

Boos, S. (2003). Abuse detection and screening as it appears in child abuse and neglect: Guidelines for identification, assessment, and case management. In M. Strachan-Peterson & M. Durfee (Eds.), *Child abuse and neglect: Guidelines for identification, assessment and case management* (pp. 7–14). Volcano, CA: Volcano Press.

Child maltreatment. (2003). U.S. Department of Health and Human Services. Available at: http://www.acf.hhs.gov/programs/cb/pubs/cm03/chapterthree.htm#types.

Connell-Carrick, K., & Scannapieco, M. (2006). Ecological correlates of neglect in infants and toddlers. *Journal of Interpersonal Violence, 21*(3), 299.

Cooke, P., & Standen, P. (2002). Abuse and disabled children: Hidden needs . . . ? *Child Abuse Review, 11*(1), 1–18.

Crosson-Tower, C. (2004). *Understanding child abuse and neglect*, 6th ed. Boston, MA: Allyn and Bacon.

Elliot, G., Cunningham, S., Linder, M., Cloangelo, M., & Gross, M. (2005). Child physical abuse and self-perceived social isolation among adolescents. *Journal of Interpersonal Violence, 20*(12), 1663.

Feerick, M., & Snow, K. (2005). The relationships between childhood sexual abuse, social anxiety, and symptoms of posttraumatic stress disorder in women. *Journal of Family Violence, 20*(6), 409.

Haskett, M., Marziano, B., & Dover, E. (1996). Absence of males in maltreatment research: A survey of recent literature. *Child Abuse and Neglect, 20*(12), 1175–1182.

Illinois Dept. of Children and Family Services. (2003). A manual for mandated reporters. Available at: http://www.state.il.us/DCFS/docs/MANDATED2002.pdf.

Liang, B., Williams, L., & Siegel, J. (2006). Relational outcomes of childhood sexual trauma in female survivors: A longitudinal study. *Journal of Interpersonal Violence, 21*(1), 42.

Mignon, S., Larson, C., & Holmes, W. (2002). Family abuse: Consequences, theories, and responses. Boston: Allyn and Bacon.

Sedlak, A., & Broadhurst, D. (1996). Executive summary of the Third National Incidence Study of Child Abuse and Neglect. *U.S. Department of Health and Human Services Administration for Children and Families. National Center on Child Abuse and Neglect.* Available from: http://nccanch.acf.hhs.gov/pubs/statsinfo/nis3.cfm.

Statistics and Interventions. (2004). *National Clearinghouse on Child Abuse and Neglect Information 2004.* Available at: http://nccanch.acf.hhs.gov/pubs/factsheets/fatality.cfm.

Turner, H., Finkelhor, D., & Ormrod, R. (2006). The effect of lifetime victimization on the mental health of children and adolescents. *Social Science & Medicine, 62*(1), 13.

William Gladden Foundation. (1989). *About child sexual abuse.* York, PA: William Gladden Foundation.

Mike Olivero

ADD/ADHD.   Today, ADHD is one of the most frequently occurring diagnoses in child and adolescent psychiatry. The typical symptoms of ADHD are attention difficulties, short attention span, motor hyperactivity, restless behavior, impulsivity, temper outbursts, and being distractible in different degrees. The above-mentioned symptoms start early in childhood and often interfere with social integration within the child's family as well as in the extra-family context. This includes social integration in nursery schools, elementary and secondary schools, and, consequently, with adequate social integration and education in general. In some cases, children and adolescents are truant from school for a number of reasons related to their ADHD. They act aggressively both physically and/or verbally; their reactions are unpredictable and out of context; they frequently exhibit violent behavior; and they show little or no response to educational methods or to punishment. These children are often expelled from school(s). Children and adolescents with ADHD/ADD often demonstrate hostile attributional biases, meaning they have a tendency to interpret ambiguous social cues as having hostile intent. This often leads to problems in their social environment.

It is important to mention that children and adolescents diagnosed with these disorders often have certain characteristic risk factors in their family system, including a broken family background, early exposure to parental violence, family discord, physical abuse by their parents, callousness, high levels of stress from living in a violent home, frequent family change, low parental support, parental psychopathology and criminality, insecurity or avoidant attachment, inconsistent and arbitrary educational methods, lack of education of their parents, and emotionally overstrained single parents. It should be mentioned that some research studies show certain evidence for genetic influence on the development of ADHD/ADD.

Educationally, individuals with ADHD/ADD are less likely to reach the level of achievement that is expected on the basis of their intellectual abilities. This increases the risk for them to be sent to special schools for the disabled or special schools for children with conduct disorders, which often limits their chances to find an apprenticeship or vocational training. It also increases the risk of unemployment and frequent job changes so that an occupation, which is important for the social status and social integration of a person, becomes a factor of instability.

Children with ADHD often have other disorders and social and emotional disturbances. Characteristic comorbid disturbances/disorders are conduct disorders, learning disabilities, tics or Tourette's syndrome, anxiety disorders, affective disorders, alcoholism, substance abuse, incapacity to love, and personality disorders like impulsive personality disorder (IPD) and antisocial personality disorder (APD). Children and adolescents with ADHD/ADD, in connection with the comorbid disturbances/disorders, are at high risk of becoming criminal offenders. It is difficult to clearly differentiate between the risk factors that have their origin in ADHD/ADD and the risk factors that originate in the widespread comorbid disorders. Higher rates of serious motor vehicle accidents have also been linked to ADHD. Characteristic crimes for comorbid disorders, like alcoholism and substance abuse, are drug-related robbery and theft. Violent crimes are also related to personality disorders, such as impulsive personality disorder.

FURTHER READING

Barkley, R., & Murphy, L. (1998). *Attention-deficit hyperactivity disorder. A clinical workbook.* New York: Guilford.

Biederman, J., Parone, S., Spencer, T., Willens, T., Norman, D., Lapey, K., Mick, E., Lehman, B., & Doyle, A. (1993). Pattern of comorbidity, cognition, and psychosocial functioning in adults with attention deficit hyperactivity disorder. *American Journal of Psychiatry, 150,* 1792–1798.

Jensen, P., Martin, D., & Cantwell, D. (1997). Comorbidity and ADHD: Implications for research, practise, and DSM-V. *Journal of the American Academy of Child and Adolescence Psychiatry, 36,* 1065–1079.

Mannuzza, S., Klein, R., Bessler, A., Malloy, P., & LaPadula, M. (1993). Adult outcome of hyperactive boys: Educational achievement, occupational rank, and psychiatric status. *General Psychiatry, 50,* 565–576.

Piatigorsky, A., & Hinshaw, S. (2004). Psychopathic traits in boys with and without attention-deficit/ hyperactivity disorder: Concurrent and longitudinal correlates. *Journal of Abnormal Child Psychology, 32* (5), 535–550.

Plizska, S. 1(998). Comorbidity of attention-deficit/hyperactivity disorder with psychiatric disorder: An overview. *Journal of Clinical Psychiatry, 59* (supplement 7), 50–58.

Rösler, M., Retz, W., Retz-Junginger, P., Hengesch, G., Schneider, M., Supprian, T., Schwitzgiebel, T., Pinhard, K., Dovi-Akune, N., Wender, P., & Thome, J. (2004). Prevalence of attention deficit/ hyperactivity disorder (ADHD) comorbid disorder in young male prison inmates. *European Archives of Psychiatry and Clinical Neuroscience, 254,* 365–371.

Sprengelmeyer, P. (1997). *Individual, family, and peer characteristics of juvenile offenders exposed to interparental violence.* Dissertation presented at the University of Missouri-Columbia, UMI Dissertation Services, Ann Arbor, Michigan.

Wender, P. (1995). *Attention-deficit hyperactivity disorder in adults.* New York: Oxford.

Woodward, L., Pergusson, D., & Horwood, J. (2000). Driving outcomes of young people with attentional difficulties in adolescence. *Journal of the American Academy of Child and Adolescent Psychiatry, 39,* 627–634.

Ruth Erken

AFRICAN AMERICANS AND JUVENILE VIOLENCE.

Juvenile violence has been prevalent in poor, African-American communities since the early- to mid-twentieth century, especially in urban ghettos, yet much of the scholarly attention during this period focused on understanding delinquent behavior among white ethnic, immigrant youth. African-American cultural and literary critics, such as Gordon Parks, Claude Brown, and James Baldwin, generally examined juvenile violence and related activities in African-American communities, as well as their underlying causes.

Violence became a principal concern among African-American activists and civil rights leaders in the 1980s, after the sharp increase in youth-related crimes. Interestingly, violent offenses, such as sexual assaults, robbery, and non-firearm assaults, and nonviolent offenses associated with drug use and distribution have been similar among whites and African-American youth. Yet what stood out in poor, African-American communities was the disturbing increase in gun-related offenses during this decade.

The number of firearm deaths among African-American youth between the ages of 15 and 19 increased from about 700 in 1985 to over 2200 in 1993 (an increase of 214 percent). Among African-American youth and young adults between the ages of 15 and 24, homicide resulting from gun violence was the leading cause of death. The increase of gun violence had a disproportionate impact on African-American males living in urban ghettos, and much of this violence was intra-racial or what is known as "black-on-black" crime. Between 1980 and 1997, African Americans consisted of 15 percent of the juvenile population, but homicide rates were five to seven times greater among African-American youth compared to their white counterparts. These crimes tended to invite more punitive responses, and lawmakers have used them to legitimate the passage of laws transferring juveniles to adult prisons.

There are numerous explanations for the rise in serious violent crimes among African-American youth: the elimination of safety net programs in poor communities; the intensification of poverty among African-American children and families; the loss of manufacturing jobs in urban centers that left working-class youth and young adults isolated from stable employment industries; and the breakdown of the black family and the growth of single-parent (primarily female-led) homes. Most social scientists and community activists also attributed the escalation of violence to the over-participation of poor, African-American youth in the drug culture. More specifically, the mushrooming of the **crack cocaine** trade ignited competition between rival drug **gangs**, comprised primarily of unemployed and underemployed African-American youth.

Juvenile violence points to larger, unresolved problems concerning African-American youth who grew up after the end of the civil rights movement. An important concern for civil rights groups is whether they can develop effective programs that can reduce juvenile violence. A host of community organizations, health care professionals, social service providers, civil rights and faith-based groups have developed antiviolence prevention strategies and programs to curtail this trend. For example, in the mid-1990s, the Children's Defense Fund's Black Student Leadership Network (BSLN) and the NAACP Youth Council developed national days of action promoting antiviolence initiatives.

Another concern is the substantial number of African-American youth incarcerated in secure detention facilities. African-American youth, despite their minority status, make up the largest percentage of youth confined in **detention centers**. Many policymakers attribute this to the involvement of African-American youth in gun and drug-related offenses. Youth advocates, on the other hand, contend that disproportionate sentencing between African-American and white youth is related to systemic racism in the juvenile justice system. The Youth Law Center's Building Blocks for Youth Initiative found that African-American youth who commit violent crimes are incarcerated for longer sentences than white youth who commit similar crimes.

Civil rights groups and youth organizations have raised additional concerns that the **media's** portrayal of African-American youth promotes stereotypes regarding their involvement in violent crimes. They claim the media unfairly depicts African American youth as prone to crime, violence, and lawless behavior. In recent years, several youth groups have shed light on the unequal treatment of African-American youth by the mainstream media. We Interrupt This Message, a prominent media advocacy group, organized several media studies to examine the coverage by news' organizations of African-American (and Latino) youth. Two of these studies, cosponsored by the Youth Force of the South Bronx and the Youth Media Council in the San Francisco Bay Area, evaluated the media coverage of African-American and Latino youth by *The New York Times* and KTVU Channel 2 in the Bay Area. They found biases in the coverage of these youth, which tended to focus on their involvement in criminal activities with little mention of their participation in politics, civic life, education, sports, and recreation.

Unfortunately, juvenile violence will remain a persistent problem in the African-American community unless activists and policymakers develop and lobby for effective prevention and antipoverty programs. Civil rights groups must also create public education campaigns that are able to combat the racialization of juvenile violence and the negative stereotypes of African-American youth in the media.

FURTHER READING

Hoyt, E., et al. (2002). *Pathways to juvenile detention reform: Reducing racial disparities in juvenile detention*. Baltimore, MD: Annie E. Casey Foundation.

McFate, K. (1991). Urban violence: Drugs, gangs, and juveniles. Mimeographed.

Mendel, R. (2000). *Less hype, more help: Reducing juvenile crime, what works—and what doesn't*. Washington, DC: American Youth Policy Forum.

Poe, E., & Jones, M. (2000). *And justice for some: Differential treatment of minority youth in the justice system*. Washington, DC: Youth Law Center's Building Blocks for Youth Initiative.

Snyder, H. (2003). Juvenile Arrests 2001. *Juvenile Justice Bulletin*. Washington, DC: Office of Juvenile Justice and Delinquency Prevention.

We Interrupt This Message. (2001). *Soundbites and cellblocks: An analysis of the juvenile justice media debate & a case study of California's Proposition 21*. San Francisco: We Interrupt This Message.

Youth Force. (2000). *In between the lines: How the New York Times frames youth*. New York: We Interrupt This Message.

Youth Media Council. (2001). *Speaking for ourselves: A youth assessment of local news coverage*. San Francisco: We Interrupt This Message.

Sekou Franklin

AGING OUT. Aging out is a term criminologists use to refer to people's tendency to decrease criminal activity as they age. All crime statistics, including official and self-report surveys, indicate that juveniles are arrested at a rate that is disproportionately higher than their representation in the population, and this disproportion has remained stable over time. The groups with the highest crime rates tend to fall into the 15 to 18 age range, but this can differ slightly depending on the crime type. Moreover, these figures can differ across race, gender, socioeconomic status, and other demographic factors. Regardless, the overall peak age for most property crimes is 16, while it is roughly 18 years of age for violent crimes.

There are a number of potential explanations for the aging out phenomenon, mostly theoretical in nature. One group of explanations centers on the powerlessness of juveniles in society and their natural tendency to rebel and to seek money and other resources typically unobtainable for them. Another group of explanations falls under a deterrence perspective, contending that juvenile punishments, or at least juveniles' perceptions of punishments, are low. Indeed, research has indicated that juveniles have lower expectations of punishment than do college students.

FURTHER READING

Sampson, R. (2003). Life-course desisters? Trajectories of crime among delinquent boys followed to age 70. *Criminology 41*: 555–592.

Brion Sever

ALCOHOL. The type of alcohol normally ingested for its psychoactive properties (known as ethanol, ethyl alcohol, or grain alcohol) comes in a variety of forms, such as beer, whiskey, wine, and vodka. Alcohol can be produced from several natural foods, such as grain, fruit, and honey, and is believed to be the single oldest substance synthesized by humans, with beer having been brewed in Egypt as early as 3700 B.C. Alcohol is a depressant that affects the chemistry of the brain, releasing dopamine and serotonin. Consequently, the user experiences a variety of sensations, inclusive of a general sense of well-being, a reduction of behavioral inhibitions, a slowing of the spinal cord reflexes, and (when an excessive quantity is consumed) dizziness, drowsiness, nausea, and memory loss.

Owing to the addictive properties of alcohol, alcoholism is considered to be a disease. The experience of alcoholism has been described as a transformation and division of the self, wherein the alcoholic suffers from a psychological conflict between the parts of the psyche that recognize the detrimental impact that alcohol has on the individual's life and the parts of the psyche that crave the effects of alcohol. In addition, the regular consumption of alcohol has been proven to damage vital organs (e.g., heart, liver) and to increase the likelihood of several diseases (e.g., cardiovascular disease, cancer).

In contrast to many psychoactive drugs (e.g., **cocaine**, **heroin**, **marijuana**), alcohol can be legally produced and consumed in many nations. Owing to its widespread availability, alcohol arguably poses a greater threat to the world population than any other psychoactive substance. Research conducted in the United States, for instance, shows that alcohol is the most commonly used drug among young people age 12 to 20 and is the leading contributor to violent deaths (homicide, suicide, and motor vehicle crashes) among youths. Moreover, research indicates that the brain continues to develop until a person is in his/her early twenties and that heavy drinking during adolescence and young adulthood can negatively impact intellectual development and increase the likelihood of alcohol dependency. Concisely stated, alcohol poses a serious risk to the physical, psychological, and social well-being of the world's juvenile (and adult) population.

FURTHER READING

Brown, Sandra A., Tapert, Susan F., Granholm, Eric., & Delis, Dean C. (2000). Neurocognitive functioning of adolescents: Effects of protracted alcohol use. *Alcoholism: Clinical and Experimental Research 24*, 164–171.

Denzin, N. (1993). *The alcoholic society: Addiction and the recovery of the self.* New Brunswick, NJ: Transaction Publishers.

Liska, K. (1997). *Drugs and the human body with implications for society*, 5th ed. Upper Saddle River, NJ: Prentice Hall.

Substance Abuse and Mental Health Services Administration. (2003). *Results from the 2002 national survey on drug use and health: National findings.* Rockville, MD: Department of Health and Human Services, Office of Applied Studies, Substance Abuse and Mental Health Services Administration.

Ben Brown

ANOMIE/STRAIN THEORY. Beginning with Emile Durkheim's contributions, anomie or strain theories have provided a framework for examining crime and delinquency for more than one hundred years. Durkheim wrote during the late 1800s and early 1900s and is most famous for coining the term anomie. He is also credited with being the first French sociologist.

Durkheim's work focused on the relationship between individuals and society. He was the first theorist to view society's institutions as structures that use boundaries, or laws, to maintain equilibrium. Durkheim contended that if this equilibrium was disturbed, institutions and society would be thrown into a state of lawlessness, or anomie. He therefore saw laws as society's glue, because they defined sanctioned conduct, reflected the society's common consciousness, and prescribed punishment.

Durkheim also recognized that anomie could occur at the individual level. In his study of suicide, Durkheim proposed that the loss of cohesion in modern society and the absence of suitable moral norms by which to orient oneself can result in confusion and vulnerability, which ultimately may lead to deviant behavior, crime, and higher rates of suicide. Thus, individual anomie is also caused by social structures. It is this idea that was used as the foundation for modern strain theory.

Modern Strain Theory

The first modern theorist to develop Durkheim's ideas was Robert Merton. Merton's theory has probably played the most important role in the development of modern-day juvenile delinquency theory and subsequent legal interventions. Referred to as anomie theory or classical strain theory, it purports to explain some forms of crime, deviance, and drug use.

Like Durkheim, Merton sees social disorder as the cause of strain. However, the two theorists disagree on the causes of social disorder—Durkheim blames social disorder on sudden social change, while Merton cites social competition or the need to "keep up with the Joneses'."

Merton contended that everyone in society was socialized to accept the American dream as their life goal. The American dream is a commonly recognized group of goals based on material success, such as owning a big house, early retirement, and so on. Not everyone in society has the means or the opportunities to achieve the American dream, however. According to Merton, anomie, or strain, was experienced by individuals who felt a disjuncture between the goals of society and the means to achieve them.

In response to strain, Merton proposed that people could adopt any of five modes of behavior: conformity, innovation, ritualism, retreatism, or rebellion. Conformity, the most common response, occurs when an individual accepts both the means and the ends prescribed by society. Innovation is the second form of adaptation and the most frequently adopted nonconformist mode of adaptation. Innovators do not accept that prescribed goals are limited to those with access to appropriate means, so they try to invent new and illegitimate ways to achieve goals. Examples of innovators include youth gangs that participate in economic deviance, organized crime families, rackets, and drug dealers.

The third form of adaptation to strain is ritualism, where people give up the unrealistic struggle to get ahead and concentrate on retaining what has been achieved by zealously sticking to norms and rules. In essence, they water down cultural ends and means. Retreatism is the fourth mode of adaptation and occurs when people abandon both the prescribed goals and the legitimate ways to achieve them. Retreaters are society's dropouts and no-hopers, such as alcoholics, drug addicts, and vagrants.

The fifth and final mode of adaptation is rebellion. In this mode, both the means and the ends prescribed by society are rejected and replaced by new goals and means. This mode is usually collective rather than individual and can be deviant as well as criminal. Religious cult groups, Green Peace, militia groups, and Neo-Nazis are modern-day examples of rebellious groups.

Other strain theorists proposed different causes of strain than Merton's. In his book *Delinquent Boys* (1955), Albert Cohen suggested that the inability to gain status and acceptance in society produced strain. Cohen wrote that status deprivation or status frustration was especially acute among lower-class males, because unlike members of the middle and upper classes, they were often not in positions that allowed them to gain status and acceptance from peers and adults. Further, they did not have the means to conform to middle-class standards, even in such everyday things as dress and appearance. As a result, lower-class males suffered from feelings of failure, diminished self-worth, and status frustration. Cohen maintained that delinquent subcultures were born out of a reaction formation to this strain.

Richard Cloward and Lloyd Ohlin further developed strain theory by proposing that when people experience strain, they react depending on the types of opportunities they are presented. They called their theory **Differential Opportunity**. They argue that individuals will pursue legitimate or illegitimate opportunities contingent on which are more readily available. Further, individuals who experience the same types of strain and have the same opportunities may band together to form subcultures.

Cloward and Ohlin identified types of delinquent subcultures that strained youth may form. First is a criminal subculture that is found primarily in lower-class neighborhoods and is organized around stable adult criminal patterns. The second subculture is conflict groups, typified by fighting gangs found in lower-class, socially disorganized neighborhoods with fitful illegal opportunities and fewer legal opportunities. Status is achieved in these subcultures by acts of aggression and violence. The third type of subculture is retreatist and is focused primarily on the consumption of drugs and alcohol. Members of such gangs have given up on all types of goals and means and are failures in both legitimate and illegitimate worlds.

As a result of Cloward and Ohlin's research, the Mobilization for Youth program was established in several New York communities during the 1960s. The program provided youth with education, job training, and conventional role models. Variations are still used today, such as Big Brother and Big Sister programs.

See also Gang Involvement, Theories on; General Strain Theory (GST); Mentoring

FURTHER READING

Cloward, R., & Ohlin, L. (1960). *Delinquency and opportunity*. New York: Free Press.

Cohen, A. (1955). *Delinquent boys*. New York: Free Press.

Durkheim, E. (1951). *Suicide*. (J. A. Spaulding & G. Simpson, Trans.). New York: Free Press. (Original work published 1897).

———. (1984). *The division of labour in society*. (W. D. Halls, Trans.). New York: Free Press. (Original work published 1893).

Merton, R. (1938). Social structure and anomie. *American Sociological Review, 3,* 672–682.

———. (1957). *Social theory and social structure*. Glencoe, IL: Free Press.

Ritzer, G., & Goodman, D. (2004). *Modern sociological theory,* 6th ed. New York: McGraw-Hill.

Monica L. P. Robbers

AROUSAL THEORY. Arousal theory is an attempt to link the propensity for violent behavior to biologically based preferences for arousal. Arousal is a psychological and physiological state involving the autonomic nervous system (involuntary functions), somatic nervous system (voluntary functions), and the endocrine system (involuntary release of hormones). Normally, the body tends to maintain an internal state, a process known as homeostasis. Similar to the operation of a thermostat, homeostasis attempts to maintain the body at a constant, optimal (or preferred) level. This preferred internal state of arousal is maintained through the regulation of the previously listed bodily systems. Under arousal theory, then, human behavior is driven by an attempt to achieve or maintain this optimal level of arousal. For example, if a person's arousal levels are too high, which might be caused by exposure to too many new or intense experiences, the person may experience stress and anxiety. This would result in the drive to get away from intense experiences, thereby reducing stress and anxiety, resulting in homeostasis. If a person's arousal levels are too low, which might be caused by exposure to too few new experiences, the person may experience boredom. This would result in the drive to have new experiences, thereby reducing boredom, resulting in homeostasis.

A central premise of arousal theory is the idea that individuals vary on what is considered an optimal level of arousal. That is, people vary in terms of how they react to new and intense experiences (such as committing a violent act), with the same experience eliciting more or less arousal, depending on the individual in question. While there is little disagreement that brain functioning is different from individual to individual, arousal theorists maintain that it is this variation that explains why some people are more prone to violence and crime than others. Critics of arousal theory maintain that this variation is not enough to explain the large differences in behavior among those committing violence and those who do not.

In order to illustrate how the variation in arousal may lead to differences in violent behavior, the three general possibilities that exist for an individual's base rate of arousal will be represented by three different people (A, B, C). First, we have individual A, who is optimally aroused under ordinary circumstances. This is what we would expect to find in the majority of people, according to arousal theory. Committing violence would be too arousing for individual A, especially if there was a sizable risk of being punished. Thus, individual A would not be driven to commit violence. Instead, there would be a drive to avoid exposure to that intense of an experience. Second, we have individual B, who is overly aroused under ordinary circumstances. This person's behavior is directed to reduce arousal most of the time. For this person, even the thought of violence would be too arousing. Thus, individual B would be driven to avoid exposure to even thinking about violence. Finally, we have individual C, who is underaroused under ordinary circumstances. This person's behavior is directed to increase arousal most of the time. For this person, the committing of a violent act, possibly even upon themselves, would be pleasurable, as it would alleviate boredom. Thus, individual C may be driven to think about and commit violent acts in order to achieve optimal levels of arousal.

While violent behavior is arousing, there are other ways to achieve this arousal. Some are also destructive, such as drug use and risky sexual behaviors. Others are more creative, such as skateboarding and mountain climbing. Dr. Marvin Zuckerman, a prominent arousal theorist, has suggested that such behavior is characteristic of individuals who are at the high end on the trait of sensation seeking, which typically peaks in adolescence and diminishes in adulthood. For Zuckerman, these are individuals who risk physical, social, legal, and financial risks for the opportunity to have varied, novel, and intense experiences. Through the examination of fraternal and identical twins raised in the same or different families, he has found strong evidence that high-sensation seeking has a genetic component. Zuckerman has also found evidence that high-sensation seekers also have low levels of *monoamine oxidase* (MAO), an enzyme in the blood that seems to regulate neurochemicals associated with arousal. While the role that MAO plays in behavior is still unclear, low MAO levels seem to be associated with high-sensation seeking behaviors and increased risk of criminal behavior. High MAO levels seem to be associated with depression and bipolar disorders. Additional support for arousal theory is found through studies that demonstrate lower resting heart rates and skin conductance activity for people who are criminally prone than those who are not. Such physiological findings seem to confirm that those who are criminally prone are more under-aroused than those who are not criminally prone.

A question remains as to what differentiates high-sensation seekers who are violent or destructive and those who are creative in their behavior. Arousal theory is limited in that it does not address this question. Instead, the focus of arousal theory is on the propensity for violent behavior to occur, not the effect that upbringing, personal experience, and other environmental factors might have on the expression of high-sensation seeking behavior. It is possible that high-sensation seekers who develop in stable family settings would use their need for sensation-seeking more positively and creatively than those born into disorderly and unpredictable family settings.

See also General Theory of Crime; Neurological Theories; Trait Theories

FURTHER READING

Ellis, L. (1996). Arousal theory and the religiosity-criminality relationship. In P. Cordella & L. Siegel (Eds.), *Readings in contemporary criminology theory* (pp. 65–84). Boston, MA: Northeastern University Press.

Raine, A. (1993). *The psychopathology of crime: Criminal behavior as a clinical disorder*. San Diego, CA: Academic Press.

Zuckerman, M. (1994). *Behavioral expression and biosocial bases of sensation seeking*. New York: Cambridge University Press.

Dave D. Hochstein

ASIANS AND JUVENILE VIOLENCE. While a sharp upswing in crimes committed by youth was globally experienced, juvenile violence in Asia has been increasing at alarming rates since the outset of the last decade. In a number of countries in Asia, including Japan, China, Korea, and Singapore, the outburst of some serious delinquent acts has demonstrated the need for a resolution. As juvenile crime is a complex phenomenon caused by diverse cultural, socio-economic, ethnic, and demographic factors, no single strategy will suffice to prevent it. Although the growing rate of Asian youth delinquency was lower than that of adult crime, public concern has been generated about a series of immoral deeds and offensive lifestyles led by juveniles, such as organized crime, alcoholism, drug abuse, prostitution and sex work, rape, robbery, and theft. More critically, violence perpetrated by Asian youth living abroad has become another source of concern.

While the decade-long economic malaise in Far East, East, and Southeast Asian countries has engendered many unemployed, depressed juveniles being vulnerable to offenses, chronic poverty and wider disparity in wealth and privilege go hand-in-hand with youth crimes in the nations of South Asia. The lack of involved legal and organizational orders, as well as the changing climate due to the forces of globalization, further heightens the challenges to resolving the issue. Population growth and migration creating dysfunctional families, fragile family ties, intergenerational conflict, as well as the nature and degree of parental relationships are some significant considerations in Asian juvenile violence. Peer delinquency is also one of the vital contributing components in self-reported delinquency among the four major ethnic groups in Asia including Chinese, Korean, Vietnamese, and Japanese American. Peer groups may even be more important for Asians owing to their adoption of collectivistic cultural values that place group superiority beyond individual autonomy and representation. There is further a reciprocal relationship between commitment to school and delinquency. In Japan, for example, in 1997, a fourteen-year-old boy in Kobe killed an eleven-year-old child and left the severed head in front of his school with a written message threatening to kill again in order to claim his "revenge against the compulsory education system and the society that has designed it." The boy, who came from an ordinary middle-class family, was regarded as sensitive and cheerful. But after entering his junior high school, a strict, test-oriented institution, he reportedly grew isolated and frustrated. The youngster was first bullied and then regrettably became a bully himself.

A closer look at the Asian experience demonstrates that the latest juvenile violent crimes are not simply scattered occurrences, but rather the outbreak of delinquency has its deeper roots in the continuing societal dislocation spurred by the profit motive in both richer and poorer Asian economies, which has left thousands of youngsters insecure, diverted, and, to some extent, acutely agitated. Asia's cracked juvenile justice framework is also responsible for hundreds of victimized children and for minor crimes, as incarcerated youth survive immense tragedy and hardship in crowded jails where they are allegedly abused by adult inmates and prison guards.

Regarding juvenile violence among Asian youth in the United States, according to a 2003 report of the U.S. Census Bureau, Asian Americans represent one of the fastest growing ethnic minority groups in the country, with current tabulations at about 12.5 million Asians. Most of the Asian immigrants are now well settled in metropolitan areas, including New York, Los Angeles, and Chicago, and have formed organized ethnic enclaves throughout the nation. The socioeconomic situation, immigration status, culture of origin, place of settlement, entrenchment in U.S. society, among other factors, are components influencing the degree to which Asian adolescents engage in criminal behavior. For instance, due to divergent social structures, assimilation paradigms, and practical exposures, Chinese, Vietnamese, and Filipino youth have the highest arrest rates over the years, whereas Japanese Americans, Asian Indians, Laotians, and Cambodians have the lowest. However, as the rate of youth crimes, including murder cases, in the United States has comparatively been much higher than in other developed nations, there is a need for further improvement of its juvenile justice system. More specifically, more steadfast steps can be accelerated toward reducing victimization, school-based violence, and the frequency of domestic delinquency involving Asian youth.

FURTHER READING

Choi, A., & Tit-Wing, L. (2004). *Fighting youth crime: Success and failure of two little dragons.* Singapore: Times Academic Press.

Foljanty-Jost, G. (Ed.). (2003). *Juvenile delinquency in Japan: Reconsidering the 'crisis.'* Leiden, Japan: EJ Brill.

Paymar, M. (2005). *Teens in South Korea (Teens around the world).* Hersteller, CA: Lucent Books.

Sheu, C. (1986). *Delinquency and identity: Juvenile delinquency in an American Chinatown.* New York: Harrow and Heston.

Song, J., Dombrink, J., & Geis, G. (1992). Lost in the melting pot: Asian youth gangs in the United States. *Gang Journal 1*, 1–12.

Monir Hossain Moni

ASSAULT. There are two types of assault: simple and aggravated. Simple assault, generally defined, is an unlawful attack by one person on another. It does not involve the use of a weapon. Simple assault is the most common of all crimes against persons and generally occurs approximately five times more frequently than aggravated assault. Aggravated assault is more serious; it is categorized as a Part I offense in the **Uniform Crime Reports (UCR)**. It involves an unlawful attack involving the use or display of a weapon or in which the victim suffers obvious severe damage, such as broken bones, loss of teeth, or internal damages. As noted in other entries, official data, such as the UCR and the National Crime Victimization Survey (NCVS), may not accurately reflect the number of assaults because of their numerous flaws.

In 2002, UCR data show a total of 894,348 aggravated assaults. They tend to occur with greater frequency in metropolitan areas and in the most populous areas of the South. Most aggravated assaults involved personal weapons, which generally includes hands, fists, or other body parts. Firearms were used in 19 percent of the aggravated assaults in 2002, and knives and other articles were used in 17.8 percent. Police made arrests in just over one-half—56.5 percent—of all reported aggravated assaults in 2002. Of these, only 1.8 percent involved only persons under the age of 18, although others might have involved a young person as either victim or offender. Males constitute almost 80 percent of arrests for aggravated assault.

Between 1980 and 1994, arrests of juveniles for aggravated assault more than doubled. According to the **Office of Juvenile Justice and Delinquency Prevention** (OJJDP), which defines "juvenile" as under age 18, juvenile arrests for aggravated assault increased 150 percent between 1980 and 1999. While rates for males increased, arrest rates for males increased even more dramatically, 270 percent compared to 120 percent. Many criminologists and policymakers, such as John DiIulio of the Brookings Institute and James Alan Fox, dean of Northeastern University's College of Criminal Justice, cited this increase as evidence of a coming wave of "Juvenile Superpredators." Media publicized these claims, with *People* featuring the headline "KIDS Without a Conscience" and *Time* and *U.S. News & World Report* warning of "Teenage Time Bombs." These claims never came true, as assault rates plummeted even though the number of teenagers in the population grew. Interestingly, aggravated assault rates for females continued to rise throughout the 1990s. Noted criminologist Franklin Zimring of the University of California at Berkeley maintains this increase was generally due to two factors: the availability of guns and changes in police practice. According to Zimring, only one in eight assaults perpetrated with a gun ends in death, so the remaining 87.5 percent are either called attempted murder or aggravated assault. In addition, police changed the way they classified aggravated assault, which increased the likelihood of arrest. Others maintain that efforts to crack down on gang activity inflated these rates, as police aggressively arrested alleged gang members. Further, juveniles may be more likely caught for crimes against the person than adults. Race also seems to be a factor. Arrests of black juvenile males for aggravated assault were significantly greater than for white males or for white and black juvenile females.

Assaults by juveniles are most likely to occur in specific locations or contexts. Assaults involving a family member, at school, within a gang, or in some form of confinement (prison or detention center) are the most common, as these are the locations where juveniles spend the majority of their time.

In schools, students may assault other students, or they may assault teachers or administrators. Assaults on students may occur in the form of a fight (with or without weapons), or it may occur in the course of athletic or club **hazing**. While these forms of school violence have received a great deal of attention in recent years, most notably assaults with weapons, in reality school is still one of the safest places for people of all ages. Rates of school violence have been steady since 2002 and continue to be half what they were in 1992. In 2003, students between the ages of 12 to 18 were victims of 740,000 reported violent crimes in school, with 9 percent of those classified as aggravated assault. People in that age group are twice as likely to be violently victimized in any setting outside of school. In 2003, one-third of high school students said they had been involved in a fight somewhere, while 13 percent said they had been involved in a fight at school. Research has shown that approximately 1.5 million high school students are hazed each year, with 22 percent experiencing dangerous hazing. Dangerous hazing often involves some form of physical assault. Violent victimization of teachers is also more rare than the public has been lead to believe; between 1995 and 1999, only three in 1,000 teachers were the victims of serious violent crimes.

Aggravated assault is among the more commonly reported crimes among gangs. Of all the serious violent crimes reported in the early 1990s, one-half involved groups of offenders, most likely in gangs. Most commonly, a rival gang member is the target of the assault, which might include a drive-by shooting. Gang violence tends to occur in spurts and most frequently involves firearms. Like other forms of assault, gang-related violence increased through the 1980s and early 1990s, although there are great concerns over what is classified as "gang-related."

Research shows that juveniles are more likely than adults to be the victims of violent assaults, whether perpetrated by peers or by adults. Based on National Crime Victimization Survey (NCVS) data from 2000, people ages 12 to 17 are 2.7 times more likely than adults to be the victims of an aggravated assault. Finkelhor, Ormrod, Turner, and Hamby (2005) found in one large study of youth ages 12 to 17 that over 50 percent had experienced some physical assault in the past year of study. In addition, those who had been victimized once had a 69 percent chance of experiencing victimization in another year. In the family, juvenile assaults are often in self-defense or in response to abuse. In the mid-1990s, 10 percent of juveniles admitted hitting their parents, although the reasons for this behavior are not clear. Likewise, many assaults that occur in institutions are for self-defense or out of a perception that being aggressive will prevent attacks by others. In 2003, there were at least 300 attacks in California's Stark Youth Correctional Facility alone. In addition, there were 52 assaults on staff members, although it is not clear whether these were provoked or in response to abusive treatment. In addition, fights between gangs in prisons or detention centers are not uncommon and, in fact, may sometimes be encouraged by correctional authorities, as Sanyika Shakur documents in his autobiography, *Monster.*

See also Bullying; Gang-On-Gang Violence; Gang Violence, against Bystanders; Gun-Related Violence, Rates of; Gun-Related Violence, Types of

FURTHER READING

Cannon, A., & Beiser, V. (2004, August 9). Juvenile injustice. *U.S. News & World Report, 137*(4), 28–32.

Englander, E. (2003). *Understanding violence,* 2nd ed. Mahwah, NJ: Lawrence Erlbaum Associates, Publishers.

Finkelhor, D., Ormrod, R., Turner, H., & Hamby, S. (2005). The victimization of children and youth: A comprehensive national survey. *Child Maltreatment, 10*(1), 5–25.

School Violence Fact Sheet. (2004). *National Youth Violence Prevention Resource Center.* Available at: www.safetyyouth.org/scripts/facts/school.asp.

Shakur, S. (1993). *Monster: The autobiography of an L.A. gang member.* New York: Penguin.

Thomas, D. (2005). School Safety Report Released. U.S. Department of Education. Available at: www.ed.gov/news/pressreleases/2005/11//11202005.html.

Laura L. Finley

BIOCHEMICAL THEORIES. There are a number of biochemical theories that have been used to explain juvenile violence. Some involve exposure, either prenatal, postnatal, or both, to environmental contaminants. Others suggest our diets may influence our proclivity toward violence. Another part of biochemical research involves examining the role hormones play in shaping violent behavior. In particular, hormonal research has focused on explaining gender differences.

Environmental Contaminants

To date, exposure to lead has received the most attention. Research examining lead concentrations in the air found that the areas with the most lead also had the highest homicide rates. Other research done with teenagers found that those arrested for crimes had lead levels four times higher than those without criminal records. Even low levels of exposure have been linked to aggression and other behavioral problems. Rick Nevin conducted a study of U.S. crime rates and lead consumption in 2000. He found that gasoline lead exposure between 1879 and 1940 explained approximately 70 percent of the variation in murder rates between 1900 and 1960, and exposure between 1941 and 1986 explained approximately 90 percent of the variance in violent crime rates between 1960 and 1998. Nevin concluded that only childhood exposure had a significant effect. Earlier research has linked lead exposure to lowered IQ, so the impact on behavior may be indirect.

Dietary Explanations

A high intake of artificial food coloring and an excessive consumption of sugar and caffeine have all been associated with violent behavior. Other food additives, such as monosodium glutamate and artificial flavorings, have also been linked in some research.

In addition, intake of foods with little nutrient value takes away from a person's ability to consume needed nutrients. Some research has shown a correlation between deficiencies in certain nutrients and violent behavior. For instance, a study by British researchers found that inmates who received a vitamin supplement were 25 percent less likely to break prison rules than those who received a placebo. Essential fatty acids seem to be a key nutrient in constraining violet behavior, as they build and maintain bran cells. Research has repeatedly linked depleted levels of Omega 3 fatty acids, most commonly found in fish, with higher rates of depression, bipolar disorder, and suicide. In addition, B vitamins and magnesium are critical in the production of neurotransmitters, like serotonin and dopamine, which affect peoples' moods. Other research has suggested that either an undersupply or an oversupply of certain vitamins, including C, B3, and B6, may be linked to restlessness and antisocial behavior among young people.

Longitudinal research published in 2004 by scholars at the University of Southern California found that certain vitamin deficiencies in the first three years of life are connected to behavioral problems later in life. Children deficient in zinc, iron, vitamin B, and protein at age three were more likely to be irritable and pick fights at age eight. At age eleven, these same children were more likely to swear, cheat, and get into fights, and at seventeen these children stole, bullied others, and were more likely to use drugs. Those with a greater degree of nutrient deficiency were more antisocial. Stephen Schoenthaler conducted randomized, controlled studies with elementary school students, teenage delinquents confined in detention centers, and confined adult felons. Those receiving dietary supplements equivalent to a diet with more fruit, vegetables, and whole grains exhibited significantly less violent and nonviolent antisocial behaviors when compared to control groups. Some researchers posit that the link may be indirect: poor nutrition is linked with lower IQ, which is then linked with school frustration and antisocial behavior. Studies of children and teens in four countries and in California, Arizona, Missouri, and Oklahoma found those taking dietary supplements had IQ scores sixteen points higher than those receiving a placebo.

Food allergies might also be linked to violence. Milk, citrus fruit, chocolate, corn, wheat, and eggs all swell the brain of an allergic person, which then reduces the person's learning ability and may be indirectly linked to delinquency.

Hormonal Explanations

Hormonal rates are said to help explain antisocial behavior and violence, as both peak during adolescence. High levels of testosterone in the uterus have been connected with later aggressive behavior. Further, the notion that steroid use, which is an addition of testosterone to the body, leads to aggressive behavior is well documented.

Criticisms

The biggest criticism of these theories is that it is difficult, if not impossible, to isolate the effects of biochemical factors. The specific studies conducted to date are often criticized for failing to control for all the appropriate factors. Regarding excessive consumption of caffeine and sugar, it is unclear whether these substances cause more aggressive behavior or whether more "excitable" people are drawn to them.

Policy Implications

There are important policy implications of these theories. If it is true that environmental contaminants are linked with violent and criminal behavior, then governments have an even greater incentive to ensure these contaminants are not spread to land, water, and air. This might require additional laws or better enforcement of existing laws. In addition, governments will need to be more diligent in cleaning up environmental contaminants. Experts advocate checking all children at age one or two for high lead levels. Further, schools could offer extra support for kids identified with high levels of lead. If diet is truly linked to crime and violence, then more efforts to educate the public will be necessary. Parents will need to ensure that their children have access to adequate nutrients and that they limit their children's intake of items such as sugar and artificial colors. Movements are already in place in many schools, driven by obesity concerns, to provide students with more healthy lunch and snack alternatives. Clearly these will need to continue and expand.

FURTHER READING

Fishbein, D. (1996). Selected studies on the biology of antisocial behavior. In J. Conklin (Ed.), *New perspectives in criminology* (pp. 26–28). Needham Heights, MA: Allyn & Bacon.

Lawson, W. (2003). Fighting crime one bite at a time: Diet supplements cut violence in prisons. *Psychology Today, 22*(1) [Online edition].

Poor diet linked to bad behaviour. (2004, November 22). *BBC News.* Retrieved February 23, 2006 from: www.bbc.co.uk.

Roberts, M. (2005, February 19). Lead 'turning children to crime.' *BBC News.* Retrieved February 23, 2006 from: www.bbcnews.co.uk.

Schauss, A. (1980). *Diet, crime, and delinquency.* Berkeley, CA: Parker House.

Schoenthaler, S., & Bier, I. (2000). The effect of vitamin mineral supplementation on juvenile delinquency among American schoolchildren: A randomized, double-blind placebo-controlled trial. *The Journal of Alternative and Complementary Medicine: Research on Paradigm, Practice, and Policy, 6,* 7–18.

Stretesky, P., & Lynch, M. (2001). The relationship between lead exposure and homicide. *Archives of Pediatric Adolescent Medicine, 155,* 579–582.

Laura L. Finley

BIOSOCIAL THEORIES. Biosocial theories examine the relationship between biological and social factors to understand juvenile delinquency. These theories are useful when trying to understand juvenile crime because adolescents deal with an interaction of transforming biological and social factors.

Biological theorists look at behavior as caused by something internal to the person. They also focus on physical differences between criminals and those who are not criminals. In contemporary times, most do not feel physical characteristics will definitely cause someone to become a criminal, but they believe certain characteristics can affect a person's chances of exhibiting criminal behavior. Social theorists look at society outside of the individual and how a person's environment may help lead that person toward crime or violent behavior. Biosocial theories try to combine these two theoretical perspectives, and they look at how a predisposition toward violent behavior may be carried out when paired with the right social environment. This approach is often used to try to explain juvenile delinquency, since during adolescence many changes occurring internally to the person happen in conjunction with social environments that can be hard to handle.

Adherents of this perspective find it nonsensical to look at only biological or environmental factors; rather, they believe both need to be looked at within the same context. Discoveries now show that it is not only nature (biology) or nurture (environment) that affects a person's outcome, but both together. Developmental biology has shown that a person is not predetermined and fixed to be a certain way, but that from the earliest stages of development, they are constantly being affected by their environment. Contemporary neuroscience research indicates that the relationship between biology and environment may be more complex than it seems, and many feel more research is needed on the subject. However, many feel it is the best explanation of violent behavior thus far, explaining aggression better than just biological or social explanations alone.

Some environmental factors that can contribute to juvenile delinquency are a low socioeconomic status, an unstable family, peers, and stress. These can interact with biological predispositions, such as a low heart rate, hormones, or biological defects. Some suggest that living in a neighborhood with a high amount of crime influences a predisposition toward being antisocial. According to this argument, these environmental factors coincide with factors of cognition and temperament, resulting in antisocial behavior.

Biosocial theories have shown that the interaction between brain deficiencies and a lack of good parenting during early development can lead to continual criminal offending. For example, there has been evidence of the combination of delivery difficulties and the rejection of a mother resulting in male violence, especially adolescent violent arrests. It has also been shown that some people's brains do not react correctly to threatening situations or environments. The same areas of the brain seem to process fear and aggression, and while many people may react to a threat with fear, people with brains unable to regulate these emotions may react with aggressive behavior. Other offenders, which usually include antisocial children, have lower resting heart rates, possibly resulting in a lack of fear. This lack of fear could make these children lack inhibition to engage in violent encounters and could account for their lack of response to punishment. Another explanation for this is that they may be under-aroused, which could account for them trying to find situations that will increase their level of arousal, usually including violent or aggressive situations.

A significant relationship has been found between certain individual characteristics and processes of social development. Signs of depression, a lack of concentration, antisocial attitudes, and introversion have amplified the chances of a juvenile becoming a part of antisocial interaction. It also decreased their interaction skills and their chances of being involved in prosocial activities.

Hormones are another biological factor than can be influenced by the environment. Hormones can create a propensity toward aggression, especially in adolescent males, and then the environment can determine the instances in which that aggression is used. It has also been suggested that testosterone determines how the social environment is perceived, so it helps to determine a reaction to that environment.

Complex traits develop and mature with the aid of both internal factors and the environment. For example, temperament is affected by the environment. A child will exhibit a certain temperament and, in response to others' reactions to that temperament, will keep it the same or change it. If the child is met with negative reactions, it could lead to negative behavior from the child, and this can shape the child's temperament into the future. This same interaction occurs with other behaviors. Environmental factors, including social exchanges, have lasting consequences on the neurobiological processes that trigger behaviors. In other words, positive interactions between biological factors and environmental factors lead the person to behave in a manner accepted by society. In the same way, negative interactions lead to negative behaviors, including violence and delinquency.

Biosocial theorists believe that intervening with either the biological or environmental problem would help prevent criminal behavior because both factors are necessary for the delinquency to occur. Some people have biological traits that could encourage them to antisocial behavior, but their environment lacks the opportunities to carry out this behavior, so they do not engage in it. This helps to show that the interaction between biology and social environment is important and that one on its own may not cause the behavior.

See also Arousal Theory; Biochemical Theories; Hormonal/Chemical Explanations for Gender Differences; Neurological Theories

FURTHER READING

Brennan, P. (1999). Biosocial risk factors and juvenile violence. U.S. Courts website. Available at: www.uscourts.gov/fedprob/1999decfp.pdf#search='biosocial%20perspective%20to%20juvenile%20violence'.

Farrington, D. (Ed.) (2005). *Integrated developmental & life-course theories of offending.* New Brunswick, NJ: Transaction Publishers.

Niehoff, D. (1999). *The biology of violence.* New York: Free Press.

Shoemaker, D. (2005). *Theories of delinquency: An examination of explanations of delinquent behavior,* 5th ed. New York: Oxford University Press.

Sharon Thiel

BOOT CAMPS. In the early 1990s, the use of boot camps for juvenile offenders was believed to be the answer to solving the juvenile crime issue, promising lower operating costs and less recidivism. This directly coincided with the belief that intermediate sanctions in corrections were the new remedy for an overburdened juvenile correctional system. Boot camps are highly structured residential programs generally modeled after military basic training. They emphasize rigorous physical exercise, regimented activities, strict supervision and discipline, and military drill and ceremony. Military-style battle dress uniforms and boots are the standard uniforms for offenders, who are often referred to as "cadets," as well as staff. The cadets are expected to learn and use basic military courtesy, drill, and ceremony. This expectation of military courtesy and discipline are continued throughout the stay of the cadet at the boot camp, with the belief that it will continue outside of the boot camp.

The use of boot camps for juveniles is a relatively new phenomenon, rising out of earlier programs, such as "shock probation" and "scared straight." The initial use of boot camps for juveniles was a way to provide order, structure, and discipline, while alleviating the need for placement in already overcrowded juvenile detention centers. The blend of rigid format and deliberate strictness found political and public support. This short sanction was tough enough to satisfy those who wanted harsher sanctions, and it was believed to be a way in which to reform hardened juveniles who were not being helped by traditional juvenile punishments. While the trend of using boot camps by government agencies has dwindled in the 1990s and into the twenty-first century, they have found a new surge of use by parents who are looking to cure their "troubled teens."

The Internet has a large number of websites that are designed to assist parents who are looking for military-type options for out-of-control teens that parents feel may need structure and discipline. Participation in these programs is not sanctioned by the courts or the juvenile justice system but they are often seen by parents as a last resort for teenagers who are acting out. While boot camps that are used by the court usually are seen as a short-term sentencing option, private boot camps may house children for a year or longer, depending upon the parents and the treatment team recommendation. Many boot camps, whether they be privately owned and operated or run by the government, only accept willing participants, as boot camps are an alternative to incarceration; it is believed that true success in any form of rehabilitative effort must come from an individual's own personal willingness to change. While the promised benefits of using boot camps for juveniles were large, there is still debate regarding the overall effectiveness of juvenile boot camps.

Critics of juvenile boot camps often cite abuse and mistreatment as their primary concern. According to the National Mental Health Association (NMHA), a confrontational model employing tactics of intimidation and humiliation is counterproductive for most youth in the juvenile justice system. The NMHA also contends that juvenile boot camps are not cost-effective and do not reduce recidivism rates among juveniles. The NMHA believes that changes that often occur in the boot camp setting do not last when juveniles are returned back into the community. Critics see the demand for discipline and adherence to rules characterized by the military model as rigid, dehumanizing, humiliating, and breaking the spirit. Opponents believe that juveniles should be allowed to talk at the dinner table, teaching them proper etiquette and conversational skills. Does the strict regimentation and paramilitary style teach people to listen, to control their bodies, and to pay attention, as it is intended? Research about the effectiveness of juvenile boot camps has found mixed results, and their popularity has faltered as the reduced recidivism it has promised is called to question. Further, many have questioned whether boot camps are abusive to juveniles. In particular, the death of fourteen-year-old Martin Lee Anderson in 2006 at a Florida boot camp called attention to this issue. That camp will be closed and the remaining four in the state are to be improved. Despite criticisms, proponents still maintain that intermediate sanctions are important sentencing options for juvenile offenders and the use of boot camps for juveniles.

FURTHER READING

Boot camps for teens. (n.d.). Available from: http://www.bootcampsforteens.com.

Fins, A. (Ed.). *Juvenile and adult boot camps*. New York: American Correctional Association.

Juvenile boot camps. (n.d.). Available from: http://www.nmha.org/children/justjuv/bootcamp.cfm.

Szalavitz, M. (2006). *Help at any cost*. New York: Riverhead.

Kelly Cheeseman

BOSTON YOUTH STRIKE FORCE. Perhaps more appropriately known as the Boston Youth Violence Strike Force, this multiagency, coordinated law enforcement team was created as a unit within the Boston Police Department's Special Operations Division. An interagency working group of criminal justice practitioners initially formed the strike force. Members of this strike force traditionally include local police, parole, and probation officers, affiliates of other law enforcement agencies, such as the Massachusetts State Police, as well as the Bureau of Alcohol, Tobacco and Firearms, local clergy members, and other youth service workers. Utilizing three approaches to crime control and deterrence, the Boston Youth Violence Strike Force incorporates prevention, intervention, and apprehension into their mission. Common goals include strict law enforcement and a decrease in violent assault rates and homicide.

During the late 1980s, Boston's youth violence and homicide rates increased dramatically. Much of the violence was attributed to gang activity. To reverse such trends and deter violent crime, the city of Boston initiated a comprehensive community-based approach targeting at-risk and violent youths. The strike force became a primary law enforcement entity behind crime control strategies employed throughout the city of Boston, namely **Operation Ceasefire**. In order to better understand the workings of the Boston Youth Violence Strike Force, the following synopsis is offered.

Enforced by the Boston Police Department's Youth Violence Strike Force, Operation Ceasefire was first implemented in May of 1996 and was the primary tactic employed throughout Boston to combat youth violence. The Boston Youth Violence Strike Force first set up formal and informal meetings with violent and at-risk youths. A zero-tolerance message was delivered, expressing that the consequences of violent actions would result in the use of intensive law enforcement tactics. Defiant youths were targeted, and delinquent acts, such as illegal drinking and motor vehicle violations, were strictly enforced.

Shortly after the implementation of Operation Ceasefire, researchers from Harvard University's Kennedy School of Government noticed a significant reduction in the annual rates of youth homicides. A formal evaluation of Operation Ceasefire revealed that the intervention enforced by the Boston Youth Violence Strike Force was associated with a significant decrease in the monthly number of youth homicides, as well as a significant decrease in the monthly number of gun assaults.

The Boston Youth Violence Strike Force continues to be a leading enforcement agency behind prevention, intervention, and apprehension programs throughout Boston. Prior to the Boston Youth Violence Strike Force, law enforcement and criminal justice agencies operated independently of one another and not as a multiagency system. The Boston Youth Violence Strike Force and initiatives such as Operation Ceasefire are examples of this multiagency approach, collaborating crime-combating elements used to address the complexities associated with youth crime.

See also Gun-Related Violence, Rates of; Gun-Related Violence, Types of

FURTHER READING

Braga, A., Kennedy, D., & Tita, G. (2001), New approaches to the strategic prevention of gang and group-involved violence. In R. Huff (Ed.), *Gangs in America,* 3rd ed. Newbury Park, CA: Sage.

Eagley, A., Maxson, C., Miller, J., & Klein, M. (Eds.). (2005). *The modern gang reader,* 3rd ed. Los Angeles: Roxbury.

Emily I. Troshynski

BRAZIL, NATHANIEL. On May 26, 2000, thirteen-year-old Nathaniel Brazil shot and killed his thirty-year-old, seventh-grade language arts teacher, Barry Grunow, with a .25 caliber gun. Earlier that day, Nathaniel was suspended for throwing water balloons in the school cafeteria. He returned later in the day and asked Mr. Grunow if he could speak to two students. When his request was denied, he pointed the gun at Mr. Grunow's head and pulled the trigger. The single gunshot killed Mr. Grunow and, in an instant, Nathaniel's case was thrust into the national spotlight.

The prosecutor transferred Nathaniel's case to the adult criminal court. In Florida, prosecutors (as opposed to judges) have the authority to decide if a juvenile should be charged as an adult. The trial was wrought with a great deal of controversy because of Nathaniel's age and the severity of his crime. According to reports, there were three critical points in the trial. The first critical point, which had a chilling effect on the jury, was the jury's viewing of the school surveillance tape showing the actual shooting of Mr. Grunow. The second critical point occurred when the jury viewed Nathaniel's three-hour police interview tape where he confessed to the shooting, helping the jury to find that this murder was not premeditated. The final pivotal point was Nathaniel's testimony and subsequent cross-examination, where he was perceived as emotionless, cold, and calculating.

On May 16, 2001, Nathaniel was convicted, as an adult, of second-degree murder. The jury failed to convict him of first-degree murder because they did not find sufficient evidence that the crime was premeditated. Under Florida's sentencing laws, the judge was required to impose a sentence of twenty-five years to life. On July 27, 2001, at the age of fourteen, Nathaniel was sentenced to twenty-eight years in prison without the possibility of parole. Following his twenty-eight-year sentence, he will serve a mandatory two-year house arrest, followed by five years' probation.

There are two sets of questions that crimes such as this raise: why do children commit violent crimes, and what should be done about it? There are a multitude of theories that are helpful in understanding juvenile delinquency. There are, however, perhaps two theories that may be relevant for Nathaniel's crime. **Social control theory** proposes that serious and violent juvenile crime happens because of the weak social bonds to prosocial entities, such as schools or parents. Despite Nathaniel's status as an honor student, his bonds to school were likely tenuous, since he had an undiagnosed learning disability. In addition, his bond to his family may have been weak since his family background included witnessing the domestic abuse of his mother.

A second potentially relevant theory is based on **social disorganization**. This theory proposes that children's likelihood of involvement in delinquent behavior increases when they grow up in areas of social decay marked by high levels of community-level violence, unemployment, and physical deterioration. Consistent with this theory, Nathaniel's background was such that he grew up in an impoverished area where he was exposed to the environmental conditions that were conducive to his participation in delinquent behavior, including easy access to a gun.

It is perhaps equally important to understand what legal statutes guide the punishment of juveniles and how they have changed in the recent era. The arrest rates for violent crimes among juveniles increased at an unprecedented and rapid pace during the 1980s and 1990s. In response, forty-five states began constructing new penalties and reforms to address the problem. A chief response was to increase the penalties associated with both nonviolent and drug offenses as well as violent offenses, thus making the offenders eligible for prosecution in the adult criminal justice system, a process known as a **waiver**.

Proponents of adult punishment for juvenile offenders contend that the intent of harsher sentences is to deter crime by holding juveniles accountable for their actions, especially those who commit serious and/or violent crimes. Advocates for juvenile offenders, however, contend that these punishments are often arbitrarily implemented, not focused on rehabilitation as their primary goal, and affect minorities disproportionately.

The proponents of adult punishment for serious and/or violent juvenile offenders feel that the punishment that Nathaniel received was lenient, in that he was not charged with first-degree murder and thus did not receive a life sentence or the death penalty. Their view is that, irrespective of age, individuals should be held accountable for their actions, and the need for these young offenders to receive treatment should not override the need to punish them for the severity of their crimes. As such, they consider the issue of punishment to be one of protecting the public from potential harm.

Finally, but not exhaustively, proponents of adult punishment for serious and/or violent juvenile offenders also point to the fact that juvenile crime, overall, has declined in the last decade as punishment has increased.

Advocates for juvenile offenders who oppose the use of adult punishment for adolescents point to the original justification for the implementation of the juvenile court; namely the issues of maturity, judgment, and competence. These advocates contend that adolescents do not possess the same levels of maturity nor the same capacity for judgment as adults. The issues of maturity and judgment are related not only to the decisions the offenders made as they engaged in crime, but also their understanding of the legal proceedings. Finally, these advocates question the ability of adolescents to effectively participate in a court trial.

Finally, but not exhaustively, youth advocates are concerned with the increased frequency with which juvenile offenders have been remanded to adult prisons. In the past twenty years, we have seen more than a 300 percent increase in the numbers of juvenile offenders in adult prisons. This is problematic because of the increased likelihood of physical and sexual abuse as well as a reduced likelihood of rehabilitation in adult facilities. Thus, adult prisons may boost the criminal tendency of youth who are released after confinement in an adult prison.

FURTHER READING

Building blocks for youth. Available at: http://www.buildingblocksforyouth.org/issues/transfer/studies.html.

Cullen, F., & Agnew, R. (2003). *Criminological theory: Past to present*, 2nd ed. Los Angeles: Roxbury Publishing Company.

Potter, M. (2001, May 2). Friend says she saw teen-ager pull trigger. *CNN.com*. Available at: www.cnn.com/2001/LAW/05/02/teacher_shooting.03/index.html.

Randall, K. (2001, August 3). Another Florida teenager receives harsh adult prison sentence. *World Socialist Web Site*. Available at: www.wsws.org/articles/2001/aug2001/flor_a03.shtml.

Paula Smith

BULLYING

Types of Bullying

Bullying may be defined in other contexts as "sexual harassment," "gay (queer) bashing," or homophobia. In the present sense, bullying can be defined as any intentional, hurtful act that typically involves a recurring pattern of harassment and typically entails an imbalance of strength or power. Bullies can include children, adolescents, and sometimes adults, such as teachers. Bullying is distinguished from fighting or "roughhousing." Fighting between equal parties is "merely" escalated conflict. Roughhousing is normal, aggressive play. Bullying occurs when there is an imbalance in power exploited by the bully over the victim. The goals of a bully are to increase his or her power, social capital, or status.

The most common form of bullying is physical. However, bullying has been categorized into three forms: physical, relational, and verbal. It is further classified as being mild, moderate, and severe. Generally, bullying progresses from mild to more severe levels unless stopped. Physical bullying includes hitting, shoving, and violation of the victim's personal space. Verbal bullying involves name-calling, threats, and intimidation. Finally, relational bullying involves an attempt at exclusion through leaving others out and manipulating friendships.

Bullying is widely prevalent. Both rural and urban schools indicate the presence of bullying, and significant numbers of students have experienced it prior to their senior year in high school. Some research suggests that bullying is on the rise. Research also suggests that the issue is a global phenomenon with many countries finding bullying to be problematic.

Who Bullies

Bully profiles seem to be mixed. Some children who bully have low school bonding and adjustment, which is associated with poor educational performance and truancy. Researchers also suggest that bullies are more likely to be involved in self-destructive or antisocial behaviors, including fighting and getting in trouble with the law. Other studies suggest that bullies can also be popular, seek social status, be intelligent, and so on. In any case, it would appear that boys of all ages are more likely to be involved in physical forms of bullying. Further, race/ethnicity and urban/rural environments may play significant but minor roles in predicting bullying.

The Impact of Bullying

Bullying can have negative physical, emotional, and social ramifications for bully victims. These include somatic symptoms, such as problems with sleeping, bed-wetting, headaches, stomachaches, and so on. The victims may experience low self-esteem, anxiety, depression, and suicidal ideation or an increased risk of suicide, as well as feeling rejected or isolated from their peers. Repeated victimization can cause harm to a child's physical and emotional development. In fact, while there are physical damages resulting from bullying, most of the harm is emotional in nature.

Victimization from bullying has also been linked as a contributing factor in famous incidents of school violence. In some instances, victims have brought guns to school and shot their tormentors. Possibly the most high-profile case was the **Columbine High School massacre**, where the actions of the two killers were attributed to the result of their being bullies and a failure by school officials to intervene. The social climate at Columbine was described as being horrific for students who were anxious and shy. Athletes or "jocks" were known to bully other students and were specifically sought out for shooting during their murder spree.

Interventions

There exists a host of intervention strategies to manage bullying in the schools. Some involve anti-bully education workshops in the classroom setting, including the teaching of strategies for conflict resolution. **Zero tolerance** policies have grown in popularity, but there is little evidence that they have deterred bullying. Some schools seek to train faculty to intervene and provide counseling for individual victims and bullies. Other schools have trained and empowered peer group members to intervene and avoid bystander reinforcement for bullying.

Recent Developments

Two of the most recent developments stemming from bullying issues include "Cyberbullying" and school litigation. Cyberbulling includes bullying through the sending of harassing emails, cell phone text messages, unwanted pictures through camera phones, and embarrassing or humiliating postings on blogs. School districts have been successfully sued for failing to deal with bullying and harassment.

FURTHER READING

Brown, B., & Merritt, R. (2002). *No easy answers: The truth behind death at Columbine.* New York: Lantern Books.

Brown, S., Birch, D., & Kancherla, V. (2005). Bullying perspectives: Experiences, attitudes, and recommendations of 9- to 13-year-olds attending health education centers in the United States. *Journal of School Health, 75,* 384–393.

Conn, K. (2004). *Bullying and harassment: A legal guide for educators.* Alexandria. VA: Association for Supervision and Curriculum Development.

Kroll, J. (2006, January). Bullies can be beat. *Current Health, 29,* 18–23.

Leff, S., Patterson, C., Kupersmidt, J., & Power, T. (1999). Factors influencing teacher identification of peer bullies and victims. *School Psychology Review, 28*(3), 505–517.

Mulrine, A. (1999). Once bullied, now bullies, with guns. *U.S. News & World Report, 126,* 24–26.

O'Connell, P., Pepler, D., & Craig, W. (1999). Peer involvement in bullying: Insights and challenges for intervention. *Journal of Adolescence, 22,* 437–452.

Olweus, D. (1994). Bullying at school: Long-term outcomes for the victims and an effective school-based intervention program. In L. R. Huesmann (Ed.), *Aggressive behavior: Current perspectives* (pp. 97–130). New York: Wiley.

Packman, J., Lepkowski, W., Overton, C., & Marlowe, S. (2005). We're not gonna take it: A student driven anti-bullying approach. *Education, 125,* 546–557.

Salmivalli, C. (1999). Participant role approach to school bullying: Implications for interventions. *Journal of Adolescence, 22,* 453–459.

———. (2001). Peer-led intervention campaign against school bullying: Who considered it useful, who benefited? *Educational Research, 43*(3), 263–278.

Stevens, V., De Bourdeaudhuij, L., & Van Oost, P. 2002. Relationship of the family environment to children's involvement in bully/victim problems at school. *Journal of Youth and Adolescence, 31*(6), 419–428.

Twemlow, S., & Fonagy, P. (2005). The prevalence of teachers who bully students in schools with differing levels of behavioral problems. *American Journal of Psychiatry, 162,* 2387–2390.

U.S. Department of Education. (1998). Preventing bullying: A manual for schools and communities. Washington, DC: U.S. Department of Education. Available at: www.cde.ca.gov/spbranch/ssp/bullymanual.htm.

Mike Olivero

CARNEAL, MICHAEL. Michael Carneal is currently serving a life sentence for the shooting deaths of Jessica James, 17, Kayce Steger, 15, and Nicole Hadley, 14, as well as five counts of attempted murder and one count of burglary. On December 1, 1997, just one month after Luke Woodham shot and killed three and wounded seven fellow classmates at Pearl High School in Mississippi, Carneal opened fire on a prayer group in the lobby of Heath High School located in Heath, Kentucky. Carneal, who was fourteen years old at the time of the incident, pleaded guilty but mentally ill to all charges. The families of the three dead girls brought suit against Carneal as well as twenty-one media companies, claiming that Carneal had been desensitized to violence by his frequent exposure to video games and violent movies. Although their suit against the companies was ultimately dismissed, it did spark a national debate on violence in the media.

By all accounts, Carneal was a normal fourteen-year-old freshman who had been at Heath less than a semester when the shooting occurred. His sister Kelly, a senior, was a member of the marching band, the choir, and a regular contributor to the school newspaper. His parents, John and Ann, were heavily involved in the school community and often accompanied the band on trips and volunteered at the concession stand. John, an unemployment compensation and injury lawyer, and Ann, a homemaker with some postgraduate education, were also actively involved in their church and local community. Carneal's home life was one that valued education and service.

Although Carneal's sister excelled academically, his grades had begun to slip while he was in middle school. Additionally, Carneal's career in the marching band was less than successful, as he was relegated to the sidelines during competitions. Furthermore, he was self-conscious and uncomfortable in the often harsh high school social world and was a frequent target of bullying and teasing because of his small size. He was interested in video games and computers, and much of his time was devoted to using the Internet, visiting chat rooms and answering e-mail. After his arrest, the police seized his hard drive and uncovered a stash of pornographic and violent materials. Fellow students reported that Carneal often sold or gave away such materials at school in an effort to impress the "Goths," a group whose long black coats and other trappings of Goth clothing and makeup made them unconventional participants in Heath's social scene.

Several weeks before the shootings, Carneal stole a .38 special from his parents' bedroom. He later claimed that he had considered committing suicide, but brought the gun to school instead, where he showed it to several classmates and offered to sell it. An older student demanded that Carneal sell him the gun or he would alert the police; Carneal handed over the gun but never received payment. A few days before Thanksgiving, Carneal broke into a friend's father's garage and stole a .22 caliber pistol and ammunition, both of which he brought to school in an effort to impress his friends. Additionally, he warned many students that "something big" was going to happen and to stay away from the school's lobby the following Monday. His classmates claimed that Carneal had made empty threats on previous occasions and therefore did not take his warnings seriously. Nor did they report the gun to school authorities.

Over the Thanksgiving weekend, Carneal loaded a duffle bag with two shotguns and two .22 rifles he retrieved from his parents' gun locker. He placed the stolen pistol and hundreds of rounds of ammunition in his backpack. On December 1, 1997, Carneal entered the lobby of Heath High School and opened fire on a prayer group that met each morning before classes began. After firing eight shots, Carneal noticed Nicole Hadley lying in a pool of blood and placed the gun on the ground. Bill Bond, the school's principal, rushed out of his office and led Carneal to a conference room.

Carneal was charged with three counts of murder, five counts of attempted murder, and one count of burglary. Although just fourteen at the time of the shootings, Carneal was charged as an adult in accordance with Kentucky statutes that allow juveniles accused of murder to be waived for trial in criminal rather than juvenile courts. The day before his trial was set to begin, Carneal's defense team agreed to a plea bargain. Carneal pleaded guilty but mentally ill to all charges and received a life sentence with the possibility of parole after twenty-five years.

Following his conviction in October 1998, the families of the girls he killed filed a $33 million lawsuit against Carneal, his family, the school, the students who failed to report him, and several media companies, including AOL Time Warner, Nintendo, and Sega. The families alleged that Carneal's parents, his classmates, and the school knew of the dangers he posed and failed to take action to prevent the shootings. Additionally they blamed the entertainment industry for inciting Carneal's violent behavior. All of the cases, with the exception of that against Carneal, were dismissed before trial. In August 2000, Carneal entered a settlement with the families for $42 million, an amount the parents of the slain girls are unlikely ever to see.

See also Music, Juvenile Violence and; Television, Juvenile Violence and

FURTHER READING

Harding, T. (2001). Fatal school shootings, liability, and sovereign immunity: Where should the line be drawn? *Journal of Law and Education 30*, 162–170.

Kimmel, M., & Mahler, M. (2003). Adolescent masculinity, homophobia, and violence: Random school shootings, 1982–2001. *American Behavioral Scientist 46*, 1439–1458.

Messerschmidt, J. (2000). *Nine lives: Adolescent masculinities, the body, and violence*. Boulder, CO: Westview Press.

Moore, M., Petrie, C., Braga, A., & Mc Laughlin, B. (Eds.). (2003). *Deadly lessons: Understanding lethal school violence*. Washington, DC: National Academies Press.

Newman, K., Fox, C., Harding, D., Mehta, J., & Roth, W. (2004). *Rampage: The social roots of school shootings*. New York: Basic Books.

Angela Winkler Thomas

CENTER FOR THE PREVENTION OF SCHOOL VIOLENCE (CPSV).

Established in 1993 as one of the nation's first school safety centers, the Center for the Prevention of School Violence serves as a resource center and think tank for efforts that promote safer schools and foster positive youth development. The Center's efforts in support of safer schools are directed at understanding the problems of school violence and developing solutions to them. The Center focuses on ensuring that schools function so that every student who attends does so in environments that are safe and secure, free of fear, and conducive to learning. Positive youth development efforts are emphasized as the Center focuses beyond the school into the community and works to prevent juvenile violence and in support of youth-serving programs and agencies that target the development of attitudes, behaviors, and conditions that enable youth to grow and become productive members of their communities.

The Center began with the purpose of providing information, program assistance, and research and evaluation expertise. Its initial clientele were members of the education and law enforcement communities. As time passed, the Center was able to develop expertise on the many issues that fall into the realm of school violence. The Center established a widely recognized definition of school violence (any behavior that violates a school's educational mission or climate of respect or jeopardizes the intent of the school to be free of aggression against persons or property, drugs, weapons, disruptions, and disorder) and put into words its vision for safer schools (Every student will attend a school that is safe and secure, one that is free of fear and conducive to learning.). The Center's Safe Schools Pyramid was developed, and its emphasis of comprehensive approaches to school safety that rely on data-driven processes rather than quick-fix programs was molded. Because it was one of the nation's first state school safety centers, it was increasingly turned to as a resource by people outside the state of North Carolina.

The Center's placement in 2000 into North Carolina's Department of Juvenile Justice and Delinquency Prevention allows it to refine its purpose and continue to meet needs. Emphasizing safer schools and positive youth development and serving as a think tank about issues related to these efforts enable the Center to continue putting into practice its long-standing philosophy of service and support to the ever-increasing number of stakeholders concerned about school safety and youth development. The provision of information and technical assistance to schools and communities continues to be the task pursued by the Center, but it now also serves as a resource for the Department of Juvenile Justice and Delinquency Prevention and its initiatives. As part of the Department, it also pursues and emphasizes early prevention efforts that include focusing upon violence prevention for younger children, precursor behaviors that lead to violence, and the modification of adult attitudes and actions. The Center also serves as a facilitator of collaborative efforts that are needed to ensure that schools are safe and all youth are provided opportunities to develop in positive ways.

FURTHER READING

Website: www.cpsv.org

Joanne McDaniel

CENTERS FOR DISEASE CONTROL (CDC).

The Centers for Disease Control is probably the most respected governmental agency in the United States. This respect is due to the agency's track record of investing scientifically to find cures for all diseases, including violence. Surveillance is the agency's backbone in the **public health** approach to youth violence. It reveals the magnitude of a problem, tracks the magnitude over time, and uses the information gained from such monitoring to help shape actions to prevent or combat the problem. It is CDC's position that youth violence is widespread in the United

States and typically involves children, adolescents, and young adults between ages 10 to 24, who may become the perpetrator, the victim, or both.

The CDC is particularly concerned with school violence, dating violence, and other violent victimization of juveniles. CDC data shows that 877,700 young people ages 10 to 24 were injured from violent acts and 1 in 13 required hospitalization in 2004. Overall, the agency claims that homicide was the second leading cause of death among young people ages 10 to 24. Furthermore, in 2001, 5,486 youths in the same age group were murdered for an average of fifteen each day.

CDC funds programs and research in several centers, including the University of California in Riverside and San Diego. The agency is relentless in developing new, innovative, and empirically sound strategies to prevent juvenile and all violence and injuries. CDC has credibility not only because of the agency's dedication to the prevention of juvenile violence but also because of the fact that it has successfully conquered several potentially destructive diseases around the world.

CDC uses two approaches to measuring the magnitude of youth violence. The first relies on official crime statistics and the second approach surveys young people. In fact, evidence makes it clear that most crimes by young people do not reach the attention of the justice system. Self-reports are well suited to helping researchers understand the proportions, types, volume, and trends of youths violence. These questions and many others are the thrust of CDC's research-minded investments across the globe.

FURTHER READING

Anderson M. A., Kaufman, J., Simon, T., Barrios, L., Paulozzi, L., Ryan, G., et al. (2001). School associated violent deaths in the U.S., 1994–1999. *Journal of the American Medical Association, 286*, 695–702.

Centers for Disease Control and Prevention. (2005). Web based injury statistics query and reporting system (WISQARS). Available from: www.cdc.gov/ncipc/wisqars.

Department of Health and Human Services. (2004, May). Youth violence: A report of the surgeon general. Available from: www.surgeongeneral.gov/library/youthviolence.

Uniform crime reports. (n.d). The Federal Bureau of Investigation. Available at: http://www.fbi.gov/ucr/ucr.htm.

Evaristus Obinyan

CENTRAL PARK JOGGER CASE

General Description and Significance of the Case

The Central Park Jogger case was a significant event in American criminal justice, bringing a number of concerns to the attention of the general public. Although the brutal beating and rape of a female is by no means a trivial event in any city, the surrounding issues of this case seemed to take on gravity beyond that of the crime or the harm done to the victim. In fact, the identity of the victim was not even known during the media circus that followed the case through the arrest, prosecution, and sentencing of the defendants.

The Central Park Jogger case brought a number of criminal justice issues to the center stage of American media. For instance, the case did much to demonstrate the polarization that exists between many minorities and nonminorities on issues of race and criminal justice.

Public opinion surrounding the treatment of the defendants in this case differed significantly based on race, the largest controversy having to do with the police net used to round up suspects and then the controversial use of interrogation tactics to acquire confessions from the defendants.

This case also highlighted what many criminologists had been studying for decades: the impact of the **media** on fear of crime. The frenzy surrounding the case eventually brought the media behavior under the microscope of theorists interested in the sensationalism following criminal justice cases. Many argued that media hype surrounding the case was causing more damage via the spread of fear than the actual damage done by the crimes.

Description of the Case

The crime that became known as the Central Park Jogger case was actually the culmination of a series of attacks, all occurring on the night of April 19, 1989. According to police, about forty teenagers between 14 and 16 years of age entered Central Park on that night at 110th Street and 5th Avenue between 8:30 and 9:00 p.m. Many of these teens later admitted that they intended to assault and rob people that they encountered, with the term "wilding" being later used by the media to describe this activity. There were at least nine attacks that night, ranging from badly beaten and robbed joggers to others who were merely threatened and harassed. The worst of the attacks occurred to a female jogger who was found brutally beaten, raped, and unconscious at 1:30 a.m. The evidence at the scene indicated that she had been initially assaulted on a jogging trail at 102nd Street and then dragged two hundred feet into the woods where the major attack occurred.

Police responded to a number of calls regarding the attacks and quickly arrested two suspects, Raymond Santana and Kevin Richardson, based upon eyewitness descriptions of the night's events. Another defendant, Anthony McCray, voluntarily turned himself in without being contacted by police, and two final suspects, Kharey Wise and Yusef Salaam, were arrested after being implicated by other suspects. Although five other suspects were arrested in relation to the events of that night, only these five suspects were charged with the assault on the Central Park jogger. Four of these defendants were convicted of assault, riot, robbery, and rape, while Kharey Wise was found guilty of only sexual abuse.

The major controversy surrounding police activity involved the confessions received from the defendants in the case, which they later revoked. It is alleged by some that officers created an atmosphere in which the teens felt they would be immune to punishment if they just corroborated the theory of the police about the attacks. Accordingly, police provided the defendants with too much information surrounding the attacks and should have seen the inconsistencies in the teens' stories as evidence that they were not being truthful in their admissions. The police countered with a panel that found that the inconsistencies in testimony were outweighed by the many consistencies between the teens' description of the basic events of the night, as well as some of the details surrounding the victim that police had not provided.

Recent Developments

The controversy of the Central Park Jogger case was revisited in 2002 when the DNA evidence found on the defendant was matched with a sixth defendant who had been previously unknown. Matias Reyes's DNA matched the DNA found on the victim, and even more significantly, he claimed that he undertook the assault on the Central Park Jogger by himself. Based on this new evidence, the five defendants were released from their prison sentences.

This new evidence has not settled the controversy, however, as the police still maintain that these five defendants participated in the assault of the Central Park jogger. Although the jogger, who has now been identified, has no memory of the attacks, police cite as evidence the teens' statements describing the jogger as well as the hair, blood, and semen analysis found on the defendants' clothing.

Despite the controversial nature of the Central Park Jogger case, it did manage to alter departmental policy within the New York Police Department and other departments with regard to interrogation of suspects. The size and comfort of interrogation rooms, the taping of interrogations, and the administrative oversight of the interrogations were all part of the focus of change. Moreover, this case continues to serve as a reminder of the potential panic that the media can create as well as the struggles still apparent in the relations between minority populations and the police.

See also African Americans and Juvenile Violence; Assault; Hispanics and Juvenile Violence; Sexual Violence, Rates of; Sexual Violence, Types of

FURTHER READING

Benedict, H. (1993). *Virgin or vamp? How the press covers sex crimes.* New York: Oxford University Press.

Hancock, L. (2003, January). Wolfpack: The press and the Central Park jogger. *Columbia Journalism Review, 38,* pp. 38–42.

Kassin, S., Meissner, C., & Norwick, R. (2005). I'd know a false confession if I saw one: A comparative study of college students and police investigators. *Law and Human Behavior, 29,* 211.

Shepherd, R. (2003). Wolfpack: The press and the Central Park jogger false confessions: How they happen. *Juvenile Justice Update, 9,* 9–20.

Smith, J. (1996). And the blood cried out. *Journal of Criminal Law and Criminology, 87,* 362–363.

Sullivan, T. (1992). *Unequal verdicts: The Central Park jogger trials.* New York: Simon & Schuster.

Brion Sever

CHICAGO AREA PROJECT. **Social disorganization** theorists Clifford Shaw and Henry McKay attempted to put theory into practice in the early 1930s by establishing the Chicago Area Project (CAP). Through social disorganization theory they argued that delinquency was the result of economically deteriorated neighborhoods that were too mobile and ethnically heterogeneous to establish informal control mechanisms against delinquency. They argued that in these poverty-stricken neighborhoods, delinquency attitudes, characters, and behaviors were transmitted to younger generations in a process they termed cultural transmissions. Youth that were living in these lower socioeconomic neighborhoods were learning the criminal trade from older more experienced criminal generations.

The Chicago Area Project was the first community-based delinquency prevention program in the United States. It was an attempt to eliminate the conditions that caused delinquency through: (LL) (a) the use of recreational activities, summer camps, workshops and respective facilities; (b) the renovation and restoration of physically decayed neighborhoods and schools; (c) enhancing communication between troubled youth and law enforcement with the assistance of citizen participation and mediations; and (d) educating youth on the importance of obtaining an education. The project offered over twenty different programs to Chicago youth, including counseling services, mentoring services, discussion groups, tutoring, hobby groups, and recreational activities.

The Chicago Area Project was implemented under the idea that the community should assist in the development of its youth, as opposed to simply abandoning them to the juvenile justice system. Through the assistance of professional individuals and volunteers in the community, the program's mission was to eradicate juvenile delinquency. The Chicago Area Project has always solicited the assistance of individuals that have been in contact with the criminal justice system. It is believed that these individuals understand many of the problems facing youth and are able to relate to them through their personal experiences. Many of the projects current volunteers have been former participants of the Chicago Area Project in the past.

From its inception, the program focused on neighborhoods that had high delinquency and crime rates. The program was initiated in three areas of Chicago: South Chicago, the Near North Side, and the Near West Side. The program has grown to twenty-two area projects throughout the city, and several others have been established throughout the state of Illinois.

In 2004, the Chicago Area Project celebrated its 70th year in operation. The program is still fighting delinquency using Shaw and McKay's original three-pronged approach: direct service, community organization, and youth advocacy. Even though the program has been criticized for not dealing with the most serious forms of delinquency, it has been successful in many other areas, such as increasing youth activities, having communities solve their own problems, and building a partnership between the youth and its community. However, the program's most noteworthy success has been the reduction of juvenile delinquency through the use of the community and its resources.

FURTHER READING

Shaw, C., & McKay, H. (1942). *Juvenile delinquency in urban areas*. Chicago: University of Chicago Press.

The Chicago Area Project. Available at: www.chicagoareaproject.org.

Georgen Guerrero

CHILD ABUSE PREVENTION AND TREATMENT ACT (CAPTA). The Child Abuse Prevention and Treatment Act (CAPTA) is the most significant piece of legislation enacted on **child abuse** in the United States. The general purpose of CAPTA is to provide funding through the federal government to public agencies in support of the suppression of emotional, sexual, and physical abuse and neglect of children. Specifically, federal funds are provided to agencies that support the treatment, prevention, investigation, and prosecution of child abuse and neglect. Moreover, funding is also provided for research examining the causes of child abuse and neglect and evaluating prevention strategies undertaken by agencies.

CAPTA was originally enacted in 1974 and has been refined on a number of occasions, being extensively restructured in 1988 and amended as recent as 2005. In addition to serving as a funding source, CAPTA disseminates literature on child abuse and neglect strategies and consults states on their child abuse programs. It also created the National Clearinghouse on Child Abuse and Neglect Information, which collects various statistics on child abuse. Due to the impact of CAPTA legislation, many states have their own CAPTA programs designed to provide state funding for abuse and neglect initiatives.

FURTHER READING

About CAPTA: A legislative history. (2004). *National Clearinghouse on Child Abuse and Neglect Information*. Available at: http://nccanch.acf.hhs.gov/.

Davidson, H. (1999). Child protection policy and practices at century's end. *Family Law Quarterly*, *33*, 765–774.

Brion Sever

CHILD SAVERS. The second half of the nineteenth century, from about 1850 until 1890, is sometimes known as the era of the Child Savers. What differentiated the child-saving movement from earlier efforts was the widespread recognition that significant social, political, and economic reforms were needed. At the same time, these reformers sought to preserve the existing class system and distribution of wealth, which, in general, favored them. Child-savers saw delinquents both with contempt and with benevolence. Delinquents were less than human, an idea derived from nativist and racist ideologies of the time, including the criminological theory of Cesar Lombroso and the Social Darwinism of Herbert Spencer. Criminals were described as "creatures" who lived in "burrows" and as "little Arabs" who were "shiftless," "ignorant," and "indolent." Progressive child-savers based their strategies on two contradictory notions: while assigning families the primary role for socializing children, progressives also advocated greater state involvement to oversee this socialization.

The most common form of action by any social service agency in the 1900s was removal of the child. In the winter of 1873, Etta Wheeler, a church worker in Hell's Kitchen, New York, was informed about a case of child cruelty involving a young girl named Mary Ellen Wilson. At that time, there were no child protection laws and agencies to assist her, so Etta Wheeler decided she would use the next best thing—legislation prohibiting cruelty against animals. This successful attempt to remove Mary Ellen from her abusive parents led to the 1875 creation of the New York Society for the Prevention of Cruelty to Children. In that same year, the New York state legislature authorized the establishment of branches of the organization in every county in the state. Just over a decade later, similar laws and agencies were passed in the United Kingdom. Agents of child-saving organizations, such as the Children's Aid Society, also urged urban youth to submit to being placed with farm families.

Lucy Flower and the Chicago Women's Club helped create the Protective Agency for Women and Children in 1887. The agency provided legal assistance, housing, and employment to women and girls who had been swindled, violently beaten by fathers or guardians, or sexually assaulted. This effort was in stark contrast to the predominant view that women and girls were carriers of disease, temptation, and immorality

These efforts are generally seen as a dramatic departure from earlier times. Historians claim, however, that there was some recognition in the previous century that children were treated poorly by parents and that at least some mechanisms were in place to condemn and punish parents and to remove children. Others contend that historians simply desire to represent the progressive era and the "child savers" as fundamentally different than those before them. While reformers were certainly concerned about the welfare of children, the real concern was that neglected and abused children had become an eyesore.

See also Parens Patriae

FURTHER READING

Feld, B. (1999). *Bad kids: Race and the transformation of the juvenile court.* New York: Oxford University Press.

Ferguson, H. (2004). *Protecting children in our time: Child abuse, child protection and the consequences of modernity.* New York: Palgrave MacMillan.

Grossberg, M. (2002). Changing conceptions of child welfare in the United States, 1820–1935. In M. Rosenheim, F. Zimring, D. Tanenhaus, & B. Dohrn (Eds.). *A century of juvenile justice* (pp. 3–41). Chicago: University of Chicago Press.

Platt, A. (1977). *The child savers: The invention of delinquency,* 2nd ed. Chicago: University of Chicago Press.

Laura L. Finley

CHILDREN IN NEED OF SERVICES (CHINS). Children in Need of Services, also known as CHINS, is a legal option developed in the early 1970s to intervene in a child's life before more serious interventions are required. Specific CHINS purposes and procedures vary by state, but in general, a CHINS petition may be filed if a child is truant, runs away, is disruptive at home or school, lives in a dangerous circumstance, or is injured by a parent. CHINS offenses are considered those that harm the child as opposed to harming society. Thus, CHINS are noncriminal proceedings intended to determine helpful services for the child.

A CHINS petition is filed by an interested party, such as a parent, truant officer, or the police, and alleges that the child's behavior or condition is a significant threat to his or her well-being. The court then determines whether the child is in need of services. If so, the child becomes eligible for a variety of support services, including a family needs assessment, crisis counseling, parent education, and substance abuse evaluations. CHINS has been criticized because many CHINS children become delinquents anyway, parents lose control over decision-making for their children, and the services provided are often inadequate, disorganized, and poorly funded.

See also Policing Juveniles

FURTHER READING

Citizens for Juvenile Justice. CHINS Report Card: The Unfinished Agenda [Online, May 2005]. Citizens for Juvenile Justice Website: www.cjjj.org.

Melanie Moore

CHILDREN'S AID SOCIETY. Founded in 1853 in New York City, the Children's Aid Society (CAS) serves the needs of disadvantaged children and their families. Today, the CAS operates from approximately forty sites located throughout metropolitan New York and administers more than one hundred programs related to its mission.

Founded by Charles Loring Brace and like-minded social progressives, the CAS was conceived as a more compassionate and efficacious alternative to the almshouses and orphan asylums that, in the middle of the nineteenth century, provided the only safety net for parentless, homeless, and severely impoverished children. In its outreach efforts, the CAS emphasized the establishment of more secure and healthful home environments, the expansion of educational opportunities, and the availability of meaningful employment. At the time that he established the CAS, Brace estimated that there were between 30,000 and 40,000 homeless children in New York City.

Because the number of children in need in New York continually increased as immigration increased, the CAS began to sponsor "orphan trains." Trainloads of orphans would be transported to preselected communities throughout the American heartland. At each stop, children would be adopted into families that could provide the sort of wholesome home life that the CAS saw as the most fundamental factor in a child's developing into a productive adult. Between 1853 and 1929, the CAS, in conjunction with agencies such as the New York Juvenile Asylum and the Orphan Asylum Society of the City of New York, placed approximately 150,000 of these children with new families in some forty-five states, as well as in Canada and Mexico.

The "orphan trains" were not without their critics. Some observers charged that some of the "upright" families with whom orphans were placed were actually abusive, that some of the children were simply being exploited as "indentured" labor, and that, in any case, there was too little follow-up investigation of the conditions under which the children were living. However valid such charges may have been, the "orphan trains" are viewed today as a precursor to the foster-care system. In addition, the program produced many unquestionable successes, with many orphans achieving considerable success in their new communities as businessmen, educators, and political figures, including at least two governors and a U.S. congressman.

Over the last century and a half, the CAS has taken the lead in the development of industrial education, free-lunch programs, parenting education, visiting nurses' services, kindergartens, nurseries for preschoolers, support services for working women, rural summer camps for urban children, convalescent facilities for seriously ill and injured children, and educational opportunities for children with physical and mental limitations. The accomplishments of the CAS in New York encouraged the establishment of parallel agencies in urban areas throughout the United States.

FURTHER READING

Clarke, H. (2001). *Orphan trains and their precious cargo: The life's work of Rev. H. D. Clarke.* Bowie, MD: Heritage.

Inskeep, C. (1996). *The Children's Aid Society of New York: An index to the federal, state, and local census records of its lodging houses, 1855–1925.* Baltimore, MD: Clearfield Co.

Langsam, M. (1964). *Children west: A history of the placing-out system of the New York Children's Aid Society, 1853–1890.* Madison, WI: State Historical Society of Wisconsin for the Department of History, University of Wisconsin.

Patrick, M., & Goodrich, E. (1997). *Orphan trains to Missouri.* Columbia: University of Missouri Press.

Martin Kich

CHILDREN'S DEFENSE FUND. The Children's Defense Fund (CDF) was created in 1973 to ensure that all children, especially the most vulnerable, have a healthy and safe start. The CDF is a private, nonprofit organization supported by foundations, corporate sponsors, and individual donations; it receives no government monies. Fifteen regional CDF offices are located throughout the country.

Because children cannot vote or lobby for themselves, the CDF acts as their voice, educating Americans about children's needs and supporting child-centered programs and policies.

Through their research, media campaigns, political lobbying, and program development, the CDF has lessened the rate of neglect, illness, poverty, pregnancies, and gun deaths in children. Additionally, the CDF has increased children's access to health care, Head Start, mental health resources, and protections in the social service and criminal justice systems. In terms of juvenile violence, the CDF emphasizes the role and cost-effectiveness of prevention programs that include quality housing, education, child care, nutrition, and family and community supports, such as living wages, tax credits, and after-school programs. To this end, the CDF officially opposes the 2006 Budget Resolution that reduces funding for such programs.

FURTHER READING

Children's Defense Fund Website: www.childrensdefense.org.

Melanie Moore

CHIVALRY HYPOTHESIS

General Description

The chivalry hypothesis refers to a theoretical explanation for the disproportionately lower involvement of women in the criminal justice system. The theory is based on the concept of "chivalry," which began as a term depicting the benevolent nature of knights toward common people during the Middle Ages. It has since been popularized to describe the protective nature of men toward women. Although many perceive the idea of chivalry as an archaic stereotype of women, chivalrous behaviors, such as men opening doors for women, allowing women to take an open seat on a bus, and the notion of women and children first during a crisis, are still common in modern-day society.

The chivalry hypothesis was a popular theory relating to female criminality in the middle of the twentieth century, but has lost some of its influence because of gender research over the past thirty years. The hypothesis holds that because criminal justice is a male-dominated institution, women who come under the focus of criminal justice personnel for their criminal behavior will receive less severe punishment due to men's penchant for protecting women. Therefore, female involvement in the criminal justice system may be somewhat misleading in relation to the actual amount of their criminal behavior.

Chivalry as an Explanation of Gender Differences in Crime

The potential for chivalry exists in the discretionary power of criminal justice personnel at every stage of the criminal justice system. This includes law enforcement, prosecution, sentencing, corrections, probation, and parole. Just as criminologists who study race and crime often argue that each step of the process is unfavorable to minorities, chivalry theorists contend that each step has the opposite impact on females.

Perhaps the group in criminal justice that has been accused most of partaking in chivalrous behavior is the group that has the most contact with the public. Indeed, since law enforcement is the most male-dominated and generally least-educated group of the criminal justice practitioners, their discretionary decisions have received much attention from researchers. The stereotype has been that they are more lenient on women, particularly those who are attractive, because they want to protect them from the rigors of the criminal justice system. Perhaps this idea has been amplified by the popularity of stories surrounding attractive women receiving no ticket for violations when being pulled over by a male officer.

Although prosecutors and judges typically have more education and less discretion than law enforcement officers, they have also come under the focus of chivalry theorists. Indeed, women convicted of crimes are generally less likely to receive prison terms than men and are given lesser sentences when they are incarcerated. Many attribute these differences to chivalry in the charging decisions of male prosecutors as well as the sentencing decisions of male judges.

While it has been challenging to offer statistical proof of chivalry in police decisions, decisions within the court process are less difficult to document. For instance, there has been research indicating that prosecutors offer females better plea offers than male defendants. Moreover, other researchers have found that judges are more lenient on women in sentencing and more likely to consider mitigating factors for women, such as marital status, family background, and dependent children, than for men.

Legacy of the Chivalry Hypothesis

The chivalry hypothesis has lost a great deal of popularity over the past thirty years, with many suggesting that it is an outdated theory containing only historical importance. Indeed, some researchers point toward increasing female arrest rates as a sign that police are exercising chivalry less frequently, particularly those of the newer generation.

Some criminologists critique the simplistic nature of the chivalry hypothesis as a theory of gender differences, adding that it does not recognize the contextual nature of the sentencing of female offenders. Research has indicated that police are actually tougher on some females than males, often depending on the nature of the crime and the image that the offender portrays. For instance, females who resemble men or who participate in male-oriented violent crime and gang involvement have been less likely to receive chivalry from police and judges. Also, police are typically tougher on female runaways than males.

Ethnicity has been found to have an impact on the treatment of females as well, and racial differences may have an effect on the criminal justice practitioners' perceptions of the female involved in crime. Research has supported this idea in that minority females have been found in a number of studies to receive tougher penalties than nonminority females.

Finally, the impact of chivalry has also been examined on females working in the field of criminal justice, and many argue that women in criminal justice face an uphill battle due to chivalry. Others have contended, however, that women have been able to use the chivalry of offenders effectively, particularly in policing and corrections. In theory, male offenders are less likely to attack female officers, and thus female officers have been successful in calming down situations that may have escalated with only male officers present.

Although many would argue that chivalry remains in the criminal justice system, the future of the chivalry hypothesis is uncertain. Common thoughts hold that as women continue to make up a greater proportion of personnel within the criminal justice system, the notion of chivalry will become less valuable as an explanation of gender differences in crime.

See also Gender, Frequency of Perpetrating Violence by; Gender, Frequency of Receiving Violence by; Gender, Types of Violence Perpetrated by; Gender, Types of Juvenile Violence Received by; Liberation Hypothesis

FURTHER READING

Avekame, E., & Fyfe, J. (2001). Differential police treatment of male-on-female spousal violence: Additional evidence on the leniency thesis. *Violence Against Women, 7*, 22–45.

Crew, K. (1991). Sex differences in criminal sentencing: Chivalry or patriarchy? *Justice Quarterly, 8*, 59–83.

Goethals, J., Maes, E., & Klinkhamers, P. (1997). Sex/Gender-based decision-making in the criminal justice system as a possible (additional) explanation for the underrepresentation of women in official criminal statistics: A review of international literature. *International Journal of Comparative and Applied Criminal Justice, 21*, 207–240.

Leiber, M., & Mack, K. (2003). The individual and joint effects of race, gender, and family status on juvenile justice decision-making. *Journal of Research in Crime and Delinquency, 40*, 34–70.

Brion Sever

CHRONIC 6 PERCENT. The label "chronic 6 percent" has become a famous phrase in delinquency research. Representing an empirical breakthrough in 1972, Wolfgang, Figlio, and Sellin found that, in a given year, a small proportion of arrested juveniles perpetrate most of the delinquent acts. This reinforced prevention efforts in the identification of youth who engage in numerous offenses compared to delinquents who are not chronic offenders (those who commit only a few offenses).

The study examined a cohort of juveniles (9,945 boys) born in the same year and monitored their police arrest documents. Chronic offenders were boys with five or more police arrests, further subdivided into types. Delinquents were boys arrested infrequently for nonserious offenses. Serious offenders engaged in violent crimes (homicide, rape, robbery, assault, and sexual assault) and more serious property crimes, such as theft and arson, while violent offenders were arrested for only violent offenses.

The key finding was that 6 percent of the chronic offenders and 18 percent of the delinquents perpetrated 52 percent of Philadelphia's juvenile arrests in a given year. It underscored the fact that a smaller number of delinquents (chronic) are much more frequent in their offense rates compared to most delinquents (not chronic). This has tremendous policy implications today, as both preventative and law enforcement efforts should target those most likely to be multiple offenders.

See also Aging out; Delinquency in a Birth Cohort; Developmental Theories

FURTHER READING

Loeber, R., & Farrington, D. (Eds.). (1998). *Serious and violent juvenile offenders: Risk factors and successful interventions.* Thousands Oaks, CA: Sage.

Wilson, J., & Howell, J. (1993). *A comprehensive strategy for serious, violent and chronic juvenile offenders.* Washington, DC: Office of Juvenile Justice and Delinquency Prevention.

Wolfgang, M., Figlio, R., & Sellin, T. (1972). *Delinquency in a birth cohort.* Chicago: University of Chicago Press.

James Steinberg

COCAINE AND CRACK COCAINE. Cocaine is an illicit stimulant and psychoactive drug in a powder form that can also be chemically processed to produce a solid resin called crack cocaine. Cocaine made its way to the United States by the 1970s and was used by middle- and upper-class users. Initially thought to be nonaddictive, it became glamorized as a high-status drug in comparison to marijuana. By the early 1980s, crack cocaine began appearing in Miami, Detroit, Los Angeles, and later in New York. This solid form popularized smoking the drug, as it had more immediate and intense euphoric effects. An unanticipated cultural turn in crack use led to the recognition of abuse and addiction and the shift in use and trafficking from the middle and upper classes to the lower social classes.

Being a stimulant, cocaine increases blood pressure and heart rate and generates increased alertness while reducing appetite and the need for sleep. Large doses and chronic use of either form of cocaine may produce cravings and addiction. This is to offset uncomfortable side effects of irritability, paranoid ideation, and mood swings. Using cocaine with **alcohol** or other illegal substances creates a synergistic effect and speeds up physical problems and addiction. Medical problems include heart arrhythmias, respiratory failure, digestive disorders, malnourishment, and the risk of AIDS in IV users. Youth involved in dealing and using crack have a risk addiction, especially if they begin use before fourteen years of age.

The presence of crack in economically depressed inner cities in the 1980s resulted in increased use, abuse, addiction, trafficking by singletons and some youth gangs, criminal activity, and violence. The crack epidemic became a very serious social problem. Trafficking mushroomed as minorities faced fewer employment opportunities, took up the crack trade, and armed themselves with guns for status and protection. Two forms of criminality emerged; territorial disputes among trafficking gangs and increased crimes by users to purchase the drug or as a defensive tool by dealers. The presence of guns led to increased rates of youth homicide, drive-by shootings, and tragic bystander fatalities. By the 1990s some researchers found a link between gun violence, prior drug convictions, and dealing crack; however, major trafficking is by adult organizations. The policy response to the crack epidemic included increases in prison sentences for gun and drug convictions, prevention and treatment programs, drug screening, confiscation of the property of drug dealers, and prosecution of low-level dealers—all aimed at deterring the spread of crack and illicit drugs.

In the **Monitoring the Future: National Results of Drug Use Survey (MTF)**, annual self-reports of high school youth show cocaine use peaked during 1980–1987 when 11 to 13 percent reported use in the last twelve months. By the 1990s, crack use dropped 10 percent, showing a steady 2 to 3 percent annual use rate; thirty-day use rates, moreover, were considerably lower. The MTF found 95 percent of seniors have disapproved of crack use since the early 1990s. Although crack remains a threat, as do all illicit drugs, increased public awareness of the damaging effects of drugs and their severe consequences combined to contain its use.

See also Drug Enforcement Agency (DEA); Gang-On-Gang Violence: Gun-Related Violence, Rates of; Gun-Related Violence, Types of; Stimulants

FURTHER READING

Agar, M. (2003). The story of crack: Towards a theory of illicit crime trends. *Addiction Research and Theory, 11*(1), 3–29.

Howell, J., & Decker, S. (1999, January). The youth gangs, drugs, and violence connection. *OJJDP Bulletin*. Washington, DC: U.S. Department of Justice, Office of Juvenile Justice and Delinquency Prevention.

James Steinberg

COGNITIVE THEORIES. A psychology-based approach, cognitive theories focus on mental processes as the source of delinquency. Specifically, the way people perceive and make sense of their world and how they solve problems is said to shape their delinquent involvement. Like **developmental theories**, cognitive theories tend to utilize a life course perspective. In contrast to most life course theories, which largely address criminal desistance, cognitive theories are more interested in why delinquent behavior persists.

Building on the work of Jean Piaget, cognitive theorists look first at childhood, as this is when reasoning processes are developed. Piaget posited there are four stages of cognitive development that begin at birth. By age twelve, most have entered the fourth stage, called the formal operational stage, and are able to use logic to solve problems and understand abstract concepts. Although Piaget did not specifically discuss delinquency, those who apply his work have maintained that delinquent youth are "stuck" in stage three, the concrete operational stage, characterized by dualistic morality. These juveniles are unable to recognize ambiguity, seeing the world and their decisions as "black or white."

Another influential cognitive theorist, Lawrence Kohlberg, addressed the mental processes involved in moral development. Kohlberg suggested that there are six stages of moral development and that offenders may have a different moral orientation than law-abiding people. The first of Kohlberg's stages involves making decisions based on obedience or to avoid punishment and the second involves making decisions to meet one's own needs. Evaluations of Kohlberg's work have found delinquents are more likely in these first two stages, whereas nondelinquents were more likely to put themselves in others' shoes (stage three), maintain rules that are needed for the benefit of a group or society (stage four), recognize that rules and laws are part of a social contract (stage five), or apply principles of justice to their decision-making (stage six). The most hard-core delinquents are said to be stuck in stage one.

Kohlberg, as well as many psychologists and sociologists, has been accused of being androcentric. That is, his work is based on males and designed to explain the moral reasoning of males. Carol Gilligan and others assert male moral reasoning differs significantly from that of females, who base their decisions on an ethic of justice and care. A study of 846 Dutch youth between 1991 and 1997 that measured moral reasoning three times at three-year intervals found delinquency decreased as moral reasoning developed. This study found gender differences in delinquency, but not in reported delinquency.

Another focus for cognitive theorists is in understanding the link between delinquency and information processing. Violence-prone youth, it is suggested, may not process information in the same way, may retrieve it differently, or may be too slow to make decisions. This is because they developed flawed "mental scripts" early in life that tell them how to respond and what to expect. They may have learned these mental scripts from parents and may even have been abused or neglected. In particular, women who are abused may have developed flawed mental scripts. As a child tries out violent behavior and finds little response or even positive responses, they may continue to use those same mental scripts.

Expectancy-Value theory posits that individuals choose behaviors based on the outcomes they expect and the values they ascribe to those outcomes. This theory also emphasizes that youth learn what to expect and how to value those expectations via socialization. Neo-cognitive theories are beginning to stress the ways institutions alienate youth and how that alienation may reinforce the flawed mental scripts these juveniles already hold. Research by Giordano, Cernkovich, and Rudolph with seriously delinquent adolescent females has demonstrated that offenders are agents in achieving the milestones needed for personal transformation. They identify four types of cognitive transformation: the offender's openness to change; the offender's exposure to a "hook" or set of hooks for change; the ability to envision a transformed self; and a change in the way the offender views the delinquent behavior. Their research shows that women may be more likely to have religious transformations, as well as using childbirth as a "hook" to change their views on delinquency.

Evaluations

Research has demonstrated that violent children perceive people as aggressive. Studies generally confirm that delinquent youth hold more negative attitudes toward parents, teachers, police, and the law than do their nondelinquent peers. Aggressive youth generally attribute fewer positive intentions to people when given problem-solving tasks. Further, delinquents use fewer cues to process information than do nondelinquent peers. Oftentimes, violent youth misread situations and respond violently when it is not necessary. Another study comparing incarcerated with nondelinquent youth found the delinquent group was more likely to externalize and use proactive aggression than their more educated peers, but not more likely to do so than their nondelinquent but lesser educated peers. An evaluation of Expectancy-Value theory found that delinquents do not necessarily believe aggressive behavior will be an effective way to solve their problems; rather, juveniles use aggressive behavior because they perceive no other valued options. These studies would suggest education may be the key to teaching youth to respond nonviolently. In regard to what cognitive transformations may help offenders desist, Gini Sikes's research with hard-core female gang members supports Giordano, Cernkovich, and Rudolph's contention that childbirth may lead to significant cognitive transformation for females.

Research to date has found little significant difference between delinquents and nondelinquents in regard to moral reasoning. Further, some research supports that, while moral reasoning affects delinquency, it is also affected by it—a more reciprocal relationship than generally posited.

Criticisms

Some criticize cognitive theories, asserting flaws in the basic premises. For instance, critics point out that Jean Piaget's theory was based largely on studies of his own children, hardly a representative sample. Many of the studies of moral reasoning and information processing involve small samples as well. In regard to moral reasoning and its impact on delinquency, critics note that not all delinquent behavior is clearly immoral. In addition, self-reports are the primary tool used to measure moral reasoning, information processing, and all other independent variables. Likewise, delinquency is typically measured via self-reports. These might not be very accurate measures of complex concepts. Several researchers have pointed out that the longitudinal studies used to evaluate cognitive theories often include few or no seriously violent offenders.

Policy Implications

Clearly, educating youth about alternatives to violence follows logically from these theories. Hence, **peaceable schools** and **conflict resolution** make a great deal of sense. Specifically, improving the moral reasoning of young people is a logical response if delinquency is truly due to cognitive explanations. Evaluations of a program designed to increase moral judgment and social skills, EQUIPPE, have not found it to do so.

See also Interactionist Theories; Social Development Model

FURTHER READING

Borders, A., Earlywine, M., & Huey, S. (2004, Fall). Predicting problem behaviors with multiple expectancies: Expanding Expectancy-Value theory. *Adolescence* [Online edition].

Giordano, P., Cernkovich, S., & Rudolph, J. (2002). Gender, crime, and desistance: Toward a theory of cognitive transformation. *American Journal of Sociology, 107*(4), 990–1064.

Nas, C., Oroboide Castro, B., & Kops, W. (2005). Effects of the EQUIPPE programme on the moral judgement, cognitive distortions, and social skills of juvenile delinquents and antisocial youth. *Psychology, Crime, and the Law, 11*(4), 421–434.

———. (2005). Social information processing in delinquent adolescents. *Psychology, Crime, and the Law, 11*(4), 363–375.

Raaijmakers, Q., Engels, R., & Van Hoof, A. (2005). Delinquency and moral reasoning in adolescence and young adulthood. *International Journal of Behavioral Development, 29*(3), 247–258.

Laura L. Finley

COMMUNITY TREATMENT. In order to fully understand community-based treatment for juvenile offenders, it is beneficial to understand individual treatment. Individual treatment attempts to identify and treat the individual in order to prevent acts of delinquency. Psychiatrists and other mental health professionals use a variety of personality and psychiatric tests to determine if a youth is in danger of getting into trouble with the law. Community-based treatments then seek to assist in the rehabilitation of a juvenile offender in lieu of incarceration.

Probation

Probation is a common method of community treatment. Probation allows the juvenile offender to complete his or her sentence in the community. While on probation, offenders must comply with various stipulations, such as attending school or maintaining solid employment. In order to make sure that the juvenile is on track, the juvenile court assigns each child a probation officer. It is the probation officer's job to oversee the youth's progress. The probation officer also acts as a liaison between the juvenile court and the minor.

Parole

Parole, also known as aftercare, is release from an institution based on the conditions set by the juvenile court. Unlike those on probation, juvenile offenders must serve part of their sentence in a **juvenile detention center**. They are then released to complete their sentence in the community. If a criminal act is performed while on parole, the prisoner may be sent back to juvenile hall to complete a full sentence. Parolees are also assigned a parole officer, who, like a probation officer, oversees the parolee and makes sure that the conditions of parole are being adhered to.

Intensive Supervised Programs

An **intensive supervised probation (ISP)** is a median between probation and institutionalization. Because some offenders may need or even want more individualized attention, they are placed with ISP probation officers assigned by the juvenile court. These probation officers have smaller case loads than regular probation officers and can concentrate more of their time and energy on a smaller amount of clients. Ultimately, the goal of an ISP is to reduce overcrowding in juvenile detention facilities.

Group Homes/Group Care

Instead of being sent to a correctional facility or parolled, a juvenile court may send a minor to a group home where they can receive more individualized attention. There they are classified by age, gender, and severity of the crime committed. The severity of their crime also determines the level of security put in place. For example, secure care facilities are for more violent and repetitive offenders. They are indicative of a correctional facility in environment and restrictions. In these secure care facilities, offenders are encouraged to maintain communication with family and others in the community in an attempt to build a support system that is available upon completion of their time served.

Upon evaluation of the minor's progress in the secure care facility, they may be permitted to transfer into a staff-secure facility. These facilities are for nonviolent offenders who, without structured supervision, are at risk to re-offend. In both a secure care and a staff-secure facility, rehabilitative programs include drug abuse treatment, family and individual counseling, educational and vocational training, and sports.

Foster Care

In supervised foster care, nonviolent offenders are placed with trained foster care parents. This arrangement is temporary and is not a substitute for a detention center, but rather a short-term residence in lieu of adjudication or until permanent arrangements can be made. Supervised foster care does not offer rehabilitative treatment.

Day or Evening Reporting Centers

By judicial order, nonviolent juvenile offenders go to day or evening reporting centers during peak crime hours throughout the day in an effort to prevent re-offending. Day centers are supervision for those who are not enrolled in school. Evening centers are after-school alternatives for those who are enrolled in school. These centers offer alcohol, drug, and mental health counseling and vocational training. The centers operate in partnership with various social service groups that help fund them.

Home Confinement

Home confinement, also known as house arrest, is the most common alternative to the juvenile detention center. A minor released under home confinement is allowed to live at home or with relatives, but is assigned a curfew. Home confinement allows the juvenile to attend school and other activities approved by juvenile court. Those under house arrest are assigned probation officers who make scheduled visits to the youth's home and school.

Electronic Monitoring System

In the event that a nonviolent high-risk juvenile offender violates his or her probation, does not attend school or their day/evening center regularly, or fails to abide by the rules and regulations set forth by the juvenile court, he or she may be charged to wear an **electronic monitoring** bracelet. It is irremovable and is usually locked to the juvenile's ankle. The youth must live in a house under adult supervision that has a working telephone. The monitoring system is linked to a transmitter within the phone line, and if the offender ventures beyond their designated areas, it is documented and the proper authorities are notified. This violation may result in the minor being placed back in a juvenile detention facility.

Juvenile Boot Camps

Juvenile **boot camp** is an alternative to lengthy sentences within a juvenile correctional facility. It is a military-style program that emphasizes discipline as well as physical training. There are state-run and privately run camps. Minors that attend the boot camps may also be placed on a period of probation following the program. Not necessarily rehabilitative in the mental health aspect, these camps focus on the behavioral problems of the juvenile.

Wilderness Camps

Wilderness therapy, also known as adventure therapy, is the concept behind wilderness camps. Wilderness camps are the alternative to traditional military-style boot camps. Instead of a barracks-style armed forces setting, troubled youth are placed in a wilderness setting where they are encouraged to form relationships with other youth within their camp in order to perform various wilderness activities. They utilize psychological treatment through cooperative activities to build self-esteem and self-confidence.

FURTHER READING

Albanese, J. (1993). *Dealing with delinquency: The future of juvenile justice*. Chicago: Nelson-Hall Publishers.

Boot Camp Information. (n.d.). What are boot camps for troubled teens? Available from: http://www.boot-camps-info.com/bootcamps.html.

Center on Juvenile and Criminal Justice. (n.d.). Reforming the juvenile justice system. Available from: http://www.cjcj.org/jjic/reforming.php.

Circuit Court of Cook County. (n.d.). Court programs: Juvenile probation and court services department. Available from: http://www.cookcountycourt.org/services/programs/juvenile/detention.html#hc.

Kipnis, A. (1999). *Angry young men: How parents, teachers, and counselors can help "bad boys" become good men*. San Francisco: Jossey-Bass Publishers.

Lundman, R. (1993). *Prevention and control of juvenile delinquency,* 2nd ed. New York: Oxford University Press.

National Mental Health Association. (n.d.). Juvenile Boot Camps. Available from: http://www.nmha.org/children/justjuv/bootcamp.cfm.

Office of Juvenile Justice and Delinquency Prevention. (n.d.). Available from: http://ojjdp.ncjrs.org/.

Outward Bound Wilderness. (n.d.). Available from: http://www.outwardboundwilderness.org.

Dionne R. Pusey

CONFLICT RESOLUTION. There are many methods being used to address violence in schools. One of these involves implementing conflict resolution programs. Conflict resolution is based on the idea that conflict is inevitable. It is how we deal with it that matters most. Youth today are repeatedly taught that violence is the way to deal with conflict, and conflict resolution programs attempt to teach students that there are other methods to resolve conflict. Conflict resolution programs take many forms, including those that are part of a school-wide, systemic effort, to individual classroom efforts, to special programs like peer mediation. The basic premise underlying these programs is that most issues teachers and students deal with in schools are about differences of opinion and interpersonal conflict, not overt acts of violence. Further, research has demonstrated that most acts of physical violence are in retaliation for some verbal provocation. Essentially, conflict is about unmet needs. Thus students and teachers must be taught the skills needed to constructively resolve these conflicts.

An example of one curriculum modeled on conflict resolution is called Open Circle. Open Circle has been approved by the U.S. Department of Education and is designed for grades K-5. Its primary purpose is to teach communication, responsibility, cooperation, respect, and assertiveness. Open Circle also recognizes the importance of parental involvement in decreasing violence and encourages parent-teacher communication. Evaluations show Open Circle decreases violent and antisocial behavior, as well as drug and alcohol use. It is also said to improve conflict resolution skills and impulse control, although the credibility of these studies is unknown.

Another curricular program is Second Step, which has been implemented in thousands of U.S. schools. Second Step teaches the social skills of empathy, impulse control, problem solving, and anger management. All evaluations to date have found Second Step to result in decreased student suspension rates, perhaps because Second Step goes beyond teaching these skills just to students but also teaches them to all members of the faculty, even custodians.

Peer mediation is a means of resolving disputes and conflicts by using a third party. In contrast to arbitration, the third party in peer mediation remains neutral and is involved only to assist in communication between the two parties in dispute. By 1994, there were more than 8,000 peer mediation programs in schools, and there have been many more added in the 21st century. The parties in dispute are each provided the opportunity to tell their side of the story in a setting where ground rules are established and maintained. Peer mediation has been widely implemented at all levels, although it is more common at the high school level. Mediators are generally given ten to thirty hours of training and then mediate cases with a supervisor at first. Mediators are trained in active listening, paraphrasing, and eliciting information and solutions from disputants. Typically teachers select the mediators, but some schools allow students to participate in the selection process.

Evaluations have shown that peer mediation decreases disciplinary referrals as well as suspensions and expulsions. One study found 85 to 95 percent of mediated conflicts resulted in some lasting agreement between the disputing parties. Too frequently, though, schools fail to conduct any form of evaluation of their peer mediation programs. Consequently, it is not clear precisely how effective they may be. To work best, peer mediation must be thoroughly supported by school personnel, which sometimes does not occur. A 2002 study found teachers did not allocate time to peer mediation as they felt they already lacked adequate instructional time. Peer mediation works best when students are involved in all parts of the process, from organization to implementation. Ideally, peer mediation teaches students to resolve conflict nonviolently in both school and nonschool settings, although research to date has not examined whether this goal has been achieved. Further, some students may not feel comfortable using a peer mediator. Peer mediation seems to be most useful when disputes are relatively minor and does little to address the multiple forms of violence that occur in schools, such as racial violence, sexual violence, and **systemic violence**. Teachers also need to be trained in conflict resolution so they can support the mediation program, which is not always guaranteed.

The most well-known conflict resolution effort is the Resolving Conflict Creatively Program (RCCP). RCCP was started by the New York City Public Schools in 1985 and is now used at over 4,000 schools and with students at all grade levels. It is a comprehensive, multiyear strategy that involves staff, students, families, and communities in the effort to make less violent and more **peaceable schools**. The primary goal is to change the school culture so that conflict is minimized and, when it occurs, managed peaceably. These concepts are integrated into the curriculum through a variety of cooperative learning exercises. Teacher training and observation of teachers are important components of RCCP. After one year in the program, schools may begin to develop a peer mediation program as well. The Carnegie Foundation has rated RCCP one of the top ten violence prevention programs. Research by the **Centers for Disease Control (CDC)**, in conjunction with several private foundations, found great teachers and parental satisfaction with RCCP. Teachers report less physical violence in the class and an increase in student cooperation, while parents report the program increases their own communication skills. Both in and out of school suspension rates decrease with RCCP. The biggest drawback of RCCP is the cost and time investment; it runs approximately $35 per student, which may be prohibitive for some districts that could benefit from it. In addition, much of the evaluation of RCCP has come from self-reports, which have certain limitations.

The biggest problem with conflict resolution programs is that they tend to be piecemeal. They have been poorly supported and poorly funded add-on programs, expected to work wonders.

FURTHER READING

About the RCCP. (n.d.). Educators for Social Responsibility. Available at: www.esrnational.org/about-rccp.html.

Baldauf, S. (1999). Programs to prevent violence before it starts. *Christian Science Monitor, 91*: 105.

Eisler, R. (2000). *Tomorrow's children*. Boulder, CO: Westview.

Selfridge, J. (2004). The resolving conflict creatively program: How we know it works. *Theory into Practice, 43*(1), 59–67.

Webster, D. (1993). The unconvincing case for school-based conflict resolution programs for adolescents. *Health Affairs, 12*(4), 126–41.

Laura L. Finley

CONFLICT THEORIES

General Description

Conflict theorists view crime as the outcome of a class struggle between the haves and have-nots within society. Those in power use the law and criminal justice system in a subtle manner that protects their interests against those not as satisfied with the order of society or their place within that order. Thus, crime is partly the result of the focus of the law on controlling the have-not members of society, while at the same time preserving the position of the elite. Criminals are not necessarily amoral misfits or sociopaths, but often people who have not had success in life and have come under the focus of the power elite when attempting to find alternative ways to achieve that success.

Conflict theorists contend that evidence to support their ideas is quite obvious within the criminal justice system. Illegal corporate crime and corporate executives are investigated, prosecuted, and sanctioned much less severely than those who commit lower-class crime.

Accordingly, this is due to the influence that the corporate elite have on governmental decision-making as well as the economical stakes that governmental elite often have in such organizations. Similarly, conflict theorists contend that victims of crime who are wealthy and have influence receive quick reactions from criminal justice agents, while these same agents are often disinterested in crimes against the lower class.

History

The philosophical underpinnings of conflict theory can be found in the writings of Karl Marx and his successors. Marxist theorists focus on the structure of capitalist societies and, specifically, the natural crime-causing tendencies of such class structures. Part of the focus of Marxist theory is on the preferential treatment that businesses and those in the upper class receive from the government and law. Thus, Marxist theory is in complete contrast with consensus theorists, who contend that the law is designed to maintain a fair and unbiased society and is based on the consensus of thought in a democratic society. By focusing on the government's role in crime and criminal justice, Marxist ideology undeniably provides the groundings for conflict theory.

Conflict theory became a popular sociological theory during the 1960s, a time of social and political upheaval when distrust of the government was perhaps at its highest in American history. Adding to the popularity of this theory was research highlighting the weaknesses of official statistics whereby crime is represented by arrests or reported crime. Indeed, self-report studies indicated that crime was not as much a phenomenon of the lower class as had been commonly asserted. This added fuel for conflict theorists, who contended that the elite used the criminal justice system to control the lower class and maintain the status quo, rather than to provide justice in an objective and evenhanded manner.

Conflict theory began to have a strong impact on criminology in the 1970s, when new attention was being placed on white-collar crime. At this time, many criminologists split from **labeling theory**, stating that it focused too much attention on the impact that criminal justice agents have on blue-collar crime, thus causing it to be vastly incomplete. Conflict theory melded well with the attention being given to white-collar crime and helped the criminal justice system in its understanding of the incongruity between the serious negative impacts that white-collar crime has on society and the lack of focus placed on pursuing and punishing this crime type.

The Legacy of Conflict Theory

As all theories, conflict theory is not without its critics. A number of criminologists have argued that conflict theory is too general in describing the elite or the haves. For instance, are the elite a part of the government? Are they interest groups? Are they businesses? Many would argue that the elite in society is a complicated arrangement made up of a plurality of groups that is complex, ever-changing, and differs across regions. Moreover, there are questions surrounding the actual control that the elite have over the criminal justice system. In fact, some research has provided support for consensus theory by finding that police dispersion and patrol decisions have sometimes been based on the desires of constituents, many being from the lower class.

Critics also have questioned the causal order surrounding conflict theory's assertions about the attention placed on blue-collar crime. Specifically, perhaps the criminal justice system's lack of attention toward white-collar crime is not based on the motivations that conflict theorists posit. Indeed, there is much historical literature suggesting that society's focus on blue-collar crime is rooted in tradition, stretching back to a time before the industrial revolution and insurance coverage when blue-collar crimes, such as theft and burglary, were catastrophic, and white-collar crimes of industrial and corporate groups were not an issue. Such critics would contend that conflict theorists are taking a complicated phenomenon of law that is based on years of tradition and socialization and adding a simple explanation without quantifiable or historic merit.

Yet, despite the critics, it is difficult to deny the impact that conflict theory and related ideologies have had on criminology. It has increased the field's understanding of the complexities of crime and the role that society has in defining and thus shaping crime. In the beginning of the century, many groundbreaking criminological theories focused on blue-collar crime and largely ignored the creation of law and, in turn, crime. Conflict theory has helped make criminologists aware of their own subjective interpretations of crime and decreased the acceptance of official statistics and classifications of crime.

FURTHER READING

Chambliss, W., & Seidman, R. (1971). *Law, order and power*. Reading, MA: Addison-Wesley.

Mosher, C. (2001). Predicting drug arrest rates: Conflict and social disorganization perspectives. *Crime and Delinquency*, *47*, 84–104.

Petrocelli, M., Piquero, A., & Smith, M. (2003). Conflict theory and racial profiling: An empirical analysis of police traffic stop data. *Journal of Criminal Justice*, *3*, 1–31.

Pratt, T., & Lowenkamp, C. (2002). Conflict theory, economic conditions, and homicide. *Homicide Studies*, *6*, 61–83.

Brion Sever

CONTROL THEORIES. Control theory is a perspective seeking to explain the genesis of delinquent behavior. It attempts to explain why youth *refrain* from engaging in delinquent behavior. This shifts the emphasis generally used in other theories from the question "What causes delinquency?" to the question "What causes youth *not* to engage in delinquency?" There has been considerable empirical research performed that offers explanations and analysis. The key mechanism in control theory is an elucidation of various types of social and psychological controls that will stop or prohibit the onset of delinquent behavior. Consideration of youth violence would focus on the question "What factors would prevent youth from engaging in violent crimes?"

Control theories put forth certain assumptions that are held to be generalizations about delinquent and criminal behavior. First is that individual's must be restrained or controlled to reduce delinquency. Second, youthful delinquency is common, so this redirects attention to the accurate identification of factors that stop delinquency. A third assumption is that delinquents lack the particular restraint mechanisms that operate to prevent delinquency in nondelinquents. Fourth, control theories hold that society clearly delineates accepted norms, values, and laws that serve as guideposts for behavior. There are three main versions of control theory.

Psychoanalysis is an early form of control theory that proposes that humans' personalities are composed of three parts: the id, the ego, and the superego. The impulsive id requires restraint by operation of other parts of the personality and is accomplished by way of socialization. This restraint from delinquency is exercised by the ego and, most importantly, the superego. This part of the personality energizes when a potential norm violation requires a decision to restrain from inappropriate behavior. Thus, based on early learning experiences in the family and society, the superego overrides the urges from the id. Empirical tests of psychoanalysis have not been as extensive as with other control theories, as the concepts are abstract in nature.

The second control theory was offered by Reckless. It contends that low self-esteem (or self-concept) is associated with delinquency and high self esteem contains delinquency. Reckless states that there are many social and psychological inducements that make delinquency appealing. A youth's strong self-esteem is the key inner mechanism that provides them with the strength to resist delinquency. For Reckless, there are outer and inner pressures that may generate delinquency and outer and inner containments that insulate a youth from delinquency, if they are developed. Inner containment originates from strong self-esteem, which is derived from favorable socialization and child development. Self-esteem then buffers or insulates one from delinquency. Outer containment originates from primary groups and acceptance of role expectations derived from intensive group participation.

Research has shown that in some samples of delinquents, their self-esteem ratings are lower than nondelinquents. Self-report studies involve sampling youth who report delinquency but may not have been in contact with police. Self-concept may be important for its indirect effects that operate through more important causes, such as the family, peer affiliations, and social class.

Social control theory is the third version of control theory and was advanced by Hirschi in 1969. The key mechanism that restrains delinquent and criminal behavior is referred to as the social bond. There are four components of this bond: attachment, commitment, involvement, and belief. The assumption is that the absence or weakness of these bonds reflects a deficiency in juveniles compared to nondelinquents. If the social bonds are intensive and strong, this reduces the youth's inclination toward delinquent behavior.

Attachment is the strength of one's emotional connection with important individuals and groups. If a youth has ties of affection and identification with these groups, they will internalize group norms opposing delinquency. Commitment is a developed sense of investment in and orientation to reference groups that makes the potential pain of group rejection a deterrent to delinquency. The bond involvement ranges in strength from low to very strong group-orientation, based on the time spent establishing allegiance with conventional groups and individuals. Finally, belief involves the internalized endorsement by the youth to maintain conformity to legal codes. If any four of the bonds are weakened, the social bond is less controlling of a youth's behavior and more predictive of delinquency.

Considerable research has been conducted to evaluate control theory. There have been three societal processes studied: the family, school, and religion's influence on delinquency. Studies on the family that posit a breakdown in controls usually look at disorganized communities and families; however, control theories look at family structure (death and divorce) and family process (supervision, affection, cohesion, and abuse).

Research on broken homes has found some connection with delinquency; however, many studies claim a more important factor is the quality of family relationships, such as supervision, happiness, and parental involvement. In general, research finds modest confirmation between effective family supervision (time spent), reciprocal happiness in a family atmosphere, and participation in activities. All are linked with lower propensities toward delinquency. Hirschi found that attachment to school and school grades are also linked to delinquency. The connection between religious attendance and delinquency has had inconsistent findings.

Research evaluating control theories shows more application to property offenses and drug offenses than to violent crime. Research comparing the relative importance of family, abuse, and school variables has suggested that school-based variables are more important. Thus youth who are disconnected and unattached to school and teachers ostensibly are linked to juvenile violence.

Gottfredson and Hirschi offered the fourth control theory in 1990, called the **General Theory of Crime (GTC)**. Their theory states that delinquency is likely by offenders who lack self-control in concert with having opportunities to commit delinquent acts. Delinquents have faulty inner impulse control in a social context of delinquent temptations. The youth's personality can not muster the internal strength to refrain and to use moral reasoning to desist the appeal of immediate gratification and excitement-seeking. This model suggests that some delinquency is contextual and based on opportunities that override a rational cost-benefit analysis of the delinquent act.

Control theories continue to be expanded and tested in criminology today. While they may have weak power explaining youth violence, they do explain some garden-variety delinquency, such as property, drug, and status offenses.

See also Personality Theories; Psychodynamic Theory; Rational Choice Theory

FURTHER READING

Gottredson, M., & Hirshi, T. (1990). *A general theory of crime*. Stanford CA: Stanford University Press.

Hirschi, T. (2001). *Causes of delinquency*. Somerset, NJ: Transaction.

Pfohl, S. (1994). *Images of deviance and social control*, 2nd ed. New York: McGraw Hill.

Shoemaker, D. (2000). *Theories of delinquency: An examination of explanations of delinquency behavior*. New York: Oxford University Press.

James Steinberg

CORPORAL PUNISHMENT. Corporal punishment is the deliberate infliction of pain intended as correction or punishment. This type of punishment is generally held to differ from torture because it is only applied for disciplinary reasons and is therefore intended to be limited, rather than intended to jeopardize the will of the victim. Historically, parents have used corporal punishment on their children for disciplinary purposes. It has also been used by societies to curb norm violation, especially by juvenile violent offenders.

Some social scientists see corporal punishment as a disciplinary tool for incorrigible children and as a stress relief for parents. Schools use corporal punishments to deliver corrective discipline to children and youth for the purpose of socialization. One form of corporal punishment that is still used at some schools to discipline children is paddling. Every industrialized nation, except the United States, Canada, and one state in Australia, have banned corporal punishment in schools. Twenty-three states still allow corporal punishment of students, and best estimates are that almost 350,000 students are subjected to it each year. This system of punishment is also used in boot camps for violent juvenile offenders to keep them in check and in military types of discipline.

Historically, slaves received corporal punishment from their owners from instruments such as canes or whips. The goal was to assure that slaves were disciplined and put in their places. Sometimes beating them to death was said to enforce supremacy.

Colin Farrell, in *Birching in the Isle of Man, 1945 to 1976*, stated that birching was principally a punishment for boys under fifteen years of age who were convicted of larceny. Violent juvenile offenders suffered similar punishment as well. Other examples of corporal punishment include the "cat-o-nine-tails," which is an instrument consisting of leather thongs with pieces of metal inserted. It was once used in America, Britain, and by the Russians. Later on in the twentieth century, people who were locked up in prison yards or in correctional facilities were regularly beaten and flogged whenever they broke rules or became unruly. One example of this is the Parchman Prison Farm in Mississippi. The true symbol of authority and discipline at Parchman was a leather strap, three feet long and six inches wide, known as "Black Annie," which hung from the driver's belt. Whipping had a long history in the South, of course, and not only on the slave plantation.

Corporal punishment is lawful as a sentence for crime because, although the Constitution recognizes the right not to be subjected to torture or to other cruel, inhuman, and/or degrading treatment or punishment, other legislation allows for corporal punishment. Whipping is lawful as a sentence for young male offenders under the Corporal Punishment Ordinance (1889).

Corporal punishment has existed since the beginning of man. It is still regarded as a socialization and disciplinary tool. Conservative politicians are more comfortable with this tool. In the Bible there are various scriptures that mention violence against children and how children should behave: "He that spareth the rod hateth his son." This passage demonstrates how far society has evolved.

Opponents maintain the United States has elevated corporal punishment to capital punishment for youths. Corporal punishment can damage the lives of children wherever and whenever it is imposed. In severe cases, experts say children who have received corporal punishment may suffer from post-traumatic stress disorder (PTSD). Opponents argue corporal punishment is not healthy for children in any society and should be restricted if not eliminated in favor of other forms of discipline.

FURTHER READING

Crowell, D., Evans, I., & O'Donnell, C. (Eds.). (1987). *Childhood aggression and violence: Sources of influence, prevention, and control*. New York: Kluwer Academic/Plenum Publishers.

Farrell, C. (n.d.). Birching in the Isle of Man, 1945 to 1976. Available from: www.corpun.com.

Greven, P. (1990). *Spare the child: The religious roots of punishment and the psychological impact of physical abuse*. New York: Vintage.

Hyman, I., & Snook, P. (1999). *Dangerous schools*. San Francisco: Jossey-Bass.

Miller, F., Jenkins, J., & Keating, D. (2001). Social economic status, parenting practices, and childhood disturbance. In D. Williams (Ed.), *Vulnerable children*. Edmonton, Canada: University of Alberta Press.

Website on corporal punishment: www.stophitting.com.

Evaristus Obinyan

COURT APPOINTED SPECIAL ADVOCATES (CASA). A court appointed special advocate (CASA) is appointed by a judge to represent the best interests of maltreated children. These advocates help free up an overburdened legal system while providing unique attention to each child. They work closely with professionals in the educational, medical, and legal fields, reporting their findings directly to the court. They stay with each case until the child is placed in a safe and permanent home. Some states call the advocates guardians ad litem (GAL).

Concerned that he did not have the amount of information necessary to make a confident decision on the welfare of abused and neglected children, the Honorable David Soukup created the first CASA program in 1977 in Seattle, Washington. The success of the Seattle program has since been replicated across the country with now over 900 CASA programs that help over 280,000 children.

The National CASA office is headquartered in Seattle, Washington, and is not a political organization. They do not remove the children from their homes or prevent their safe return. They know there is not a universal generic solution applicable to all children.

The advocates are responsible for investigation, mediation, reporting, and monitoring. Through this process, they come to understand the child and their family, thus allowing them to make recommendations to the court that represent their best interests. Maintaining the privacy of the children is of the utmost importance.

Advocates are carefully screened and are required to complete between thirty to forty hours of training as well as attend lectures on sexual and physical abuse. They learn how to write court reports and conduct interviews. In addition, each advocate is required to attend twelve hours of national or local continuing education each year.

The U.S. Department of Justice has supported CASA since 1985 through its **Office of Juvenile Justice and Delinquency Prevention (OJJDP)**. In 1990, Congress encouraged the expansion of the CASA program with the passage of the Victims of Child Abuse Act. In 1991, CASA was declared a commendable national program in the prevention of juvenile delinquency.

In 2003, Congress approved a bill, the **Child Abuse Prevention and Treatment Act (CAPTA)**, in which CASA proposed an amendment that all GALs have appropriate training and an increase in funding for child abuse prevention and education.

The national CASA public policy is also concerned with improving educational outcomes for foster children. In some communities, CASA maintains facilities that allow supervised visitation in a homelike environment between the children and their families. Games, books, hobbies, and snacks are provided. The advocate protects the child from abuse while keeping a careful account of the encounter for the court record. In addition, parents that are going through a divorce can use the CASA house as well.

See also Child Savers; Children in Need of Services (CHINS); *Parens Patriae*

FURTHER READING

About CASA. (2005, June). CASA Website: http://www.nationalcasa.org/htm/about.htm.

National CASA 2003 Annual Report. (2005, July). CASA Website: http://www.nationalcasa.org/index-1.htm.

April C. Wilson

CURFEWS. The application of curfews on juveniles has a long history in the United States. For example, curfews were initiated during World War II to maintain control over adolescents while their parents were at war or working in the war industry. They were resumed in the 1980s and gained popularity in recent years. In 2005, seven hundred cities had and enforced teen curfews.

There is widespread support for curfews among the general population, minority communities, and politicians. Those in support of teen curfews suggest they will keep teens safe and they reduce the risk of traffic accidents. Further, supporters say curfews lessen juvenile crime, including vandalism. Others counter that curfews are unfair. Opponents argue that curfews stereotype or penalize good kids, the majority, for the actions of a few troublemakers. Some maintain they are unconstitutional. In addition, minority youth appear to be over-represented among curfew violators, and there is concern that the police will use curfews to focus upon race, ethnicity, or nonconformity.

Research has not tended to support the claims of curfew proponents. Research on curfews does not indicate a significant impact on juvenile crime. In fact, juvenile crime peaks in the late afternoon, while most curfew laws focus upon nighttime hours. However, at least one study indicated that curfews were effective in curtailing gang activity. In summary, it is very difficult to scientifically determine whether curfews are effective or ineffective. They do hold significant political support, even in minority communities where police may use the law in a discriminatory manner.

The Supreme Court has not addressed the constitutionality of teen curfews, so the consti-tutionality remains unresolved. The federal courts are not in concert as to the constitutional-ity of curfew laws, however juvenile curfews have not been judged to be inherently unconstitutional. The typical constitutional challenge to curfew laws is that they violate fundamental rights, including the First Amendment, and may also be vague. The constitu-tional rights of youth are not as expansive as those for adults. Therefore, some curfew laws hold exceptions that allow the right of association or activities protected by the First Amendment. Exceptions have also been infused into curfew laws to allow teenagers to drive during proscribed hours if they are engaged in driving associated with their employment duties. In conclusion, the issue is not whether curfews are legal, but rather an issue about the language and exceptions.

See also Policing Juveniles

FURTHER READING

Adams, K. (2003). The effectiveness of juvenile curfews at crime prevention. *The Annals of the American Academy of Political and Social Science*, 587 Annals, 136–159.

Bilchik, S. (1996, April). Curfew: An answer to juvenile delinquency and victimization? *OJJDP Juvenile Justice Bulletin*. Available at: http://www.ncjrs.gov/txtfiles/curfew.txt.

Grounded . . . every night. (2005). *Current Events, 105*(6), 3.

Indiana uses curfews to cut summer crime. (2003). *Juvenile Justice Digest, 31*(15), 3.

Kaminsky, T. (2003). Rethinking judicial attitudes toward freedom of association challenges to teen curfews: The first amendment exception explored. *York University Law Review, 78*(6), 2278.

Krull, K., & Divito, A. (1999). *A kids' guide to America's Bill of Rights: Curfews, censorship, and the 100-pound giant*. New York: Avon Books.

McCollum, S. (2005). Mall curfews: Teen discrimination? *Literary Cavalcade, 57*(4), 18–20.

Note: Juvenile curfews and the confusion over minor rights. (2005). *Harvard Law Review, 118*, 2400–2419.

Slavick, P. (1996). *Juvenile curfew and parental responsibility ordinances in Washington State*. Olympia: Washington State Institute for Public Policy.

The impact of curfew laws in California. (n.d.). Center on Juvenile and Criminal Justice. Available at: http://www.cjcj.org/pubs/curfew/curfew.html.

Zink, J. (2004, November 19). Court says no to cities' curfews. *St. Petersburg Times* (Florida), 1B.

Mike Olivero

DEATH PENALTY

Introduction

Until 2004, the United States was the only Western country, and one of only a few countries in the world, to execute juveniles. The first recorded execution of a juvenile in the United States was in 1624 in Massachusetts, where Thomas Graunger was executed after being convicted of bestiality. During this time, the death penalty was used as a punishment for a wide range of crimes, including the striking of one's mother or father. Juveniles were treated like miniature adults and were punished like adults. The recognition that juveniles did not think and make decisions like adults was the driving force behind the establishment of the juvenile justice system in the United States. However, due to **juvenile waiver** to adult jurisdictions, twenty-two juveniles have been executed in the United States since 1976, with thirteen of those executions taking place in the state of Texas.

Arguments for the Juvenile Death Penalty

Like the death penalty for adults, pro-death penalty arguments for juveniles center on retribution and **deterrence**. Deterrence is the idea that harsh punishment for murder will dissuade others from committing murder. Deterrence is based on **rational choice theory**, which assumes that individuals make rational choices to commit crime. Retribution is the notion of an eye for an eye, or payback. Often in capital cases, the victim's family maintains that the offender's execution will provide some closure.

Arguments against the Death Penalty for Juveniles

Perhaps the most compelling argument against the death penalty for juveniles in recent years has been that of differing brain functioning. Medical research has indicated that the frontal lobes, which regulate impulse control and reasoning, are the last areas of the brain to develop, and full development may not occur until the early twenties. Therefore, juveniles may not be held responsible for their actions to the same degree as adults.

Another new area of study is the relationship between childhood trauma, in the form of **abuse** or neglect, and criminal behavior. A number of studies conducted under the auspices of the Department of Justice have indicated that violent victimization can predict future violent behavior. Juveniles are unique in that they often cannot escape an abusive environment, and they may not have the maturity to adopt coping skills.

The Supreme Court and the Juvenile Death Penalty

Criminologists have argued that the Supreme Court has been slow to align its practices with overwhelmingly negative public opinion about the juvenile death penalty. Most of the legal debates have focused on Fourteenth and Eighth Amendment issues. One of the most influential Supreme Court opinions came about from a case in Oklahoma, where a sixteen-year-old boy named Eddings shot and killed a police officer and was sentenced to death. The Supreme Court ruled that the mitigating circumstances of the case, which were the petitioner's turbulent and abusive family history, the offender's emotionally disturbed state, and the offender's age, were not adequately considered in lower courts. The Supreme Court vacated Edding's death sentence. This was the first time the Supreme Court had viewed age as an important factor in determining the death sentence (*Eddings v. Oklahoma,* 455 U.S. 104, 1982).

Several years later, the Supreme Court heard another juvenile death penalty case, also from Oklahoma. In *Thomson v. Oklahoma*, the petitioner had, at age fifteen, participated in the killing of his brother-in-law and was subsequently sentenced to death. The Court debated whether the Eighth Amendment was violated because the state of Oklahoma had not set a minimum age limit for the death penalty. The Supreme Court held that executing someone who was under sixteen at the time of the offense was considered cruel and unusual, and the death sentence was again vacated (487 U.S. 815, 1988).

A third Supreme Court case that was influential in the development of the death penalty for juveniles was *Stanford v. Kentucky*. This case was also an Eighth Amendment challenge, as the petitioner claimed that sentencing a seventeen-year-old to death was cruel and unusual punishment. The Supreme Court held that it was constitutional to execute sixteen- and seventeen-year-olds and upheld the sentence. This case therefore set the minimum age limits for executing juveniles (492 U.S. 361, 1989).

Recent Supreme Court opinions set a more lenient tone for juveniles convicted in capital cases. In 2002, the Supreme Court held that juveniles who were mentally retarded could not be executed (*Atkins v. Virginia*, 536 U.S. 304, 2002). The most influential case to date was heard in 2004. In this case, Simmons was seventeen when he committed a murder in Missouri and was subsequently convicted and sentenced to death. Simmons appealed on the grounds that the death penalty for offenders under the age of eighteen was cruel and unusual. The appeal was launched on the premise of the decision in *Atkins v. Virginia*.

The Missouri Supreme Court agreed with the petitioner and vacated the death sentence. The case then moved to the Supreme Court. By a vote of 5 to 4, Supreme Court justices held that executing juveniles violated both the Eighth and Fourteenth Amendments, as both prohibit the execution of offenders who were under the age of eighteen at the time of their crime (*Roper v. Simmons,* 633 U.S. 1962). The Supreme Court opinion in this case refers often to evolving standards of decency that go hand-in-hand with evolving societies, thus justifying the shift in philosophy. This decision has ended the long-standing debate over the juvenile death penalty and has converted juvenile death sentences to life sentences without parole across the United States. However, if the pendulum in criminal justice swings again in favor of more punitive sentences, this decision could be challenged in the future.

See also Abused/Battered Children; Child Savers; Cognitive Theories

FURTHER READING

Death Penalty Information Center: http://www.deathpenaltyinfo.org.

English, D., Widom, C., & Brandford, C. (2001). *Childhood victimization and delinquency, adult criminality, and violent criminal behavior: A replication and extension.* Washington DC: Department of Justice.

Morreale, M., & English, A. (2004). Abolishing the death penalty for juvenile offenders: A background paper. *Journal of Adolescent Health, 35*, 335–339.

Oritz, A. (2004). *Cruel and unusual punishment: The juvenile death penalty, evolving standards of decency.* Washington DC: The Juvenile Justice Center of the American Bar Association.

Skovron, S., Scott, J., & Cullen, F. (1989). The death penalty for juveniles: An assessment of public support. *Crime and Delinquency, 35*(4), 546–561.

Vogel, B., & Vogel, R. (2003). The age of death: Appraising public opinion of juvenile capital punishment. *Journal of Criminal Justice, 31*(2), 169–183.

Monica L. P. Robbers

DELINQUENCY AND DRIFT THEORY

Introduction

The 1950s and 1960s was a period of social turbulence in the United States. The Korean War had ended, the Vietnam War was in full swing, the Cuban missile crisis was publicized, and there was cultural upheaval provided by the hippie and civil rights movements. During this time, sociologists David Matza and Gresham Sykes proposed a theory of social control called drift theory to explain why people change their behavior from law-abiding to lawbreaking. The drift hypothesis states that delinquents do not blindly follow delinquent cultural values, but instead are influenced by both conventional cultural values and delinquent cultural values. Therefore, such individuals find themselves drifting back and forth between the two sets of values.

The subculture of delinquency provides delinquents with values that enable them to disengage the demands of conventional society, thus allowing them to commit delinquent activities. Sykes and Matza developed a model of **techniques of neutralization** that delinquents follow when committing crime, helping them to rationalize their criminal actions.

Matza developed the idea of drift further. He proposed that individuals are capable of drifting from being completely law-abiding to being completely free of restraint. Although Matza maintained that most people live somewhere in between, some individuals move from one extreme in behavior to the other. This is not an overnight process, but is instead gradual. The very nature of the gradual drift process helps define an individual's behavior, similar to the process found in **differential association**.

Initially, when someone commits a delinquent act, he or she would feel guilty and counteract the delinquent act by behaving in a strict law-abiding manner. Then gradually he or she may drift back to delinquency. Matza describes drift as soft determinism in that the delinquent act is a combination of choice and determinism. Individuals will choose to commit crime when either preparation or desperation is present. Desperation is often involved during the first time that an offender commits a crime and is usually the result of dire circumstances. Preparation refers to the second time an individual commits a crime after the offender acknowledges that the crime was worth the risk and can be done again.

One of the most important reasons for drift from law-abiding behavior to lawbreaking behavior, wrote Matza, was a sense of injustice that a delinquent may feel. Injustice could be experienced through cognizance, competence, consistency, commensurability, and comparison. The level of injustice perceived by an individual directly affects their likelihood of drift.

Cognizance refers to the level of ownership a delinquent associates with the delinquent act. If he or she neutralizes the act, thereby taking little responsibility for it, the level of cognizance is low. Competence refers to the expertise of authority. If the delinquent feels that the person in authority is behaving unfairly toward him or her, drift toward delinquency is likely to increase, as the sense of injustice is likely to be great.

If a delinquent feels that not everyone is being treated the same, their perception of consistency in the justice system is distorted, and their level of perceived injustice will increase. Commensurability refers to whether the individual believes the act should even be punishable. Comparisons affect injustice and therefore drift when a delinquent perceives that laws apply to their group but not others. The best example of how comparison can affect perceptions of injustice and then drift is status offenses that apply to juveniles but not to adults.

Matza won the prestigious C. Wright Mills book award from the Society for the Study of Social Problems for his book on delinquency in drift in 1964.

Applications of Drift Theory

Applications of drift theory have appeared in both sociology and criminology. John Hagan and colleagues tested the premise of subterranean influences of self-interest on subcultural delinquency (the drift from law-abiding to lawbreaking behavior) and found that males were more likely to drift. Another study by Hagan and others examined Matza's ideas that adolescent friendships can add to drift toward delinquent subcultures. In this study, results indicated that girls were more affected by intimate friendships, and these friendships tend to support law-abiding behavior rather than lawbreaking behavior.

Criticisms of Drift Theory

One of the most oft-cited criticisms of drift theory is that it is difficult to empirically test. The concepts in the theory are largely cognitive, such as the sense of injustice and its impact on drift toward lawbreaking behavior. Another criticism is that the theory does not clearly specify how exactly the drift process begins. Travis Hirschi also criticized the theory, saying that it did not accurately describe delinquent behavior. He saw delinquency occurring because of a lack of social bonds and social controls, rather than a conscious decision to be delinquent.

See also Developmental Theories; Social Learning Theories; Subcultural Theories

FURTHER READING

Cullen, F., & Agnew, R. (2003). *Criminological theory: Past to present,* 2nd ed. Los Angeles: Roxbury Publishing.

Einstadter, W. (1995). *Criminological theory: An analysis of its underlying assumptions.* Fort Worth, TX: Harcourt Brace College Publishers.

Hagan, J., Hefler, G., Classen, G., Boehnke, K., & Merkens, Hans. (1998). Subterranean sources of subcultural delinquency beyond the American dream. *Criminology, 36*(2), 309–342.

Hirschi, T. (2001). *Causes of delinquency.* Somerest, NJ: Transaction.

Matza, D. (1964). *Delinquency and drift.* New York: Wiley and Sons.

Sykes, G., & Mazta, D. (1957). Techniques of neutralization: A theory of delinquency. *American Sociological Review, 5,* 664–670.

Monica L. P. Robbers

DELINQUENCY AS PROBLEM SOLVING THEORY. In many countries of the world, especially industrialized ones, juvenile delinquency is an increasing problem. All researchers agree that young people who live under difficult social and economic circumstances are most at risk of becoming delinquent. However, which particular circumstances these are and how they have to be weighted is still under discussion.

The Family

Problems in the family are identified as the ultimate source of juvenile delinquency. Cumulative family stressors significantly increase the likelihood that children develop behavioral problems. The family stressors identified include: parents having an unskilled or semiskilled job; overcrowded or large family; mother with depression or neurotic disorders; child who has been in the care of child protective services; criminal conviction of father; and marital discord. A family stressor in isolation has no significant effect on the likelihood of behavioral problems, but the interaction of two or more does, especially when the stressors tend to be chronic. Others mention further family stressors like high debts, alcohol and drug abuse of the parents, death of one or more family members, parents who suffer from psychosis, are unemployed, or are illiterate. On the other hand, research shows that children who receive careful upbringing less likely tend to start a criminal career.

In the underdeveloped world, youth often face additional stressors. Risk factors typical for underdeveloped regions of the world are HIV/AIDS and the death of parents during armed conflicts. Orphans of both are typically without a means of subsistence, housing, and other basic necessities, thus making them at greater risk for delinquency.

The consequences of a defunct family life for the juvenile can be dramatic and are best illustrated by case studies of domestic violence. Children who experience domestic violence, either as a witness or as a victim, are more likely to have psychological and cognitive problems than children raised in more stable families. Children who witness domestic violence are more endangered to develop post-traumatic stress disorder (PTSD). Symptoms of PTSD can include the reexperiencing of the trauma in their thoughts, preoccupation with the event, a reduction of normal activities, anxiety, fear, sleep problems, somatic complaints, and, what is especially important here, explosive outbursts of aggression. A recent study found children with PTSD to have greater externalizing behavioral problems than children who do not have PTSD. Witnessing violence between the father and mother, both directly and indirectly, affects the normal development of a child. These parents normally are not able to adequately accompany their child's development and address his or her everyday needs. They are also more likely to be inconsistent in their parenting style. Moreover, by witnessing spousal violence, the children may copy strategies of conflict resolution that are based on physical and verbal violence. Several studies suggest that children who observe violence in the parental environment may repeat this behavioral pattern later in life. Sons who have witnessed their father's violence are 1000 percent more likely to mirror this abusive behavior toward their partners as an adult. Moreover, children who are themselves exposed to violence in the family or in the community are at a greater risk of becoming either an offender or a victim of violence.

Children from disadvantaged families have fewer chances to find a legitimate occupation and are thus exposed to a higher risk of social marginalization, which results in their overrepresentation among perpetrators. This is especially true of boys, whereas girls are more prone to internalize behavioral problems, thus suffing greater rates of depression.

Alcohol and drug abuse as "self medication" are thought to serve a variety of functions for abused and neglected youth, including psychological and/or emotional escape from their abusive environment, alleviation of depression and anxiety, reduction of feelings of isolation and loneliness, and enhancement of self-esteem.

The Criminal Identity of Delinquents

The identity of a juvenile delinquent is complex, since it is, on the one hand, influenced by the delinquency itself and, on the other hand, by the person's ethnicity, social class, and gender. Construction of individual identity is often carried out within a peer group. The peer group plays an important role in the construction of gender roles and relations, including delinquent behavior.

Violence and conflict are constituent strategies in the construction of group and delinquent identities. Group identity and activity are established and maintained through conflict relations with other juvenile groups and society as a whole. Violence functions as a means for the integration of members into a gang, reinforcing their sense of identity, and thereby accelerating the process of group adaptation to the local environment. Those most likely to participate in delinquent activities are members of such "territorial gangs." According to statistical evidence, they commit three times as many crimes as juveniles and youths who are not gang members. Fighting, street extortion, and school violence are the most frequent offenses committed by these groups. In many cases juvenile delinquent groups are the starting point for an adult career in organized crime.

Peer groups are often ethnically based. Immigrants tend to exist at the margins of society and frequently fail to comply with social, legal, and economic standards of the majority. Thus they often seek refuge in groups that represent their social and cultural ideologies. Difference in cultural norms, as well as the acceptance of ethnic subcultures into mainstream society, results in cultural conflicts, which is linked to criminal activity. Violence can thus be seen as a means of "solving" violent conflict.

See also Abused/Battered Children; Developmental Theories; Gang Involvement, Theories on

FURTHER READING

Carlson, B. (1990). Adolescent observers of marital violence. *Journal of Family Violence, 5,* 285–299.

Cavaiola, A., & Schiff, M. (1989). Self-esteem in abused, chemically dependent adolescents. *Child Abuse and Neglect, 13,* 327–334.

Collins-Hall, L. (2001). Application of a social interactionist perspective to examine the effects of children's experiences of domestic violence on the development of juvenile delinquency and substance use. Unpublished dissertation, UMI Dissertation Services.

Dembo, R., Dertke, M., LaVoie, L., Borders, S., Washburn, M., & Schneider, J. Structural analysis among high risk adolescents. *Journal of Adolescence, 10,* 13–33.

Dembo, R., Williams, L., Getreu, A., Berry, E., LaVoie, L., Genung, J., Schmeidler, J., Wish, E., & Kern, J. (1990a). A longitudinal study of the relationship among alcohol use, marijuana/hashish use, cocaine use, and emotional/psychological functioning problems in a cohort of high risk youth. *International Journal of Addiction, 25,* 1341–1382.

Dembo, R., Williams, L., LaVoie, L., Berry, E., Getreu, A., Wish, E., Schmeidler, J., & Washburn, M. (1987). Physical abuse, sexual victimization, and illicit drug abuse: Replication of a structural analysis among a new sample of high risk youths. *Violence and Victims, 4,* 121–138.

Eth, S., & Pynoos, R. (1994). Children who witness the homicide of a parent. *Psychiatry, 57,* 287–307.

Fantuzzo, J., & Lindquist, F. (1989). The effects of observing conjugal violence on children: A review and analysis of research methodology. *Journal of Family Violence, 4,* 77–95.

Graham-Bermann, S., & Levendosky, A. (1998). Traumatic stress symptoms in children of battered women. *Journal of Interpersonal Violence, 13,* 111–128.

Ireland, T., & Widom, C. (1994). Childhood victimization and risk of alcohol and drug arrests. *International Journal of Addiction, 29,* 235–274.

James, O. (1995) *Juvenile violence in a winner-loser culture: Socio-economic and familial origins of the rise in violence against the person.* New York: Free Association Books.

Kilpatrick, K., & Williams, L. (1998). Potential mediators of post-traumatic stress disorder in child witnesses to domestic violence. *Child Abuse & Neglect 22,* 319–330.

Youth at the United Nations. World Youth Report, 2003. Available at: www.un.org/esa/ socdev/ unyin/wtr03.htm.

Ruth Erken

DELINQUENCY IN A BIRTH COHORT. Referring to a 1972 research-based book bearing this title, Wolfgang, Figlio, and Sellin's study is often called the Philadelphia Birth Cohort Study. Using a cohort sample of 9,945 adolescent males born in 1945, the researchers followed the boys from age ten to age seventeen. The entire cohort lived in Philadelphia, and records from police contacts were used to tally the number of offenses over a seven-year span. Thirty-five percent (3,475) of the boys had one or more police contacts. While this seems high, it also demonstrated that many boys did not experience police encounters. Of the subgroup with police encounters, the authors recorded 10,214 total contacts. They further examined the initiation of delinquent acts, age differences, offense seriousness and frequency, and the specialization in delinquent acts.

One-time offenders made up nearly half of the boys with police contacts (46.4 percent). This demonstrates that some boys do not continue and escalate their offenses. They are episodic in their delinquency and had no other police contact. Statistics on offenders committing two to four offenses revealed a proportion of 28 percent of the contact cohort. Finally, 6 percent of the juvenile cohort had police documents of five or more offenses. In total, this 6 percent had 5,305 police contacts, which was 52 percent of all documented offenses. The authors deemed those who had five or more police contacts chronic offenders. It is this finding that created an important social fact; a small proportion of juveniles—chronic delinquents—perpetrated a disproportionately large amount of delinquent acts. This group is often called the **chronic 6 percent**. Key additional findings were that offenders started delinquency by age fourteen and that some of them continued engaging in crime as adults.

Following this trailblazing publication, numerous studies created a new genre of delinquency research called cohort studies. These studies attempted to replicate and expand on the original findings by following juveniles into adulthood. Youth in Ohio and Wisconsin were subject to cohort studies. Overall, they confirmed the original Philadelphia Birth Cohort Study. The percentage of chronic delinquents, however, varied from 6 to 25 percent. Additional refinement in cohort research was generated with improvements in measurement and sampling.

A distinction began to be made among chronic delinquents: those committing serious offenses and those committing violent offenses. Chronic delinquents are those who are persistent offenders over a longer time period. Moreover, later studies demonstrated that chronic delinquents tend to be involved in serious offenses, violent offenses, and some in both. However, some violent and serious offenders are not chronic offenders, so an important distinction in criminology is between chronic/unchronic and serious/violent offenders.

The 2001 Philadelphia-Juvenile-Adult Career Study examined 27,160 males and females born in 1958 and examined juvenile police contacts until age twenty-six. Males were found to be much more chronic than females, and nonwhites had greater rates of chronicity. Males that were recorded as chronic delinquents are linked to adult crime involvement. Violent offenses are also predictive of some juveniles moving into adult crime. Now, many juvenile justice probation agencies engage in the identification of chronic, violent, and serious juvenile offenders and focus interventions and incapacitation toward the chronic few.

FURTHER READING

Hamparian, D., Davis, J., Jacobson, J., & McGraw, R. *The young criminal careers of the violent few.* Washington, DC: U.S. Department of Justice.

Kempf-Leonard, K., Tracy, P., & Howell, J. (2001). Serious, violent and chronic juvenile offenders: The relationship of delinquency subtypes to adult criminality. *Justice Quarterly, 18,* 449–478.

Wilson, J., & Howell, J. (1993). *A comprehensive strategy for serious, violent and chronic juvenile offenders.* Washington, DC: Office of Juvenile Justice and Delinquency Prevention.

Wolfgang, M., Figlio, R., & Sellin, T. (1972). *Delinquency in a birth cohort.* Chicago: University of Chicago Press.

James Steinberg

DETACHED STREET WORKERS. The goal of detached street or gang worker programs was to intervene in the lives of the most violent and delinquent gang members and channel their antisocial behaviors into more positive and prosocial activities. Street workers were truly detached from their office desks and spent their working hours in the gang's environment interacting with gang members in the streets, on their own turf, and in their clubhouses. Workers were expected to gain acceptance and establish a strong rapport with gang members by demonstrating empathy, understanding, and concern for each member.

Detached street workers fulfilled many functions and carried out numerous roles that required them to act as counselors, social coordinators, tutors, mentors, positive adult role models, and advocates or liaisons between gang members and the juvenile justice system. A street worker's typical day, or night, might involve planning a dance or athletic contest, trying to avert retaliatory violence against a rival gang, researching employment opportunities, facilitating a group counseling session, discussing a child's truancy with their parents, or simply hanging out with the gang members on the street corner.

The concept of the detached street worker evolved from the **Chicago Area Project**, which sought to revitalize disorganized inner-city communities by actively engaging residents in community planning, organizing, and problem solving. The New York City Youth Board began using street workers extensively in 1947, and the popularity of these programs grew considerably during the 1950s and into the mid-1960s, with street workers appearing in Los Angeles, Boston, Seattle, and San Francisco.

Research and evaluation of street worker programs, primarily studies of the Chicago Youth Development Project and the Roxbury Project, revealed that the impact and effectiveness of street worker programs was at best negligible or in most cases nonexistent. Many gang members who were assigned street workers actually incurred more police contacts, arrests, and court appearances than their counterparts who did not have an associated worker. Paradoxically, the use of street workers may have served to heighten the gang's negative reputation on the streets as only the most violent and volatile gangs were afforded street workers. Thus the gang's image, to both its members and rival gangs, may have been enhanced.

Critics have also put forth the theory that street workers unintentionally strengthened gang cohesiveness and unity through many of their organized events, which often inadvertently produced a prime opportunity for recruitment and subsequent growth in the gang's membership. The failure of street worker programs has also been attributed to poor program implementation, a lack of clearly defined goals and objectives, as well as role confusion among many of the workers who faced the dilemma of trying to build rapport while honoring their moral and legal obligation to report any criminal activities that were perpetrated by gang members.

See also Gang Sweeps; Gang Units, Police

FURTHER READING

Klein, M. (1971). *Street gangs and street workers*. Englewood Cliffs, NJ: Prentice-Hall.

Youth Gang Programs and Strategies (2005). United States Department of Justice, Office of Juvenile Justice and Delinquency Prevention. Available at: http://www.ncjrs.org/html/ojjdp/summary_ 2000_8/intervention.html.

Douglas L. Yearwood

DEVELOPMENTAL THEORIES

The Gluecks and Sampson and Laub

Many scholars and researchers maintain that the only way to truly understand juvenile delinquency and violence is to understand how it develops over time. These theorists generally use longitudinal studies to examine the life cycle of delinquent careers. Some of these are also called integrated theories, as they generally combine elements from a number of other theories. The earliest of this type of work was that of **Sheldon and Eleanor Glueck** of Harvard University in the 1930s. The Gluecks conducted a series of longitudinal studies involving known delinquents and utilized a variety of methods, including interviews and secondary analysis. Their goal was to determine which factors predicted continued offending. After comparing 500 delinquents with 500 nondelinquents, their primary conclusion was that early onset of delinquency was most linked with persistent offending. While the Gluecks identified a number of personal and social factors leading to persistent offending, they felt the most important was the family. The most vulnerable to delinquency, they determined, were children raised in large families with only one parent and with limited funds and educational access. They also found that physical and mental factors are associated with persistent delinquency, most notably low intelligence and mental disorders. In the 1980s, **John Laub and Robert Sampson** rekindled interest in the Gluecks' work, reanalyzing data found in the basement of the Harvard Law School Library. They published their book, *Crime in the Making: Pathways and Turning Points through Life*, in 1993. Sampson and Laub's analysis generally affirmed the Gluecks' findings. In recognition of the fact that different factors impact people throughout the life course, Sampson and Laub developed a theory they referred to as "sociogenic" and named Age-Graded. They assert that there are two critical life events that enable young delinquents to desist: marriage and career. Sampson and Laub also maintain that social capital, or positive relations with individuals and institutions, and social bonds can reduce the likelihood of long-term delinquency. An interesting adaptation of Sampson and Laub's work is focusing on how victimization as a child or adolescent impacts life-course offending.

The Cambridge Youth Study

Another important longitudinal study of delinquent careers followed 411 boys from London who were born in 1953. Self-reports, interviews, and psychological testing were used to identify factors involved in crime over the life-course. Persistent offenders exhibit deviant traits as early as eight, including dishonesty and aggressiveness, according to this study. Chronic offenders typically began as property offenders, were born into low-income families with criminal parents, and have delinquent siblings. As young people, the career criminals received poor parental supervision and were often dealt with inconsistently and harshly. Most chronic offenders had delinquent friends and had little educational success. They were more likely to get into fights and to have erratic work histories. The Cambridge Youth Study, as it is known, found that most career criminals do not specialize in a particular type of offense. Drawing on the results of this study, researchers attempted to identify factors that caused offenders to desist. Shy individuals, those with few friends at age eight, those having nondeviant families, and those who are highly regarded by their mothers, are least likely to persist in crime as adults.

Contemporary Developmental Theories

Contemporary developmental theories still emphasize the age of onset as a critical variable in persistent offending. Research has continued to support this notion, finding that the most serious adult offenders began very early, even at preschool age, and exhibited a variety of antisocial behavior, including truancy, animal cruelty, lying, and theft. One study found males who begin offending prior to the age of fourteen were most likely to engage in serious offending by age eighteen, and those who were involved in the most serious offenses had exhibited antisocial behavior the earliest.

Some developmental theories stress the importance of important events, or life transitions, in guiding whether an individual persists or desists in offending. Important transitions, which are supposed to occur in succession, include completing education, leaving the parents' home, entering the workforce in a career, finding permanent relationships, marrying, and beginning their own family. When transitions occur too early—as in the case of teen pregnancy—or too late—when a student fails to graduate on time—delinquency may result. Further, disruption of one transition is likely to disrupt others as well. For instance, teen pregnancy may set back graduation. Some people are more at-risk than others, thus are more susceptible to delinquent involvement when a transition is disrupted. Impoverished teens that become pregnant, for instance, are less likely to graduate and consequently are more likely to engage in delinquent activity. In contrast, positive transitions can help an individual cease being delinquent. Students who graduate and move on to college, work, or military service may cease delinquent activity.

Delinquent Pathways

One specific form of developmental theory stresses that there are multiple pathways to a life of crime. Rolf Loeber and associates used longitudinal data to develop three distinct paths: authority-conflict, covert, and overt. In the first path, stubborn behavior at an early age may lead an individual to become defiant or disobedient. That individual may then become author-ity-avoidant, doing such things as staying out late, running away, and skipping school. The covert pathway begins with minor devious behavior, such as lying and shoplifting, which escalates to property damage. The behavior then escalates to more serious criminality, such as stealing cars, dealing drugs, and breaking and entering. In the overt pathway, individuals begin by exhibiting aggressive behavior, such as annoying others or bullying peers. They next engage in physical altercations and then to criminal acts of violence, such as robbery and assault. A person might enter more than one pathway. These individuals are the most persistent offenders. Some research has supported the idea of distinct delinquent pathways.

Delinquent Trajectories

Terrie Moffitt developed a theory called Delinquent Trajectories. Moffitt posits that, for most people, antisocial behavior peaks in adolescence. She calls these people adolescent-limiteds (AL). These offenders generally engage in minor forms of delinquency considered typical of teenagers. Until the age of sixteen, the peer group is highly influential. For others, called life-course persisters (LC), offending continues into adulthood. It is the combination of family dysfunction and neurological problems, according to Moffitt, that makes some persist. Poor parenting prior to age fourteen leads these individuals to commit deviant behaviors and to become involved with delinquent peer groups, who reinforce the deviant behavior. Those who start their delinquent behavior after the age of fourteen follow a slightly different path; they first become involved with delinquent peers, who then lead them to delinquent involvement. Life-course persisters tend to have limited verbal ability, which often impacts their success in school. They seem to mature faster and thus are more prone to early sexual involvement and drug use. While adolescent-limiteds focus mostly on one form of misbehavior, such as drug abuse or shoplifting, life-course persisters tend to engage in a variety of deviant behaviors. More recently, Moffitt has adapted her theory to explain that some AL offenders may persist into adulthood if certain "snares," such as drug dependency or failure to complete an education, are present.

Criticisms

While many agree with the basic idea that any theory should explain delinquency over the life course, critics maintain these theories are too broad to have a great deal of explanatory power. Surely their predictive and explanatory power for all forms of delinquency of all age groups is somewhat limited, critics contend. Further, many of the studies testing these theories are with small, homogeneous samples. In particular, these theories may not adequately address gender differences. Loeber et al's theory, for instance, was derived from a longitudinal study of males in Pittsburgh, and the Gluecks (as well as Sampson and Laub) studied only poor white males. Longitudinal work has found that Sampson and Laub's two key factors for desistance—marriage and military service—did not explain desistance among serious adolescent female delinquents. More recent research is attempting to better discern gender differences in life-course offending.

See also Interactionist Theories; Social Development Model

FURTHER READING

Giordano, P., Cernkovich, S., & Rudolph, J. (2002). Gender, crime, and desistance: Toward a theory of cognitive transformation. *American Journal of Sociology, 107*(4), 990–1064.

Hagan, J. (2003). S/He's a rebel: Toward a sequential stress theory of delinquency and gendered pathways to disadvantage in emerging adulthood. *Social Forces, 82*(1), 53–87.

Loeber, R., Farrington, D., Stouthamer-Loeber, M., Moffitt, T., & Caspi, A. (1998). The development of male offending: Key findings from the Pittsburgh Youth Study. *Studies in Crime and Crime Prevention, 3,* 197–247.

Macmillan, R. (2001). Violence and the life course: The consequences of victimization for personal and social development. *Annual Review of Sociology, 1,*1–22.

Moffitt, T. (1993). "Life-course-persistent" and "adolescent limited" antisocial behavior: A developmental taxonomy. *Psychological Review, 100,* 674–701.

Sampson, R., & Laub, J. (1983). *Crime in the making: Pathways and turning points through life.* Cambridge, MA: Harvard University Press.

Shoemaker, D. (2005). *Theories of delinquency,* 5th edition. New York: Oxford.

Thornberry, T. (1997). *Developmental theories of crime and delinquency.* New Brunswick, NJ: Transaction.

Laura L. Finley

DIFFERENCES BETWEEN JUVENILE JUSTICE AND CRIMINAL JUSTICE.

The juvenile justice system is fundamentally different from the adult (criminal) justice system. The current American system of juvenile justice was founded on the British doctrine of **parens patriae**, or the state as parent, wherein the state intervenes as necessary according to its interest in the welfare of a child. It was based on several other underlying premises: that children are worth "saving," which can occur through nonpunitive measures; children need to be nurtured, and part of nurturing is to avoid stigmatizing labeling processes; justice must be individualized in order to reform a delinquent youth; and noncriminal procedures are necessary to address the needs of the child. Primary goals of the juvenile justice system are rehabilitation and treatment rather than punishment and deterrence, as with the adult criminal system.

There are several important distinctions between the systems. At the earliest phase of the process, juveniles can be apprehended for acts, called status offenses, that are not criminal when committed by adults. The standards for arresting a juvenile are looser as well. Access to juvenile court records is usually highly restricted, whereas adult criminal court records are open to the public. Juvenile justice is handled under a casework approach. The caseworker attempts to ensure the system acts in the child's best interest. The child attends a hearing rather than a trial. Protections for juveniles are far more limited than they are for adults. Juveniles have fewer protections against unreasonable searches and seizures, particularly in school settings, and self-incrimination provisions may vary as well. Whether juveniles can waive Miranda rights is also in question. In addition to legal facts, the hearing takes into consideration the child's specific needs and personal history. Thus, parents and others may be very involved through the entire process. Consistent with the philosophical differences, terminology differs between the courts. Rather than being "indicted," a "petition" is filed against a juvenile. Rather than being judged "guilty," as in the case of criminal offenders, juvenile offenders are judged "delinquent." Juveniles have no right to trial by jury, as adults do.

Because a juvenile's case is heard only by a judge and with far fewer formalities, juvenile cases are processed far more quickly than are adults in the criminal courts. Sentencing includes a significant rehabilitative component and is usually flexible compared to adult sentences, which are often predetermined by the nature of the offense and criminal history. Where adult defendants have the right to apply for bond or bail, juvenile offenders do not. At the discretion of law enforcement, juveniles may be held indefinitely under preventative detention (for the protection of the child and/or community). In general, however, juveniles are not held beyond their twenty-first birthday, and the most commonly assigned punishment is probation. Many juveniles are released into their parents' care, something that cannot occur in the adult system. While it was common practice for some time, juveniles are no longer to be held in facilities with adults. The use of **waivers** has muddied this issue some, and some rural areas have difficulty establishing separate facilities. Until recently, both juveniles and adults could be assigned the death penalty. The Supreme Court declared that **capital punishment** for juveniles unconstitutional in 2005.

Modern schools of thought tend to believe a preventative approach to violence is more effective than a punitive approach. Research has also shown that sending juveniles through adult criminal court rather than juvenile court does not lower recidivism. Over the past few decades, however, there has been a shift in societal opinion about the juvenile justice system. In response to a spike in juvenile violent crime during the early 1990s, there was a public outcry for reform, stating the juvenile justice system was ineffective in its response to juvenile violence. Many state legislators pushed for a "get tough" approach that would send more violent juvenile offenders through the adult criminal courts. Today, more juveniles are being tried as adults in cases of violent crime.

Research shows that, in contrast to public opinion, juveniles are not committing more violent acts. A greater number of juveniles seem to be committing violence, but these statistics may be skewed given the increase of juveniles sent through the justice system as a result of the legislation from the mid-1990s. Arrests of juveniles for violent crimes have decreased consistently since 1994. Adults still commit the large majority of violence and have higher recidivism rates than juveniles.

Some, such as Barry Feld, have called for the abolition of the juvenile justice system. They feel the trend toward making the juvenile system more like the adult system, without significantly altering the protections juveniles are afforded, is making the distinctions between the two systems obsolete. For instance, in 2000, California voters, believing juvenile crime was out-of-control, passed Proposition 21, the Gang Violence and Juvenile Crime Prevention Act. Proposition 21 seriously reduces the confidentiality in the juvenile court, limits the use of probation with certain juvenile offenders, and increases the ability of prosecutors to waive juveniles to adult courts. Critics such as Feld maintain the system cannot be fixed due to conflicting purposes and shifting priorities.

The federal government has also passed legislation that alters the role of juvenile courts. The Department of Justice Authorization Act for Fiscal Year 2003 operates on the premise that juveniles must be accountable for their crime, and thus must face swift and certain sanctions proportionate to their offense.

FURTHER READING

Feld, B. (1999). *Bad kids: Race and the transformation of the juvenile court.* New York: Oxford University Press.

Humes, E. (1996). *No matter how loud I shout: A year in the life of juvenile court.* New York: Simon & Schuster.

Krisberg, B., & Austin, J. (1993). *Reinventing juvenile justice.* Newbury Park, CA: Sage.

Mahoney, K. (2005, May). Juvenile justice tips & information. Relentless Defense Website: http://www.relentlessdefense.com/juvenile.html.

Office of Juvenile Justice and Delinquency Prevention. (2005, May). Juvenile justice: A century of change. National Criminal Justice Reference Service Website http://www.ncjrs.org/html/ojjdp/9912_2/juv1.html.

WGBH Educational Foundation. (2005, May). Juvenile vs. adult justice. Public Broadcasting System Website: http://www.pbs.org/wgbh/pages/frontline/shows/juvenile/stats/juvvsadult.html.

Adam Doran

DIFFERENTIAL ASSOCIATION THEORY

General Description

Edwin Sutherland established differential association when he took some existing theoretical ideas and formed them into a theory of criminal behavior in 1939. Sutherland believed that crime was not biologically or economically driven, but rather is learned through the processes of socialization. He argued that since crime is a socially or politically defined phenomenon, we can learn to take part in it just as we would any other socially created phenomenon.

The key premise in Sutherland's theory is that criminal behavior is learned through the same process that any other behavior is learned. It is not thought up anew by every individual, but learned from others. Accordingly, the most significant learning comes via face-to-face interaction through communication, rather than from television, movies, or media outlets. From these interactions, individuals learn techniques of crime from those around them, just as one would learn techniques to undertake any other occupation.

Differential association theory contends that people learn behavior through developing a series of definitions that are either favorable or unfavorable to carry out that behavior. These definitions can change over time because one is likely to encounter people with diverse opinions about breaking the law. A person commences criminal behavior when the ratio of definitions favorable to breaking the law outweighs those unfavorable toward breaking the law.

Another important component of this theory involves the source of the communications that one encounters. Associations that are more intense, have a longer duration, are given more priority, and are more frequent have the greatest ability to influence one's behavior. Some theorists contend that the intensity and priority of an association can outweigh other significant relationships, such as those with peers that occur with greater frequency. Therefore, definitions provided by a parent having an intense relationship with a child may still outweigh definitions provided by other children who the child is around for six hours a day.

History

Differential association theory was formed in part via early imitation theory, which focused on people's tendency to imitate and repeat behavior that they observe. These imitation theories were, in part, a response to the biological theories present at the turn of the twentieth century. These theories critiqued the notion that behavior was biologically determined and focused attention on the socialization process.

Again, Edwin Sutherland was the father of differential association, but a number of different researchers have continued and popularized his work, starting with Donald Cressey. Differential association theory is classified by some today as a social learning theory. Others see it as being separate from social learning theories, which have taken the ideas of imitation and differential association and integrated them with psychological and biological processes.

Legacy of Differential Association Theory

As with most popular theories that have existed for a significant amount of time, differential association has withstood a number of criticisms. Perhaps the most consistent criticism is that it is difficult to thresh out the impact of learning from biology in explaining violent crime. For instance, if a father abuses his wife in front of their child and that child later abuses his wife, it is difficult to determine whether the underlying cause is biologically impacted or is learned behavior. In addition, while violent criminals may learn to use certain techniques in their trade or mimic certain styles or strategies, learning still may not explain the underlying motivation to commit the attacks or the lack of conscience or neutralized conscience that it may take to undertake some of the actions. Also, while one may learn behavior from others, his or her abilities, skills, confidence, and opportunity may play a greater role in the likelihood of undertaking crime.

Despite criticism, differential association theory remains one of the most popular theories in criminology and criminal justice. Many theorists are impressed by its ability to explain white-collar as well as blue-collar crime. It also is helpful in attempts to explain individual differences in behavior between two similar children living in the same neighborhood or essentially the same environment. Differential association theory contends that everyone encounters different definitions toward law-breaking, even those living next door to one another. For instance, the definitions provided by one strong grandmother figure with an intense hold on a child may be given priority over the communications given by others in the community.

Differential association theory has also had a significant impact on criminal justice and social policy. Community revitalization plans often use the premises of this theory in pursuing stronger Boys and Girls clubs, Police Youth Leagues, Big Brothers and Big Sisters operations, and other programs that include positive **mentoring** of youth.

All one has to do is look at the popularity of the phrase "he fell in with the wrong crowd" to realize the powerful impact that differential association theory has on the beliefs of society.

Although Sutherland lived in a time before television and when the impact of the media was less obvious, future generations of researchers have now begun researching this topic. Today, policy surrounding television and movie viewing, as well as Internet activity, has been significantly impacted by differential association theory. Given this information age in which we now live, it is likely that differential association theory will be a popular theory for years to come.

See also Differential Identification Theory

FURTHER READING

Adams, M. (1996). Labeling and differential association: Towards a generalsocial learning theory of crime and deviance. *American Journal of Criminal Justice, 20,* 147–163.

Alarid, L., Velmer, B., & Cullen, F. (2000). Gender and crime among felony offenders: Assessing the generality of social control and differential association theories. *Journal of Research in Crime and Delinquency, 37,* 171–201.

Hochstetler, A., Copes, H., & DeLisi, M. (2002). Differential association in group and solo offending. *Journal of Criminal Justice, 30,* 559–573.

Merton, R. (1997). On the evolving synthesis of differential association and anomie theory: A perspective from sociology of science. *Criminology, 35,* 517–525.

Brion Sever

DIFFERENTIAL IDENTIFICATION THEORY. Differential identification theory is a learning theory of crime, first introduced in 1956 by Daniel Glaser as an extension to Edwin Sutherland's **differential association theory**. Differential identification embraces a differential association learning perspective on criminality; however, Glaser's theory posits that the process of learning criminality may begin before an individual is directly exposed to others who exhibit patterns of criminal behavior. According to differential identification theory, the criminal learning process starts when an individual self-identifies with real or imaginary criminal role models. Thus, in differential identification theory, the process of becoming a criminal is primarily guided by a set of psychological factors that steer an individual's desires toward emulation of criminal roles rather than noncriminal role interpretations.

Differential identification recognizes a preliminary or anticipatory phase of socialization where an individual actively seeks potential mentors from among a range of groups with whom he or she wishes to be associated. The differential identification process not only guides the selection of associates but also affects the impact and potential influence of any given association on individual behavior.

Differential identification theory also emphasizes that potential role models need not be physically proximate or even real to be effective in the learning process. Individuals can just as easily identify with distant figures or mass media personas as they can with real people in interactive social settings. This aspect of differential identification makes the theory practical for use in explaining the impact of television, comic books, video games, and other media on juvenile violence.

Critics of differential identification theory argue that the theory is limited because it interprets the learning process as primarily autistic as opposed to social and interactive. Other critics argue that identification is neither necessary nor sufficient for a learning process to be effective.

FURTHER READING

Glaser, D. (1956). Criminality theories and behavioral images. *American Journal of Sociology, 61*, 433–444.

Glaser, D. (1960). Differential association and criminological prediction. *Social Problems, 8*, 6–14.

Laub, J. (1983). *Criminology in the making: An oral history.* Boston: Northeastern University Press.

Williams, F., & McShane, M. (2004). *Criminological theory.* Upper Saddle River, NJ: Prentice Hall.

Edward L. Powers

DIFFERENTIAL OPPORTUNITY THEORY. Building on concepts from social disorganization, strain, differential association, and subcultural theories, Cloward and Ohlin propose three primary ideas about delinquency. First, from **social disorganization theory**, Cloward and Ohlin maintain that crime is largely focused in lower-class neighborhoods. Second, from Robert Merton's **strain theory**, Cloward and Ohlin maintain that economic opportunities are severely limited, at least in conventional institutions, for some Americans. Blocked aspirations cause people to have low self-concept and to become frustrated. Third, they assert that these frustrations lead to delinquency, more specifically, gang subcultures. This is learned behavior, as Edwin Sutherland pointed out in his **differential association theory**.

Cloward and Ohlin proposed four categories of lower-class, delinquent youth. Type I youth seek to improve their economic position by moving toward the middle class. Type II youth wish to improve their status, but are not improving their economic position. Type III youth are working on improving their economic position but are not interested in attaining middle-class membership. Type IV youth reject both middle-class membership and improvement of their economic position. According to Cloward and Ohlin, Type III youth are the most serious delinquents. They prefer conspicuous consumption—fancy cars and clothes, for instance—yet they are not interested in adopting middle-class means to get them.

Cloward and Ohlin then identified three types of gangs that Type III youth will form. A criminal gang is primarily involved in theft, a conflict gang is most prone to be violent, and a retreatist gang is mostly involved in drug-related behaviors. The formation of a specific type of gang is dependent on neighborhood characteristics. Individuals in different neighborhoods learn to adjust to the frustrations of "position discontent" in distinct ways.

Criminal gangs are generally formed when there is highly organized adult criminal activity in a lower-class neighborhood. Here, the criminal adults become role models for youth, as well as their tutors in "how to" commit specific offenses. Cloward and Ohlin propose that, in this type of neighborhood, there is a stable relationship between the criminal adults and the conventional adults. Some even operate between the two, acting as "fences" in which they sell illegal goods through conventional businesses. Further, law enforcement and politicians in the area often look the other way or even accept bribes from the criminals. The effect is that gang activity in these communities tends to be more businesslike and thus is more likely to involve theft than violence—more like the common notion of organized crime. Youth learn to adjust to the frustrations of blocked goals by serving as apprentices to adults.

Other lower-class communities that also legitimate opportunities are characterized by far less stability and seem to have no form of adult role models. In these communities, youth form conflict, or violent, gangs as a means of obtaining some form of status and success. Violence is expressive, not instrumental. Those adult criminals who do reside in these communities are generally involved in low-skill, disorganized, and typically unsuccessful efforts.

Retreatist gangs are referred to as "double failures," those who succeed in neither the legitimate nor criminal world. Some will not become complete failures; rather, they will take the position of "corner boys." Many times, retreatist gangs are the result of failed involvement in either of the two other forms.

Evaluations

Interviews with lower-class youth, including gang members, do not typically support the notion that they feel their aspirations have been blocked. What seems to matter is whether aspirations and expectations are similar. Research has found the most delinquent youth are those with both low aspirations and expectations, rather than those with high aspirations and low expectations. Some research supports that the relationship is actually the reverse—that the delinquency occurs first, and this leads to blocked aspirations and opportunities.

Research has offered more support for the notion that different types of gangs form in different communities, although some find different types than those outlined by Cloward and Ohlin. Some research supports a "parent delinquent subculture" that explains all gangs and from which specific gang subcultures emerge. In sum, evaluations tend to confirm Cloward and Ohlin's ideas on what gangs do, but not on why they form.

Criticisms

One problem with research assessing differential opportunity theory is how the concepts of aspirations, expectations, and opportunities are measured. Self-reports on questionnaires may simply be inadequate to measure these complex concepts. Further, most tests of differential opportunity theory, as well as other anomie or strain theories, involve the use of official government statistics that may not be valid or reliable. Like many strain-related theories, Cloward and Ohlin are criticized for focusing only on lower-class delinquency.

Policy Implications

There are really two primary types of interventions that follow strain-related theories: reducing aspirations and increasing opportunities. Many are leery of reducing aspirations in any organized fashion, asserting this would be far too close to a caste system. Consequently, most programs are intended to increase opportunities.

In the 1960s, delinquency prevention programs founded on differential opportunity and other strain and social disorganization-related theories were popular and received federal funding. Robert Kennedy, then attorney general, read Cloward and Ohlin's book and asked Lloyd Ohlin to help craft federal policy regarding delinquency. The result was the Juvenile Delinquency Prevention and Control Act of 1961, which was intended to improve education, create job opportunities, organize lower-class communities, and provide services to those in need. The 1961 legislation was a precursor to Lyndon B. Johnson's "War on Poverty." One of the more ambitious programs was New York City's Mobilization for Youth (MOBY), which received more than $50 million in federal funding. MOBY was intended to create employment opportunities, increase job skills of youth, help minorities overcome workplace discrimination, coordinate social services, and sponsor social action groups in the sixty-seven-square-block area of Manhattan. MOBY also spawned at least seventeen similar programs in the early 1960s. Despite what sounds like a great deal of money, MOBY was always underfunded, and many question whether any of the goals were ever truly achieved. Some assert that MOBY and programs like it were simply too radical for the politicians who initially supported them and not radical enough to effect the dramatic social change needed to reduce delinquency rates. Poor citizens did begin to support changes, including rent strikes, legal action for welfare recipients, and the collection of data about discrimination and housing code violations. Unfortunately, these participants were often denounced as "Commies." In other cases, once a movement began, it was taken over by bureaucracies to serve their own interests. According to criminologist Richard Quinney, the idea that a mass movement of the poor might be gaining momentum scared the powers that be. Richard B. Nixon dismantled these programs when he became president in 1968.

FURTHER READING

Cloward, R., & Ohlin, L. (1960). *Delinquency and opportunity: A theory of delinquent gangs.* New York: Free Press.

Helfgot, J. (1981). *Professional reforming: Mobilization for youth and the failure of social science.* Lexington, MA: Heath.

Shoemaker, D. (2005). *Theories of delinquency,* 5th ed. New York: Oxford.

Vold, G., Bernard, T., & Snipes, J. (1998). *Theoretical criminology,* 4th ed. New York: Oxford.

Laura L. Finley

DIVERSION. In 1967, The President's Commission on Law Enforcement and the Administration of Justice set forth a call for local communities to create options for addressing the needs of youthful offenders. In large measure, the recommendation was driven by concerns that experiences in the traditional juvenile justice system may invite effects that are more harmful than beneficial. Scholars particularly contended that the juvenile justice system stigmatized young people for relatively minor violations of the law. Diversion programs, as a consequence, were developed as an alternative means of attending to the needs of youths facing legal charges. The general purposes of diversion programs are to focus on bettering young people's social skills, self-concepts, and attitudes; to educate youths about the legal system while appropriately redressing offenses; and to reduce the likelihood of continued involvement with illegal activity.

Although not confined to such populations, diversion program officials often work with first-time offenders who are charged with relatively petty crimes. Examples of well-known models include detention diversion, such as The Key Program, Inc. based in Boston, Massachusetts, and **teen courts** that exist throughout the nation. When creating diversion programs, agencies are urged to consider the following questions: (1) What ages will be included? (2) Which crimes will be included and excluded? (3) How will parents, guardians, and families be included? (4) What linkages, if any, will exist with other stakeholder organizations? (5) How long will the program last, including follow-up procedures? and (6) How will the program be evaluated?

Supporters of diversion initiatives argue that youth participation meets a variety of needs ranging from those of the young people involved to the elements of the juvenile justice system. For example, scholarly investigations suggest that a program's success is influenced by several key factors. On one level, professionals are assigned fewer cases in comparison to officials with the juvenile court system. The reduced load enables individuals to work closely and intensely with the young people in their charge. Diversion initiatives, on a second level, frequently target nonviolent crimes. Hence, alternative arrangements work to alleviate overcrowding in traditional courts and detention facilities that are assigned the responsibility of working with individuals who have committed serious offenses. Critics, however, contend that youth services suffer from an inadequate number of agencies to meet current needs. Such limitations may give rise to a number of unintended consequences, such as net widening, in which diversion aims are subverted by increasing rather than decreasing the number of young people in the juvenile justice system.

Additionally, researchers have developed serious concerns regarding patterns of differential treatment based on race. To date, a number of studies provide compelling evidence that youths of color are less likely to be diverted to alternative programs than whites. Discrepancies in diversion rates, social scientists argue, seem to demonstrate that people of color are processed and retained through the juvenile justice system at elevated rates. Further, people of color are more likely sentenced to detention and incarceration. Data gathered from studies of diversion programs have led some authors to conclude that disproportionate incarceration rates among African Americans, in particular, are linked with an absence of diversion options.

Despite a growing knowledge base focused on the role of diversion programs, researchers continue to possess a narrow understanding of such efforts from the perspectives of program participants themselves. Future scholars are encouraged to forge new directions in their work by conducting robust qualitative studies that capture the experiences and perspectives of program officials, families, and, of course, youths themselves. Studies conducted in this vein would mark an important step toward identifying ways to best meet the needs of juveniles in local communities.

FURTHER READING

Chernoff, Nina W., & Watson, Bernadine H. 2000. *An investigation of Philadelphia's youth aid panel: A community-based diversion program for first-time youthful offenders.* Philadelphia, PA: Public/Private Ventures.

Office of Juvenile Justice and Delinquency Prevention. 1999. *Detention diversion advocacy: An evaluation.* Washington, DC: Office of Justice and Delinquency Prevention.

Carla R. Monroe

DRUG ENFORCEMENT AGENCY (DEA). The Drug Enforcement Agency (DEA) is a law enforcement agency that concentrates on deterring the sale, manufacture, and distribution of illicit drugs. It was formed in 1973 by the Department of the Treasury and the U.S. Department of Health, Education and Welfare and has since coordinated with other federal and state agencies to deter the supply and demand for drugs. The resources and mission of the DEA have expanded considerably since its inception, with the number of special agents and total employees more than tripling in a little over thirty years. Today, the DEA is involved in the investigation of major violations of drug laws, investigation of drug gangs, drug intelligence, drug seizure and forfeiture, training other governments in suppression strategies, and liaison work in international drug control programs. Moreover, the DEA is increasing its presence in aviation control, computer forensics, money laundering, and border control. Although often lauded for its highly organized and high-tech response to drug abuse, the DEA has also come under much scrutiny by critics of the drug war and proponents of drug policy change.

FURTHER READING

Lock, E., Timberlake, J., & Rasinski, K. (2002). Battle fatigue: Is public support waning for war-centered drug control strategies? *Crime and Delinquency, 48,* 380–398.

U.S. Department of Justice Website: http://www.usdoj.gov/dea/.

Brion Sever

EDUCATIONAL OPPORTUNITY AND JUVENILE VIOLENCE. In

Moral Education, Emile Durkheim talked about the importance of circular education, especially as it relates to children. Durkheim's position is that education is the vehicle through which members of society, especially youths, are socialized to meet the needs of our values and culture. When that same society decides that a segment of its citizens are not worth the exposure to this mechanism of socialization, the society must blame itself for the consequences of such a decision. Several researchers are clear on the fact that when society isolates a segment of the population, that group becomes bound to set their own values, which may not be consistent with those of the popular culture.

Race socialization is one of the tools used to separate one's group values from those of the dominant group. African-American youths are usually in the middle of this debate. Research has shown, however, that the lack of understanding of youths of color is responsible for their behavior more frequently being defined as aggressive, violent, or delinquent. Educational opportunity and quality education are necessary to fight the problem of youth violence. It was not too long ago, in *Brown v. Board of Education*, that African Americans were legally allowed access to legitimate education that had been available to most Americans for many decades. Some minority groups distrust the political and economic systems of the society and therefore any institution within them. The past denial to quality educational opportunities is seen by many scholars as a crucial contributor to youth violence, especially among minority groups and particularly African Americans. There is what some refer to as an achievement gap among various groups.

In addition, there is significant poverty in the United States, particularly in minority communities. Ten years ago, child poverty reached epidemic proportions within the United States. Over fourteen million children, according to the Bureau of the Census, were living in poverty. Eighteen percent of them experience extreme poverty. This situation interacts with the lack of quality education and is a constant correlate of juvenile violence. In impoverished homes, single parenthood dominates family arrangements. Youths who are raised in impoverished, single-parent homes, who are unsupervised, and who are denied educational opportunity or quality education may experience low self-esteem and are more prone to violence.

A series of violent criminal events in our schools has shown legislators across the country that they must find solutions to juvenile violence. Some of our nation's schools are referred to as "persistently dangerous," and some believe that our public schools have become the most dangerous environment in our society. Researchers have verified that long-term public education campaigns on violence prevention, family education, alcohol and other drug prevention, and gun safety curriculums in school are effective strategies to help prevent juvenile violence. A significant number of youths in our public schools fear victimization to and from school. Some research indicates that almost one-fifth of our nation's students are afraid to use school bathrooms because they are often sites for assaults and other forms of victimization.

Studies show that from 1998 to 2002, teachers were the victims of approximately 234,000 nonfatal crimes at school, including 144,000 thefts and 90,000 violent crimes. The U.S. Department of Education School Safety Report indicates that more than 6,000 teachers are threatened each year, and 200 are physically injured by students. This type of environment is not conducive to a quality education.

Unfortunately, many communities in the country are plagued with disorganization. **Social disorganization** is more likely to be found in minority communities where poverty, violence, and delinquency interact. Children who are raised in disorganized communities are more likely to be poor, unsupervised, and exposed to drug use and violence, and experience inadequate education and a lack of proper nutrition and clothing. Research has shown that birth weight, nutrition, housing quality, and access to health care contribute to the relationship between Socioeconomic status (SES) and educational outcome. Many children come to school hungry, dirty, and angry, and they lack enough sleep. These kids can be disruptive in class and are usually punished by those who supervise them. The inadequate response to the children's cry for help was manifested in several violent criminal events across the country. Furthermore, **bullying** and sexual harassment has increased tremendously on our public school grounds.

While no school can claim to be without violence, some schools are safer than others. This safety is dependent on the presence or absence of a variety of characteristics, including school-based risk factors of poor design and use of school space, overcrowding, lack of caring but firm disciplinary procedures, insensitivity and poor accommodation to multicultural factors, student alienation, rejection of at-risk students by teachers and peers, and anger and resentment at school routines and demands for conformity. Characteristics of safer schools include a positive school climate and atmosphere with social and emotional learning, clear and high performance expectations for all students, inclusionary values and practices throughout the school, strong student bonding to the school environment and the schooling process, high levels of student participation and parent involvement in schools, and provision of opportunities for skill acquisition and social development.

In sum, violence is preventable as several causal factors have been indentified: poverty, institutionalized and individual racism, intolerance of differences, abuse, lack of parental involvement, and the breakdown in family structures. Youth violence is fueled by lack of hope, a disjuncture between an individual's dream and the American dream, including the belief that there is nothing to lose. Involving youth and developing community consensus is essential to an effective public education process to deal with the problem of educational opportunity and juvenile violence.

FURTHER READING

Dedman, B. (1999). Government team seeks explanation for violence. *Register Guard* (Iowa) 8A.

Jones, N., & Martinez, S. (2005, October). The violence prevention initiative: Accomplishments, challenges and lesson learned. Available from: www.tcwf.org/pub_lesson.

National Center on Education, Disability, and Juvenile Justice. (n.d.). Available at: www.edjj.org.

Office of the United Nations High Commissioner on Human Rights. (n.d.). United Nations guidelines for the prevention of juvenile delinquency. Available at: www.ohchr.org/english/law/juvenile.html.

Smith, B. (2000). Marginalized youth, delinquency, and education: The need for critical-interpretive research. *Urban Review, 32*(3).

U.S. Department of Education. (1993). Annual report on school safety 2004. Washington, DC: American Psychological Association.

Evaristus Obinyan

FAMILY RELATIONS AND JUVENILE VIOLENCE. Families are the major socializing agent for children. Positive family relations, therefore, can minimize the risk of juvenile violence, while negative family relations can promote antisocial behavior, violence, and delinquency. Research on family relations shows that juveniles who lack parental supervision and appropriate punishment and who are not attached to prosocial family members are more likely to be violent. Negative family relations often must be found in combination with other risk factors to produce actual violence.

Other terms used to describe the concept of family relations include "family functioning," "family control," "parental efficacy," and "family process." Regardless of terminology used, there are several key dimensions of the concept. They are attachment, support, and parental control (**See Control Theory**). Family relations are dynamic by nature and how relations affect juvenile violence may change over time, yet there are some relatively consistent findings on these key dimensions.

Research shows that attachment to parents and parental morals and values are important. Juveniles who are positively attached to parents with prosocial attitudes are less likely to be antisocial, violent, or delinquent. Positive attachments to parents also insulate juveniles from the temptations of peers. Juveniles who are positively attached to parents who do not hold conventional morals and values, however, are at greater risk for violence.

The home environment is an integral piece of the family relations/juvenile violence link. Parents who provide emotional support and instrumental resources to their children, who are involved in their children's lives, and who demonstrate caring are a buffer against juvenile violence. The lack of a caring and supportive environment is associated with juvenile violence. Yet research also shows that juveniles from highly enmeshed families have higher rates of violence and delinquency. There is, then, a balancing point of appropriate family support and cohesion that minimizes the risk of violence. That balancing point may differ by demographics.

Age, sex, ethnicity, and class have been associated with violence, but research findings are not consistent across studies. For example, some research points to an age-graded effect of family relations on juvenile violence, in which family relations are correlated with violence at younger ages. Other research suggests that family relations have more of an effect on juvenile violence as juveniles mature. Overall, more research on demographic differences and juvenile violence needs to be conducted in order to understand these influences.

Violence in the family of origin also must be taken into account. Juveniles who have been maltreated, who have witnessed family violence, or who have families with excessive conflict, have higher rates of violence than those juveniles whose families do not display such characteristics. In addition, juveniles exposed to multiple forms of family violence are more likely to be violent than those who have not been exposed to violence or those who have been exposed to only one form of violence.

Parental management, or parenting style, can influence juvenile violence. Juvenile violence is more likely to occur in families where parents are either too lenient or too harsh. Generally, research has found that an authoritative parenting style in which parents set clear standards, ensure supervision, give appropriate consequences, and provide a caring environment is a protective factor against violence. Violence by juveniles can alter parenting styles, but studies have shown that parents also can adjust to such behavior changes and apply appropriate parenting techniques.

The mechanisms by which family relations affect juvenile violence are filtered through the juvenile's own perceptions. A juvenile's perceptions of such things as rules, support, and attachment play a role in violence. For example, some research has found that girls are monitored more closely by parents than boys, but because of the negative perceptions of such monitoring by the girls themselves, parental monitoring is a risk factor for violence, not a protective factor.

Other research points to the importance of family structure, but family structure variables are often mediated by the dimensions of family relations. Juvenile violence has been correlated with female single–parent-headed households. When controls for the decreased lack of supervision and family financial strain have been included in studies, the effects of female-headed households on violence often disappear. Similarly, some research shows that the more children in the household, the greater the likelihood of juvenile violence. The ability to monitor and punish is decreased with more children. Once this is controlled for in studies, the effects of family size are diminished almost entirely.

The impact of family relations on juvenile violence also operates indirectly. Ample evidence suggests that family relations influence the juvenile's personality, which, in turn, influences the selection of peers. Juveniles from disorganized, high-conflict homes select peers from the same backgrounds. Family relations then combine with peer influences to increase the risk of violence.

Juvenile violence prevention and intervention measures need to address family issues, particularly at the parental level. Areas of parental focus include parenting skills that encourage good child-rearing practices, recognition and appropriate punishment of violent behavior, and techniques to enhance family cohesion. Because family relations can produce juvenile violence in combination with other factors, some of the most effective juvenile violence intervention efforts, such as multi-systemic therapy or functional family therapy, focus on influencing the major spheres of juveniles' lives: family, individual, peer, school, and community.

FURTHER READING

Center for the Study and Prevention of Violence. Available at: http://www.colorado.edu/cspv.

Flannery, D., & Huff, R. (Eds.). (1999). *Youth violence, prevention, intervention, and social policy.* Washington, DC: American Psychiatric Press.

Hawkins, J., Herrenkohl, T., Farrington, D., Brewer, D., Catalano, R., Harachi, T., & Cothern, L. (2000). *Predictors of youth violence.* Washington, DC: Office of Juvenile Justice and Delinquency Prevention.

Loeber, R., & Southamer-Loeber, M. (1986). Family factors as correlates and predictors of juvenile conduct problems and delinquency. In M. Tonry & N. Morris (Eds.). *Crime and justice: An annual review of research* (pp. 129–149). Chicago: University of Chicago Press.

Wright, J., & Cullen, F. (2001). Parental efficacy and delinquent behavior: Do control and support matter? *Criminology, 39,* 677–705.

Erika Gebo

FILM, JUVENILE VIOLENCE AND. Shortly after its inception at the turn of the twentieth century, the medium of film attracted the ire of child-saving reformers for allegedly inspiring juvenile delinquency. In the United States, nickelodeon theatres ("cheap nickel dumps" to their detractors) located in urban slums became gathering spots for youth gangs, as well as thrill-seeking adolescents more generally. However, these objections soon receded before concerns about the content of violent films and their effect on adolescent behavior. Such anxieties became especially pointed after World War II, when films made all over the world (but especially in the States) began to depict adolescent as well as adult characters engaged in all manner of violent acts.

Films featuring juvenile violence can be broken into three broad and sometimes overlapping categories: "social problem" films showcasing adult concerns; "teenpics" marketed to young viewers; and what can be called "nonconformist" films offering multiple perspectives and appealing to diverse audiences. This last set has grown in number in recent decades, reflecting the work of a generation of filmmakers working independently of previously extant industry and government restraints and a growing awareness of the complex roots of delinquent behavior emerging from theories of the social and behavioral sciences. At the same time, recent murders on school campuses have reinvigorated old criticisms of movies; observers have blamed *The Basketball Diaries* (U.S., 1995) for inspiring the mass murders at Columbine High School and *Battle Royale* (Japan, 2002) for eliciting "copycat" murders throughout Japan.

Social problem films typically present juvenile violence from an adult perspective. For example, in *The Blackboard Jungle* (U.S., 1955), we see a multiracial, multiethnic group of inner-city students at the dilapidated North Manual Trades High School through the eyes of their reform-minded teacher, Richard Dadier. The film depicts numerous episodes of youth-on-adult violence: the attempted rape of a female teacher; a vicious beating of Dadier and another teacher by a gang of students; the smashing of one teacher's collection of jazz records; and a climactic showdown between Dadier and a knife-wielding student. After suggesting numerous socioeconomic reasons for the students' violent behavior, the film resolves improbably with Dadier forging a personal connection with most of his students. This theme of middle-class uplift of "dangerous" adolescents would resurface in subsequent American films (*Up the Down Staircase*, 1967; *To Sir With Love*, 1967; *Dangerous Minds*, 1995), although recent treatments of this subject offer darker outcomes (*The Substitute*, 1996; *One Eighty-Seven*, 2002).

By contrast, *Los Olvidados / The Young and the Damned* (Mexico, 1950) portrays Mexican slum youth in an objective, naturalist fashion. Poverty, parental neglect, and a criminal street culture overwhelm any chance that Jaibo or Pedro, the two youthful lead characters, may rise out of their circumstances. The film depicts street kids who rob and even kill, but reserves its harshest indictments for adults and adult society, offering no tidy resolution. A similar tone, albeit with far more graphic violence, is struck in *City of God / Cidade de Deus* (Brazil, 2002), which shows the path of gun-toting adolescent gangsters in the slums of Rio de Janeiro from the 1960s to the 1980s. See also *My Name is Harlequin / Menya Zovut Arlekino* (Russia, 1988), featuring a neo-fascist youth gang that preys on commuters in Minsk. As these examples illustrate, American "social problem" films about juvenile violence tend to place greater faith in Horatio Alger-like narratives of upward mobility than do their counterparts in the international cinema, where redemption comes less often or easy. One notable exception, *Colors* (U.S., 1988), depicts black and Latino youth gangs in Los Angeles through the eyes of two white cops.

The influence of Hollywood upon filmic representations of juvenile violence becomes apparent when one considers "teenpics," pioneered by American filmmakers and popular in

Western societies in the mid-to-late 1950s. Aimed at a growing teenage market, these films told stories of peer pressure, youth culture, and generational rebellion. In "JD films" such as *Rebel Without a Cause* (U.S., 1955), *Die Halbstarken / Teenage Wolfpack* (West Germany, 1956), or *The Cool and the Crazy* (U.S., 1957), corrupt or incompetent adults prove unable to prevent adolescents from becoming embroiled in violence. By the 1970s and 80s, violent teenpics omitted parents altogether; compare the uncomprehending parents in *I Was a Teenage Werewolf* (1959) to the invisible ones in "slasher" films like *Friday the Thirteenth* (1980) or *I Know What You Did Last Summer* (1997).

As youth-oriented films moved away from the generational conflicts that had helped define the teenager as a cultural category, they began offering more complex explorations of juvenile violence. Films such as *A Clockwork Orange* (England, 1971) and *Heathers* (U.S., 1989) punctuate satires of their respective societies with stunning scenes of brutality and murder. In the United States, long-ignored social groups began to tell their own stories of gang violence. Films such as *Boyz n the Hood* (1991), *Juice* (1992), *Menace II Society* (1993), and *Mi Vida Loca / My Crazy Life* (1993) give shocking yet sensitive portraits of African-American and Latino youth coming of age amid drive-by shootings, easily acquired drugs, lethal codes of respect, and a dominant white society that prefers to act as if they did not exist. The drive for authentic representation of misunderstood groups that motivated these important films has animated independent productions such as *Kids* (U.S., 1995), *La Haine / Hate* (France, 1995), *Thirteen* (U.S., 2002), the aforementioned *City of God* (Brazil, 2002), *Elephant* (U.S., 2003), and *Certi Bambini / A Children's Story* (Italy, 2004). Several of these recent films employ a documentary realism that forces viewers to see violent or delinquent youth through their own eyes in ways never imagined by the purveyors of commercially oriented "teenpics" or reform-minded social problem films. Although still controversial, juvenile violence on film is less a Hollywood phenomenon than in past years and is less likely to offer comforting answers for viewers of any age group.

See also Music, Juvenile Violence and; Television, Juvenile Violence and

FURTHER READING

Arai, A. (2003). Killing kids: Recession and survival in twenty-first century Japan. *Postcolonial Studies,* *6*(3), 367–379.

Considine, D. (1985). *The cinema of adolescence.* London: McFarland.

Doherty, T. (2002). *Teenagers and teenpics: The juvenilization of American movies in the 1950s,* 2nd ed. Philadelphia, PA: Temple University Press.

Goldstein, R., & Zornow, E. (1980). *The screen image of youth: Movies about children and adolescents.* Metuchen, NJ: Scarecrow Press, Inc.

McGee, M., & Robertson, R. (1982). *The J.D. films: Juvenile delinquency in the movies.* London: McFarland.

Shary, T. (2002). *Generation multiplex: The image of youth in contemporary American cinema.* Austin: University of Texas Press.

Bill Bush

GANG INVOLVEMENT, THEORIES ON.

GANG INVOLVEMENT, THEORIES ON. Some theories on gang involvement focus on social factors such as poor housing and unemployment, while others stress attitudes and behaviors. There are many subcategories to these theories, but the foundational arguments remain the same.

Biochemistry

The theories of biochemistry blame the biological makeup of a criminal for their predisposition toward criminal activity. One who is in a gang is predisposed to do so by their genetic makeup. Those wanting to join a gang are prone to criminal behavior, thus joining others with the same biological makeup.

Conflict Theory

The **conflict** theorist perspective says that gangs are a byproduct of a capitalist culture that creates social and racial inequality. Minority populations, in an effort to survive in a capitalist society, must resort to criminal activity. At an attempt to make money because of the lack of jobs caused by jobs moving overseas, one would become involved in a gang in an effort to accumulate money. Due to capitalism, conflict theorists would argue that money has been taken out of community establishments, such as schools, police stations, and parks, letting gangs become the predominant social order.

Control Theory

The basis of **social control theory** is that the failure of adequate social control accounts for criminal behavior; crime happens because there is a lack of social mechanisms in place for youth to become bonded (i.e., families, youth groups, sports teams, jobs). The lack of jobs, school funding, and after-school activities creates a void in the opportunities available for children to become engaged, therefore leaving them open to other forms of distraction. Also, with the breakdown of the home, where consistent social control is enacted, youth look outside of the home for family-like relationships.

Cultural Deviance Theory

Cultural deviance theory states that deviance is directly related to one's environment. In socially decaying areas, gangs create an idio-culture that is attractive to an individual within a lower-class environment as they rebel against cultural norms set by the upper classes. The desire to be in a gang and conform to their cultural values is greater than the desire to conform to the idea of being a part of middle-class society.

Labeling Theory

Those who support the labeling theory might ask what constitutes a group being called a gang. They are concerned with the labels that we place on groups of individuals and the effect of these labels. Perhaps being labeled "at-risk" for gang involvement may actually propel individuals to pursue that type of behavior.

Learning Theory

According to social learning theory, one learns delinquent behaviors the same way one learns to become anything else: through watching the actions and behaviors of those individuals that are in their surroundings. It is probable that youth living in a community with a strong gang presence will have interactions with gang members throughout their daily activities. These interactions are said to aid in the formation of beliefs and attitudes about gang behavior that propel these youth to actually become a part of a gang.

Psychological Theories

Psychological theories aim to prove that criminal behavior has to do with functions of the mind. The predisposition to commit crime has nothing to do with the biological makeup of the individual, but rather their psychological aspects, such as IQ, a personality disorder, or a mental reaction to stress.

Social Disorganization Theory

Social disorganization theorists believe the likelihood of gang involvement is directly related to a community's characteristics (i.e., poverty, unemployment, inadequate housing, poor schools). The most significant use of the social disorganization theory as a way to solve the creation of gangs was done by a group called the Chicago School, namely because they were a group of professors from the sociology department of the University of Chicago during the 1920s and early 1930s. Mapping out where most of the crime within Chicago took place, they soon found that in areas lacking strong social institutions (i.e., families, schools, local governments, hospitals), a subculture of criminality emerged, replacing traditions and values once held.

Rational Choice Theory

Rational choice theory proposes that crime is a product of rational choices one makes everyday. There is a rationality of belonging to a gang in the lower classes. Although youths may rationalize the dangers of belonging to a gang, their cost-benefit analysis says it is more profitable to be a part of this group, regardless of delinquent behaviors, than to uphold moral beliefs learned at institutions such as church and school. They weigh the costs of abiding by the law, which they may not have seen enacted on their behalf, and they find the benefits of camaraderie found within the gang outweigh the risks of imprisonment and/or death.

Strain Theory

Anomie is a state in which norms, values, and expectations of conduct are blurred. Emile Durkheim came up with the anomie theory as a way to explain deviance found in society. His thought was that with norms and expectations not fully outlined, deviance is eminent. Robert Merton applied Durkheim's theory to modern-day societies, creating the **strain theory**. He theorized that individuals involve themselves in criminal behavior in an effort for economic gain due to high levels of social ills within their perspective communities. These forms of deviance are tolerated due to the lack of strong institutions and the need to meet the goal of material success set by a capitalist society. Gangs become an alternative social institution, therefore setting the standards and values of their community and providing alternate sources of capital gain.

See also Biochemical Theories; Differential Association Theory; Differential Opportunity Theory; Gang Types; Gangs, Female

FURTHER READING

Collins, K. (2003). Anomie and strain theory. International Encyclopedia of Justice Studies. Available at: http://www.iejs.com.

Coser, L. (n.d.). The function of theory is to provide puzzles for research. In *Crime theories*: *MegaLinks in criminal justice*. Retrieved January 26, 2006 from http://faculty.ncwc.edu/toconnor/rest.

Curry, D., & Decker, H. (2003). *Confronting gangs: Crime and community*. Los Angeles: Roxbury Publishing Company.

Shelden, R., Tracy, S., & Brown, W. (2004). Youth gangs in American society. Belmont, CA: Thomson and Wadsworth.

Thabit, W. (n.d.). How did East New York become a ghetto? In *Social disorganization theories of crime*: *MegaLinks in criminal justice*. Retrieved January 28, 2006 from: http://faculty.ncwc.edu/toconnor/rest.

Vigil, J. (1993). Gangs, social control and ethnicity: Ways to redirect. In S. Brice-Heath & M. McLaughlin (Eds.), *Identity and inner city youth: Beyond ethnicity and gender* (pp. 94–119). New York: Teachers College Press.

Dionne R. Pusey

GANG SWEEPS. Conducted by police to break up gangs, sweeps are efforts focused on arresting, prosecuting, convicting, and incarcerating gang leaders. Some specialized police gang units also conduct curfew and truancy sweeps. Los Angeles police have long been known for their gang sweeps, in which they will swarm gang-infested areas with more than 1,000 officers. Officers are supposed to intimidate gang members as well as show the neighborhood they care. The LAPD's "Operation Hammer" was a preannounced sweep. Almost 1,500 people were arrested, but 1,350 were released without charge. Many accused the operation as being "all for show."

In the mid-1990s, federal antigang efforts were limited. Responding to criticisms, the FBI created seventy-three special gang task forces. The terrorist attacks of September 11th diverted much of this work to homeland security efforts. In 2004, the LAPD and the FBI collaborated to conduct a sweep involving 400 officers and agents intended to target the Bounty Hunters, an ultra-violent gang terrorizing a housing project in Watts. The sweep led to fifteen federal indictments. Some are critical of the FBI's involvement, saying they should be focused on the war on terror. Director Robert Mueller responded that, "Outside of New York, al Qaeda isn't killing people [in the United States]; gang violence is" (Ragavan, Guttman, & Elliston, 2004, p. 20).

To date, gang sweeps have not been terribly effective in the long term, although some research shows a short-term decline in gang-related crime. However, little research about the effectiveness of gang crackdowns has been conducted. Some assert gang sweeps will never work with gangs that focus on drugs, as they operate more like organized crime. Research has demonstrated that targeted, or "hot spot," policing is effective, so it may be that gang sweeps are too broad in their mission and need to be focused on a specific type of crime, such as gun crime. Other experts, such as Malcolm Klein, professor emeritus of the University of Southern California, maintain that responding to the gang problem with only law enforcement tactics will never be very effective.

Critics also contend that gang sweeps are targeted at minorities who are most likely to reside in the public housing projects where sweeps are common. In addition, some maintain the FBI pressured Immigration and Naturalization Services (INS) officers to deport immigrants caught via gang sweeps in Los Angeles, despite little evidence that most were "hardcore" gang members. Rarely do sweeps lead to the apprehension and conviction of gang leaders. This is especially true in the case of curfew and truancy sweeps, which generally catch young, lower-level members. These youth may then be labeled and harassed by police.

See also Detached Street Workers; Gang Units, Police

FURTHER READING

Decker, S. (Ed.). *Policing gangs and youth violence.* Belmont, CA: Wadsworth.

Juvenile curfews and gang violence: Exiled on Main Street. (1994). *Harvard Law Review, 107*(7), 1693–1710.

Klein, M. (2006). *Street gang patterns and policies.* New York: Oxford.

Klein, M., Maxson, C., & Miller, J. (2001). *The modern gang reader*, 2nd ed. Los Angeles: Roxbury.

Ragavan, C., Guttman, M., & Elliston, J. (2004). Terror on the streets. *U. S. News & World Report, 137*, 20.

Laura L. Finley

GANG TYPES. The earliest gang researchers concluded that gangs vary tremendously based on characteristics of members, types of leaders, the organization of leadership, their activities, and how they are regarded in the community. Gang researchers in the 1950s and 1960s continued describing many types of gangs. In the 1980s, research continued to identify numerous types, but began to stress that some gangs are highly organized. By the 1990s, critics asserted that most gangs were actually not very organized. While early gang research generally identified white members, by the 1970s, approximately 80 percent of gang members identified by law enforcement were black or Hispanic, up to 90 percent in the 1990s. Close to half of all gangs in the mid-1990s had multiethnic members.

One major indicator of the number and type of gangs is the National Youth Gang Survey (NYGS), which has sampled over 3,000 law enforcement agencies since its inception in 1996. The NYGS does not provide respondents with a definition of a gang; rather, respondents are to use their own definitions. The characteristic of a gang most commonly cited on the 1998 survey was "commits crimes together."

Today, the following nine types of gangs constitute the broad category of "street gangs": hedonistic/social gangs, party gangs, instrumental gangs, predatory gangs, scavenger gangs, serious delinquent gangs, territorial gangs, organized/corporate gangs, and drug gangs. Hedonistic/social gangs generally spend their time getting high and hanging out. They are not typically involved in crime, especially not violent crime. Party gangs also spend most of the time using drugs, but may also sell them. Party gangs also engage in vandalism. Instrumental gangs are generally found to commit property crimes. Predatory gangs and serious delinquent gangs are involved in serious crime, but predatory gangs are far more involved with seriou drug abuse. Scavenger gangs commit petty crimes, generally as a means of survival, although they will occasionally engage in violence for fun. These gangs are loosely organized and generally include members with the poorest education. Territorial gangs are associated with specific areas, or turf. Organized/corporate gangs are very involved in the use and sales of drugs but, in contrast to other types, they run much like a business focused on discipline and merit. Drug gangs are the smallest and most cohesive type, focused solely on the drug business. Two other groups that are often called gangs are stoners and taggers. Stoners are generally white youth who form in groups much like cults. They tend to be of higher socioeconomic status and of greater intelligence than other gang members, although many are nonachievers who never complete their education. Stoners are largely involved in drug abuse. Taggers are groups of youth who are known for graffiti. Rather than identifying turf, taggers use graffiti to express themselves. Most engage in underage drinking and some in recreational drug use, but, for the most part, taggers are not violent.

In addition, some gangs have joined together, often for protection, to form what has been called "supergangs" or "nations." For example, the People and Folks joined together in Illinois prisons as a form of protection. Other gangs are so large they are broken into sets. The most famous of this sort are the Los Angeles Bloods and Crips. Another type of gang is the hybrid gang. First identified by Thrasher in the 1920s, early hybrid gangs were racially or ethnically mixed. Today, hybrid gangs are still racially or ethnically mixed, and they also tend not to have an identifiable gang color, may co-opt the symbols of other gangs, and may change names or merge with other gangs. Also, hybrid gang members may shift affiliations between gangs or claim multiple affiliations. Most researchers agree that the spread of gangs to rural and suburban areas has escalated the creation of hybrid gangs. Another type of gang, albeit one that includes other forms, is the prison gang.

Another way to classify gangs is to look at the racial and ethnic composition of members. Some of the oldest gangs in the United States are Chicano gangs from Southern California, often referred to as *cholos* (marginalized). Family and community are most important to these gang members, most of whom live in the impoverished barrios. Members of these Chicano gangs generally see each other as brothers. Chicano gangs are known for their hypermasculine front and are said to be more involved in "turf-related" offenses. Asian-American gangs are more commonly involved in property offenses, and when they do commit violence, it is typically instrumental, rather than expressive, and generally impacts fellow Asians. Asian-American gangs are known to be highly secretive, and, because members act polite and respectful, police often find members difficult to apprehend. African-American members are more commonly involved in entrepreneurial activities and are likely to advertise their gang affiliation through distinctive dress, slang, and gestures. The Bureau of Indian Affairs documented over five hundred gangs on Indian reservations with over 6,000 members at the start of the twenty-first century. Research has demonstrated that white youth are only about 10 percent of all gang members in the United States, although some argue this is due to racist definitions and classification of members. Skinheads are perhaps the most widely known type of white gang. Contrary to public perception, there are both racist and non-racist skinheads. Non-racist skinhead groups may have members of many different ethnic groups. Some skinheads are political in nature and are strong critics of the U.S. government, while others are survivalists who seek to be alone and denounce government involvement. Skinheads are generally involved in violent activity, with racist groups committing **hate crimes**.

Researchers have identified eight types of gang members, ranging from those most attached to and involved in the gang to those with little attachment or involvement: regulars/hard core members, peripheral members, temporary members, situational members, at-risk members, wannabe members, veteranos/O.G.s, and auxiliary members. Regulars or hard-core members participate regularly and have few non-gang attachments. Peripheral members, or associates, are strongly attached but participate with less regularity as they have some interests outside the gang. Temporary members are not nearly as committed, tend to join later and leave earlier, and are less intensely involved. Situational members join the group for specific activities, avoiding the most violent ones. At-risk members are actually not members but those who have expressed interest and may fantasize about involvement. They may have family members already involved in the gang. Wannabes admire gang members and may emulate their dress and talk. Some may join the gang upon invitation, while others never participate. Veteranos, or Original Gangsters (O.G.s), are in their twenties or older but still participate occasionally in gang activities. Chicano gangs prefer the term Veteranos, while African-American gangs more frequently call these members O.G.s. Auxiliary members hold limited responsibilities, perhaps because they have a fairly active life outside the gang. **Female gangs** or female members of mixed-gender gangs have often been said to hold auxiliary roles.

See also African Americans and Juvenile Violence; Asians and Juvenile Violence; Hispanics and Juvenile Violence; Native Americans and Juvenile Violence

FURTHER READING

Howell, J. (2004). Youth gangs: An overview. In F-A. Esbensen, S. Tibbetts, & L. Gaines (Eds.), *American youth gangs at the millennium* (pp. 16–51). Long Grove, IL: Waveland Press.

Shelden, R., Tracy, S., & Brown, W. (2004). *Youth gangs in American society*, 3rd ed. Belmont, CA: Wadsworth.

Starbuck, D., Howell, J., & Lindquist, D. (2004). Hybrid gangs. In F-A. Esbensen, S. Tibbetts, & L. Gaines (Eds.), *American youth gangs at the millennium* (pp. 200–214). Long Grove, IL: Waveland Press.

Worth, R. (2002). *Gangs and crime*. Philadelphia, PA: Chelsea House.

Zatz, M., & Portillos, E. (2004). Voices from the barrio: Chicano/a gangs, families, and communities. In F-A. Esbensen, S. Tibbetts, & L. Gaines (Eds.), *American youth gangs at the millennium* (pp. 113–141). Long Grove, IL: Waveland Press.

Laura L. Finley

GANG UNITS, POLICE. Generally, local police departments are responsible for gang control. Most typically, police departments use suppression techniques to respond to gangs. Under the suppression approach, law enforcement sees their primary responsibility as responding to gang crime. Based on deterrence theory, suppression techniques assume that swift apprehension and severe punishments for gang crimes, like assault, drug sales, drive-by shootings, and even graffiti, will reduce gang activity. In addition, suppression is said to reduce gang membership. Prevention is not a priority.

There are three primary types of police units that deal with gangs. One is through youth service programs, in which police personnel assigned to youth units also deal with gangs. The second is through gang details. Here, one or more police officers, again generally from youth units or perhaps detectives, are given exclusive control over gang activity. These two forms were more common until the 1980s. The third form of police gang control is the specialized gang unit formed solely to deal with the problem of gangs.

A 1992 national assessment found that fifty-three of the seventy-two police departments they surveyed had separate gang units. By 1999, over 55 percent of the large police departments in the United States had a specialized gang unit, with more than 85 percent formed since the late 1980s. These units have at least one of the following four functions: intelligence, suppression, investigation, and prevention. Departments vary regarding which of these functions receives priority, although research has found that over 80 percent stress intelligence first. Intelligence involves gathering and disseminating information about gang members, including their street names, legal names, addresses, known associates, photographs, and gang affiliation. Research about the activities of police gang units has found most to be highly selective regarding the cases they choose to investigate. Investigations are only conducted on cases where officers feel there is a high probability of obtaining an arrest, valuable information, or those gang members considered high profile. In most cases, the decision regarding which cases to investigate is not made by superior officers or based on a specific mission or goal. Suppression and enforcement activities tend to take up the most time and receive the most public attention. Suppression techniques generally involve directed patrol of known gang areas, most often public housing districts, parks, and parking lots. **Gang sweeps** are a form of suppression. Most specialized units perform some form of prevention, generally speeches at local schools and to community groups, although prevention generally receives the lowest priority of the four functions. Community relations divisions of police departments are generally responsible for presenting the educational program **Gang Resistance Education and Training (GREAT)**, rather than the gang unit. Specialized units generally have different administrative structures than the rest of the department and typically feature officers with specific training. Approximately 85 percent of the units provide personnel with specialty training about gangs.

The rapid growth in specialized police gang units can be explained by four main theories. Contingency theory maintains that police gang units are a rational response to the growth of gangs and gang-related crime in the 1970s and 1980s. Constructionist theory asserts that, like many policy initiatives, specialized police gang units are in response to a moral panic about gangs and gang crime more than a serious and growing gang problem. Advocates of this theory express concern that specialized gang units, if not really needed, will crack down on other, less serious offenses, even those committed by non-gang members. Institutional theory maintains specialty police gang units are the result of pressure from important community stakeholders. They are needed to maintain a positive public image and to convince the public that police are indeed responding to the problem of gangs. Following resource dependency theory, specialized police gang units were created in order to allocate federal grant monies. Many units were formed upon receiving support from the **U.S. Department of Justice**, Office of Community Oriented Policing Services' (COPS) Anti-Gang Initiative.

The Chicago police department has one of the larger specialized gang units, with over four hundred officers. Officers identify gang members and enter them into a computerized database that provides all officers in the department with an alert if a member is arrested. The Chicago gang unit also coordinates community activities, presents lectures at schools, and offers counseling and assistance to parents and community organizations.

Another specialized gang unit that received a great deal of attention was the LAPD's Community Resources Against Street Hoodlums (CRASH) unit. Many said the unit dramatically cut down on gang-related crime with their aggressive tactics, but the unit was dissolved in March 2000 amid tremendous scandal. One officer, Rafael Perez, implicated seventy antigang cops for corruption, excessive force, and planting and falsifying evidence when he was arrested in 1998. In all, eight officers were indicted. Los Angeles Chief of Police Bernard Parks replaced CRASH with Special Enforcement Units, which had had very restrictive rules.

Some police units today are seizing new technology to help them identify and apprehend gang members involved in criminal activity. In Florida, one police agent is spending fifteen to twenty hours per week scanning websites and chat rooms for information about local gangs, as many gangs have now taken to "Netbanging." Gangs are using the Web to recruit, as well as to communicate and sometimes even to pick online fights with other gangs. Police in Boston and Texas have broken up fights that were scheduled on gang websites. The sites are also useful to police in identifying new gang symbols, language, and dress.

Specialized police gang units have been criticized in a number of ways. First, specialized units tend to be isolated from other units in the department, generally by their own choice. This isolation reduces the department's ability to share information. The FBI recommends that all officers receive training on gang awareness and identification. Because the units often operate autonomously, there is greater risk that officers will abuse their powers as there are fewer checks to ensure their accountability. Units tend to develop distinct subcultures that may not be positive. For instance, the aforementioned CRASH unit of the LAPD Rampart Division was found to have created their own culture and maintained their own rules with little oversight, which contributed to the group's corruption. Further, specialized units are often isolated from the community, thus some communities see them as unresponsive to their needs.

Many criticize gang units for overemphasizing suppression techniques they say are racist. Policing only public housing projects, for instance, will likely result in more arrests of poor minorities. As noted in a number of other gang-related entries in this volume, critics also complain that how these units define and identify gangs is based on race; they assert that groups of white youth who commit crimes are generally not defined as a "gang" and thereby do not receive the same treatment.

In addition, many gang experts maintain that more emphasis needs to be on prevention in order to truly disrupt gang activity. Gang units are not likely the best method to achieve this end. In particular, prevention requires collaboration between police, schools, and other community organizations, yet, as noted above, specialized units tend to be very isolated and to act largely alone. **Boston's Youth Violence Strike Force** is a good example of a multiagency, collaborative effort.

FURTHER READING

Briscoe, D. (2006, March 13). "Netbangers," beware; Street gangs are going online to compare notes and pick fights. But the cops are right behind them. *Newsweek*, 31.

Decker, S. (Ed.). *Policing gangs and youth violence*. Belmont, CA: Wadsworth.

Langston, M. (2003). Addressing the need for a uniform definition of gang-involved crime. *The FBI Law Enforcement Bulletin, 72*(2), 7–12.

McCarthy, T. (2001, September 3). L.A. gangs are back. *Time, 158*, 46.

Schaefer, D. (2002). Police gang intelligence infiltrates a small city. *Social Science Journal, 39*(1), 95–109.

Laura L. Finley

GANG VIOLENCE, AGAINST BYSTANDERS

Preliminary Concerns

In understanding gang-related violence, it is important to examine several critical issues, including how membership is determined and how violence is measured. Depending on whether a jurisdiction applies a "gang membership" definition, which involves classifying incidents committed by known members as gang violence, or a "gang motivated" definition, which requires that a gang-related purpose be the motivation for a violent incident, one ends up with estimates of the volume of gang violence that are either "twice as great" or "half as great." The Los Angeles Police Department generally uses a membership-based definition, while the Chicago Police Department uses a gang-motivated definition. Only 50 to 60 percent of the gang-related homicides in Los Angeles would meet the more restrictive definition used in Chicago. There are flaws with each. Gang-membership definitions generally assume that gang-member databases are accurate, which certainly may not be true. In some areas, police gang units may devote a great deal of time to collecting and classifying members, whereas in other locations there may not be a specialized gang unit. Motive-based definitions require more complicated investigations into an offender's purpose, which is always tricky.

Measuring homicide rates also presents difficulties, as it is often done from databases maintained by law enforcement. Not only do these data suffer from the same definitional issues described above, but crime rates are often tallied for only one city or police agency. Further, because of intimidation, information from witnesses is often incomplete. Both measurement and definitional problems do not always result in valid estimates of gang violence, let alone gang violence against innocent bystanders.

Gang Homicides

Acknowledging the shortcomings presented above, Maxson and Klein developed a survey in 1992 to assess the number of homicides involving gang members. They analyzed data from 792 cities that reported gang activity. Of those, 60 percent reported no gang homicides in the previous year. Of the remaining 299 with gang homicides, more than 80 percent had fewer than ten incidents. Twelve cities reported 40 percent of the total number of gang homicides for 1991. Eight of the twelve were located in California. Research from Chicago using the Illinois Criminal Justice Information Authority (ICJIA) homicide data from 1965 to 1995 has found that gang-motivated homicides represented an increasing percentage of all homicides in the city. Gang homicides averaged about 5 percent through the 1970s, just under 9 percent in the 1980s, then spiked to 17 percent through the early 1990s. In 1994 and 1995, gang homicides were more than a quarter of all Chicago homicides. Los Angeles experienced a similar increase in the proportion of homicides attributed to gangs, recording 805 gang-related murders in 1995. The mid-1990s started a drop in gang-related violence, with Los Angeles documenting two hundred gang-related murders in 1996. None of these projects, however, measured the number of innocent bystanders who were victims. It is presumed that the bulk of these homicides involved fellow gang members.

Innocent Bystanders

Gang violence in general, and gang violence involving innocent bystanders, typically involves firearms. Greater rates of violence in the last few decades can, in part, be traced to greater access to high-powered weapons. Bystanders might also be injured as part of gang initiation requirements, which might require robbery or assault of a nonmember. In 1997, gang members slashed the faces of at least 135 innocent New Yorkers as part of their initiation rites. In 1989, the *U.S. News & World Report* reported that gangs were increasingly victimizing innocent bystanders, citing a wheelchair-bound man killed in gang crossfire in Miami and a three-year-old in Brooklyn who was used to shield a drug dealer. The article cites a report from the Crime Control Institute documenting that the number of bystanders injured or killed by gangs had tripled in just three years in New York, Los Angeles, Boston, and Washington DC. They documented 135 incidents of gang violence against bystanders in 1989. At the time, criminologist Lawrence Sherman maintained that these gangs differed from the more organized violence of the mafia in that the young gangsters made no efforts to avoid harming innocents; rather, they took pride in it. While this may be an oversimplification, first-person accounts, such as Sanyika Shakur's ("Monster" Kody Scott) autobiography do highlight that, to some gangs, violence against bystanders may gain a member the respect of his peers.

Since there are no good national measures of the number of innocent bystanders killed, it is difficult to discern whether this trend has reversed. Surges in gang violence do lead to surges in bystanders being injured or killed, though. Los Angeles experienced this type of surge between January 2004 and June 2005, when gang violence killed forty-four people, half of whom were said to have no gang affiliation. Canada has been experiencing greater gang activity in the twenty-first century. Officials blame the surge in gang violence on greater access to guns. Officials argue the new gangs like the attention they receive when innocent bystanders are involved, as was the case when seven bystanders but no intended victims were shot in Toronto on Boxing Day.

Media Sensationalism

Part of the issue is that, even though the number of innocent bystanders wounded or killed by gangs has always been relatively low, they receive a great deal of attention when they occur. For example, the death of blond-haired, blue-eyed Stephanie Kuhen in 1995 in Los Angeles spawned outrage and led to the creation of a citywide task force. In November 2004, the gang-related shooting of Louis Olander in Brooklyn received a great deal of attention. He and two others received wounds that were not life-threatening, but because Olander made it through a year of service as an army medic in Baghdad, Iraq, the media publicized the irony of his domestic injuries. These reports make it appear that no one is safe from gang violence. They also garner support for a number of antigang measures, such as those listed below.

Interventions

A number of strategies have been proposed to reduce gang violence in general and to minimize the effects on innocent bystanders. **Police gang units** gather intelligence, arrest gang members, and educate the public on gang awareness. **Gang sweeps** involve aggressive efforts to arrest gang members for any type of offense. The **Boston Youth Strike Force** and **Operation Ceasefire** are often held up as examples of how to reduce gang violence through collaborative efforts. Some maintain that more severe sanctions would act as a deterrent, although this seems unlikely given that gang members convicted of these crimes often are given lengthy prison sentences already. In some cases, gang members who kill innocent bystanders have received death sentences. Many maintain that bystanders will be injured as long as the social conditions that prompt youth to join gangs remain unchanged and the access to lethal weapons remains relatively easy.

See also Gang Types; Gun-Related Violence, Rates of; Gun-Related Violence, Types of

FURTHER READING

A slaughter of innocents. (1989, July 10). *U.S. News & World Report, 107*, p. 12.

Dillon, N. (2005, November 24). Survives Iraq only to be hit on B'klyn St. *New York Daily News*, p. 8.

Edwards, P. (2005, December 31). Fewer killings than 1991, but bystanders more at risk now. *Toronto Star*, p. E03.

Egley, A., Maxson, C., Miller, J., & Klein, M. (2006). *The modern gang reader*, 3rd ed. Los Angeles: Roxbury.

Garvey, M. (2005, December 17). L.A. county targets racial gang war. *Los Angeles Times*, p. B4.

Maxson, C. (2004). Gang homicide: A review and extension of the literature. In F-A. Esbensen, S. 1Tibbetts, & L. Gaines (Eds.), *American youth gangs at the millennium* (pp. 275–296). Long Grove, IL: Waveland Press.

Maxson, C., Gordon, M., & Klein, M. (1985). Differences between gang and non-gang homicides. *Criminology*, 23(2).

Maxson, C., & Klein, M. (1990). Street gang violence: Twice as great, or half as great? In R. Huff (Ed.), *Gangs in America: Diffusion, diversity, and public policy*. Newbury Park, CA: Sage Publications.

Mays, L. (1996). *Gangs and gang behavior*. Chicago, IL: Nelson-Hall Publishing Company.

Thompson, C., Young, R., & Burns, R. (2003). Representing gangs in the news: Media constructions of criminal gangs. In T. Calhoun & C. Chapple (Eds.), *Readings in juvenile delinquency and juvenile justice* (pp. 206–219). Upper Saddle River, NJ: Prentice Hall.

Worth, R. (2002). *Gangs and crime*. Philadelphia, PA: Chelsea House.

Emily I. Troshynski and Laura L. Finley

GANG-ON-GANG VIOLENCE. According to Lewis Yablonsky's seminal work on gangs in 1962, there are three types of gangs: delinquent gangs, violent gangs, and social gangs. Violent gangs are the most persistent and problematic. They tend to form in response to safety threats and are perceived by initiates to offer a form of protection for members. While all gangs may commit acts of violence against rivals, violent gangs do so with greater frequency. Gang-on-gang violence is said to be more common on Native American reservations than in other areas.

Although gangs may use violence for a number of reasons, the most common is in response to actual or perceived threats to the gang's territory. Honor is of utmost importance to gangs, and violence in response to actual or perceived threats demonstrates that a gang is not to be messed with. Consequently, gang members see gang-on-gang retaliatory violence as rational and purposeful acts.

Contrary to media presentations, most victims of gang violence are members of a gang themselves, not the so-called **"innocent bystander."** A study of gangs in Chicago revealed that violence is more frequently turf-related than it is drug-related and that most of the non-lethal, nondrug offenses by gangs were violent assaults, most frequently perpetrated on rival gangs. In further support that gang-on-gang violence is turf-related, gang-related shootings tend to be concentrated in specific regions of a given city. By the end of the 1980s, however, some cities had seen an increase in gang-on-gang violence connected to the distribution of crack. Research has demonstrated that the threat of violence from a rival gang serves a positive function, as it actually increases solidarity between members. Increased gang membership in the 1980s, as well as increased rivalry among factions within a particular gang, increased gang-on-gang violence.

A gun is the most commonly used lethal weapon in gang-related homicides, which tend to occur in bursts. Increased availability of high-powered assault weapons in the 1980s had a dramatic effect on the amount of gang-on-gang violence. The number of gang-related homicides committed with an automatic, semiautomatic, or high-caliber nonautomatic weapon in Chicago increased from 24 to 70 percent between 1987 and 1990.

One of the more common and more publicized means of gang-on-gang violence is the drive-by shooting. A drive-by involves a member or, more typically, multiple members of one gang, driving into a rival gang's area and shooting at someone. Drive-bys also happen when gang members arrive in a location by car, but leave the car to chase and assault a rival gang member. The percentage of gang assaults that were drive-by shootings increased dramatically through the 1980s, from 23.7 percent in 1981 to 41.8 percent in 1988. The goal of a drive-by may not always be to kill or even injure; some drive-bys are intended to send a message instead. Parties are often targeted so that a gang can demonstrate their willingness to attack a large group.

Drive-bys often occur after a gang has hung out at a party, become intoxicated and/or high, and then decides to make a "hit." Drugs and alcohol are not the only explanation for a drive-by, however, as most gang members are "drunk and loaded" a vast majority of the time. Some drive-bys happen somewhat spontaneously. Gang members may be driving around with weapons in the car, when a member says something to a rival out the car window, typically an insult or challenge. In other cases, the target initiates the assault by saying or doing something to antagonize those in the car. In another form of the drive-by, the assault is prompted when a rival gang is seen driving through another's turf, and the home gang mobilizes to attack the drivers. Other drive-bys occur with no direct precipitation by the target, such as when a rival gang defaces another's *placaso*, or gang signature. The responding gang then decides to execute a drive-by at a specified time.

Gangs, like any other group, have norms. While it is acceptable to execute a drive-by on a dwelling where non-gang members may be inside, it is typically not acceptable to single out innocent family members of a rival gang. Gangs tend also to demonstrate remorse when innocent children and women are killed, although they generally see this as a natural consequence of their gang warfare.

The drive-by is a type of hit-and-run attack that originated with gangs shortly after World War II. Called "japping," it was derived from some of the unorthodox strategies used by Japanese soldiers in the war. Prior to the introduction of hit-and-run tactics, the most frequent type of gang-on-gang violence was the rumble, exemplified in films like *West Side Story*. Early hit-and-run assaults were often made on foot or even via public transportation. Use of automobiles for the hit-and-run began on the West Coast, where neighborhoods were farther apart and less densely populated, and public transportation was scarce.

While seemingly a sneaky and nefarious tactic, drive-bys are actually one method to keep episodes of gang-on-gang violence brief and may be far less lethal than if rival gangs were to line up, arsenal in tow, opposed to one another. Drive-bys are difficult for law enforcement to control, as a car driving through a particular area is not particularly suspect. Police efforts to help gang members cool off after an incident tend only to prolong the retaliation.

Despite their support for and use of violence, gangs tend to be surprised when one of their own is severely wounded or hurt in a drive-by. Those who have maimed or killed others in a drive-by talk about it as though it was an act of bravery. Further, to have executed a drive-by typically raises a gang member's status in the group, as not all members have the mettle to carry out such an assault.

While there are growing numbers of **female gang members**, research to date has found females commit fewer acts of violence of all types than do males. It seems this type of violence is less critical to maintaining or increasing a female member's status than a male's. In fact, it is fairly common that a male gang member will commit an act of violence against a rival member in defense of a female member's virtue or in retaliation for an assault or rape of the female member.

One difficulty in discerning how frequent gang-on-gang violence occurs lies in how gangs are defined. In some locations, anyone who was related or even acquainted with a known or suspected gang member was classified as a member themselves. Consequently, tallies of gang violence would be skewed upwards.

See also Assault; Gang Types; Gun-Related Violence, Rates of; Gun-Related Violence, Types of; Native Americans and Juvenile Violence

FURTHER READING

Decker, S., & van Winkle, B. (1996). *Life in the gang: Family, friends, and violence*. Cambridge: Cambridge University Press.

Dudley, W., and Gerdes, L. (Eds.). (2005). *Gangs: Opposing viewpoints*. Farmington Hills, MI: Greenhaven Press.

Hernandez, A. (1998). *Peace in the streets: Breaking the cycle of gang violence*. New York: Child Welfare League of America.

Miller, J., Maxson, C., & Klein, M. (2001). *The modern gang reader*, 2nd ed. Los Angeles: Roxbury.

Shakur, S. (1993). *Monster: The autobiography of an L.A. gang member*. New York: Penguin.

Shelden, R., Tracy, S., & Brown, W. (2003). *Youth gangs in American society*. Belmont, CA: Wadsworth.

Sikes, G. (1997). *8-ball chick: A year in the violent world of girl gangsters*. New York: Anchor.

Laura L. Finley

GANGS, FEMALE. Historically, female gang members were not the focus of gang studies. Girls, it seemed, were "invisible." Early accounts of female involvement came from male members, were given to male researchers, and publicized by male academics. In the mid-1970s, female gang members were classified into three groups: auxiliary subgroups affiliated with male gangs, independent or autonomous gangs, or part of a mixed-gender gang. When they are involved with gangs, researchers have generally stressed females' auxiliary role, and autonomous female gangs were said to be rare. For instance, girl gangs generally emerge after a male gang has been formed and often take a feminized version of the male name, such as the Vice Queens, whose name came from the Vice Kings. Recent research, from the late 1990s to the present, is more likely to find autonomous and mixed-gender gangs. One study found 92 percent of gang youth claiming their gang had both male and female members. Further, the role of female members seems to vary by race and ethnicity. Chicana/Latina gangs are most likely to describe themselves as affiliated with male groups, while African-American females more commonly describe their gangs as mixed-gender. The autonomous female gangs identified to date are more likely to be African-American as well. In addition, more recent research has found that female auxiliary gangs are more independent than previously thought, as many maintain their own rules for membership and other autonomous actions.

Numbers of Female Members

Research in the late 1990s was more likely to find female members, in particular in known gang localities. Because definitions of gang membership vary tremendously, as do methodologies to discern membership, it is difficult to get precise numbers on membership of either males or females. Interview and survey research in a number of cities in the 1990s found as few as 8 percent of known members were female and as many as 46 percent in other cities.

Surveys of law enforcement tend to show smaller numbers of female gang members, perhaps due to definitional issues, differential policing practices, and gender biases. One study found that some police agencies in the early 1990s purposely excluded females from their gang count. Some maintain that police simply do not see female gangs as a priority, perhaps because females in general are viewed as less threatening. Also, female gang members tend to be younger, in part because females leave gangs earlier than do males. Thus, if researchers are taking samples from older youth, they may reflect a different number of female members than if they were to sample a younger group.

Reasons for Joining

Regarding why young people join gangs, research has identified engaging in sexual activity and having delinquent peers to be important to both male and female members, although sexual activity was less important to females. Other research tested twenty-six risk variables, with eighteen identified for males and eleven for females. Males shared eight of the eleven characteristics with females, including poor performance in school, access to and positive attitudes toward drugs, and delinquent involvement. Neighborhood integration was important for females but not for males. Also unique as a risk factor for females was low parental involvement. Another study found females are more likely to join for socialization reasons, while males join for protection, for excitement, and for the opportunity to belong. Qualitative research with female members has demonstrated that they often join as a way to cope with a bleak existence in which they are economically marginalized and subordinated to males. Female members are more likely to come from homes with significant problems, including abuse and regular drug use. Some research has found female members have lower self-esteem and are more socially isolated than male members, although other research has not found these to be significant variables regarding gang membership.

Initiation Rites

Like males, females generally go through some form of initiation into the gang. Being beaten or kicked by members, participating in a violent crime like a drive-by shooting or robbery, getting tattooed, fighting multiple members at once, having sex with multiple male members, engaging in a stealing spree, or some form of mental test are all ways a recruit may be initiated. One study found that female recruits might be asked to fight a male member. In some gangs, a female recruit rolls a pair of dice and must have sex with the number of males she rolls, an initiation process called rollins.

Gang Violence

As a whole, gang youth are more delinquent than their non-gang peers. Gang females are more delinquent than non-gang boys. Most research has found female members commit fewer serious, violent crimes than do male members, although at least one study found they commit more serious, violent offenses. There is tremendous variation between gangs and locales regarding the number and type of crimes committed. Female gang members generally do not seek out violence; rather, when violence occurs, it is simply an acceptable part of their daily existence. Male and female gangs are about equally likely to engage in alcohol use, drug sales, extortion, and property damage. Most studies confirm that gun use is far more prevalent among male gangs. In some mixed-gender gangs, males purposely exclude females from some activities, such as drive-by shootings. One analysis of the GREAT project found that majority female or all female gangs were the least delinquent, followed by all-male gangs, while other research has found all-male groups to be the most delinquent. Many gang girls do not consider victimless offenses to be criminal, and they use a variety of **techniques of neutralization** to differentiate themselves from serious, "crazy" criminals. Similarly, other studies have found female gang members feel more guilt about committing violent crimes than do male members.

Risks of Membership

In contrast to the argument that gangs provide members protection, there is substantial evidence that members are at higher risk for victimization. Research has found gang girls more likely to be sexually assaulted, threatened with a weapon, or stabbed and more likely to have witnessed stabbings, shootings, drive-bys, and other homicides, than nonmembers.

Female Gangs as Liberating

Some scholars have maintained that, because gang activities generally defy gender stereotypes, female gang involvement is a form of **liberation**. Little research backs up that conclusion. Even all-female gangs operate within a male-dominated street culture. Gang girls face social sanctions for their gender inappropriate actions, both within and outside the gang. Girls who are "too hard-core" risk offending other members and have limited dating prospects among nonmembers. While females, by and large, want to be respected by male gang members, they are often seen as possessions, used only for sexual purposes. Male members often have "respectable," non-gang girlfriends. Gang girls do, however, often see themselves as different from non-gang females. Qualitative studies have found that gang girls see their involvement as a rejection of community norms.

Leaving the Gang

Female members are at greater risk for a number of problems after leaving the gang. While legitimate work opportunities are often severely limited in gang areas to begin with, having been involved with a gang further reduces a person's chance at gainful employment. Research with Chicano/a gangs in Los Angeles found three categories of ex-gang members: *tecatos*, *cholos*, and squares. Approximately 25 percent of the sample were *tecatos*, or heroin addicts, although males were far more likely in this group. About one-third of the males and even more females were *cholos*, who persisted in gang activity into adulthood. These people rarely had stable jobs or marriages. About 40 percent of the men and fewer women lived conventional lives, called squares. Several qualitative studies have found childbearing prompts females to desist gang involvement and that female members value being a good mother.

See also African Americans and Juvenile Violence; Gang Types; Gender, Frequency of Perpetrating Violence by; Gender, Frequency of Receiving Violence by; Gender, Types of Violence Perpetrated by; Gender, Types of Juvenile Violence Received by; Hispanics and Juvenile Violence

FURTHER READING

Chesney-Lind, M., & Hagedorn, J. (Eds.). (1999). *Female gangs in America*. Chicago: Lake View Press.

Maxson, C., & Whitlock, M. (2002). Joining the gang: Gender differences in risk factors for gang membership. In R. Huff (Ed.), *Gangs in America* (pp. 19–36). Thousand Oaks, CA: Sage.

Miller, J. (2002). The girls in the gang: What we've learned from two decades of research. In R. Huff (Ed.). *Gangs in America* (pp. 175–198). Thousand Oaks, CA: Sage.

Miller, J., & Brunson, R. (2004). Gender dynamics in youth gangs: A comparison of males' and females' accounts. In F. A. Esbensen, S. Tibbetts, & L. Gaines (Eds.), *American youth gangs at the millennium* (pp. 163–190). Long Grove, IL: Waveland Press.

Shelden, R., Tracy, S., & Brown, W. (2004). *Youth gangs in American society*, 3rd ed. Belmont, CA: Wadsworth.

Sikes, G. (1997). *8-ball chicks: A year in the violent world of girl gangsters*. New York: Anchor.

Laura L. Finley

GENDER, FREQUENCY OF PERPETRATING VIOLENCE BY.

There are a number of ways to explore the frequency of perpetrating violence for juveniles in general and, more specifically, based on gender. Juvenile violence takes many forms and can include simple assault, aggravated assault, carrying a weapon, domestic violence situations, murder, and manslaughter. It is crucial to realize that there are a number of ways to define violence, and when dealing with juveniles, violent acts could very well include schoolyard fights or other instances that are unaccounted for in arrest statistics. Given this, it becomes difficult to acquire a perfect idea of the frequency of perpetrating juvenile violence by gender. One other issue to consider is the way in which boys and girls commit violent acts as juveniles. This, in turn, could affect the frequency of the violent behavior. Boys may be more prone than girls to be involved with peers who are likely to engage in violent behavior. In some instances, boys belong to gangs or groups in which violence is more likely to occur. Official data on gangs reveals that upward of 95 percent of the members are male and that half of the gang membership is under the age of eighteen. Minorities make up nearly three-quarters of gang members, with Hispanics making up the majority of the minority representation followed by blacks and Asian-Americans. Black juvenile males have been overrepresented in the officially recorded arrest data for violent crimes. During the mid-1990s black juvenile males were significantly more likely to be arrested for murder, robbery, and aggravated assault than white juvenile males, as well as white and black juvenile females.

The idea that girls are violent or would act in a violent manner contradicts gender norms within society. Girls are not necessarily perceived as being violent, and when they do engage in violent behavior, it may be perceived more negatively than when a boy engages in similar behavior. However, it must be noted that girls have seen more activity as part of gang-related offenses in recent years, and this can contribute to some of the explanations for the increase of arrests in the mid-1990s for girls who were involved in certain types of assaults.

Girls and boys perpetrate violence at different rates. Frequency of perpetrating is measured through arrest rates of juveniles and through the use of self-report surveys. Since the 1980s, arrest records indicate that there was a significant increase in the number of arrests for violent crimes for both juvenile males and females, with some decline coming since the late 1990s. However, when it comes to juvenile females and males who were arrested for aggravated and simple assault from 1993–2002, statistics indicate that juvenile males saw a decline in the numbers of arrests, while juvenile arrests involving females remained near their highest levels. Boys are much more likely than girls to be arrested by the police for violent crimes on the whole. Discretion of the police could also affect the amount of juvenile violence that is officially reported, given that the police may or may not arrest someone depending upon the severity of the violent behavior. Official data on arrests show us one aspect of violent behavior on the part of juveniles, while self-report data gives us a deeper understanding of the frequency of perpetrating. When examining self-report surveys, such as the National Youth Survey, one finds that juvenile males are more likely to indicate that they have been involved in violence-related activities, such as carrying a handgun, involvement in gang activity, aggravated assaults, hitting students in school, and sexual assault, than their female counterparts. Trends in the self-report survey data show the amount of physical fighting that takes place has declined in the past decade for both juvenile males and females.

As the twenty-first century progresses, it is uncertain as to whether or not there will be a rise in violent behavior perpetrated by juveniles, either male or female. However, there is some indication of a downward trend in the frequency of perpetrating violence for both juvenile males and females. A number of factors must be considered when assessing the future of juvenile violence. These include the amount of gang involvement by male and female juveniles, the issue of violent peers and their influence, the amount of school violence that takes place, and the overall rates of violence in the country, which could give rise to the amount of violence perpetrated by juveniles.

See also Assault; Gang-On-Gang Violence; Gender, Types of Juvenile Violence Received by; Gender, Types of Violence Perpetrated by; Gun-Related Violence; National Youth Survey

FURTHER READING

Belknap, J., Holsinger, K., & Dunn, M. (1997). Understanding incarcerated girls: The results of a focus group study. *Prison Journal, 77*, 381–405.

Chesney-Lind, M., & Sheldon, R. (2004). *Girls, delinquency, and juvenile justice*. Belmont, CA: Wadsworth.

Steffensmeier, D. (1993). National trends in female arrests: 1960–1990: Assessment and recommendations for research. *Journal of Quantitative Criminology, 9*, 411–437.

Dale J. Brooker

GENDER, FREQUENCY OF RECEIVING VIOLENCE BY. Compared with adults, juveniles are more than twice as likely to be the recipients of violence (rape, sexual assault, robbery, and simple or aggravated assault). More specifically, statistics show that individuals from ages 12 to 19 are most at risk for being the victims of violent crimes than any other age group. Homicide victimization decreased for juveniles in the late 1990s. One group of juveniles that saw an increase in homicide victimization since the late 1990s was black juvenile (ages 14 to 17) females. Juvenile males are more likely than girls to be officially receiving violence.

It is crucial to understand the dynamics in which the frequency of receiving violence occurs. Juvenile females, despite recently (last two decades) reported increases in gang involvement, are less likely to be on the receiving end of such violence that includes aggravated assault, simple assault, and murder. It is the juvenile male who is most at risk for being the recipient of a violent act, but it must be recognized that one violent act alone is the exception to this—sexual assault. The majority of juvenile victims of sexual assault are females, according to official statistics and self-report victimization surveys such as the National Crime Victimization Survey (NCVS).

There are four major dimensions that must be considered when assessing gender and the frequency of receiving violence. They are (1) involvement in gang activity, (2) sexual assault,

(3) family violence, and (4) school violence. Juvenile males are more likely to be involved with gangs than juvenile females, and this fact alone creates a dynamic whereby they will be more prone to receiving violence. Gang-related homicide and assaults have been on the increase over the past two decades and have accounted for an increase in the victimization of juvenile males. While gang involvement is not restricted to one gender, the majority of those individuals that make up the gang membership are males; females, on the other hand, are often viewed as taking an auxiliary role in the gang organization, although this has changed somewhat in the recent past with girl gangs coming to be examined in the criminal justice literature. Therefore, it is the gang lifestyle and the gang involvement that may account for some of the fluctuation in the frequency of receiving violence between the genders.

The one major difference in the frequency of receiving violence is for sexual assault. Females, according to official data, are three times more likely than juvenile males to be the victims of sexual assault. Within this context it must be noted that a great number of cases of sexual abuse can go unreported if the offender was a family member. In terms of self-report surveys that focus on receiving violence, juvenile girls indicate that they have been the victims of sexual abuse or sexual violence at much higher rates than their male counterparts. To further this point, the family dynamic must be noted as having some influence on the amount of receiving violence for juveniles. Family violence can, and oftentimes does, include violence against juvenile boys and girls. Furthermore, approximately one-third of all sexual assaults of juveniles are committed by a family member. The victim-offender relationship reveals more about the receiving of violence in that girls, more than boys, are likely to be sexually assaulted by a family member, especially those under twelve years of age.

Finally, when assessing the frequency of receiving juvenile violence, school violence must be explored with emphasis on the differences in gender. Male students are more likely to be the recipient of a violent act in the school setting than female students. This, of course, is inclusive of the idea that boys are more likely to be in fistfights that are reported to school officials. Juvenile males are also more likely to bully other boys in a violent manner, which could account for more frequently occurring instances of receiving violence. It is quite possible, however, that girls receive a great deal of violence at school that goes "under the radar" because it takes less traditional forms.

The twenty-first century looks questionable in terms of how much violence juveniles will face. However, there are indications that juveniles will be less victimized based on data that indicates a decrease in family violence as well as an overall decrease in the amount of violence on the part of adults. Major cities across the United States are working to reduce the amount of violent gang activity and therefore can reduce the amount of juvenile victims that are the result of such violent behaviors. School violence may very well decrease given the last decade's refocus on school safety. This, in turn, would lead to less violence experienced by both juvenile males and females.

See also Assault; Gang-On-Gang Violence; Gender, Types of Violence Perpetrated by; Gun-Related Violence, Rates of; Gun-Related Violence, Types of; National Youth Survey

FURTHER READING

Bottcher, J. (2001). Social practices of gender: How gender relates to delinquency in the everyday lives of high-risk youths. *Criminology, 39*, 893–932.

Chesney-Lind, M., & Sheldon, R. (2004). *Girls, delinquency, and juvenile justice.* Belmont, CA: Wadsworth.

Herrera, V., & McCloskey, L. (2003). Sexual abuse, family violence and female delinquency: Findings from a longitudinal study. *Violence and Victims*, *18*, 319–334.

Dale J. Brooker

GENDER, TREATMENT OF, IN THE JUVENILE JUSTICE SYSTEM. The

juvenile justice system attempts to treat both males and females successfully; however, researchers speculate that there may be gender-related differences in juveniles' needs that could result in varying degrees of treatment effectiveness for both males and females. This may create the need for gender-specific programming. To date, however, there are generally not gender-specific treatment programs that are used in the juvenile justice system. This is because males have traditionally been more delinquent than females, and treatment in the juvenile justice system has been tailored to meet their needs. Treatment of females thus far has fallen under a "one size fits all" model.

Recently, though, research on the gender-related concerns, differences, and treatment in the juvenile justice system has begun. This has revealed that, among other factors, juvenile female offenders are more likely to have been abused, depressed, engaged in suicidal or self-inflicted harmful behaviors, and become pregnant early, while male juveniles are more likely to be violent, destructive, and exhibit behavior problems both in and out of school settings. Because of these differences, it appears that females benefit from treatments that provide supportive, nonconfrontational, and noncompetitive environments, utilize cognitive behavioral therapies, provide educational programs, and are based on social learning models. Males also benefit from cognitive behavioral and educational treatments based on social learning models, as well as behavior modification techniques, and some types of individual and group counseling.

Treatment in the juvenile justice system is provided in both institutional and community-based settings. Juvenile treatment programs vary across states and jurisdictions. Generally, however, the treatment modalities used in the juvenile justice system fall under six types of treatments, including individual and group counseling, behavioral, group-centered, educational, multimodal, and deterrence-based treatment programs. Incorporated in these are individual and group psychotherapy, transactional analysis, role-playing, reality therapy, behavior modification, therapeutic communities, guided group interaction, cognitive therapy, family therapy, drug and alcohol interventions, boot camps, and scared straight programs.

Psychotherapy, transactional analysis (TA), and role-playing are types of counseling programs that can be conducted in an individual or group setting. Psychotherapy provides an opportunity for children to talk about their thoughts, feelings, and past personal experiences with a therapist or clinician. Because of its focus on feelings, this type of therapy has been more effective for females than males. Transactional analysis (TA) is a counseling program that attempts to make youth aware of the types of interaction they have with others around them. Juveniles learn to identify when they are engaging in childlike and parental behavior, while striving to engage in mature, adultlike interactions with others. Role-playing provides an opportunity for juveniles to act out their emotions and is therefore considered a type of psychodrama.

Behavior modification and reality therapy are types of behavioral treatments used in the juvenile justice system. Behavior modification uses either operant or classical conditioning techniques to change a delinquent's behavior by manipulating the elements in their environment that reinforce antisocial behaviors. These treatments are based on the assumption that the environment influences an individual's behavior and that changing the contingencies in the environment may change a person's behavior. Most research to date has focused on the effectiveness of behavior modification techniques on delinquent boys' behavior. Reality therapy asserts that respect and social relations are basic human needs that, when not met, cause a child to behave inappropriately. This treatment approach trains adolescents to focus on their current behaviors and the consequences of those actions and teaches them how to fulfill their basic needs in prosocial ways.

Guided group interaction and therapeutic communities are group-centered treatment modalities that are used most often in institutional settings. These approaches focus on how the institutionalized community, or a group of juveniles living in close quarters, can set boundaries, make rules, and reinforce appropriate behavior. Because they are based on the social learning model and attempt to provide a supportive and prosocial environment, these types of treatment modalities have been most effective with female juveniles, although they are also used with and are effective for male juveniles. Guided group interaction gives decision-making power to the residents, while therapeutic communities focus on making the environment conducive to social therapy.

Educational and substance abuse programs are used in community and institutional settings. Substance abuse programs help youths identify their chemical dependencies and they also provide youths with information about the harmful effects of drug addiction. Educational programs help juveniles obtain diplomas or certificates, such as their GEDs. Both males and females benefit from educational programs, but substance abuse programs have shown to produce varying degrees of effectiveness.

Cognitive behavioral and family therapies are multimodal types of treatments used in the juvenile justice system. Cognitive behavioral therapy teaches juveniles to identify their dysfunctional thinking patterns, take responsibility for their actions, and understand how their thinking errors lead to inappropriate behavior. This treatment modality teaches juveniles to think and, subsequently, act differently. Family therapy focuses on teaching effective communication and problem-solving skills to both parents and children. It also teaches parents how to be more consistent and effective in their disciplinary techniques.

Deterrence-based treatment programs include boot camps and scared straight programs. Most research to date has examined the impact of these programs on male juvenile offenders, while very little research has been conducted with female juvenile offenders. **Boot camps** teach youth the value of discipline and hard work and operate on the assumption that punishments teach juveniles that there are consequences to their actions. Scared straight programs attempt to scare a juvenile from engaging in delinquent behaviors by exposing them to harsh realities of confined or institutional living conditions. These have typically been used with males.

See also Chivalry Hypothesis; Gender, Frequency of Perpetrating Violence by; Gender, Frequency of Receiving Violence by; Gender, Types of Violence Perpetrated by; Gender, Types of Juvenile Violence Received by

FURTHER READING

Bartollas, C., & Miller, S. (2001). *Juvenile justice in America*, 3rd ed. Upper Saddle River, NJ: Prentice Hall.

Ellis, R., O'Hara, M., & Sowers, K. (1999). Treatment profiles of troubled female adolescents: Implications for judicial disposition. *Juvenile and Family Court Journal*, 25–87.

Lipsey, M., & Wilson, D. (1999). Effective intervention for serious juvenile offenders: A synthesis of research. In R. Loeber & D. Farrington (Eds.), *Serious and violent juvenile offenders: Risk factors and successful interventions* (pp. 313–345). Thousand Oaks, CA: Sage.

Emily Wright

GENDER, TYPES OF JUVENILE VIOLENCE RECEIVED BY. The most common terminologies used to describe violence as it differs by gender are "gender violence," "gender-based violence," "partner violence," or "domestic violence." The ultimate key to understanding the types of violence received by gender and why this differs lies in understanding the concept of gender. Juvenile gender-based violence takes many forms—physical, sexual, emotional, and psychological. The behavior occurs in both the public and private realm.

Males are more likely to both perpetrate and be the victims of violent crime. The 2004 FBI data show that older juveniles were at higher risk of being murdered. For both male and females, the murder risk was relatively high during the first year of life but increases during the teenage years. In 2004, males comprised 82.2 percent of arrestees for violent crime. The 2004 **Unified Crime Report (UCR)** figures indicate that of the 15,935 murders in which police made arrests, males were responsible for 10,262 and females were responsible for killing 1,130 victims. The juvenile data indicate that of the 854 victims of juvenile violence of murder, juvenile males were responsible for 794, while female juveniles were responsible for 59 victims. Violent crimes committed by girls differ significantly from boys' offenses in that boys are two to three times more likely to carry weapons, and girls are more likely to use knives than guns. Girls are more likely than boys to murder someone as a result of a conflict rather than during a crime and to murder and fight with family members. Research indicates that adolescent girls are less likely than boys to be arrested for violent crimes of homicide, forcible rape, aggravated assault, burglary, and arson. Females are now outpacing males in all offense categories, according to **Office of Juvenile Justice and Delinquency Prevention (OJJDP)** data. OJJDP data indicate simple assault cases increased for both males and females more than any other offense.

Academic literature on juvenile gender-based violence suggests that a major gender-based problem is boys' violence toward girls. The focus in academia is on relationship violence, primarily on the battery of girls or women by boys or male partners. The National Association of Social Workers defines gender-based violence as the perpetration or threat of emotional, verbal, or physical violence or sexual assault targeted toward adolescent girls within the context of a dating relationship. Advocates for youths tell us that female teenagers are more likely to suffer dating violence and are more likely to be injured as a result of dating violence. Girls are three times more likely to suffer a beating and to suffer emotionally than their male peers. A 1997 study indicated that nearly one in five high school young women report having been physically or sexually abused. The **Centers for Disease Control** defines violence as a disease and in 2000 determined that "although partner violence transcends all racial, ethnic, and socioeconomic groups, African American teenage girls are more likely to report being slapped or hit by a boyfriend." Furthermore, the Commonwealth Fund (1999) tells us that "the impact of intimate partner violence on the overall health and well being of young girls is significant . . . dating violence has severe consequences . . . in addition to physical injuries that may be sustained, young women are three times more likely to report severe emotional trauma when a violent episode occurs in a dating situation . . . other long term consequences can include continued or chronic health problems, increased use of medical services and hospitalizations, and poor self-rated health status." A single act of physical violence increases the impact of subsequent threats of violent behavior and other psychologically abusive acts.

Rape is another crime primarily committed against girls and young women, and adolescents are considered to be at highest risk for sexual assault, with more than half of reported assaults occurring in dating situations. Research has shown that age fourteen is a young woman's year of greatest risk of sexual assault. The Centers for Disease Control in 2000 found that 12.5 percent of young women in grades nine through twelve reported being forced to have sexual intercourse.

Sexual harassment, particularly in school settings, is also an issue that disproportionately affects adolescent girls, though often it is not reported. When boys are the recipients of sexual harassment, they are even less likely to report it to officials or authorities.

The types of violence received by gender is rooted in the gender differences of masculinity and femininity and the prescribed norms and definitions of what it means to be a man or a woman. These gender differences allow for or encourage violent behavior within a context of assumed privilege and hierarchical power for certain groups of men. Included in the literature as factors that provide for this phenomenon are the influence of childhood experiences and family dynamics, social institutions, gender socialization, and especially socially permissive attitudes.

Gender-based violence is an articulation of, or an enforcement of, power hierarchies and structural inequalities that are informed by belief systems, cultural norms, and socialization processes. It is grounded in patriarchy, a system that positions men over women (and other men) and instills a sense of entitlement and privilege in many men. Patriarchy also institutionalizes the social, cultural, and legal contexts that permit gender violence. But gender violence is also based in the pressures, fears, and stifled emotions that underlie "hegemonic masculinity," or many of the dominant forms of manhood espoused in cultures around the world. Added to this are the personal experiences of violence for individuals—being nurtured in a culture of violence—and learning and experiencing violence from the environment, including the family, the media, and the community.

The scope and effect of gender-based violence are profound. Gender-based violence plagues every society in every region of the world. No one group, regardless of the culture, class, or location, is immune to its devastation. It incapacitates families and partnerships and the ability for many to relate to themselves or others with love, compassion, or respect. In a macro sense, gender-based violence restricts the achievement of development, peace, and freedom.

Because women in U.S. society experience systematic oppression, they have fewer options in responding to abusive behavior in their intimate relationships. Moreover, abusive behavior by men toward their female partners further reinforces men's dominant position in relationships and maintains the oppression of women. African-American women are even more affected by this phenomenon due to their status as both women and African Americans.

See also Gender, Frequency of Perpetrating Violence by; Gender, Frequency of Receiving Violence by; Gender, Types of Violence Perpetrated by

FURTHER READING

Butts, J. (1994). Delinquency cases in juvenile court 1992. *Office of Justice Programs*. Available at: www.ncjrs.gov.

FBI Uniform Crime Report (2004). Available at: www.fbi.gov/ucr.

Girls and violence: Is the gender gap closing? (2005, October). Available at: www.hamfish.org/topics/gender_violence.

Kwong, M., & Bartholomew, K. (1999). Gender differences in patterns of relationship violence in Alberta. *Canadian Journal of Behavioral Sciences, 31*(3), 150–160.

Evaristus Obinyan

GENDER, TYPES OF VIOLENCE PERPETRATED BY. Males perpetrate all forms of physical violence with greater frequency than females. This is true of adults as well as juveniles and across a variety of settings. It is also important to note that, with the exception of sexual assault, males are more likely to be violently victimized than females (see the entry on Gender, Types of Juvenile Violence Received by). Two specific types of violence that stand out regarding the gender of perpetrators are sexual violence and school violence. Many theories have been proposed to explain these gender differences, ranging from purely biological to purely sociological in their emphasis. It is important to understand the incidence and types of offenses perpetrated by each gender, as well as why there are differences. If there are indeed different reasons why males and females become violent, then gender-specific interventions might be required.

Official Crime Data

Males are far more likely to commit murder than females. The 2001 **Uniform Crime Report (UCR)** data shows that 508 males under the age of eighteen were arrested for murder compared to 69 females. When females do commit murder, it is far more likely against a family member (32 percent) or a very young victim. Twenty-four percent of females who murdered victimized someone under the age of three, compared to just 1 percent of boys. When girls commit murder, they are more likely to kill alone, whereas boys are more commonly joined by an accomplice. The primary motive for murder by girls is interpersonal conflict.

Using the same 2001 UCR data, males under the age of eighteen were also more frequently arrested for robbery (11,695 compared to 1,104 for girls) and burglary (44,560 compared to 6,896 for girls). Many have pointed to the fact that female arrests for aggravated **assault** increased, going from 6,325 in 1992 to 7,814 in 2001, which suggests that females are becoming more "like males" in terms of violent offending. This is known as the **liberation hypothesis**. While it is true that there was a 23.5 percent increase in female arrests, males are still arrested for aggravated assault almost four times more often. Some researchers point out that the increase in females arrested for assault may be a function of relabeling certain offenses. For instance, a girl hitting her mother was once labeled "incorrigible" and dealt with largely by the family. In the early 1990s, some states relabeled this as an assault and dealt with it in the juvenile or criminal justice systems. In addition, police practices and recommendations may have changed, leading to more arrests of females. For example, some police advised parents of "unruly girls" to block the doors when their daughters attempted to leave, then to call in law enforcement if the young woman pushed past them. In sum, official crime data continues to verify that females constitute a very small portion of those arrested for violent crimes.

Self-Reports

While there are valid criticisms of the UCR, self-report data confirm that males are more involved in physical violence. For instance, the 2001 Youth Risk Behavior Survey showed that 43.1 percent of males under the age of eighteen had been involved in a physical fight, compared to 23.9 percent of females. Only 2.7 percent of females reported being injured in a physical fight, while 5.2 percent of boys reported injury. The primary reason for fights between juvenile females, according to qualitative research, has to do with boys. Other things that prompt girls to fight include rumors and name-calling. Males are more prone to respond violently to verbal attacks on their competence or their sexuality. Occasionally, girls fight boys. This is, most typically, the result of sexual harassment or misconduct, either real or perceived.

Sexual Violence

One of the most striking differences between juvenile male and female offending is in the commission of sexual violence. Once again drawing on UCR data from 2001, juvenile males arrested for rape outnumber juvenile females arrested for rape 2,312 to 30. National Crime Victimization Survey (NCVS) data generally shows that 99 percent of rapists are males, while National Incident Based Reporting System (NIBRS) data from 1997 and 1998 indicated 92 percent of sexual assault offenders were male. Studies with college-aged males have found that many would not rule out rape if they could guarantee they would not be caught and punished. One study found one in twelve college-aged males had committed an offense that met the legal definition of rape or attempted rape, yet did not call themselves rapists.

School Violence

Male shooters have perpetrated all of the high-profile school shootings from the 1990s to the present. The primary motive for the Pearl, Springfield, Jonesboro, and Littleton shootings seems to have been revenge against those who had rejected and alienated the young men. Survey research has found that students of all types tend to define aggressive boys as popular, whereas only other girls who are violent rate aggressive girls as popular. When girls are involved in school violence, it tends to involve indirect aggression, such as verbal abuse, gossip, and social exclusion. Some have argued, however, that these forms of violence are every bit as damaging as physical forms. Although both genders are involved in **hazing** in high school, males are involved more frequently and in more serious, violent forms.

Theories Regarding Gender Differences

The field of criminology has long been androcentric, first ignoring female criminality altogether, then chalking it up to pathology. Some even argued that females were every bit as deviant as males, they were simply more devious and secretive, hence they "got away with it." In his seminal text on gangs in Chicago, Thrasher spends approximately one page out of 600 on females. **Social disorganization theory**, which emerged from the University of Chicago in the 1930s, was founded on analyses of male delinquency rates. Sutherland's **differential association theory** could be applied to females, although Sutherland, too, focused on male case studies to formulate the theory. There is support, however, for the contention that females who have greater contact with deviant females engage in more deviant acts themselves. Many delinquency theorists in the 1950s and 1960s clearly stated that they were explaining behavior by males. Likewise, Travis Hirschi created his **social bond theory**, arguably the most cited theory in criminology, by studying males. Even into the 1980s, major research projects, like the Philadelphia longitudinal study, included only males. Some theories pose obvious problems when gender is considered. For instance, Merton's **strain theory**, which proposes that individuals offend when they cannot reach socially desirable goals through socially desirable means, would seem to suggest that females should offend at greater rates, as they experience more strain due to blocked opportunities.

More recently, theorists have made efforts to consider gender when formulating and testing theories. Many point to gender role socialization, asserting that females are socialized to be passive and nurturing, while males are socialized to take risks and to be aggressive. Being aggressive is simply part of "doing" masculinity. Cases like the sexual assault in **Glen Ridge, New Jersey** and those perpetrated by the **Spur Posse** highlight this idea. Hagan's **power-control theory** maintains that patriarchy is the root cause of male offending. The workplace is still patriarchal, so males are still in a dominant role structurally. Relations in the family mirror relations in the workplace. Because patriarchal families monitor girls more closely while providing males more opportunities for risk-taking, boys are more delinquent. Hagan's theory retains remnants of the liberation hypothesis, as he maintained that when more women are in the workplace and have more egalitarian relationships, females will be more prone to delinquency.

See also Gender, Frequency of Perpetrating Violence by; Gender, Frequency of Receiving Violence by; Gender, Types of Juvenile Violence Received by

FURTHER READING

Alder, C., & Worrall, A. (Eds.). (2004). *Girls' violence: Myths and realities.* Albany: State University of New York Press.

Artz, S. (1999). *Sex, power, & the violent school girl.* New York: Teachers College Press.

Chesney-Lind, M., & Pasko, L. (2004). *The female offender: Girls, women, and crime*, 2nd ed. Thousand Oaks, CA: Sage.

Messerschmidt, J. W. (1993). *Masculinities and crime.* Lanham, MA: Rowman & Littlefield.

Rabrenovic, G., Kaufman, C., & Levin, J. (2004). School violence: Causes, consequences, and interventions. In S. Holmes & R. Holmes (Eds.), *Violence: A contemporary reader* (pp. 115–132). Upper Saddle River, NJ: Prentice Hall.

Simmons, R. (2002). *Odd girl out: The hidden culture of aggression in girls.* New York: Harcourt.

Laura L. Finley

GENERAL AND SPECIFIC DETERRENCE THEORY

Introduction

Deterrence theory first appeared in classical criminology in the late 1700s in the writings of Cesare Beccaria (1738–1794). Beccaria believed that people wanted to choose pleasurable experiences over painful ones. Crime could provide pleasure, and so Beccaria maintained that punishment for committing crime must be just severe enough to outweigh the pleasure. Beccaria's ideas were extended by philosopher Jeremy Bentham (1748–1833), who called for proportionality of punishments to crimes.

The principle behind deterrence theory is that punishments are set in order to deter or dissuade people from committing crime, rather than punishment being about vengeance or retribution. However, in order for punishments to deter more serious criminals, they must be proportionate to the crime. For example, if the punishment for burglary was execution and the punishment for murder was execution, a criminal might not think twice about murdering someone during a burglary.

Another essential element to deterrence theory is the certainty and swiftness of punishment. If a criminal feels that there is very little chance that he or she will be caught and convicted for a crime and that apprehension may take years, the deterrent effect of a punishment is weakened considerably.

Classical criminology became popular again in the 1970s after rehabilitative approaches to punishment were criticized. Much of the loss of faith in rehabilitation came after a study conducted by justice policy analyst Martinson, who concluded that, "nothing works."

Types of Deterrence

There are two main types of deterrence: general and specific. General deterrence is used when policy makers want to deter the general public from committing crimes. This means that people are fearful of the punishment and do not commit the crime. For example, the threat of capital punishment is supposed to deter everyone from committing murder. Another example would be the threat of legislative **waiver** for juveniles, which is designed to deter juveniles from committing serious or violent offenses.

Specific deterrence occurs when punishments are given to individual offenders to try to prevent them from committing future criminal acts. For example, a juvenile may be sentenced to an indeterminate community-based sentence so he or she can be monitored, with the threat of more severe punishment upon subsequent criminal acts.

Both types of deterrence can be absolute or marginal. Absolute deterrence occurs when a punishment stops a crime altogether. This is difficult to achieve. An example of this would be if police ticketed every speeding driver on a particular road. Everyone who was speeding has been punished, and the crime would be stopped, if only for a brief period. Marginal deterrence occurs when a proposed punishment for an offense will provide some reduction in crime. For example, the threat of chemical castration in sex offenders is likely to deter some sex offenders from committing sex offenses.

Research on Deterrence

There have been a number of studies on the deterrent effect of the death penalty. The premise tested in these studies is that if the death penalty is an effective general deterrent, the homicide rate should decrease after a publicized execution. This decrease is expected because potential murderers will be reminded that the punishment for homicide is execution. Empirical evidence collected by a number of researchers actually indicates that the murder rate increases after a publicized execution, thus providing little support for the deterrence argument. Other studies that have examined the murder rates across different countries have also found that the threat of capital punishment has little impact on the murder rate as many countries that do not have the death penalty have lower murder rates than those countries that do have it. However, Bentham may argue that execution is too severe a punishment and therefore has little deterrent effect. Others may argue that it takes too long to execute someone on death row to be an effective deterrent.

Other researchers argue that deterrence works better for other types of crimes. For example, when one is given a speeding ticket on a particular stretch of road, one is likely to slow down on that stretch in the future. Punishments for drinking and driving offenses, such as stiff fines and loss of one's driver's license also provide an effective deterrent.

Critics of deterrence theory maintain that punishment based on this principal will not work because none of the other circumstances surrounding the crime are addressed, for example, the criminal's reasons for committing the crime. If the prison environment is better than the community environment where the offender lived, there is no deterrent. Further, if the culture is such that incarceration adds to one's reputation, there is also no deterrent effect.

Despite strong criticism, deterrence theory remains one of the most popular foundations for modern criminal sanctions.

See also Death Penalty; Delinquency and Drift Theory; Rational Choice Theory

FURTHER READING

Cullen, F., & Agnew, R. (2003). *Criminological theory: Past to present*, 2nd ed. Los Angeles: Roxbury Publishing.

Einstadter, W. (1995). *Criminological theory: An analysis of its underlying assumptions*. Fort Worth, TX: Harcourt Brace College Publishers.

Pogarsky, G., Piquero, A., & Paternoster, R. (2004). Modeling change in perceptions about sanction threats: The neglected linkage in deterrence theory. *Journal of Quantitative Criminology, 20*, 4, 343–360.

Schuck, A. (2005). American crime prevention: Trends and new frontiers. *Canadian Journal of Criminology and Criminal Justice, 47*, 2, 447–463.

Monica L. P. Robbers

GENERAL STRAIN THEORY (GST). Robert Agnew wrote the general strain theory (GST) in 1985 in response to several criticisms of classic strain theories. Agnew proposed that the inability of classic strain theories to cite more than one cause of strain limited their theoretical application. Agnew suggested that strain could be produced by different circumstances, with delinquency just one in a number of adaptations to strain. The second criticism of traditional strain theories that Agnew cited was that they looked to macro causes of strain, such as social institutions, and did not focus on individual experiences of strain.

Where Durkheim's concept of strain refers to a state of disorder in society, Agnew's concept of strain refers to aversive situations and environmental adversity, suggesting that Agnew conceptualized strain as an emotional, frustrated state, similar to the modern conceptualization of stress. As GST continues to be refined, the terms stress and strain are becoming synonymous. GST has been used extensively in juvenile justice literature to help explain gender differences in delinquency, different community crime rates, and even young white-collar delinquency.

Agnew's GST identifies three types of strain-producing situations. First is the failure to achieve goals, which is the traditional notion of strain seen in Merton's strain theory. This type of strain also extends to the disjuncture between expectations and achievements or fair outcomes and actual outcomes. An individual's response to the failure to achieve goals could include anger, frustration, depression, or withdrawal. Second is the removal of positively valued/desired stimuli or other significant changes in life circumstances. The loss or anticipated loss of positively valued stimuli may lead to delinquency, particularly if the individual tries to prevent the loss or seeks revenge.

A third strain-producing situation occurs when individuals are confronted with other people's negative actions, such as victimization at school or physical abuse at home. Negative stimuli may lead to delinquency as the adolescent tries to escape, alleviate, or seek revenge against the source of the stimuli.

Agnew maintained that responses to strain can vary and can be delinquent or nondelinquent. Nondelinquent responses include depression, deflection, escapism (this can also be delinquent), frustration, or catharsis through sports. Nondelinquent options are often limited by legal constraints, which may preclude the juvenile's escape from the strain-producing situation; for example, exposure to negative stimuli such as sexual abuse in the home. Delinquent responses are most likely to occur when a juvenile reacts to strain with anger toward other people or social structures. Mediating factors, such as peer associations, moral values, self-efficacy, sports involvement, and religious beliefs, can all influence an individual's response to strain.

Criminologists initially viewed GST with skepticism, claiming it did not offer different or new insights than other leading perspectives. In response to these claims, Agnew revised the theory in 1992 to distinguish GST from both **social control/social learning theories** and **differential association**. Agnew claimed that several factors differentiate GST from social control theories. First, social control theories cite a lack of valued relationships with significant others and social institutions as the cause of delinquency, and no special motivation is needed to commit delinquent acts. When social controls are minimized, people will act deviantly. GST, however, maintains that negative relationships, or situations in which juveniles feel they are treated badly, may lead to delinquent actions. Second, social control theories focus on why individuals conform to social norms, whereas GST focuses on negative coercion toward delinquency.

According to Agnew, the differences between GST and differential association are clear-cut. Differential association maintains that adolescents model their behavior on the behavior of others. Modeling is usually based on the behavior of individuals with whom adolescents spend the most time and whose behavior they accept as normal. When accepting behavior, adolescents do not consider whether the behavior conflicts with societal norms. Thus, delinquency is a learned behavior, and juveniles who spend their time in the company of a delinquent gang are more likely to commit delinquent acts. GST views delinquency as an adaptation to strain, which is produced by different circumstances. Where differential association emphasizes cognitive processes, strain theory looks to emotional responses.

In 2000, Agnew redefined GST to fit the context of school violence and delinquency. In the school setting, Agnew proposed four strain-producing situations. The first is negative peer relations, such as being picked on, bullied, or any other interpersonal conflicts between students. In the school setting, a student victim may be picked on in a public forum, which adds to the victim's experience of strain. The second form of strain Agnew cited is negative teacher relations, such as teachers who show an open disrespect for students and/or who have low expectations of students. Negative teacher relations may have an especially strong effect on a student if the student values the teacher's opinion and is motivated by the teacher's encouragement. The third strain-producing situation is low grades. Students who are diligent and strive to maintain high grade point averages can be greatly affected by poor grades. Last, Agnew proposed that school dissatisfaction could also cause strain. Students who feel that school is a waste of their time, materials learned have no relevance to the real world, and have few school bonds, experience this type of strain. Agnew notes that these students are likely the very ones that have a great deal of trouble learning.

GST continues to evolve. In 2002, Agnew and colleagues extended the original GST to include the conditioning effects of personality traits on strain, specifically negative emotionality and constraint. Findings from this study indicated that juveniles who had high levels of negative emotionality and low constraint were far more likely to respond to strain with delinquency.

See also Gender and Juvenile Violence entries

FURTHER READING

Agnew, R. (1985). A revised strain theory. *Social Forces, 64*, 151–167.

Agnew, R. (1986). Work and delinquency among juveniles attending school. *Journal of Crime and Justice, 9*, 19–41.

Agnew, R. (1992). Foundation for a general strain theory of crime and delinquency. *Criminology, 30*(1), 47–87.

Agnew, R. (2001). Building on the foundation of general strain theory: Specifying the types of strain most likely to lead to crime and delinquency. Unpublished paper.

Agnew, R., Brezina, T., Wright, J., & Cullen, F. (2002). Strain, personality traits, and delinquency: Extending general strain theory. *Criminology 40*(1), 43–71.

Agnew, R., & White, H. (1992). An empirical test of general strain theory. *Criminology, 30*(4), 475–498.

Akers, R. (2000). *Criminological theories: An introduction and evaluation*, 3rd ed. Los Angeles: Roxbury.

Monica L. P. Robbers

GENERAL THEORY OF CRIME. Authored by Michael Gottfredson and Travis Hirschi, the general theory of crime (GTC) is the most widely cited trait theory. It builds on Hirschi's control theory and integrates elements from biosocial and psychological theories, as well as rational choice and routine activities theories. In general, the theory considers the offender to be separate from the act, and the interplay of the two is what matters. Further, Gottfredson and Hirschi asserted that their theory could explain all forms of crime or delinquency, hence the word "general" in the title.

Drawing on rational choice and routine activities theories, Gottfredson and Hirschi posit that delinquency is rational and predictable. It is the result of an offender weighing the costs and benefits of his or her actions and deciding to do that which he or she perceives as being advantageous. Following this logic, the threat of punishment should be a **deterrent**.

From the biosocial and psychological theories, Gottfredson and Hirschi draw the notion that some delinquents are predisposed to offend. While these juveniles are not constantly offending—much of their time is spent like that of other juveniles, attending school, after-school activities, working, and the like—when an opportunity for delinquency arises, these individuals are more prone to seize it. According to GTC, an individual's propensity to be delinquent remains stable throughout their lifetime; rather, it is the opportunities to offend that change.

The trait that Gottfredson and Hirschi assert makes one delinquent-prone is self-control. Those with limited self-control are more impulsive and adventuresome, tend to be physical risk-takers and be active physically, are often insensitive to the feelings of others, are short-sighted, and often do not have well-developed communication skills. Further, they tend to lack perseverance. They often feel little shame when they engage in various forms of delinquency, instead finding them pleasurable. As these individuals get older, they are more likely to be involved in dangerous behaviors, such as drinking, reckless driving, and smoking, and they tend to have unstable work patterns and relationships. Since delinquent acts often involve stealth, agility, speed, and power, individuals with low self-control are more likely to get involved and find enjoyment in them. In sum, these individuals seek short-term gratification.

People are not born with low self-control, these authors argue. Rather, self-control is developed, generally by age eight, through socialization. The root cause of inadequate self-control is poor child rearing, according to Gottfredson and Hirschi. Parents might be inadequate in a number of ways. They might fail to or do a poor job of monitoring their child's behavior. They may not punish deviant behavior when it occurs; in fact, many parents do not even recognize deviant behavior in their children. Children of deviant parents are even less likely to develop adequate self-control. GTC maintains that male delinquency rates are higher than female's because males have less self-control; likewise, certain racial groups offend more frequently because they, too, lack self-control. In addition to families, schools are a key source for the development (or lack thereof) of self-control. Further, individuals with low self-control are prone to seek out peers who also lack self-control.

Gottfredson and Hirschi maintain that their theory explains why some with low self-control never offend (the opportunities are not presented) as well as why those with high self-control still might offend (they are presented with too many and/or too enticing opportunities).

Evaluations

Many researchers have attempted to evaluate GTC. One method involves identifying measures of impulsivity and self-control, then assessing whether these correlate with delinquency rates. Some research from the United States and other countries has supported this correlation. Further, research has demonstrated that those who begin delinquent patterns early in life are less likely to be helped by rehabilitation or treatment, suggesting a fixed trait. One study analyzing youth from four countries (United States, Hungary, the Netherlands, and Switzerland) also affirmed the connection between self-control and delinquency. Few research studies have focused on testing the link between child rearing and self-control.

Criticisms

Ronald Akers has been one of the most vocal critics of GTC, asserting it is tautological, that is, the only way to determine if someone lacks self-control is by measuring their "low self-control behaviors." Critics maintain that there are significant differences in the way impulsivity and self-control have been measured, thus research using one definition or one form of measurement may differ significantly from research using different terms or measures. Further, most measures of impulsivity and self-control come from self-reports, which may not be accurate. Some also argue that impulsivity interacts with other characteristics, such as anger. Critics also maintain there is little support that males are more impulsive than females or that certain racial groups lack self-control. Using arrests rates to measure delinquency may simply reflect racial or gender biases in policing, rather than an individual's traits. GTC also underestimates people's power to change and to control their own impulsivity, according to critics. Some are also leery of any theory that purports to explain "all" crime and delinquency.

FURTHER READING

Colder, C., & Stice, E. (1998). A longitudinal study of the interactive effects of impulsivity and anger on adolescent problem behavior. *Journal of Youth and Adolescence, 27*(3), 255–275.

Forde, D., & Kennedy, L. (1997). Risky lifestyles, routine activities, and the general theory of crime. *Justice Quarterly, 14*, 265–294.

Gibbs, J., Giever, D., & Martin, J. (1998). Parental management and self-control: An empirical test of Gottfredson and Hirschi's general theory of crime. *Journal of Research in Crime and Delinquency, 35*, 40–70.

Gottfredson, M., & Hirschi, T. (1990). *A general theory of crime*. Stanford, CA: Stanford University Press.

Grasmick, H., Tittle, C., Bursik, R., & Arneklev, B. (1993). Testing the core empirical implications of Gottfredson and Hirschi's general theory of crime. *Journal of Research in Crime and Delinquency, 30*, 5–29.

Shoemaker, D. (2005). *Theories of delinquency*, 5th ed. New York: Oxford.

Laura L. Finley

GENETIC THEORIES. Historically, many have asserted that violence and aggression are passed on genetically. It is believed that behavioral characteristics and mental disorders making one prone to crime and violence are passed along in the same way that height and eye color are inherited traits. The earliest theories focused on specific families as delinquency-prone and stemmed from Cesare Lombroso's claim that he could identify a "born criminal." One of the more popular family studies was Richard Dugdale's analysis of the infamous Jukes family of New York in the late nineteenth century. Dugdale concluded that the large number of criminals and prostitutes in the Jukes family was evidence that crime was inherited. In the early twentieth century, H. H. Goddard followed in Dugdale's footsteps, using "family tree" research to pronounce a link between genetics, feebleminded-ness, and crime.

Recent genetic research often involves studying siblings and even identical twins. Since families are also the primary socialization agent of young people, it is difficult to discern precisely the role of genetics, even in studies of twins and adopted children. Further, genetic theories are always controversial, as they bring up important social control questions and concerns. The work of Dugdale and Goddard helped usher in the policy of eugenics, whereby those deemed feebleminded were subject to coerced sterilization in the name of societal betterment. Minorities and the poor were disproportionately subject to forced sterilization, and today genetic theorists are often accused of racism. In addition, the eugenics movement was an important influence in Adolf Hitler's development of the final solution. In 1992, researchers attempted to hold an interdisciplinary conference on genetic theories and the social policy implications. The meeting was cancelled when it was denounced for being racist, then rescheduled in 1995 for a smaller and more remote location. Nonetheless, protesters arrived at the conference.

Twin Studies

Comparing twins with similar non-twins is a common method to explore possible genetic explanations for crime and violence. The agreement in behavior among pairs of individuals is called concordance rates. Twins are still brought up in the same household, however, so researchers have compared monozygotic (MZ) (identical) twins, who share 100 percent of their genetic makeup, with dizygotic (DZ) (fraternal) twins, who share only 50 percent of their genetic makeup. Studies like this have found that identical twins are closer in many personal characteristics, including intelligence. Most studies of this nature have found iden-tical twins have more similar antisocial behavior patterns and delinquency rates than do fraternal twins. A meta-analysis of thirty-eight published twin studies concluded that there is some genetic influence on delinquency, but it is much smaller than previously thought.

One problem is that few twin studies have been conducted with juveniles. One study of 340 pairs of same-sex twins found that adult criminality may be genetically inherited, but that juvenile delinquency, especially among females, is largely due to social factors. Critics also contend that since identical twins are more likely to look and act alike, so they are more likely treated similarly as well. Thus, nurture, not nature, may still be the explanation.

Other studies have looked at identical twins reared separately. The most famous of these studies, from Minnesota, found that identical twins reared apart are quite similar in personal style and behavior. In contrast, fraternal twins reared apart are rarely similar in these qualities.

Adoption Studies

Another method used to explore the role of genetics in shaping delinquent behavior is to compare adopted children with their biological parents. The idea is that if the child's criminal behavior is similar to their biological parent, whom they never met, and not similar to their adoptive parent who raised them, then the behavior is likely inherited. Studies have shown that adoptees share behavioral and intellectual characteristics with their biological parents. In one study, researchers found that 31 percent of the biological fathers of adjudicated delinquent youths had criminal records, compared with just 13 percent of the adoptive fathers. Further, adoption studies have highlighted the fact that heredity and delinquency may be indirectly linked. For instance, adopted hyperactive children are more likely to have hyperactive biological parents. Other forms of learning disabilities may be genetically inherited and thus provide an indirect genetic link to delinquency. Another important indirect link between heredity and delinquency may be intelligence, since intelligence, as well as success in school, are both linked with delinquency. Current genetic research is largely focusing on the heritability of conduct disorders, ADHD, and other temperamental traits.

Criticisms

Critics point out that genetic theorists have tended to oversimplify delinquency, assuming that there is a specific gene linked to crime and violence. This has simply not been proven to date. Further, critics note that genetic theorists assume any genetic trait causing delinquency or violence must be abnormal or aberrant. Even genetic researchers admit that simply possessing a particular gene is not problematic; what matters is whether that gene is expressed. In addition, twin studies are often criticized in a number of ways. Most twin studies involve small samples that are not generalizable. It is not always clear whether twins are DZ or MZ, so researchers may be making faulty assumptions. As noted earlier, it is difficult to control for all possible environmental factors. Also, most twin studies begin by identifying at least one of the pair who has been involved in crime or delinquency, generally using police records. This assumes that police records are an accurate measure of delinquency. A more accurate method is to first identify sets of twins, then trace their delinquent behavior. Researchers who used this technique in Norway found slight differences between DZ and MZ twins, but they were not statistically significant.

Recent research examining genetic explanations for crime and violence is more sophisticated. Advances in understanding genetic markers in the late 1980s and 1990s have helped in addressing some of the early criticisms of genetic theories. In 1993, researchers identified a genetic marker and then a gene they thought to be associated with aggression in male members of a Dutch family. The affected gene produces monoamine oxidase A (MAOA), which is involved in metabolizing serotonin, the neurotransmitter associated with impulse control. A longitudinal study of youth by researchers from New Zealand in 2002 supported the importance of MAOA, but concluded that it was indirectly linked. Low levels of MAOA failed to protect young people from the psychological effects of abuse or maltreatment, making them more vulnerable to the effects of that maltreatment.

See also ADD/ADHD; Biochemical Theories; Biosocial Theories; Neurological Theories; Trait Theories

FURTHER READING

Bouchard, J., Lykken, D., McGue, D., Srgal, N., & Tellegen, A. (1990). Sources of human physiological differences: The Minnesota study of twins reared apart. *Science, 250*, 223–228.

Rowe, D. (1995). *The limits of family influence: Genes, experiences, and behavior.* New York: Guilford.

Shoemaker, D. (2005). *Theories of delinquency*, 5th ed. New York: Oxford University Press.

Walters, G. (1992). A meta-analysis of the gene-crime relationship. *Criminology, 30*, 595–613.

Wasserman, D. (2004, Spring). Is there value in identifying individual genetic predispositions to violence? *Journal of Law, Medicine, and Ethics, 32*(1), 24–34.

Laura L. Finley

GLEN RIDGE, NEW JERSEY (1989). On March 1, 1989, a mentally disabled teenage girl (who will be called Christina in this entry for purposes of protecting her privacy) was raped in the basement of a home where two high school athletes lived with their parents in the city of Glen Ridge, New Jersey. This crime, known as the Glen Ridge Rape, was prosecuted and the suspects brought to trial in 1993. Four of the seven defendants indicted on various criminal charges were convicted; three served detention sentences. Two other defendants made plea bargains with the prosecutor's office, and one other had the charges against him dropped. This crime brought national attention to juvenile sexual violence and to the vulnerability of disabled teens.

On March 1, 1989, Christopher Archer lured Christina, a seventeen-year-old girl with an IQ of 64 and the mental capacity of an eight-year-old, from the park where she was playing basketball and into the basement of the home where twins Kyle and Kevin Scherzer lived. Christina was promised a date with Archer's brother, Paul, if she went to the basement. When she arrived, she found several other teenage boys waiting.

The Archer brothers, the Scherzer brothers, Richard Corcoran, Peter Quigley, and Bryant Grober proceeded to command Christina to perform sex acts on herself and on them as several other boys watched. The attack also involved using a broomstick and a fungo bat (a baseball bat used for practice) to sexually assault Christina. After the attack, was over, the boys threatened to tell her mother what happened if she discussed the attack with anyone.

Even though Christina did not tell about the attack for several days, rumors were rampant at the boys' school that some type of rape had occurred. One student, Charles Figueroa, complained to school officials and was met with skepticism. Christina, who attended a different school that had programs for mentally disabled students, finally chose to tell her swimming coach. After the disclosure, the police were notified of the attack. Officers questioned Christina and the suspects in the case. After it was determined that Corcoran had been present, his father, a lieutenant for the Glen Ridge Police Department, was removed from the investigation. On the morning of May 24, 1989, the Scherzer twins, Peter Quigley, and the Archer brothers were arrested and charged with various crimes. Corcoran was arrested a few months later.

The time in between the arrests and the trial was difficult for the victim and the city in which she lived. The crime left Glen Ridge, an affluent upper-class neighborhood, largely in denial that this type of crime could occur in their city. Many citizens blamed Christina for what happened, citing her history of inappropriate sexual behavior as reason to doubt the truthfulness of her story. Students at Glen Ridge High School openly defended their classmates, and one tried to trick Christina into admitting the sexual acts were consensual. Other citizens defended Christina and asserted that it was well known she was mentally disabled. It has since been discovered that several of the boys involved had histories of violence and misbehavior, with some incidents involving Christina.

Prior to the trial, Christopher Archer and Peter Quigley accepted plea bargains and agreed to testify for the prosecution against the other defendants. The trial took five months to complete, during which time jury members heard graphic testimony from Christina about what happened to her in the Scherzers' basement. The defense strategy focused on proving that Christina was a sexually active teenager who was not forced to participate in the crimes the defendants were accused of committing. The prosecution argued that Christina was so mentally disabled that she could not give informed consent. The Glen Ridge trial marked the first time that evidence about rape trauma syndrome was permitted to be entered into evidence in New Jersey.

After twelve days of deliberation, a jury of seven women and five men convicted each of the defendants on various charges. In the summer of 1997, Christopher Archer and the Scherzer twins were remanded to jail for the first time since a jury found them guilty in 1993. They were classified as young adult offenders and sentenced to detention facilities with looser restrictions than those that govern prisons and jails.

Kyle Scherzer was scheduled to be released from prison on parole December 6, 1999. Corcoran, who was never tried and won $200,000 in a lawsuit against the Essex County prosecutor's office for malicious prosecution, shot his wife and another man and then killed himself near Fort Bragg, North Carolina, where he was stationed as a Special Forces soldier (Associated Press, 2005). No further information is available on Kevin Scherzer and Chris Archer.

FURTHER READING

Associated Press. (2005, February 7). Man from Glen Ridge rape case kills self in bloodbath. *New York Daily News*.

Greenberg, K., & Hall, M. (1989, May 26). Assault case shakes affluent New Jersey town. *USA Today*, 3A.

Hanley, R. (1997, July 1). 3 men are jailed in Glen Ridge sexual assault case. *The New York Times* [Online edition].

Laufer, P. (1994). *A question of consent: Innocence and complicity in the Glen Ridge rape case*. San Francisco: Mercury House.

Lefkowitz, B. (1997). *Our guys*. New York: Vintage Books.

Man jailed for rape in Glen Ridge is paroled. (1999, October 30). *The New York Times*.

Wendy Perkins

GLUECK, SHELDON AND ELEANOR. Sheldon and Eleanor Glueck were two of the most influential researchers in life course criminology during the twentieth century. In what is now considered a classic study in juvenile delinquency, they examined the careers of 500 delinquent and 500 nondelinquent boys in a longitudinal study while working at Harvard in the 1930s. Entitled *Unraveling Juvenile Delinquency*, the study was designed to examine the early onset of delinquency as a precursor to crime in adulthood. They examined various biological, psychological, and social causes to delinquency; focusing on sociocultural, somatic, intellectual, and emotional-temperamental origins.

Sheldon and Eleanor followed a delinquent population from Westboro, Massachusetts to determine what factors contributed to their offending behavior. The population was matched to a nondelinquent youth population from the Boston, Massachusetts area. The two cohorts of juveniles were matched by age, ethnicity, intelligence, and area of residence.

Original data were collected through psychiatric interviews with subjects, their parents, reports from their teachers, and official records from police departments, court systems, and correctional agencies. The subjects were followed and their activity was measured. Measurements were taken through the years of 1940–1948 (Time I), the years of 1948–1956 (Time II), and the years of 1954–1963 (Time III).

Their findings included several social and personal causes of delinquency that would change over an individual's life course. At the psychological level, they found that an individual who suffered from mental disease was more likely to commit delinquent acts than an individual who did not.

At the social level, family structure was found to be the single most important factor related to criminal offending. The child that was raised in a large, single-guardian household without a solid economic and educational foundation was more likely to commit delinquency.

At the biological level, they found that one of the major attributes related to delinquency was the subject's physical body type. Their findings supported William Sheldon and his somatotype theory. His theory stated that the mesomorph, the individual who is athletic and muscular, is more likely to commit delinquent activity than the endomorph (soft and round) and the ectomorph (thin and fragile).

Finally, they noted that if an individual was a delinquent early in life, the chances of becoming a criminal as an adult were greater. Initially their work was well received in the field, but was harshly criticized after their deaths, as it became popular to criticize any research that linked criminal behavior to biological or psychological traits.

The Gluecks and the life course perspective returned to the forefront of criminology in 1993, when famed criminologists **Robert Sampson and John Laub** published their book entitled *Crime in the Making: Pathways and Turning Points through Life*. The data that were used for this book originated from the initial study conducted by Sheldon and Eleanor Glueck in the 1930s, after the researchers found it in the basement of the Harvard Law School Library.

FURTHER READING

Glueck, S., & Glueck, E. (1950). *Unraveling juvenile delinquency*. New York: The Commonwealth Fund.

Glueck, S., & Glueck, E. (1968). *Delinquents and non-delinquents in perspective*. Cambridge, MA: Harvard University Press.

Laub, J.H., & Sampson, R.J. (1993). *Crime in the making: Pathways and turning points through life*. Cambridge, MA: Harvard University Press.

Georgen Guerrero

GOLDEN, ANDREW (AND MITCHELL JOHNSON)

General Description and Significance of the Case

This shooting was one of the few juvenile school shootings in American history that involved more than one lone shooter and was a precursor to the Columbine shootings by **Eric Harris and Dylan Klebold** just one year later. It established a new level of fear and outrage among Americans due to the youth of the shooters and the methodical and deliberate nature of their acts.

This act occurred during the high point of school shootings in America, the late 1990s, and a time of fear and sometimes sweeping policy changes. A number of issues came under the microscope of officials, parents, and the media during this time period, including stricter penalties for gun-owners whose weapons are accessible to others, particularly juveniles. Similarly, some officials and policy makers were facing new concerns surrounding the protection of children in schools. A number of schools implemented metal detectors and additional **school resource officers**, while others created programs that would be more proactive in recognizing warning signs in youth.

Description of the Case

On March 24, 1998, Mitchell Johnson and Andrew Golden, ages thirteen and eleven, opened gunfire at students and teachers at the middle school they attended in Jonesboro, Arkansas. The boys' plan had begun earlier that morning, when both boys skipped school and acquired transportation and weapons. Mitchell Johnson stole his stepfather's van and drove it to Andrew Golden's house, whose parents were at work. The boys then attempted to break into the cache of guns and weapons stored in the house, but were only successful in taking three short-range guns. Since they needed long-range weapons to carry out their attack, they then drove to Andrew Golden's grandparents' house and broke in, stealing a number of rifles.

After loading the guns into the van, the boys then drove to Westside Middle School, parking and walking up to a hill above the school facing the schoolyard. Andrew Golden then proceeded to walk down to the school and pull a fire alarm, quickly running back up and taking his place a short way away from Mitchell, setting up a cross fire. The two boys, both dressed in camouflage, waited for students to exit the school and began to open fire on them after enough had entered the schoolyard.

The attack lasted less than five minutes, but four students and one teacher were killed and another ten were injured. Police responded immediately to the shootings and quickly threw a net over the area, trying to block off any escape for the two shooters. They captured the two boys trying to exit the woods and make it to their van, where they later discovered over a dozen weapons and a sizeable stock of ammunition. Both boys were charged as juveniles and placed into juvenile institutions.

Aftermath and Explanations of the Shootings

As would be expected, outrage and shock followed the shootings, and Jonesboro was said to be a town that was torn apart. The search for answers began, and some details about the two boys soon emerged. Although Mitchell Johnson was seen by many to be a normal, respectable thirteen-year-old who was even a choirboy in his church, others had seen warning signs. There were some instances where he deliberately defied authority and then made threats when scolded. For instance, he once wore a hat into class and had to have it forcibly removed, and on another occasion he wrote out threats during detention, stating that his English class may no longer exist in the future.

Mitchell had recently experienced a breakup with his girlfriend and was said to be enraged at her. He also was reported to have made threats toward her on a number of occasions. Many claim that the warning signs for Johnson were visible, and they simply were not given any credence because of a disbelief that such a thing could occur in Jonesboro. Golden, the younger of the two, was considered to be more of the follower, but some contended he was not simply a naïve child who was led into the acts. In fact, some parents living in his neighborhood stated that he acted so strangely that they would not allow their children to play with him.

Although this attack had similarities with the Columbine shootings that occurred a year later (i.e., there were two shooters with one leader and a follower), there were also major differences between the two shootings. This is not surprising due to the age difference between the two sets of shooters, one involving high school seniors and the other middle school students. Rather than being aggravated or bullied by schoolmates, the Jonesboro shooters, particularly Mitchell Johnson, were considered more as bullies than the bullied. Moreover, **suicide** did not seem to be an option for the Jonesboro shooters, while many psychologists have concluded that it was one of the central motivations behind the Columbine shooting. Both shootings, however, shared similar accusations made in hindsight about missed warning signs during a period of unsuppressed threats and rage by the students leading up to the attacks.

Because both Mitchell Johnson and Andrew Golden were prosecuted and sentenced as juveniles, they both can only be held until their eighteenth birthdays under Arkansas law. Federal prosecutors used federal gun charges, however, to increase their release age to twenty-one. On August 12, 2005, amid heavy criticism from the Jonesboro community, Mitchell Johnson was released from a Tennessee facility, his record wiped clean because he is no longer a juvenile. Johnson does not plan to live in Arkansas. Andrew Golden is scheduled to be released in 2007.

FURTHER READING

Burns, R., & Crawford, C. (1999). School shootings, the media, and public fear: Ingredients for a moral panic. *Crime, Law and Social Change, 32*, 147–169.

Clete, S., Bailey, C., Carona, A., & Mebane, D. (2002). School crime policy changes: The impact of recent highly-publicized school crimes. *American Journal of Criminal Justice, 26*, 269–288.

Newman, K. (2004). *Rampage: The social roots of school shootings.* New York: Basic Books.

Ruddell, R., & Mays, L. (2003). Examining the arsenal of juvenile gunslingers: Trends and policy implications. *Crime and Delinquency, 49*, 231–252.

Brion Sever

GREAT. Conceptualized by the Bureau of Alcohol, Tobacco, and Firearms (ATF) and the Phoenix, Arizona Police Department in 1991, the Gang Resistance Education and Training (GREAT) program was first implemented in 1992. It is a school-based, law enforcement-instructed program intended to help minimize delinquency and violence among youth, as well as to prevent youth involvement in gangs. The program teaches young people life skills and problem-solving strategies that can replace violence as a response and that can reduce the inclination for involvement with gangs. In 1999, in response to evaluation data, the program was revamped to include more active learning.

Today, there are four components of GREAT: An elementary school program, a middle school program, a summer program, and a program for families. The elementary school program is designed for fourth and fifth grade students and consists of six 30- to 45-minute lessons. The middle school program is more extensive. It includes thirteen 45- to 60-minute lessons designed for sixth and seventh grade students. These lessons are skills-based and are meant to effect knowledge, attitude, and behavioral change. They have also been designed to integrate national English/language arts and health curriculum standards. Interested students can enroll in the GREAT summer program closest to their neighborhood. Summer programs vary in length and specifics, but all include educational and recreational activities, such as field trips, sporting events, and community service. There are two parts to the GREAT program for families. One part is a six-session family curriculum designed for implementation with 10 to 14 year olds. The other part is a resource guide for GREAT facilitators.

GREAT officers are trained at one of five regional sites in LaCrosse, Wisconsin; Philadelphia, Pennsylvania; Orlando, Florida; Portland, Oregon; and Phoenix, Arizona.

GREAT is supported by the **United States Department of Justice (USDOJ)**, the Federal Law Enforcement Training Center, and the Bureau of Alcohol, Tobacco, Firearms and Explosives. Full-time, sworn officers with at least one year of experience must complete a one-week (40 hours) training session. They must also have teaching or public speaking experience or hold elementary or secondary teaching certification. To date, more than 8,000 officers have been trained.

All fifty states and the District of Columbia had implemented GREAT programs by 1997. To date, more than four million students have graduated from a GREAT program. Evaluations have found GREAT to be somewhat successful. A five-year longitudinal evaluation in 1995 found those who completed the training experienced lower levels of victimization, held more negative views of gangs,but more positive views of police, reported decreased risk-taking behavior, and had more positive associations with peers in prosocial activities. A 1999 evaluation of eleven sites including surveys of 5,935 eighth grade students found those who completed the program reported less drug use and less total delinquency, but found no difference in current or previous gang membership, selling of drugs, or commission of status offenses. This evaluation has been critiqued for not using pretests to assess baseline characteristics of students. A 2001 evaluation that did use pretests and surveyed over 3,500 students found those who completed GREAT engaged in fewer property offenses, but did not find significant change in gang membership, drug use, violence against persons, or status offenses.

FURTHER READING

Esbensen, F-A., & Osgood, D. (1999). GREAT: Results from a national evaluation. *Journal of Research in Crime and Delinquency, 34*(2), 194–225.

Esbensen, F-A., Osgood, D., Taylor, T., Peterson, D., & Freng, A. (1999). How great is GREAT? Results from a longitudinal, quasi-experimental design. *Criminology and Public Policy, 1*(1), 87–118.

GREAT officer training. (n.d.). Available at: http://www.great-online.org.

History of the GREAT program. (n.d.). Available at: http://www.great-online.org.

Programs that work. (n.d.). Promising Practices Network. Available at: http://www .promising practices.net.

Welcome to the GREAT Web site. (n.d.). Available at http://www.great-online.org.

Laura L. Finley

GUN-RELATED VIOLENCE, RATES OF.

Concerns about violence among juveniles stemming from the use of firearms and other weapons are well founded. Mirroring the drop in juvenile violence from 1994, the prevalence or rate of weapon carrying has declined among high school students from 1991 (26.1 percent) to 2003 (17.1 percent), according to the National Youth Risk Behavior Survey, 2004. Research indicates, however, that juveniles have relatively easy access to firearms, and youth involved in delinquent acts are more likely to carry weapons than nondelinquent-involved youth. According to data from the **Centers for Disease Control and Prevention (CDC)**, the leading cause of death among all youth ages 7 to 17 is firearms (48.1 percent). Among the same age group (7 to 17), firearms were the cause of death in approximately 75 percent of all homicide cases. The type of violent crime is related to the presence of a weapon. For example, robbery is more likely to involve a weapon than sexual assault. Sources of information on rates of weapon-related violence are drawn from large national survey data such as the **National Crime Victimization Survey (NCVS)**, health behavior data from the CDC, official records from the Federal Bureau of Investigation's

Uniform Crime Reporting (UCR) system, and studies by university researchers using self-reports.

Although a number of factors have been identified, relatively little is known about what drives some youth to be involved in weapon-related violence and not others. Demographic factors related to weapon carrying show that males are more likely than females to carry weapons. There is evidence that weapon choice is influenced by gender, resulting in men more likely to carry guns and women knives or mace. Youth from urban settings report higher levels of weapon carrying than youth from suburban and small town areas. Other behavioral and interpersonal variables have been found to be associated with weapon carrying and subsequent violence. These variables include gang affiliation, peer misbehavior, marijuana and other drug use, selling drugs, physical fighting, sexual activity, and low levels of family attachment and perceived social support. The involvement of gangs in selling drugs, physical aggression, and the need for self-protection have been found to be primary determinants of weapon carrying among gang-involved youth. Youth who report lower levels of family attachment and perceived social support are also more likely to carry a weapon. This is thought to be due to the importance that interpersonal social networks—parents, caregivers, friends, teachers, and coaches—play in exerting positive control and attachments. Findings are revealing that multiple pathways exist to the carrying of weapons and that these pathways are interrelated and influence overall rates.

See also Center for the Prevention of School Violence (CPSV); Gun-Related Violence, Types of; Public Health Approach

FURTHER READING

Bureau of Justice Statistics. Available at: www.ojp.usdoj.gov/bjs/.

Centers for Disease Control and Prevention. Available at: www.cdc.gov.

Gaensbauer, T., & Wauboldt, M. (2000, January 5). Facts about gun violence. *American Academy Of Child and Adolescent Psychiatry*. Available at: www.aacap.org/info_families_NationalFacts/coGunviol.htm.

Office of Juvenile Justice and Delinquency Prevention. (n.d.). Promising strategies to reduce gun violence. Available at: http://www.ojjdp.ncjrs.org/pubs/gun_violence/contents.html.

Michael G. Vaughn

GUN-RELATED VIOLENCE, TYPES OF.

Violence generated by gun use or gun possession by a juvenile includes a range of violent crimes, such as armed robbery, gang-related shootings, homicides, and attempted homicides. Accidents may also be classified as unintentional firearm deaths that are negligence-related. Concealed gun carrying for nonsporting purposes is a nonviolent illegal act and is included in weapons violations by juveniles in the **Uniform Crime Reports (UCR)**. Injury, death from homicide, bystander homicide, suicide, and threat of injury caused by the actual brandishing of a gun during a crime is gun-related violence.

Reasons for Carrying

Self-report studies on gun carrying are helpful in identifying motives for carrying a gun and the frequency of carrying a gun. Longitudinal studies that examine gun carrying individuals at different ages can determine the trends in carrying and reasons and circumstances of gun carrying. Gun carrying trends show that the 1990s was the peak of youth gun carrying. The major reason that juveniles report gun carrying is for self-protection from other juveniles; however, it can lead to offensive use during a situation of opportunity or strain. The statistics on gun carrying are not the equivalent to gun-related violence, as fewer youth use the weapon. Gun carrying for sport was not found to be connected to crime, focusing the risk on gun carrying in general and bringing a gun to school. The percentage reported for gun carrying has declined since the peak rates of 18 percent to current statistics of 3 percent (carrying in the last month), which is similar to statistics for carrying a gun to school.

Gangs and Guns

Longitudinal studies of gangs report that while some future members carry a gun, most important is that a large increase in carrying is reported when youth join a gang. Thus membership increases gun possession for reasons of protection. Gun carrying is short-term, which is up to a half-year. When a youth leaves the gang, gun ownership decreases. Crimes linked to gangs that involve guns include homicide, drug dealing, and nonviolent serious crimes. The crack cocaine epidemic has been given as a reason for increases in gun-related violence. There is partial evidence that drug markets may contribute to homicides, but it does not account for all of the murders.

Gangs in many metropolitan areas maintain neighborhood regions. As automobiles gained use among gang youth, gun discharging—the infamous drive-by shooting—became a tragic problem. Homicide caused by discharging a firearm from a motor vehicle at a person outside the vehicle gained national attention. Offenses, such as gun threats in car-jackings, firing at a dwelling, a motor vehicle, an airplane, or a recreational camper, include legal responsibility by the driver and occupants. By specifying laws on drive-by shootings, three-strikes laws, targeted enforcement, and gun exchange and turn-in programs, the frequency of shootings has declined. Random gun violence is a continuing problem in major cities and receives aggressive enforcement and prosecution. Prevention programs to reduce gun carrying involve intensive unscheduled police visits of high-risk gang youth on probation.

Guns and Homicides

The late 1980s and the 1990s showed a considerable increase, both in the number of juvenile victims killed with firearms and the number of juveniles arrested for homicide. Overall, about 60 to 80 percent of homicides involved a firearm. This increase is even greater than self-reports of violent behavior, showing that this trend was the key violence problem of the 1990s. By 2002, the murder rates that were perpetrated by a juvenile dropped to 1984 levels. The UCR subdivides homicides into three types: a juvenile acting alone, a juvenile acting with at least one other juvenile, and a juvenile acting with an adult (usually under twenty-four years of age). Overall, homicide levels dropped considerably; proportionately, half are solos, a third act with an adult, and a tenth act with another juvenile.

Currently, juveniles perpetrate a tenth of murders (approximately 1,300 victims annually). Two-thirds of the victims were killed (by males) with a firearm. A third of female offenders used a gun and consistently have about 200 victims annually. Demographically, most victims are male, half are white and nearly half are black, and they are concentrated in urban cities over one million in population. Characteristics of homicides are that victims are nonfamily members or acquaintances with the perpetrator using a handgun to murder them. The scenario of homicide involves either a family or friendship dispute or the murder of a victim during the commission of another crime, such as robbery, rape, arson, and assault. While juveniles perpetrate firearm violence, adult criminals' prevalence in homicides is much greater.

Guns and Suicides

Youth suicide rates peaked in the 1990s and recently leveled off, so for every two youth victims of a homicide there is a youth who commits suicide. Black males showed the greatest increases (nearly tripling) in firearms suicides, followed by white males (growth by a third). Current rates have decreased and are stable. Increased gun availability has been argued as a cause; however, where amounts of guns are limited, other methods of suicide are used, which diminishes this argument.

Guns and Schools

Juveniles' involvement in violent crimes involving a firearm show a similar temporal pattern with adults. Peak gun violence is reported between 9 p.m. and 10 p.m., however some gun violence appears from after school to 9 p.m. In comparing school and nonschool days, there is no difference when gun violence is recorded. Schools, however, are involved in reporting weapons laws violations during all hours of the school day. Security measures in schools, such as random locker searches, metal detectors, and security professionals, are used to prevent gun contraband.

See also Assault; Gang-On-Gang Violence; Suicide

FURTHER READING

Braga, A. (2003). Serious youth gun offenders and the epidemic of youth violence in Boston. *Journal of Quantitative Criminology, 19*(1), 33–54.

Lizotte, A., & Sheppard, D. (2001). *Gun use by male juveniles: Research and prevention.* Washington, DC: Office of Juvenile Justice and Delinquency Prevention.

Snyder, H., & Sickmund, M. (2006). *Juvenile offenders and victims: 2006 national report.* Washington, DC: National Center for Juvenile Justice.

James Steinberg

HALLUCINOGENS. As the term hallucinogens implies, "Hallucinogens are drugs that cause hallucinations—profound distortions in a person's perception of reality" (National Institute on Drug Abuse, 2001, p. 1). Different hallucinogens affect the brain in different ways, but the primary impact of hallucinogens is a disruption of the neurotransmitter serotonin. One of the best-known hallucinogens, LSD, was discovered by Dr. Albert Hoffman in the 1940s. Then, during the 1960s, young people throughout the United States began using LSD based on the belief that LSD expands human consciousness. This belief was best elaborated by Dr. Timothy Leary (1968), a popular social philosopher of the mid-to-late twentieth century who used LSD and conducted a variety of experiments with the drug, inclusive of giving it to prison inmates based on the dubious speculation that LSD could rehabilitate criminals by broadening their consciousness. LSD use declined during the late 1970s and 1980s, but other hallucinogens gained popularity. By far the most dangerous is PCP which, in addition to being a hallucinogen, has depressive, stimulative, and anesthetic properties and can produce extremely violent behavior. Fortunately, PCP use has significantly decreased since the 1980s. Nonetheless, hallucinogens remain popular among young people.

Most recently there has been an increase in the use of MDMA, a hallucinogen amphetamine derivative which produces energy, peaceful feelings of euphoria, and mild hallucinations (usually a distortion of light). The Merck pharmaceutical company in Germany first manufactured MDMA in the early 1900s, and over the next several decades the drug was experimented with and prescribed by psychotherapists for a variety of disorders. During this time it acquired the nickname Adam because of the peaceful feelings of innocence it induces. MDMA gained popularity as a recreational drug during the 1980s among young people who frequented dance clubs in Austin and Dallas, Texas, and came to be known as Ecstasy. Since that time, MDMA has continued to gain popularity among the youth populations of Europe, the United States, and the United Kingdom. In particular, MDMA is popular among youths who frequent dance clubs and parties known as Raves. There is no evidence that MDMA causes violent behavior, but there is a risk of death from heat stroke, especially when the drug is taken at a Rave wherein the user may dance for hours and be unaware of the rise in body temperature and dehydration that are occurring.

FURTHER READING

Beck, J., & Rosenbaum, M. (1994). *Pursuit of ecstasy*. Albany: State University of New York Press.

Leary, T. (1968). *High priest*. New York: World Publishing Company.

Liska, K. (1997). *Drugs and the human body with implications for society,* 5th ed. Upper Saddle River, NJ: Prentice Hall.

Hallucinogens and dissociative drugs. (2001). National Institute on Drug Abuse. Bethesda, MD: U.S. Department of Health and Human Services, National Institutes of Health, National Institute on Drug Abuse.

Ben Brown

HARRIS, ERIC (AND DYLAN KLEBOLD)

Introduction

On April 20, 1999, many people sat watching their televisions, horrified at the events that unfolded at Columbine High School in Littleton, Colorado. Two students, Eric Harris, aged eighteen, and Dylan Klebold, aged seventeen, marched into Columbine High School armed with shotguns that they had sawed the barrels off, a semiautomatic handgun, and a dozen or so homemade bombs. The two went on a rampage and killed twelve students and one teacher. Both then committed suicide. According to journal entries from blogs and websites, Harris and Klebold had been planning the attack on the town of Littleton and Columbine High School since April of 1998.

Events at the school were going to begin at 11a.m., when the largest number of students would be in the cafeteria and, therefore, the most harm could be inflicted. The two had chosen April 20 because it was the anniversary of Adolf Hitler's birthday. In addition to the weapons that the boys had on their persons, they had planted bombs around the school and around the town of Littleton. The largest bomb was placed in the school cafeteria, but fortunately it did not detonate. The Jefferson County Sheriff's Department estimated that there were twelve detonations around Littleton, but none caused any injuries.

Background

Since the Columbine incident, a great deal of information about Harris and Klebold has been released to the public, not all of which is accurate. It does appear, however, that there were warning signs of the attack, although no one could have foreseen its scope. Some months before the attack, a deputy at the Jefferson County Sheriff's office was directed to Harris's website by the father of a schoolmate of Harris. The website outlined a plan of mass murder in Littleton, including the use of explosives. The website also touted racist messages and anti-homosexual rhetoric and had material depicting hatred of teachers at Columbine High School and people in Littleton. There was even evidence on the website that the two boys were building and experimenting with pipe bombs. An affidavit for a search warrant was written, but it was never filed.

Another hint at the boys' potential for violence was found in a video that Klebold and Harris made as part of a school project. The video showed them with fake firearms, killing students, and acting as hired hit men. The video was not shown to other students after a teacher decided it was too graphic.

The two boys planned the Columbine incident while in a youth violence prevention program that served as a **diversion** program for juvenile, Harris and Klebold were assigned diversion when they were caught breaking into a van. This was the first time that either Harris or Klebold had been in trouble with the law, but it was not the first time that either had undergone counseling.

Eric Harris came from a startlingly normal middle-class family. His father was an ex-air force pilot, and his mother worked for a catering company. The family moved around due to military requirements and settled in Littleton in 1993. Eric wanted to join the Marine Corps, but shortly before April 20, 1999, the Corps turned him down because he was undergoing drug therapy and psychiatric counseling for depression and was in anger management classes. His father was worried about his son, and when he heard about the attack on the high school, he immediately called police and expressed fear that his son was involved.

Dylan Klebold grew up in Littleton. His father was a geophysicist, and his mother worked for the State Consortium of Community Colleges. Many say that Klebold was greatly influenced by Harris and that his behavior changed for the worse after he became good friends with Harris. The two had a common interest in computers and computer games, although Harris appeared to be the most talented in this arena, designing and writing software for video games. Harris wrote software for the game *Doom*, which is still available.

Both Harris and Klebold were suspected of being members of the Trench Coat Mafia, but members of this group claim that the two were actually only acquaintances with students in the group. Classmates do claim that the two boys were picked on by other students, particularly the athletes, but they were not singled out, and, therefore, unlike other school shootings, the main motivation behind the attack does not seem to be repeated victimization at school.

An FBI clinical psychologist has proposed that Klebold was hurting inside, while Harris externalized his pain by wanting to hurt people. Harris has been dubbed a psychopath by a number of psychologists. This diagnosis was made based on his inability to feel empathy; he did not quite understand love, hate, or fear. It is the opinion of many experts that Harris was the driving force behind the attack.

Robyn Anderson, an eighteen-year-old student at Columbine High School made the straw purchase of two shotguns for Harris and Klebold. She was never charged with this offense. The semiautomatic handgun was one of several firearms purchased by Mark Manes and Philip Duran for the boys. These two were charged.

In the aftermath of the Columbine incident, controversial filmmaker Michel Moore released the documentary film *Bowling for Columbine*. The film's title comes from Harris and Klebold's class schedule, which had them in bowling class on the morning of the attack. In his documentary, Moore tackles many of the post-Columbine issues, such as the influence of Marilyn Manson's music on Harris and Klebold. In an interview with Manson, Manson says that his appearance provides people with a fitting image of fear, but blaming the incident on his music is about as ridiculous as blaming the incident on bowling. Manson suggests that the failure to listen to Harris and Klebold, and the inability to provide effective solutions to their teenage problems, was more likely the cause of the incident.

See also Biochemical Theories; Biosocial Theories; Center for the Prevention of School Violence (CPSV); Conflict Resolution; Diversion; Gun-Related Violence, Rates of; Gun-Related Violence, Types of; National School Safety Center (NSSC); Peaceable Schools

FURTHER READING

Center for the Prevention of School Violence. Available at: http://www.juvjus.state.nc.us/cpsv/cpsvrroom.htm.

Columbine High School massacre. (n.d). Wikipedia Free Encyclopedia. Available at: http://en.wikipedia.org/wiki/Columbine_High_School.

DeVoe, J., Ruddy, S., Miller, A., Planty, M., Peter, K., Synder, T., et al. (2002). *Indicators of school crime and safety, 2002*. Washington, DC, Department of Education and Department of Justice. NCJ 196753.

Owens, Bill. (2001). Governor's Columbine review commission report. Denver, CO: State of Colorado Governor's Office. Available at: http://www.state.co.us/columbine.

Monica L. P. Robbers

HATE CRIME. Also known as "bias crime" and "ethnoviolence," the term "hate crime" was first used in the 1980s in reference to a racial incident in the Howard Beach section of New York City, where a black man was killed while trying to evade a mob of white teens. Specifically, hate crime refers to crimes committed against individuals, groups, or property based on real or perceived race, religion, gender, sexual orientation, disability, national origin, or ethnicity of the victim. While certainly hate crimes have occurred throughout history, it wasn't until Congress passed the Hate Crime Reporting Statute in 1990 that any systematic form of tracking was put into place. In the 1990s, the federal government, as well as most states, enacted various forms of hate crime laws. By 1995, thirty-seven states and the District of Columbia had one or more of the following four types: sentence enhancements; substantive crimes; civil rights statutes; and/or reporting statutes.

Sentence enhancements, which add penalties for offenders convicted of hate crimes, are the most common form of hate crime law. The 1994 Violent Crime Control and Law Enforcement Act mandated a sentence enhancement of three levels above the base sentencing level in hate crime cases. Hate crime statutes that define new offenses are referred to as substantive offenses. These might include crimes like "intimidation" and "institutional vandalism." There is great variation between the states regarding what prejudices hate crime laws cover. For instance, Washington, DC includes discrimination based on personal appearance, family responsibility, and matriculation, while a few states include political affiliation and marital status of the victim. Most hate crime laws are predicated on the notion that hate crimes are more harmful than other offenses with different motivations. In contrast to other countries like Great Britain, France, Canada, and Germany, the United States does not prohibit hate speech.

Critics contend these laws are not the most useful way to address hate crimes. They maintain that there is no conclusive data to show that hate crimes are worse than other offenses, that "protected" groups are receiving unfair treatment, and that police and prosecutors are not well-prepared to apply hate crime laws. Further, critics maintain that those committed to engaging in hate-related offenses are not very deterrable.

According to data collected through the National Incident Based Reporting System (NIBRS), there were 5,855 hate crime incidents between 1995 and 2000. In 2003, the FBI counted 7,489 incidents. The most common form of hate crime offense is race-related, specifically, against blacks. In 2003, anti-black hate crimes represented 34 percent of all hate crimes reported. Offenders are more commonly Caucasian. Between 1997 and 1999, 62.3 percent of all offenders were white. Geographically, California, New York, New Jersey, Michigan, and Massachusetts accounted for almost 50 percent of all recorded hate crimes.

People under the age of eighteen represented 29.1 percent of the total number of offenders, the largest proportion of all age groups. The most common hate crime scenario involves a juvenile victim and a juvenile offender; between 1997 and 1999, this accounted for 64 percent of reported hate crimes. When juveniles commit violent hate crimes, they are far more likely to use a knife or other blunt object than a firearm, according to NIBRS data.

From 1997 to 1999, juveniles (under the age of eighteen) were 23 percent of the victims of hate crimes, compared to 11 percent of victims of all other types of crime. Between 1995 and 2000, NIBRS data showed that people between the ages of 25 and 39 were more likely to be victims of a hate crime, 30.6 percent compared to 26.7 percent. Males are far more likely to be both victims and perpetrators. Between 1997 and 1999, males constituted 69 percent of all victims. Males under the age of eighteen were 81 percent of the victims. Hate crimes against juveniles tend to be more serious; between 1997 and 1999, 63 percent of hate crimes against juveniles involved simple or aggravated assault, in contrast to 39 percent of hate crimes with adult victims. Other differences between juveniles and adults are the locations of the hate offenses and the relationship between victim and offender. While 10 percent of all other types of crimes occur at school, 21 percent of reported hate crimes between 1997 and 1999 occurred there. Thirty-nine percent of adult victims of hate crimes knew their offender, whereas 56 percent of juvenile victims did.

In addition to hate crime laws, many efforts have been taken to prevent and respond to hate crimes, both in general and specific to juveniles. In 1992, the Juvenile Justice and Delinquency Prevention Act required states to include hate crime efforts in their juvenile justice plans. It also authorized and funded a national assessment of hate crimes, as well as provided grant monies for curricular efforts addressing hate crime. The Anti-Defamation League recommends alternative sentencing and rehabilitation of juveniles convicted of hate offenses. They have sponsored a nine-week **diversion** program called Learning about Discrimination, which involves lessons on racism, anti-Semitism, the Holocaust, and civil rights. Partners against Hate, a collaborative effort among several civil rights groups, has prepared a middle school program guide for teaching about hate crimes. Since research has shown that children ages five to eight begin to identify similarities and differences among people and that, by fourth grade, students have largely formed their racial attitudes, it seems early efforts at teaching the importance of diversity are critical.

Others maintain that, while these efforts are important, until broader structural problems are addressed, hate will continue in the United States and so will hate crimes. Research has demonstrated, for instance, that poor young people, in particular jobless males, are more likely to relate to the message of hate organizations such as the Aryan Nations. Hence, some argue that addressing youth unemployment and poverty would also help address the problem of hate crimes.

See also Gun-Related Violence, Rates of; Gun-Related Violence, Types of;

FURTHER READING

Ezekial, R. (1995). *The racist mind*. New York: Penguin.

Hate crimes against juveniles reported to police. (n.d.). University of New Hampshire Crimes Against Children Research Center. Available at: www.unh.edu/ccrc/factsheet/hatecrimes.html.

Jacobs, J., & Potter, K. (1998). *Hate crimes: Criminal law & identity politics*. New York: Oxford.

Levin, J., & McDevitt, J. (2002). *Hate crimes revisited: America's war on those who are different*. Boulder, CO: Westview.

Laura L. Finley

HAZING. Acts of hazing occur when groups seek to make initiation difficult for new recruits. Acts that are intended to humiliate and degrade the newcomers through physical and emotional means are considered hazing, even if the recruits agree to participate. Hazing is most common when the "group" can be clearly defined and there is little or no question as to whether someone is in the group. For example, athletic teams and clubs are known for the commitment required for participation, and, as such, rookies are often subjected to hazing before they can be considered "true" members.

Commonly, hazing is used to establish an order of status among group members, with the most senior, or important, group members directing new initiates through often barbaric rites. Among athletic teams, such rites as freshmen carrying water bottles to the practice field are generally not considered hazing, although they met official definitions of hazing. Acts that are intended to humiliate and degrade newcomers are considered to be hazing by all groups. According to experts (see stophazing.org), there are three levels of hazing that occur. Subtle hazing is used to demonstrate the imbalance in power among group members and is endured by newer members who believe that it is inevitable for group membership. Subtle hazing includes denying privileges to newcomers, assigning menial tasks, calling newcomers by insulting nicknames while demanding they refer to older members in reverent terms, and socially isolating newcomers. Harassment hazing involves causing undue stress and frustration through threats, verbal abuse, sleep deprivation, and being forced to simulate sexual acts. Newcomers may also be denied the right to clean themselves for long periods. Finally, violent hazing has the potential to cause serious harm, whether physically, emotionally, or psychologically (and often would result in a combination of all three). These include beating or paddling recruits, forcing them to consume alcohol, forcing them to be naked in public (and even to touch each other's bodies), kidnapping, and tying up newcomers.

Participants often defend hazing (including those being hazed), as do coaches and communities, under the guise that it is "tradition" that bonds members together and clearly defines status among group members. While group membership is often a positive experience for teenagers, it can come with negative consequences, such as when enduring hazing is requisite for membership. A study from Alfred University revealed that 48 percent of high school students who belonged to groups had been hazed (about 1.5 million students per year) and 43 percent had suffered humiliating activities in the process. Typically, students who had been hazed suffered their first experience before the age of fifteen. Male students tended to haze and be hazed more often than females (although members of both genders are at risk), and students with lower grade point averages were hazed more than better students. The study also revealed that hazing is not limited to athletic teams and clubs: Of students involved in church-related clubs, 24 percent had been hazed to gain entry.

Even at the college level, as another study from Alfred University revealed, hazing occurs frequently, and there is little effort to stop it. Results of the study indicated that 80 percent of college athletes had been subjected to at least one of the three levels of hazing, and, in spite of this, many coaches and athletic directors did not identify hazing as a problem among their teams (see www.alfred.edu for more on these important studies).

Perhaps the most egregious example of hazing in recent years comes from an incident at a preseason football camp for Mepham High School in Long Island, New York. Sixty players had traveled to western Pennsylvania to practice for five days. While there, three players, aged 15, 16, and 17, used broomsticks, pine cones, and golf balls to sodomize three freshmen players. The assailants allegedly brought the broomstick with them, as well as stereos that were used to drown out the boys' cries for help. Other young players were sprayed with shaving cream, had powder and gel put in their eyes and hair, and had their hair ripped from their legs and buttocks with duct tape. The coaches claimed to have no idea that these events were occurring. Upon returning home, the victims initially remained silent, but then they had to tell their parents as they suffered persistent bleeding from the attacks. The school board voted to cancel the football season before it got underway because so many players knew the events occurred and did nothing to intervene or to inform the coaches. The assailants were later charged with a range of crimes, including aggravated assault, kidnapping, and unlawful restraint.

A similarly nasty event occurred among females at an off-campus Powderpuff football game between seniors and juniors from Glenbrook North High School (near Chicago, Illinois). Thirty-one seniors were expelled after they punched, kicked, and beat members of the junior class, even dousing the victims in urine, paint, fish guts, trash, pig intestines, and feces. One victim needed stitches and another suffered a broken ankle. The event was videotaped and the world watched in shock at the behavior of girls from a school that many considered elite.

In lieu of hazing initiates, groups can, and should, consider team activities that will bond members in a positive manner. Many respondents to the Alfred University study indicated they had participated in initiation rites, including maintaining a minimum grade point average, going on trips (such as camping), dressing up formally for events, attending banquets and picnics, mentoring new members, and taking part in group singing, cheering, or chanting.

FURTHER READING

High school hazing. (n.d.). Alfred University Hazing Site. Available at: www.alfred.edu/hs_hazing/.

Nuwer, H. (2000). *High school hazing: When rites become wrongs*. New York: FranklinWatts.

Nuwer, H. (2004). *The hazing reader*. Bloomington: Indiana University Press.

Sports hazing. (n.d.). Alfred University Hazing Site. Available at: www.alfred.edu/sports_hazing/.

Stop Hazing. www.stophazing.org.

Peter S. Finley

HEROIN. Heroin is an addictive opiate that releases dopamine into the brain, causing an intense rush followed by hours of euphoric drowsiness. Heroin can be inhaled, smoked, injected into a muscle, or injected directly into the bloodstream. It is unknown how much heroin a human can use, as some addicts could inject quantities that would kill an inexperienced user, but the potential for taking a lethal dose is considerable even among addicts. The Bayer pharmaceutical company coined the name "heroin" in 1898. At this time, they used the drug in a cough syrup. During the early 1900s, heroin was commonly used for treating morphine addiction, the result being that morphine addicts became heroin addicts. Heroin eluded the notice of legislators in the United States until 1924, when it was classified as an illegal substance; as a consequence, heroin addicts (many of whom had become addicted while under the care of physicians) were forced to resort to illegal means of obtaining the drug.

Since that time heroin, has achieved a unique mystique, having been glamorized and vilified perhaps more than any other drug. For instance, heroin has been used by a number of famous entertainers, such as Billie Holiday, Ray Charles, Courtney Love, and Robert Downey, Jr., and been featured in numerous entertainment productions, such as the movies *The French Connection* and *Trainspotting*, the Rolling Stones' song "Brown Sugar," and the HBO miniseries *The Corner*, which was adapted from Simon and Burns' (1997) ethnographic study of heroin addicts. But perhaps the best indicator of heroin's cultural significance is the fact that the term "junkie" was derived from heroin's street name "junk."

There is no evidence that heroin causes violent behavior, but owing to heroin's debilitating and addictive properties, many addicts have difficulties holding legitimate jobs and resort to illegal activities (e.g., theft, prostitution) in order to obtain money to purchase heroin. In addition, the practice of sharing hypodermic syringes and needles for the purpose of injecting heroin has resulted in a high transmission of HIV among heroin addicts. Fortunately, the use of heroin among adolescents is uncommon. Recent research indicates that only a small minority (fewer than 2 percent) of high school students have used heroin, that the majority of heroin users do not try the substance prior to the age of eighteen, and that the bulk of heroin users are adults age twenty-six and over. Nonetheless, owing to the potential for addiction, heroin continues to pose a threat to the youth population.

FURTHER READING

Alter, J. (2001, February 12). The war on addiction. *Newsweek, 137,* 36–39.

Heroin and drug addiction. (2005). *National Institute on Drug Abuse.* Bethesda, MD: U.S. Department of Health and Human Services, National Institutes of Health, National Institute on Drug Abuse.

Rudgley, R. (2000). *The encyclopedia of psychoactive substances.* New York: St. Martin's Press.

Simon, D., & Burns, E. (1997). *The corner.* New York: Broadway Books.

Ben Brown

HISPANICS AND JUVENILE VIOLENCE. While juveniles of all races/ethnicities engage in and are subject to violent actions, research suggests that Hispanic youths engage in and are the victims of violent activities at disproportionately high rates. With respect to school violence, for instance, research indicates that Hispanic youths are more likely than white youths to be involved in fights on school grounds and to carry firearms to school. To provide another example, there is evidence to suggest that Hispanic youths are more likely than white youths to engage in weapon-related violence and that Hispanic youths are more likely than youths of all other races/ethnicities to report gang activity in schools and to participate in gang activity.

As to victimization, prior to the late 1990s, victimological research consistently showed that Hispanics were victimized at disproportionately high rates, but in recent years there has been a lack of consensus among scholars as to whether Hispanics are disproportionately victimized. Whereas some research shows that victimization rates are disproportionately high in Hispanic communities, analyses of recent **National Crime Victimization Survey (NCVS)** data show few differences in the rates of victimization of Hispanics and non-Hispanics. Nonetheless, analyses of NCVS data show that Hispanics age twelve to seventeen are victimized at substantially higher rates than Hispanics of all other age groups. In addition, reports from the **Centers for Disease Control** show that homicide is the second leading cause of death among Hispanics age fifteen to thirty-four.

Although it is not clear why Hispanic youths are disproportionately likely to engage in and be the victim of violent activities, any plausible explanation would need to incorporate three interrelated variables: education, poverty, and immigration. As to the first two variables, education and poverty, it is necessary to acknowledge the facts that (1) Hispanics have the lowest rate of educational attainment of any racial/ethnic group in the United States; (2) Hispanics are a disproportionately impoverished demographic group, and (3) Persons with limited education and/or persons of low socioeconomic status are more likely to be arrested, incarcerated, and victimized than persons with a high school or postsecondary education and/or persons in the middle or upper socioeconomic tiers. With respect to the issue of immigration, it is important to consider the facts that (1) Approximately half of all immigrants who entered the United States since the 1980s (legally or otherwise) have been of Latin

American origin and that by the early 2000s there were an estimated 15 million Hispanic immigrants residing in the United States; (2) Hispanic immigrants are more likely to be poorly educated and impoverished than native-born U.S. citizens; (3) Hispanic immigrants are disproportionately concentrated in impoverished urban neighborhoods (areas where crime tends to be concentrated), and (4) Hispanic immigrants constitute the bulk of the migrant labor force in the United States. Consequently, many Hispanic immigrants and their descendants feel themselves to be isolated from mainstream America and unable to access the educational and economic opportunities in the United States, which, in turn, may affect their likelihood of victimization and likelihood of engaging in crime. Some scholars have gone so far as to employ the term "choloization" to describe the process of Hispanic youths being marginalized from mainstream American society and resorting to gang activity as a means of developing a sense of community, a cultural identity, and a connection to their Latin American heritage.

It is essential to note, however, that violence and victimization among Hispanic youths are poorly understood phenomena and that studying these issues has proven difficult. One problem is that Hispanics are often classified as an ethnic group rather than a racial group by government researchers. Thus, in many government reports pertaining to racial differences in rates of arrest and victimization, Hispanics are classified as whites and/or separate analyses are conducted for ethnic differences in rates of arrest and victimization wherein people of all races are classified as being either Hispanic or non-Hispanic. Another issue to consider is that many Hispanic immigrants do not speak English and are concerned about contact with government officials. In addition, many Hispanic immigrants work as migrant laborers and spend much of each year moving throughout the United States as the seasons (and need for agricultural labor) change. It is therefore likely that Hispanic immigrants are underrepresented in survey research projects and that many Hispanic immigrants are unwilling or unable to contact law enforcement agencies to request assistance, which means that many crimes committed against Hispanics go unreported. In brief, much of the data pertaining to violence and victimization among Hispanics are of uncertain validity.

See also Educational Opportunity and Juvenile Violence; Family Relations and Juvenile Violence; Gang Types

FURTHER READING

Alaniz, M., Cartmill, R., & Parker, Robert. (1998). Immigrants and violence: The importance of neighborhood context. *Hispanic Journal of Behavioral Sciences, 20*, 155–176.

Davis, R., & Erez, E. (1998). *Immigrant populations as victims: Toward a multicultural criminal justice system* (NCJ 167571). Washington, DC: U.S. Department of Justice.

Egley, A. (2002). *National Youth Gang Survey Trends from 1996 to 2000* (FS 200203). Washington, DC: U.S. Department of Justice.

Lopez, D., & Brummett, P. (2003). Gang membership and acculturation: ARSMA-II and choloization. *Crime and Delinquency, 49*, 627–642.

McNulty, T., & Bellair, P. (2003). Explaining racial and ethnic differences in serious adolescent violent behavior. *Criminology, 41*, 709–748.

Peacock, M., McClure, F., & Agars, M. (2003). Predictors of delinquent behaviors among Latino youth. *Urban Review, 35*, 59–72.

Rennison, M. (2002). *Hispanic victims of violent crime, 1993–2000* (NCJ 191208). Washington, DC: U.S. Department of Justice.

Ben Brown

HOME CONFINEMENT/ELECTRONIC MONITORING.

Electronic monitoring and home detention have become the latest methods to alleviate jail and prison overcrowding. These methods occur whenever an offender is ordered to stay in his or her home in lieu of being confined in a correctional facility. Often this can occur as part of an offender's **probation** or parole requirement. In other cases, however, an individual can be ordered to wear an anklet even before he or she is found guilty. Some celebrities, such as Charlie Sheen and former heavyweight boxing champion Riddick Bowe, have been forced to wear electronic anklets rather than serve lengthy jail sentences. The business guru Martha Stewart was also forced to wear an electronic anklet following her release from the federal prison system. The sixty-three-year-old Stewart even spent time with fans online complaining that her anklet was uncomfortable and interfered with daily exercise routines. Other celebrities, including Robert Blake, have been subjected to home confinement. After being acquitted of killing his wife, Blake made a public display by cutting off his electronic monitoring ankle bracelet in front of media cameras.

While home confinement is occasionally utilized as a means to monitor celebrities who break the law, it is more often used for everyday criminals. Juvenile delinquents can also be sentenced to home detention. Because juvenile offenders tend to be very impulsive and unpredictable, some officials believe that twenty-four-hour-a-day monitoring can keep these clients from committing further crimes. In some states, such as California, juvenile offenders are tracked by sophisticated mapping software via the Internet. This technology can be used to locate an offender within thirty feet. In addition to this, additional programs can be utilized in order to determine whether or not a juvenile offender refrains from drinking alcohol. Sobrietor is one type of alcohol monitoring service that administers random breath tests to juvenile delinquents in their homes. Generally, companies such as Sobrietor administer these tests by installing unobtrusive devices inside the offender's telephone receivers. These devices are capable of detecting the presence of alcohol anytime the client talks into his or her telephone.

If an offender commits a particularly heinous crime, such as sexual assault, it increases the chance that he or she will be required to wear an electronic anklet. These bands tend to be extremely durable and are usually the size of a cell phone. It is not unusual for offenders to be required to pay for the anklets themselves. Occasionally, an offender is unable to afford this and opts to serve his or her sentence in a correctional facility instead. Generally, clients must shower and sleep with these anklets, and the band is not to be removed at anytime. In most jurisdictions, if a client attempts to remove his or her anklet, a signal will be sent to officials. Once officials are notified, the client can be apprehended by local authorities. If an offender persists in tampering with his or her electronic anklet, it increases the likelihood that he or she will be sent to a correctional facility.

Juvenile offenders who are sentenced to home confinement generally are allowed to work, attend classes, and participate in religious services. All of these exceptions must be made in writing before a client is granted home confinement in lieu of incarceration in a correctional facility. In most cases, a client who is sentenced to home confinement is not even permitted to go to the grocery store or visit a neighbor's house unless he or she has official permission. A task that seems very innocent and mundane, such as getting a haircut, is seldom permitted. Also, some technology enables officials to implement safeguards that will notify authorities if a client encroaches upon a restricted area. For example, if a sex offender on home confinement comes within a certain distance of a daycare center or school, some jurisdictions have software that will immediately notify the police of his or her presence.

Home confinement can undoubtedly be stressful for juvenile offenders, but it may also be difficult for the delinquent's family members as well. They too must endure frequent contacts that are designed to ensure that the client is indeed staying in one designated area. Sometimes these contacts may be made by a probation or prison official who arrives unannounced at the juvenile's home. In many cases, this may be embarrassing for family members, especially if they themselves have never been in any type of trouble with the law. In other instances, random phone calls generated by a computer may be made to a juvenile's home. This has the potential to be inconvenient and intrusive to other members of the juvenile client's family. If a juvenile is sentenced to home confinement, his or her family members may feel as though their lives are also being monitored, even if they themselves have not committed any type of a crime.

Not all juveniles who are sentenced to home confinement are forced to undergo electronic monitoring. In any case, if an offender is required to stay at home, he or she may understandably become plagued with boredom or "cabin fever." This is especially true for the juvenile offender who is forced to wear an electronic anklet. This individual will generally not have the option of attending social functions, such as dances, athletic events, or other extracurricular activities that teenagers and young adults typically enjoy. Juveniles sentenced to twenty-four-hour supervision may also feel humiliated by having to wear the device and may even be subjected to ridicule by their peers. There is also the potential that the client will be labeled in a negative manner by teachers and school administrators. In spite of these shortcomings, however, home confinement and electronic monitoring are cost-effective alternatives to incarceration. It is very likely juveniles will continue to be sentenced to this form of punishment in lieu of jail time.

FURTHER READING

Bartollas, C., & Miller, S. (2005). *Juvenile justice in America,* 4th ed. Upper Saddle River, NJ: Pearson Education, Inc.

Gibbons, S., & Rosecrance, J. (2005). *Probation, parole, and community corrections.* Boston, MA: Allyn and Bacon.

McCarthy, B. (1987). *Intermediate punishments: Intensive supervision, home confinement, and electronic surveillance.* New York: Criminal Justice Press.

Robert Worley

HOMELESSNESS AND YOUTH VIOLENCE. American social science attention to the homeless, generally, and to their criminality, specifically, dates to the sociological ethnographies of the 1920s. Research on the homeless through the 1970s continued an ethnographic orientation to the phenomena, but assumed a critical and conflict approach. While the majority of sociological and criminological attention to the homeless has focused on adults, there is also an established knowledge base on the criminality of homeless youth, generally, and on their violence, specifically. Homeless youth are generally considered those youth that have run away or been expelled from their homes and spend some or all of their time in public areas.

In 2003, the homeless youth population was estimated at being between 1.3 million and 1.5 million, an alarming figure likely much higher than what most Americans might think. A fundamental focus of research on the topic has been generating a knowledge base regarding the causes, activities, and consequences of homelessness. Research has shown that there is a link between homelessness and a number of social problems and deviance, ranging from property crime for survival purposes to various forms of youth violence. While the exact nature of the homelessness and violence link is still debated within the field, with background effects and related behavior prior to homelessness status being complicating issues, family dysfunction is widely acknowledged as a primary contributing factor. Such dysfunction ranges from various forms of parental neglect, including physical and sexual abuse, substance abuse in the home, and firsthand observation of violence, to daily assaults and minor confrontations commonly associated with "throwaway youth" and "latchkey kids": typically lower-class youth in marginally stable living situations largely left to fend for themselves. With little opportunity to form conventional, prosocial bonds, many marginal youth eventually become homeless. They enter this situation following codes of violence wherein social capital is measured in terms of physical toughness. Such social learning is a precedent to cyclical violence, a point partially evidenced by the fact that homeless youth are typically victims of violent crime as well as being perpetrators.

Background Effects and Violence

Homeless and street youth have life paths that are characterized by violent experiences. Many have histories of both physical and sexual abuse that began at home, and they have been exposed to domestic violence within their families. Exposure to these acts of violent victimization in the home may make youth more likely to model these types of behavior and use violence as a way of injuring others and gaining respect on the street, essentially behavior predicted by both cultural transmission, **social learning**, and imitation theories. Witnessing coercive discipline to solve problems in one's family can lead to the creation of definitions favorable to violence, which then make these youths more prone to violent forms of delinquency. However, despite these negative predisposing background variables, many researchers argue that street youth participate in crime as the result of the homeless experience itself.

Conditions of Homelessness Conducive to Violence

It appears that youth who are homeless face a heightened risk of criminal involvement regardless of their backgrounds. Various theories have been invoked to explain this link, including **strain**, economic deprivation and poverty, peer variables, development of **subcultural values**, **routine activities**, and substance abuse effects. However, subcultural values seem to be the tie that binds all of these ideas together. Street youth acquire values that are supportive of violence through deviant peer associations, living in adverse socioeconomic conditions that produce social isolation and shield them from positive interactions, and through victimization experiences that produce a desire to fight back. While subcultural theories provide a logical explanation as to why street youth commit crimes involving violence, they do not provide a complete explanation. The link between homelessness and youth violence is very complex and is still being researched to determine exactly what factors play a role in mediating the relationship.

Overall, it appears that aspects of predisposing background variables, the street subcultural lifestyle, structural and economic factors, and victimization all work together to explain street youth violence. Violence among street youth is produced by a combination of belonging to certain groups, having certain values, and living in certain situations. All of the researchers on this topic produce implications for policy, intervention strategies that focus on the issues of homelessness itself, and the factors leading to youth violence and their various interaction effects. A particular policy-relevant finding addresses the role of co-offending. Homeless youth, much like delinquent youth generally, commit a wider range of offenses and do so with greater frequency than in an independent context.

See also Educational Opportunity and Juvenile Violence

FURTHER READING

Anooshian, L. (2005). *Violence and aggression in the lives of homeless children: A review*. Lincoln: University of Nebraska Press.

Bandura, A. (1962). Social learning through interaction. *Aggression and Violent Behavior, 10,* 129–152.

Baron, S. (2003). Street youth violence and victimization. *Trauma, Violence, & Abuse, 4,* 22–44.

Baron, S. (2004). General strain, street youth, and crime: A test of Agnew's revised theory. *Criminology, 42,* 457–483.

Baron, S., & Hartnagel, T. (1998) Street youth and criminal violence. *Journal of Research in Crime and Delinquency, 35,* 166–192.

Baron, S., Kennedy, L., & Forde, D. (2001). Male street youths' conflict: The role of background, sub-cultural, and situational factors. *Justice Quarterly, 18,* 759–789.

Chambliss, W. (1964). A sociological analysis of the law of vagrancy. *Social Problems, 12,* 67–77.

Cohen, A. K. (1955). *Delinquent boys: The culture of the gang*. New York: Free Press.

Fleisher, M. (1995). *Beggars and thieves*. Madison: University of Wisconsin Press.

Kipke, M., Unger, J., O'Connor, S., Palmer, R., & LaFrance, S. (1997) Street youth, their peer group affiliation and differences according to residential status, subsistence patterns, and use of services. *Adolescence, 32,* 655–669.

McCarthy, B., & Hagan, J. (1991). Homelessness: A criminogenic situation? *British Journal of Criminology, 31,* 393–410.

McCarthy, B., & Hagan, J. (2005). Homelessness and criminal behavior. In R. Wright & J. M. Miller (Eds.), *Encyclopedia of Criminology*. London: Taylor and Francis.

Miller, W. (1958). Lower class culture as a generating milieu of gang delinquency. *Journal of Social Issues, 14,* 5–19.

J. Mitchell Miller with research assistance from Casey Bowers

HORMONAL/CHEMICAL EXPLANATIONS FOR GENDER DIFFERENCES.

Hormonal theories of juvenile violence try to show the ways in which hormones may affect an individual's levels of aggression and violence. Hormonal theories examine differences between genders in relation to juvenile delinquency by mainly focusing on the male hormone testosterone and its connection to aggression in males.

The connection between testosterone and aggression or violent behavior is a complex one, filled with controversy and inconsistent results. Many feel that hormones are not directly related to aggression and that more research is needed in this area. Also, a lot of experiments done on testosterone levels have been carried out on rodents, which can be flawed when trying to relate the results to humans.

Testosterone is a hormone made in the testicles of males that leads to the development of secondary sex attributes, including muscular growth, the growth of facial and pubic hair, maturity of the penis, and the deepening of the male voice. Testosterone is often used to show that males engage in more violent behavior than females because the hormone is linked with aggression. Hormonal theories are especially used to account for juvenile violence, since adolescent males have increased levels of testosterone and exhibit the most aggression. Although females produce some testosterone, males produce much more than females.

Males make up most of all juvenile arrests and are more likely to be arrested for more violent crimes, such as murder and robbery, than female juveniles, who are more likely to be arrested for offenses such as prostitution and running away from home. Males tend to be more violent than females in general. They are more likely to have antisocial personality disorder, to become rapists, stalkers, mass murderers, and serial sexual killers, and to commit **suicide**. Some research has correlated males with higher levels of testosterone with more violent crimes, such as murder or rape, as opposed to theft or burglary. Some studies have shown that female rodents, when exposed to testosterone, show levels of aggression close to that of males. This helps to show that testosterone can lead to aggression without other factors involved, although the results could be different on humans than on animals.

Modern biological explanations for delinquency and violence use testosterone to account for the age-crime curve, which states that violent crime appears in preadolescence, drastically increases during adolescence, and decreases slowly with age. This explanation says that there has been a positive correlation between physical violence and testosterone, with significant increases of testosterone from early to late adolescence and decreases during adulthood, following the same pattern as the amount of violent crime in each age group.

A number of studies have been done that link testosterone to aggression by taking testosterone out of various male animals. With less testosterone, time and again, the male animals are much calmer, and when given testosterone, they become aggressive. However, those with previous fighting knowledge continued to be aggressive after a reduction in their testosterone levels. This suggests that environmental factors are in play with hormones in relation to aggressive behavior. In relation to humans, hormonal levels seem to correspond to levels of violence as well, but experiments have not always come to this conclusion.

Although some dispute that testosterone directly causes violent behavior, some arguments find testosterone to be indirectly related to violence. Hormones may cause a person to have a stronger predisposition toward aggressive behavior in response to certain events. Some arguments find that hormones work together with a person's external environment, saying that hormones react to environmental factors. One argument claims that testosterone is important in male sexual behavior, which may lead to issues of status, power, and a desire to win that could result in violence. Testosterone can rise and fall in relation to changes in a person's social environment. Winning seems to stimulate testosterone, as losing lowers it, so confrontation over dominance and winning can turn into physical aggression. Further support for this idea is that psychological experiments have shown that sexual maturity causes rodents to become more aware of external signals. This helps to show how testosterone can be connected to perceptions and reactions to them. Another way environment can affect hormones is through responding to a threat. Studies noticed that instead of starting the aggressive behavior, testosterone caused adolescent males to respond to certain threatening situations, or situations where they were provoked, in magnified ways. Testosterone works with neurotransmitters, chemicals in the brain that carry messages between nerves, in this threat-perceiving and responding process. During puberty, strong hormonal changes react with the brain's first mature responses to threatening situations. Before this time, a child will run and hide from a threat. After this time, a person will decide whether or not to fight. So testosterone can cause an adolescent to become aggressive when faced with a threatening situation.

Although a number of studies have pointed at hormones to explain the gender difference in aggressive behavior, the results are not always consistent, and many argue that this explanation is lacking. One argument against using hormonal theories to explain juvenile delinquency is that they fail to account for levels of female violence and delinquency. This side argues that although female juveniles may not engage in as much violence as males, they do account for a significant amount of juvenile violence, and this should not be ignored. Hormonal theories do not account for this.

See also Gender, Frequency of Perpetrating Violence by; Gender, Frequency of Receiving Violence by; Gender, Types of Violence Perpetrated by; Gender, Types of Juvenile Violence Received by

FURTHER READING

Archer, J., Willard W., & Tremblay, R. (Eds.). (2005). *Developmental origins of aggression*. New York: Guilford Press.

Krohn, M., & Thornberry, T. (Eds.). (2003). *Taking stock of delinquency: An overview of findings from contemporary longitudinal studies*. New York: Kluwer Academic/Plenum Publishers.

Niehoff, D. (1999). *The biology of violence*. New York: Free Press.

Sharon Thiel

ILLINOIS JUVENILE COURT. The first juvenile court in the world was established in Chicago, Illinois on July 3, 1899. The court was established by the Illinois Juvenile Court Act and was formed to supervise the treatment of children ages sixteen years and younger who were neglected, dependent, or delinquent. Until that time, children were adjudicated in the adult system.

Juvenile courts mostly handled cases of delinquency, status offenses, and child abuse and neglect. Juvenile delinquency cases are acts committed by minors, which, if committed by adults, would be crimes. On the other hand, status offenses are noncriminal acts that are illegal only for minors.

The Illinois Juvenile Court Act provided judges broader control in dealing with children and changed the way they were treated. Some of the changes included focusing on rehabilitation rather than punishment, separating juveniles from adults in facilities, making juvenile records confidential, providing civil proceedings rather than criminal proceedings to avoid the stigma of criminality, providing a more informal system of *parens patriae*, and eliminating the formal rules of procedure found in the adult system.

The **child-savers** movement was the impetus for treating children different than adults in regards to various social issues, including labor practices and the care of neglected and orphaned children. The philosophy of the juvenile court was based upon *parens patriae*, which can be traced back to England. *Parens patriae* meant that the state could act as the parent when a child violated the law or their parents were believed to be unfit.

Juvenile courts spread quickly, and by 1925 only two states had not passed legislation to create a separate court. By 1950, every state had a juvenile court system. Juvenile courts are not without their critics. In the 1960s it was found that courts were not standardized throughout the states, and judges often were either too harsh or too lenient in sentencing. As a result of several court cases, the juvenile system today closely resembles the adult system. Supreme Court cases such as *Kent v. United States* (1966) and *In re Gault* (1967) applied many of the same due process protections formally guaranteed only to adults.

Today, every state has at least one juvenile court. Some states refer to these courts as family or probate courts. In 2000, juvenile courts handled approximately 1.6 million delinquency cases, with the majority of the cases being property offenses.

See also Differences between Juvenile Justice and Criminal Justice

FURTHER READING

Fox, S. (1998). A contribution to the history of the American juvenile court. *Juvenile and Family Court Journal*, *49*, 4.

Hurley, T. (1977). *Origin of the Illinois Juvenile Court Law*. New York: AMS Press, Inc.

Puzzanchera, C., Stahl, A., Finnegan, T., Tierney, N., & Synder, H. (n.d.). Juvenile court statistics, 1999. National Center for Juvenile Justice. Available at: www.ncjrs.org/pdffiles1/ojjdp/209736.pdf.

Shepherd, R. (1999). The juvenile court at 100 years: A look back. *Juvenile Justice, VI,* 2.

The juvenile court: One hundred years in the making. (n.d.). Building Blocks for Youth. Available at: www.buildingblocksforyouth.org/juvenile_court.htm.

Nicolle Parsons-Pollard

IN LOCO PARENTIS. Translated, *in loco parentis* means "in place of the parent." This term is used to describe the legal authority by which public or private institutions take the place of the parent within proscribed boundaries. For the most part, the practice of *in loco parentis* has centered on the degree to which public and private schools function in regard to punishment and disciplinary guidelines.

American schools adopted the custom of *in loco parentis* in part from European colleges, where higher education was integrated with residential living. William Blackstone, writing in 1765, is nominally credited with the earliest American recognition of the validity of *in loco parentis* in noting that a father "may also delegate part of his parental authority, during his life to the tutor or schoolmaster of the child; who is then *in loco parentis.*" For the most part, American courts in the eighteenth and nineteenth centuries refused to hear challenges to the practice. When they did, for example in *State v. Pendergrass* (1837) and *Pratt v. Wheaton College* (1866), they affirmed educational institutions' rights to stand in place of the parent regarding guidelines for and sanctions against behavior and conduct.

In loco parentis was not seriously challenged until the 1960s. In the early 1960s, students were expelled from the Alabama State College for their role in sit-ins related to the civil rights movement. This decision was eventually overturned in *Dixon v. Alabama State Board of Education.* In the later 1960s, the practice was also challenged, both formally and informally, as students demanded increased rights concerning their own behavior as well as a stronger voice in administrative decisions. The expansion of suffrage to eighteen-year-olds in 1972 furthered the notion that students were now adults not subject to the extension of parental authority once given to colleges.

The whittling away of *in loco parentis* did not last long, however. By the mid-1980s, universities and colleges adopted new arguments in favor of the practice, due in part to several highly publicized deaths related to drinking and the liability issues that ensued from these deaths. This argument was bolstered by the de facto change in drinking age from eighteen to twenty-one in 1987. This change put colleges in a stronger position to police the activities of their students, and many colleges have since developed policies of informing parents of drug or alcohol use, based in part on changes made in 1998 to the Family Educational Rights and Privacy Act.

By the 1990s, colleges were also arguing that mental health problems and increasing rates of depression and **suicide** furthered the need for increased supervision over students' lives. A well-publicized incident in 2000 at MIT, where a student set herself on fire, brought national attention to the apparent inability of colleges to adequately address mental health issues. Today, while *in loco parentis* is not as totalizing as it once was, it has gained significant support once again through the implementation of student codes of conduct, increased parental notification, and counseling for students who evidence problems with alcohol, drugs, and depression. It has been used as a justification for greater **surveillance** of students and for policies like **zero tolerance laws.**

See also Parens patriae

FURTHER READING

Lonte, A. (2000). *In loco parentis*: Alive and well. *Education, 121*(1), 195.

Nuss, E. (2003). The development of student affairs. In S. Komives & D. Woodard (Eds.), *Student services: A handbook for the profession*, 4th edition (pp. 65–88). San Francisco, CA: Jossey-Bass.

William R. Wood

INTENSIVE AFTERCARE. Intensive Aftercare Programs (IAP) are highly structured and specialized twenty-four-hour-per-day court-ordered service programs. It is a juvenile court program intended to protect the community, youths, and families. Intensive aftercare reintegrates juvenile offenders who are released from institutional placement into the community, much like parole in the adult system. Research has indicated that surveillance and intensive monitoring through, for example, drug testing, employment training, supervision, group or foster homes, **electronic monitors**, and graduated progress/sanctions, can reduce and control recidivism.

Intensive aftercare is a multiphase program offered to juveniles in some jurisdictions that may include assessment, classification and evaluation, survey, development of strategic model, training and technical assistant delivery. It usually targets those youths who are deemed to pose the highest risk of recidivism when released to their communities. In some of these programs, youths are placed in a designated residential treatment program where an intensive aftercare worker, liaison, and residential staff member work to develop an aftercare plan for successful transition of these youths back to the community.

Other intensive aftercare programs include some form of graduated progress program whereby, after release from residential aftercare, the youth may graduate to a community phase system in which intensive contacts, services, and supervision is emphasized. These programs vary slightly in origin, design, and approach, but all share the aftercare concept: incarceration and a follow-up period characterized by surveillance and the provision of community services. Some examples of these include the Philadelphia Intensive Probation Aftercare Program, the Juvenile Aftercare in Maryland Drug Treatment Program, the Skillman Intensive Aftercare Project, and the Michigan Nokomis Challenge Program.

Success in these programs is measured by their performance in areas such as family and peer relations, education, jobs, substance abuse, mental health, and recidivism without negatively affecting the community. Evaluations of these programs have produced mixed results, mostly because of poor program design and implementation rather than a faulty concept.

There are five pillars or elements that are crucial in developing, implementing, and evaluating IAP: risk assessment and classification, individualized case planning, a mix of intensive surveillance and services, a balance of graduated incentives and consequences, and links with community resources and social networks.

To maximize its potential for crime reduction, IAP focuses on high-risk offenders. Jurisdictions intent on implementing the IAP model need to use a validated risk-screening instrument to accurately identify high-risk youth.

Individualized case planning must incorporate family and community perspectives to develop a plan to address everyone's needs during incarceration, transition, and community aftercare.

Although the IAP model offers close supervision and control of high-risk offenders in the community, it also emphasizes the need for intensive services and treatment. This dual approach requires both a sufficient number of qualified staff to keep caseloads small and funds to support the provision of services. Ideally, IAP services parallel those that are initiated in institutional care.

The IAP model requires the use of sanctions to punish inappropriate behavior or program infractions and rewards to encourage compliance and mark progress. Because intensive supervision programs are intrusive, numerous technical violations are likely to occur. Instead of relying on a one-size-fits-all solution, the IAP model requires a range of graduated sanctions that are directly and proportionately tied to the seriousness of the violation.

To meet the broad range and depth of services required for high-risk, high-need parolees, the IAP model creates alliances and partnerships among a host of departments, agencies, and organizations. Because interventions focus on family, school, peer, and community issues, case managers and service agencies need to create strong working relationships among these social networks.

The most current review of intensive aftercare programs by Spencer and Jones-Walker (2004) indicates support for these programs, but they add that high levels of intensive structure, program duration of nine or more months, clear expectations and consequences, sensitivity to interpersonal dynamics and cognitive-behavioral skills orientation are characteristics required for a successful intensive aftercare.

The problem with the system is that the probation officers who are in constant interaction with the youths ordered by the court to participate in the intensive aftercare are not well paid. In fact, the beginning salary for such positions in many jurisdictions is between $25,000 and $30,000 annually. These officers are often swamped with too many cases, reducing their ability to provide the best care and services.

FURTHER READING

Altschuler, D., & Armstrong, T. (1994). *Intensive aftercare for high-risk juveniles: A community care model.* Washington, DC: Office of Juvenile Justice and Delinquency Prevention.

Armstrong, T. (Ed.). (2002). *Intensive interventions with high-risk youths: Promising approaches in juvenile probation and parole.* Washington, DC: Office of Juvenile Justice and Delinquency Prevention.

Spencer, M., & Jones-Walker, C. (2004). Interventions and services offered to juvenile Offenders reentering their communities: An analysis of program effectiveness. *Youth Violence and Juvenile Justice, 2,* 88–97.

Evaristus Obinyan

INTENSIVE SUPERVISED PROBATION (ISP).

Intensive Supervised Probation for juveniles is an alternative to lengthy commitment in a **detention center**. It is a community-based sentencing option for seriously at-risk juvenile offenders who can be safely managed in the community. The purpose of the program is to provide meaningful intervention with juvenile offenders by addressing major areas of risks and needs and, at the same time, providing more intense supervision for juvenile recidivists, lowering the cost of commitment, providing intervention locally, and giving juveniles a voice in corrections. It is frequently used for a variety of purposes and affects a significant number of juveniles within the juvenile justice system. Juvenile **probation** is the most often used medium through which a plethora of court-ordered services are delivered.

When the court orders probation as a dispositional, alternative, community-based corrections program, the juvenile offender remains in the community and is allowed access to regular activities, such as school and work. The juvenile probationer must be in compliance with court-stipulated conditions of the probation. This can either be by mandate or with voluntary compliance. Over 60 percent of juvenile probationers are on mandatory probation placement. The specialized, school-based probation program is regarded as an intensive probation in which the officer works directly in the school rather than using traditional methods of monitoring.

Intensive probation supervision ensures personal responsibility and public safety. It is said to reduce recidivism through increased juvenile offender monitoring and use of appropriate sanctions to induce treatment and rehabilitation, as the offender's needs are identified and addressed through programming and community referrals. Furthermore, **restorative justice** is emphasized in certain cases, and retribution through fines, **restitution**, **curfews**, drug counseling, weekend confinement, community service, and full-time employment and/or full-time educational programming are sometimes required.

Juvenile ISP differs from regular probation in that surveillance is more intensive, there is a higher availability of treatment services, and caseloads are usually smaller. The term for probation can be for a specific number of months or years until the youth is eighteen years old and could even be open-ended. Each juvenile case on probation is reviewed periodically to enforce compliance and monitor progress. The court terminates the case if conditions are not met during the probation period, or probation can be revoked if conditions are violated, leading to harsher sanctions. In 2002, 55 percent of the 1.1 million delinquency cases received probation orders. Though a large number of juveniles adjudicated delinquent and placed on probation were property offense violators, those placed on mandatory probation were more likely to be drug and public order cases (i.e, drunkenness, curfew violations). White juveniles were more likely than African-American youths to be placed on probation.

There is an alarming increase in the number of juveniles on probation for drug law violations, as evidenced in the current (2004) national report on crime in the United States. In some jurisdictions, such as Texas, intensive supervision probation is a program that specifically provides services as an intermediate, community-based alternative for juveniles requiring a higher level of control. The cost per probationer in Texas is $14.34, but costs vary across jurisdictions. Furthermore, because of the continuing problem of overcrowded juvenile facilities across the country, it is no wonder that ISP is a popular alternative. Krisberg and Howell (1998) surveyed research using a meta-analytic approach and concluded that "alternatives to secure confinement for serious and chronic juveniles are at least as effective in suppressing recidivism as incarceration, but considerably less costly to operate."

Opponents argue that the relative lack of punishment, increased risk to the community, and increased social costs seem to be persistent problems of juvenile ISP. Research shows that the recidivism rate among offenders assigned to intensive probation supervision programs is only about one-quarter to one-half of that among offenders who do not participate in such a program. Successes in some jurisdictions can be attributable to smaller caseloads, lack of bureaucratic impediments, whites supervising whites and blacks supervising blacks, and emphasis on rehabilitative services. The Juvenile Justice Evaluation Center summary of evaluations of community-based programs agrees that the outcomes of surveyed programs were positive, showed improvements, and reduced recidivism rates.

FURTHER READING

Abadinsky, H. (2003). *Probation and parole: Theory and practice*, 9th ed. Upper Saddle River, NJ: Prentice Hall.

Austin, J., Johnson, K., & Weitzer, R. (2005, September). *Alternatives to secure detention and confinement of juvenile offenders*. Available from: www.ncjrs.gov/pdffiles/ojjdp/208004.pdf.

Cauffman, E., & Steinberg, L. (2000) (Im)maturity of judgment in adolescence: Why adolescents may be less culpable than adults. *Behavioral Sciences and the Law, 18,* 741–760.

Champion, D. (2001). *Probation, parole, and community corrections,* 4th ed. Upper Saddle River, NJ: Prentice Hall.

Juvenile Justice Evaluation Center. (2004). Summary of community-based program evaluations. Available at: www.jrsa.org/ijec/programs/community/index.html.

Krisberg, B., & Howell, J. (1998). The impact of juvenile justice system and prospects for graduated sanctions in a comprehensive strategy. In R. Loeber & D. Farrington (Eds.). *Serious and violent juvenile offenders* (pp. 346–66). Thousand Oaks, CA: Sage.

Petersilia, J. (2001). *Reforming probation and parole in the 21st century.* New York: American Correctional Association.

Rittenour, M., & Miller, L. (2005, October 25). *Crawford County Common Pleas Court: Intensive Supervised Probation.* Available from: www.crawfordcocpcourt.org/ISP.

Evaristus Obinyan

INTERACTIONIST THEORIES. The interactionist perspective, founded by George Herbert Mead (1863–1931), is typically used as an explanation for social deviance. The central idea of this theory is that delinquency cannot be understood simply by examining the individuals who commit delinquent acts. Instead, those acts must be examined through the context of what is defined as delinquent behavior and what is defined as a delinquent individual. A social deviant is characterized as an individual who is not only different from the majority in society, but different in a way that causes society to treat that individual in a negative manner. A key aspect of this theory is that there is no such thing as an intrinsically deviant act. It only becomes deviant if observers label it as being deviant. For instance, the majority of people typically view violence against others as deviant. However, there are cases, such as sporting events, in which violence is not labeled as deviant.

Interactional theory's approach to understanding criminal and delinquent behavior is through the combination of three distinct foci: the developmental change in the individual, the interaction between that individual and their environment, and the individual's method of defining their place or role in the world. This makes interactional theory different from theories of criminality and delinquency that only focus on static or unchanging variables, such as **trait** or integration theories.

Developmental change in the individual is considered essential, which is made evident by the differing causal models of criminality required by this theory to explain criminality over the course of development. Three general causal models, based on the research of Terence Thornberry and others, suggest that criminal behavior, in general, follows a pattern during development. This pattern starts around ages twelve or thirteen (initiate phase), rapidly increases by ages sixteen or seventeen (maintenance phase), and then ends in the mid-twenties (termination phase). One of the advantages of this approach is that it allows for different causal factors to have more or less influence, depending on the age of the individual. For instance, unemployment as a causal factor may be more reasonable for a twenty-year-old than for a twelve-year-old. Parental influences, on the other hand, may be more influential for the twelve-year-old than the twenty-year-old.

The second focus of interactionist theory is the dynamic between individuals and the environment. Over time, individuals interact with others, thereby affecting other people's behavior. In turn, interactionist theory states that the behavior of those other people is not only changed, but it also changes the behavior of the original individual. The whole interaction pattern is circular, with the situation and the individual influencing one another at the same time. To illustrate this, imagine a child gets reprimanded at school (a negative impact on behavior) for delinquent behavior involving a teacher. Once the parent is informed of that reprimand, the parent's behavior is presumably going to be negatively impacted by this knowledge. In turn, the way that the parent interacts with the child is also presumed to be impacted negatively. The child's behavior, then, is not only affecting the relationship with the teacher and parent, but is also indirectly having effects on how those individuals are going to interact with the child in the future. This can lead to a cycle of behavior, where the child in the prior example commits more delinquent or even violent behavior in response to the continued negative interactions with these individuals. A static model of delinquency, as opposed to interactionist theory, would predict that the child's initial delinquent behavior would cause repercussions with the teachers and the parents, but the effects of the initial delinquent behavior would end there.

The third focus of interactionist theory is on how individuals define their own place or role in the world. The child in the prior example may define their role in the world based on the feedback that labeled them as delinquent. Based on this, delinquent behavior during the initiate phase may lead to the child identifying with a peer group that is also considered delinquent. Once this occurs, interactions with that peer group will result in the child impacting that peer group's behavior and the peer group impacting that child's behavior. One key idea here is that while we know that people have an effect on other's behavior, people also often choose which people they will be near to and thus affected by. This emphasis on the choices people make allows interactionist theory to offer a method of preventing or reducing violent or delinquent behavior. For example, an examination of the interactions that juveniles have with others may reveal the beginnings of the labeling of that child as a delinquent or self-identification of the child with delinquent peer groups. This may result in opportunities to intervene in the previously described cycle of delinquency, emphasizing to the child more positive labeling or different interpretations of prior interactions.

A criticism of interactionist theory is that the description of delinquent behavior being influenced by as much as it influences peer groups is too simplistic. For example, while interactionist theory emphasizes the effects that peer groups and delinquent behavior have on each other, other theories, such as integrated theory, go a step further and suggest that exposure to a delinquent peer group more often leads to delinquent behavior than the other way around. One advantage to interactionist theory is the focus on following individuals through the span of development. Relatively few studies have done so. Thus, interactional theory may spur more research into this area, which will benefit our understanding of criminal behavior, regardless of theoretical orientation.

See also Developmental Theories; Labeling Theory

FURTHER READING

Blumer, H. (2004). *George Herbert Mead and human conduct.* Walnut Creek, CA: AltaMira Press.

Lillyquist, M. (1980). *Understanding and changing criminal behavior.* Englewood Cliffs, NJ: Prentice-Hall.

Thornberry, T. (1996). Empirical support for interactional theory. In J. Hawkins (Ed.), *Delinquency and crime* (pp. 198–235). New York: Cambridge University Press.

Dave D. Hochstein

JUVENILE DETENTION CENTERS. The first placement decision made by the juvenile justice system involves whether a youth should be held in a juvenile detention center. Juvenile detention centers are short-term, secure facilities that hold youths at various points during the juvenile court process. Juvenile detention centers hold juveniles awaiting their adjudication hearing. Two generally accepted uses of preadjudication detention are to ensure that a juvenile will appear for an upcoming hearing and to maintain public safety. The Supreme Court upheld preventive detention for violent juvenile offenders in *Schall v. Martin* (1984). In *Schall*, the court upheld New York's preventive detention statute, which allows detention before hearings for juveniles who present a serious risk of committing another offense. In the decision, the court ruled that the juvenile's due process rights may be subordinated to the state's ***parens patriae*** interests of promoting the welfare of the child as well as protecting society. However, the case also established a due process standard for detention hearings that included notice and a statement of facts/reasons for the detention. Despite these procedural safeguards, opponents argue that preventive detention deprives juveniles of their freedom since guilt has not been proven. They also argue that it is unfair to punish youths based on a prediction of what they may do in the future.

Detention centers also hold juveniles who have been adjudicated delinquent and are awaiting residential or institutional placement. Juveniles may also be detained for evaluation purposes. Unlike the adult court system, juveniles may also be detained for their own protection (i.e., to protect the child from an abusive parent or neglectful home or to prevent a child from harming himself or herself). Federal law and many states bar the confinement of status offenders in secure detention facilities, although exceptions allow for the placement of youths who have committed such offenses. These exceptions include youths who have violated a valid court order or juveniles who are already on probation. On the other hand, use of detention centers as a separate disposition or punishment is becoming increasingly popular. Although detention centers are intended as preadjudication holding facilities, they are increasingly being used for postadjudication purposes.

The Advisory Commission on Accreditation for Corrections provides that placement in a juvenile detention center should not exceed 30 days. Approximately 20 percent of formally petitioned juveniles are held in a detention center until the final disposition of their case. A large number of youths will be released at detention intake or after a few days. This practice explains why the average length of stay for all detained youths is about 15 days. Federal law requires that holding in police lockups is of very short duration and that youth should be moved to an appropriate juvenile facility as soon as possible. Further, this law requires strict "sight and sound" separation of juveniles from adult offenders.

Juveniles were detained in 20 percent of the cases processed in 2000, compared to 21 percent of the cases processed in 1985. Although the percent of cases processed is quite similar, the number of cases processed between 1985 and 2000 increased 41 percent, from 234,600 to 329,800. Of all juvenile delinquency cases resulting in detention in 2000, 28 percent were offenses against persons, 33 percent were for property offenses, 11 percent were for public order offenses, and 11 percent for drug offenses.

Racial minorities, especially African American youths, are overrepresented in juvenile detention centers. Although African American youths were involved in 28 percent of all delinquency cases in 2000, they represented 35 percent of the detained cases. The Juvenile Justice and Delinquency Prevention Act of 1988 requires states to reduce the overrepresentation of minorities in secure facilities and, beginning in 1995, states applying for federal funding for juvenile justice programs must show in their proposal that attempts are being made to deal with disproportionate confinement of minorities. Research demonstrates that youths who have been in detention are more likely to be formally processed and receive more punitive sanctions at disposition than those not placed in detention, after controlling for demographic and legal factors.

Nearly one-half of public detention centers in the United States were filled above capacity in 2000. Consequences of overcrowding in detention center include affects on the provision of basic services such as education and medical treatment, in addition to creating unsafe conditions for juveniles and staff. Overcrowded conditions have been found to be associated with increased altercations between juveniles and staff and increased injuries to juveniles. The overcrowded conditions in many detention centers and the negative affects of being detained have led to investigations of alternatives to detention. Research on alternatives to secure detention have, to date, not found them to pose greater risks to the public than secure detention. In addition, such alternatives tend to be less costly.

See also Community Treatment; Restorative Justice

FURTHER READING

Frazier, C.E., & Bishop, D.M. (1985). The pretrial detention of juveniles and its impact on case dispositions. *The Journal of Criminal Law and Criminology*, *76*(4), 1132–1152.

Frazier, C.E., & Cochran, J. K. (1986). Detention of juveniles: Its effect on subsequent juvenile court processing decisions. *Youth and Society*, *17*(3), 286–305.

Krisberg, B. (2005). *Juvenile justice: Redeeming our children*. Thousand Oaks, CA: Sage.

Puzzanchera, S., Stahl, A., Finnegan, T., Tierney, N., & Snyder, H. (2004). *Juvenile court statistics 2000*. Washington, D.C.: Office of Juvenile Justice and Delinquency Prevention.

Rust, B. (1999). Juvenile jailhouse rocked. *Advocacy*, 1–16.

Shelden, R.G. (1999). *Detention diversion advocacy*. Washington, D.C.: Office of Juvenile Justice and Delinquency Prevention.

Snyder, H., & Sickmund, M. (1999). *Juvenile offenders and victims: 1999 National Report*. Washington, D.C.: Office of Juvenile Justice and Delinquency Prevention.

Wordes, W., & Jones, M. (1998). Trends in juvenile detention and steps toward reform. *Crime and Delinquency*, *44*(4), 544–560.

LaVerne McQuiller Williams

JUVENILE JUSTICE AND DELINQUENCY PREVENTION ACT, 1974 (JJDPA).

The JJDPA of 1974 was the first legislation to provide an integrated national program addressing juvenile delinquency prevention and control within the context of law enforcement and criminal justice efforts. The JJDPA replaced the Juvenile Delinquency

Prevention and Control Act (JDPCA) of 1968, which was responsible for the creation and implementation of juvenile delinquency plans for states that received federal funds.

The JJDPA stipulated that juveniles could no longer be placed in any institution in which they may have regular contact with adults that have been convicted of criminal charges. States that participated in the JJDPA were ordered to remove status offenders from secure detention and correctional facilities within two years.

The JJDPA was also responsible for creating a National Advisory Committee, a Federal Coordinating Council, and the National Institute for Juvenile Justice and Delinquency Prevention. The JJDPA was authorized for three years with a budget of $350 million. Discretionary funds were used to support programs developed by public and private agencies for America's youth.

See also Juvenile Justice Reform Act, 1977; National Institute of Justice (NIJ)

FURTHER READING

The Juvenile Justice and Delinquency Prevention Act of 1974 (n.d.). Available at: http://www.ncjrs.org/.

April C. Wilson

JUVENILE JUSTICE REFORM ACT, 1977.

The Juvenile Justice Act of 1977 established rules pertaining to procedures in the juvenile justice system, the juvenile court system in particular. Under this act, the juvenile court system added some of the procedural methods commonly found in the adult system and expanded its scope. This was particularly true for the trial system, which took on some of the procedures found in the adult court of the time. It also addressed pertinent issues already considered in the adult court, such as the child's capacity to understand the procedures as well as the process used to attend to this issue.

Under this new system there were also changes in the personnel responsible for various procedures impacting the juvenile process. For instance, prosecutors instead of probation officers were now responsible for charging decisions, based on the juvenile's prior record and the strength of the particular case. Moreover, juveniles were now to be adjudicated in order to determine whether the accusation for which they were accused was accurate. While this act resulted in some new procedures for the juvenile system, many of the traditional protections for juvenile defendants remained.

See also Juvenile Justice and Delinquency Prevention Act, 1974 (JJDPA)

FURTHER READING

Krisberg, B. (1998). The evolution of an American institution. *Crime and Delinquency, 44,* 1–5.

Brion Sever

JUVENILE VIOLENCE, 1600–1800 (COLONIAL ERA).

In order to understand the state of juvenile justice and violence during colonial times in America, it is important to frame it within the context of the social mores of that time. Juvenile justice, as it exists today, has evolved throughout most of the nineteenth and twentieth centuries into a model wherein juvenile offenders are generally thought of as youths in need of treatment and rehabilitation, not as adults who must be incapacitated from further offending. This is an important distinction to consider when examining the model of juvenile justice and violent crimes committed by juveniles during colonial America.

Attitudes Toward Children

Children, from a relatively young age, were expected to assume adult culpability for crimes they committed. Punishments for children rivaled those for adults. Juveniles in colonial times did not have the same luxuries as contemporary juveniles. For example, they were forbidden to engage in playtime, leisure, or idleness—activities thought to be works of the devil. The colonies, within one decade of their founding, had passed laws demanding children obey their parents. In 1648, Massachusetts prescribed the death penalty for any child over sixteen who "shall curse, or smite their natural father or mother." Colonial America's favored punishment for juvenile offenders was to have parents "beat the devil" out of their child if he or she committed a crime. Since fathers were held accountable for their children's actions and had full authority to punish them, fathers could be required by the community to publicly execute, whip, or even banish their children if society found them to be criminally liable. Due process for juvenile offenders simply did not exist in the same way as it exists today.

These harsh disciplinary responses were deemed necessary to maintain compliance with social and religious mores, to transmit educational information, and even to expel evil spirits that were thought to possess children, as was most evident during the Salem Witch Trials. The control of family, church, and community over colonial children was complete; no legal machinery was necessary.

Punishment of Delinquents

In early colonial times, children who committed serious, violent offenses were jailed with adults. Courts generally subjected children to the same punishments as adults. Punishment for juveniles who misbehaved fell within the realm of the family, the community, and the church. However, those who defied internal familial controls, and who were accused of certain criminal actions, were adjudicated in the British common law tradition. The justice system considered that children between the ages of one and seven were not responsible for commission of a crime; those between seven and fourteen *were* responsible for their actions and received appropriate punishment decided in an adult court; those older than fourteen were believed capable of the act (*Actus Reus*—the actual criminal act) and of the intent to commit the act (*Mens Rea*—able to understand the intent of the act) and were eligible for more severe punishment. Another category of criminal behavior was created exclusively for children. Either parents or the community could punish colonial youth who engaged in what was then considered to be immoral conduct like rebelliousness, disobedience, playing ball in public streets, or sledding on the Sabbath.

School Violence

Unlike the school-related violence endemic in our modern society, in colonial America most young children were taught at home. Those who did attend school, however, were just as prone to be disorderly as today's youths (although certainly not at the level of the Columbine shooting). Teachers kept problem children in line with corporal punishments that are illegal today: They tied children to whipping posts and beat them or branded them for their crimes—a "T" for thievery, a "B" for blasphemy. For the most part, common punishments for children were whipping and caning. The exception was execution of juveniles. The first recorded state execution of a condemned juvenile was in 1642, when Thomas Graunger was put to death in Plymouth Colony, Massachusetts. Graunger was "indicted for buggery with a mare, a cow, two goats, divers sheep, two calves, and a turkey, and was found guilty, and received sentence of death by hanging until he was dead."

In sum, juveniles who committed serious and/or violent crimes in colonial America faced the same harsh punishments as adults did. For less serious trespasses, the juvenile was subject to family- or church-controlled punishments.

FURTHER READING

www.djs.state.md.us/history.html

http://en.wikipedia.org/wiki/Criminal_justice

http://www.ferrum.edu/kmccreedy/jdlinks.htm

Aviva Twersky-Glasner

JUVENILE VIOLENCE, 1861–1865 (CIVIL WAR ERA).

Reliable juvenile violence rates during and after the Civil War years (1860–1890) are unknown. There was no uniformly collected criminal data on adults or juveniles during this period. Information about crime and juvenile violence during the Civil War period comes from historians, U.S. census reports, and police records from a few cities. These sources indicate that there was an increase in overall crime after the Civil War and that the increase stabilized after the war through the end of the nineteenth century. While the sources cannot be relied on to document juvenile crime rates, they do provide a good indication of society's responses to social problems at the time.

Until 1820, American juveniles were imprisoned with adults. This began to change in 1824 when the Quakers developed the House of Refuge. It was an institution to help juveniles and separate them from adult offenders, and it was partly prison, school, and job training. In 1825, the State of New York enacted legislation that provided funding for the first House of Refuge. Twenty-five years after New York's House of Refuge opened, it had transformed into a reformatory where secured custody, rather than help, became its main purpose. By 1860 there were twenty, and by 1885 there were forty-five, juvenile reformatories in the United States.

The reformatories held a disproportionate share of Irish immigrants, and in some states, black youth were not allowed in them unless there was room in a limited number of segregated dormitories. When there was no room, they were sent to adult prisons.

An increase in crime during the Civil War has been attributed to complex changes in the American social structure. In addition to the problems of slavery and the war, the country was becoming industrialized, and economic conditions were changing. Families frequently moved from rural to urban living situations and vice versa. The authoritarian method many families used to control youth was challenged by the loss of fathers and older brothers who went to fight in the war. It is also estimated that between 250,000 and 450,000 boys, and a few girls, under the age of fourteen fought in the Civil War.

The 1850 U.S. Census reports numbers of people (including juveniles) imprisoned in poorhouses and prisons, which total around 18,000. By 1890, census reports state that there were 14,840 (11,535 male and 3,311 female) inmates in juvenile reformatories. The ages of the juveniles ranged from under age five to twenty-nine years. The average age of inmates was fourteen. Less than three hundred inmates were over the age of twenty. The problems of putting younger juveniles with the older, more hardened juveniles were apparent to prison officials at the time. Officials saw the need to separate them, but lacked funding for separate facilities.

The 1890 census report compares the number of juveniles incarcerated in 1880 with the 1890 number and indicates a slight increase in the rate of juvenile inmates in reformatories over the decade. In 1880, 11,468 juveniles were incarcerated, compared to 14,846 incarcerated in 1890. The resulting rate was 229 per million of the total population in 1880 and 238 per million in 1890.

Out of the 14,846 juvenile offenders, only 308 were incarcerated for violent offenses, which included 16 homicides, 16 rapes, 1 kidnapping, and 275 assaults. The remaining juvenile offenders were imprisoned for offenses "Against the government," "Against society," "Against property," and "Miscellaneous," which included twenty-one children under the age of five. Twenty-nine older juveniles were "Held as witnesses."

After offenses against property, which 4,515 juveniles were imprisoned for, the next largest group of 4,069 was imprisoned for "incorrigibility." In addition to being imprisoned for this vague offense, over 2000 juveniles were imprisoned for other social reasons, including 1,760 for being poor, 196 for not having a home, 22 for unfit parents, 102 for exposure to criminal contagion, 230 for juvenile delinquency, and 79 who had vicious habits.

The issue of imprisoning juveniles for social problems, and not crimes, was determined unconstitutional in 1870 by the Illinois Supreme Court case in *People ex rel. v. Turner*, 55 Ill. 280 (1870). The court found the state had violated a teenager's due process rights when it imprisoned him for "misfortune," which included being a "vagrant, destitute of parental care, growing up in mendicancy, ignorance, idleness or vice." This case was part of the impetus for establishing juvenile courts, which Cook County, Illinois did first in 1899.

During the Civil War period, several cities, including New York, collected police department data, including some arrest and conviction statistics of juveniles. New York City was especially plagued by social problems because of an expanding and newly diverse population and a lack of social support for people. Thousands of children, estimated between 5,000 and 30,000, lived on the streets during the nineteenth century. Some juveniles became involved in gangs, but most of their criminal behavior concerned theft, not violence, and most of the theft in New York City concerned juveniles. In 1854, 80 percent of felony indictments and 50 percent of petty offenses for larceny were for juveniles under age twenty-one. A review of indictment samples between 1859 and 1876 for pickpocketing shows only 19 percent of the youth were accused of being physically aggressive, for instance, by snatching a purse or wallet and then running away with it. Despite the lack of violence involved in most crimes committed by juveniles, New York increasingly imposed harsh sentences on them. Before 1873 it never sent more than six juveniles a year to prison, but in 1874 and 1876, fifty teenagers were sent to Sing Sing Prison.

FURTHER READING

A reformatory for juvenile criminals. *Annual report of the board of directors and of the superintendent of the state's prison, for the year ending December 31, 1894*. Available from: http://docsouth.unc.edu/nc/prison1894/prison1894.html.

Conward, C. (2004). There is no justice, there is "just us": A look at overrepresentation of minority youth in the juvenile and criminal justice system. *Whittier Journal of Child and Family Advocacy, 4*, 35–63.

Gilfoyle, T. (2004). Street-rats and gutter-snipes: Child pickpockets and street culture in New York City, 1850–1900. *Journal of Social History, 37*, 853–882.

Inciardi, J., & Faupel, C. (Eds.). (1980). *History and crime: Implications for criminal justice policy*. Beverly Hills, CA: Sage.

Lane, R. (1997). *Murder in America*. Columbus: Ohio University Press.

Murphy, J. (1990). *Boys' war: Confederate and union soldiers talk about the Civil War*. New York: Clarion Books.

Reef, C. (2002). *Childhood in America: An eyewitness history*. New York: Facts on File.

Stone, R. (2005). History and philosophy of the juvenile court. *Florida Juvenile Law and Practice*. Tallahassee, FL: Florida Bar Continuing Legal Education.

Sutton, J. (1983). Social structure, institutions, and the legal status of children in the United States. *American Journal of Sociology, 88*(5), 915–947.

Sutton, J. (1988). *Stubborn children: Controlling delinquency in the United States, 1640–1981*. Berkeley: University of California Press.

Tonry, M. (1999). Rethinking unthinkable punishment policies in America. *UCLA Law Review, 46*, 1752–1791.

U.S. Census Bureau. *Compendium of the Seventh Census: 1850, Part I. Analysis, 1854*. Available from: http://www.census.gov/prod/www/abs/decennial/1850.htm.

U.S. Census Office. *Report on crime, pauperism, and benevolence in the United States*. Eleventh Census: 1890, Part I. Analysis. Available from: http://www.census.gov/prod/www/abs/decennial/1890.htm.

Wolcott, D. (2003). Juvenile justice before juvenile court. *Social Science History, 27*(1), 109–136.

Lorenn Walker

JUVENILE VIOLENCE, 1865–1899 (RECONSTRUCTION AND LATE 1800s).

In colonial America, no distinction was made between juvenile offenses and adult offenses. Not only did courts treat juveniles harshly, but parents were taught that they must as well, following the "spare the rod, spoil the child" philosophy. Both common law and custom assumed that a child accused of some type of mischief was automatically guilty.

Reforms began in the late eighteenth century. So-called **"Child Savers"** were responsible for many reforms, most importantly the recognition that children were in need of protection and guidance.

Types of Crimes

The industrial era brought new challenges as cities grew rapidly. Many families, immigrants in particular, struggled financially. Some children were abandoned by families in times of hardship and turned to gangs for protection and a sense of belonging. Immigrant gangs, such as the Irish Dead Rabbits, popularized in the film *Gangs of New York*, were common in some areas. The most notorious gang of the time period was the Five Points Gang, named for their home turf in the Five Points section of Manhattan. The Five Points Gang was essentially a feeder system for the mafia, and it spawned perhaps the most notorious mobster, Al Capone. Mexican street gangs were common in the West.

In addition to gang activity, juveniles were most likely to be arrested for crimes, in contrast to adults who were more commonly arrested for public order offenses, like drunk and disorderly. It might be, however, that police dealt informally with juveniles committing public order offenses, thus records may not accurately reflect the actual incidence of crimes. Most of the arrests of young boys were for crimes against property, rather than violent crimes. Boys typically stole relatively insignificant items and rarely used or threatened to use violence.

Violent offenses seem to have been quite rare; in Detroit, for instance, they were less than 10 percent of the arrests of juveniles. Many of the arrests of young boys in this time period were for status offenses or offenses that were not actually criminal, such as incorrigibility.

Racial violence was a major problem, as the country worked to recover from the Civil War. Lynching of black males, especially younger ones who had been accused of sexual violence involving white women, occurred with some frequency. The law allowed for the execution of men convicted of rape, a punishment disproportionately given to black males.

Punishments

Based on Christian principles that eschewed idleness, child savers started reform schools for delinquent and pre-delinquent youth. The first, the New York House of Refuge, opened its doors in 1825. Despite their popularity with historians, houses of refuge were never the primary means of dealing with wayward youth, as they could generally only house small numbers at a given time. These houses were criticized for their paternalistic and often harsh, even abusive, approach, and by 1890 foster homes for delinquent juveniles were created in some states as an alternative

The Role of Police

Police had the primary duty of maintaining order among children and teens in many cities. Police were also charged with enforcing state compulsory education laws. It was believed that truants would become criminals if not addressed promptly. Police often used truancy laws as a guise to arrest those they felt were *likely* to be delinquents. Police, as they do today, had a great deal of discretion in handling juveniles. Many juveniles were simply discharged to parents or other family members.

Juvenile Justice

In the 1870s, states further recognized the need to protect juveniles in trouble. Massachusetts was the first state to mandate separate court hearings for juveniles, with other states following soon thereafter. Some states began to prohibit the incarceration of juvenile and adult offenders together, although the practice remained common. In 1899, Illinois became the first state to create a separate juvenile court. The court was built on recognition of the differences between adults and juveniles, and it thus used new terminology and different procedures. The Illinois court had jurisdiction over three classes of children: dependent children, neglected children, and delinquent children. The juvenile courts were based on the principle of *parens patriae*, or the state as parent. Since juveniles were handled less formally and actions taken were allegedly in their best interests, they were not afforded the due process rights given to adults, a point of some controversy today. Other states soon added juvenile courts, and in 1938, the federal government established a law much like the one in Illinois. By 1945, every state had some type of juvenile court.

Explanations for Crime

Prior to the 1870s, few criminology textbooks were available in the United States. Theorists early in this time period were influenced by the work of Cesare Lombroso, who saw criminality as a genetic phenomenon. Richard Dugdale followed Lombroso's lead, examining inmates incarcerated in New York and arguing there was a family link. Also popular were theories addressing the link between intelligence and crime and violence. Newly developed intelligence tests were used to demonstrate that some delinquents were intellectually inferior and thus could not be rehabilitated. This led to policies like eugenics that sterilizied those dubbed "feeble-minded" under the rationale that this would, among other things, prevent a new breed of delinquents.

In the early 1900s, Freudian ideas added a challenge to the notion that criminality is innate. Freud asserted that environmental influences in the form of childhood socialization experiences influenced later delinquency. These ideas helped shape the budding juvenile justice system. Lombroso and Freud, as well as Freud's followers, were reflective of their time in that they rarely addressed female delinquency. Lombroso did briefly, maintaining that female offenders were atavistic and hysterical. Because of these biases, little is known about the incidence or reasons for female violence or delinquency.

In the 1920s, new theories, more sociological in nature, were being developed. Many of the new ideas emanated from Chicago and postulated that crime and violence are the result of social disorganization. In places experiencing rapid change, people may not feel connected to or invested in their communities. Consequently, minor crimes and acts of violence may occur. These then escalate into more serious incidents, as social controls also tend to break down.

FURTHER READING

Hwang, A., Lafond, R., Hansen, E., & Robinson, P. (2002). Is juvenile delinquency and aggression produced by permissive parenting: Re-evaluating 50 years of research. Paper presented at the American Association of Behavioral and Social Sciences National Convention. Available from: http://aabss.org/journal2002/Hwang.htm.

Mennel, R. (2003). Origins of the juvenile court: Changing perspectives on the legal rights of juvenile delinquents. In T. Calhoun & C. Chapple (Eds.), *Readings in juvenile delinquency and juvenile justice* (pp. 72–81). Upper Saddle River, NJ: Prentice Hall.

Platt, A. (2003). The rise of the child-saving movement. In T. Calhoun & C. Chapple (Eds.), *Readings in juvenile delinquency and juvenile justice* (pp. 82–99). Upper Saddle River, NJ: Prentice Hall.

Wolcott, D. (2003). Juvenile justice before juvenile court: Cops, courts, and kids in turn-of-the-century Detroit. *Social Science History, 27*(1), 109–136.

Laura L. Finley

JUVENILE VIOLENCE, 1900–1910

Historical Introduction

On December 17, 1900, Ellis Island reopened as the official immigration station. During this second mass wave of migration, society's attitude toward foreigners had changed. For instance, in 1907, although many Japanese had already migrated to America, President Theodore Roosevelt banned the immigration of Japanese laborers. Similarly, Congress enacted one of the first "No Fly Zones" because a German individual flew a zeppelin around the U.S. Capitol dome in Washington. The influence of these sanctions served to reinforce the fear of foreigners on American soil and to further segregate diverse populations.

Additionally, the industrial revolution influenced American's views of immigrants. Between 1901 and 1909, eight million immigrants arrived in the country. The big cities were becoming overcrowded, leaving only the slums available to ethnic populations. Similarly, these ethnic groups were taking job opportunities. Americans were beginning to harbor resentment toward all ethnic populations. With the influx of immigrants into America, most families settled in the big cities, such as Chicago, New York, Los Angeles, and San Francisco. These cities provided the greatest opportunity for wealth. However, with this opportunity came the cost of discrimination and segregation for most immigrant families. New York experienced a mass migration of Irish, Germans, Scandinavians, and Italians. These families longed for the traditions and values of their homeland and found it difficult to relate to American values. Ethnic segregation occurred, further alienating these populations from American mainstream society. Disputes often broke out between neighborhoods, hence the formation of the first territorial gangs in New York City.

Adult and Juvenile Gangs

The most notorious of these street gangs became known as the Five Points Gang. This gang gave birth to the modern gangster and was a turning point in the history of gang violence. The leader of this gang was an Italian who was able to mingle with the socialites and developed great wealth and reputation. Although the Five Points Gang consisted primarily of adults, this elite club fed the poverty-stricken youth by providing small jobs, such as running numbers for gambling operations, delivering letters of extortion, and working as lookouts for the speakeasies. The enamored youth learned from these gangsters and were later accepted into many of the Five Points Gang's smaller divisions. One of the most famous of these teenagers was Al "Scarface" Capone.

Other Types of Juvenile Crime and Violence

During the industrial revolution, with fewer than half of the juvenile population able to go to school, boys and girls as young as seven years old worked in factories and in the coal mines. Many of these children were immigrants. Some had lost their parents during the war. Others were separated from their parents due to the discriminatory implementation of the 1907 immigration laws. These orphans, if jobless, parentless, and homeless, found ways to survive by banding together, committing delinquent acts such as petty thievery and pickpocketing. The pickpocket gangs were notorious during this era and divided territories, often with the knowledge of the police.

Truancy was actually a form of delinquency offense prior to the establishment of the juvenile courts. It was used with some regularity; of the children jailed at the Bridewell (Chicago House of Correction) in 1898, one-quarter were there for truancy. It was thought that truancy reflected poor parenting and was a precursor to more serious delinquency. Yet only two of the 178 children tracked for school absence in 1906 were found to be truly incorrigible.

Responses to Juvenile Crime and Violence

Police behavior was shaped by the values of the society. With no formal training, police often acted as catalysts for violence and enforced the violent acts committed by gangs.

In 1899, the State of **Illinois** established the first juvenile court system. This system provided for confidential and protective measures to treat the offender as a child and not an adult. The confidentiality of the youth was to ensure that rehabilitation could be accomplished without a tarnished name. The family was also allegedly protected from society's judgment. Houses of Refuge were used as homes to rehabilitate and deter delinquents. Juveniles who were fourteen were treated as adults and housed in prison. Another major addition to the juvenile court was the installation of psychiatric clinics, the first being the Juvenile Psychopathic Institute in Chicago in 1909.

The case of *Commonwealth v. Fisher* in 1905 was an early challenge to the constitutionality of the new courts. Frank Fisher had been committed to the Philadelphia House of Refuge, and his attorney maintained his incarceration was unlawful on three grounds: (1) Fisher had not received due process in the way he was brought to court; (2) he was not provided a jury trial; and (3) his indeterminate sentence to the reformatory was a form of age-based discrimination. The appellate court of Pennsylvania rejected these arguments. The appellate court rejected the discrimination claim, contending that ***parens patriae*** allows the court to exercise its power over children, just as a parent exercises restraint of their children.

In the early twentieth century, civic groups began to pay attention to the "girl problem." Local organizations, such as PTAs and women's clubs, began sponsoring lectures and discussions about female delinquency and began to sponsor organizations to address the problem, including girls' clubs, the YWCA, and even the Girl Scouts. In Chicago between 1899 and 1909, 59 percent of boys appearing before the court received probation compared to 37 percent of girls. Fifty percent of the girls were committed to reformatories in contrast to 20 percent of the boys.

The laws in the early 1900s did not generally hold children under the age of fourteen responsible for crimes. Parents or guardians were held as neglectful, and having delinquent children gave the family a bad name. Police acted as surrogate parents for orphans by disciplining these children, often beating them. Many believed this was more of a deterrent than arrest and incarceration. The decade also saw the introduction of probation, which was used widely by the end of the decade.

FURTHER READING

Dohrn, B. (2002). The school, the child, and the court. In M. Rosenheim, F. Zimring, D. Tanenhaus, & B. Dohrn (Eds.), *Juvenile justice century* (pp. 267–309). Chicago: University of Chicago Press.

Tanenhaus, D. (2002). The evolution of juvenile courts in the early twentieth century: Beyond the myth of immaculate construction. In M. Rosenheim, F. Zimring, D. Tanenhaus, & B. Dohrn (Eds.), *Juvenile justice century* (pp. 42–73). Chicago: University of Chicago Press.

Tompkins, V. (Ed.). *American decades, 1900–1910*. Detroit, MI: Gale Research Group.

Celene Andreano

JUVENILE VIOLENCE, 1910–1919

Historical Introduction

This decade was a period of unrest and reform. In addition to the immigration of large numbers of Italians, Poles, Greeks, Russians, and Jews, the black population from the South was migrating north and west to pursue unskilled labor opportunities. Simultaneously, America was dealing with the Mexican Revolution and the buildup to World War I. In the West, Los Angeles, San Francisco, California, and El Paso, Texas were experiencing a population growth from Mexican immigrants.

In the early years of this decade, two publications influenced an already segregated society where large immigrant populations were fighting over territories and jobs. *Heredity in Relation to Eugenics* essentially promoted racial purity by advocating sterilization, controlled breeding, and executions of those populations that were darker, smaller in stature, and allegedly prone to immorality. In 1907, Pennsylvania passed the first coercive sterilization law. Many well-known progressives, including birth control advocate Margaret Sanger, supported coerced sterilization. Mental testing was conducted in reformatories, starting in the 1910s, in order to discern which inmates were so inferior they were to be sterilized.

The Dillingham Commission Reports, published in 1910–1911, claimed that the immigrant population increased social and economic problems in America. These publications further isolated all ethnic populations and validated the fears and disdain of the native American population. These reports also created justifications for one immigrant population to use another as scapegoats for social and economic instability. During the decade, there were a number of race riots in response to several decades of mob lynchings across America, yet another illustration of the racial tensions.

In 1914, the Harrison Narcotics Act, a tax on narcotics, was the first step toward criminalizing most drug use.

Adult and Juvenile Gangs

During this decade, territorial and scavenger groups evolved into organized gangs. Street gangs were common in most immigrant populations, mostly to protect their territories. However, in the big cities, the mafia was forming from smaller groups like the Five Points Gang in New York and Chicago. The mafia became highly structured and organized crime by utilizing smaller "clubs" for its profits. It infiltrated the political, social, and economic realms of society and solicited juveniles to work for the members of the organization. In 1915, the Ku Klux Klan (KKK) was re-established. This occurred five years after the first legalization of segregated neighborhoods in America. The KKK is essentially a gang of white supremacists, and they were responsible for many lynchings across the states. Members consisted of disgruntled farmers, politicians, and even police officers. Many of their recruits were youth that were easily influenced by adult conversation and so became close observers of the KKK's affairs, even attending mob lynchings. The KKK was similar to the mafia in that both gangs were glorified and feared. These organized gangs provided juvenile recruits with training, money to provide for their families, and a sense of belonging.

Other Types of Juvenile Crime

Most juvenile crime in the decade involved minor incidents. Twenty-five percent of the cases heard by the New York Children's Court in 1914 were for petty offenses and another 38 percent were for children in need of care. Of the 37 percent of "serious offenses," the most common was burglary.

Responses to Juvenile Crime and Violence

Progressives of the era began to advocate for children as a national resource, following key publications, such as Denver Juvenile Court Judge Ben Lindsey's *Children in Bondage* in 1913. They were now to be protected against harm in many institutions. Most notably, child labor laws were passed in a number of locations.

To deal with what was perceived to be a growing youth gang problem, by 1910, thirty-two states had juvenile court systems. The laws provided for ***parens patriae***, or the state as parent. This meant that the state was to act in the best interest of youth under eighteen and was given full power and responsibility for the juveniles' and society's well-being. The progressive movement during this decade concluded that juveniles lacked mens rea, or criminal intent, were easily influenced by immoral ideas, and therefore could not be held responsible for delinquent activity and charged in an adult manner.

The decade between 1910 and 1920 saw the opening of twenty-three new facilities for female delinquents, in contrast to just five that were opened in each of the decades prior since 1850. In 1913, the Juvenile Protection Association reported that one-third of the girls in the Cook County jail were African American.

FURTHER READING

Schlossman, S. (1977). *Love and the American delinquent*. Chicago: University of Chicago Press.

Schlossman, S., & Wallach, S. (1998). The crime of precocious sexuality: Female juvenile delinquency in the progressive era. In P. Sharp & B. Hancock (Eds.), *Juvenile delinquency: Historical, theoretical, and societal reactions to youth*, 2nd ed. (pp. 41–63). Upper Saddle River, NJ: Prentice Hall.

Tompkins, V. (Ed.). *American decades, 1910–1919*. Detroit, MI: Gale Research Group.

Celene Andreano

JUVENILE VIOLENCE, 1920–1929

Historical Introduction

On January 16, 1920, Prohibition began. The temperance movement called the Eighteenth Amendment's prohibition of alcohol a great success, even though they had already influenced more than half of the forty-eight states by 1916 to prohibit alcohol. The Eighteenth Amendment banned the manufacture, sale, and transport of alcohol. This meant that possession and consumption was still legal. As a consequence, many of America's politicians and social elites kept alcohol in their homes and offices. The public found these politicians, even Presidents Harding and Coolidge, to be hypocrites in trying to enforce a policy that they violated. Police were the primary enforcement agencies, but laws prevented them from entering speakeasies or other establishments by force. Often, these agents ended up working for organized crime gangs. Prohibition created contempt for the law and fostered corruption throughout American society. The enforcement of Prohibition was influential in the emergence of violence and weapons into the psyche of young gang members. Also evolving within the gang culture were new concepts of respect, reputation, and revenge. Each member earned each of these traits in order to gain higher status within their "club."

The invention of the Ford automobile in 1908 originally provided mobility only to the elite at a cost of $1,000. By 1920, the assembly line decreased costs to less than a $400 purchase price. Gangsters relished in the opportunities provided by this new mobility. Drive-by shootings began, transporting of liquor across state lines was made convenient, and kidnapping for ransom became common. Liquor was in such high demand that hijackings would occur. The "hijacking gangs" formed to boost profits for organized crime. These hijacking gangs often used the infamous Thompson machine gun, which became known as the gun to hold up or murder opposing liquor runners. For gangsters, revenge became easy, earning one a national reputation of violence and power. Juvenile gang members waited for opportunities to make a name for themselves, allowing for a profitable return to provide for their families.

By the mid-1920s, a recession began that led to the Great Depression beginning in 1929. Taxes and tariffs were exceedingly high and President Calvin Coolidge chose not to aide those families that lost their livelihoods. Americans, depleted of energy, life savings, and hopeful futures, turned toward the gangsters that were still thriving well into the thirties.

Adult and Juvenile Gangs

By the 1920s, America was a melting pot of cultures. Juvenile gangs existed in all corners of the United States. In the big cities, New York, Chicago, and Boston, for instance, many of the juvenile gang members of the earlier 1900s had evolved into organized crime leaders. Many of these gangsters provided opportunities for juveniles during the Prohibition era. These youth were trained under the guidance of adult gangsters and often made "little members" for these organizations. Juveniles participated in crimes such as driving getaway vehicles, being lookouts at the speakeasies, and running messages regarding racketeering, gambling, bribery, or death threats to prostitutes, politicians, or any member of society that was involved. Juveniles were also involved in transporting alcohol, burglary, robbery, and working the trains, which were privatized by the Esch-Cummins Transportation Act of 1920.

The enforcement of prohibition proved nearly impossible in the 1920s. By 1925, six states banned local police from investigating violations. Bootleggers, speakeasies, moonshine, bathtub gin, and rum runners outnumbered and outpaced law enforcement. Essentially, enforcement would cost too much money. Organized crime was reaping the benefits of Prohibition, while the American economy was beginning to suffer.

The Irish and Jewish gangs that existed in the earlier decades in New York were overrun by the Italian mafia, and Chicago was nicknamed the crime capital of the world. The Hispanic gangs had a stronghold from California to Texas. These gangs survived with little or no leadership and committed crimes such as burglary, armed robbery, and vandalism. With the influence of Prohibition, an underground alcohol trade was rampant across state lines, bringing opportunity and money to Hispanic immigrants from Texas to California. The youth, influenced by bootlegging, speakeasies, and profits, were easily lured in to helping any side that could provide financial security for their family.

The 1920s brought the beginning of African-American gangs. These gangs surfaced from Los Angeles to Harlem, primarily as a means to portray the tough guy image during Prohibition and in contrast to the growing white supremacy movement in the South. In 1922, the Ku Klux Klan, a white supremacist gang, named Hiram Evans as its Imperial Wizard. Membership in this gang grew to nearly four million members by 1925. Many of its members became politicians from as far south as Texas to as far west as Oregon. Other African-American gangs in the big cities were formed with friends and family to operate small-time criminal activities, such as prostitution and robbery. The African-American juvenile gangs were not territorial and existed with little or no leadership.

Other Types of Juvenile Crime and Violence

In May of 1924, the nation was stunned by the murder of a fourteen-year-old by two wealthy teens. Leopold and Loeb, two incredibly smart young men, murdered a boy they barely knew in an attempt to commit "the perfect crime." They were caught quite easily and were tried for a capital offense. Famous defense attorney Clarence Darrow succeeded in obtaining life sentences, as opposed to death, for the boys.

Responses to Juvenile Crime and Violence

In 1909, President Theodore Roosevelt invited a number of social service professionals to the White House Conference on the Care of Dependent Children, the first national effort to promote a social services agenda. Their primary determination was that the federal government should establish a national agency devoted to children. In 1912, the Children's Bureau was created for this purpose. In 1920, the Child Welfare League of America was founded with a similar mission.

Like today, many alleged there were race, gender, and social class biases in the juvenile justice system. In 1923, 16 percent of the girls at the Geneva Reformatory in Cook County, Illinois were black, yet they were only 2 percent of the Illinois population at the time.

FURTHER READING

Baughman, J. (Ed.). *American decades, 1920–1929*. Detroit, MI: Gale Research Group.

Dohrn, B. (2002). The school, the child, and the court. In M. Rosenheim, F. Zimring, D. Tanenhaus, & B. Dohrn (Eds.), *A Century of Juvenile Justice* (pp. 267–309). Chicago: University of Chicago Press.

Krisberg, B., and Austin, J. (1993). *Reinventing juvenile justice*. Newbury Park, CA: Sage.

Platt, A. (1998). The child-saving movement and the origins of the juvenile justice system. In P. Sharp & B. Hancock (Eds.), *Juvenile delinquency: Historical, theoretical, and societal reactions to youth*, 2nd ed. (pp. 3–17). Upper Saddle River, NJ: Prentice Hall.

Watkins, J. (1998). *The juvenile justice century*. Durham, NC: Carolina Academic Press.

Celene Andreano

JUVENILE VIOLENCE, 1930–1939

Incidence and Types of Offenses

In general, violent offenses by youth were relatively rare in this decade. For instance, in Massachusetts during the years 1930–1932, violent offenses made up 2.6 percent of all the offenses of boys and girls aged fourteen, fifteen, and sixteen. The term "violent" in this case includes vicious attacks on persons, crimes against property that involve force or violence, or fear against the personality or body of another. Among children aged eighteen, the rate rose to 3.9 percent.

It is interesting to note the gender differences of these youthful offenders. During this two-year period, Massachusetts statistics show that only 384 seventeen-year-old girls were brought into court for any offense—and only three of those 384 offenders were deemed violent. Out of 5,715 seventeen-year-old boys who were brought into court for any offense, 205 of them were deemed violent.

Because of the Great Depression, youth gangs were growing very rapidly across the country. In large cities, especially in the West, Pachucos, often referred to as "Zoot Suiters," were gangs of Mexican Americans that formed for protection as well as criminal enterprises. The next decade would see riots involving these gangs, largely on the West Coast.

Juvenile Justice

Since its inception in the nineteenth century, the American juvenile justice system has seen myriad changes. By the year 1925, all but two states in the country had created juvenile courts. Juvenile courts generally focused on treatment rather than punishment for youthful offenders. The period between 1930 and 1940 is one in which the courts worked to refine their mission and procedures.

From the fifty-year period between 1925–1975, most of the country's juvenile courts held exclusive jurisdiction over all youthful offenders under the age of eighteen who were accused of committing criminal crimes. If the juvenile court relinquished its jurisdiction over a case, only then could the youth be relocated to a criminal court to be tried as an adult. These decisions were made on a case-by-case basis, using *parens patriae*, or the state as parent, as justification. In the 1930s, youthful offenders were often granted more leniency than mature offenders. In general, in cases where there was no penal policy guiding the judge, the child offender was treated more mercifully regarding his/her sentence.

Between 1930–1932, several Massachusetts court officials asked if raising the juvenile court age would help to diminish violent youth offender numbers. But raising the court age of juveniles would not lower the crime rates themselves; it would merely illustrate lower numbers for that age group, while the older offenders would be thrown into the criminal court system instead of staying in the juvenile court system. In 1936, the FBI reported that the average age of criminals was nineteen.

It is important to note that the juvenile courts did not control every aspect of the judicial process at this time. The police had a great deal of discretion when dealing with youthful offenders. When a juvenile crime was committed, it was the police alone who held the discretionary power to decide which cases should be referred to the juvenile courts. At that time the police—not the courts—decided if they would hold youthful offenders until their scheduled court dates. Therefore, the police could discipline juvenile criminals in whatever way they saw fit.

Prevention Efforts

Many social programs sprung up in this time period as well, which seemed to help keep youthful offenders out of the criminal court system. An annual report from the decade observed that during routine visits to foster homes, social workers took more time out of their visit to study the foster child's emotional status. Because of this, four times as many children were taken to "child guidance clinics" in 1935 than in 1934. In Connecticut, several town police departments, as well as juvenile courts, began referring children to the Connecticut Children's Aid Society instead of sending them straight to reform school.

The **Chicago Area Project** (CAP) was pioneered in 1934, and to this day it is the most widely known juvenile delinquency prevention program in our country's history. Organized by sociologist Clifford R. Shaw, CAP focused on the poorest neighborhoods of Chicago. CAP strove to improve the quality of life in poor communities by helping youth and their families solve difficult problems.

On the other side of the country, social groups were hoping to lower the rate of juvenile violence by establishing crime prevention groups. The Los Angeles Coordinating Councils (LACC) broke new ground when it focused on the "community approach to crime control." The LACC advocated social programs and focused on the environmental factors contributing to youth crime, which differed greatly from the federal war on crime in that era.

FURTHER READING

Alper, B. (1939). Teen-age offenses and offenders. *American Sociological Review, 4*(2), 167–172.

Appier, J. (2005). The Los Angeles Coordinating Councils during the Great Depression. *Journal of Urban History, 31*(2), 190–218.

Males, M. (1999, November 21). Generation gap: For adults, "today's youth" are always the worst. *L. A. Times.*

Shulman, H. (1932). A statistical study of youthful offenders in New York City. *Journal of the American Statistical Association, 27*(177), 19–29.

Snyder, H., & Sickmund, M. (1999, December). Juvenile justice: A century of change. *1999 National Report Series, Juvenile Justice Bulletin.* Available at: http://www.ncjrs.gov/html/ojjdp/9912_2/ juv1.html.

Whittaker, D. (2001, Winter). *Chicago Area Project Newsletter.* Available at: www.chicagoareaproject.org/ publications.

Wolcott, D. (2001). "The cop will get you": The police and discretionary juvenile justice, 1890–1940. *Journal of Social History, 35*(2), 349–371.

Kristin Emanuel

JUVENILE VIOLENCE, 1940–1949

Incidence and Types of Offenses

The end of the Great Depression did not bring an end to juvenile violence. Economic tensions caused by the Great Depression extended to the 1940s and into the World War II era. Racial tensions also aided in high juvenile crime rates in the 1940s. In the fall of 1941, a series of muggings in the Central Park area perpetrated by black youths from Harlem attracted nationwide attention. Newspaper headlines claimed there was a crime wave, and most citizens believed it because of the widespread repetition in the print media. There really was no crime wave among black offenders in 1941. In fact, the number of offenses committed by blacks in 1941 Harlem was only slightly greater than in the corresponding period of 1940. Juvenile delinquency rates among New York blacks were much higher than whites at the time. These high juvenile crime rates in New York are often attributed to poverty and parental neglect.

Whereas the gangs of the 1930s were predominantly white, major American cities in the 1940s saw the growth of all-black gangs who were constantly fighting over neighborhood turfs. In 1943, Mexican gang members, known for wearing "zoot suits," clashed with white soldiers in what is now called the zoot suit riots. These riots highlighted the growing racial tensions around the country. Another event that demonstrated the nation's racism was the misidentification and trial of several Chicano teenagers for murder in Sleepy Lagoon in 1942. One of the earliest Chicano gangs, the White Fence, formed in the 1940s as a form of protection against racist bullying. The White Fence is said to be one of the first to use chains and guns as weapons. In the Northeast, the massive influx of Puerto Ricans into New York City spawned the creation of Puerto Rican gangs, as depicted in the musical and film *West Side Story.*

Explanations for Juvenile Violence

One possible explanation for the rise in youth crime in this era is that with so many fathers leaving home to fight for their country, families were left broken and without a strong male role model in the home. In the first three months after the United States entered World War II, juvenile delinquency among all races in New York City increased 10 percent over the corresponding three months of the year previous.

Yet another explanation for youth crime lies in economic status alone. Gustav L. Schramm, a wartime juvenile court judge, cited one case in which the juvenile delinquent in question, Richard, was sent to court for excessive truancy. The boy's reasoning was clear: his father was dead, and his mother, who was left to raise eight children on her own, needed money. Richard's only brother still living at home was responsible for providing the family's total income. Richard firmly believed that by quitting school he could get a job to help bring in more money to support his family.

Policing Juveniles

Because law enforcement perceived a wave of youth crime, police began to arrest increasing numbers of youth in the early 1940s. For instance, the Federal Bureau of Investigations (FBI) reports that arrests for girls went up 55 percent between 1941 and 1942, although these arrests were generally not for violent offenses. Rather, they were an attempt to police females' sexuality, as there was great concern that adolescent females were "cruising" for soldiers. Caseloads for boys also increased by about one-third between 1942 and 1943.

Juvenile Justice

By 1950, all fifty states as well as Washington, DC, had juvenile court systems in place. The movement of all states to create specialized juvenile courts spread quickly because it offered a new approach to handling youthful offenders who were previously dealt with in criminal courts. Social change advocates liked the new juvenile court system because it was extremely informal (compared to criminal court) as well as personal, accounting for the unique circumstances of each case. Juvenile court judges liked the new system because it made it possible for them to take the time to talk to every offender brought into court. Probation officers could (ideally) thoroughly inspect each juvenile delinquent's home life. Due process protections for accused youths were seen as unnecessary because the court was to always follow the best interests of the youth.

Unfortunately, this informality of the juvenile courts sometimes posed a problem. Because juvenile court judges were allowed to sit privately with each offender and discuss the youth's offenses, these judges would sometimes abuse their discretionary power. Judges, too, held biases that might come out in their dealings with poor and racially diverse youth. There were more problems with the juvenile justice system, problems that stemmed from the social reformers' "excessive idealism." Justine Wise Polier reports that by the 1940s "youths charged with offenses sat for hours in airless waiting rooms. Noisy verbal and physical battles had to be broken up by court attendants. The hard benches on which everyone was forced to sit and the atmosphere, like that in lower criminal courts, resembled bullpens more than a court for human beings" (Butts & Mitchell, 2000, p. 76).

World War II brought about some significant changes to the juvenile justice system. One new program that began during the war involved boys who had already been through the juvenile court system and who had improved their situations while on probation. These young men volunteered for the armed services, and if they were honest about their prior records to recruiting officers, the juvenile courts would usually allow them to join the service. Those offenders whose records prohibited from joining the service oftentimes slipped back into delinquent behaviors.

Other Prevention Efforts

New social programs were still being created during this war-time era. In 1941, the California Youth Authority (CYA) was founded in hopes of rehabilitating juvenile delinquents. The CYA is committed to treating "juveniles as individuals who are still capable of changing their behavior, their thinking, and their lives if the correct outside influence is provided." Programs that had already been in play for years were still active during wartime as well. For instance, in 1946, the Connecticut Children's Aid Society encountered a 67 percent increase in requests for help.

FURTHER READING

Blanshard, P. (1942). Negro delinquency in New York. *Journal of Educational Sociology, 16*(2), 115–123.

Butts, J., & Mitchell, O. (2000). Brick by brick: Dismantling the border between juvenile and adult justice. *Journal of Criminal Justice, 2*, 167–213.

California Youth Authority. (1994). State/local juvenile corrections in California—A systems perspective. *Little Hoover Commission, 127.*

Carmichael, B. (2004). Urban change and criminal patterns: An historical context. *National Social Science Journal, 21*(2), 8–15.

Mihailoff, L. (2004). Youth gangs. Available at: http://parenting.families.com/youth-gangs-916-917-ecc.

Schramm, G. (1942). The juvenile court in wartime. *Journal of Educational Sociology, 16*(2), 69–81.

Snyder, H., & Sickmund, M. (1999, December). Juvenile justice: A century of change. *1999 National Report Series, Juvenile Justice Bulletin.* Available at: http://www.ncjrs.gov/html/ojjdp/ 9912_2/ juv1.html.

Kristin Emanuel

JUVENILE VIOLENCE, 1950–1959

Incidence and Types of Violence

Although the economic strains of the Great Depression and World War II had lifted somewhat, Americans still saw a rise in juvenile crime rates in the 1950s. Perhaps the most prevalent type of juvenile crime in this decade was the growth of street gangs. During this time, gangs in New York seemed to overrun low-income housing projects. The gangs spent their time committing random acts of vandalism and violence. They experimented with drugs, drank cheap alcohol, and sometimes maimed and killed one another.

Explanations for Juvenile Violence

One possible reason for this rise in youth crime could be attributed to **television**. The "Nifty Fifties" was the decade when the majority of American families bought their first home television set. Whereas in previous decades gang violence was confined to the country's larger cities, television helped to bring gang activity to even the quietest of suburbs.

One might argue that television programs of the 1950s were, for the most part, wholesome in nature. Shows like *The Adventures of Ozzie & Harriet, I Love Lucy,* and *Leave It to Beaver* portrayed solid families with good American moral values. But a closer examination shows subtle influences, even in shows such as these. Take, for instance, how angry Ricky Ricardo would get at his dramatic wife, Lucy. Ricky often yelled and fumed at Lucy. One has to ask whether constant exposure to the heated arguments the Ricardos often had actually had a negative effect on youths' perceptions of relationships.

Other popular programs, such as *Gunsmoke* and *Bonanza,* also modeled violence. It is true that in shows like these Americans watched the "good guys" battle it out with the "bad guys," yet this too could be blamed for the rise in youth violence. Television shows like these show violence in a positive light—that it is perfectly all right, even expected—for the "good guys" to use excessive (i.e., deadly) force to defend their way of life.

For families in more rural areas of the country, television was their link to the larger world. While the more discerning viewer may be able to differentiate between real-world and fictional situations, perhaps some of the more rural American viewers had no idea that what television portrayed was not actual reality in the big city. Further, if adults have such problems discerning truth from fiction on television, it must be even harder for children. A study done much later, in 1969, revealed that television is an important source of "incidental learning" from which children learn "a variety of concepts, ideas, and attitudes."

Juvenile Justice

Even more so in the 1950s than in previous years, many Americans began to worry about the state of our juvenile court system. People began questioning the juvenile court's ability to rehabilitate juvenile offenders. The basic philosophy behind the juvenile court system was not in question, but professionals had legitimate concerns about the escalating number of youth who had been institutionalized indefinitely.

During the 1950s, youth advocates and legal activists started challenging the broad discretionary powers given to juvenile court judges. A particularly significant law review article in 1957 questioned whether juvenile courts were completely benevolent, arguing that "an adjudication of delinquency, in itself, is harmful and should not be capriciously imposed" (Butts & Mitchell, 2000, p. 176). Yet another article, published in 1960, accused juvenile courts of violating essential principals of equal protection and made a case that juveniles deserved real trials with real due process guarantees.

Other Prevention Efforts

At a time when the judicial system was getting so much flak from legal and social advocates, social welfare groups became even more imperative. During the 1950s, the number of children who needed "emergency permanent placement" into alternative homes grew rapidly. In Connecticut, for example, the Hartford Orphan Asylum merged with the Connecticut Children's Aid Society. A second merger occurred not much later with the Family Service Bureau of Norfolk. The children that came to the Connecticut Children's Aid Society would stay at the Children's Village between six months and two years.

FURTHER READING

Butts, J., & Mitchell, O. (2000). Brick by brick: Dismantling the border between juvenile and adult justice. *Journal of Criminal Justice, 2,* 167–213.

Carmichael, B. (2004). Urban change and criminal patterns: An historical context. *National Social Science Journal, 21*(2), 8–15.

Delgado, C. (1997). Teens rebel against authority. *Borderlands, 15,* 14.

Hwang, A., Hansen, E., Lafond, R., & Robinson, P. (2002). Is juvenile delinquency and aggression produced by permissive or punitive parenting: Re-evaluating 50 years of research. Paper presented at The American Association of Behavioral and Social Sciences National Convention.

Snyder, H., & Sickmund, M. (1999, December). Juvenile justice: A century of change. *1999 National Report Series, Juvenile Justice Bulletin.* Available at: http://www.ncjrs.gov/html/ojjdp/9912_2/juv1.html.

Sykes, G., & Matza, D. (1957). Techniques of neutralization: A theory of delinquency. *American Sociological Review, 22,* 664–670.

Taylor, H., & Dozier, C. (1983). Television violence, African-Americans, and social control, 1950–1976. *Journal of Black Studies, 14*(2), 107–136.

Kristin Emanuel

JUVENILE VIOLENCE, 1960–1969

Historical Overview

Many people who specialize in juvenile justice or delinquency regard the 1960s as the age of youth, as 70 million children from the postwar baby boom reached adolescence and became teenagers and young adults during the decade. Child labor laws had previously excluded youth in general from the labor force, and compulsory education laws ensured that youth began to create peer cultures in unprecedented numbers. A movement away from the conservative fifties eventually resulted in new ways of thinking, which led to social movements across the United States. Due to these and other factors, the number of juveniles incarcerated increased steadily until the end of the decade. Juveniles also increased the frequency of drug use as well as experimentation with different types of drugs.

Explanations for Violence

New theories such as Sykes and Matza's (1957) **delinquency and drift** influenced the field of criminology. Sykes and Matza contended that the great majority of juveniles are engaged in normal law-abiding behavior most of the time. Juveniles may drift into occasional delinquency when social control is weakened, but most "age out" (grow out of) of delinquency entirely as they approach adulthood. Based on the work of Wolfgang, Figlio and Sellin, scholars began to look to **subcultural** explanations for juvenile crime and violence. Also popular during the 1960s were a variety of learning theories, each in some way positing that delinquency, like other behaviors, is learned. Included were Burgess and Akers' **differential association-reinforcement** and Daniel Glaser's **differential identification**. As people became concerned about the impact of punitive methods of social control, **labeling theories** also began to have influence in the field of juvenile justice. At the end of the decade, **conflict** or **critical** theories emerged from the work of Karl Marx and Friedrich Engels. Travis Hirschi's **social bond** theory, posited in 1969, was widely used to explain delinquency into the 1970s and beyond.

As all forms of media became more available to youth, scholars began to recognize the influence media may have on the developing minds of youths, prompting societal debates regarding the relationship to juvenile violence. The media also played an important role in juvenile violence during the 1960s by portraying violent images of youth.

Incidence and Types of Violence

During this decade, the crime rate outpaced population growth, 4 to 1. There were 160.9 violent crimes per 100,000 citizens during this decade. Police records of violent youth show that young Americans between the ages of thirteen and twenty-four were involved in homicide, robbery, and aggravated assault. The 1960s set the stage for the evolution of juvenile violence to the extent that, following this decade, arrests for persons under eighteen years of age for eight serious crimes increased more than 231 percent. From 1960 until the mid-1990s, juvenile crime escalated. Juveniles were responsible for as much as 84 percent of homicides, and overall rates for violent crimes perpetrated by juveniles against individuals increased 1,200 percent between 1960 and 1993.

Violence was just one of the crimes associated with the youth. Strong social movements led thousands of young Americans to experiment with illicit drugs. Many of the drugs had specific neurological effects. Accordingly, teenage drug arrests in the United States rose to 1,451 percent by 1965.

Juvenile Justice

The 1960s also saw the beginning of the so-called court unification. Juvenile court processing became more like adult court processing than the original design that utilized the concept of *parens patriae*. The U.S. Supreme Court in this decade began to alter the direction and shape of the juvenile justice system. The first full-scale alteration began with *Kent v. U.S.* (1966), when a sixteen-year-old rapist was transferred for trial in adult criminal court. The court ruled that **waivers**, or transfers, should be accompanied by a special hearing, the assistance of counsel, access to records by such counsel, and a written statement of reasons for the transfer. In the same decade, the court, in *In re Gault* (1967), ruled that juveniles deserve the right against self-incrimination, adequate notice of charges, the right to confront and cross-examine accusers, assistance of counsel, and the rights of sworn testimony and appeal. The system became much more adversarial and less informal. These drastic erosions of the traditional juvenile justice system were possible because of the explosion in crime during the decade. Further, new criticisms of the juvenile court suggested that juveniles had "the worst of both worlds," that is, they received none of the protections of adult court yet virtually all of the same punishments.

Many writers were very critical of landmark cases, blaming the decline in morality and the subsequent upsurge in crime in the country on a so-called liberal Supreme Court. Teen pregnancies, drug abuse, juvenile violence, and many other deviant and immoral behaviors were blamed on certain Supreme Court decisions, including *Engel v. Vitale, Abington Township v. Schempp*, and *Murray v. Curlett*, that expanded or extended civil rights to juveniles. The upsurges in crime, delinquency, and violence that characterized the 1960s, some argued, may not have occurred until the Supreme Court decisions of 1962–1963. Others maintained that these decisions were critical to empower young people in a democratic nation.

The 1960s also saw furious fights for civil rights for African Americans, women's rights activism, protests against the Vietnam War, increased drug use, the appearance of hippies, and more juvenile gang violence. There was racial tension, which turned deadly in the riots at Watts and elsewhere. In the first nine months of 1967 alone, there were 164 urban race riots. It is very important to note that African Americans were not allowed access to legitimate or legal education until the Supreme Court decision in 1954 in *Brown v. Board of Education*. Even then, especially in the southern states, minorities continued to be denied equal access to services. Juveniles are not robots. They too can see, feel, hear, and touch. They began to rebel against the middle-class values imposed on society at large, as they saw their parents do. Perhaps because of this rebellion, in the beginning of the 1960s, most studies regarding juveniles indicated that discipline was a key concern among parents and teachers. The Gilbert research survey indicated that the number one complaint of teachers regarding juveniles was lack of courtesy and respect for elders. Others, however, maintain that juveniles were not nearly as bad as critics suggested, and that they were simply expressing themselves in many cases.

Social Factors

It is pertinent to note that America embarked on several wars just prior to and during the 1960s, drug use increased during the 1960s, divorce rates increased, tension between races became very nasty, tension between citizens and law enforcement was very deadly, and segregation in education and housing as well as high poverty rates, particularly among immigrants and blacks, paralyzed some communities. As a result, a crime wave of vast proportions overwhelmed large cities like New York and Chicago. In New York, for example, between 1960 and 1968, robbery increased over 825 percent and burglary by 480 percent according to Uniform Crime Reports (UCR) 1973. Another important phenomenon that fostered violence in the 1960s was corruption that particularly engulfed political campaigns and strengthened organized crime. While not specific to juveniles, these trends most certainly impacted juvenile crime and violence.

FURTHER READING

Burgess, R., & Akers, R. (1966). A differential association-reinforcement theory of criminal behavior. *Social Problems, 14*, 363–83.

Chambliss, W. (1973). The Saints and the roughnecks. In D. Henslin (Ed.). *Down to earth sociology* (pp. 180–194). New York: The Free Press.

Cohen, L., & Land, K. (1987). Age structure and crime: Symmetry versus asymmetry and the projection of crime rates through the 1990s. *American Sociological Review, 52*, 170–183.

Glaser, D. (1956). Criminality theories and behavioral images. *American Journal of Sociology, 61*(5), 433–44.

Hirschi, T. (1969). *Causes of delinquency.* Berkeley, CA: University of California Press.

Layman, R. (1994). *American decades, 1960–1969.* Detroit, MI: Gale Research Group.

Shannon, L. (1998). *Alcohol and drugs, delinquency and crime: Looking back to the future.* New York: Palgrave Macmillan.

Sykes, G., & Matza, D. (1957). Techniques of neutralization. *American Sociological Review, 22*, 664–670.

Wolfgang, M., Figlio, R., & Sellin, T. (1972). *Delinquency in a birth cohort.* Chicago, IL: University of Chicago Press.

Evaristus Obinyan

JUVENILE VIOLENCE, 1970–1979

Historical Introduction

The 1970s were a transitional period in regard to crime and violence; that is, they were less explosive than the tumultuous 1960s but predated the crime surge of the mid-1980s. Major concerns included the growing population of teens and young adults as baby boomers came of age, as well as the economic woes many faced in light of a global oil crisis.

Researchers were also developing new theories and using new research methods. Further, the federal government established measures helpful in tracking crime and violence. The 1970s was a period of widespread concern that *parens patriae* was a failure and that juveniles must also face stiff punishments for their actions. Consequently, it was the start of a more punitive phase in juvenile justice, one that has not abated to the present.

Types of Violence

Gang membership grew tremendously in the 1970s and had become more violent. In Los Angeles and Chicago, the well-known gangs—the Bloods, the Crips, the Surenos (all in Los Angeles), the Latin Kings and the Gangster Disciples (Chicago)—had formed and were becoming organized. Many of these gangs spread through the prison system.

While not unheard of, violence in schools generally took a form different than the sensationalized images of school shooters many have today. Reports of assaults, robberies, and vandalism at schools were on the rise in the late 1960s and early 1970s, but seemed to level off by 1975. Recent research has demonstrated that schools today are no more violent than they were in the 1970s, but suspension and expulsion are far more common today.

Contrary to popular opinion, drug use was a far greater problem in the 1970s than in the 1960s and 1980s. Several new nationwide surveys began in the 1970s and still play an important role in measuring drug use among juveniles and adults. The Monitoring the Future study was established in 1975 by a team of researchers at the Institute for Social Research. When it began it only measured drug use among high school seniors, but later college students and eighth and tenth grade students were added. Its primary benefit is the huge sample used—between 15,000 and 20,000 young people—and the high response rate. **The National Household Survey on Drug Abuse** was started in 1971. Sponsored by the federal government, this survey involves interviews with randomly selected people over the age of twelve.

Drug use rose sharply in the early 1970s, reached a peak in the late 1970s and early 1980s, and declined again in the 1980s. For instance, 31 percent of respondents to the Monitoring the Future survey in 1975 had used one or more illegal drugs in 1975. By 1979, 39 percent had done so. Adolescent attitudes about drugs have changed as well. The proportion of young people who thought marijuana use was harmful and disapproved of its use was quite low in the 1970s. This proportion rose until the early 1990s, when it declined again. There is little evidence, however, that the drug use of the 1970s was associated with an increase in juvenile violence.

As the feminist movement gained speed in the 1970s, both female and male scholars expressed concern that prior theories and research did not adequately address violence by and to females. Scholars like Freda Adler proposed that, as females gained more freedom and had greater access to work, education, and other social institutions, they would commit more crime. Known as the **liberation hypothesis**, this notion was widely accepted but has not seemed to bear out in research. The 1970s was also a critical time period in the recognition of violence against females, in particular, various forms of sexual and domestic violence.

Changes in Juvenile Justice

Several critical court decisions came out of the decade as well. While many provided greater protections for juveniles, some contributed to the trend of making juvenile justice more like criminal justice for adults. In the late 1960s, the *Gault* case established that juveniles, too, must be provided due process throughout the court process. In 1970, *in re Winship* established that a juvenile's guilt must be established beyond a reasonable doubt, as in the adult courts, if the juvenile faces detention. Juvenile courts were still allowed to use the lower standard, a preponderance of evidence, with status offenders. In 1971, in *McKeiver v. Pennsylvania*, the high court ruled that juveniles have no right to a jury by their peers. In 1974, Congress passed the **Juvenile Justice and Delinquency Prevention (JJDP) Act**. JJDP provided for federal grants to states and cities wishing to improve the way they handled juvenile offenders. To accept federal monies, states had to agree to house juveniles in facilities separate from adults and to deinstitutionalize status offenders.

Research Studies and Methods

In 1972, Marvin Wolfgang, Robert Figlio, and Thorsten Sellin published their seminal study, *Delinquency in a Birth Cohort*. They had followed a cohort of almost 10,000 boys born in Philadelphia from their birth until age eighteen. Their most significant discovery was that of the chronic offender, known today as the chronic 6 percent. William Chambliss published his famous "Saints and Roughnecks" work in the early 1970s as well. Based on **labeling theory**, Chambliss's work addressed how societal reaction impacts juvenile delinquency.

In 1972, the Bureau of Justice initiated the **National Crime Victimization Survey (NCVS)**. Intended to account for weaknesses in the **Uniform Crime Reports (UCR)**, the NCVS surveys households about victimization, rather than asking police to report arrest rates. It is less useful in measuring juvenile victimization, however, as it only addresses those over twelve. Use of self-reports became a popular means to study violence and delinquency. The National Youth Survey, initially surveying 1,725 adolescents about their delinquency, debuted in 1977.

Theories about Crime and Violence

The perceived failure of the War on Poverty and other social programs rooted in **strain theories** prompted many to challenge some of the sociological theories forwarded in the 1960s. **Control theories** were popular, in particular Hirschi's social bond theory. This theory posits that we all have the potential for crime, so we need to study why people do *not* offend, rather than why they do. Hirschi further posited that there are four critical social bonds that constrain people from committing crime and violence: attachment, commitment, involvement, and belief. Labeling theories were also popular. These theories suggest that how a society reacts to an offense is important in shaping future delinquency; thus, the label "delinquent" may become a self-fulfilling prophecy. Learning theories, such as Bandura's social learning theory, were also widely accepted.

As noted above, feminists began to establish theories and conduct research that included women. In another trend, **conflict-based theorists** were further articulating their beliefs that the economic structure of the United States contributed to crime, delinquency, and violence.

FURTHER READING

Goode, E. (2003). Drug use in America: An overview. In T. Calhoun & C. Chappel (Eds.), *Readings in Juvenile Delinquency and Juvenile Justice* (pp. 238–246). Upper Saddle River, NJ: Prentice Hall.

Savelli, L. (2000). Introduction to east coast gangs. *National Alliance of Gang Investigators Associations*. Available from: www.nagia.org/east_coast?gangs.htm.

Siegel, L., Welsh, B., & Senna, J. (2003). *Juvenile delinquency: Theory, practice, and law*, 8th ed. Belmont, CA: Wadsworth.

Laura L. Finley

JUVENILE VIOLENCE, 1980–1989

Historical Introduction

The 1980s was a turning point for the juvenile justice system and the evolution of juvenile violence. Although delinquency and violence were reoccurring problems throughout the twentieth century, the 1980s experienced a sharp increase in violent crimes among juveniles. Juvenile justice advocates argued that comprehensive prevention programs could be used to curb youth violence. Others, however, believed zero-tolerance policies and incarceration could remedy juvenile violence.

Incidence and Types of Juvenile Violence

There were some noticeable trends about juvenile violence in the 1980s that caught the attention of juvenile justice advocates and lawmakers. First, girls "began" to perpetuate some of the same types of violent behavior as boys. In fact, there is some evidence that violent crimes among girls were beginning to increase at a faster rate than boys. Second, because of continued patterns of racial segregation, much of the serious violent offenses were intra-racial—that is, the perpetrators and victims tended to be of the same race. Third, **suicide** rates or self-inflicted violence also increased in the 1980s. Fourth, the hysteria over juvenile violence led to new methods of policing schools, such as heavy police presences on school campuses and the use of metal detectors in public schools. Fifth, rural communities also experienced a sharp increase in juvenile violence.

Interestingly, the most serious offense among juveniles—homicide victimization—peaked in the first two years of the decade, stabilized shortly afterwards, and dramatically increased in the late 1980s. It is difficult to explain why this occurred. One plausible explanation is that, throughout the 1970s and early 1980s, gangs institutionalized their influence in central cities. This may have laid the groundwork for the spike in juvenile violence in the latter part of the decade.

The illegal drug trade—more specifically, the explosion of **crack cocaine**—also contributed to the sharp increase in juvenile violence. This sparked violent competition between rival gangs over the control and distribution of the drug trade. Invariably, those young people who were among the most isolated and alienated in these communities were also the most likely to fall prey to the drug culture, gun violence, and other types of juvenile violence.

Juvenile Violence and Guns

The proliferation of guns in vulnerable communities, especially high-powered assault weapons and poor gun control policy, were also viewed as major reasons why there was an increase in juvenile violence. Groups such as the Children's Defense Fund and the Violence Policy Center believed poor communities were disproportionately targeted by gun manufacturing industries, which increased their production in the 1980s in order to boost slumping gun sales.

Whether gun manufacturing industries intentionally targeted poor youth is debatable and perhaps will never be fully verified. Nonetheless, the point remains that the rise in gun production significantly contributed to the rise of illegal gun re-sales on the street. In fact, the increase in gun production, along with juvenile gun violence, crack cocaine proliferation, and poverty, and their collective impact upon primarily poor African-American and Latino youth, was unprecedented in the twentieth century. Moreover, it led to record increases of drug-related arrests among poor youth and the increase in the overrepresentation of African-American youth in the juvenile justice system.

Responses to Juvenile Violence

The rise of juvenile violence also caught the attention of Congress. Beginning in the early 1980s, congressional representatives from the Judiciary Committee's Subcommittee on Juvenile Justice and the Subcommittee on Criminal Justice held a series of hearings investigating juvenile delinquency and violence in urban jurisdictions throughout the country. These hearings drew upon the testimony of local law enforcement officials, district attorneys, ex-gang members, activists, and policymakers.

Although proponents of zero-tolerance began to reassert their influence in the 1980s, Congress passed some important measures, which, if utilized properly and given the appropriate enforcement power, could be used to combat juvenile violence in selected areas. Congress passed the Civil Rights of Institutionalized Persons Act of 1980 (later reauthorized in 1997). This allowed the U.S. Justice Department to investigate abuses in public institutions, including juvenile facilities that can become laboratories of violent activities. In 1980, it reauthorized for the second time the **Juvenile Justice Delinquency Prevention Act** that initially created a unified national program to deal with juvenile delinquency and prevention and created the Office of Juvenile Justice and Delinquency Prevention. The 1980 reauthorization provided for the removal of juveniles from adult jails and lockups after five years from the date of the enactment of the legislation. This was particularly important for juvenile offenders who committed violent crimes, since they were often transferred to adult courts. Congress reauthorized the act in 1988.

See also Gun-Related Violence, Rates of; Gun-Related Violence, Types of; Rural Juvenile Violence; School Police Officers; Suicide; Surveillance in Schools; Urban Juvenile Violence; Zero Tolerance Laws

FURTHER READING

Black Community Crusade for Children. (1994). Saving our children from the violence: The ounce of prevention. *Necessary: News of the Black Community Crusade for Children, 2*(3), 6.

Canada, G. (1995). *Fist, stick, knife, gun: A personal history of violence in America.* Boston, MA: Beacon Press.

Howell, J. (1995). *Guide for implementing the comprehensive strategy for serious, violent, and chronic juvenile offenders.* Washington, DC: Office of Juvenile Justice and Delinquency Prevention.

Miller, W. (2001). *The growth of youth gang problems in the United States: 1970–1998.* Washington, DC: Office of Juvenile Justice and Delinquency Prevention.

Snyder, H., & Sickmund, M. (1999). *Juvenile offenders and victims: 1996 national report.* Washington, DC: National Center for Juvenile Justice.

Snyder, H., & Sickmund, M. (2006). *Juvenile offenders and victims: 2006 national report.* Washington, DC: National Center for Juvenile Justice.

Surgarmann, J., & Rand, K. (1994). *Ceasefire: A comprehensive strategy to reduce firearms violence.* Washington, DC: Violence Policy Center.

Sekou Franklin

JUVENILE VIOLENCE, 1990–1999

Incidence and Types of Juvenile Violence

Juvenile violence followed two divergent patterns in the 1990s. The period of 1990–1993 was the nadir for juvenile justice advocates, because youth violence, firearm deaths, and homicide victimization rates reached an all-time high. Yet, by the end of the decade, juvenile violence experienced a sharp decline. In 1993, over 4,300 youth under eighteen years of age were arrested for homicide, but by 1999, this number declined to about 1,800. In addition, juvenile arrests for violent crimes, such as firearm use, **rape/sexual assault**, and burglary, decreased by over 35 percent in the same time period.

Explanations for Juvenile Violence

There was no universally shared viewpoint among criminologists and advocates that explained the decline of juvenile violence in the late 1990s. Some attributed this phenomenon to the entrenchment of **zero-tolerance** policies and longer periods of confinement for chronic offenders (those arrested multiple times). Others believed the economic growth during Bill Clinton's presidency gave at-risk youth better access to jobs. Still another argument contends that central cities, with the highest crime rates in the 1980s and early 1990s, underwent a phase of depopulation, due to rising housing prices and the demolition of public housing. This may have forced poor youth to relocate to communities that lacked the high-density poverty clusters of their original neighborhoods.

Notwithstanding the reduction of juvenile violence, it remains a major problem for juvenile justice advocates and the poor communities that produce at-risk youth and juvenile offenders. During the 1990s, youth in their mid-teenage years were more likely to be victimized by violence than adults in their late twenties and early thirties. These youth were more likely to commit crime and violent acts between 3:00 and 5:00 p.m. during the school year and 11:00 p.m. during the summer months.

Research on juvenile violence further revealed that most youth—over half in some studies—have been involved in violent activities of some type, such as school yard or neighborhood fistfights. Yet there was a distinction between these minor acts of violence and serious violent offenses. Serious violent offenses, such as the use of firearms, were primarily carried out by chronic offenders. Estimates suggest that 5 to 15 percent of the youth in impoverished neighborhoods fall within this category or will be involved in serious violent offenses.

Furthermore, because of continued patterns of racial segregation, peer-to-peer violence in the 1990s was mostly intra-racial. Black, Latino, and white youth were more likely to harm other youth in their respective racial/ethnic groups. However, it was not uncommon for violent offenses to occur between racial/ethnic groups who live in close proximity to each other.

Moreover, juvenile violence was a principal concern among youth during the decade. A 1994 nationwide survey of 421 youths (ages eleven to seventeen), conducted by the Children's Defense Fund's Black Community Crusade for Children and the Peter G. Hart Research Associates, Inc., found that among youth surveyed for the poll, 70 percent indicated that gun distribution was among their greatest concerns. Another 64 percent indicated a deep concern about gun violence in their schools.

Responses to Juvenile Violence

Throughout the 1990s, lawmakers, activists, and intellectuals debated juvenile violence and remedies to this phenomenon. They also investigated the relevance of the juvenile justice system and its ability to combat juvenile delinquency and violence. Not surprisingly, there was a concerted effort by lawmakers to implement "get-tough" measures as correctives to violent (and nonviolent) juvenile offenders. Some states enacted "blended sentencing" policies that combined juvenile and adult sentences. Congress further considered legislation such as the Violent Crime Control and Law Enforcement Act of 1994, the Violent Youth Predator Act of 1996, and the Consequences for Juvenile Offenders Act of 1999.

In the mid-to-late 1990s, lawmakers were heavily influenced by the research of political scientist and criminologist John Dilulio, who popularized the term "super-predators" to describe violent youth. "Super-predators" depicted chronic juvenile offenders as menacing preys who were uncontrollable and committed to a life of violence—similar to the monster creature in Arnold Schwarzenegger's 1987 film, *The Predator*. The assumption was that these super-predators could be tamed only by harsh, zero-tolerance policies.

Dilulio's commentary angered many civil rights groups and African-American activists, despite the fact that **African-American youth** were not specifically identified as the super-predators. Civil rights groups believed the concept was racially coded or implicitly linked to Africa-American youth and feared it might be used to justify harsh policies that had a disparate impact on poor African Americans. Although Dilulio later apologized for popularizing this concept, its underlying rationale was used to promote a series of zero-tolerance policies at the national and state levels.

During the late 1990s, a new cadre of activists, youth organizers, and legal advocates attempted to mobilize their communities against what they perceived as the unequal treatment of youth by the juvenile justice system. This included groups such as the Maryland Juvenile Justice Coalition, the Juvenile Justice Project of Louisiana, the Prison Moratorium Project, and the Justice 4 Youth Coalition in New York and California's Books Not Bars, all of whom reflected a renewed interest in juvenile justice policies among grassroots activists.

These activists brought attention to the epidemic of violence in America's youth detention centers, such as the Tallulah correctional facility in Louisiana, the Cheltenham and Hickey facilities in Maryland, New York City's Spofford detention center, and in the California Youth Authority. All of these institutions were known for their high incidences of violence. In fact Human Rights Watch, an international human rights organization, investigated the harsh conditions and violence in Tallulah. The U.S. Justice Department also opened up investigations of Tallulah and both of the Maryland facilities, and investigated physical, mental, and sexual abuses in over eighty-five other juvenile detention centers.

See also Gun-Related Violence, Rates of; Gun-Related Violence, Types of; Hispanics and Juvenile Violence

FURTHER READING

Casamento Musser, D. (2001). Public access to juvenile records in Kansas. *Corrections Today, 63*(3), 112–113.

Cavanaugh, S., & Teasley, D. (1998, February 5). *Juvenile justice act reauthorization: The current debate.* CRS Report for Congress.

Howell, J. (1995). *Guide for implementing the comprehensive strategy for serious, violent, and chronic juvenile offenders.* Washington, DC: Office of Juvenile Justice and Delinquency Prevention.

Mills, K. (1994, May 27). Black adults found to be pessimistic on children's futures. *Philadelphia Inquirer*, A03.

Snyder, H. (1998). Juvenile arrests 1997. *Juvenile Justice Bulletin*. Washington, DC: Office of Juvenile Justice and Delinquency Prevention, 1–12.

Snyder, H., & Sickmund, M. (1999). *Juvenile offenders and victims: 1996 national report*. Washington, DC: National Center for Juvenile Justice.

Snyder, H., & Sickmund, M. (2006). *Juvenile offenders and victims: 2006 national report*. Washington, DC: National Center for Juvenile Justice.

Youth Violence Statistics. (n.d.). Rockville, MD: National Youth Violence Prevention Resource Center. Available at: http://www.safeyouth.org/scripts/facts/docs/statistics.pdf.

Sekou Franklin

JUVENILE VIOLENCE, 2000 TO DATE

Incidence and Types of Juvenile Violence

Juvenile violence has declined significantly across the United States since 1993, as evidenced by downward trends in arrest rates, victimization data, and hospital emergency room records. In 2003, the last year for which complete data is available, the Juvenile Violent Crime Index arrest rate was at its lowest since 1980 and was 48 percent below the peak year of 1994. 2003 represented the ninth consecutive year that the juvenile arrest rate for violent crimes declined. However, 2003 data shows that juveniles are both more likely to commit crimes in groups and more likely to be arrested than adults.

In 2003, U.S. law enforcement agencies made approximately 2.2 million arrests of persons under the age of eighteen. According to the Federal Bureau of Investigation (FBI), juveniles accounted for 16 percent of all arrests and 15 percent of violent crime arrests that year. The juvenile arrest rate for each of the following has declined steadily since the mid-1990s: murder, forcible rape, robbery, and aggravated assault. The juvenile arrest rate for murder, specifically, fell 77 percent from its peak in 1993. Of all violent crimes cleared by arrest in 2003, juvenile offenses accounted for 5 percent of murders, 12 percent of forcible rapes, 14 percent of robberies, and 12 percent of aggravated assaults. In 2003, 20 percent of juvenile arrests involving youth eligible for processing in their states' juvenile justice systems were handled within law enforcement agencies, while 71 percent were referred to juvenile court and 7 percent were referred directly to criminal court. In general, the proportion of youth sent to juvenile court increased from 58 percent in 1980 to 7 percent in 2003.

Between 1980 and 2003, juvenile arrest rates for simple assault increased 269 percent for females and 102 percent for males. Arrest rates for aggravated assault indicate a similar inconsistency: female rates increased 96 percent while male rates increased 13 percent. Although male juvenile arrests for assault fell from the mid-1990s through 2003, female juvenile arrests for assault remained at their highest levels. Females accounted for 24 percent of all juvenile arrests for aggravated assault and 32 percent for other assaults in 2003. This may not, however, represent an increase in female offending as much as it might represent a change in police arrest policies.

Twenty-nine percent of 2003 juvenile arrests involved females, and arrest trends show females account for an increasing proportion of the juvenile justice population. A disproportionate involvement of minorities in juvenile arrests persists, although the black-to-white disparity in violent crime arrest rates declined substantially between 1980 and 2003 (from 6-to-1 in 1980 to 4-to-1 in 2003). Juvenile arrests in 2003 accounted for 11 percent fewer than the number of arrests in 1999.

School Violence

School violence has consistently increased in frequency since the 1990s, with **bullying** being one of the main indicators of such violence. In 2003, 7 percent of students ages twelve to eighteen reported they had been bullied in the last six months, up from 5 percent in 1999; 9 percent of students in grades 9 through 12 reported being threatened or injured with a weapon on school property. One-third of high school students reported having been in a physical fight that year, and 13 percent reported having been in a fight on school property. Students aged twelve to eighteen were victims of approximately 684,000 nonfatal violent crimes in 2002. While exact statistics on the number of school shootings since 2000 are unavailable, **gun-related violence** continues to occur in schools across America.

According to the 2003 Criminal Victimization Survey, youth are one of three groups historically most vulnerable to violent crime and continue to be victimized at higher rates than other groups of people. Although violent crime fell significantly (16.6 percent) from 2000–2001 to 2002–2003 for persons aged twelve to fifteen and fell 7.4 percent for persons aged sixteen to nineteen, persons aged twelve to nineteen as a whole experienced violence at higher rates than those aged twenty-five and above. An estimated 1,550 juveniles were murdered in 2003, the lowest since 1984. Of those murdered, 40 percent were under the age of five, 68 percent were male, 50 percent were white, and 45 percent were killed with a firearm. **Suicide** was the third leading cause of death for youth ages ten to twenty-four in 2004, accounting for approximately 12 percent of all deaths in that age group. The suicide rate has increased slightly in recent years, following six consecutive years of decline in the 1990s and a steady rate in 2000. Juvenile suicide rates have tripled since 1970, and suicide continues to be a significant factor in juvenile mortality rates.

FURTHER READING

Catalano, S. (2004, September). Criminal victimization, 2003. *Bureau of Justice Statistics National Crime Victimization Survey*. Available from: http://www.usdoj.gov.

Crews, G., & Montgomery, R. (2001). *Chasing shadows: Confronting juvenile violence in America*. Upper Saddle River, NJ: Prentice Hall.

DeVoe, J., et al. (2004). Indicators of school crime and safety: 2004. *U.S. Departments of Education and Justice*. Washington, DC: U.S. Government Printing Office.

Snyder, H. (2005, August). Juvenile arrests 2003. *Juvenile Justice Bulletin*. Office of Juvenile Justice and Delinquency Prevention. Available from: http://www.ojjdp.gov.

Allison Wright Munro

JUVENILES IN ADULT PRISONS. Since 1985, there has been a proliferation of juveniles (i.e., anyone under the age of eighteen) being committed to adult corrections (e.g., jails and prisons) as a result of increased juvenile participation in violent and serious crimes and policy changes. In 1985, there were 3,400 juveniles admitted to state prisons and 1,629 admitted to adult jails. By 1997, the admittance rate had more than doubled to 7,400 juveniles in state prisons and 9,105 in local jails, representing a yearly 2 percent increase in admittance rate. Overall, at year-end 1997, there were 14,500 juveniles incarcerated in adult facilities, including local jails (9,100) and adult prisons (5,400) nationwide. The demographic profile of these juveniles indicated that most are male (92 percent), black or Hispanic (73 percent), and seventeen years old (79 percent). The majority (61 percent) was convicted of violent offenses, which represents a 52 percent increase since 1985.

Public perception has also played a role in the increased incarceration rate of juveniles in adult corrections. As a result of the steady rise in crime in the 1970s, there was a public outcry for stricter punitive sanctions for violent juvenile offenders that resulted in the **Juvenile Justice and Delinquency Prevention (JJDP) Act of 1974**. The Act governed the placement of juveniles in adult correctional facilities and required that certain conditions be met before juveniles can be incarcerated in adult institutions. The original mandates of the JJDP Act of 1974 were reaffirmed with the JJDP Act of 2002 reauthorizations. Initially, the goals of the Act provided assistance to states and local governments in the prevention and control of juvenile delinquency, provided protection for youth placed in adult facilities, and assisted in the facilitation of community-based treatment for offenders. With the reauthorization in 2002, status offenders were deinstitutionalized (DSO) (e.g., children who commit an offense that would not be criminal if committed by an adult, such as truancy or running away), ensuring that they will not be placed in secure detention or correctional facilities. Further, the reauthorization required separation from adults by sight and sound, and removal of delinquents from adult jails and lockups. The jail removal provision allowed for detention or confinement in adult jails and lockups for up to six hours (the "rural exception" allows for up to 48 hours confinement in rural localities) for processing, identification, interrogation, appearance in court, release to parental custody, and transfer to a juvenile facility. Reaffirmation of the JJDP Act also addressed disproportionate minority contact in the juvenile justice system with the goal of reducing disparity by requiring states to develop and implement strategies for delinquency prevention and system improvement initiatives for compliance. Eligibility for grant funding for states is based on compliance with these core requirements.

Juveniles are at risk of victimization when placed in adult correctional facilities. In an effort to comply with the sight and sound mandate of the JJDP Act, juveniles are placed in solitary confinement when housed with adults, which can have a psychological impact that may lead to the increased potential for suicide. Research indicates that juveniles confined in adult jail facilities are five times more likely to commit **suicide** than other offenders. Additionally, these juveniles are eight times more likely to commit suicide than their counterparts housed in traditional juvenile facilities. Juveniles in adult correctional facilities are also more likely to be victims of rape and sexual assault. Research indicates that sexual assault is five times more likely to occur in prison than in traditional juvenile facilities. Additionally, 47 percent of juveniles in adult prisons suffer violent victimizations as compared to 37 percent of those in juvenile facilities.

Traditionally, juveniles who commit crimes are generally processed in the **juvenile justice system** and placed in juvenile facilities that are more conducive to providing resources for mental, physical, psychological, and educational rehabilitation. In 1997, however, all states allowed provisions mandated by state legislation for juveniles under certain circumstances to be **waived (transferred) to adult court** for adjudication (trial and sentencing) where they are subject to punishment in adult correctional institutions. Based on these provisions, most states allow certain categories of offenders under eighteen to be incarcerated in adult prisons and housed with older offenders. Furthermore, since 1992, forty-nine states have enacted or amended legislation that is more expedient for prosecuting juveniles as adults and thereby sentencing them to confinement in adult correctional institutions.

FURTHER READING

Austin, J., Johnson, K., & Gregoriou, M. (2000). *Juveniles in adult prisons and jails: A national assessment*. Washington, DC: Bureau of Justice Assistance.

McShane, M., & Williams, F. (2003). *Encyclopedia of juvenile justice*. Thousand Oaks, CA: Sage Publications.

Office of Juvenile Justice and Delinquency Prevention. (2003). *Guidance manual for monitoring facilities under the JJDP Act*. Washington, DC: United States Department of Justice.

Sickmund, M. (2003). Juveniles in court. *Juvenile Offenders and Victims: National Report Series Bulletin*. Office of Juvenile Justice and Delinquency Prevention. Washington, DC: United States Department of Justice.

Sickmund, M. (2004). Juveniles in corrections. *Juvenile Offenders and Victims: National Report Series Bulletin*. Office of Juvenile Justice and Delinquency Prevention. Washington, DC: United States Department of Justice.

Strom, K. (2000). Profile of state prisoners under age *19*, 1985–97. *Bureau of Justice Statistics*. Washington, DC: United States Department of Justice.

Urban, L., St. Cyr, J., & Decker, S. (2003, November). Goal conflict in the juvenile court: The evolution of sentencing practices in the United States. *Journal of Contemporary Criminal Justice*, *19*(4). Available from: http://ccj.sagepub.com.proxy.library.vcu.edu/cgi/reprint/19/4/454.pdf.

Patricia Hylton Grant

K

KINKEL, KIP. Kip Kinkel is the infamous fifteen-year-old school shooter who, after murdering his parents, killed two students and wounded twenty-five others at Thurston High School in Springfield, Oregon on May 21, 1998. Kinkel's spree was the last student-conceived rampage in a school year marred by high-profile shootings in Pearl, Mississippi (October 1, 1997), West Paducah, Kentucky (December 1, 1997), and Jonesboro, Arkansas (March 24, 1998).

By all accounts, Kinkel was a mildly problematic child in an otherwise stable middle-class family. Kinkel was born August 30, 1982, the second child of Bill and Faith Kinkel, two well-respected high school Spanish teachers. As a young child, Kinkel struggled with verbal tasks in school and was diagnosed with a learning disability in the fourth grade. Kinkel's junior high school years were marked by several delinquent episodes, including using the Internet at school to order books on how to build bombs (seventh grade), an arrest for shoplifting (eighth grade), and throwing rocks at cars from a highway overpass (eighth grade). The rock-throwing incident inspired Kinkel's parents to send him to counseling where he was treated for depression. Psychological treatment continued for six months but was discontinued in July 1997 when Kinkel was assessed to be significantly improved.

During Kinkel's junior high years, his fascination with guns and bombs also became noticeable. According to Kinkel's older sister Kristen (from a post-rampage interview), Kinkel had expressed high interest in guns and bombs from the time he was a little boy. Kristen notes, "He was not interested in violence. He was interested in guns—how they worked, what made them have the power that they had" (PBS, Frontline Transcript). In a 1997 school assignment, when given the option to make a speech on a topic of his choice, he chose, "How to Make a Bomb." In an attempt to redirect Kinkel's interests into a positive hobby of recreational target shooting, Kinkel's father helped purchase a 9mm Glock and Ruger .22 semiautomatic. These guns were purchased with the understanding that they would only be used with adult supervision and that Kinkel's father would control them until Kinkel turned twenty-one years old. Unbeknownst to his parents, Kinkel also purchased another handgun from a friend during this period.

Most accounts indicate that an arrest and suspension from school were the key precipitating events to the ultimate shootings. On the morning of May 20, 1998, Kinkel was caught at school in possession of a stolen handgun he had recently purchased from another student. Kinkel was arrested, taken to the police station, and charged with both possession of a firearm in a public building and receiving a stolen weapon. He was released to the custody of his father, who took him home. According to Kinkel's confession transcript, once they arrived home, Kinkel went upstairs, found and loaded the Ruger semiautomatic, and, without further provocation, sneaked up behind his father and murdered him with a single shot to the back of the head. Approximately three hours later, Kinkel's mom returned home after work. Kinkel met her in the garage and shot her six times.

After spending the night in the house with his parents' corpses, Kinkel put on a trenchcoat, loaded his backpack with ammunition, grabbed three guns, and drove himself to school in his parents' Ford Explorer. At approximately 7:55 a.m., Kinkel entered Thurston High School, walked toward the cafeteria, shot two students along the way, then entered the cafeteria and shot off what remained of the Ruger semiautomatic rifle's 50 round clip. Kinkel was eventually wrestled to the ground by five other students but not until he had killed two and injured twenty-five others.

In September 1999, Kinkel plead guilty to four counts of murder and twenty-six counts of attempted murder. In November 1999, he was sentenced to 111 years in prison without the possibility of parole. By accepting the plea bargain agreement, Kinkel waived his right to the insanity defense. However, during the sentencing phase of Kinkel's trial, substantial evidence was presented by child psychologist Orin Bolstad suggesting that Kinkel "suffered from a psychotic disorder with major paranoid symptoms, potentially some form of early onset schizophrenia" (PBS, Frontline Transcript).

FURTHER READING

Dwyer, K., Osher, D., & Warger, C. (1998). *Early warning, timely response: A guide to safe schools.* Washington, DC: U.S. Department of Education. Available at: http://cecp.air.org/school_violence.asp.

Oregon Supreme Court, 2003, ruling on Kinkel's appeal. Available at: http://www.publications.ojd.state.or.us/A108593.htm.

PBS, Frontline documentary. (2000). *The killer at Thurston High.* Associated resources including transcripts available at: http://www.pbs.org/wgbh/pages/frontline/shows/kinkel/.

Edward L. Powers

LABELING THEORY. Labeling theory is an approach to the study of criminology and deviance that focuses on the social construction of deviance and the effects of negative labeling and stigmatization. Alternatively called social reaction theory, labeling theory argues that individuals acquire certain labels or stigmas through social interaction and that negative labels in turn often lead to deviance and crime.

Within criminology and studies of deviance, labeling theory emerged in the 1950s and 1960s, partially as a critical response to structural-functional analyses of crime and deviance and, later, in relation to the radical social changes of the late 1960s. Whereas the structural-functional approach emphasized various functions of crime and deviance, labeling theory represented a shift toward the study of the effects of negative labels such as "troublemaker," "delinquent," "drug user," "criminal," and so forth. Drawing from the symbolic-interactionist theories of American sociologists Charles Horton Cooley and George Herbert Mead, early proponents of labeling theory argued that crime and deviance are not fixed within any given social order, but are rather conferred through social interactions. Labeling theory may then be considered a "micro-theoretical" approach, as it is concerned primarily with the effects and consequences of social interactions, the use of social control in daily life, and the manner by which people acquire and adopt negative labels.

For labeling theorists, no act is inherently deviant or criminal, but rather becomes so through interaction with others who are in a position to apply labels, for example, teachers, police officers, psychologists, and social workers. Howard Becker has referred to people who are in such a position as "moral entrepreneurs." One strength of labeling theory is that, as a micro-theoretical approach, it nevertheless recognizes larger social structures that enable differential relationships of power and social control. Its primary focus, however, remains rooted in the understanding of how individuals make sense and meaning out of these structures in their daily lives.

While labeling, both positive and negative, occurs frequently within social interactions, labeling theorists are more concerned with labels that have the power to cause negative long-term or permanent effects for the individual who is labeled. One crucial element is the relationship between those being labeled and those doing the labeling. Negative labels from those with whom the individual has a close relationship (for example, parents) may be far worse than labels from peers. Likewise, negative labels from those able to make substantial decisions about one's future or direction (for example, teachers) are also crucial. Moreover, labeling theorists argue that negative labels often emerge not only from deliberate acts on the part of the individual, but often from conditions outside of the person's control: rumors or suspicions, associations, or medical conditions (including mental illness).

Labeling theorists, however, do not see the attachment of labels as occurring haphazardly. Rather, labeling mirrors larger inequalities of social relations. Those with less personal power are more likely to be negatively labeled through processes of "differential enforcement." For example, poorer children are often at greater risk than middle- or upper-class children for being arrested in relation to criminal and status offenses. The official label of criminal or deviant, argue proponents of this theory, often begets further labeling, as well as internalizing of the label on the part of the individual. Edwin Lemert has called this process "secondary deviance." While most individuals engage from time to time in "primary deviance," or minor deviant acts, secondary deviance occurs when others around an individual begin to apply a particular negative label (i.e., thief, drug user, cheater) that eventually serves as a type of stigma. The movement from primary deviance to secondary deviance and stigma is often achieved through "degradation ceremonies," such as a court trial, expulsion or incarceration where public shame is evident, and a high level of permanence is attached to the label. At this point, stigmatized individuals find their legitimate opportunities limited and, having internalized the label to a lesser or greater extent, often join with others sharing similar stigmas.

One consequence of the work of labeling theorists is the recognition that deviants and criminals may be, at least in part, created by the very social agencies designed to prevent or dissuade such behaviors. Primary education, for example, includes not only formal education that leads to greater opportunities, but also processes of negative labeling from teachers and peers. Policing agencies and the juvenile justice system, which function in part to rehabilitate or correct deviant juvenile behavior, may in fact create "delinquents" through the attachment of secondary labels.

Labeling theory provides important insights into how people may become identified as deviants or criminals, but it has also been criticized by sociologists and criminologists for several reasons. Notably, critics of labeling theory argue that this approach fails to take into account well-established relationships between crime and environment. For example, if crime is an outcome of negative labeling, why do particular crimes occur with more frequency in warmer climates or in summer months? Other critics have pointed out that negative labels may have positive effects, for example, in the use of reintegrative shaming, where labeling may be used in conjunction with techniques designed to reintegrate juvenile offenders back into their families and communities. Finally, labeling theory is often criticized for failing to articulate initial conditions of deviant or criminal behavior.

Today, labeling theory is not as commonly used or cited in sociological literature as it once was. However, it remains a useful and necessary theory insofar as criminological literature, particularly studies of juvenile crime, routinely identify the problems associated with labeling and social control agencies, such as schooling, juvenile justice systems, and social welfare programs. Moreover, where labeling theory has been less successful in delineating root causes or conditions of criminal behavior, it has become more useful as a means of understanding how differential enforcement is enacted through social interactions, particularly in the case of the poor and minorities, once they are labeled.

See also Interactionist Theories

FURTHER READING

Becker, H. (1963). *Outsiders: Studies in the sociology of deviance*. New York: Macmillan.

Garfinkle, H. (1956). Conditions of successful degradation ceremonies. *American Journal of Sociology, 61*, 420–424.

Lemert, E. (1951). *Social pathology*. New York: McGraw-Hill.

William R. Wood

LIBERATION HYPOTHESIS. First proposed in 1975, the liberation hypothesis posits that as women become more liberated they will engage in crimes traditionally associated with males. This notion emerged from the women's movement, which grew in popularity and strength across the nation throughout the 1970s. Women's movement reformers advanced new ways of thinking that challenged the androcentrism in the theory and research of prior decades. Specifically, feminists maintained that criminology theretofore had involved male researchers studying male subjects and developing theories to explain male violence and delinquency. Further, the liberation hypothesis is derived from sociological theories of crime and violence popular at the time. If social opportunities were what made males more likely to commit violent offenses, then females should begin to offend in similar ways and at greater rates as social opportunities became available. Like all sociological theories, the liberation hypothesis rejects the notion that males are inherently more violent than females.

Rita Simon was perhaps the first to offer this viewpoint in her 1975 text, *Women and Crime.* Simon felt that women's greater participation in the workplace would lead to greater involvement in white-collar crimes. She did not feel, however, that violent crimes by females would be altered by their increased presence in the workplace. While women may feel violent urges due to their exploitation and subservience in society, their participation in the workplace would offset any inclination to act on those urges.

Freda Adler more clearly articulated the liberation hypothesis in 1975 with the publication of her book, *Sisters in Crime: The Rise of the New Female Criminal.* Adler cited skyrocketing arrest statistics for a number of offenses to argue that women were indeed engaging in more and different types of crime. For instance, between 1960 and 1972, female arrests for burglary went up 168 percent, and for robbery, embezzlement, and larceny, they increased 277 percent, 280 percent, and 300 percent, respectively. In later studies, Adler claimed to have found support for her thesis in England, Canada, Norway, Germany, Japan, India, and Poland. She harshly criticized prior criminological thought, which, when it addressed females at all, tended to presume they were hysterical, biological aberrations. Further, Adler maintained that competition in the workplace required women to take more risks and to be more aggressive. Interestingly, antifeminists promoted the theory to enforce their argument that women should stay in the home.

There are three primary criticisms of the liberation hypothesis. First, many assert that statistics from the era really do not reflect the dramatic change Simon and Adler described. In addition, because arrest rates for females were generally so low, any change might appear significant but is really not. While arrest rates for females did rise in this time period, they rose for males as well. Further, the most dramatic changes were in arrests for nonviolent crimes, those more typically associated with females, which is inconsistent with Adler's claims. Second, the notion that females' participation in the workforce would prompt them to commit more crime seems in contrast to what was and is still known about most female offenders. That is, female offenders are more likely to come from the subgroups least involved in the workplace—the poor and otherwise economically marginalized. Steffensmeir, Steffensmeir, and Rosenthal (1979) maintained that the greatest increases in the time period Adler referenced were for larceny, check forgery, and fraud—all offenses more likely committed by impoverished females. Some have asserted that, rather than increase women's criminal involvement, equality might decrease it. Research has shown that support for feminism did not connect to greater participation in delinquency; in fact, incarcerated females tend to advocate more traditional gender roles. Third, radical feminists criticized Adler, Simon, and others for under-theorizing the role of patriarchy in women's oppression. Liberal feminists like Adler and Simon, these critics contend, were too quick to accept incremental legal change instead of demanding dramatic overhaul of patriarchal institutions. Critics maintain that Adler falsely assumed attitudes about female equality had changed along with legal changes. Regardless of these criticisms, proponents of the liberation hypothesis were instrumental in the effort to develop a criminology that considered females and that denounced earlier pathological explanations.

The 1990s saw a revival of the liberation hypothesis, albeit sometimes titled differently. Again, academics cited statistics showing rapidly growing arrests for females to assert that females were offending like males. Between 1978 and 1988, female arrests for violent crime went up 41.5 percent. Department of Justice statistics showed the violent crime rate for women more than doubled between 1987 and 1994. Arrests for girls for all violent crimes grew 12 percent between 1992 and 2001, with the biggest increase, at 23.5 percent, in arrests for aggravated assault. Juvenile females constituted 16 percent of arrests for violent crime. Deborah Prothrow-Stith, professor of public health at Harvard University, maintained that it was no surprise females were committing more violent crimes in a society that equates violence with power. Prothrow-Stith also pointed to the increasing number of violent females in video games and movies, such as Lara Croft in the video and film *Tomb Raider*. Further, Prothrow-Stith speculated that "we have socialized girls to solve problems like boys" (Beaucar, 2001).

Regardless of whether factual evidence supports it, the liberation hypothesis became one of the media's favorites. Rather than based on academic theories, however, much of the coverage of the supposed female violent crime spike seemed to be based on fear that females were no longer just "sugar and spice and everything nice." In this iteration, the main focus was on females' increased involvement in gangs, stressing not only that girls were joining in record numbers, but that they, like their male counterparts, were hyper-violent. In 1992, CBS aired an episode called "Girls in the Hood" on its program *Street Smarts*. The program began with a voice-over announcing, "Some of the politicians like to call this the Year of the Woman. The women you are about to meet probably aren't what they had in mind. These women are active, they're independent, and they're exercising power in a field dominated by men" (cited in Chesney-Lind & Pasko, 2004, p. 32). In addition, these **female gang members** supposedly joined and committed violence not out of need, but out of desire to own fancy things. As in the 1970s, conservatives pointed the finger at women's liberation.

Once again, critics contend that the issue is far more complex than simply girls going bad. Changes in police practices, for instance, may lead to more arrests but do not necessarily indicate an increase in the incidence of offenses. Further, while it may be true arrests for girls for violent offenses have increased over specific time periods, the fact remains that males still commit the vast majority of violent offenses. Despite decreases, boys were still 89 percent of arrests for murder and nonnegligent manslaughter, 91 percent of robbery arrests, and 76 percent of aggravated assault arrests over the last decade.

See also Assault; Gangs, Female; Gender, Frequency of Perpetrating Violence by; Gender, Frequency of Receiving Violence by; Gender, Types of Juvenile Violence Received by; Gender, Types of Violence Perpetrated by; News, Juvenile Violence and

FURTHER READING

Adler, F. (1975). *Sisters in crime: The rise of the new female criminal.* New York: McGraw-Hill.

Adler, F. (Ed.). (1981). *The incidence of female criminality in the contemporary world.* New York: New York University Press.

Artz, S. (1999). *Sex, power, & the violent school girl.* New York: Teachers College Press.

Beaucar, K. (2001, August 8). Spike in female juvenile violence prompts multitude of explanations. *Fox News*. Retrieved May 1, 2006 from: www.foxnews.com.

Chesney-Lind, M., & Pasko, L. (2004). *The female offender: Girls, women, and crime,* 2nd ed. Thousand Oaks, CA: Sage.

Cullen, F., & Agnew, R. (1999). *Criminological theory: Past to present.* Los Angeles: Roxbury.

Hanna, C. (1999). Ganging up on girls: Young women and their emerging violence. *Arizona Law Review, 41,* 93–141.

Leventhal, G. (1977). Female criminality: Is "women's lib" to blame? *Psychological Reports, 41,* 1179–1182.

Smart, C. (1979). The new female offender: Reality or myth? *British Journal of Criminology, 19*(1), 50–59.

Steffensmeir, D., Steffensmeir, R., & Rosenthal, A. (1979). Trends in female violence. *Sociological Focus, 12*(3), 217–227.

Laura L. Finley

LOUKAITIS, BARRY

Introduction

On February 2, 1996, fourteen-year-old honor student Barry Loukaitis walked into Frontier Junior High School in Moses Lake, Washington, dressed as the man with no name from the film *Fistful of Dollars* and armed with a high-powered hunting rifle and two pistols. He went into his algebra class, took the class hostage, killed two students, Manual Vela, Jr. and Arnie Fritz, and his algebra teacher, Leona Caires, and seriously wounded several other students. He was eventually overpowered by physical education teacher Jon Lane, who managed to talk his way into the classroom. This shooting was the first of a series of multiple victim homicides perpetrated by students on school grounds. Many consider the Frontier Junior High School incident as the one that triggered copycat-type incidents around the country.

Mitigating Factors?

Because Loukaitis was fourteen years old at the time of his offense, a hearing was held in juvenile court to assess in what jurisdiction he should be tried. The juvenile court judge declined jurisdiction over the case because of the severity of the crimes. Loukaitis was **waived** to adult criminal court where he was tried on multiple counts of murder. This case brought up a number of issues for juveniles, such as age, accountability, mental illness, and genetic predispositions toward violence.

As the Loukaitis trial unfolded, so did details of Loukaitis' bizarre family life. Loukaitis' parents were divorced, and his mother told him repeatedly that she was going to take his father and his father's lover hostage, tie them up, and force them to watch her kill herself. She told Loukaitis she was going to do this on Valentine's Day. Loukaitis tried to talk her out of her plan. The court eventually heard that both parents' families had long histories of depression.

Life at school for Loukaitis did not appear to be much better than it was at home. In his trial, a number of his classmates testified that one of Loukaitis' victims, Manual Vela, often taunted Loukaitis at school, calling him a faggot in front of other students. It appears that Vela was the intended target of the attack. Other students also ridiculed Loukaitis, and classmates testified that he was an easy target because of his seriousness, gangly build, and the cowboy outfits that he frequently wore.

This case also reignited speculation and research about copycat media violence. Among Loukaitis' personal effects recovered from his home was a copy of the book *Rage* written by Stephen King. This book was one of Loukaitis' favorites, and its plot has an uncanny resemblance to what happened at Frontier Junior High School. The protagonist in *Rage* is a high school student who is victimized and bullied and eventually goes insane. He goes to school, holds his class hostage, kills his teacher, and takes revenge for prior mistreatment. *Rage* is the only novel that Stephen King has publicly regretted publishing, given its connection to this case and other school shootings.

Loukaitis also seemed to be preoccupied with the film *Natural Born Killers*. Records indicated that he had rented the film numerous times, and classmates said he could quote the film's lines by heart. The third factor discussed at the trial was Loukaitis' obsession with Pearl Jam's song *Jeremy*, which is about a boy who shoots his classmates after repeatedly being taunted by them. This song has also appeared in connection to other school shootings.

Loukaitis entered a plea of not guilty by reason of insanity. Legal experts for the state argued that the precise nature by which Loukaitis planned the attack, down to details of his costume, indicated a rational thinker. Defense experts argued that Loukaitis' planning was part of his psychosis as he was living in a fantasy world. The jury rejected the insanity plea and found Loukaitis guilty of aggravated first-degree murder and a number of other offenses. He was sentenced to life without possibility of parole. In 1999, the Washington State Court of Appeals denied his request for a new trial.

One factor about this case that has been discussed in legal circles was Loukaitis' defense counsel. As many as five contracted defenders were assigned to Loukaitis at some point, but the attorney who defended Loukaitis for most of his trial, including his juvenile court hearing, was Guillermo Romero. A number of agencies are investigating Romero, including the Washington State Bar Association, for providing inadequate legal council following numerous client complaints. Garth Dano sought to defend Loukaitis at public expense after reviewing two hundred of Romero's cases and finding little evidence of any kind of case preparation. Loukaitis expressed little confidence in Romero's ability to defend him, and the social worker, the psychiatrist, and the corrections expert in the Loukaitis case shared his sentiments.

The Effects of the Incident

The Moses Lake community is a small community and relied heavily on community social support as a coping mechanism. Immediately after the shootings, the school closed temporarily, and the area of the school in which the shootings occurred was renovated so students would not be constantly reminded of the incident. The families of some of Loukaitis' victims filed wrongful death suits against the school district, citing poor school security, and failure to monitor Loukaitis' strange behavior. With the latter, they argue that Loukaitis displayed warning signs of possible criminal behavior in his poems that detailed his enjoyment of killing classmates.

The school district has since implemented a strict dress code, has increased security, and has guards at some schools. They have also added money for recreational and after-school programs to keep students occupied.

One positive outcome of this incident was a renewed interest in school bullying prevention programs and a reexamination of how school administrators deal with threatening behavior, including written threats.

See also Biosocial Theories; Bullying; Center for the Prevention of School Violence (CPSV); Conflict Resolution; Gun-Related Violence, Rates of; Gun-Related Violence, Types of; National School Safety Center (NSSC); News, Juvenile Violence and; Peaceable Schools; Surveillance in Schools; Television, Juvenile Violence and; Waivers to Adult Court

FURTHER READING

Center for the Prevention of School Violence. Available at: http://www.juvjus.state.nc.us/cpsv/cpsvrroom.htm.

DeVoe, J., Ruddy, S., Miller, A., Planty, M., Peter, K., Synder, T., et al. (2002). *Indicators of school crime and safety, 2002*. Washington, DC: Department of Education and Department of Justice. NCJ 196753.

Ericson, N. (2001). Addressing the problem of juvenile bullying. *Office of Juvenile Justice and Delinquency Prevention (OJJDP) FactSheet, 27*.

Fox, J., Elliot, D., Kerlikowske, R., Newman, S., & Christenson, W. (2003). Bullying prevention is crime prevention. Washington, DC: Fight Crime: Invest in Kids. http://www.fightcrime.org/reports/BullyingReport.pdf 2003.

Monica L. P. Robbers

MARIJUANA. Marijuana is produced in all fifty states and is the most commonly used illegal drug in the United States. Roughly 60 percent of juveniles who use drugs use marijuana exclusively. Marijuana use among juveniles dropped 11 percent from 2001 to 2003, the largest decline in juvenile drug use in more than ten years. While recent studies indicate decreasing trends in use among juveniles, more than half of teenagers say they could obtain marijuana easily if they wanted to. First-time users of marijuana are predominantly under eighteen years of age. During the late 1960s, less than 50 percent of those using marijuana for the first time were juveniles. Now, that figure has increased to more than 65 percent. More than half of juveniles who use marijuana get it for free or share it with someone else. The vast majority obtain the drug from a friend.

A product of the hemp plant, cannabis sativa, marijuana is green to greenish-gray in color and is composed of shredded leaves, stems, seeds, and flowers that have been dried. It is usually smoked in the form of hand-rolled cigarettes called "joints" and cigars called "blunts" or by using glass pipes. Marijuana is also smoked in larger quantities by groups using water pipes or large glass containers called "bongs." The active ingredient that gives marijuana its intoxicating characteristics is delta-9-tetrahydrocannabinol (THC). THC causes marijuana to act as a depressant in the user's system, similar to alcohol. The levels of THC in marijuana manufactured in the United States have continued to increase over the past twenty years, making it more potent.

Research shows an association between marijuana use and violence among juveniles. Data obtained by the National Household Survey (U.S. Department of Health and Human Services) in 1994–1996 indicated juveniles with a higher frequency of marijuana use were more likely to attack others or destroy property. A report by the U.S. Substance Abuse and Mental Health Services Administration revealed that juvenile marijuana users themselves said they were more likely than nonusers to attack other teens or destroy property. The same report indicated juvenile marijuana users were four times more likely than nonusers to engage in violence. The majority of youths who engage in violence also report using marijuana. However, violence and aggression usually precede the use of drugs as part of a dangerous lifestyle developed over time.

FURTHER READING

Marijuana and teens: Fact sheet. (2004, August 24). Office of National Drug Control Policy National Youth Anti-Drug Media Campaign. Retrieved May 9, 2005, from: http://www.mediacampaign.org/marijuana/kids_and_marijuana.html.

Marijuana and youth violence. (2003). Alcohol and Drug Information Clearinghouse. Nebraska Department of Health and Human Services, Office of Mental Health, Substance Abuse and Addiction Services Website. Retrieved August 14, 2005, from: http://www.prevlink.org/getthefacts/facts/marijuanaviolence.html.

NIDA InfoFacts: High school and youth trends. (2004, December). *National Institute on Drug Abuse.* Retrieved May 9, 2005, from: http://www.nida.nih.gov/infofacts/HSYouthtrends.html.

ONDCP drug policy information clearinghouse fact sheet. (2004, February). Office of National Drug Control Policy. Retrieved May 9, 2005, from: http://www.whitehousedrugpolicy.gov/publications/factsht/marijuana.

Teen drug use and violence. (n.d.). *National Youth Violence Prevention Resource Center.* Retrieved May 15, 2005, from: http://www.safeyouth.org/scripts/teens/drugs.asp.

Adam Doran

MENTORING. Activists, juvenile justice advocates, and policymakers have created a host of mentoring programs for at-risk youth in almost every city and county that experienced juvenile violence since the 1980s. These mentoring programs typically fell under seven categories: initiatives sponsored by intergenerational and youth-based organizations, identity-based programs that appeal to youth based on their specific identities or unique experiences (i.e., gender, race/ethnicity, immigrant status), large-scale community organizing campaigns, diversionary and aftercare programs, public-private partnerships involving government agencies and community activists, mentoring projects inside of juvenile detention centers, and cultural initiatives.

Intergenerational and youth-based programs are the most widely used mentoring initiatives. These programs offer leadership development seminars and rites of passage programs, and many groups develop anticrime or deterrence projects for at-risk youth. These programs usually target the most marginalized youth, including ex-offenders and gang members, some of whom have previously committed violent offenses. Some examples of these programs are the San Francisco Bay Area's Omega Boys Club, founded by Joe Marshall and Jack Jacqua in 1987; Boston's Ten Point Coalition, founded by a coalition of clergy leaders in the 1990s; Dante Wilson's Reclaiming Our Children and Communities, Inc. in Baltimore, Maryland; Hall of Fame football player Jim Brown's Amer-I-can organization in Los Angeles County; the Southwest Youth Collaborative in Chicago; the Youth Justice Coalition/Free LA organization; and Al-Malik Farrakhan's Cease the Fire, Don't Smoke the Brothers and Sisters in Washington, DC.

The Juvenile Justice Project of Louisiana (JJPL) also sponsors two mentoring programs: Families and Friends of Louisiana's Incarcerated Children (FFLIC) and the Youth Empowerment Project (YEP). FFLIC offers a support network for parents and family members of incarcerated youth and helps them facilitate mentoring programs for youth exiting juvenile facilities. YEP assists and mentors youth and young adults ages twelve to twenty-one who are leaving the state's juvenile facilities.

Identity-based mentoring is another approach used to assist juveniles and at-risk youth. This approach identifies youth who may be victimized by violence and crime because of their racial/ethnic background, immigrant status, gender, or sexuality. It attempts to reduce discriminatory and abusive practices that are specifically tailored to harm these youth. This approach further emphasizes consciousness-raising activities as a tactic for addressing inferiority and improving self-esteem among these youth.

One example of identity-based mentoring is exhibited in several programs developed for Lesbian, Gay, Bisexual, and Transgendered (LGBT) youth, who are frequent targets of physical harassment and abuse inside and outside of juvenile facilities. The Gay Youth Project of the Urban Justice Center and the Audre Lorde Project in New York City; the Nelly Velasco

Project, sponsored by the Center for Young Women's Development in San Francisco; and the North Carolina Lambda Youth Network, are examples of programs that mentor LGBT youth.

Furthermore, the children of undocumented workers or illegal immigrants have been the disproportionate targets of violence. Since the 1990s, mentoring programs for Latino and Asian immigrants have been formed by the Committee Against Anti-Asian Violence (CAAAV) of New York City, the ESPINO organization in California's Central Valley, the Community Youth Organizing Campaign in Philadelphia, Calpulli Tlapalcalli/Esperanza Unida in Brownsville, Texas, and the Providence (Rhode Island) Youth Student Movement. These groups also have an expansive interpretation of violence that includes not only physical harassment and assault, but also deportation, detainment, and work in unhealthy and hazardous conditions.

Another form of identity-based mentoring focuses on at-risk girls. In fact, there has been a noticeable increase in violent acts perpetuated by and against young females. Much of the violence against girls occurs in the home and in personal relationships and results from sexual or domestic abuse. The Women and Girls Leadership Project in Chicago, Brooklyn's Sista II Sista program, Washington, DC's Sister to Sister/Hermana a Hermana program, and Sisters in Action for Power in Portland, Oregon are some of the well-known gender-based mentoring programs.

The third type of initiative is the development of large-scale organizing campaigns that mentor and attempt to improve the environment that shapes the daily experiences of marginalized youth. An innovative project that existed in the 1990s was the Democracy Multiplied Zone developed by the Youth Force of the South Bronx (New York City). The DMZ was a strategically targeted area in the South Bronx, delineated by marked neighborhood boundaries that functioned as a safe zone for youth. The youth living in this zone received special attention, mentoring, and developmental resources. This initiative resembled a similar project called the Harlem Children's Zone that was created in 1970.

Another initiative that offers mentoring, conflict resolution, and violence prevention activities is the Community Conferencing Center in Baltimore founded by a Johns Hopkins University professor, Laura Abramson. It mediates conflicts between juvenile (and adult) offenders and the victims of crime through a process that it calls "conferencing." From 1994 to 2003, the Community Conferencing Center mediated conflicts involving over 4,000 people.

Community activists have developed transnational mentoring programs. Michael Zinzun, a former member of the Black Panther Party and a Los Angeles gang counselor, has organized several trips for gang and ex-gang members to London, England and Rio de Janeiro's (Brazil) *favelas* (ghettos). The trips offer a cross-cultural exchange where youth can learn about different mentoring strategies from similarly situated youth throughout the world.

The fourth and fifth types of mentoring initiatives are **diversionary** and **aftercare programs**, as well as public-private partnerships between government agencies and community-based organizations. Diversionary and aftercare programs monitor at-risk youth or juveniles exiting juvenile facilities. Policymakers in Missouri have developed the most successful diversionary and aftercare programs in what is known in juvenile justice circles as the Missouri Model.

Public-private partnerships have also been successful throughout the country. Community justice and **youth courts** have been formed throughout the country to deter juvenile offenders from violent crimes. The Community Conference Center has partnered with the Baltimore police department, the school system, and the Departments of Juvenile Services and Social Services to develop diversionary programs. Boston also has a public-private partnership called Alternatives to Incarceration Network that involves the police, probation officers, and service providers. The initiative counsels youth offenders exiting **juvenile detention centers**.

A pioneering project is the Juvenile Detention Alternative Initiative developed by Bart Lubow of the Annie E. Casey Foundation. Although the initiative focuses on reforming the entire juvenile justice system, it has a prevention and aftercare component in which community-based organizations work with juvenile services. This initiative has been implemented in Cook County, Illinois; Multnomah, Oregon; Sacramento, California; and to a lesser extent, in New York City.

Another type of mentoring initiative occurs inside of juvenile detention centers. Cameron Miles, the Community Outreach Director for the Maryland Juvenile Justice Coalition, formed a program called Mentoring Male Teens in the Hood. Part of this program entails working with juveniles in Baltimore's Gay Street Detention Center. The Youth Force of the South Bronx developed a mentoring program in the Spofford Juvenile Detention Center called Ujima Productions. The Center for Young Women's Development also offers support services to incarcerated girls in San Francisco's juvenile facility.

Finally, community activists have used cultural activities to mentor youth. This includes the use of hip-hop, poetry, and media/film and is designed to educate youth about the negative consequences of violence.

See also African Americans and Juvenile Violence; Asians and Juvenile Violence; Conflict Resolution; Gang Units, Police; Hispanics and Juvenile Violence; Native Americans and Juvenile Violence; Quantum Opportunities Program (QUP); Restorative Justice

FURTHER READING

Boston Police Department. (1996). *Youth violence: A community-based response: One city's success story*. Washington, DC: National Institute of Justice.

Checkoway, B., Figueroa, L., & Richards-Schuster, K. (2003). Democracy multiplied in an urban neighborhood: Youth force in the South Bronx. *Children, Youth and Environments*, *13*(2), 1546–2250.

Feinstein, R., et al. (2001). *Justice for all? A report on lesbian, gay, bisexual and transgendered youth in the New York juvenile justice system*. New York: Urban Justice Center.

Franklin, S. (2005, April 7–10). *Policing and protesting juvenile (In)justice*. Panel presentation at the Midwest Political Science Association Annual Conference, Chicago, Illinois.

Miao, V., et al. (2005). *Pipeline*. New York: Funders' Collaborative on Youth Organizing.

Stein, N. (1997). The gang truce: A movement for social justice. *Social Justice, 24*(4), 258–268.

Sekou Franklin

METHAMPHETAMINES. Methamphetamine is a stimulant that affects the central nervous system and increases the levels of the neurotransmitter dopamine, causing an increase in attention capacity and energy and a suppression of the appetite. Methamphetamine can be orally ingested, smoked, snorted, or injected and is known by a number of street names, such as "meth," "ice," and "crank." The primary danger of methamphetamine is the high potential for addiction. Because of the increased energy methamphetamine provides, addicts go through a "binge and crash" cycle, wherein they may stay awake for several days, sleep for a day, and then restart the cycle. The combination of the drugs' effects and the accompanying food and sleep deprivation can result in psychotic behavior, including paranoia, hallucinations, and repetitive behaviors (stereotypy), such as hours spent pacing.

Methamphetamine is unique among the so-called "hard drugs" (e.g., **cocaine**, **heroin**) in that methamphetamine is relatively easy to produce using substances that can be legally purchased in the United States. Thus, whereas trafficking in drugs such as cocaine and heroin (i.e., drugs produced from plants that do not fare well in the United States) requires a combination of foreign suppliers, international smugglers, and regional distributors virtually anyone can produce methamphetamine in their own home. As a result, methamphetamine use has spread rapidly, even in isolated rural areas where other hard drugs are somewhat difficult to obtain. For instance, research conducted in Nebraska shows that cocaine use is more common among urban denizens than residents of rural areas, but methamphetamine use is as common in rural areas as in urban areas.

Another danger is that methamphetamine production involves combustible materials. Consequently, numerous methamphetamine producers (many of whom are themselves addicts) have been killed in explosions while attempting to manufacture the drug. And, because many clandestine methamphetamine laboratories are operated by inexperienced methamphetamine producers, there is extreme variation in the composition of methamphetamine. This has no doubt contributed to the more than 10,000 methamphetamine-related admissions to hospital emergency rooms that occur in the United States every year. Finally, although research suggests that methamphetamine use is decreasing among adolescents, analyses of recent data show that more than 6 percent of high school students have used methamphetamine, which indicates the drug poses a serious risk to the adolescent populace.

FURTHER READING

Herz, D. (2000). *Drugs in the heartland: Methamphetamine use in rural Nebraska.* Washington, DC: U.S. Department of Justice, Office of Justice Programs, National Institute of Justice.

Liska, K. (1997). *Drugs and the human body with implications for society,* 5th ed. Upper Saddle River, NJ: Prentice Hall.

National Institute on Drug Abuse. (2002). *Methamphetamine abuse and addiction.* Bethesda, MD: U.S. Department of Health and Human Services, National Institutes of Health, National Institute on Drug Abuse.

National Institute on Drug Abuse. (2004). *High school and youth trends.* Bethesda, MD: U.S. Department of Health and Human Services, National Institutes of Health, National Institute on Drug Abuse.

Ben Brown

MONITORING THE FUTURE. Surveying attitudes and drug use patterns of students and adults each year, Monitoring the Future (MTF) has reported trend data on high school seniors since 1975. Based at the University of Michigan's Institute of Social Research, the principal researchers are Lloyd Johnston, Jerald Bachman, John Schulenberg, Patrick O'Malley, and John Wallace. The MTF study has obtained representative samples of students from which to report student and adult prevalence rates for various types of licit and illicit drugs. A total of 50,000 randomly selected students are used for the study. The study measures prevalence three ways: lifetime use, use in the past year, and use in the last thirty days. Use of representative samples enables users of MTF research to apply the rates to the U.S. student and adult population (until the age of forty-five).

Each year the study releases a two-volume National Survey Results. The first looks at trends in drug use for students in eighth, tenth (started in 1991), and twelfth grade. The second volume follows previously sampled students as college students and adults from age nineteen to forty-five years of age. Additional publications such as an overview of key findings and press releases, focus on particular trends, such as teen smoking. Social scientists, educators, and policymakers use the study to keep track of the ebbs and flows of drug use. When drug use rates increase or new drugs of abuse are found, this illustrates problems that need to be addressed in prevention, research, and policy. The survey also addresses ease of access, a critical concern in substance abuse prevention.

Being funded by the National Institute of Drug Abuse, the research program maintains an Internet website that provides many publications for consumers, including topical press releases. The website reviews the purposes, research design,and methods of sampling and explains how the survey is administered.

There are other studies that attempt to track drug use, but MTF does so in a unique way. **The National Survey on Drug and Health** (changed from the National Household Survey of Drug Abuse) links drug abuse with measures of mental health. It provides details on the prevalence and correlates of individuals who use drugs and manifest mental problems. The Core Alcohol and Drug Survey focuses primarily on alcohol and other licit and illicit drugs reported by college students. The MTF study provides a longer trend line and also studies early adolescence, the age when the onset of drug use is initiated.

Beginning in 2000, the Monitoring the Future study revealed some declines in illicit drug use among youth. The 2004 MTF National Results on Adolescent Drug Use reported declines in cigarettes, marijuana, LSD, steroids, and ecstasy. Hallucinogens other than LSD, heroin, cocaine and crack, and tranquilizers are reported as stable. Two drugs show increases, especially for eighth graders: inhalants and OxyContin (a narcotic **prescription drug**). Most illicit drugs have monthly use rates considerably less than 10 percent of students. Monthly prevalence rates for alcohol were 48 percent for high school seniors, and 30 percent reported binge drinking in the last two weeks. Cigarette smoking in the last month was 23 percent while marijuana's rate was 19.9 percent.

Perceived risk and personal disapproval toward specific drug use is also assessed by the MTF and reveals students increasingly view illicit drugs and binge drinking as unacceptable. These attitudes influence drug use behavior.

FURTHER READING

Bachman, G., O'Malley, P., Johnston, L., Merline, A., Ludden, A., & Schulenberg, J. (Eds.). (2002). *The decline of substance use in young adulthood*. Mahwah, NJ: Lawrence Erlbaum Associates.

Johnston, L., O'Malley, P., Bachman, J., & Schulenberg, J. (2005). *Monitoring the future: National results on adolescent drug use, overview of key findings, 2004*. Bethesda, MD: U.S. Department of Health and Human Services.

James Steinberg

MUSIC, JUVENILE VIOLENCE AND. Although various forms of media have long been blamed for violence, recent events have drawn greater attention to the role violent motion pictures, television, music, and video games might play. It is clear a number of the school shooters of the 1990s and 2000s enjoyed a variety of forms of violent media; what remains unclear is the degree that their viewing, listening, and playing might have influenced their actions. In 1999, shortly after the Columbine shooting, President Clinton asked the Federal Trade Commission to study whether the motion picture, music, computer, and video game industries market and advertise violent material to children and teens and whether the current rating and labeling systems are effective at controlling young people's access to violent material. The commission found that only the video game industry specifically prohibited marketing products rated as violent to young people, yet it still happens. They also concluded that marketing and media plans were most likely to reach people under the age of seventeen, as they are advertised on the most popular television shows, websites, magazines, and even in sporting goods and other stores.

Over one thousand studies have been conducted addressing the effect of media violence, and groups such as the American Medical Association, the American Academy of Pediatrics, and the National Institute of Mental Health have all pronounced there is a relationship between violent media and violent actions. What research has not definitively answered to date is whether the relationship is causal or correlational. Most of these studies, however, have addressed viewing violent television or film, rather than listening to music. A few studies have focused on the role of music. One Swedish study found those who developed an early interest in rock music were more likely to be influenced by their peers. Another study of college students found those who listened to more antisocial music were more accepting of antisocial behaviors. Yet another study found that, after listening to "tense music"—music with no lyrics but that was dubbed intense—people wrote more unpleasant stories.

Regardless of the actual impact of media on violent behavior, polls repeatedly show the U.S. public is concerned about media violence. Even teens themselves often recognize there is a correlation; A Time/CNN poll found 75 percent of teens age thirteen to seventeen think the Internet is partly to blame for violent crime, 66 percent think movies, television, and music are, and 56 percent think video games are partly to blame.

Music is of concern because teens are voracious consumers. Research has demonstrated the average teen listens to 10,500 hours of rock music between seventh and twelfth grade. Teens listen to more than 40 hours of music each week, some of which likely contains violent messages.

Those who express concern point to a number of cases in which the violent act followed listening to violent music or watching violent videos. There were 144 law enforcement officers shot on duty in 1992. Interviews with the killers revealed that violent music, such as Ice T's "Cop Killer," made them feel powerful and gave them a sense of purpose. Some were reported to have sung this and other violent, antipolice songs at the police station when they were arrested. A seventeen-year-old was charged with stabbing a fourteen-year-old girl in front of a satanic altar he had built. He reportedly had watched a Marilyn Manson video with a similar altar.

Even when no specific incident is recorded, many express concern over the potential for some violent lyrics to lead to actual violence. Nine Inch Nail's song "Big Man with a Gun," for instance, glorifies a sexual assault at gunpoint. Marilyn Manson asks in one of his songs, "Who says date rape isn't kind?" Tool has a song called "Jerk Off," which states, "I should play god and shoot you myself." Other musicians or groups who have received much attention for their violent lyrics are Jay Z, Limp Bizkit, Cypress Hill, NWA, Eminem, and Ice Cube. Another concern is that violent content leads teens to commit suicide. A Marilyn Manson song says, "I throw a little fit, I slit my teenage wrist." Teen suicide was the major issue in the 1980s, after several so-called "epidemics." The lyrics of Ozzy Osbourne, Judas Priest, and Metallica were all under fire and prompted the creation of the Parents Music Resource Center, led by Tipper Gore.

Most studies have not found an effect of listening to violent lyrics. Recently, however, the American Physicians Association announced results of a study indicating that listening to violent lyrics leads to an increase in aggression-related thoughts and emotions. Violent videos represent another concern, as they combine the issue of violent lyrics with violent imagery. One analysis found thirty-six instances of weapon carrying and/or violence in just one song by the Beastie Boys and one song by Guns-N-Roses.

Many argue, however, that blaming violent music for teens' actions is unfair and overlooks the realities teens face that are the primary cause of their actions. These people posit that any relationship is correlational and that violent teens may be drawn to more violent music. Research also supports this contention. One study found a preference for heavy metal music was a marker for alienation, substance abuse, psychological disorders, suicide risk, sex-role stereotyping, and risk-taking behavior. Teens themselves tend to adhere to this view. They often say that the music they listen to simply reflects reality. Others contend that listening to violent music is cathartic for teens; that is, as Freud posited, we all have violent urges for which we need outlets. The catharsis notion has never borne out in research, however. Further, many times a listener cannot discern the content of specific lyrics nor do they pay attention to them, thus some maintain they cannot possibly impact a juvenile's behavior.

The notion that listening to violent music is a factor in violent behavior is rooted in learning theories. Interventions, then, should also be based on learning theory as well. Recognizing that it is difficult to completely eliminate violent media, the American Academy of Pediatrics recommends a nationwide media education program.

Those who are convinced that media plays a primary role in juvenile violence often go overboard in their response. While many organize boycotts of controversial musicians, others have gone so far as to ban the wearing of clothes depicting a group or artist. In one area, local law enforcement recommended educators carefully monitor any teen interested in rap or heavy metal music and even search their lockers. Parents were told to take their kids in for psychological assessments. In August 2005, a judge overturned the expulsion of a fourteen-year-old who had written violent and profane rap lyrics for a school assignment. The judge determined the lyrics were expression, not true threats.

See also Film, Juvenile Violence and; News, Juvenile Violence and; Television, Juvenile Violence and; Victims in the Media

FURTHER READING

Freedman, J. (2002). *Media violence and its effects on aggression: Assessing the scientific evidence.* Toronto: University of Toronto Press.

Gerdes, L. (Ed.). (2003). *Media violence: Opposing viewpoints.* New Haven, CT: Greenhaven.

Grossman, D., & DeGaetano, G. (1999). *Stop teaching our kids to kill: A call to action against T.V., movie, and video game violence.* New York: Crown.

Rich, M., Woods, E., Goodman, E., Emans, S., & Durant, R. (1998). Aggressors or victims: Gender and race in music video violence. *Pediatrics, 101*(4), 669–674.

Sternheimer, K. (2003). *It's not the media: The truth about popular culture's influence on children.* Boulder, CO: Westview.

Laura L. Finley

NATIONAL CENTER FOR JUVENILE JUSTICE. Perhaps the most prolific assembler or compiler of juvenile justice qualitative and quantitative information is the National Center for Juvenile Justice (NCJJ). The Center tracks state juvenile justice issues, reforms, and innovations and publishes descriptions of the organizational and administrative structure of state delinquency services. The agency is a nonprofit private organization. The National Center for Juvenile Justice is the research division of the National Council of Juvenile and Family Court Judges and was established in 1973.

The Center has been an information source for those interested in research related to juvenile justice. NCJJ is the only national, private research organization that has juvenile justice as their exclusive subject matter. The agency established its own budget and is responsible for its own upkeep. In order to remain operating, the agency must generate its own operating funds.

NCJJ is composed of three departments, including systems research, applied research, and legal research. The goal of the applied research division is to assist the nation's juvenile and family courts and juvenile probation departments in solving their daily problems. The goal of the legal research division is to conduct comparative analyses of state juvenile codes, model acts, national standards, and family law. The goal of the systems research division is to provide policymakers, justice professionals, the media, and the public with the most current statistical information available on children as both victims and offenders and about the juvenile justice system. Through the three departments, the Center has developed resources and capacities that make it unique in the juvenile justice field with substantial support from both public and private sources.

"The mission of the National Center for Juvenile Justice is effective justice for children and families . . . our primary means of accomplishing that mission is through research and technical assistance" (NCJJ, 2005). The agency's services to the public include but are not limited to: law/statute analysis, statistical research (creates data files and custom analysis), program planning and evaluation, facility evaluation and/or planning, court services and administration, technical assistance, and information dissemination. The Center deals with issues such as confidentiality, crime statistics, the death penalty, delays in the justice system, detention, family court, female offenders, legislation, parental responsibility, probation, and transfers to criminal/adult courts.

The Center compiles juvenile justice information about all of the states in the United States. The Center also compiles lists of initial contacts and summary information from NCJJ's own records, state and local suppliers to national juvenile court data archives, various published directories including the National Directory of Children and Youth Services, the American Correctional Association's National Juvenile Detention Directory, probation and parole directories, directories of juvenile and adult correctional departments, institutions, paroling authorities, and various state court and state juvenile corrections agency websites and annual reports. The Center can also answer questions regarding each state's organizational and administrative services.

FURTHER READING

Cohill, B. (n.d.). National center for juvenile justice: Celebrating 30 years. Available from: http://ncjj.servehttp.com.

Snyder, H. (1999). Juvenile arrests, 1998. Washington, DC: Office of Juvenile Justice and Delinquency Prevention.

Snyder, H., & Sickmund, M. (1999). *Juvenile offenders and victims: 1999 national report*. National Center for Juvenile Justice. Available from: www.ojjdp.ncjrs.org.

Evaristus Obinyan

NATIONAL COUNCIL ON CRIME AND DELINQUENCY. The National Council on Crime and Delinquency (NCCD) is a nonprofit organization that aims to promote fairer and more economically sound solutions to family and community problems of crime and delinquency. In order to achieve this mission, the NCCD makes connections not only with individuals, but also other public and private organizations and the media in order to prevent and reduce criminal activities and delinquency.

When the juvenile court system began to expand in the early twentieth century, the NCCD was established in 1907. Working to prevent children from facing the perils of the country's criminal justice system, the NCCD's earliest mission was to develop and lobby for new systems of determent and punishment for children and youths, including probation and parole. A strong organization from the beginning, the NCCD was influential in many states and was able to promote and help establish their first juvenile court systems. Additionally, the NCCD interested itself in promoting the rehabilitation of all offenders, not just children and youths, without making them face the harsh realities of incarceration.

As the organization progressed, it began to reach out more to citizens. In 1954, it established a program to better incorporate citizens into its attempts at reform. The involvement program not only had a research component to gather information about criminal justice reform awareness, but also a consultation component to seek out potential citizen support. The Ford Foundation sponsored the program, and the NCCD was able to establish citizen committees in twenty-one states. The citizen committees concentrated themselves upon the NCCD's traditional goals of reform and improvement of criminal justice from their beginning and have remained and expanded to other states.

Other foundations began to also support the NCCD throughout the 1960s and 1970s, including the Mary Babcock Reynolds Foundation, the Rockefeller Brothers Fund, and the National Institute of Mental Health, allowing the NCCD to better promote awareness and to become a stronger organization. With this new financial power, a council of judges was established to research and lobby for reform. Once again, the Ford Foundation strongly supported the NCCD, allowing it to solicit more nationwide contributions to the new council. Soon, the NCCD became influential enough to gain the full attention and support of the presidency. In 1967, President Lyndon B. Johnson was strongly in favor of the establishment of the National Emergency Committee (NEC), also supported by the NCCD. The NEC went on to propose and hold many conferences in cities nationwide and involved business leaders who wished to discuss and debate new methods for justice reform and crime reduction.

More recently, the NCCD inaugurated its Children's Research Center (CRC) in 1991, which aims to influence juvenile and child protection systems and standards nationwide by working with relevant state and local agencies. Through all of its work, the NCCD has gained not just national influence, but also an international reputation for working for improvement and reform of the criminal justice system. As the organization has become more powerful, it is able to propose and support the implementation of new standards in the areas of women and justice, violence prevention, and community-based crime action plans. To this day, the NCCD works to ensure that punishment is never the only solution.

FURTHER READING

Home. (n.d.). National Council on Crime and Delinquency. Available from: http://www.nccd-crc.org/nccd/n_index_main.html.

Mission. (n.d.). National Council on Crime and Delinquency. Available from: http://www.nccd-crc.org/nccd/n_mission_main.html.

More about NCCD: Our history. (n.d.). National Council on Crime and Delinquency. Available from: http://www.nccd-crc.org/nccd/n_more_history.html.

Arthur Holst

NATIONAL CRIME VICTIMIZATION SURVEY (NCVS). Started in 1973, the National Crime Victimization Survey is distributed and administered by the U.S. Census Bureau for the Bureau of Justice Statistics. It is the authoritative source of information on crime victimization in the United States. Goals of the survey include gathering detailed information about victims and consequences of crime, estimating the volume and types of crimes that have not been reported to law enforcement, providing a uniform system of measuring specific, select crimes, and allowing accurate comparisons over time of the different types of crimes and areas in which they occur.

The survey is taken twice yearly from a nationwide representative sample of about 100,000 people age twelve years and older. Due to the age range of survey participants, a valid criticism is that juvenile victimization is likely underreported. Mainly, the National Crime Victimization Survey tracks crime rates and trends. In contrast to the **Uniform Crime Reports (UCR)**, it reveals figures on crimes not reported to police and illustrates the frequency, characteristics, and consequences of being a crime victim. Taken from the victim's perspective, it avoids police bias and more accurately reflects specific characteristics (race, gender, context of the crime, etc.) of the victim, offender, and crime. The survey intends to indicate the likelihood of victimization for the U.S. population as a whole and for special populations, such as women, the elderly, minority groups, rural residents, and urban residents.

Crimes listed on the survey are categorized as either "personal" or "property" crimes. Personal crimes include: rape, sexual assault, robbery, aggravated and simple assault, and purse-snatching/pickpocketing. Property crimes include: burglary, theft, motor vehicle theft, and vandalism.

The National Crime Victimization Survey serves as an informational resource for law enforcement, lawmakers, policymakers, administrators, and researchers. Information gained from the survey is utilized to place emphasis on reducing and preventing chronically problematic crimes. By tracking crime and victimization trends, governmental administrators can prioritize policies and operations by importance with regard to the existing needs of victims and communities. With regard to juvenile violence, an effort can be made to reduce the number of juvenile victims of specific crimes. In the past, the National Crime Victimization Survey has revealed such specific trends in crime victimization as what hours of the day were the highest risk for juveniles in being the victim of a violent crime. This information has been used by teachers and school administrators to create policies and programs that reduce the risk during specific times of the day, thus reducing overall risk to potential juvenile victims.

FURTHER READING

National Crime Victimization Survey. (2005, June). Data sets: Crimes & victims. *Center for Criminology & Criminal Justice Research*. University of Texas at Austin Website. Available at: http://www.la.utexas.edu/research/crime_criminaljustice_research/index.html.

National Crime Victimization Survey Resource Guide. (2005, June). *National Archive of Criminal Justice Data*. University of Michigan Website. Available at: http://www.icpsr.umich.edu/NACJD/NCVS/.

Adam Doran

NATIONAL HOUSEHOLD SURVEY ON DRUG ABUSE. The National Household Survey on Drug Abuse, recently renamed the National Survey on Drug Use and Health (NSDUH), is administered by the federal Department of Health and Human Services in order to research and summarize the pervasiveness and consequences of drug and alcohol abuse among the U.S. citizenry. It is the federal government's main source of nationwide information on drug and alcohol abuse and has been conducted since 1971. Performed and analyzed annually, roughly 70,000 citizens of the fifty states and the District of Columbia above the age of twelve participate in the survey every year. This report, once published, is available to the public online.

Information is collected from households and noninstitutional establishments, such as shelters, dormitories, and military bases. Certain groups of people are excluded from the survey, including those who are in prison, on active military duty, or on long-term hospital stays. Data is solicited from all fifty states based upon an independent and multistage probability sample. Interestingly, data samples collected from the eight largest states are substantial enough to draw conclusions and make estimates about drug and alcohol abuse in those states.

Concerning sampling, youths and young adults are over-sampled in order to provide a more equal distribution of age ranges. These three groups are youths from twelve to seventeen years old, young adults from eighteen to twenty-five years old, and adults from twenty-six and older.

Data collection methodology involves many in-person interviews performed at their home or place of residence. Before the introduction of the computer-assistant system used currently, a paper-based interviewer method was used, known as PAPI methodology. Since 1999, CAPI and ACASI methodology has been used, incorporating computers to allow for a more confidential way of answering the questions presented by the survey. As a result, many researchers at the NSDUH believe that the survey attained a new level of confidentiality and honesty.

The survey not only inquires about a subject's current drug and alcohol use, but also about use during the last year and the entire lifetime. Since current use only refers to consumption during the last month, these inquiries allow the survey to cover a much larger time frame. Nine classes of drugs are researched and analyzed, made up of marijuana, cocaine, inhalants, hallucinogens, heroin, and misused prescription drugs that are dealt with individually as pain relievers, tranquilizers, stimulants, and sedatives. For alcohol, abuse is categorized as binge use, which is five or more drinks on one occasion, and regular heavy use. Additionally, inquiries are also made about tobacco use.

Processing the data, NSDUH performs numerous edits, consistency checks, and conducts statistical imputation to replace missing data. Survey controls are placed upon non-responses, sample populations, and extreme responses only when absolutely necessary. Lastly, the sampling error is calculated and reported before final analysis and publication is undertaken. Currently, the final survey report is made public by the Substance Abuse and Mental Health Services Administration, an agency of USDUH.

FURTHER READING

About SAMHSA. (n.d.). SAMHSA: U.S. Department of Health and Human Services. Available from: http://www.samhsa.gov/Menu/Level2_about.aspx.

National Survey on Drug Use and Health (NSDUH). (n.d.). Office of Applied Science: U.S. Department of Health and Human Services. Available from: http://www.oas.samhsa.gov/2k3/NSDUH/nsduh.htm.

SAMHSA. Department of Health and Human Services. (n.d.). National Survey on Drug Use and Health methodology reports and questionnaires. Available from: http://www.oas.samhsa.gov/nhsda/methods.cfm#2k4.

Arthur Holst

NATIONAL INSTITUTE OF JUSTICE (NIJ). The National Institute of Justice (NIJ) originated in 1968 as part of the Omnibus Crime Control and Safe Streets Act. Congress formed the Institute to act as a federal criminal justice research agency. The NIJ was designed as a progressive effort, assisting local governments with the improvement of police services, courts, and corrections. Research conducted by the NIJ also seeks to reveal new information and understandings of criminal behavior. The main goal of the organization is to create critical knowledge in the fields of crime and justice, then share and implement that knowledge.

The NIJ is an agency of the U.S. Department of Justice, overseen by a director who is appointed by the president and approved by the Senate. In addition to conducting new research, the NIJ continuously evaluates modern governmental programs and offers grants to independent researchers for new information on crime and justice. The Institute seeks to find objective, independent, and evidence-based information in order to best guide policy and practice in the justice system.

In order to reduce costs and improve efficiency, the NIJ was reorganized in 2003. Today, the Institute manages such programs as the National Criminal Justice Reference Service (a clearinghouse of criminal justice information), the National Commission on the Future of DNA Evidence (seeks to maximize the value of DNA evidence to the justice system), Mapping and Analysis for Public Safety (authority on crime-mapping), and Violence Against Women and Family Violence Research. The information these and other programs have produced is disseminated through numerous publications that provide up-to-date research and statistics as well as suggested policies and practices. The NIJ plays a significant role in the fight against juvenile violence, acting as an important source of research and information. The Institute releases reports frequently on topics including school safety, juvenile gangs, and monitoring juvenile drug abuse. Some recent examples of the agency's work to prevent juvenile violence are: *Evaluating* GREAT *A School-Based Gang Prevention Program* (NIJ Report, June 2004),

Youth Gangs in Rural America (NIJ Journal Article, July 2004) and *Toward Safe and Orderly Schools: The National Study of Delinquency Prevention in Schools* (NIJ Research In Brief, November 2004).

FURTHER READING

About NIJ. (n.d.). National Institute of Justice. Available at: http://www.ojp.usdoj.gov/nij/about.htm.

Programs. (n.d.). National Institute of Justice. Available at: http://www.ojp.usdoj.gov/nij/programs.htm.

Publications. (n.d.). National Institute of Justice. Available at: http://nij.ncjrs.org/publications/pubs_db.asp.

Adam Doran

NATIONAL SCHOOL SAFETY CENTER (NSSC). The National School Safety Center (NSSC), an organization that advocates safe and peaceful schools, not just in the United States but also worldwide, is located in Westlake Village, California. In order to achieve its goals, NSSC acts as a resource for school communities and those who work in conjunction with school districts to provide information, resources, training, and consultations for the improvement of school safety. Going further, NSSC develops and promotes its own strategies that it in turn shares with school districts and school safety personnel.

This mission to create a safe and peaceful learning environment is based upon NSSC's belief that the feeling of being "safe" is essential to a successful learning and growth environment. The security that NSSC aims to promote creates more effective schools free from violence and other distractions.

To achieve this vision and mission, NSSC offers a variety of programs and services to school districts and education personnel. First, it advocates for school safety not as the only solution to bettering schools worldwide, but as part of a more holistic approach where safety is only one component of an effective school. It offers training to everyone who has an impact upon school safety, particularly educators, law enforcement officials, and other professionals who work at schools. It is active at school safety conferences and workshops, often delivering keynote addresses on particular aspects of school safety, depending on hot topics, trends, or strategies. Every strategy or program offered to a certain school is customized by NSSC to meet specific needs. Lastly, it provides on-site technical assistance to schools and communities who request it when they are facing rather significant and demanding crises.

Additionally, NSSC performs on-site assessments of school safety, provides international leadership and research on school safety, publishes media commentaries, resources, and an informative website. Most often, schools and communities utilize videos and publications produced by NSSC to develop their own strategies in conjunction with NSSC's suggestions. It is also an active participant during "Safe Schools Week" that occurs annually in October.

Most recently, NSSC has been busy preparing and presenting its programs and strategies geared toward the issue of terrorism and school safety. It offers two programs to address this issue: "Safeguarding Schools against Terror" and "Managing Schools Under the Threat of Terror." Within each program, NSSC explains the Department of Homeland Security's risk alert status color-coded scheme, details why schools are at risk for potential terrorist attacks, and offers assistance in finding the appropriate actions and responses to these troubling and demanding issues. Advocating safe and secure schools, NSSC offers up-to-date services and programs to schools worldwide in order to achieve its vision of a peaceful learning environment.

FURTHER READING

NSSC Homepage. (n.d.). National School Safety Center. Available from: http://www.nssc1.org/index2.htm.

Students Against Violence Everywhere: Safe School Week. (n.d.). SAVE. Available from: http://www.nationalsave.org/main/safe%20schools%20week.php.

Arthur Holst

NATIONAL YOUTH SURVEY. The National Youth Survey (NYS) is a longitudinal probability study of 1,725 adolescents between the ages of eleven and seventeen that began in 1976. It is an influential study utilized by many disciplines whose focus is on attitudes and behaviors of the respondents on such topics as education, family relationships, and conditions of their neighborhoods. The survey is concerned with subject matter about career goals, family and community involvement, and violence, drugs, and social values. Currently, the survey has data on three generations.

Del Elliott is the creator and founder of the NYS. Since the beginning of the survey, participants have been interviewed in all fifty states and the District of Columbia. The respondents for the National Youth Survey were randomly chosen from across the United States and are thought to represent views, attitudes, and behaviors of other American inhabitants of roughly the same demographic characteristics.

The gender distribution is 53 percent male and 47 percent female. The majority of participants are white (79 percent), with 15 percent African Americans, 4.5 percent Latino or Hispanic, 1 percent Asian American/Pacific Islander, and less than 1 percent is Native American. As of 1992, over 80 percent of the original respondents have continued participating with the survey.

Information collected on the demographics of the respondents includes gender, ethnicity, date of birth, age, marital status, and employment. Marital status and employment of the parents of the participants are included as well. All interviews were originally conducted with the young respondents, as well as one of their parents.

Beginning in 1993, the survey included a section on the original respondent's family, interviewing not only the original respondent, but their children and partners as well. To accommodate this expansion, the study changed its name to the National Youth Survey–Family Study (NYS–FS) in 2000. This was to account for the aging of the participants and the growth of their families. The NYS–FS includes questions about the respondent's family and their careers.

Currently, interviews last approximately ninety minutes. The respondents are interviewed about their attitudes, values, and beliefs on both conventional and deviant behavior. This includes disruptive events in the home, problems in their neighborhood, parental aspirations for the participants, labeling, integration of family and peers, deviance, parental discipline, involvement in their community, drug and alcohol use, victimization, pregnancy, depression, outpatient services, spousal violence, and sexual activity.

There have been eleven waves conducted thus far for the NYS–FS, beginning with the original cohort in 1976 and continuing through the year 2004. In the year 2002, they started collecting DNA of the respondents for the first time. Currently the research labs for the NYS–FS are located at the University of Colorado in Boulder. The Institute of Behavioral Science and the Institute for Behavioral Genetics collaborate on data collection efforts.

FURTHER READING

National Youth Survey (NYS) Series. (n.d.). National Archive of Criminal Justice Data. Available at: http://webapp.icpsr.umich.edu/cocoon/NACJD-SERIES/00088.xml.

National Youth Family Study. (n.d.). University of Colorado. Available at: http://www.colorado.edu/ibs/NYFS/.

April C. Wilson

NATIVE AMERICANS AND JUVENILE VIOLENCE.

After conquest by European immigrants, Native Americans and their youth have been stripped of their cultural identity, colonized, oppressed, and discriminated against. Native American youth were eventually forced into military-style boarding schools where they were forced to speak English and give up traditional ways. While the practice of boarding schools has diminished, the educational experience for Native youth remains poor. Today, around 30 percent of native students drop out annually, reflecting the highest dropout rate of all ethnic groups.

In addition to problems with education, Native youth experience significant other social problems. The **suicide** rate for Native American youth is three times that of the national average. Native American youth represent 1 percent of the population. They also reflect 2 to 3 percent of the youth arrested for larceny-theft and liquor law violations. Native Americans between the ages of twelve to twenty stand a 58 percent higher risk of becoming crime victims than whites and blacks. Native American and Alaska Native children have twice the rate of death caused by injuries or violence as do other children. Indians under fifteen years of age are murdered at twice the rate of white teenagers. Native Americans ages fifteen to twenty-four have alcohol-related deaths seventeen times higher than the national average. Alcohol-related deaths are more than ten times higher among Indian teens than those of other races. Discrimination against Native Americans is associated with early onset of substance abuse with Indian children.

There is a disparate number of Native American youth in secure confinement when compared to their representation in the population in twenty-six states. For example, South Dakota's Native American youth population is approximately 13 percent, and represented approximately 45 percent of the youth incarcerated at the South Dakota State Training School in 2000. By 2001, the number of Native American youth in the Federal Bureau of Prisons system increased by 50 percent. In midyear 2000, Native American youth represented nearly 16 percent of inmates in custody in Indian country facilities.

A current concern in Indian country is the spread of gangs. A survey of Indian communities in 2000 revealed that 23 percent indicated the presence of active gangs. These gangs were primarily Native American gangs (78 percent). The Native American gangs spawned on reservations include Thug Rida, Red Pride, Eastside Brown Dawgs, Brown Tribe Krew, Born Strictly Rotten, and Everybody Killers. Imported gangs, like the Crips and the Bloods, were brought onto reservations by tribal members who lived in urban areas and then returned home. Gangs accounted for one homicide in 14 percent of the cases and two or more homicides in 8 percent of the instances. In 2000, the Bureau of Indian Affairs estimated that there were 520 gangs on Indian reservations, with a total of more than 6,000 members.

Various approaches have been used to bring a halt to the problems that plague Native American youth. These include traditional spirituality or culturally relevant and sensitive approaches to therapy or social work.

See also Educational Opportunity and Juvenile Violence; Gang Types; Weise, Jeff

FURTHER READING

Arrillaga, P. (2001, April 15). 'Stuck between two worlds': Tribal youth ravaged by violence, drug abuse, depression, culture. *Los Angeles Times*, B1.

Associated Press. (2004, August 10). Program targets Natives' drinking. *Lincoln Journal Star*, 02.

Associated Press. (2000, July 14). Crime rate rises among Indian youth. *Denver Post*, A06.

Beiser, V. (2000, July 10/July 17). Boyz on the rez. *New Republic*, 2/3, 15–17.

Bighorn, E. (2005, August 4). Suicide 'epidemic' grips reservations: Young American Indians gather in Montana to find ways to stop the trend. *Orlando Sentinel*, A12.

Building Blocks for Youth. (n.d.). Native American youth fact sheet. Available from: http://www.buildingblocksforyouth.org/issues/nativeyouth/facts.html.

Clark, J. (1996). No reservations about gangs: Urban youth-crime problem infects Indian country. *Law Enforcement News*, *447*, 1.

Clemmons, L. (2001). We find it a difficult work. *American Indian Quarterly*, *24*(4), 570–602.

Creno, C. (1995, July 11). Seeds of hope from cultural roots: Native American woman guides at-risk youths and others in spiritual journey to sense of identity. *Arizona Republic*, D1.

Duarte, C. (2002, November 24). Gangs find new land. *Arizona Daily Star*, A1.

Henderson, E., Kunitz, S., & Jerrold, L. (1999). The origins of Navajo youth gangs. *American Indian Culture and Research Journal*, *23*(3), 243–264.

Kurilovitch, M. (1998, February 8). After school program helps Tuscarora students walk tall. *News Niagara Correspondent*, NC1.

Lincoln, J. (2000, March 13). School not for them, many Indian youths feel an academic star that is unhappy that his Ho-Chunk peers resent his success: The drop out rate for Native American students is higher than any other ethnic group. *Lincoln (Neb.) Journal Star*, 1A.

Listug-Lunde, L. (2004). A cognitive-behavioral treatment for depression in Native American middle-school students. Doctoral dissertation. University of North Dakota.

Major, A., Egley, A., Howell, J., Mendenhall, B., & Armstrong, T. (2004, March 4). Youth gangs in Indian country. *Office of Juvenile Justice and Delinquency Prevention, Juvenile Justice Bulletin*. Available at: http://www.ncjrs.org/html/ojjdp/jjbul2004_3_1/contents.html.

Office of Juvenile Justice and Delinquency Prevention. (2003, May 30). Native Americans, violent crime, children and youth. *Juvenile Justice Digest*, *31*(10), 4.

Piere, R. (2004, March 31). Northwest tribe struggles to revive its language: Project a challenge for Klallam, others as Native speakers age. *Washington Post*, A3.

Shillinger, S. (1995). "They never told us they wanted to help us": An oral history of Saint Joseph's Indian Industrial School. Doctoral dissertation. University of Pennsylvania.

Strickland, D. (1995, May 16). Reservations trying to chase gangs away—Washington tribes turn to counseling, increased vigilance to combat problem. *Seattle Times*, A1.

Whitebeck, L., McMorris, B., Xiaojin, C., & Stubben, J. (2001). Perceived discrimination and early substance abuse among American Indian children. *Journal of Health and Social Behavior*, *42*(4), 405–425.

Wright, G. (2000, November 24). Gangs lure Native Americans, Indian youths mirror urban blacks, Latinos who search for identity. *Detroit News*, 18.

Youth violence: A report of the Surgeon General. (n.d.). Available at: www.surgeongeneral.gov/library/youthviolence/chapter2/sec12.html.

Mike Olivero

NEUROLOGICAL THEORIES. Neurological theories focus on the role of the brain and nervous system in explaining violent behavior. Empirical tests of these theories generally involve the use of medical technology to measure brain waves, heart rate, arousal levels, skin conductance, and attention span. In other cases, psychological tests and even standardized tests are used to measure cognitive ability and specialized learning. Most commonly, these theories involve a deficiency or damage to some part of the brain. Sometimes this is the result of a genetic defect. Brain damage in utero and in early childhood have also been correlated with increased tendencies toward both youth and adult violence. Some of history's most notorious serial killers, including David Berkowitz (better known as "The Son of Sam"), Kenneth Bianchi, and John Wayne Gacy, all suffered childhood head trauma.

The Neuroendocrine System

This view asserts that an imbalance in the neuroendocrine system, which controls brain chemistry, may be linked to antisocial behavior. Research has demonstrated a connection between abnormalities in the way the brain metabolizes glucose and substance abuse. This may develop while a fetus is developing. The fetus requires a steady stream of glucose in order for the brain to grow. If the mother is not providing the fetus with adequate nutrition, the brain may not receive the needed amounts of amino acids and proteins that produce serotonin and dopamine. Low levels of serotonin, a neurotransmitter that provides for communication with the brain, may also be the result of genetic error. In addition, studies have shown that inadequate nurturing early in life can lead to a deregulation of these processes.

Depleted serotonin levels can reduce inhibitions, thus making an individual more impulsive and perhaps more likely to act out violently. The combination of high noradrenaline and low serotonin is the most likely to lead to impulsive forms of behavior. When noradrenaline and serotonin are both low, the individual may be more prone to high-risk behavior as they seek to be aroused. Low levels of serotonin are correlated with suicidal tendencies, violence and aggression, depression, alcoholism, and impulsive behavior. Studies have demonstrated that individuals diagnosed with violent personality disorders have both low serotonin levels and high testosterone levels, which might explain **gender differences in violent crime rates among juveniles.**

Neurological Dysfunction

Another neurological theory posits that neurological dysfunction, rather than an imbalance, causes violent behavior. Some research has supported this view, in that some children who act violently have minimal brain damage (MBD) or an abnormality in the brain structure. MBD can significantly alter a person's cognitive abilities and even their IQ. Both cognitive ability and IQ are associated with delinquency. Other behaviors correlated with brain dysfunctions or abnormalities include poor impulse control, limited social ability, hostility, temper tantrums, destructiveness, and hyperactivity. MBD can be inherited or can occur during traumatic labor or from accidents later in life. Some research has found that 95 percent of all serious head injuries are the result of **child abuse**. Babies born with low birth weight are also more likely to suffer from MBD. Research has linked brain damage to mental disorders, such as schizophrenia and depression. In one of the most significant attempts to empirically test the role of neurological damage in regard to violent behavior, researchers found habitually aggressive youth had, on average, a 57 percent abnormality rate on an electroencephalogram (EEG), compared to an average 12 percent abnormality rate for youth who had committed only one violent act. A 1986 study examined the neurological histories of fifteen death row inmates and found that every member of the experimental population had experienced severe head injury prior to incarceration. Similarly, every one of a sample of fourteen juveniles on death row in 1988 had sustained a serious head injury.

Similarly, dysfunctions in the frontal lobe of the brain have been linked with delinquency. The frontal lobe is responsible for the brain's ability for abstract thinking, planning, and self-monitoring, all of which might be connected to a juvenile's violent behavior. Some researchers have said that frontal lobe damage is a key factor in the development of sociopathic, "cold-blooded" criminals. Dysfunctions in the brain's left hemispheres have been linked to low IQ, which is itself linked to delinquency.

Learning Disabilities

Research has demonstrated that teens that are arrested and incarcerated are more likely to have learning disabilities than those in the general population. Estimates are that approximately 10 percent of all American youths have some form of learning disability, but rates for adjudicated delinquents ranged from 26 percent to 73 percent. Other research has shown that between 28 and 43 percent of incarcerated youth have special education needs, with learning disabilities the most common form. Research on adolescent females with learning disabilities shows they are also more likely to be delinquent. More recent research has focused on the specific learning disability of **ADHD**, which has been linked with higher risk for aggressive behavior, family violence, low academic achievement and academic retention, substance use and abuse, emotional problems, and antisocial behavior. Boys are five to seven times more likely to be diagnosed with ADHD, a fact that could help explain why males are over-represented for violent crimes.

While it is not clear precisely how learning disabilities (LD) connect with delinquency, there are two main lines of thought. One is that the effects of learning disabilities, including impulsivity and inability to pick up on important social cues, are what lead to delinquency and violence. The other argument is that frustration from the learning disability leads to school failure, and thus the student may act out both inside and outside of school. LD students may be more easily frustrated, and the rigid expectations of traditional public school education may make it difficult for them to feel successful. Thus, **educational opportunity** may be the critical variable.

Some maintain, however, that these rates do not necessarily tell us who is committing acts of violence; rather, they tell us who is getting caught for them. Further, biases may lead to greater focus on these young people in schools, by police, and in other institutions. Additionally, when other sources are used, such as self-reports, there seems to be no difference in violent behavior between LD and non-LD youth. Critics also are concerned that neurological explanations for delinquency serve to minimize if not completely ignore social factors. Critics maintain that these theories easily become deterministic; that is, if a person has sustained a serious head injury, for instance, then they will automatically become violent. Clearly, this is not the case. Research has shown, for instance, that many issues related to serotonin can be addressed through nurturing.

See also Arousal Theory; General Theory of Crime (GTC); Trait Theories

FURTHER READING

Brown, G. L., et al. (1982). Aggression, suicide, and serotonin: Relationships to CSF metabolites. *American Journal of Psychiatry, 139*, 741–746.

Karr-Morse, R., & Wiley, M. (1997). *Ghosts from the nursery*. New York: Atlantic Monthly Press.

Lewis, D. O., et al. (1986). Psychiatric, neurological, and psychoeducational characteristics of 15 death row inmates in the United States. *American Journal of Psychiatry, 143*, 838–845.

Monroe, R. (1987). *Brain dysfunction in aggressive criminals*. Lexington, MA: D.C. Heath.

Seguin, J., Pihl, R., Harden, P., Tremblay, R., & Boulerice, B. (1995). Cognitive and neuropsychological characteristics of physically aggressive boys. *Journal of Abnormal Psychology, 104*, 614–24.

Winters, C. (1997). Learning disabilities, crime, delinquency, and special education placement. *Adolescence, 32*(126), 451–463.

Laura L. Finley

NEW YORK HOUSES OF REFUGE. Houses of Refuge were early juvenile facilities that housed delinquents and neglected, abused, poor, and orphaned children. These houses were managed by superintendents who focused on moving away from a family-style upbringing and toward a societal-style religious upbringing with an emphasis on education and hard work. Even though these early institutions were designed to replace the family and provide a religious atmosphere, they were quickly organized and managed much like authoritative penal institutions.

The first house of refuge housed eight children, which included three females housed separately from the males, and was opened in New York City on January 1, 1825. The house of refuge concept quickly spread to other states and was duplicated in Rochester, New York in 1849. These houses were established with strong religious convictions. The religious influence promoted the notion that all the residents were intrinsically evil and needed to be reformed toward goodness.

Originally, the development of the houses of refuge was a movement away from housing juveniles with adult offenders. These houses were intended to prevent young delinquents from learning criminal trades from their adult counterparts and falling into a life of crime. Upon entry to the houses, parents, who were looked down upon by society for their inability to raise their children, would give total control and responsibility of the child's upbringing to the superintendent of the house. The superintendent provided strict discipline to his residents. Even the smallest infractions would result in vigorous whippings with the use of a cat-o'-nine-tails.

A usual day consisted of waking up at sunrise and following a rigorous schedule that included daily chores, religious worship, education, and work. Even though religious and educational activities were performed twice a day, the main focus at the houses of refuge was physical labor. In the summer months the children could be expected to work up to fourteen hours a day. The children were required to learn a trade in preparation for an apprenticeship upon their release. Trades for the males included the manufacturing of commercial goods, such as chairs, brass nails, brushes, and shoes. The females focused on domestic duties, such as sewing uniforms and doing laundry. Upon the completion of their chores, schooling, worship, and work, children would return to their cells and remain silent throughout the night. Harsh work conditions and strict discipline resulted in numerous children running away.

In accepting wayward children into the houses of refuge and taking the responsibility to raise and care for them away from the parents, these houses of refuge were initiating a juvenile justice concept that would later become known as ***parens patriae***, or in the best interest of the child. Under this medieval English concept, the king (the state in America) would assume control of the child and act as its parent. Despite criticism of harsh treatment of the children, the New York concept of houses of refuge lasted for over one hundred years.

See also Child Savers; Juvenile Detention Centers

FURTHER READING

Sharp, P., & Hancock, B. (Eds.). (1998). *Juvenile delinquency: Historical, theoretical, and societal reactions to youth*, 2nd ed. Upper Saddle River, NJ: Prentice Hall.
Vito, G., & Simonsen, C. (Eds.). (2004). *Juvenile justice today*, 4th ed. Upper Saddle River, NJ: Prentice Hall.

Georgen Guerrero

NEWS, JUVENILE VIOLENCE AND. Violent crimes committed by juveniles receive extensive coverage by the news media. As a result, the general public tends to believe that rates of juvenile violence are increasing, irrespective of the fact that violent juvenile crime has been steadily decreasing for at least a decade. It is surmised that many citizens use the media as their primary source about crime and form opinions based upon what the news media reports, regardless of inaccuracies.

The general public has long had its fears about juveniles driven by the media. In the 1950s, people were deeply concerned that unflattering media portrayals of youth could influence their children to behave in the same undesirable ways. These fears were furthered by the government's attention to the rise in juvenile delinquency after World War II. These fears continued in the 1970s, as the perception prevailed that younger children were involved in a large amount of violent crime. The development of national news networks, cable television, and other advances in media technology has also contributed to the nature of citizens' fears. For instance, it is now permissible to cover stories that were once considered unfit for public consumption or that could not be covered due to location. These developments have turned what would once only be local news into national news stories with extensive coverage.

With stories of criminal activity on every television, in every newspaper, and in many newsmagazines, society's fear has come to include the threat of juvenile violence. Some accuse the media of fearmongering through the way stories are framed and delivered and contend media coverage of violent juvenile crimes contributes to "moral panic." A moral panic occurs when people experience intense fear as a result of the shaping of events by people who are presumed experts on a subject. The experts contributing to most news stories about crime are the police. Many officers and other officials refer to juvenile violence when making statements to the media, emphasizing it as a social issue in the minds of the public.

Studies about fear of crime indicate that most people believe juvenile violence is increasing, when in fact there have been steady declines since 1994. Statistics from the Office of Juvenile Justice and Delinquency Prevention demonstrate that juvenile arrest for violence has reached its lowest rate since 1983. Media reports of juvenile violence are frequently out of proportion to the amount of juvenile violence that actually occurs. Juveniles commit more property crime than violent crime, but property crimes committed by anyone are rarely reported in the news.

Several factors, such as age and gender of the suspect and/or victim, have been found to influence media reporting of juvenile violence. Younger violent juveniles tend to receive more reporting coverage than older juveniles, and violent crimes involving juvenile female offenders tend to receive more coverage than violent crimes committed by adult females. In addition, while juveniles account for a very small percentage (10 percent) of suspects arrested for murder, television news stories about juvenile murderers are significantly out of proportion to what really occurs across the nation.

Another factor that is believed to influence reporting of juvenile violence is the race of the suspect and victim. There is some indication that if the suspect and the victim are both black, news coverage occurs less frequently. It has been suggested that because a vast amount of crime occurs with black victims and suspects, crimes of this nature are not perceived as novel by the police or as newsworthy by the media. Others, however, believe that black suspects are overrepresented in the media, creating incorrect public visions of minorities.

Further contributing to the images of juvenile violence that people have is the couching of stories in past events, such as school shootings. These, like much other criminal activity reported in the news, are relatively rare events. However, they became important on a national level because of the extensive attention they received by national news media. By keeping these rare events in the forefront of society's mind, the media seemingly "cultivates" crime in the minds of its consumers. Only further research will determine the extent of the media's impact in the future.

See also Film, Juvenile Violence and; Music, Juvenile Violence and; Television, Juvenile Violence and; Victims in the Media

FURTHER READING

Boulahanis, J., & Heltsley, M. (2004). Perceived fears: The reporting patterns of juvenile homicide in Chicago newspapers. *Criminal Justice Policy Review, 15,* 132–60.

Feld, B. (2003). The politics of race and juvenile justice: The "due process revolution" and the conservative reaction. *Justice Quarterly, 20,* 765–800.

Gilbert, J. (1998). Mass culture and the fear of delinquency: The 1950s. *Journal of Early Adolescence, 5,* 505–16.

Glassner, B. (2004). Narrative techniques of fear mongering. *Social Research, 71,* 819–26.

Laub, J. (1983). Trends in serious juvenile crime. *Criminal Justice and Behavior, 10,* 485–506.

Sacco, V. (1995). Media constructions of crime. *Annals of the American Academy of Political and Social Sciences, 539,* 141–54.

Snyder, H. (2005). Juvenile arrests 2003. *Juvenile Justice Bulletin.* Office of Juvenile Justice and Delinquency Prevention, U.S. Department of Justice.

Welch, M., Fenwick, M., & Roberts, M. (1997). Primary definitions of crime and moral panic: A content analysis of experts' quotes in feature newspaper articles on crime. *Journal of Research in Crime and Delinquency, 34,* 474–94.

Yanich, D. (2005). Kids, crime, and local television news. *Crime and Delinquency, 51,* 103–132.

Wendy Perkins

OFFICE OF JUVENILE JUSTICE AND DELINQUENCY PREVENTION (OJJDP).

The Office of Juvenile Justice and Delinquency Prevention was established by Congress in 1974 under the Juvenile Justice and Delinquency Prevention Act. The OJJDP seeks to improve juvenile justice policies and practices, conduct relevant research, and provide funding for research and programs directed at preventing juvenile violence and improving juvenile justice and the welfare of America's youth. Through the dissemination of current information and financial support via federal grants, the OJJDP works toward providing better public safety, better accountability of juvenile offenders, and more effective programs that meet the needs of youth, families, and communities.

The OJJDP is part of the **U.S. Department of Justice**, Office of Justice Programs. The organization consists of five divisions and is overseen by an administrator. Some of the programs the OJJDP coordinates include the Gang Reduction Program, Internet Crimes Against Children Task Force Program, Juvenile Justice Evaluation Center, and Safe Start: Promising Approaches for Children Exposed to Violence. The OJJDP releases numerous publications, including a bimonthly newsletter, regular bulletins, journals, fact sheets, reports, and research summaries covering topics of youth development, gangs, education issues, families, and youth violence prevention.

FURTHER READING

About OJJDP. (2005, June). Office of Juvenile Justice and Delinquency Prevention. Available at: http://ojjdp.ncjrs.org/about/about.html.

Programs. (2005, June). Office of Juvenile Justice and Delinquency Prevention. Available at: http://ojjdp.ncjrs.org/programs/index.html.

Publications. (2005, June). Office of Juvenile Justice and Delinquency Prevention. Available at: http://ojjdp.ncjrs.org/publications/index.html.

Adam Doran

OPERATION CEASEFIRE.

Operation Ceasefire was part of a coordinated problem-solving policing enterprise seeking to deter illegal gun possession and gun violence by targeting high-risk youths and violent juvenile offenders from the ages of eight to eighteen.

Operation Ceasefire was part of a collaborative and comprehensive strategy that was developed over a two-year span (1994–1996) and implemented in Boston, Massachusetts in May 1996 to address Boston's escalating crime rates. The Boston Gun Project—gun suppression and prohibition—and Operation Night Light—a police-probation partnership—accompanied Operation Ceasefire's gang abatement approach. There are two components to the Ceasefire strategy: direct attack on illegal gun traffickers and deterring gang violence.

The Boston Police Department's **Youth Violence Strike Force (YVSF)**, a multiagency task force working in collaboration with several agencies and institutions from all levels of government, developed the strategy. Agencies participating consisted of volunteers from the Boston Police Department; Massachusetts Department of Parole; the Suffolk County District Attorney; the United States Attorney's Office; Bureau of Alcohol, Tobacco, and Firearms (ATF); Massachusetts Department of Youth Services; Boston School Police; gang outreach programs; and Boston Community Centers Program.

The primary goal of Operation Ceasefire was to warn gangs that violence would no longer be tolerated or the full weight of law enforcement and criminal justice agencies would be brought upon them. This was accomplished by targeting noncomplying gangs with enforcement any outstanding warrants and probation surrenders. The zero tolerance message quickly spread among the other gangs. The logic behind Ceasefire was a "pulling levers" deterrence strategy that focused criminal justice attention on chronically offending gangs that were responsible for many of the homicides in Boston.

Operation Ceasefire was a concerted effort between researchers, practitioners, law enforcement, and prosecution. The concentrated focus was aimed at recovering illegal guns, prosecuting dangerous felons, increasing public awareness, and promoting public safety. The objectives were to assemble an inter-agency working group of line-level criminal justice and other practitioners; to use research techniques in creating an assessment of the nature and dynamics of youth violence in Boston; to develop an intervention that would impact youth homicide; and the ability to evaluate the impact of this intervention.

Boston experienced an epidemic of youth homicide between the late 1980s and early 1990s. Homicides averaged forty-four per year between 1991 and 1995. Since Operation Ceasefire, Boston has witnessed a dramatic decrease in homicides. This is most likely due to a combination of the three strategic programs as well as neighborhood policing, tougher youth offender laws, and more prevention and intervention programs.

The outcomes of this strategy resulted in a citywide collaboration that informed communities, allowing Boston to become a national model for the reduction in youth gun violence. The Boston Police Department won the Innovations in American Government award from the Ford Foundation in 1997, as well as the Herman Goldstein award for the best program using problem-solving strategies.

See also Gun-Related Violence, Rates of; Gun-Related Violence, Types of; Policing Juveniles; Urban Juvenile Violence

FURTHER READING

Kennedy, D. (1997, March). Juvenile gun violence and gun markets in Boston. *National Institute of Justice.* Available at: www.ncjrs.gov/pdffiles/fs000160.pdf.

Kennedy, D., Braga, A., & Peihl, A. (2004). *Reducing gun violence: The Boston gun project's Operation Ceasefire.* New York: Diane Publishing Co.

Operation Ceasefire. (n.d.). Program in Criminal Justice Policy and Management. Available from: http://www.ksg.harvard.edu/criminaljustice/research/bgp.htm.

April C. Wilson

OREGON SOCIAL LEARNING CENTER (OSLC). The Oregon Social Learning Center (OSLC), an independent research center, identifies factors that lead to juvenile delinquency. Based in Eugene, OSLC focuses on family, peer group, and school experiences that influence social adjustment in the home, school, and community during childhood. OSLC Community Programs, a division of OSLC that became independent in 1999, implements treatment and prevention programs that were developed according to OSLC research.

OSLC formed to help communities prevent antisocial behavior by juveniles. Since an increasing number of states place young delinquents in group homes or in boot camps, OSLC researchers conducted studies to judge the effectiveness of such programs. Psychologists at OSLC examined the development of a group of two hundred boys over five years. They discovered that rule-breaking children trained others in misconduct. Boys who did not use alcohol or drugs before age thirteen, but who became friends with boys who did, became substance abusers two years later. The boys who received deviant training admitted to acts of delinquency. In conclusion, OSLC recommended that young delinquents should not be housed together because doing so magnifies the problem of juvenile delinquency.

Ineffective parenting strategies help create juvenile delinquents. Accordingly, OSLC examined parental responses to temper tantrums. Temper tantrums in preschool children can be an indication that a pattern is developing in which the children will become increasingly disobedient, rebellious, and aggressive as they grow older. Researchers studied aggressive boys in angry families. They found that when an angry exchange between a child and other family members lasts longer than eighteen seconds, the family had an increased chance of becoming violent. When talking or yelling continued, it often led to hitting. The child responds aggressively, the aggression is rewarded when the attacker withdraws, and the child learns to repeat such tactics.

To treat seriously emotionally disturbed children, OSLC developed several specialized foster care programs that were tested in Oregon in the 1980s. In the "Transitions" program, foster parents implemented a daily treatment plan that was similar to a school individual educational plan. A chart set out a child's daily schedule, with specific expectations about self-care, chores, school performance, and social behaviors. Completion of an activity earned points that could be traded for small prizes and special privileges. Points could also be lost for problem behaviors. Children who participated in the program had more success in adjusting outside of a hospital setting than children in a control group. In the "Monitor" program, teenagers with a history of chronic delinquency, who have been placed or who are at risk for placement in the state training school, are treated in foster care with systematic behavior management programs. The teenagers were subsequently incarcerated less frequently and for shorter periods of time than comparison youths. The specialized foster care programs have been operated by OSLC Community Programs since 1999.

See also Educational Opportunity and Juvenile Violence; Mentoring

FURTHER READING

Chamberlain, P., & Weinrott, M. (1990). Specialized foster care: Treating seriously emotionally disturbed children. *Children Today, 19*(1), 29–36.

OSLC Community Programs. (n.d.). Oregon Social Learning Center. Available from: www.oslccp.org.

Caryn Neumann

PARENS PATRIAE. Originating in medieval England, *parens patriae* is a doctrine that considers the king to be the benevolent father of the country. It then authorized the Crown to intervene in a family's affairs when a child's welfare appeared to be threatened.

Parens patriae was established as precedent in the states by the 1838 *Ex Parte Crouse* case, when Mary Ann Crouse was committed to the Philadelphia House of Refuge. Crouse's mother committed her for "vicious conduct" without the knowledge of her father. The court rejected the claim that Mary Ann's incarceration without a jury trial was a violation of the Sixth Amendment. In doing so, they determined that houses of refuge were primarily educational institutions, not punitive places. A key idea that emerged from the case was that the government can incarcerate children in order to prevent delinquency. The state, it was said, will act "in the child's best interest."

Although the concept of *parens patriae* was intended to protect children, it did not affect all types of children in the same way. Slave children were generally not offered the protections of *parens patriae*. Further, the vast majority of children taken from parents belonged to the lower socioeconomic classes. In addition, once a child was removed from his or her "incapable" parents and incarcerated in a reformatory, it was quite difficult for the parents to convince the courts they were actually able.

The concept of *parens patriae* was critical in the formation of juvenile courts that are distinct from criminal courts. The more central role of the judge, the less formal procedures, and the involvement of more players in the adjudication process all stem from the idea that children should be treated in court as an "ideal" parent might treat them outside of court. Hence the terminology differences—youth involved in juvenile justice are "delinquents," not criminals, and they are "adjudicated," not guilty. In addition, the idea that the state should not only respond to delinquency but can work to prevent it led to the establishment of status offenses, or acts that are only prohibited because of the offender's age. Under-age drinking and **curfew laws** are examples.

Critics contend that *parens patriae* is typically invoked as a form of elitism. Who gets to decide what is in a child's best interest? Critics maintain that the juvenile court today is far more like the adult criminal justice system in regard to procedures and punishments, but that juveniles are not afforded the same due process as adults. Further, many do not see the juvenile justice system as helpful to young people but as a way to control and label them.

See also Differences between Juvenile Justice and Criminal Justice; Illinois Juvenile Court; *In Loco Parentis*

FURTHER READING

Schlossman, S. (1977). *Love and the American delinquent.* Chicago: University of Chicago Press.

Watkins, J. (1998). *The juvenile justice century.* Durham, NC: Carolina Academic Press.

Laura L. Finley

PEACEABLE SCHOOLS. In recent years, there has been great concern over violence in schools. In actuality, schools are still among the safest places for young people. Experts put the risk of dying in a school shooting at one in two million. Yet the public has demanded that schools provide a safe place for students to be educated, and they want to see districts take obvious measures to this end. These demands have largely been addressed via technological and punitive responses. Schools have increasingly used a variety of surveillance methods intended to deter students from being violent, such as metal detectors and school police officers. A number of legal and disciplinary responses have also been implemented with the goal of making schools safer, including zero tolerance laws, dress codes, and drug testing. In essence, these interventions are focused on controlling student behavior, which is often ineffective and may bring about greater violence.

These measures, however, do very little to address the climate or culture of the school, which contributes significantly to the amount of violence that will occur. Nor do they address **systemic violence**; violence against students that is built into the way schools operate. Examples of systemic violence include tracking programs that create unnecessary hierarchies that limit some students and promote elitism, discipline policies that treat all students as though they are bad, and teaching practices that do not allow students creativity and power. Concurrent with the trend of implementing greater security measures, however, has been a powerful but less visible movement toward creating peaceable classrooms and peaceable schools.

Peaceable classrooms are places where peace-related themes are integrated into the curriculum. More than that, though, they are classrooms where teachers share power with students, where hierarchical relationships are minimized and cooperative endeavors are emphasized, where all people are treated with respect and all views are welcomed, and where conflict is positively managed. Students do not simply work in groups, but do so in ways that stress the important and unique contribution of each individual. Peaceable schools use these same concepts on a broader scale, integrating them into schoolwide policies and practices. The notion of peaceable schools goes well beyond just violence reduction. Peaceable schools are places where everyone feels important and where all students have ample opportunity to explore their learning potential. More than simply teaching about peace and justice, peaceable schools recognize that students learn from the way schools are structured and the methods used. Social justice, then, is an important component of peaceable schools. In sum, peaceable schools are a comprehensive approach that uses multiple strategies to address the multiple facets of students' lives.

The foundation of a peaceable school is the community. Schools alone cannot eliminate violence. Communities can support the goal of developing a peaceable school by establishing community approaches stressing nonviolence, both for juveniles and adults. This ensures that what is being taught at school is reinforced elsewhere. Community efforts are most successful when they involve young people in creating and maintaining services. Further, communities must recognize peacemaking as a long-term effort.

Creating a peaceable school requires commitment by staff and staff training in **conflict resolution** as well as student involvement. All involved must understand that conflict is inevitable and learn to manage it, not through force and domination but by reason and understanding. Another important component of peaceable schools is the notion of emotional intelligence; that is, all people have a need to express their emotions, and schools must be designed to allow this expression. If students cannot express emotions, and schools do not work with students on appropriate ways to express their feelings, violence may occur. Peaceable schools operate in ways that provide multiple, diverse means for students to express themselves. Peaceable schools also use controversy in a constructive manner, helping students to hone their critical thinking skills.

The concept of peaceable schools has been implemented at all levels, but is more common in elementary schools. Peer mediation programs are more popular with middle and high schools, although these are limited in that they tend only to affect the mediators and those being mediated, not the entire school.

Little evaluation of the peaceable schools movement has occurred to date. One state that has widely embraced the notion is Tennessee, where 75 percent of schools are involved in creating a peaceable setting. From 1997 to 2000, these schools saw a 14 percent drop in suspension rates, suggesting peaceable schools are effective. Some districts saw up to 80 percent reductions. Further, students in the state have increased critical thinking skills.

Evaluations of programs similar in nature, such as the Resolving Conflict Creatively Program (RCCP), widely used in New York, have found that students retain more positive behaviors throughout the school year in comparison with students not exposed to the program. Teachers who have been trained in and are working toward creating peaceable schools remark that, while it does not eliminate problems, problem behavior is minimized. Teachers report that students take responsibility for resolving their problem behavior much quicker than those without the skills provided through the peaceable schools initiative. Teachers report using discipline as a learning experience, rather than as a punishment. Research with students has shown they feel as though adults care more about them in a peaceable school setting. They also feel more comfortable expressing themselves. In sum, they felt that not only student-to-student violence had been decreased, but **systemic violence** as well.

FURTHER READING

Brock-Utne, B. (1985). *Educating for peace: A feminist perspective*. New York: Pergamon Press.

Caulfield, S. (2000). Creating peaceable schools. *Annals, AAPSS, 567,* 170–185.

Deutsch, M. (1993). Educating for a peaceful world. *American Psychologist, 48*(2), 510–517.

Eisler, R. (2000). *Tomorrow's children*. Boulder, CO: Westview.

Laura L. Finley

PERSONALITY THEORIES. Personality, typically defined as characteristic ways of thinking and behaving, plays an important role in understanding individual differences in violence among juveniles. Unlike sociological theories of juvenile violence, which focus attention on groups, communities, and societies, personality theories focus on individuals. Personality theories relevant to the study of juvenile violence can be organized into two broad categories: structural models and syndrome-specific models.

Structural models of personality attempt to capture the whole of human personality into a set of domains or factors and are thus thought of as universal, in the sense that everyone can be located within its structure. There are four examples of these universal structural models that are important for understanding violent and antisocial behavior among juveniles. These include the Five Factor Model (FFM) of personality, Cloninger's temperament and character model, Eysenck's three-factor model, and Tellegen's three-factor model.

The FFM of personality consists of neuroticism (i.e., emotional stability), extraversion (i.e., sociability), openness to experience (i.e., trying or considering new things), agreeableness, and conscientiousness. Cloninger's model is comprised of three temperament factors: novelty seeking, harm avoidance, and reward dependence, as well as four character domains: persistence, self-directedness, cooperativeness, and self-transcendence (i.e., spiritual activities). Eysenck's model includes psychoticism (i.e., callous, unemotional, and impulsive), extraversion, and neuroticism factors. Finally, Tellegen's model consists of positive emotionality, negative emotionality, and constraint (i.e., self-control). As one can readily see, there is significant overlap in the contents of these structural models. Likewise, all four have achieved good reliability and validity in multiple studies. With respect to antisocial behavior, all four models contain certain factors, such as agreeableness, psychoticism, novelty seeking, and negative emotionality, that have been shown to be related to a range of problem behaviors. However, it should be noted that the majority of these studies were with samples of adults. These models are likely to be useful with juveniles but may require some modification.

Syndrome-specific models, exemplified by the study of psychopathic personality (sometimes termed sociopathic personality or antisocial personality disorder), have emerged in recent years with a flurry of empirical investigations of juveniles. Although many descriptions of psychopathic personality have been put forth, most assert that psychopathic personality consists of individuals who are mostly male, aggressive, self-centered, callous, guiltless, impulsive, sensation-seeking, interpersonally exploitive, deceptive, low in fear, and unable to learn socially approved ways of satisfying immediate needs. One rationale for studying psychopathic traits in childhood and adolescence is that a small number of offenders, **the Chronic 6 Percent**, commit a noteworthy number of violent crimes, and early identification of these juveniles might forestall lengthy and costly patterns of violent behavior. In addition, past research on psychopathic personality traits among adults has shown considerable success in predicting future violence. It seems probable that psychopathic personality traits are recognizable in childhood and adolescence and do not appear suddenly in adulthood. Identification of psychopathic personality traits in children and adolescents could facilitate targeted prevention and intervention efforts to these youth.

Research on violence and adolescent psychopathic traits has found consistent positive associations between measures of violence and psychopathic traits in numerous studies of juveniles. As such, findings from these studies of juveniles parallel findings in the adult psychopathological literature. The proliferation of juvenile psychopathy studies has not involved cross-national samples outside of North America. However, differences between ethnic groups have been reported. Overall, there is a trend in the evidence suggesting that the construct applies to all ethnicities.

Some theories pertaining to the origins or etiology of psychopathic personality traits include frontal lobe dysfunction theory (seat of executive governance and self-control), genetic theory, lateralization theory (processing emotional meanings related to language differently than non-psychopaths), and low fear. Despite numerous unresolved theories as to the origins of psychopathic personality, few theories have attempted to integrate the study of psychopathic traits into a general theory of delinquency and antisocial behavior. Recent applications of psychopathic personality to juveniles have met with controversy when used as a basis for decision-making in the juvenile justice system. The concern raised by clinical or juvenile justice applications of this personality syndrome involves the potentially harmful labeling effects on youth.

Supporters of psychopathic personality assessment believe that appropriate uses of the model are predicated on its reliable and valid measurement. The most widely accepted current measure of psychopathy is the *Psychopathy Checklist: Youth Version* (PCL: YV). The disadvantages of this measurement instrument are the amount of time necessary to administer it (i.e., up to three hours) and the required access to sensitive legal and psychiatric case file information. There are two primary approaches to assessing psychopathic personality traits among adolescents. The first is to use existing personality inventories, such as the instrument that assesses personality based on the five-factor model previously described, the NEO-PI-R or Cloninger and colleagues' (1993) Temperament and Character Inventory (TCI). This approach is consistent with the theory that psychopathic personality, like other personality disorders, can be characterized as extremes of common personality traits. The second approach involves the use of the PCL:YV or other recently developed self-report measures.

See also Biosocial theories; Chronic 6 Percent; Cognitive Theories; Psychodynamic Theories; Trait Theories

FURTHER READING

Edens, J., Skeem, J., Crusie, K., & Cauffman, E. (2001). Assessment of "juvenile psychopathy" and its association with violence: A critical review. *Behavioral Sciences and the Law, 19*, 53–80.

Hare, R. (1993). *Without conscience: The disturbing world of the psychopaths among us*. New York: Simon & Schuster.

Miller, J., & Lynam, D. (2001). Structural models of personality and their relation to antisocial behavior: A meta-analytic review. *Criminology, 39*, 765–798.

Vaughn, M., & Howard, M. (2005). The construct of psychopathy and its role in contributing to the study of serious, violent, and chronic youth offending. *Youth Violence and Juvenile Justice: An Interdisciplinary Journal, 3*, 235–252.

Michael G. Vaughn

POLICING JUVENILES. Police handling of juveniles has undergone several major changes in philosophy and practice throughout history. As the gatekeepers of the juvenile justice system, the decisions an officer makes while in contact with a juvenile sets the stage for other decision-making points in the juvenile justice system, making police a critical component of this process. Policing juveniles should not be equated with arresting juveniles. While juvenile arrests accounted for 16 percent of all arrests and 15 percent of all violent crime arrests in 2003, police officers spend a lot of their time with juveniles resolving situations in which no law has been broken, such as quieting noise. In addition, police officers are also responsible for helping children who have been victims of crime or who may need other services.

The practice of policing juveniles has undergone vast changes over the past several decades. Police have evolved from treating juveniles the same as adults to developing specialized units to process juveniles. Many juvenile matters that are now considered criminal or status offenses (behavior that is not illegal but that may be dangerous to the child or the public) were ignored or handled informally until the late 1800s and early 1900s **child**

saving movement. At this point, police officers began to handle offenses they previously ignored on a more formal level. Female police officers were often hired in police departments as specialists who tended to juvenile matters.

Until the 1960s, the response to juvenile crime was primarily reactive and juveniles were denied many due process rights. While juveniles gradually gained many of the same rights as adults, policing juveniles was still primarily reactive in nature. It was not until the community policing era emerged that police officers began to take a more proactive approach with juveniles in the community.

With the continuing development of new policing strategies, police departments and individual officers have become more proactive in their efforts to stop juvenile delinquency before it starts. Officers in community-oriented units believe that becoming closer to the juveniles in their patrol areas ultimately helps them prevent juveniles from committing crimes. They also believe a hands-on approach helps police enforce laws because juveniles are willing to share information about area crime. **School police officers** are used in many areas to help bring police departments closer to the juvenile populations they serve. Officers are able to informally handle many cases, resolving issues without formally processing the juvenile of interest. Some police departments are partnering with probation offices to help monitor juveniles on probation to provide more supervision in an effort to prevent recidivism.

Another goal of the hands-on approach with juveniles is to improve juvenile opinions about the police. Juveniles tend to be more negative or neutral in their opinions about police than adults. Opinions about the police seem to vary according to race and gender. This is important information to consider because one factor influencing the police decision to arrest juveniles is suspect demeanor. A more negative demeanor toward police officers increases the chances of being arrested.

Police officers also provide services to juvenile victims of crimes. Most crimes against juveniles are not reported to the police, and the crimes that are reported present special issues. Children are most frequently victimized by someone they know, often a family member. This necessitates that police coordinate with other service agencies, such as child protective services, to determine the proper course of action. School resource officers are now a prime resource for children who experience criminal victimization of all types. This is important given the high level of violence experienced by children at school or en route to or from school. Officers also enforce some laws, such as curfew, to protect children from harm. After several juveniles had been violently victimized in Indianapolis, police have been citing juveniles with curfew violations in efforts to protect them. Other police departments do the same, demonstrating the variety of activities involved in policing juveniles.

FURTHER READING

Bazemore, G., & Senjo, S. (n.d.). Police encounters with juveniles revisited: An exploratory study of themes and styles in community policing. *Policing*, 20. Available from Proquest Database.

Finn, P., McDevitt, J., Lassiter, W., Shively, M., & Rich, T. (2005). *Case studies of 19 school resource officer programs*. Document Number 209271. Washington, DC: U.S. Department of Justice.

Hurst, Y., Frank, J., & Browning, S. (2000). The attitudes of juveniles toward the police. *Policing: An International Journal of Police Strategies and Management*, 23, 37–53.

Myers, S. (2004). Police encounters with juvenile suspects: Explaining the use of authority and provision of support, executive summary report. Washington, DC: U.S. Department of Justice.

Office for Victims of Crime. (2002). *Reporting school violence*. Washington, DC: U.S. Department of Justice.

Office of Juvenile Justice and Delinquency Prevention. (1996). *Juvenile offenders and victims: 1996 update on violence*. Washington, DC: U.S. Department of Justice.

Piliavin, I., & Briar, S. (1964). Police encounters with juveniles. *American Journal of Sociology, 70*, 206–14.

Platt, A. (1999). The triumph of benevolence: The origins of the juvenile justice system in the United States. In B. Feld (Ed.), *Readings in juvenile justice administration*, pp. 20–35. New York: Oxford University Press.

Snyder, H. (2005). Juvenile arrests 2003. *Juvenile Justice Bulletin*. Washington, DC: Office of Juvenile Justice and Delinquency Prevention, U.S. Department of Justice.

Taylor, T., Turner, K., Esbensen, F., & Winfree, L. (2001). Coppin' an attitude: Attitudinal differences among juveniles toward police. *Journal of Criminal Justice, 29*, 295–305.

TheIndyChannel.com. (n.d.). IPD to step up enforcement of youth curfew. Available from: www.theindychannel.com.

Wendy Perkins

POWER-CONTROL THEORY. Power-control theory, as formulated by sociologist John Hagan, mixes elements of conflict, control, and feminist theories and contends that criminal behavior is highly influenced by family structure, a structure that is reflective of the patriarchal nature of the greater society. Issues of class and gender and their relation to delinquency are at the core of Hagan's structural criminology.

Theories based on power are conflict approaches in which it is posited that there are unequal levels of power in relationships, such as employee/employer associations. Control theories normally focus on patterns of conflict within the institution of family. Hagan synthesizes these two institutional concepts in his sociological theory of deviance behavior.

According to the theory, individuals, especially juveniles, are products of various levels of control that are exercised by their families. In his analysis, Hagan differentiates between two types of family patterns: patriarchal and egalitarian. The former type is traditional and assumes that there are two separate spheres that govern behavior. The men's sphere positions the adult male in families as being the undisputed head of the household and focuses on men's role as the provider, therefore seeing the male as oriented toward occupational aspects of life. The women's sphere places adult females in subservient roles, occupying a subordinate status to males and an orientation to family, reproduction, and household concerns.

In egalitarian families, which have become more prevalent only in recent decades, there is a general sharing of familial responsibilities, a narrowing of the division of labor based on gender status and less emphasis placed on specific gender roles. Patriarchal families are still the norm in most modern societies, while egalitarian families are less common.

In Hagan's theory, types of control over boys differ from that of girls, especially in patriarchal families. Boys have lower levels of parental control while the actions of girls are dominated more closely through techniques used to limit their freedom. Due to more direct and consistent contact with the children, it is normally mothers, rather than fathers, who apply the controls and perpetuate the ideology of the separate spheres for males and females. Borrowing a typology from social psychologist Carol Gilligan, Hagan states that the two types of control exerted on children are either relational (referring to control measures that involve affective or relationship ties) or instrumental (referring to control strategies that involve surveillance and restrictions on freedom). Families of the patriarchal type will have higher rates of male delinquency due to the relative freedom allowed boys and lower rates of female delinquency due to higher levels of social constraint from their families. This has traditionally been the case in Western society. As social changes have developed in which married women are now more prevalent in the occupational sphere, an egalitarian structure has emerged in some families, and in these families, it is expected that there will be less differentiation in male and female delinquency rates. It is due to this greater level of freedom for girls that they will experience similar risk factors, resulting in higher delinquency rates for girls.

Hagan conceptualizes three levels, moving from a micro to macro level of analysis. The first involves the social-psychological process that accounts for the juvenile behavior under study. The second level refers to the social positions that are reflective of gender and delinquency status. The last level is the class structure in which families are organized, based on the prevailing cultural structure as designated by the state.

Generally, Hagan's theory assumes that social norms governing gender power relations, especially as it relates to power derived from employment and financial status, will be passed down to individual families, who in turn use certain methods to control the behavior of the adolescent children. Delinquency is fun, according to Hagan, and is basically an expression of freedom. In patriarchal families, these expressions are allowed for young males, who frequently go further than society allows in pursuit of enjoyment. At this point, delinquency occurs. Girls, having fewer options for pursuing these pleasurable and risky activities, are less likely to engage in acts deemed by society to be deviant.

In an elaboration of the theory, Hagan added two other elements that have caught the attention of other sociologists and criminologists. He suggests that adolescents often experience "deviant role exits" in which teens attempt to deal with the pressures that extend from the resistance of familial control; the situation is especially grave for females who often turn to suicidal ideation or ideas about running away from home. Later, Hagan expanded the role exit concept to age as well as gender stratification, adding a developmental aspect to the concept. The other element is "vulnerability to crime," which refers to the phenomenon that victimization and offending behaviors are linked. As it affects females, an implied contract exists in which women in traditional families trade freedom for protection from victimization while women in more egalitarian families trade a level of protection for increased freedom, whereby they increase both their chances for offending and being victimized.

Hagan tested his theory in Canada and found empirical support for power-control theory. Other researchers have tested the power-control theory but have obtained mixed results. Recently, Hagan has broadened the theory by suggesting that offending behavior by juveniles has its basis in stressors from developmental and social processes. The resulting stress manifests itself in differential consequences; the consequence for females is depression and for boys, it is the excessive use of intoxicants. He further proposes that the despair that is related to the developmental stage of adolescence has implications into later life that could lead to various types of failure.

FURTHER READING

Blackwell, B., Sellers, C., & Schlaupitz, S. (2002). A power-control theory of vulnerability to crime and adolescent role exits revisited. *Review of Sociology and Anthropology, 39,* 199–219.

Hagan, J. (1989). *Structural criminology.* New Brunswick, NJ: Rutgers University Press.

Hagan, J., McCarthy, B., & Foster, H. (2002). A gendered theory of delinquency and despair in the life course. *Acta Sociologica, 45,* 37–47.

Leonard Steverson

PRESCRIPTION DRUGS. Prescription drugs have the capability to alter brain activity and lead to addiction. Given this potential and the rise of prescription drug abuse, there are well-founded concerns about these drugs contributing to juvenile violence. One of the major ways to track the drug use trends of American youth is a large national survey known as the **Monitoring the Future Study (MTF)**. According to data from the 2003 MTF survey, approximately 10 percent of high school seniors reported nonmedical use of the opioid hydrocodone. To place this figure in perspective, the use of hydrocodone was the third most-abused illicit substance, next to marijuana and amphetamines. Findings indicate that girls and boys abuse prescription drugs equally.

Prescription drugs fall into three broad classes: opioids, central nervous system (CNS) depressants, and central nervous system (CNS) stimulants. Opioids include such medications as morphine and codeine and are also termed narcotics. Other common opioids abused by youth are oxycodone (OxyContin), hydrocodone (Vicodin), propoxyphene (Darvon), and hydromorphone (Dilaudid). These drugs are prescribed for their analgesic or pain-relieving properties. CNS depressants work by decreasing brain activity and are used to treat anxiety, sleep disorders, and other stress-related disorders. It is common for the abuse of these drugs to occur in tandem with other drugs of abuse, such as alcohol, marijuana, and cocaine. Examples of CNS depressants include barbiturates and benzodiazepines. Benzodiazepines are more commonly abused and include diazepam (Valium), alprazolam (Xanax), and chlordiazepoxide (Librium). CNS stimulants work by increasing brain activity. Thus, attention and alertness are heightened. Commonly abused prescription stimulants are methylphenidate (Ritalin) and the amphetamines Dexedrine and Adderall. Ritalin and Adderall are typically prescribed for attention deficit-disorder (ADD) and attention deficit-hyperactivity disorder (ADHD).

Either through physical dependence or compulsive taking, all three classes of prescription drugs can have serious health consequences. Opioid misuse, for example, depresses breathing and can lead to death. Like opioids, CNS depressants are physically addictive. These drugs also have the potential to cause seizures and death, particularly when mixed with alcohol or other prescription medications. With respect to stimulant abuse, dangerous increases in body temperature and heart rate are possible.

The relationship between prescription drug abuse and juvenile violence is poorly understood. Although it is known that there is an association between substance abuse and violent behavior, the mechanisms, both physiological and social, are unresolved. Because prescription drug abusers also tend to use other drugs, it is difficult to sort out the direct association between a prescription drug and a violent episode. For stimulant abuse, the potential for violent behavior can be a result of heightened feelings of hostility and paranoia.

See also Alcohol; Cocaine and Crack Cocaine; Heroin; Marijuana; Methamphetamine; National Household Survey of Drug Abuse; Stimulants

FURTHER READING

Colvin, R. (1995). *Prescription drug abuse: The hidden epidemic.* Omaha, NE: Addicus Books.

Johnston, L., O'Malley, P., & Bachman, J. (2004). *Monitoring the future: National results on adolescent drug use; Overview of key findings, 2004.* National Institute on Drug Abuse, Department of Health and Human Services.

Roberts, J. (2000). *Prescription drug abuse.* New York: Rosen.

Michael G. Vaughn

PRIDE SURVEYS. Pride Surveys is an independently owned company created to produce a low-cost and effective means of collecting self-report evaluation measures of juvenile participation in drug, alcohol, and tobacco use. The activities of Pride Surveys were once part of the National Parents' Resource Institute for Drug Education (P.R.I.D.E.), a nonprofit organization devoted to drug abuse prevention through the education of parents and youth. Pride Surveys split off as its own company in 1998.

The original Pride Survey was created in 1982 in an effort to bridge the gap between national drug and alcohol usage data and local level substance abuse-related issues. The first surveys were administered to students in grades six through twelve. Shortly thereafter, in 1988, the survey was expanded to include students in grades four through six, and eventually parents as well as faculty and staff were participating in the questionnaire process. The initial survey was further expanded to measure a wide range of youthful behavioral influences that impact student learning, including family, discipline, gang involvement, violence, and safety concerns.

The objective of Pride Surveys is to help schools, school districts, and other community-based organizations evaluate and understand the activities that juveniles are participating in, with particular emphasis on drug, alcohol, and tobacco usage. Juvenile participation in drug and alcohol experimentation and usage has been a concern for decades, with much of the empirical data suggesting a general increase in participation and a general decline in the age of involvement. Measurement techniques and prevention efforts are widespread and take many forms throughout the United States. In 1998, Pride Surveys was designated by federal law as an official measurement of adolescent drug use in the United States.

Pride Surveys allow for the collection of strictly anonymous data from four population groups: students in grades four through six, grades six through twelve, parents, and faculty and staff. The grades four through six surveys ask students to respond to questions pertaining to usage within the past year, tolerance for drug usage, accessibility of drugs, conduct at school, family life and discipline, violent behavior, and more. The survey most often used is the grades six through twelve questionnaire, which asks respondents about the age of onset of usage, perceived risks, ease of obtaining, location of usage, family life, academic achievement, and more.

The parental survey is designed to facilitate parental involvement in the school-based survey. The parent questionnaire asks respondents to report information about their child and their child's peers at school, in the home, and in the community. Parents are asked to reflect on their child's behaviors and their own perceptions about drug usage. The faculty and staff questionnaire asks teachers and staff questions pertaining to their perception of student drug use, school safety, knowledge of school drug policies, and more.

Pride Surveys provide all necessary questionnaires to be disseminated to a population of juveniles in school. The surveys take approximately twenty minutes to complete and are then returned to Pride Surveys by the contracting agency for thorough analysis. Results are then reported and are compared nationally, across states, and over time.

FURTHER READING

Greenfield, T. K., & Rogers, J. D. (1999). Who drinks most of the alcohol in the U.S.? The policy implications. *Journal of Studies on Alcohol, 60*(1) 78–89.

Pride Surveys. (n.d.). *Measuring student behavior.* Pride Surveys Website: http://www. pridesurveys .com/index.htm.

2002–2003 National Summary, Grades 6 through 12. (2003). *Pride surveys.* Available at: http://pridesurveys.com/main/supportfiles/ns0203.pdf.

Jeffrey A. Walsh

PROBATION. One of the first efforts at addressing the dehumanizing conditions used with youth in criminal justice was the introduction of probation in 1841. Massachusetts was the first state to use probation with juveniles in an effort to help them avoid prison, and all but Wyoming had juvenile probation laws by 1927. By 1890 probation was a mandatory feature of the court. The use of probation was an important precursor to the development of the juvenile justice system, which recognizes the developmental differences between youth and adults and was designed to help, not punish, delinquent youth.

Probation today involves the assignment of an offender to the control of the county probation department with a set of rules and conditions to follow. Those who do not follow the rules and conditions may have their probation revoked and may be incarcerated. Probation is supposed to emphasize treatment and is based on the idea that the offender is not a threat and can be better rehabilitated in the community than in jail or prison. Juveniles on probation can be placed in a number of different community programs, including drug treatment, counseling, and anger management. Further, youth on probation typically face conditions such as mandatory school attendance and curfew restrictions, as well as restrictions on where they must reside and with whom they can associate. Conditions might also include restitution or some type of reparation. Probation is the most commonly used sentence for juveniles who are adjudicated delinquent.

Despite the "get tough" trends of the 1980s and 1990s, use of probation with youth has only expanded. The nature of probation has become more conservative, however, focusing less on rehabilitation and more on control. Generally, this has meant additional conditions and more restrictive penalties.

Probation officers play a critical role throughout the entire juvenile justice process. They are involved at four different stages: intake, predisposition, post-adjudication, and post-disposition. During the intake process, probation officers are the primary screening mechanism in determining whether a case needs to be referred for judicial action or to a community service agency. The officer has discussions with the offender and his or her family to discern whether the situation would best be handled in court or elsewhere. During predisposition, the probation officer helps guide the decision to release or detain a juvenile. This is done largely through the predisposition report, a clinical diagnosis of the youth's problems and needs submitted to the court. Included in the report are the juvenile's feelings about the incidence, as well as a summary of relations with peers and family, success in school, and a number of other environmental factors that might affect the way the youth should be handled. At post-adjudication, the probation officer helps the court to reach their decision regarding disposition. The largest amount of a probation officer's time is spent in the post-disposition phase, where he or she supervises juveniles placed on probation. Sometimes the probation officer is a source of counseling, but more typically makes referrals to other agencies for needed services. Further, recommendations from probation officers typically dictate when an offender's probation is terminated, as well as when probation is revoked.

There are a number of forms of probation. Juvenile **intensive supervised probation** involves treating a special group of serious offenders who would normally have been sent to a secure treatment facility. The main goal of intensive supervised probation is to keep these juveniles out of jail, and an officer with a small caseload checks in with juveniles on an almost daily basis. A secondary goal is control; the more frequent and intense scrutiny helps ensure these offenders are not a danger to the community. Third, intensive supervision is intended to help juvenile offenders establish community ties and work toward reintegration. An important facet of reintegration is completing education, something far easier for a juvenile in intensive or traditional probation than one who is incarcerated. Research has offered mixed results about intensive probation programs. The failure rate does tend to be high, although it is unclear if that is because of the youth or because the conditions are too harsh. Younger offenders who commit petty crimes are the most likely to fail in intensive programs. A study from Mississippi also found intensive probation to be less cost-effective than traditional probation or a special cognitive behavioral treatment. Further, many probation officers assert that intensive probation caseloads are still too high for it to be truly effective.

Another innovation used in conjunction with probation is that of house arrest, whereby an individual may be allowed to stay in the community rather than jail but is confined to his or her home for specific periods and may only leave for specified reasons, such as school or work. Offenders on house arrest can be monitored via home visits, random phone calls, and/or **electronic devices**.

Balanced probation is another form of probation. Balanced probation seeks to integrate community protection with holding the juvenile accountable and meeting his or her individualized needs. Here the probation officer establishes a specific program to help the offender while also helping the offender take responsibility for his or her actions. Balanced approaches have met with great success in a number of places. In Florida, juvenile offenders on probation help create shelters for abused, abandoned, and HIV-positive infants. The California 8% Solution is a comprehensive, multiagency program run by the probation department and directed at the most **chronic offenders**. The program provides those identified as at-risk with outside schools, transportation to and from school, drug and alcohol abuse counseling, employment preparation and job placement, and intensive family counseling.

Wilderness probation is another form of probation designed to use outdoor activities to help juvenile offenders improve social skills as well as self-esteem and self-control. Wilderness programs are often modeled on **boot camps**. Evaluations have produced mixed results, but more research is needed, as few programs have been evaluated to date.

Proponents of probation assert that it is an appropriate disposition for nonviolent offenders. They also maintain it allows the court to tailor the program specifically to the offender, allowing for greater chance of rehabilitation and better opportunity for reintegration. Further, probation is far cheaper than incarceration. Finally, keeping youth out of jail or prison decreases the chance they will socialize with and learn from other offenders. Evaluations have found it to be effective when adequate surveillance and supervision are included.

Opponents express a number of concerns. Some are opposed to the notion of probation, seeing it as too lenient and a danger to the community. Others express concern with the administration of probation services. First, there is much concern that probation caseloads are far too large to be effective. Second, since probation is often assigned for an indefinite period, probation officers have a great deal of discretion in making length of assignment and revocation decisions. This provides great potential for abuse. The great variation in the probation conditions a youth might be assigned can also result in bias. Research has found that probation officers are more likely to consider delinquency among black youth a feature of internal attributes rather than environmental factors, and consequently black youth serve longer terms with stricter rules and conditions. Appellate courts have invalidated probation conditions that are cruel or unfair.

FURTHER READING

Abadinsky, H. (2003). *Probation and parole: Theory and practice*, 9th ed. Upper Saddle River, NJ: Prentice Hall.

Champion, D. (2001). *Probation, parole, and community corrections*, 4th ed. Upper Saddle River, NJ: Prentice Hall.

Getis, V. (2000). *The juvenile court & the progressives*. Urbana: University of Illinois Press.

Petersilia, J. (2001). *Reforming probation and parole in the 21st century*. New York: American Correctional Association.

Laura L. Finley

PROBLEM BEHAVIOR SYNDROME (PBS). Problem behavior syndrome (PBS) is the phrase used to describe the tendency for a number of distinct negative characteristics of youth and adolescents to cluster together. As youth engage in negative behavior in one characteristic, they are more likely to be involved in other negative characteristics as well. The study of a series of problem behaviors in adolescence originated with Jessor and Jessor's pioneering longitudinal studies on the onset and combining of selected problem behaviors among youth in 1977. Since then, research has mushroomed, and the number of problem behaviors included in studies varies from three to over ten characteristics. One challenge is to determine actual measures of problem behavior in studies.

Common types of PBS clusters include a basic scheme of three items: problem drinking, cigarette smoking, and general delinquency. A four-item scheme generally includes serious delinquency, drug use, poor academic grades, and externalizing behavioral problems, such as hyperactivity and aggression. The five-item scheme presented in problem behavior theory is problem drinking, marijuana use, other illicit drug use, cigarette smoking, and general deviant behavior. Items are measured separately, and in some research, the items form a cumulative measure referred to as the multiple problem behavior index. A ten-item scale has also been used with some of the same behaviors: alcohol, smoking, marijuana, hard drugs, sexual activity, major delinquency, minor delinquency, direct aggression, indirect aggression, and gambling.

Problem behaviors are generally prohibited conduct for youth, and being considered unacceptable, violation will lead to punishment. In the family and in school environments, these problem behaviors are counterbalanced with conventional behaviors, such as getting strong grades, church and civic involvement, and refraining from deviance.

The longitudinal research method is used to study the emergence of these problem behaviors among cohorts of youth who are reinterviewed as they move through youth, adolescence, young adulthood, and adulthood. Each phase is called a wave, and by examining the onset and extent of problem behaviors, researchers can determine the age that problem behaviors begin, the number of problem behaviors reported, and the persistence of these problem behaviors into adulthood.

Samples for PBS studies are self-report questionnaires administered in schools or questionnaires sent to the home. Cohort samples may be a random selection of youth prior to problem behaviors or focused on at-risk youth.

A theoretical model forms the basis of problem behavior syndrome. Problem behavior theory is an extensive theoretical explanation of human development of problem behaviors. The model posits that problem behaviors are a function of the effects of socio-environmental and context variables and social psychological variables. Both of these variables can generate risk factors leading to problem behaviors and protective factors reducing problem behaviors and increasing conventionality.

Initial research findings using youth samples showed that problem behavior reveals a clustering that is deemed a syndrome, a simultaneous existence of multiple problem behaviors at nearly the same time. An examination of problem behaviors (not including delinquent behavior) over two time periods has been a standard approach, assessing subjects once in adolescence and once in adulthood over ten years later. The same youth are compared in measures of problem behavior and conventionality. Research generally finds that the problem behavior cluster in adolescence is still found when the adolescents mature and, as adults, reveals a conventional (avoid problem behaviors) or unconventional (engage in problem behaviors) response to problem-solving. Other research did not incorporate all variables in problem behavior theory; as a consequence, the term PBS has limited use and has generally been replaced with the term problem behaviors (PB).

Other research developments examine co-occurrence of problem behaviors, comparing serious delinquency, school problems, drug use, and mental health problems. Overlap in PBs would be shown by a high percentage of the sample involved in most of the PBs. The findings showed that most problem behavior is temporary, lasting less than a year. Persistent PBs were shown in approximately 9 percent of the sample (three years of serious delinquency), which correlates to juvenile violent behavior, particularly in assault and robbery. While the connections among persistent PBs are statistically significant, most serious delinquents are not drug users and do not have school problems and mental health problems. The research shows that persistent delinquent youth may not have additional PBs in all cases. However, youth showing PBs of mental health, school, and drug problems that also are seriously delinquent range from a third to half, further diminishing the applicability of the medical term "syndrome."

The weakness of PBS is that it is deterministic in suggesting that the display of one problem behavior invariably links with other problem behaviors. While PBs show clustering, it is not inevitable nor is it demonstrated in every case. Few studies adopt the comprehensive problem behavior theory model; rather, most modify it for their own purposes. While the PBS-based studies are useful for intervention approaches, it also may be used as a tool to stereotype youth with multiple problems as hardened personalities, so they may be unresponsive to services and treatment. The assumption of PBS research underscores prevention and intervention, but it does not address concerns about adjudication and sentencing of youth. Although some studies show co-occurrence in PBS, the persistence may be short-lived, perhaps less than several years. Finally, not all the problem behaviors co-occur; select items may co-occur in pairs or more but not necessarily all at once.

PBS represents an extensive multidisciplinary research stream that has produced trailblazing developmental studies on the onset of delinquency. It promotes interventions that can prevent violence and delinquency more effectively than punitive measures.

See also Developmental Theories; Personality Theories; Social Development Model

FURTHER READING

Donovan, J., Jessor, R., & Costa, F. (1988). Syndrome of problem behavior in adolescence: A replication. *Journal of Consulting and Clinical Psychology, 56*(5), 762–765.

Jessor, R. (Ed.). (1998). *New perspectives on adolescent risk behavior.* New York: Cambridge University Press.

Jessor, R., & Jessor, S. (1977). *Problem behavior and psychosocial development: A longitudinal study of youth.* New York: Academic Press.

Willoughby, T., Chalmers, H., & Busseri, M. (2004). Where is the syndrome? Examining co-occurrence among multiple problem behaviors in adolescence. *Journal of Consulting and Clinical Psychology, 72*(6), 85–92.

James Steinberg

PSYCHODYNAMIC THEORY. The term *psychodynamic* refers to a broad range of psychological theories that explore the influence of instinctive drives, forces, and developmental experiences on one's personality. Psychodynamic theories range in focus from unconscious motives, unconscious conflicts, conscious experiences and their interaction with the unconscious to the impact of social factors on the human psyche. Accordingly, psychodynamic theorists argue that juvenile violence can be understood by examining internal processes, personality development, motivation, drives, and childhood experiences.

Psychodynamic theories emerged from Freudian psychoanalysis, which emphasizes the unconscious components of one's personality. Sigmund Freud proposed that childhood sexuality and unconscious motivations influence personality. Therefore, mental illness/personality disorders are caused by unconscious and unresolved conflicts in the mind that arise in early childhood. This conflict impedes the balanced development of three systems that constitute the human psyche: the id, the ego, and the superego. These concepts were first presented by Freud in his book, *The Ego and the Id* (1923). The id is a completely unconscious reservoir of primitive energy that strives to satisfy basic sexual and aggressive drives. The ego is the part of the id that is in touch with reality because it has been influenced by the external world. It mediates and maintains psychic balance between the unconscious id and the conscious superego. The superego is the part of the ego that is our conscious. It is an abstract representation of cultural, ethical, and moral values that imposes standards of behavior. The superego translates the drives of the id into appropriate social behaviors.

Some of Freud's students, Alfred Adler and Carl Jung, broke away but maintained a basic element of Freudian theory, the unconscious. They assumed that much of our mental life is unconscious. We are often experiencing inner struggles among our wishes, fears, and values. What differentiates these theorists from Freud is the view that childhood experiences, not sex, shape personalities and ways of becoming attached to others.

Alfred Adler's (1870–1937) theory proposes that we are all born with and experience feelings of inferiority as children. We are constantly trying to overcome this feeling. We strive for superiority. Therefore, juveniles participating in violent behavior are utilizing violence as a means to overcome feelings of inferiority and achieve feelings of superiority to others.

Carl Jung (1875–1961) built upon Freud's theory of the unconscious. He agreed that the unconscious was essential in understanding the human psyche. However, he argued that there was much more to the unconscious than Freud had theorized. Jung believed that there are fears, behaviors, and thoughts that are universal and generational. He called them the collective unconscious. This collective unconscious influences personality, which is made up of many parts. In order to study juvenile violence from this perspective, one would have to investigate the unconscious negative side of a personality.

Erik Erikson (1902–1994) is another theorist most often associated with the psychodynamic perspective. Erikson built upon Freud's concept of ego. He saw the ego as a positive driving force in personality development. The ego helps establish and maintain a sense of identity. According to Erikson, a person with a strong identity has a sense of uniqueness, belonging, and wholeness. Erikson also focused on the impact of early caregiving on personality development. He theorized that children who experience sensitive, loving parenting will have a strong sense of security, identity, and basic trust. He also theorized that personality develops in distinct stages. Failure to successfully complete a stage impedes one's ability to complete further stages. This will result in an unhealthy personality and sense of identity. Hence, juvenile violence is a symptom of an unhealthy personality, a poor sense of identity, and deficient caregiving.

No matter which theory is used to understand juvenile violence, there are basic assumptions of psychodynamic theories. Primarily concerned with internal psychological processes, psychodynamic theories assume that the causes of behavior have their origins in the unconscious and are motivated by instinctual drives. Different parts of the unconscious are assumed to be in constant struggle. Another assumption of psychodynamic theories is the existence of ego and superego.

There are a number of strengths and weaknesses of psychodynamic theories. Major strengths are the significant impact they have had on the discipline of psychology, development of the case study method, some experimental support (widely used outside psychology), and the ability to tie together varied aspects of experiences. Major weaknesses of psychodynamic theories include little or no predictive value, unscientific methods of data collection, and unreliability, and they are also primarily androcentric, meaning they are male-focused.

See also Abused/Battered Children; Family Relations and Juvenile Violence; Personality Theories

FURTHER READING

Geen, R. (1998). Aggression and antisocial behavior. In D. Gilbert, S. Fiske, & G. Lindzey (Eds.), *The handbook of social psychology* (pp. 317–356). Oxford, UK: Oxford University Press.

Gilligan, J. (1996). *Violence: Our deadly epidemic and its cause*. New York: Grosset/Putnam Books.

Myers, D. (2005). *Exploring psychology*, 6th ed. New York: Worth Publishers.

Pollack, W. (1998). *Real boys: Rescuing our sons from the myths of boyhood*. New York: Owl Books.

Schellenberg, J. (1978). *Masters of social psychology*. Oxford, UK: Oxford University Press.

Joanne Ardovini

PUBLIC HEALTH APPROACH. The public health approach contends that juvenile violence is not solely a law enforcement issue, but an epidemic that must receive the same treatment and comprehensive care as infectious diseases or injuries. Thus, remedies to juvenile violence and delinquency should focus on preventive measures rather than punishment. Accordingly, this approach suggests that community activists, physicians, nurses, psychologists, and mental health professionals are as instrumental to violence deterrence and prevention as are social service providers and law enforcement officials.

The linkage between public health and juvenile violence was first discussed in the late 1970s and early 1980s. Mark Rosenberg, the director of public health services for the **Centers for Disease and Control (CDC)**, urged the U.S. Surgeon General to incorporate community violence in the nation's public health agenda. A year later, the Federal Alcohol, Drug Abuse and Mental Health Administration organized a symposium of physicians, psychiatrists, psychologists, and academicians to look at the intersection between public health and violence. Five years later, Surgeon General C. Everett Koop sponsored a conference on this subject, and the secretary of the U.S. Department of Health and Human Services' Task Force on Black and Minority Health published a report that examined homicides among African-American youth and young adults.

The public health approach is popular among community activists and child advocates. The traditional approach to violence deterrence, which is opposed by public health proponents, gives law enforcement agencies and prosecutors the primary responsibility for combating juvenile crime. It focuses on punishment, the incarceration of at-risk youth and juveniles, "get-tough" measures, and **zero tolerance policies**. Advocates of the public health approach maintain these methods are ineffective at curbing juvenile violence and are actually detrimental to juveniles.

Public health professionals have used a number of intervention strategies to reduce juvenile violence. One of the most widely used strategies is Multisystemic Therapy (MST), which closely monitors the settings—family/home, community, neighborhood, peer group, school—into which youth come in contact on a daily basis. Parental training and school-based counseling are also instrumental to the MST strategy. This strategy has been particularly useful for reducing violence among youth with acute conditions, such as mental illnesses.

Additionally, the public health approach has been used to promote dialogue among professionals and advocates who come into contact with violent offenders in their various agencies and departments, such as mental health professionals, educators, juvenile justice officials, and social workers. Advocates in Louisiana created the Youth Enhanced Services (YES) to encourage cooperation between the New Orleans' Department of Education, the child welfare system, mental health services, and juvenile services. Prior to this, these departments and agencies rarely shared information about their youth populations or engaged in cross-agency collaborations.

In the early 1990s, juvenile justice and child advocates were heavily influenced by Deborah Prothrow-Stith's book, *Deadly Consequences: How Violence is Destroying Our Teenage Population and A Plan to Begin Solving the Problem*, which reflected much of the thinking of Mark Rosenberg a decade earlier. Prothrow-Stith's research also insisted that poverty, racism, and the violent images portrayed in the media contribute to delinquent behavior among juveniles. Hence, her research integrated antipoverty and public education initiatives into the public health approach.

Prothrow-Stith's research and activism altered community activists and educators' perceptions of juvenile violence. During the 1990s, she worked closely with municipal leaders and child advocacy groups in developing comprehensive antiviolence measures. She collaborated with the **Children's Defense Fund**, the nation's leading advocacy group for children, and served on the Black Community Crusade for Children's Task Force on Violence.

Despite attention given to the public health approach in the last two decades, it has run into some difficulties. One challenge is whether this approach can be successful in rural, poor communities that have a shortage of health care professionals, advocates, community organizations, and physicians. In addition, legislators have been less receptive to this approach than activists and health care professionals. In fact, this approach gained popularity among activists at the same time lawmakers were endorsing "get-tough" measures and zero tolerance policies.

Support among lawmakers may very well determine the success of the public health approach in the next decade. Members of Congress and state legislators control funds and budgets that can support the comprehensive intervention strategies promoted by advocates who utilize this approach. Yet lobby groups that support zero tolerance policies—prosecutors, the gun lobby, and the prison industr—tend to have more influence in the legislative arena than public health professionals and juvenile justice advocates. This may impede the progress that proponents of the public health approach have made since the late 1970s.

See also Community Treatment; Film, Juvenile Violence and; Mentoring; Music, Juvenile Violence and; News, Juvenile Violence and; Television, Juvenile Violence and

FURTHER READING

Louisiana YES. (2003, August 3). *Comprehensive community mental health services for children and adolescents with serious emotional disturbances and their families.* A Proposal to the Department of Health and Human Services Center for Mental Heath Services for the Child Mental Health Services (CMHS) Initiative RFA No. SM-03-009. Louisiana Department of Health and Hospitals, Louisiana Office of Mental Health.

Mendel, R. (2000). *Less hype, more help: Reducing juvenile crime, what works—what doesn't.* Washington, DC: American Youth Policy Forum.

Prothrow-Stith, D. (1991). *Deadly consequences: How violence is destroying our teenage population and a plan to begin solving the problem.* New York: HarperCollins Publishers.

Satcher, D. (2001, January). *Youth violence: A report of the Surgeon General.* Washington, DC: U.S. Department of Health and Human Services, Office of the Surgeon General, SAMHSA.

Sekou Franklin

QUANTUM OPPORTUNITIES PROGRAM (QOP). A form of **mentoring**, the Quantum Opportunities Program (QOP) is one of the most successful programs to use mentoring to prevent and address juvenile delinquency. Originating in 1989, the primary goal of QOP is to improve the life opportunities of disadvantaged high school youth who are at-risk for delinquent involvement. Goals include increased graduation rates, decreased pregnancy rates, and decreased violent behavior. There are three "quantum opportunities" stressed in the program: educational activity, including peer tutoring, computer-based instruction, and assistance with homework; service activities in the community; and developmental activities, including curricula that focuses on life and parenting skills, as well as career planning. Specific curricula varies by program site. Students are also offered incentives to carry out the above activities, with the idea that they will stimulate motivation. Incentives include cash and college scholarships. Staff involved in the program can also receive incentives and bonuses if they keep youth in the program.

QOP was implemented in five cities: Milwaukee, Oklahoma City, Philadelphia, Saginaw (Michigan), and San Antonio. At each cite, twenty-five students were recipients of the program and another twenty-five served as a control group for comparison. Students selected had all completed the eighth grade, and their families had received public assistance. The program ran for four years or until the students graduated. Rather than end the program each summer, its services were provided continuously. On average, participants spent 1300 hours involved in the program.

One evaluation of the program, conducted six months after it ended, found significantly lower arrest rates for those involved in the program. Follow-up evaluations two years later found QOP participants were more likely to graduate from high school and more likely to be enrolled in some type of postsecondary education. Participants were three times as likely to attend a four-year college and twice as likely to attend a two-year college than was the comparison group. They were also more likely to have been involved in community service. Pregnancy rates also decreased, as did the likelihood of fathering a child. While these evaluations did not focus on violence per se, it seems as though QOP was helpful in reducing violence rates as well. It should be noted, however, that the most significant effects were found at the Philadelphia site. In 1996, the **Center for the Study and Prevention of Violence (CSPV)** initiated a program called Blueprints for Violence Prevention. Their goal was to identify the most successful youth violence prevention efforts in the United States and replicate these programs. They identified eleven model programs out of the more than five hundred they reviewed, referring to them as "Blueprints." One of the programs on that list is QOP.

Other evaluations of mentoring programs, however, have found less positive results. The most important variable for success seems to be the one-on-one attention afforded students in programs like QOP that allows staff the opportunity to form critical social bonds with at-risk students. Critics also express concern over the way students come to be labeled "at-risk." Some see this as another example of elitism, whereby lower-class youth, often minorities, are prejudged.

FURTHER READING

Hahn, A., Leavitt, T., & Aaron, P. (1994). *Evaluation of the quantum opportunities program: Did it work?* Waltham, MA: Brandeis University.

Quantum Opportunities Program. (2002, January 29). *Guide to effective programs for children and youth.* Available from: www.childtrends.org/Lifecourse/programs/QuantumOpportunitiesProgram.htm.

Siegel, L., Welsh, B., & Senna, J. (2003). *Juvenile delinquency: Theory, practice, and law*, 8th ed. Belmont, CA: Wadsworth.

Laura L. Finley

RATIONAL CHOICE THEORY

Introduction

Rational choice theory focuses on behavior choices that people make after weighing the risks and benefits of different actions. The theory is derived from expected utility theory in economics that emphasizes maximizing profits while minimizing losses. Rational choice theory is linked with **deterrence theory** and is usually classified as a branch of deterrence theory. The main difference between the two is that deterrence theory is based on events, and rational choice is based on economics.

Rational choice theory has a number of underlying assumptions. First is that all individuals have goals, or they strive for utility, such as wealth. The second assumption is that individuals behave and live within their means when working toward their goals. Third, the rational choice is the choice that best achieves the goal using the least means.

Notions of rational choice first appeared in criminology in the late eighteenth century when Cesare Beccaria applied Enlightenment thinking to crime and punishment. Beccaria maintained that individuals had free will to choose to commit criminal acts, and decisions to commit crime would be based on a rational assessment of the risks and benefits of the act. He wrote that people want to experience pleasure and avoid pain, and while criminal acts can bring pleasure of various sorts, possible punishment can bring pain. Thus, Beccaria said that in order for the risks of crime to outweigh the benefits, punishment must be certain and swift.

Rational choice theory was popular in criminology and sociology during the 1960s and was referred to as exchange theory. Later, the principles in rational choice theory appeared in **control theory** and routine activities theory. Since the mid-1970s, there has been a marked loss of faith in rehabilitative approaches to crime policy in the United States, and policymakers began to look again to classical explanations of crime. This was fueled by James Q. Wilson's proposal that punishment was not certain or swift, and so criminals thought that crime did pay.

Applying Rational Choice to Crime

One of the best illustrations of applying rational choice theory to crime is burglary. Assume a juvenile is part of a burglary ring that is planning to break in and rob a home. According to rational choice theory, the juvenile will have to assess the expected benefits or utility of the crime by weighing the odds of detection, arrest, and conviction, the severity of the punishment if convicted, and other variables, such as different ways to make money, opportunity costs, social consequences of conviction, his or her own belief system, material costs of committing the crime, and so forth. The benefits of the crime will then be weighed against the risks. Benefits can extend beyond financial gain and may include psychological pleasure, excitement, revenge, and reputation. The calculation of pleasure versus pain can also be applied to crimes like drug dealing, white-collar crime, prostitution, and other property crimes.

Criticisms of rational choice theory have focused on the tendency of humans to make only partially rational decisions. Typically, other factors such as emotion, tradition, or even conformity may influence decision-making. For example, a violent crime may be inspired by a passionate response to an event, rather than the rational process of cost-benefit analysis.

Research on Rational Choice Theory

There have been a number of studies conducted on criminal behavior from a rational choice perspective, with varying results. One study of repeat property offenders found that offenders did weigh the expected costs of the crime, particularly the odds of serving prison time. Subjects in this study felt that they probably would not be caught, and if they did, their sentences would be short. They also reported that they thought the benefits of the crime, that is, the financial gain, was greater than the risk of arrest and conviction. This study provides some support for rational choice theory; however, subjects in this study also reported knowing at least one other offender who did not weigh the risks of arrest and conviction against the benefits of the crime. Another study of burglars conducted in 1991 indicated partial support for rational choice theory.

Policy Implications

Rational choice theory has practical policy implications. The principle that punishment must be severe enough so that it outweighs the benefits of crime is the one from rational choice theory that is most reflected in criminal justice policy. The use of capital punishment, indeterminate sentences, "three strikes and you're out" sentences for repeat offenders, and tougher sentences are all examples of policies where the intent was to make potential criminals think about the consequences of criminal behavior. In the juvenile justice system, juvenile waivers to adult jurisdictions, whether automatic, judicial, or prosecutorial, also reflect increased severity of sentences.

Special programs have been developed for juveniles based on principles of rational choice theory. For example, the Scared Straight program, first established in Rahway Prison, New Jersey, was an effort to show juveniles what prison was really like and what their lives would be like if they continued to offend. In this program, juveniles who had committed minor offenses spent the night in an adult prison. Again, the intent of this program was to make the risks and consequences of crime far outweigh the benefits.

See also Routine Activities Theory; Waivers to Adult Court

FURTHER READING

Cromwell, P., Olson, J., & Avary, D. (1991). *Breaking and entering: An ethnographic analysis of burglary*. Newbury Park, CA: Sage.

Felson, M., & Clarke, R. (1998). Opportunity makes the thief: Practical theory for crime prevention. *Police Research Series, Paper 98*. London, UK: Policing and Reducing Crime Unit.

Tunnell, K. (1992). *Choosing crime: The criminal calculus of property offenders*. Chicago: Nelson-Hall.

Monica L. P. Robbers

RESTITUTION. Restitution, broadly defined, is the process by which offenders provide money or services to victims to compensate for their damages. Although the idea of restitution has ancient origins, the concept was mostly absent from the formal criminal justice system prior to the 1960s, when the growing victims' rights movement renewed interest in remedying the harm to victims of crime. In 1982, the President's Task Force on Victims of Crime recommended that restitution be customary in all criminal cases. The Victim/Witness Protection Act of that same year mandated that federal judges provide written justification in cases in which they did not impose full restitution. Currently, nearly all fifty states have restitution legislation; many states require mandatory restitution sentencing, regardless of an offender's ability to pay.

Restoring the Victim

A popular rationale for restitution involves restoring victims. In fact, victims are frequently influential advocates for restitution legislation. Victims often experience pain, suffering, difficult times, and financial losses at the hands of their offenders. Thus, many believe every effort should be made to restore victims as much as possible to their pre-victimized state. Receiving money or services from the offender can be beneficial to victims by helping to diminish some of the victim's losses and by giving the victim the opportunity to address their offender. For victims, being able to face offenders and detail how the crime has impacted them is believed to be psychologically beneficial and may assist in the healing process.

Rehabilitating Offenders

Some suggest that the process of restitution can be beneficial for offenders and prevent future crime. Rather than simply receiving punishment, offenders must come to terms with the pain they have caused others. Confronting the reality of their crimes and attempting to correct their wrongs is thought to be rehabilitative for offenders. In addition, some believe that making restitution diminishes any gains offenders receive from their crime. By returning property or repaying money, the offender is returned to his/her pre-crime state and thus is left with no benefits from the crime. Taking away the benefits of crime is believed to deter offenders from committing future offenses.

An Alternative to Incarceration

Consistent with the rationale of rehabilitation, another justification for restitution is that other sentence types, such as incarceration, are too severe for some offenders. The underlying thought is that the conditions and stigma associated with incarceration is detrimental for offenders and may increase the likelihood of further criminal behavior. Thus, juveniles and low-level or first-time offenders may be better served by the community-based process of restitution. Often these individuals, particularly juvenile offenders, receive restitution in addition to community service and other types of restorative treatments. Rather than condemning them (or, alternatively, simply excusing their offenses), restitution both holds people accountable for their actions and allows them to "correct" their wrongdoings and reintegrate back into the community.

Evaluating Restitution

Studies suggest that there are several obstacles to enforcing restitution. One difficulty is determining who is responsible for collecting restitution payments. The responsibility of restitution compliance varies across jurisdictions, including specialized governmental departments, probation offices, clerks of court, and other agencies. Often, there is little communication or coordination across agencies, hindering effective monitoring of restitution orders. Furthermore, the success of restitution collection can vary significantly across administrations. In particular, research reveals that agencies in which restitution was a top priority were more aggressive in their efforts and subsequently yielded more successful collection rates. Thus, victims in some jurisdictions are more likely than similar victims in other areas to receive restitution payments.

Another factor troubling restitution collection involves the imposition of restitution with other punishments. Individuals sentenced in the criminal justice system tend to be disproportionately from lower socioeconomic conditions. Many offenders have no, unsteady, or low-paying employment. Often, these offenders do not have the means to make restitution payments. Moreover, the fact that restitution is frequently imposed in addition to other costs and fines makes the completion of restitution orders even more daunting.

Research on recidivism and restitution has yielded mixed results. Early studies found that offenders who completed restitution orders were less likely to be rearrested than those who received incarceration. However, critics argue that such findings may merely reflect selection bias; that is, prosecutors and judges perceive restitution as a less severe penalty than incarceration and thus may pursue restitution sentences in lieu of incarceration for offenders who commit lesser crimes or seem most amenable to rehabilitation. Those individuals who successfully complete restitution orders tend to be primarily low-level and first-time offenders; some suggest these offenders are least likely to re-offend anyway, regardless of any particular sanctioning.

Furthermore, critics argue that restitution is antithetical to the purpose of the criminal justice system. The United States has a state-centered system of justice, in which crimes are considered crimes against the state rather than against the individual. Therefore, incorporating restitution into sentencing focuses attention on the victim rather than the state and detracts from the purpose of the criminal justice system. Restitution orders change that criminal court system from a society orientation to an individual orientation. Critics believe that restitution essentially involves individuals seeking compensation, and such matters are more appropriately handled under civil litigation.

Despite criticism and mixed research findings, restitution remains an increasingly popular sentencing tool. Recommendations for improving restitution include making the practice mandatory nationwide, increasing victim awareness of their right to receive restitution, improving monitoring, and increasing penalties for offender noncompliance. In addition, a number of governmental organizations and victims' rights groups advocate for increasing victims' authority to seek restitution orders by having the right to petition the court regarding any unordered restitution or to dispute the payment schedule or amount.

See also Community Treatment; Restorative Justice

FURTHER READING

Bright, C. (2004, October 16). Restitution. *Restorative Justice Online*. Available at: www.restorative justice.org/intro/tutorial/outcomes/restitution.

Caputo, G. (2004). *Intermediate sanctions in corrections*. Denton, TX: University of North Texas Press.

National Crime Prevention Council. (1995). Strategy: Restitution by juvenile offenders. Available at: www.ncpc.org/Topics/Strategy_Restitution_by_juvenile_Offenders.php.

Office for Victims of Crime. Available at: http://www.ojp.usdoj.gov/ovc/.

Mindy S. Bradley

RESTORATIVE JUSTICE. Restorative justice (RJ) is an approach to crime that seeks to "restore" the harms caused to victims and the community. Although utilized in both criminal and juvenile justice, in the United States this approach is more commonly associated with juvenile courts. The basic philosophical premise of RJ is that current justice systems in the United States and other nations are not effective in addressing the effects of crime for all parties involved, focusing instead primarily on prosecution and punishment of the offender. In the conceptualization of crime merely as the breaking of laws, the current system neglects to address injuries to crime victims, cycles of victimization and violence, and long-term community effects and reactions to crime.

Restorative justice advocates often argue this approach is rooted in ancient or indigenous systems of justice, although there is considerable debate about this point. What is more clear, however, is the convergence in the 1970s of victims' rights movements, family group conferencing, victim offender mediation, and other approaches in Canada, New Zealand, and the United States that sought to bring together offenders, victims, family members, and community members for purposes of addressing the roots and effects of specific crimes. Somewhat retroactively, this grouping has become known as "restorative justice."

As an approach to criminal justice, RJ currently functions both within and outside of governmental justice agencies. Many earlier restorative approaches were private or nongovernmental, working outside or in conjunction with adult and juvenile courts. Today, the macro organization of RJ is decidedly mixed and encompasses private, quasi-public, and public organizations. It is not uncommon, for example, for a juvenile court to work with an outside organization to conduct mediations between victims and offenders. Notably, however, there is considerable disagreement among practitioners regarding the appropriate relationship of RJ to the criminal justice system, with purists arguing that RJ risks being co-opted by the state, and pragmatists arguing that RJ is most needed within a justice system that has turned toward increasingly punitive sanctions.

Approaches to restorative justice differ substantially but share several key characteristics. Victims are encouraged to voice the effects of crime in their lives to the court, community members, and the offender. These effects are often integrated with sentencing recommendations including **restitution**, community service, and personal service to the victim. Offenders are asked not only to admit guilt, but to take accountability for harm by means by restitution, service, and self-reflection, including, where necessary, counseling and treatment. This process serves a dual function of restoring harm caused to victims, as well as reintegrating the offender back into the community. Finally, community members are often asked to participate in restorative practices in order to give support to the victim, to help offenders understand the importance of making amends, and to actively engage in the construction of local justice expectations and policies.

Today, RJ approaches are quite varied. One commonly used practice in restorative justice is victim offender mediation (VOM). This technique brings together offenders, victims, and mediators with a primary goal of allowing the victim a means by which to explain the harm the offender has caused, to inquire into the motives of the offender, and to address further concerns the victim may have regarding personal safety. A secondary and not uncommon goal of VOM is the forging of an agreement between the victim and the offender regarding restitution and other appropriate means of redress. Numerous studies have shown that victims find this process meaningful, particularly in resolving unanswered questions regarding their victimization, the motives of the offender, and concerns about safety or retaliation. VOMs are usually conducted by staff trained in mediation techniques and occur only after both victims and offenders have been screened for appropriateness.

One variation of VOM is called family group conferencing, which extends participation to family members of offenders and victims, as well as other affected parties. This approach is most common in juvenile cases, where the family of the juvenile plays an important role in ensuring that he or she understands the effects of their actions and successfully fulfills their obligation to the court and the victim.

Another common RJ approach is the use of community restorative boards. These boards are comprised of community members trained in RJ goals. Offenders appear in front of these boards as a condition of their sentence. Community boards are often used when there is no identifiable victim of a crime (i.e., drug possession) or when victims cannot participate in VOMs. Normally, community boards seek to help the offender understand how his or her actions affect the community, and they often decide upon a course of action by which the offender can make amends through the setting of an agreement between the board and the offender.

A third approach is often referred to as a sentencing circle. This approach is most closely aligned with indigenous practices of justice that stress a multi-tiered method of culpability and reintegration for the offender and support for the victim. Unlike VOM, sentencing circles often involve several meetings leading up to the large circle meeting that includes victims, offenders, family members, community members and leaders, prosecutors, and other vested parties. Prior to this meeting, the offender may be asked to meet with members of the circle to admit blame and explain possible means by which to restore harm. Victims as well usually meet with members of the circle to receive support and guidance. Finally, prior to the meeting of all parties, members of the circle meet to decide upon a sentencing plan and meeting agenda.

Research is varied on the effectiveness of RJ. Meta-studies have shown that RJ can reduce recidivism in offenders; however, proponents also argue that recidivism is not an appropriate indicator for measuring the full effects of RJ. Victim satisfaction is a commonly cited indicator in the literature, and several studies exist that suggest RJ is more beneficial to victims than current practices of victim contact and support. One problem facing RJ researchers is the development of benchmark indicators that allow researchers to compare studies of different RJ programs.

While RJ has grown in the United States since the 1970s, it is not without its critics who argue that this approach leads to wildly different sentences for similar crimes, deflects decision-making away from prosecutors and judges, and cannot be applied to more serious violent crimes.

See also Victims of Juvenile Violence, Treatment of

FURTHER READING

Braithwaite, J. (2002). *Restorative justice and responsive regulation*. New York: Oxford University Press.

Department of Justice, Canada. (2001). *The effectiveness of restorative justice practices: A meta-analysis*. Research and Statistics Division Methodological Series.

Zehr, H., & Toews, B. (Eds.). (2004). *Critical issues in restorative justice*. Monsey, NY: Criminal Justice Press.

William R. Wood

ROCHESTER YOUTH DEVELOPMENT STUDY. The Rochester Youth Development Study is a continuing inquiry into the causes and manifestations of antisocial behavior. Housed at the Hindelang Criminal Justice Research Center at the School of

Criminal Justice of the University of Albany, the study is directed by Marvin D. Krohn in collaboration with co-directors Alan J. Lizotte and Carolyn A. Smith.

In 1988, initial interviews were conducted with a group of 1,000 high-risk adolescents and their parents. The adolescents were enrolled in the seventh and eighth grades at the time. The sample included 729 boys and 271 girls, with the much larger percentage of boys reflecting the higher incidence of antisocial behavior among boys. Similar reasoning led the researchers to include a disproportionate percentage of children who lived in high-crime areas. Over the subsequent decade, a dozen further interviews were conducted with these individuals, semi-annually from 1988 to 1992 and annually from 1994 to 1997. Of the original 1,000 subjects, 846, or 85 percent, remained involved in the study until the end. A slightly lower percentage of parents, 83 percent, remained involved.

Researchers gathered data from child interviews, parent interviews, observations of the interactions between children and parents, and the public records of schools, social service departments, and law enforcement agencies. Subsequent funding of the study has allowed for five annual assessments of the data gathered on the oldest participants in the study, emphasizing the ways in which antisocial behavior may be transmitted from one generation to the next and the factors that may mitigate that sort of transmission.

The study has produced data on the following influences on delinquency: familial relationships, educational performance, peer relationships, gang affiliations, socioeconomic background, community of residence, and access to and use of firearms. The study also produced data on such consequences of delinquency as high school dropout rates and the incidence of teen pregnancies. Drug abuse was considered as both a cause and an effect of delinquency. The study has quantified the dramatic increase in the likelihood of delinquency as strong familial influences are replaced by strong gang affiliations.

The study has prompted a great deal of analysis and synthesis of its data. By April 2003, sixty-eight books, chapters in books, federal bulletins, and articles in refereed journals had been published on the study, as well as another twenty-four reports and twelve doctoral dissertations. The most widely reprinted of these secondary sources remains Terrence P. Thornberry's article on the study's rationale and initial findings, "Toward an Interactional Theory of Delinquency," originally published in 1987 in the journal *Criminology* (25: 863–891). It has been reprinted in a number of collections and has even been translated for publication in collections in other languages, including Chinese.

See also Interactionist Theories

FURTHER READING

Battin-Pearson, S., Thornberry, T., Hawkins, J., & Krohn, M. (1998). Gang membership, delinquent peers, and delinquent behavior. *Juvenile Justice Bulletin.* Washington, DC: Office of Juvenile Justice and Delinquency Prevention, U.S. Department of Justice.

Huizinga, D., Loeber, R., & Thornberry, T. (Eds.). (1994). *Urban delinquency and substance abuse: Initial findings.* Washington, DC: Office of Juvenile Justice and Delinquency Prevention, U.S. Department of Justice.

Huizinga, D., Loeber, R., Thornberry, T., & Cothern, L. (2000). *Co-occurrence of delinquency and other problem behaviors.* Washington, DC: Office of Juvenile Justice and Delinquency Prevention, U.S. Department of Justice.

Lizotte, A., & Sheppard, D. (2001). *Gun use by male juveniles: Research and prevention.* Washington, DC: Office of Juvenile Justice and Delinquency Prevention, U.S. Department of Justice.

McCluskey, C. (2002). *Understanding Latino delinquency.* New York: LFB Scholarly.

Thornberry, T. (Ed.). (1997). *Developmental theories of crime and delinquency*. New Brunswick, NJ: Transaction.

Thornberry, T., & Krohn, M. (Eds.). (2003). *Taking stock of delinquency: An overview of findings from contemporary longitudinal studies*. New York: Kluwer Academic/Plenum.

Thornberry, T., Krohn, M., Lizotte, A., Smith, C., & Tobin, K. (2003). *Gangs and delinquency in developmental perspective*. New York: Cambridge University Press.

Thornberry, T., Wei, E., Stouthamer-Loeber, M., & Van Dyke, J. (2000). *Teenage fatherhood and delinquent behavior*. Washington, DC: Office of Juvenile Justice and Delinquency Prevention, U.S. Department of Justice.

Martin Kich

ROLLAND, KAYLA, SHOOTING OF. On February 29, 2000, the nation was once again stunned by an act of school violence. In contrast to the incidents in the 1990s that garnered national media coverage, which all involved teenaged perpetrators, this time both the perpetrator and the victim were in elementary school. The shooting of six-year-old Kayla Rolland prompted national discussions about how best to respond to crime by young people, as well as heated debate about gun control and the role poverty plays in explaining violent juvenile crime.

Kayla Rolland, known as "Kay-Kay," was a happy first grade student at Buell Elementary school in Mt. Morris Township, home to some 25,000 people and adjacent to the north side of Flint, Michigan. Friends, neighbors, and her teachers described her as a nice girl who seemed to get along with everyone, who enjoyed playing with Barbie dolls, and who prayed before lunch. On February 29, 2000, a young classmate with whom she had quarreled shot her with a .32 caliber handgun he took from his uncle's house, where he was staying since his mother and siblings had been evicted from their home. The shooting occurred when the classroom teacher had let a few students, including Kayla and the shooter, stay behind in the classroom while she took the others to the computer room. The boy claims he only brought the gun to school to frighten Kayla, who was killed by the single shot. She died approximately thirty minutes after the shooting.

Classes were canceled the days after the shooting as the community and people all over the nation dealt with the tragedy. The school building remained open, however, so that students and community members could meet with counselors. The shooter and his siblings were immediately removed from their mother, Tamarla Owens, and the Michigan Family Independence Agency (FIA) threatened to take permanent custody of the children. The shooter was not charged with any crime, as prosecutors agreed he was too young to understand his actions. The boy's uncle and two others were charged with weapons violations later in 2000. Jamelle Andre James was charged with involuntary manslaughter, as he admitted to providing the boy access to the gun. In 2004, Kayla Rolland's mother, Veronica McQueen, filed a suit against the Beecher School District, the district superintendent, the principal of Buell Elementary School, Kayla's first grade teacher, and several other teachers claiming they were negligent to have left Kayla and the shooter unattended.

In trying to explain the incident, many people examined the role of poverty. Flint itself, a former booming industrial city, has suffered tremendous economic woes since the closure of the General Motors plant in the 1980s. Many of the people residing in the Beecher School District are especially poor; at the time, 87 percent of the students were receiving free and reduced lunch at school. Tamarla Owens, some say, was a victim of the 1996 Personal

Responsibility and Work Opportunity Act pledged by President Clinton to "end welfare as we know it." The goal of the legislation was to reduce welfare rolls by limiting the time an individual could receive aid (five years) and by mandating that recipients work or go to school a total of thirty hours per week. Michigan was one of the states that most aggressively implemented the welfare-to-work mentality, and results indicated that fewer people were on welfare rolls as a result. On the other hand, critics contend that people were still impoverished; now they just had no assistance. Further, many states did not help those complying with the work or school requirements find adequate day care for their children. In Tamarla Owens' case, her eighteen-year-old daughter often watched the younger siblings while she worked, often at two jobs. Because she did not have reliable transportation, she was taking a bus to her job at a store in the Great Lakes Crossing mall in affluent Auburn Hills. To get there, she often had to leave the home at 7:30 a.m. and returned at 11:00 p.m. Because she had gotten delinquent on rent payments, Owens and her family were evicted eight days before the shooting. It was then that she let her son stay with her brother in what many claim was a crack house. Perhaps the most vocal critic of welfare reform at the time was filmmaker and author Michael Moore, who included coverage of the shooting in his award-winning documentary, *Bowling for Columbine.*

Moore and others also used the shooting to prompt debate about gun control. Moore criticized National Rifle Association (NRA) leader Charlton Heston for coming to Flint for a pro-gun rally shortly after the shooting. Others accuse Moore of misleading, asserting that the NRA rally was over a half a year later.

Others expressed concern that the school and the family missed critical warning signs that the boy was at risk. Prior to the shooting, he had been suspended for fighting and had repeatedly told people he "hated everyone." Further, some maintain that he was the victim of a dysfunctional family. Tamarla Owens was convicted in 1992 of child abuse, and the boy's father, Dedric Owens, had fathered six children by three different mothers. He was not really in the picture at the time of the shooting, as he was incarcerated for a parole violation.

See also Gun-Related Violence, Rates of; Gun-Related Violence, Types of; Homelessness and Youth Violence; Victims of Juvenile Violence, Very Young

FURTHER READING

Brehm, E. (2000, April 28). Michigan school shooting a tragic consequence of U.S. welfare "reform." World Socialist Website. Available at: www.wsws.org/articles/2000/apr2000/welf-a28.shtml.

Kozlowski, K., & French, P. (n.d.). Tribute to Kayla Rolland. *VisionFusion.net.* Retrieved April 10, 2006 from: www.visionfusion.net/kayla_rolland.

Moore, M. (2002). *Bowling for Columbine* [Motion Picture]. New York: MGM Studios.

More indictments in school shooting. (2000, March 16). *CBSNews.com.* Retrieved April 10, 2006, from: www.cbsnews.com/stories/2000/02/29/nationalmain166184.shtml.

Laura L. Finley

ROUTINE ACTIVITIES THEORY. Routine activities theory is a perspective in criminology that has aroused much interest since the late 1970s. This theory, also called lifestyle theory, derives its name from the proposition that the "routine activities" of people in their everyday lives place them in greater positions for criminal victimization. These recurrent activities occur at home, at work, and other venues away from home and consist of family activities, leisure activities, other social activities, employment, and activities involving the general provision of food and shelter, such as shopping.

Using a temporal and spatial (time and location) approach, the theory attempts to target the conditions that tend to make criminal victimization a probable event. Drawing on rational choice perspectives that posit that criminal behavior is a result of conscious choice by offenders, routine activities theory, as proposed by Lawrence Cohen and Marcus Felson (and also later advocated by Ronald Clarke), states that due to structural changes in American society, especially those occurring during the 1960s and 1970s, conditions became highly amenable to criminal activity. The authors use demographic data to theorize reasons for rising theft-related offenses during this period and provide some insights into prevention of criminal activity.

The theory is based upon the idea that in order for crime to occur, three elements or variables must be present: a desired object or potential victim, a person or persons motivated to commit a crime involving the valued object, and the absence of a capable guardian. Examples of desired objects are valued possessions, such as a diamond ring, a luxury automobile, or a drawer containing cash. Objects can even be people, such as a potential rape victim or an elderly person who is victimized by scam artists. Examples of motivated offenders are an adolescent wishing to break into a liquor store, a gang member who is attempting to harm a person traveling through town, or a child molester who is pursuing children. Examples of capable guardians are the police, a neighborhood watch program, an in-store camera, a watch dog, a metal detector, or any such entity that would likely prevent the crime from occurring. Although law enforcement agencies would normally be considered the ideal guardian since they are the primary social control agents in society, this in fact is usually not the case, as police officers normally appear after the victimization has occurred.

While Felson and Cohen analyzed the micro-level situations of people involved in their daily affairs, they also adopted a macro-level of reference by reviewing crime trends and relating these trends in a social-cultural context. For example, using crime data, they compared crime rates from 1960 to 1971 and found a sizable increase in criminal behavior, especially those crimes involving theft. The researchers also examined demographic data and changes in product design and manufacture from the same period as well; these changes reflected cultural changes in a larger social milieu. The data revealed that several routine activities removed people from their households during the day and at night, for example, employment, college attendance (especially by females), out-of-town travel, and long vacation times, much more in 1971 than in 1960. An increase in being away from the home, it was hypothesized, was related to the higher level of victimization by theft. The more the occupants were away from their homes and the more predators realized that the homes were unoccupied resulted in an increase in victimization rates.

Another trend during this period was the increase in technological advancements that aided in the routine activities of the general population. The greater use and increased monetary value of vehicles during the period made them highly desired objects for motivated offenders. Another by-product of technological advancements was a general decrease in the size of electronic durable goods, such as televisions, household appliances, radios, and so on, making them easier to illegally obtain, conceal, and transport. Increased financial and social value combined with easier access to and theft of these items resulted in higher rates of criminal theft.

The researchers offer several policy and social changes that they believe will thwart victimization rates. For example, they propose increasing guardianship, especially through "environmental design" strategies that make it difficult for victimization to occur, for example, placing a high fence or installing a security alarm system at a residence. Another strategy involves using "target hardening" techniques to make it difficult to obtain, damage, or injure the object, for instance, packaging that makes it difficult to conceal the object or that can be detected if it leaves a store without payment occurring. Another measure involves taking personal actions to ensure safety, for example, avoiding places that are known to be dangerous, refraining from going out late at night, or using ATM machines or gas stations that are well lighted. It is posited that these strategies will have a marked effect on levels of victimization.

Cohen and Felson (and later Felson and Clarke) have reported empirical validation for their theory and, as noted, suggest that policies should be promulgated that increase capable guardianship, especially in the form of situational prevention measures. Critics of the theory maintain that the routine activities approach fails to explain criminal motivations and that increasing guardianship simply allows displacement, that is, offenders simply going to areas where such guardianship is not present. The theory, which is primarily a theory of victimization rather than crime causation, has been supported by some studies but not by others. Its greatest value lies in its examination of crime prevention efforts.

See also General and Specific Deterrence Theory; Rational Choice Theory; Situational Crime Prevention

FURTHER READING

Clarke, R., & Felson, M. (1993). Introduction: Criminology, Routine Activity and Rational Choice. *Advances in Criminological Theory*, 5, 1–14.

Cohen, L., & Felson, M. Social change and crime rate trends: A routine activities approach. *American Sociological Review*, 44, 588–608.

Felson, M. (1994). *Crime and everyday life*. Thousand Oaks, CA: Pine Forge Press.

Felson, M., & Clarke, R. (1997). *Business and crime prevention*. Monsey, NY: Criminal Justice Press.

Leonard Steverson

RURAL JUVENILE VIOLENCE.

RURAL JUVENILE VIOLENCE. Arrest statistics indicate that the overall rate of juvenile violence has continued to decline since the early 1990s. However, it seems that public awareness of juvenile violent crime and punitive attitudes toward these offenders has increased throughout this time. This seems particularly true of rural violent juvenile offenses for a variety of reasons, including the occurrence of some extremely violent recent incidents involving juveniles living in rural areas, media portrayals of a growing menace among rural youth, and a greater presence of rural gangs. Though the rate of juvenile violence in cities continues to surpass that of regions with rural populations, in the absence of sufficient criminological research on rural juvenile violence, perceptions of growing rural juvenile violence have incited various reactions aimed at decreasing this particular social problem. There is a lack of agreement, however, on the precise actions the juvenile justice system should make in order to prevent, treat, and punish violent rural juvenile offenders.

Juvenile Arrests

Arrest statistics for juvenile offenders show that juveniles as a whole account for approximately 15 percent of all violent crime arrests in 2003. For nine consecutive years, juvenile arrests for murder, forcible rape, robbery, and aggravated assault have steadily declined. In fact, the murder rate for juveniles has dropped 77 percent since 1993. There is much less information available on the breakdown of rural versus urban juvenile arrests for violent crimes. Traditionally, juvenile violence has been assumed to be an urban phenomenon, so most studies on this social problem have tended to be centered in these areas. Only recently have studies expanded to try to discover qualities of rural juvenile violence. An examination of rural juvenile violence rates over time suggests that rural areas today experience substantially less violent crime than their urban counterparts but that they are also experiencing more juvenile violence than they did in the past, which may create some troubling problems. Juveniles arrested for violent crimes appear to be treated similarly by the justice system in rural and urban areas, with 71 percent of rural juveniles and 70 percent of urban juveniles being dealt with in juvenile court.

Prominent Episodes

Rural juvenile violence in America became an extremely prominent issue in the late 1990s when three highly publicized rural school shootings occurred. In October 1997, a sixteen-year-old teenager killed two girls and injured seven others at Pearl High School in Pearl, Mississippi. In December of that year in Paducah, Kentucky, a teenage boy shot and killed three girls and injured five others. Four months after that, in March 1998, two boys in Jonesboro, Arkansas brought guns to their school to kill four classmates and a teacher and injure eleven others. Similar incidents of extreme juvenile violence have followed, creating various degrees of moral panic throughout the United States. Since these very visible acts of juvenile violence, U.S. policymakers have been searching for answers about kids who kill and who are especially violent, particularly in rural towns.

As shocking as these cases are, however, they are not typical of juvenile delinquency in general. The truth is that they run contrary to recent juvenile homicide trends and represent more of a deviation from the norm. Juvenile homicides have fallen sharply over the past few years and are still extremely rare in rural communities. According to FBI data, juvenile homicide arrests dropped approximately 30 percent since 1994. It seems that the primary difference in juvenile violence between rural and urban settings pertains to the nature of the events; while there are clearly more perpetrators involved in urban juvenile violence, it is more likely that there are multiple victims in rural shootings.

Media Portrayals

Several studies suggest that the media's portrayal of juvenile delinquency has been a major contributor to the notion that juvenile violence is a growing threat to rural communities. Although recent reports indicate that serious juvenile violence is about twice as likely to occur in urban areas than in rural places, the media's focus on violent rural aberrations gives the appearance that these are much more common occurrences than they actually are. Many episodes of rural juvenile violence are reported in the media because their rural nature makes them newsworthy. In content analyses of news stories on juvenile violence, it has been concluded that violent juvenile episodes are much more prominently highlighted when they have occurred in rural settings. Instances of urban violence were generally viewed as more expected and therefore not deemed as newsworthy.

Rural Juvenile Gangs

In rural counties, residents widely agree that juvenile gang violence is a growing problem. Statistics indicate that rural gangs are proliferating and becoming more violent, thus creating more concern among those living in these areas. Attitudes of rural citizens vary widely, though, in terms of the most appropriate way of dealing with these juvenile gang offenders.

The nature of juvenile gangs in rural and urban settings appears to be similar. In both settings, illegal drug use and gun ownership contribute to gangs' proclivity for violence. Research suggests that although the rates of drug use are comparable across rural and urban settings, the types of drugs that juveniles are using may be different. This may be one reason why the violence associated with drug use is much lower in rural communities than in urban cities. On the other hand, gun ownership continues to be much more prevalent in rural areas than in cities. However, crime statistics indicate that guns are much more likely to be used during the commission of a crime among urban gang members. It has been argued that guns have different social meanings in rural areas, resulting in less use during violent acts. Despite the fact that gang activities appear to be similar in rural and urban areas and that pressure to join juvenile gangs is similar in both settings, urban juveniles are significantly more likely to say that they have friends in gangs or had been threatened by gangs, resulting in greater concerns for personal safety and violence in their schools and communities.

See also Gangs Types; Gun-Related Violence, Rates of; Gun-Related Violence, Types of; News, Juvenile Violence and

FURTHER READING

Bouley, Jr., E., & Wells, T. (2001). Attitudes of citizens in a southern rural county toward juvenile crime and justice issues. *Journal of Contemporary Criminal Justice, 17*, 60–70.

Donnermeyer, J. (1993). Rural youth usage of alcohol, marijuana, and "hard" drugs. *International Journal of Addictions, 28*(3), 249–55.

Evans, W., Fitzgerald, C., Weigel, D., & Chvilicek, S. (1999). Are rural gang members similar to their urban peers? Implications for rural communities. *Youth & Society, 30*, 267–282.

Fischer, C. (1980). The spread of violent crime from city to countryside, 1955 to 1975. *Rural Sociology, 45*, 416–434.

Goldstein, A., & Soriano, F. (1994). Juvenile gangs. In L. Eron, J. Gentry, & P. Schlegel (Eds.), *Gangs in America* (pp. 315–333). Newbury Park, CA: Sage.

Lowry, R., Powell, K., Kann, L., Collins, J., & Kolbe, L. (1998). Weapon-carrying, physical fighting, and fight related injury among U.S. adolescents. *American Journal of Preventive Medicine, 14*, 122–130.

Maxson, C. (1993). Investigating gang migration: Contextual issues for intervention. *Gang Journal, 2*, 1–8.

Triplett, R. (1996). The growing threat: Gangs and juvenile offenders. In T. Flanagan & F. Longmire (Eds.), *Americans view crime and justice: A national public opinion survey*. Thousand Oaks, CA: Sage.

Weisheit, R., Falcone, D., & Wells, L. (1996). *Crime and policing in rural and small-town America*. Prospect Heights, IL: Waveland.

Weisheit, R., & Wells, L. (1996). Rural crime and justice: Implications for theory and research. *Crime & Delinquency, 42*, 379–397.

Wood, R., Zalud, G., & Hoag, C. (1996). Opinions of rural mid-western principals toward violence in schools. *Education, 116*(3), 397–403.

Kelly Welch

SAFE AND DRUG FREE SCHOOLS ACT. The Safe and Drug Free Schools (and Communities) Act (SDFSC) was originally authorized by the America's Schools Act of 1994, addressing the seventh goal that called for the elimination of all illegal drugs and violence from schools by the year 2000. SDFSC was reauthorized as Title IV, Part A of the No Child Left Behind Act (NCLB) of 2001. The SDFSC provides federal funding for the prevention of illegal drug use and violence in and near schools.

Based on the premise that academic achievement is optimized in schools with no drug use, violence, firearms, and illegal tobacco and alcohol use, the SDFSC funds programs and research in local school districts. In addition to programs that increase awareness about the consequences of illegal drug use and violence, funded activities include character education, law enforcement services, emergency intervention after traumatic events, parent and community involvement, youth suicide warning trainings, and various mentoring and referral programs. The Safe and Drug Free School Program in the Office of Elementary and Secondary Education (OESE) offers model violence and drug prevention programs for schools, related research results, a variety of publications, and applications for SDFSC prevention grants.

See also Center for the Prevention of School Violence (CPSV); National School Safety Center (NSSC)

FURTHER READING

No Child Left Behind Website: www.ed.gov/nclb/landing.jhtml?src=pb.

The Safe and Drug Free Schools Program Website: www.ed.gov/about/offices/list/osdfs/index.html? src=oc.

Melanie Moore

SAMPSON AND LAUB'S ANALYSIS OF GLUECKS' DATA. **Sheldon and Eleanor Glueck**, a husband-and-wife team of researchers at Harvard University, performed a number of crime-related studies over a forty-year period. Their purpose was to obtain a better understanding of juvenile delinquency and the development and maintenance of criminal careers. The Gluecks produced four major databases on crime and juvenile delinquency; the most famous of these culminated in a book entitled *Unraveling Juvenile Delinquency* in 1950.

The Gluecks maintained a multidisciplinary focus during their research projects and never wed themselves completely to any one academic discipline. As a result, they did not focus exclusively on biological, psychological, or sociological perspectives; their main goal was uncovering or "unraveling" the complex causes of juvenile delinquency and determining the effectiveness of programs designed to thwart delinquent behavior. They conducted their research by interviewing not only their subjects (500 juveniles determined to be "delinquents"), but also parents, teachers, and others involved in the juveniles' lives. In addition to these interviews, the Gluecks reviewed police, court, and detention data. They utilized a control group (of 500 "nondelinquents") whose subjects were closely matched with characteristics thought to be correlated with crime, such as age, racial and ethnic background, intelligence, residence, and income. The Gluecks' approach was also longitudinal as they re-interviewed the delinquents again between 1949 and 1965. Their conclusion was that there are several variables associated with delinquency in youth, especially age and family process. In fact, according to the Gluecks, the primary difference between the delinquents and nondelinquents was the child-rearing practices of their families.

In the 1990s, two professors at Harvard, **John H. Laub and Robert J. Sampson**, found much of the Gluecks' data in a basement at Harvard Law School. They were generally impressed with the large data sets generated in the early studies and reviewed and reanalyzed the data using a refined computer system. Despite criticisms of the Gluecks' data collection and analysis by key social scientists of the day, notably sociologist Edwin Sutherland, the two believed that the Gluecks' data was in many ways superior to many contemporary longitudinal data sets and that the information could be of great value to the study of delinquency.

In a now famous article, Laub and Sampson confirmed the Gluecks' findings that certain family process variables, that is, supervision, attachment, and discipline, are the primary determinants of serious and persistent delinquent behavior. In addition, their analysis of the Gluecks' data also suggested that appropriate family functioning has a mediating effect on delinquency. The two researchers proposed that two other underestimated variables—parental deviance and alcoholism—were key determinants of delinquency. Laub and Sampson concluded the article with a call for other researchers to analyze the Gluecks' data.

FURTHER READING

Glueck, S., & Glueck, E. (1950). *Unraveling juvenile delinquency*. New York: Commonwealth Fund.

Laub, J., & Sampson, R. (1988). Unraveling families and delinquency: A reanalysis of the Gluecks' data. *Criminology, 26*, 355–380.

Sampson, R., & Laub, J. (1993). *Crime in the making*. Cambridge, MA: Harvard University Press.

Leonard Steverson

SCHOOL CRIME VICTIMIZATION SURVEY. The School Crime Victimization Survey is administered in selected years as a supplement to the annual **National Crime Victimization Survey**. The National Crime Victimization Survey has been conducted since 1973 on a representative sample of 42,000 households in the United States and collects information on the frequency, characteristics, and consequences of crimes, including those not reported to the police. All persons over the age of twelve in a selected household are interviewed about crimes in which they were the victim during the six-month period preceding the interview.

The School Crime Victimization Survey, also known as the School Crime Supplement, is designed specifically to collect data on crime victimization in schools. It is conducted by the Bureau of Justice Statistics within the U.S. Department of Justice and was administered in 1995, 1999, 2001, 2003, and 2005. The School Crime Victimization Survey is administered to persons within households included in the National Crime Victimization Survey who are aged 12 to 18 years (12 to 19 years in 1989 and 1995), who attended school at any time in the previous six months, and who are enrolled in an academic program leading to a high school diploma. The following types of questions are included in the School Crime Victimization Survey: (1) time, date, and location of crimes that occurred within a school building, on school grounds, or on a school bus; (2) the type of school, the distance from the student's home, the school's attendance and monitoring policies, and the student's attendance in the previous six months; (3) violence and availability of drugs within the school and school response and student reactions to rule violations; (4) demographic characteristics of household members, such as age, race, sex, and employment. Data from the School Crime Victimization Survey is available for download from the National Archive of Criminal Justice Data website housed at the University of Michigan within the Inter-University Consortium for Political and Social Research. Besides the data itself, this archive includes a brief description of the School Crime Victimization Survey, codebooks, data collection instruments, SAS and SPSS data definition statements, and references (and sometimes links) to analyses that use School Crime Victimization Survey data. Online data analysis is also available through both the Bureau of Justice and the National Archive of Criminal Justice Data websites, so that basic analyses may be conducted without downloading the data and bringing it into a statistical analysis program.

FURTHER READING

National Archive of Criminal Justice Data: The Source for Crime and Justice Data. Available at: http://www.icpsr.umich.edu/NACJD/.

Riedel, M. (2000). *Research strategies for secondary data: A perspective for criminology and criminal justice*. Thousand Oaks, CA: Sage.

U.S. Department of Justice, Office of Justice Programs, Bureau of Justice Statistics. (2005). *Indicators of school crime and safety, 2005*. Available at: http://www.ojp.usdoj.gov/bjs/abstract/iscs05.htm.

Sarah Boslaugh

SCHOOL POLICE OFFICERS. A school police officer is a law enforcement official whose duties center on enhancing school security and the welfare of primary and secondary school students. To adequately conceptualize school police officers as public servants who are distinct from other law enforcement officials, it is essential to bear in mind the fact that juvenile students are a partially institutionalized demographic group; they are legally required to attend school and are subject to greater limitations on their basic freedoms than the general population. For example, while at school a youth may be subject to a dress code, be subject to screening by metal detectors, be denied the liberty of possessing items that he/she would be free to possess while away from school (for example, cell phone, pocketknife), and have his/her personal movements restricted (for example, times during which a student may go to the bathroom).

Thus, school police officers function in a manner somewhat similar to correctional officers or attendants in drug rehabilitation facilities insofar as school police officers tend to a captive clientele who are subject to numerous restrictions on their basic liberties. It is necessary to clarify, however, that school police officers are different from school security guards/officers in that school police officers have the same legal authority as any local law enforcement agent; they are sworn law enforcement officers with special powers of arrest that exceed those of the ordinary citizen. And in the United States, school police officers normally carry sidearms, whereas school security guards/officers do not carry firearms.

As to the origins of the school police officer, it is clear that the concept originated in the United States, but it is not clear precisely when and where the first school police officer served. Suffice it to say that although some school districts developed security services as early as the 1930s, prior to the 1990s there were relatively few school police officers serving in the United States or anywhere else in the western hemisphere. During the 1990s, however, the number of school police officers rapidly increased, and by the early 2000s there were more than 20,000 school police officers serving throughout the United States.

The most common types of school police officers in the United States are the school resource officer and the school district police officer, with the distinction between the two being based on the type of agency for which the officer works. In some states (for example, Arizona and Florida) municipal police officers and/or county deputy sheriffs may be assigned to serve in the schools, while in other states (for example, California and Texas), school districts can maintain independent police departments. This is similar to the practice of universities maintaining independent police departments. School police officers who are employed by a local law enforcement agency are usually referred to as school resource officers and school police officers who are employed by an independent school district police agency are generally known as school district police officers. In the United Kingdom, there is no substantive evidence that any schools have developed independent police/constabulary agencies, but there are a number of police/constabulary agencies that assign officers the task of serving in the schools. These officers are known as school liaison officers.

With regard to the responsibilities of school police officers, the officers tend to a plethora of duties. The sample job description for a school resource officer (serving at the high school level) prepared by the National Association of School Resource Officers contains a list of duties inclusive of, but not limited to traffic supervision at the beginning and end of the school day; patrolling school grounds throughout the school day to maintain a visible law enforcement presence; gathering intelligence on criminal activities in the schools and sharing the intelligence with local criminal justice officials; attending teacher-parent meetings; attending faculty meetings; giving presentations at faculty in-services, parent-teacher gatherings, and community meetings; attending extracurricular school activities, such as dances and athletic competitions; traveling with athletic teams to away games; assisting with delinquency prevention programs, such as Drug Abuse Resistance and Education (D.A.R.E.); and providing a positive role model for students. Moreover, some of the school district police departments in metropolitan areas have officers who perform specialized duties. The Los Angeles School District Police Department, for instance, has a canine unit and a paramilitary response team (that is, a SWAT team). It is important to note, however, that school police officers in the United Kingdom focus on the provision of social services, such as programs designed to increase juvenile awareness of road safety and the hazards of drug use, rather than tending to the general law enforcement and patrol duties that occupy much of the time of school police officers in the United States.

See also Surveillance in Schools

FURTHER READING

Avon and Somerset Constabulary. (2002). *What is schools liaison?* Avon and Somerset, UK: Avon and Somerset Constabulary. Retrieved October 15, 2004 from: http://www.n-somerset.gov.uk.

Beger, R. (2002). Expansion of police power in public high schools and the vanishing rights of students. *Social Justice, 29,* 119–130.

Benigni, M. (2004, May). The need for school resource officers. *FBI Law Enforcement Bulletin, 73*, 22–24.

Burke, S. (2001, September). The advantages of a school resource officer. *Law and Order, 49*, 73–75.

Girouard, C. (2001). *School resource officer training program* (FS 200105). Washington, DC: Office of Juvenile Justice and Delinquency Prevention.

Hopkins, N., Hewstone, M., & Hantzi, A. (1992). Police-schools liaison and young people's image of the police: An intervention evaluation. *British Journal of Psychology, 83*, 203–220.

Jackson, A. (2002). Police-school resource officers' and students' perception of the police and offending. *Policing: An International Journal of Police Strategies and Management, 25*, 631–650.

Johnson, I. (1999). School violence: The effectiveness of a school resource officer program in a southern city. *Journal of Criminal Justice, 27*, 173–192.

Ben Brown

SEDUCTIONS OF CRIME THEORY. The seductions of crime approach is a relatively new theoretical perspective that focuses attention on psychological variables, especially the highly pleasurable benefits that are associated with criminal activity. As such, it has special association with younger offenders to whom the "thrill" of crime is often highly noticeable.

The originator of this "seduction theory" of crime, Jack Katz, is of the opinion that most theories of crime causation do not adequately address the importance of the internal gratification of criminal behavior. Therefore, his focus is on the seductive nature of potential criminal acts and the rewards experienced by the offenders. In fact, according to Katz in his prominent work *Seductions of Crime: Moral and Sensual Attractions in Doing Evil*, the primary motivation to offend is the crime itself. In this work, Katz advances his ideas through the use of comments from victims and perpetrators of crime obtained from ethnographic sources.

Most theories of criminology, according to the seduction theory, pay too much attention to "background" forces or those biological, psychological, or sociological conditions that compel people to commit criminal acts. The "foreground" or the enticements that people experience when considering a particular criminal act constitute the pulling force to deviate from social norms. Since the background of a person does not change, Katz is concerned with the experiential motivators and how the actors respond to these motivators. Katz notes that general descriptions of criminal acts leave out the sights, sounds, tactile, and other sensory experiences of the person committing the act. He feels the visual images and sounds of someone being physically attacked, for instance, must be considered in order to fully understand the tempting influences of crime. The "sensual dynamics" of crime account for a vast array of behaviors, from the stealing of items in a store to the extreme act of taking another person's life.

According to the theory, people delight in their actions of deviance but are often severely shamed and humiliated when caught in these acts. The humiliation turns to rage, often erupting into violent episodes of anger. People handle this humiliation differently and, as is often the case within adolescent gangs, games are created in which the juveniles perform a series of aggressive rituals against those they determine are their enemies: rival gangs. The fear of humiliation is in itself exciting and seductive.

In his theoretical perspective, Katz espouses a symbolic interactionist paradigm in that he focuses on the micro-level interactions and the idea that phenomena are socially constructed. Within this framework, meaning is constructed through interactions via the use of symbols, verbal and physical, that communicate meaning, often through the use of metaphors. This is evident in Katz's metaphorical descriptions of the stimuli that describe criminal behavior as "seductive," "thrilling," "sensuous," and "magical." The criminal actions are termed "righteous slaughter," "sneaky thrills," and "doing stickup." Terms describing the perpetrators of criminal activity include "badasses," "street elites," and "hardmen."

Adolescents who commit delinquent acts play a prominent role in Katz's work. He describes the thrills experienced by delinquents when they engage in behavior such as minor theft and vandalism as "sneaky thrills." He also examines the more serious violent offenses committed by juveniles. His term "badass" is used to describe those adolescents who have succumbed to the lures of aggressive criminal behavior and who use a number of techniques to maintain their "badness." These techniques include the use of certain types of clothing, scars, tattoos, sunglasses, aloofness, mumbling, angry facial gestures, guttural sounds, cursing, and gang signs. Members of adolescent gangs do not consider themselves members of "gangs" but of groups with a collective identity; however, those in opposing gangs *are* considered gang members. Katz describes different types of American gangs (African-American, Latin American, middle-class white adolescents) as well as gangs of other countries in his analysis.

Those adolescents who take on mythical omnipotence in their gang activity are referred to as the "street elites." These teens have a unique posture that is intended to elevate them to a higher status than others. Violence is a key aspect of being a street elite and has the power to symbolically elevate their lived experiences to those of "glorious combat," to promote a façade of independence and respectability, and to maintain their personae in spite of the obvious dangers of their urban environments. Although the image of street gangs is normally one of constant turf warring, in reality one of the major characteristics of gang life is boredom. Often to alleviate feelings of boredom, gang members will formulate means of dealing with the unpleasantness, such as walking in unison in an intimidating manner throughout different areas of town in an activity called "parading."

One common characteristic of adolescent gang members is the resistance, and often outright defiance, of authority. What makes gang membership seductive, according to Katz, is the potential that exists for the street elites to reveal the mundane absurdity of the world fueled by a fantasy that gives the gang members a superior position to others around them.

Katz takes issue with many of the sociological theories of deviant behavior, especially the **strain theory** as proposed by Robert K. Merton. Katz believes this perspective fails to capture the meanings given to the crime by the criminal. For example, the criminal "innovator" in Merton's theory is a nonconformist who uses illicit means in order to obtain socially favored goals. Obviously, many types of inner-city crime are perpetrated with no intent to obtain the "American Dream." It has been difficult to explain the etiology of white-collar and corporate deviance in similar terms as to what Katz terms "ghetto deviance." However, the seduction hypothesis provides a means of understanding that a deviant act has the same psychological reward structure for the inside trader and the inner-city bank robber as it does for the adolescent gang member who finds a genuine delight embarrassing a teacher with threats and intimidation.

While Katz's theory is provocative and is included in most juvenile delinquency textbooks, it has not generated empirical testing. This may be a result of the difficulty of testing the basic premises of the theory or a variety of other reasons.

FURTHER READING

Ferrell, J. (1995). Culture, crime, and cultural criminology. *Journal of Criminal Justice and Popular Culture, 3*(2), 25–42.

Katz, J. (1988). *Seductions of crime: Moral and sensual attractions in doing evil.* New York: Basic Books.

Leonard Steverson

SEXUAL VIOLENCE, RATES OF. Rates of juvenile sexual offending and victimization are likely underestimated because crimes against juveniles are highly under-reported. While rates of juvenile sexual violence vary because of differences in data used to estimate offending and victimization, two important pieces of information have emerged from the data collected thus far. First, juveniles are at a high risk for sexual victimization by adults and by other juveniles. Second, there are differences between male and female juvenile victimization and offending experiences.

Based upon data from the **Uniform Crime Reports, the Office of Juvenile Justice and Delinquency Prevention** has determined that the arrest rate for forcible rape committed by juveniles has steadily declined since 1993, reaching its lowest point in 2003. This does not mean that the number of juveniles committing sex offenses has decreased or that the number of juvenile-perpetrated sex offenses has decreased. Rather, these rates indicate that the number of juveniles arrested for the crime of forcible rape has declined. Juveniles who sexually offend victimize other juveniles 95 percent of the time, and the majority of these assaults involve acquaintances.

While juveniles represent 12 percent of all crime victims in the NIBRS (National Incident Based Reporting System, a national crime statistics database), they comprise over 70 percent of all victims of sexual assault. Children under the age of fifteen are the most at risk for being sexually victimized by adults or other children, and half of all victims of violent sexual assaults are under age twelve. Most child victims of sexual assault are victimized by family members or acquaintances.

Juveniles are more susceptible to sexual violence than are adults, and juvenile females are more likely to be sexually assaulted than juvenile males. Juvenile females represent at least three-fourths of the victims of sexual assaults. However, most male victims of sexual assault are juveniles, creating a unique victim population. Juvenile sexual offending also demonstrates gender differences. Ninety-two percent of all juvenile sexual assault victims were victimized by males in 1997 and 1998. Eight percent of all sexual assault victims were victimized by females during that same time period. Since females are most likely to commit crimes against other females, it is likely that the victims of these sexual offenders were primarily female. The low arrest rate for female sex offenders and lack of information about their victims makes it difficult to determine trends. Regardless, it is clear that gender differences exist in the sexual victimization and offending experiences.

See also Sexual Violence, Types of

FURTHER READING

Finkelhor, D., & Ormrod, R. (2000). *Characteristics of crimes against juveniles.* Washington, DC: Office of Juvenile Justice and Delinquency Prevention, U.S. Department of Justice.

McCurley, C., & Snyder, H. (2004). *Victims of violent juvenile crime.* Washington, DC: Office of Juvenile Justice and Delinquency Prevention, U.S. Department of Justice.

Snyder, H. (2001). *Law enforcement and juvenile crime.* Washington, DC: Office of Juvenile Justice and Delinquency Prevention, U.S. Department of Justice.

Wendy Perkins

SEXUAL VIOLENCE, TYPES OF. Juveniles who commit sexual violence are a diverse group. They may commit nonsexual criminal behavior, such as aggravated assault, or display signs of antisocial behavior. Sexually abusive behaviors can range from offenses involving no contact to those involving actual penetration. Sexual aggression has been reported in children as young as three and four, with the most common age of onset between the ages of six and nine.

Sexual violence poses a serious problem, the cost of which is considerable to victims and society. The scope of the problem may be underestimated because juvenile sexual offenders are known only when they are introduced into the criminal justice system. For treatment to be successful, it is of the utmost importance that a program should work at stopping the abusive behavior.

It is thought that those juveniles who commit crimes of sexual violence share many of the same characteristics as those who commit crimes of nonsexual violence. For example, juveniles who have committed sexual violence differ on victim and offense characteristics, histories of maltreatment, sexual knowledge and experiences, and level of academic and cognitive functioning, as do their nonsexual offending counterparts.

Because of these differences, it is difficult to classify them into groups. Some types of offenders can be thought of as naïve experimenters, sexually aggressive, child molesters, or rapists. Others exhibit deviant sexual arousal and antisocial behaviors, whereas others may not fit into any category.

A history of child abuse and its role in sexual violence is a complex issue. Some studies have found that physical abuse, neglect, and the witnessing of family violence are associated with sexual violence, whereas others have found no difference in childhood abuse history between sexual offenders and nonsexual offenders.

Some characteristics observed in abused children, such as a lack of empathy, the inability to feel compassion or to recognize appropriate emotions in others, and the inability to hold another person's perspective, may have some bearing on juvenile sex offenders. Impulse control disorders, conduct disorders, antisocial traits, and depression have also been observed in young sex offenders.

Family instability and violence may be prevalent among juveniles who commit sexual violence. Many offenders have stated that they experienced physical and/or emotional separation from one or both of their parents. These juveniles may exhibit a lack of social competence and social skills, resulting in poor relationships with their peers and experiencing social isolation.

Many young sex offenders have had consensual sexual experiences, which at times exceeded those experienced by nonsexual offending juveniles. Some juveniles expressed that sex was used as a demonstration of love or caring or for feelings of power and control; it was also used to dissolve anger, to hurt, degrade, or punish. Problems with sexual dysfunction, such as impotence and premature ejaculation, have been reported.

The role of pornography in sexual violence is unclear. A small portion of juvenile sexual offenders claimed they did not use pornographic materials, whereas others stated they were exposed to pornography before they committed sexual violence.

Some of these juveniles have academic difficulties that may or may not stem from neurological impairments. Other juveniles are considered above average. In addition, some of these sexual offenders may experience cognitive distortions, for example, blaming the victim for the sexual violence.

Evidence on the role of substance abuse is not adequate enough to claim drugs or alcohol as a causative factor in sexually violent behavior, although drugs and alcohol can have a disinhibiting effect. Substance abuse should be differentiated from normal experimentation that is part of the adolescent developmental process.

Recently, research has found a higher incidence of sexual violence committed by girls than previously thought. These incidents may be underestimated more for girls than for boys, due to the reluctance of society to acknowledge that girls can be capable of committing sexual violence. Characteristics of female offenders have shown that they tend to be younger than their male counterparts and less likely to have committed acts of rape. Girls are also more likely to have experienced sexual abuse.

Victims of very young offenders tend to be girls between the ages of four and seven, who may be victimized by their siblings, friends, or acquaintances. These very young offenders tend to have experienced higher rates of sexual victimization and neglect compared to their adolescent offenders. Many preadolescent sexual offenders have also been found to experience academic and learning difficulties, as well as impaired relationships with their peers.

There remains the same problem with classifying preadolescent sexual offenders as there is with adolescent offenders. Some are classified as sexually reactive, sexually aggressive, highly traumatized, or rule breakers. As with the adolescent sexual offenders, the sexual behaviors range on a continuum of gradually excessive and abusive sexual behaviors.

Research has shown that a small group of juveniles who have committed sexual violence are later charged with another sex crime. However, there are a few characteristics thought to be associated with sexual recidivism: psychopathy, deviant arousal, truancy, a prior sex offense, blaming the victim, and the use of threat or force. Problems associated with the accuracy of predicting sexual recidivism arise from the infrequency and hidden nature of sexual offenses, resulting in inadequate information needed to predict recidivism.

Treatment programs have proliferated during the past decade that address community safety and the prevention of further victimization, while helping the juveniles to control their abusive behaviors and to stop further development of psychosexual problems. This is accomplished by increasing prosocial interactions that helps them to develop age-appropriate relationships.

The National Task Force on Juvenile Sexual Offending states that individualized interventions with periodic assessment are necessary to treat these offenders. Treatment approaches may include individual, family, and group interventions. They focus on sex education, correcting cognitive distortions, empathy training, clarifying values, anger management, controlling impulses, social skills training, reducing deviant arousal, and relapse prevention.

See also Abused/Battered Children; Central Park Jogger Case; Family Relations and Juvenile Violence; Glen Ridge, New Jersey; Sexual Violence, Rates of

FURTHER READING

Myers, W. (2002). *Juvenile sexual homicide*. New York: Academic Press.

Righthand, S., & Welch, C. (2005). *Juveniles who have sexually offended: A review of the professional literature*. Washington, DC: Office of Juvenile Justice and Delinquency Prevention.

April C. Wilson

SITUATIONAL CRIME PREVENTION. Situational crime prevention is the prevention of crime by reducing the opportunity to offend. The importance of situational crime prevention is the ability to target specific types of offenders, geographic areas, and/or certain crime targets with increased scrutiny and/or penalties. Situational crime prevention has been used by criminal justice, and specifically physical security, professionals for many years and can generally restrict the access of perpetrators to an area. For example, the U.S. Secret

Service (and many other law enforcement agencies) routinely controls entrances and specific portions of facilities in order to control the access of unauthorized people and potentially an assassin.

With respect to juveniles, situational crime prevention is used routinely to *displace* certain types of crime. For example, harsher penalties exist for possessing or selling illicit drugs within a certain geographic area of a school. The reality of using such a policy to control drug sales near schools is that such control encourages drug dealers to find new locations to commit their crime. An important example of situational crime prevention addressing juvenile violence is to examine a trend within schools across the United States during recent years. In many states (and the District of Columbia), juveniles have been robbed, assaulted, and even killed by juveniles in order to obtain high-priced designer clothing (for example, sneakers and coats) and jewelry. Many schools have responded to this violence by instituting mandatory uniform policies for students to reduce the opportunity for this type of violence. This aspect of situational crime prevention is known as *diffusion*, meaning that in this case, schools have attempted to reduce violent crime against juveniles, but this practice of uniform clothing might also help prevent other types of crime (for example, kidnapping by adults) against these same juveniles due to their being more visible than normal.

See also Rational Choice Theory; Routine Activities Theory

FURTHER READING

California Attorney General's Crime and Violence Prevention Center. (n.d.). *Creating a drug free zone*. Available at: http://www.stopdrugs.org/drugfreezone.html.

Homel, R. (1996). *The politics and practice of situational crime prevention*. Monsey, NY: Criminal Justice Press.

La Vigne, N. (1997). *Visibility and vigilance: Metro's situational approach to preventing subway crime*. Washington, DC: U.S. Department of Justice, Office of Justice Programs, National Institute of Justice.

Newman, G., Clarke, R., & Shoham, S. (1997). *Rational choice and situational crime prevention: Theoretical foundations*. New York: Ashgate.

Protection. (n.d.). *United States Secret Service*. Available at: http://www.secretservice.gov/protection_works.shtml.

Von Hirsch, A., Garland, D., & Wakefield, A. (2000). *Ethical and social perspectives on situational crime prevention*. Oxford: Hart.

Wortley, R. (2002). *Situational prison control: Crime prevention in correctional institutions*. New York: Cambridge University Press.

David R. Montague

SOCIAL DEVELOPMENT MODEL. The social development model is a general theory of human behavior that attempts to explain and predict both prosocial and antisocial behaviors. Antisocial behaviors, such as stealing or abusing drugs, are considered deviant because they run contrary to behaviors that are accepted and viewed as normal by society. Prosocial behaviors, on the other hand, are normative behaviors that are accepted by society. This might include respecting other's possessions by not stealing them and not using drugs deemed harmful and illegal. The social development theory focuses on the socialization processes of children and adolescents and incorporates the effects of both risk and protective factors when explaining the development of antisocial behavior. Risk factors are aspects of a person's life that may arise from within themselves, their family, friends, school, or community environments, and increase the likelihood of that individual engaging in antisocial behavior during their lifetime. Having antisocial values, beliefs, attitudes, and peers are some risk factors that may lead to antisocial behaviors. Protective factors are aspects in a person's life that reduce the impact of such risk factors and therefore reduce the likelihood that a person will engage in antisocial behavior during their lifetime. This might include close bonds with parents and family members or involvement in a religious youth group.

The social development model hypothesizes that children learn patterns of behavior, whether prosocial or antisocial, from "socializing agents," such as their peers and the family, school, and religious and community institutions. It further predicts that an individual's behavior will be affected by and closely resemble the behavior, values, norms, and beliefs of the people to whom they are most closely bonded.

The social development model is considered to be an integrated theory of criminal behavior because it combines aspects of the control, social learning, and differential association theories. **Social control theory** asserts that antisocial behavior is a result of an individual's weak bonds to prosocial influences, such as prosocial peers or family members. **Social learning theory** asserts that antisocial behavior is learned through the reinforcement of such behavior. **Differential association theory** maintains that antisocial behavior is learned through interaction with other persons who engage in antisocial behavior. The social development model integrates the features of these theories into a theory that hypothesizes that bonds develop between a child and another socializing agent, such as the family, and that behavior is then learned and reinforced by the interaction of the child and socializing agents. The social development theory recognizes that an individual, as well as their social environments and corresponding social agents, will change over time and incorporates this variation in its explanation of antisocial behavior.

The social development model is based on a developmental perspective of behavior, which posits that behavior results from the interaction of internal and external developmental processes; such an interaction accounts for the fact that different patterns of behavior occur at different periods of an individual's development. For instance, the social development model specifies four developmental periods from birth through high school and predicts that the primary socializing agents (that is, peers, family, or school) of a child will change at each stage. While the family is the primary socializing agent of a child during the preschool period, parents, teachers, and school influences are the significant socializing agents during the elementary school period. Peers become the primary socializing agents in the middle school period and throughout the high school period.

The social development model specifies two general pathways: one pathway explains the processes that lead to prosocial behavior, while the other explains the processes that lead to antisocial behavior. An individual's pathway will be either prosocial or antisocial depending upon how strongly they are bonded to prosocial or antisocial socializing agents.

This theory was developed in 1981 and has been evaluated for its ability to predict and explain prosocial and antisocial behaviors. The social development model has been found to predict violence and drug use, as well as explain alcohol misuse of youth in the late adolescent years. Although it is a powerful predictive theory for these types of behaviors, it is most effective when using longitudinal data or data that is collected over a long period of time, which is often difficult to obtain.

See also Developmental Theories

FURTHER READING

Catalano, R., & Hawkins, J. (1996). The social development model: A theory of antisocial behavior. In J. Hawkins (Ed.), *Delinquency and crime: Current theories* (pp. 149–198). New York: Cambridge University Press.

Huang, B., Kosterman, R., Catalano, R., Hawkins, J., & Abbott, R. (2001). Modeling mediation in the etiology of violent behavior in adolescence: A test of the social development model. *Criminology*, *39*, 75–108.

Emily Wright

SOCIAL DISORGANIZATION THEORY

General Description

Social Disorganization Theory explains crime through examination of the ecology of an area. Crime will be highest in areas where there is the least organization and fewest stakes in the neighborhood. In such disorganized areas, there is a high amount of turnover, and thus, less bonding by the residents to their neighborhood. Accordingly, the goal of most community members is to leave these areas, and they become uninterested in their community, neighbors, schools, business opportunities, and on. The turnover also leads to a cycle of disinterest that makes it difficult for policies that urge community involvement in attempts to solve social problems.

Key to the ideas within Social Disorganization Theory is the deteriorated conditions found within the disorganized areas. Such conditions cause a lack of concern for the area, which leads to alienation between residents and diminished attention to neighbors, upkeep of the neighborhood, or the institutions found within. For example, residents may lose care for the adolescents within the neighborhood and view them with fear, rather than take an interest in their well being.

Perhaps even more critical is that the residents with the greatest conventional ties and values often leave these communities at their earliest opportunity, taking their connections, resources, and values with them. This makes it difficult for such communities to develop stability and overcome the cycle of disorganization and distrust often present. It also decreases the potential that such neighborhoods have in connecting with opportunities outside of their geographical limits, thus insuring their isolation from opportunities outside of the disorganized zone.

History

The roots of Social Disorganization Theory can be found in the research by Ernest Burgess and Robert Park, who were part of the Sociology Department at the University of Chicago, known as the Chicago School, in the early 20th Century. They examined the social ecology of Chicago and were able to divide the city into distinct zones in which different social groups lived with a host of diverse social patterns and problems. Their work influenced future scholars, including Clifford Shaw and Henry McKay, who focused the ideas of Burgess and Park to the specific phenomenon of crime.

Shaw and McKay examined Chicago during a time of extreme turnover in the early to mid 1900s, with a number of groups entering the city, including immigrants from foreign lands and southerners. Shaw and McKay studied distinct areas within Chicago, which included the inner city, the old city or zone of transition, the working class area, and suburbs. They found that the highest crime rates were in the inner city and the zone of transition. While inner city crime generally consisted of theft and other petty crimes, a larger variety of crimes, including violent crime, were found in the zone of transition.

Several generations of researchers have followed Shaw and McKay's work, and social disorganization has since become one of the most highly researched theories in criminology. Indeed, social disorganization theorists have expanded beyond Chicago and have examined cities with diverse structures, heterogeneity, and culture in an attempt to better understand how disorganization impacts crime in the United States and abroad.

Legacy of Social Disorganization Theory

A major criticism of Social Disorganization Theory is its limited scope. Specifically, it focuses on blue-collar crime and the mechanisms that cause it, and largely ignores crime of the middle and upper class. The theory's premises focus on explaining crime such as robbery, murder, burglary and theft, and its explanations are limited to such blue-collar crime. Moreover, most researchers who have tested the ideas found within social disorganization have used official crime measures, which are argued to disproportionately magnify the criminal activity of the lower class.

Social Disorganization Theory's impact is without question, however, and its ideas have done much to increase the knowledge within the fields of criminology and criminal justice. Perhaps the first myth that it helped quell was that immigrants and minorities were prone to commit crime due to their race or ethnicity. By focusing on the city of Chicago over time, researchers found that habitants of disorganized areas committed the most crime regardless of their race. Thus, increased criminal behavior was described as a normal response to disorganized social conditions found in the zone of transition.

A number of criminal justice policies have also been significantly influence by the premises found in Social Disorganization Theory. One popular policy in the field that falls into this category is the Weed and Seed Program. This program attempts to weed out the disorganizing influence of incivilities within a neighborhood and replace them with programs, policies, and other strategies that bring stability to the area. Such strategies include developing Boys and Girls clubs, encouraging residents with incentives to buy property, become involved in school, and on.

One final impact of Social Disorganization Theory is found in its interconnectivity to fear of crime research. Indeed, a focus of this theory has been on the impact that fear of crime has in the disorganization of the community structure. Thus, many have given Social Disorganization Theory credit for our increased awareness and understanding of the role that fear of crime, or lack thereof, has in the mental health and well being of a community. Today, many theorists and criminal justice practitioners see fear of crime as one of the leading causes of alienation within communities, and modern day theorists have increasingly combined this phenomenon into their research on disorganized areas.

FURTHER READING

Kubrin, C., & Weitzer, R. (2003). New directions in Social Disorganization theory. *The Journal of Research in Crime and Delinquency, 40,* 374–392.

Markowitz, F., Bellair, P., Liska, A., & Liu, J. (2001). Extending Social Disorganization Theory: Modeling the relationships between cohesion, disorder, and fear. *Criminology, 39,* 293–320.

Silver, E. (2000). Extending Social Disorganization theory: A multilevel approach to the study of violence among persons with mental illnesses. *Criminology, 38,* 1043–1074.

Veysey, B., & Messner, S. (1999). Further testing of Social Disorganization theory: An elaboration of Sampson and Groves's community of structure. *The Journal of Research in Crime and Delinquency, 36*, 156–174.

Brion Sever

SOCIAL LEARNING THEORIES. Social learning theory is one of the most widely used modern theories to explain violent behavior exhibited by juveniles. According to the theory, the behavior of individuals is learned and influenced primarily through their own personal experiences and relationships. Behaviors are learned by observation, imitation, and modeling, then reinforced through social rewards.

Origins of social learning theory date back to 1912 when French social theorist Gabriel Tarde introduced his three laws of imitation: close contact, imitation of superiors by inferiors, and insertion. Tarde's law of close contact attempted to explain behaviors that were passed from person-to-person and group-to-group. It simply stated that an individual is most likely to imitate those with whom they have the closest contact. The law of imitation of superiors by inferiors stated that inferiors would imitate superiors in an effort to gain the rewards enjoyed by the superiors. The law of insertion stated that the social insertion of new behaviors would either reinforce or replace old behaviors.

In 1934, Edwin Sutherland and Donald Cressey developed their **differential association theory**, stating that criminal behavior was learned, that it was a process, and that learning occurred in primary groups (peers, family, etc.). Sutherland and Cressey said individuals were subject to influences where the law was defined in both favorable and unfavorable terms. For example, parents would usually raise their children defining the law in favorable terms. However, those children would have contact with peers at school who participated in illegal activities and defined the law in unfavorable terms. Based on the ratio (differential) of associations with either criminal or noncriminal groups, individuals could be socially influenced to commit crime.

Ronald Akers and Robert Burgess introduced differential reinforcement theory in 1966, expanding Sutherland's theory to include ideas of reinforcement. Akers and Burgess added that criminal behavior could be encouraged through social and nonsocial rewards, as well as the avoidance of punishment. They said learned behavior could be explained as a function of rewards or punishment received from the environment. In other words, behavior that produced rewards would tend to increase in frequency, while behavior that resulted in punishment would tend to decrease in frequency.

Albert Bandura, a psychology professor at the Stanford University, is credited as the father of modern social learning theory. Bandura developed his theory in the early 1950s while studying for a Ph.D. at the University of Iowa. Bandura believed juveniles were especially vulnerable to learning violent behaviors and that they learned by observation, either in person or through media and the environment. Bandura claimed juveniles' aggressive behavior is strongly influenced by the behavior they witness in adults. The formulation of Bandura's theory included the well-known "Bobo Doll Experiment." For the experiment, children were seated in a room where they watched an adult on videotape interacting violently with the Bobo doll. The adult sat on the doll, punched it, threw it into the air, kicked it, beat it over the head with a mallet, and threw balls at it. The adult was then given social rewards for their behavior. After viewing the videotape, children were put into a room with a Bobo doll, and the vast majority of them (over 80 percent) exhibited similar violent behavior.

The Bobo Doll Experiment is so well known perhaps because it was one of the few attempts at empirical research in regard to social learning theory. Many sociologists have contributed to the theory through thought and reasoning, but there is little documentation of empirical studies actually testing the theory. This may be due to the difficulty of quantifying applicable data or of attempting to control specific factors affecting learning (behavior, cognitive processes, environment, and so forth).

Despite the convincing results illustrated by the Bobo Doll Experiment, Bandura said that four conditions must exist before a learned behavior can be modeled: (1) Attention (observer must pay attention); (2) Retention (behavior must be coded into long-term memory); (3) Motor reproduction (observer must have physical capability to reproduce behavior); and (4) Motivation (observer must want to demonstrate behavior through incentive). While person and environment played a role, Bandura believed violent behavior could produce its own social rewards, such as self-esteem building, financial gain, and praise from others.

Modern social learning theorists believe that while a behavior may be learned, it may or may not be exhibited by a change in behavior (modeling). A cognitive process is involved, wherein the observer considers the possible rewards and punishments for the behavior and those considerations have an influence on whether the behavior is exhibited. However, modern theorists also believe reinforcement and punishment are not the sole influencers on learning and that they only have indirect effects. Most critics of social learning theory say it is too simplistic and undermines the importance of other factors, especially biological factors such as genetics.

In sum, social learning theorists see violent behavior as a function of individual socialization, wherein the person, behavior, and environment all affect each other and the social learning process. This theory remains popular, yet controversial today. While it has support grounded in past and modern research, biological and behavioral theories do as well. This theory is still the most applied social theory to explanations of juvenile violence and is the method of thinking behind most juvenile crime prevention programs.

See also Differential Identification Theory

FURTHER READING

Learning theories of crime. (n.d.). North Carolina Wesleyan Faculty Pages. Available at: http://faculty .ncwc.edu/toconnor/301/301lect10.htm.

Ronald Akers and social learning theory. (n.d.). Florida State University School of Criminology and Criminal Justice. Available at: http://www.criminology.fsu.edu/crimtheory/akers.htm.

Social learning theory. (n.d.). Florida State University School of Criminology and Criminal Justice. Available at: http://www.criminology.fsu.edu/crimtheory/bandura.htm.

Social learning theory. (n.d). University of Texas at Austin, College of Education. Available at: http://teachnet.edb.utexas.edu/~lynda_abbott/Social.html.

The social learning tradition: Interpersonal relationships and deviant behavior. (n.d.). Socprobs .netWebsite. Available at: http://deviance.socprobs.net/Unit_3/Theory/DA.htm.

Adam Doran

SOLOMON, T. J. Anthony Solomon, known as T. J., is currently serving a sixty-year sentence, with the possibility of parole after eighteen years, after pleading guilty but mentally ill to twenty-nine criminal charges, including aggravated assault, cruelty to children, and illegal possession and use of firearms. On May 20, 1999, one month to the day following the school shootings at Columbine High School in Littleton, Colorado, Solomon opened fire in the commons area of Heritage High School in Rockdale County, Georgia, a suburb of Atlanta. Although there were no fatalities, six students were wounded, one of them critically. The Heritage High shootings were one in a series of school-related attacks that occurred throughout the United States during the later part of the 1990s.

Solomon was born in Baton Rouge, Louisiana on September 6, 1983. Five years later his parents divorced, and he moved with his mother and sister to Denim Springs, Louisiana. His mother later remarried, and the family moved to Pembroke Pines, Florida, where Solomon was diagnosed with attention deficit disorder and began taking the medication Ritalin. After another move, the family finally settled in Rockdale County, Georgia in the fall of 1996. During this period, Solomon began to display signs of depression; his grades declined, he lost interest in sports, and he failed to make friends. Solomon would later acknowledge that his parents' divorce and the abrupt separation from his father had a permanent effect on his psychological development. Furthermore, Solomon's family history indicated the presence of mental illness; his father had been institutionalized following a suicide attempt. However, by outward appearances, Solomon was a normal teenaged boy from an upper-middle-class home whose parents were actively involved in every aspect of his life. Although he was a loner who preferred hunting to organized sports and dating and his grades declined after the move to Georgia, he had never been arrested nor had he displayed patterns of serious violence.

It was not until his sophomore year that Solomon began to show signs of trouble. In the months prior to the incident, he began to express suicidal thoughts, stole a gun from his stepfather's boat, experimented with alcohol and marijuana, and became obsessed with the Columbine shootings.

On the morning of May 20, Solomon broke into his stepfather's gun cabinet and retrieved a .22 caliber rifle as well as a .357 magnum handgun. After sawing the stock off of the rifle, he concealed it inside his pants and placed the handgun in his book bag. Solomon boarded the bus for school and arrived shortly before 8:00 a.m. As he walked toward the rear entrance of the school's commons area, he removed the handgun from his book bag, which he left near some woods behind the school. When Solomon entered the commons area, he fired twelve shots from the rifle, emptying its magazine. Eight students were hit; however, two escaped injury because the bullets lodged in a backpack and a book. Two male students pursued Solomon as he exited the building. He dropped the rifle and fired several shots from the handgun before he stopped, dropped to his knees, and placed the barrel of the gun in his mouth. Two assistant principals eventually subdued him and coaxed him to put down the gun and surrender. Solomon's shooting spree had lasted twelve minutes. The police arrived four minutes later, and by 8:40 a.m. Solomon was in custody and awaiting police interrogation.

On August 2, 1999, Solomon appeared before Rockdale County Juvenile Court Judge William Schneider, whose task was to determine whether Solomon should be tried as an adult. Because the facts of the case were not in dispute, Solomon's mental state became the central issue at the transfer hearings. According to Georgia statute, a juvenile may not be transferred to superior court if the juvenile is committable to an institution for mental illness because he/she suffers from a disorder that significantly impairs judgment and behavior or poses a demonstrable risk to the safety of others or himself/herself. Defense attorneys argued that Solomon's actions were the result of a mental illness so severe that it required his involuntary committal to a mental institution. They further claimed that Solomon demonstrated suicidal tendencies and therefore posed a substantial risk of imminent harm to himself. While the court-appointed psychologist conceded that Solomon displayed signs of depression, these signs indicated only a mild dysthymic disorder, not major depression. As such, the psychologist concluded that Solomon, if kept confined and given appropriate medication, could be tried as an adult.

After three days of testimony, Schneider ruled that under the standards established by Georgia statutes, Solomon was not committable to a mental institution and waived his case to superior court. Schneider's decision was based in part on testimony provided by the prosecution that suggested Solomon's actions were a copycat of the Columbine shootings that occurred a month earlier. Schneider concluded that the viciousness of the crime and society's need to prevent such shootings outweighed Solomon's interest to remain in the juvenile system.

Fourteen months later, Solomon was indicted in superior court and entered a plea of guilty but mentally ill. During the sentencing hearing, Judge Sidney Nation relied heavily on transcripts from the transfer hearing as well as testimony provided by Solomon's parents, four of the six victims, and psychological experts for the state and the defense. Although Nation acknowledged that Solomon suffered a form of mental illness, he was not convinced that Solomon could be rehabilitated and therefore sentenced the defendant to sixty years of custody by the corrections department and forty years of probation. Solomon would be eligible for parole after eighteen years.

In May 2001, the state parole board released a statement concluding that under their guidelines, Solomon would serve a minimum of thirty-six, rather than eighteen, years before he became eligible for parole. Nation responded to this finding by reducing Solomon's original sentence so that he would serve the minimum of eighteen years as originally intended. Nation further modified his original ruling to include a requirement that Solomon submit to psychiatric treatment or risk violating his probation. The latter was a response to Solomon's unsuccessful suicide attempt shortly after arriving at Arrendale.

Solomon is currently housed at Arrendale and is eligible for parole in 2018.

FURTHER READING

Moore, M., Petrie, C., Braga, A., & Mc Laughlin, B. (Eds.). (2003). *Deadly lessons: Understanding lethal school violence*. Washington, DC: National Academies Press.

Newman, K., Fox, C., Harding, D., Mehta, J., & Roth, W. (2004). *Rampage: The social roots of school shootings*. New York: Basic Books.

Angela Winkler Thomas

SPECIALIZED COURTS

Introduction

In recent years, there has been a shift in juvenile justice toward promoting greater accountability in juvenile courts and implementing sanctions that are more meaningful and long lasting. One innovative practice in juvenile justice that accomplishes this is the use of specialized courts. Specialized courts may be established in juvenile or family court jurisdictions, and they adjudicate cases involving specific types of offenses. They sometimes handle cases involving juveniles of a certain age and background. Such courts are modeled on adult drug courts. Currently, there are a number of specialized courts for juveniles, such as drug courts, gun courts, and **teen courts**.

Drug Courts

The most common specialized court for juveniles is drug courts. Juveniles who have committed, and usually have been adjudicated for, drug or alcohol-related offenses are referred to drug courts if they meet certain criteria outlined by the jurisdiction. In these courts, intensive treatment is offered to juveniles and their families. Treatment programs combine multiple services, such as substance abuse treatment, mental health programs, basic medical care, family counseling, mentoring, and general and specific education programs. Once the juvenile has completed the program, the drug court maintains continued supervision over that juvenile for a set period. There are an estimated two hundred of these courts around the United States.

The key personnel in drug courts are similar to regular juvenile court, but also include treatment providers, evaluators, and school representatives. These additional personnel ensure that specific needs of each case are identified and treated. The judge oversees the process, but in drug courts, decision-making is more collaborative than in regular juvenile court.

Continued supervision of the juvenile is essential in the success of drug courts. Such supervision may involve regular drug and alcohol screening, monitoring of school attendance, and community service. Many drug courts have implemented incentive programs for successful compliance, such as promotion to the next treatment phase, which is normally less restrictive, awards such as vouchers or sports tickets or certificates of achievement and public recognition.

The Office of Juvenile Justice and Delinquency Prevention (OJJDP) estimates from current drug court statistics that recidivism rates for alcohol and drug-related offenses are significantly less than they are for juveniles who go through traditional juvenile court for the same type of offenses. OJJDP also report that substance use significantly declines for juveniles who go through drug courts, and school participation significantly increases.

Gun Courts

Juveniles charged with gun-related offenses, particularly first-time offenses, may be referred to a juvenile gun court. Other juveniles referred to this type of specialized court may be juveniles who have demonstrated risk factors for firearms-related offenses, such as gang members or juveniles who were charged with an offense and had a firearm in their possession.

Most juvenile gun court programs are based on early intervention, which means that the juvenile is referred before a disposition has been decided. They are typically short-term, intensive programs, lasting only a few months. Programs are designed to teach juveniles about gun safety, the effects of gun violence on victims and communities, laws regarding guns, nonviolent conflict resolutions, and the types of consequences juveniles are likely to face from the criminal justice system if they are caught with guns in their possession.

Successful gun court programs rely on a number of different personnel. The judge acts as the legal advisor and oversees the planning of the team required to work with the juvenile. The team consists of juvenile justice personnel, such as probation officers, police, detention officers, and people from the community. Research conducted by the OJJDP indicates that some of the most successful gun court programs use community members who are living with the effects of gun violence, for example, a parent who has lost a child to gun violence, a victim who copes with a gun-related injury, or a juvenile who was involved in gun violence but who has made life changes.

Recent research on gun court programs also indicates that mandatory attendance in the program results in less recidivism. Emphasis on nonviolent dispute resolution also decreases recidivism, as many juveniles carry guns for protection or self-defense.

Teen Courts

In the late 1980s, a number of teen courts were established in jurisdictions around the United States. Juveniles referred to teen courts are usually under the age of sixteen and are first-time offenders who have been charged with minor offenses, such as theft, misdemeanor assault, disorderly conduct, possession of alcohol, or vandalism.

Most teen courts are part of **diversion** programs for teens. Therefore, the teen court does not actually determine guilt or innocence; rather they sentence the juvenile. Most commonly, this sentence is community-based, with restitution to the victim in the form of money, service, or written apology included.

Specialized Court Concerns

Specialized courts are designed to offer collaborative treatment approaches to particular problems that were not being adequately addressed by traditional courts. For example, prior to the establishment of drug courts, there was a revolving door relationship between juvenile substance abusers and the juvenile justice system. Specialized courts have not been without criticisms. Critics maintain that individuals lose a certain amount of due process in specialized courts since the prosecutor and the defense work together. Further, individuals in many specialized courts can only go through programs if they plead guilty. There is also no adversarial system in specialized courts. Further, judges may be overextended in their roles as coordinators of multiple services.

The criticisms of specialized courts have been far outweighed by the courts' successes in preventing recidivism, reducing substance abuse, and reducing jail and prison costs.

See also Community Treatment; Gun-Related Violence, Rates of; Gun-Related Violence, Types of; Zero Tolerance Laws

FURTHER READING

Butts, J., Hoffman, D., & Buck, J. (1998). Teen courts in the United States: A profile of current programs. Washington, DC: Office of Juvenile Justice and Delinquency Prevention. Available at: http://www.ncjrs.org/pdffiles1/ojjdp/fs99118.pdf.

Center for Court Innovation. Available at: http://www.problem-solvingcourts.org.

Center for Substance Abuse Treatment. Available at: http://www.samhsa.gov/centers/csat/csat.html.

National Association of Drug Court Professionals. Available at: http://www.nadcp.org.

Sheppard, D., & Kelly, P. (2002). Juvenile gun courts: Promoting accountability and providing treatment. Washington, DC: Department of Justice, Juvenile Accountability Incentive Block Grants Program. Available at: http://www.ojjdp.ncjrs.org.

Monica L. P. Robbers

SPUR POSSE. The Spur Posse was a group of boys who implemented a points system to track and compare their sexual conquests. While high school students in Lakewood, California, the boys formed the group and agreed to don the jersey of a professional athlete with a number that corresponded to their point total. They would also take on the name of the athlete. Points were earned only if penetration occurred, and a girl could only count once. Thus, the goal was to engage in sexual intercourse with as many girls as possible. One member claimed to have had intercourse with sixty-seven girls over a four-year period.

The group was named for the San Antonio Spurs basketball team because a founding member was fond of David Robinson, who had been traded to the Spurs at the time. The group drew nationwide attention on March 18, 1993, when police officers entered their high school and placed nine members under arrest for various sex crimes, ranging from rape to lewd conduct with a ten-year-old. Prosecutors later dropped all but one of the charges, deeming most of the acts to be consensual. One member was convicted of engaging in lewd conduct with a ten-year-old girl and spent one year in the Kirby Juvenile Detention Center. He would later explain that he engaged in a sexual act with the girl because he needed the point to enhance his reputation and to make a name for himself.

In fact, "making a name" was the impetus for Spur Posse. They even compared their points system to participating in sports, suggesting that both are about standing out and achieving excellence. To justify their actions, they took the position that the girls they had sex with were "no-names," while they were famous for their exploits. Worse yet, they referred to the girls as whores and often engaged in group sex to rack up points. As they sought to bring additional excitement to their sexual trysts, they began to videotape themselves and to watch each other perform.

It is clear that these boys did not define their actions as criminal. In seeking to explain them, the most applicable theories seem to be those related to gender roles, as well as **techniques of neutralization**. Gender-related theories, such as Hagan's **power-control theory** and a number of feminist-originated theories, assert that the way a culture defines gender roles shapes criminality. In the United States, males are encouraged to take risks and to be "macho," which often involves demonstrating their heterosexuality. Thus some men may approach women not as equals in sexual relations, but as subordinates, leading to sexual harassment, assaults, and rape. Techniques of neutralization are the mental processes an offender goes through to rationalize his or her criminal actions. Commonly used techniques include denial of the victim and denial of harm, both applicable in this case.

Members of the group were invited to appear on a number of television shows, including *Maury Povich* and *The Jenny Jones Show*, as America fixated on the apparent decline in morals among its youth. Media attention was not limited to talk shows; members appeared on the front page of the *New York Times* and in *Newsweek, Sassy*, and *Penthouse*. While the boys basked in the light of the media attention, believing themselves to be celebrities, their hometown was saddled with the nickname "Rapewood" by those who were less than impressed. Several of the members believed that the attention they received would translate into career opportunities in entertainment. One boy wanted to be a stand-up comedian and another dreamed of being an actor or model. They believed that through their recognition as Spur Posse members, they would build a brand image that would open doors for them later.

As the media sought to define the group, the term "gang" was applied. However, the members deny that they were any more than a loose group of friends who felt compelled to become closer after their story gained national exposure. Members claimed that they would later see teens wearing Spurs gear and claiming to be members of the Spur Posse Gang. The founding members claimed that no such gang ever existed and that kids were looking for an easy way to attach themselves to a group that had achieved a minute of fame.

Contrary to the images of the Spurs on television talk shows, they were not all academic underachievers. One member, Billy Shehan, was in accelerated courses for gifted high school students and graduated with honors. However, attending college and becoming successful adults escaped most of the Spurs. Several members of the Spur Posse served jail time for unrelated offenses. The founder, Dana Belman, was sentenced to ten years in state prison for burglary and fraud. His crime spree included stealing a credit card and using it to fund a gambling trip to Las Vegas. Another member served time for assault. A third member, Chris Albert, was shot to death in a street fight.

The Spur Posse events have been compared to another sex scandal involving high school students in **Glen Ridge**, **New Jersey**. In this case, privileged athletes sexually assaulted a mentally retarded girl. Prior complaints with the boys involved had been dismissed with a "boys will be boys" mentality.

FURTHER READING

Faludi, S. (1999). *Stiffed: The betrayal of the American man.* New York: William Morrow & Company, Inc.

Peter S. Finley

STIMULANTS. One cannot say for sure when stimulants first appeared on earth, but full account of their use is recorded in both ancient and contemporary history. Stimulant is a concept used to describe several groups of drugs that tend to increase alertness and physical activity. Stimulants are substances that speed up the body's metabolism. Certain forms of stimulants occur naturally, like caffeine in coffee and nicotine in tobacco. However, a majority of stimulants are synthetic and are primarily used in the treatment of hyperactivity in children. Stimulants have also been used historically to treat asthma and other respiratory problems, obesity, neurological disorders, and a variety of other human and animal ailments.

Today, stimulants are mainly prescribed for narcolepsy, attention-deficit hyperactivity disorder, and depression that has not responded to other treatments. Some maintain the United States is far too quick to prescribe stimulants for young people. Current estimates suggest that 15 to 20 percent of boys in the United States are taking methylphenidate, or Ritalin. A 2003 study found Ritalin prescriptions for two to four-year-olds increased 300 percent between 1991 and 1995. The FDA found that, since 1994, more than 3,000 prescriptions for Ritalin have been written for children under one year of age. Many use stimulants for the euphoric effect. Stimulants are pharmaceuticals such as amphetamines and other controlled substances, including street drugs like "uppers," "speed," and **cocaine**. Ritalin has become so common as a street drug that it has been given the street names "Vitamin R," "R-ball," and "the smart drug." Undercover narcotics officers have said Ritalin is even easier to obtain on playgrounds than on the streets.

Methamphetamines are the most commonly abused stimulants in the twenty-first century. The long-term effect of stimulant use may include tolerance, dependence, violence, aggression, and malnutrition due to suppression of appetite. The 2004 crime report compiled by the FBI indicates that of the 15,416,973 arrests for abuse violations, 12.4 percent were of juveniles. During the decade of 1994–2003, law enforcement made 1.9 million arrests of juveniles for drug abuse violations. Nearly 84 percent of the juvenile arrests were for possession in 2003.

A review of the 2004 data indicates that there was a 22.9 percent overall increase for juvenile arrests for drug abuse violations. Arrests for marijuana rose 60.5 percent, but arrests for synthetic narcotics (methamphetamines, for example) rose 162.8 percent—by far the highest proportional increase. The 2004 data show that juvenile males accounted for the largest proportion of drug arrests, but females showed a higher proportion of those arrested at younger ages (fifteen and under). White juveniles accounted for 74.9 percent and black juveniles 39.4 percent for all drugs combined. For synthetic narcotics, white juveniles represented 86.9 percent and black juveniles 10.9 percent according to the 2004 data.

Self-report studies conducted in 2004 and reported in the Bureau of Justice statistics about high school seniors do not include dropouts or truants and likely underrepresent youth drug use. However, 47.8 percent and 85.8 percent of seniors could obtain marijuana and other stimulants on campus. The study indicates an increase from 2003.

All stimulants excite the central nervous system by increasing the heart rate, breathing, and blood pressure. Caffeine, known as the world's most popular drug, can be consumed in coffee and in soft drinks. Caffeine affects people differently; some may get jittery, nervous, or. Another very powerful additive stimulant that directly affects the brain is cocaine. Inhalants, volatile solvents, aerosols, gases, nitrites, ketamine, magic mushrooms, fly agaric, philocybe, hallucinogenic mushrooms, LSD, and Ecstacy are also stimulants. Juveniles' immature physical and psychological development makes them especially vulnerable and susceptible to the harmful effects of stimulants. The behavioral patterns following juvenile use of stimulants include violent outbursts, loss of control, self-degradation, disruptive conduct, and family unity disintegration that often produce tragic outcomes.

Certain juvenile violence is associated with feelings of hostility or paranoia. **OJJDP** studies show that juveniles who are high are more likely to carry guns for protection. They feel threatened and are consumed by a distorted feeling and a need to strike first and quick. National Institute on Drug Abuse (NIDA) research indicates teen drug use is associated with psychiatric disorders in later life. The Institute of Medicine report (2005) indicated that incidents of mental illness related to drug use are on the rise.

FURTHER READING

Bach, J., Bender, D., & Leone, B. (1988). *Drug abuse: Opposing viewpoints*. Westhaven, CT: Greenhaven Press.

Office of National Drug Control Policy. Available at: http://www.whitehousedrugpolicy.gov/pubs/fastfind.html.

Uniform Crime Report. (2004). Available at: www.fbi.gov/ucr.

U.S. Department of Health and Human Services. Available at: http://www.health.org/yourtime.

Walker, P., & Wood, E. (2004). *Stimulants*. New York: Lucent.

Evaristus Obinyan

SUBCULTURAL THEORIES. Subcultural theories emerged in the middle of the twentieth century as a variation of both **social disorganization theory** and **strain theory**. Social disorganization theorists had argued as early as the 1920s that crime rates could be linked to the social ecology of different types of neighborhoods. Sociologists such as McKay and Shaw found that high levels of social disorganization existed in so-called "transitional neighborhoods," where social services and constant resident turnover weakened cultural values as well as community resolve against crime. Robert Merton's strain theory argued that deviance and crime were arguably the products of two conflicting structural conditions of American life, namely culturally defined goals that promoted middle-class aspirations and socially approved means for obtaining these goals. Differing levels of strain existed, argued

Merton, among socioeconomic classes insofar as they were able to achieve cultural goals through legitimate means.

Utilizing both the findings of social disorganization theorists, as well as the strain theory of Merton, sociologists such as Albert Cohen argued that when lower-class groups were unable to achieve dominant culturally defined goals, they often responded through the formation of values and norms in conflict with those of the perceived status quo. In his well-known work, *Delinquent Boys*, Cohen (1955) labeled this conflict "status frustration" and suggested that this frustration was a causal factor in the formation of delinquent and criminal youth subcultures. Unable to adapt to "middle-class measuring rods," such as schooling and employment, Cohen argued that such youth were likely to fail at legitimate attempts to gain entry into the middle class and turned instead to varying subcultures as a means to both financial opportunity and belonging.

Cohen detailed subcultural groups common to boys and young men in lower-class neighborhoods: the corner boy, the college boy, and the delinquent boy. The corner boy Cohen saw as the most common response to middle-class rejection, typified by petty crime, recreational drug and alcohol use, and affiliation with a group of peers with which he feels a close personal connection. Mostly, these groups are not "gangs," as they lack an organized structure or hierarchy. Corner boys generally age out of their delinquent or deviant behaviors. College boys were those who embrace the values of the American dream by attempting to gain access to legitimate opportunities, usually to fail for lack of skills, education, and social norms appropriate to the middle class. Delinquent boys were those who most actively adopted values and norms in opposition to conventional society in what Cohen called "reaction formation." Delinquent boys often join street or criminal gangs, engage in violent behavior, and reject authority figures perceived to be in line with larger cultural or societal norms.

In their work *Delinquency and Opportunity*, Richard Cloward and Lloyd Ohlin (1960) argued in a similar vein to Cohen that delinquent subcultures were most likely to thrive where social disorganization was greatest and opportunity for legitimate means of success was limited. Cloward and Ohlin called this concept "**differential opportunity**," when all members of society share similar cultural goals and values (financial success, prestige, etc.), but are divided by means of legitimate opportunity. Moving beyond the work of Cohen, however, Cloward and Ohlin suggested that youth who were denied legitimate opportunity could be further divided into subcategories related to levels of community or neighborhood stability. Poorer communities that evidenced some degree of stability in terms of close personal relationships between members were most able to support or engender "criminal gangs," subcultural groups that evidenced a relatively high degree of criminal organization, including hierarchies, division of labor, and rational planning. Less stable communities, however, provided both less legitimate and illegitimate opportunity. In these areas, "conflict gangs" were more likely to form, where criminal enterprise was less organized and more emphasis was placed on violence both as a means of obtaining goods as well as a sign of status. Finally, Cloward and Ohlin argued that, in certain cases, "retreatist gangs" were likely to form when individuals were unable to achieve cultural goals either through legitimate or illegitimate opportunity. Unable to achieve success, individuals and groups thus retreat to the fringes of society, for example, by centering their lives and pursuits around drugs and alcohol, sex, music, and other forms of pleasure-seeking designed to inhibit feelings of failure or inadequacy.

Importantly, subcultural theories recognize that while shared values and norms contrary to conventional society serve to define such groups, group cohesion or organization may differ substantially between or among different subcultures. Many individuals, for example, belong to more than one subcultural group. Groups such as street gangs may be highly integrated. Other more retreatist groups may be united in their shared values, but evidence little cohesion or organization. Moreover, varying descriptions of subcultures, such as Cloward and Ohlin's criminal, conflict, and retreatist gangs, or Cohen's corner boys, college boys, and delinquent boys, suggest that no easy categorizations exist from which to explain and understand subcultures. Finally, subcultures themselves are constantly changing in relation to various political, economic, and cultural factors, leading to constant evaluation and reevaluation of previous theories and groupings.

Today, while social disorganization theory and strain theory are less common within sociology as they once were, subcultural theory remains somewhat vibrant, due at least in part to the proliferation of street gangs in the latter twentieth century. Research into street gangs continues to validate the findings of earlier subcultural theorists insofar as gang members often see their involvement as both a means to obtain opportunity and a rejection of larger cultural values. One important addition to subcultural theory has been the recognition of race, and its relationship to class, as a central feature in the formation of deviant subcultures. The work of Mercer Sullivan, for example, shows that among black, Latino, and white poorer communities in Brooklyn, white youth retained better access to legitimate means of opportunity and were thus less likely to engage in or join serious deviant or criminal subcultures.

See also Gang Involvement, Theories of; General Strain Theory (GST); Social Disorganization Theory

FURTHER READING

Cloward, R., & Ohlin, L. (1960). *Delinquency and opportunity*. New York: Free Press.

Cohen, A. (1955). *Delinquent boys*. New York: Free Press.

Sullivan, M. *"Getting paid": Youth crime and work in the inner city*. Ithaca, NY: Cornell University Press.

William R. Wood

SUBURBAN JUVENILE VIOLENCE. Recent arrest data collected by the U.S. Department of Justice show that juvenile violence has declined every year since 1994, despite the fact that the problem of juvenile violence seems to have become more salient during this time. Statistics indicate that, although juvenile violence continues to be largely an urban phenomenon, it seems to be growing in nonmetropolitan areas. While violence appears to be less common among younger suburban youth than younger urban youth, violent episodes are comparable across the groups once juveniles in suburban, urban, and rural areas become older teenagers. Though there is still relatively little research on rural juvenile violence compared to that in cities, there seems to be even less about the nature of juvenile violence in suburban neighborhoods.

Oftentimes, it seems that both rural and suburban juvenile violence is compounded into one context that is assessed against the more traditional, urban context of youth violence. A closer examination of this phenomenon indicates that the proliferation of youth gangs, guns, and drugs in suburban towns has been partly responsible for the prevalence of juvenile violence there. However, this clearly cannot entirely explain the occurrence of all suburban juvenile violence.

Columbine High School Massacre

It is likely that the public first became aware of suburban violence as a result of the violent Columbine High School murders in Littleton, Colorado in 1999. Two rural teenagers, **Eric Harris** (age seventeen) **and Dylan Klebold** (age eighteen), were responsible for using machine guns in their Denver suburb to kill twelve students and one teacher and injuring twenty-three others. This killing spree ended when the two students killed themselves in the library of their school. Graphic photos of this incident's aftermath were printed in most news media outlets. Television news programs broadcast live footage of students and faculty running for their lives as shots were heard in the background. Recorded cellular telephone calls to emergency services operators were played for the public's consumption. It was various media sources that allowed readers, viewers, and listeners throughout the nation to learn about the horrifying events of that day. Some have suggested that these events were shocking not only because the violence involved juveniles, but because they occurred in a suburban setting. While many may expect extreme juvenile violence in urban centers, few would expect it in areas with less population density.

Media Portrayals of Suburban Juvenile Violence

Many claim that media portrayals of various other acts of juvenile violence have contributed to the widespread perception that it presents a mounting menace for American suburbs. Content analyses of news media show that, during the 1990s, crime was the most common story type, with approximately two-thirds of these crime news stories focusing on juvenile violence. However, statistics indicate that juveniles are only responsible for about 15 percent of all violent crime. This skewed portrayal of juvenile violence is exacerbated by the fact that a highly disproportionate number of media stories focus on suburban juvenile violence. It has been suggested that these stories are much more prominent in the media because they are less common and, therefore, newsworthy. However, the result is that the public may incorrectly believe that suburban juvenile violence is a greater threat than is actually true.

Gangs, Guns, and Drugs

There has been some disagreement among criminologists and law enforcement practitioners regarding the definition of gangs, which is especially problematic when trying to account for gangs in a variety of regions. However, most concede that many gangs are comprised of minors and involve illegal activities, including varying degrees of violence. There is a widespread belief that gangs are a social problem mostly found in inner-city neighborhoods, though this is definitely not the case any longer. Over the last few decades, there has been a dramatic increase in the number of gang problems in smaller suburban cities and towns. In 1999, 47 percent of suburban counties and 27 percent of smaller cities reported active juvenile gangs. It appears that the gangs in suburban areas are quite different from gangs in large cities in several ways. Research indicates that they involve more members that are younger, female, and white. Suburban juvenile gangs are also more likely to have racially and ethnically diverse memberships.

The increasing number of guns and illegal drugs available in suburban communities may also increase the likelihood of juvenile violence. Studies suggest that although the presence of guns and drugs is growing, the problems that accompany their prevalence among suburban youth are intrinsically different from those facing urban and even rural juveniles. Though the available data is preliminary and somewhat limited, it seems that juvenile involvement with drugs and guns in suburban areas leads to fewer and less severe subsequent violent acts than for juveniles using drugs and guns in cities. The issue of suburban juvenile violence is in need of further research in order to provide more insight.

See also Assorted Drug entries; Assorted Gang entries; Film, Juvenile Violence and; Gun-Related Violence, Rates of; Gun-Related Violence, Types of; Music, Juvenile Violence and; News, Juvenile Violence and

FURTHER READING

Baker, D. (1999). Children and the law: How safe is your 'burb? *American Bar Association Journal, 3*, 1–5.

Glicklich-Rosenberg, L. (1996). Violence and children: A public health issue. *Psychiatric Times, 13* (3).

Miller, W. (2001). *The growth of youth gang problems in the United States: 1970–98*. Washington, DC: Office of Juvenile Justice and Delinquency Prevention.

National Youth Gang Center. (2000). *1998 National youth gang survey*. Washington, DC: Office of Juvenile Justice and Delinquency Prevention.

Snyder, H. (1997). *The prevalence of serious, violent, and chronic juvenile offenders in a delinquent population*. Pittsburgh, PA: National Center for Juvenile Justice.

Snyder, H. (2005). *Juvenile arrests 2003*. Washington, DC: Office of Juvenile Justice and Delinquency Prevention.

Weisheit, R., & Wells, L. (2001). The perception of guns as a problem in nonmetropolitan areas. *Criminal Justice Review, 26*, 170–192.

Wells, L., & Weisheit, R. (2001). Gang problems in non-metropolitan communities: A longitudinal assessment. *Justice Quarterly, 18*, 791–823.

Kelly Welch

SUICIDE. Authors in the field of juvenile suicide research agree that there is no single moment, no special event, and no single mechanism sufficient enough to explain the cause of a suicide. Research perspectives, rather, focus on a conglomeration of different factors that may prompt a biologically or psychologically vulnerable person to commit suicide, including family, peers, and broader social patterns. Psychological or physiological factors, or those found within an individual person, are called endogenous factors. Some authors, for instance, consider major depressive disorder (MDD) as biologically founded because it is associated with abnormalities of several hormonal systems. Exogenous factors are those occurring outside the individual, for instance, with the peer group, with other pupils and teachers at school, or with colleagues or superiors at work. Young people who have been arrested are also more likely to become suicidal, with those serving the lengthiest sentences and those involved in violent crimes, such as rape and especially murder of a family member or close friend, most at risk. There cannot, however, be a sharp dividing line drawn between endogenous and exogenous factors because they interact with each other in a complex manner.

The bridge between endogenous and exogenous factors is family-related factors, because this is the social environment that mingles nature and nurture. For example, a depressive mother passes on to her child genetic factors as well as special affective and attachment problems. Actual studies suggest that juvenile suicide can be correlated with changes in the structure and stability of families. Studies dealing with the family background of young suiciders found out that these youthful persons often come from families with one, some, or all of the following characteristics: intra-family discord; physical abuse by their parents or other family members; frequent family change; low parental support; insecurity or avoidant attachment; broken homes due to death and divorce; emotionally overstrained single-parent families; parental unemployment due to a lack of education in the parents; parents with mental illness like personality disorders, major depressive disorder, or psychosis; addiction (e.g., drug abuse, gambling, alcoholism); and criminality in the parents.

Involvement with a dysfunctional family brings a number of psychological stresses that might lead an individual to commit suicide. Suicidal adolescents often have some or all of the following characteristics: a pattern of unstable interpersonal relationships; inappropriate, intense anger or lack of control of anger; identity disturbance; affective instability; intolerance of being alone; physically self-damaging actions; chronic feelings of emptiness or boredom; and impulsivity or unpredictability in at least two areas that are potentially damaging, e.g., drug abuse or gambling. Further, social isolation within the peer group and criminal activity are often found in the biographical background of young suiciders.

In addition to individual suicides, young people commit various types of group suicides. Double suicide and homicide-suicide acts, amok, rampage killing, suicide by the police, and school massacres with suicides are infrequent, but some have received international attention, such as the 1999 mass killing by two students at Columbine High School in Littleton, Colorado. These types of suicides are prompted by similar factors as those involved in individual suicide, especially depression, borderline disturbances, narcissistic neuroses together with triggers like social losses, but the aggressive dynamics of homicide-suicide acts differ from that of individual suicide. The development of auto- and hetero-aggressive tendencies combined with the wish to get a form of compensation for social losses by a spectacular event can lead to homicide-suicide, such as school massacres.

See also Family Relations and Juvenile Violence

FURTHER READING

Ambrosini, P., Rabinovich, H., & Puig-Antich, J. (1984). Biological factors and pharmacologic treatment in major depressive disorder in children and adolescents. In H. Sudak, A. Ford, & N. Rushford (Eds.), *Suicide in the young*. Boston, MA: Year Book Medical Publications.

Duffy, D., & Ryan, T. (Eds.) (2004). *New approaches to preventing suicide: A manual for practitioners*. London: Jessica Kingsley Press.

Ford, A., Rushforth, N., & Sudak, H. (1984). The causes of suicide. In H. Sudak, A. Ford, & N. Rushford (Eds.), *Suicide in the young*. Boston, MA: Year Book Medical Publications.

Friedman, R., Corn, R., Aronoff, M., Hurt, S., & Clarkin, J. (1984). The seriously suicidal adolescent: Affective and character pathology. In H. Sudak, A. Ford, & N. Rushford (Eds.), *Suicide in the young*. Boston, MA: Year Book Medical Publications.

Haenel, T., & Elsässer, P. (2000). Double suicide and homicide-suicide in Switzerland. *Crisis, 21*(3), 122–125.

Hayes, L. (2005). Juvenile suicide in confinement in the United States: Results from a national survey. *Crisis, 26*(3), 146–148.

Richman, J. (1984). The family therapy of suicidal adolescents: Promises and pitfalls. In H. Sudak, A. Ford, & N. Rushford (Eds.), *Suicide in the young*. Boston, MA: Year Book Medical Publications.

Ruth Erken

SURVEILLANCE IN SCHOOLS. Surveillance in schools takes many forms, from formal methods, like the use of video cameras and metal detectors, to informal methods, such as teachers monitoring the halls during passing periods and at lunch. Schools are increasingly adopting more technological means of surveillance as concern over school shootings magnified in the late 1990s. Further, federal monies are available for these types of surveillance, which are generally supported by the Bush administration. In addition, more schools have hired **school police officers** to watch over students. In the mid-1990s, the New York City Board of Education employed more officers than the entire Boston Police Department. The federal government has allocated over $350 million per year for school police officers. Over 45 percent of public schools had an officer or security guard on campus in 2002.

The idea behind surveillance of students in schools is that it will be a **general deterrent**. That is, students will be less likely to commit acts of delinquency or violence if they know they are more likely to be caught by some type of monitor. Some forms of surveillance can also be a **specific deterrent**, as particular students who have demonstrated a proclivity to delinquency or violence can be more closely monitored to ensure they will not repeat those actions.

Metal detectors are one of the most commonly used forms of surveillance in schools. In 1998, an elementary school in Indiana was the first primary school to install a metal detector. Exact figures are not known, but it is estimated that approximately 10 percent of schools have metal detectors, while up to 37 percent of urban schools use them. Advocates maintain that detectors can reduce if not completely eliminate the number of weapons in schools, thus significantly impacting the amount of violence that may occur. Some schools use walk-through detectors, like those commonly found in airports and courthouses. All students and staff can be made to walk through this type of detector. Others cannot afford these, so they use handheld wands. These require staff members to use some form of random scanning, as it is impossible to search everyone entering the school.

Opponents of metal detectors maintain they are an inexact method, and the money spent on the equipment and supplies would be better spent elsewhere. Students committed to bringing a weapon to school can easily get around the detectors, either by passing their weapon to another student who was not selected for a random search, sneaking it in through another entry, or some other method. Several of the schools where shootings occurred had both metal detectors as well as police officers. Further, there is concern that metal detector searches are not always done randomly and that they may lead to very invasive searches. Some students have reported feeling as though they are being sexually assaulted via a search from a scanning wand.

Video cameras are another common form of surveillance in schools. Schools often spend thousands of dollars on installing video cameras, both inside the school building and in parking lots. Proponents feel these cameras cannot only prevent acts of delinquency and violence, but can assist in identifying perpetrators in the event that an act does occur. Not only do video cameras help keep students safe from other students, but they can also keep students safe from outsiders.

Opponents of video cameras tend to dislike the concept that students are constantly being watched. Depending on how many monitors a school has and where they are placed, students may have little privacy in schools. In some schools the video feed is even sent directly to the local police. Further, these cameras are expensive, with the more extensive systems running close to $100,000.

School police officers or security guards are being used in many schools to monitor students' behavior. While having a police officer on campus can deter students from committing acts of delinquency or violence, it can also make students more fearful and resentful. In addition, officers on campus may serve to "widen the net." Widening the net refers to the involvement of criminal justice and/or other social agencies in areas that would once have been dealt with informally. Little formal evaluation of the impact of school police officers has occurred to date; what has been done tends to show mixed results.

Another method of surveillance commonly used in schools is identification badges. Some schools have even experimented with innovative methods, including tracking devices that monitor students' whereabouts on campus using radio signals.

Schools employ informal means of surveillance with even greater frequency than they do formal means. Teachers are often instructed to "be visible," meaning they need to step out of their classrooms and monitor hallways during busy times, such as passing between classes and lunch. School officials are also able to search students, as well as their lockers, bags, and vehicles and items contained within lockers, bags, and vehicles, if they have a reasonable suspicion they will find something in violation of school or criminal laws. This is a lesser standard than what is needed for a police search, which requires probable cause. As more officers are assigned to campuses, courts will need to further address search standards in schools.

One advantage of informal methods is that they can help prevent violence of many sorts, from physical assaults to sexual and other forms of verbal harassment. On the other hand, teacher or administrator monitoring can easily become profiling, where certain students are targeted. Further, many are concerned that surveillance in schools, in particular the use of searches, is a violation of students' privacy rights.

Some maintain that both formal and informal means of surveillance, rather than reducing violence, are simply examples of **systemic violence** against students. That is, they harm students by limiting their potential. Rather than concentrating on the social, emotional, and academic growth of students, opponents of school surveillance maintain these means of surveillance are like micro-management in the business place and represent a form of distrust that will likely lead to student alienation or apathy.

FURTHER READING

Devine, J. (1996). *Maximum security*. Chicago: University of Chicago Press.

DiGuilio, R. (2001). *Educate, medicate, or litigate? What teachers, parents and administrators must do about student behavior*. New York: Corwin Books.

Finley, L., & Finley, P. (2005). *Piss off! How drug testing and other privacy violations are alienating America's youth*. Monroe, MN: Common Courage Press.

Hyman, I., & Snook, P. (1999). *Dangerous schools*. San Francisco: Jossey-Bass.

Spina, S. (Ed.). (2000). *Smoke and mirrors: The hidden context of violence in schools and society*. Lanham, MA: Rowman & Littlefield.

Laura L. Finley

SYSTEMIC VIOLENCE IN SCHOOLS. When people think of school violence, they tend to envision physical acts perpetrated by students, either on other students or on teachers. Most often today, the image of school violence is one of a school shooter, although in reality shootings in school are quite uncommon. School violence encompasses much more than physical acts, however. Violence in schools also takes the form of verbal harassment and bullying, sexual harassment, and racial violence. In addition, it is not just students who perpetrate violence; school faculty also commits violence against students. Some of this is physical, such as when a first-grade teacher duct-taped a student for talking too much. Much of the violence committed by faculty is verbal and harms students psychologically and emotionally.

Further, schools often commit systemic violence. Systemic violence refers to institutional practices or procedures that adversely impact individuals or groups psychologically, mentally, culturally, spiritually, economically, or physically. Award-winning Brazilian educator Paulo Freire said that any situation in which people are prevented from learning is violence. Systemic violence involves acts of violence that are embedded into the practices and procedures of daily life in schools. They are typically not done intentionally; that is, educators are not plotting to commit violence. Rather, educators often use practices harmful to students, but with the students best wishes in mind.

Systemic violence includes practices that appear neutral but result in discriminatory effects. Because systemic violence is "for their own good," sometimes victims do not even recognize what has occurred as an act of violence. For instance, tracking programs in schools are a form of systemic violence, as they merely reproduce social inequalities and limit students' potential. Yet often parents and even students support tracking, buying into the rhetoric that it is being used to help students and that any resultant inequalities are accidental. Another example is school disciplinary practices. These are said to ensure a safe learning environment, but are often conducted in discriminatory and dehumanizing ways.

One obvious example of systemic violence in schools is the use of **corporal punishment**. Contrary to popular belief, corporal punishment is still legal in twenty-three states. It is a practice banned by every industrialized nation except the United States, some provinces in Canada, and one state in Australia. Many schools within the states that still allow corporal punishment elect not to use it, yet it is by no means an uncommon practice. Official figures show almost 350,000 students endured corporal punishment in schools in the 1999–2000 school year. Corporal punishment is more common in southern states, such as Texas, Mississippi, and Arkansas. Opponents argue that corporal punishment is wrong. For one reason, it is more frequently used against minority students; Black students are hit at a rate more than twice their representation in the student population. Opponents also maintain corporal punishment teaches that violence is an acceptable means to deal with problems; that it can result in major injuries; that corporal punishment is not allowed in other institutions, such as prisons, mental hospitals, and the military; that it is ineffective in reducing violence and other disciplinary problems; that it is frequently used for minor infractions; and that there are a number of other more effective disciplinary measures. Many well-respected organizations have argued for the complete abolition of corporal punishment in schools, including the American Academy of Pediatrics, the American Bar Association, the American Medical Association, the National Education Association, and the National Association for the Advancement of Colored People.

Some of the most commonly practiced teaching methods in schools can be considered systemic violence. Students are typically regarded as passive recipients and have no voice in what they learn or how they do it. Passive teaching practices tend not to address the affective domain, stressing that knowledge is only academic, not emotional. Students who do not adapt well to these methods are punished, as the emphasis in schools is on obedience. Research with students shows they often feel that teachers ignore verbal harassment by students and that they frequently contribute to it by using put-downs, favoritism, and inconsistent and unequal punishment. Traditional pedagogy has repeatedly been shown to favor boys' learning styles, which is a form of systemic violence. In addition, despite attempts at more multicultural inclusion, most schools still teach a largely "white" curriculum. Standardization of curriculum, and the subsequent standardization of assessment, is a form of systemic violence that assumes all students can and should be able to perform at the same level at the same time. Many studies have found standardized tests to be culturally biased.

Some maintain that inflicting punishment on kids "for their own good" does little but destroy their sense of self and their belief in their personal worth. Students may respond to systemic violence in a number of ways, including defiance, neglect of duty, withdrawal, or addiction. Students may become self-destructive, sometimes ignoring opportunities. Further, those who survive a hostile environment often end up reproducing it unconsciously. They cannot seem to see an alternative to the violence they experience. While systemic violence harms all students, it is most harmful to those already disadvantaged. Those privileged by the system are also harmed, though, as they are taught their superiority, which reproduces inequalities.

Acknowledging that school violence is more than simply physical acts committed by one individual against another is an important step in reducing violence in schools and making the educational experience more positive and useful for all.

FURTHER READING

Epp, J. (1996). Schools, complicity, and sources of violence. In J. Epp & A. Watkinson (Eds.), *Systemic violence: How schools hurt children* (pp. 1–23). Albany, NY: State University of New York Press.

Finley, L. (2006, forthcoming). Examining school searches as systemic violence. *Critical Criminology*.

Hyman, I., & Snook, P. (1999). *Dangerous schools*. San Francisco: Jossey-Bass.

Iadicola, P., & Shupe, A. (1998). *Violence, inequality, and human freedom*. Dix Hills, NY: General Hall, Inc.

Watkinson, A. (1997). Administrative complicity and systemic violence in education. In J. Epp & A. Watkinson (Eds.), *Systemic violence in education: Broken promises* (pp. 3–24). Albany, NY: State University of New York Press.

Laura L. Finley

TATE, LIONEL. Lionel Tate is the twelve-year-old African-American boy who was sentenced in 2001 to life in prison for the 1999 murder of a six-year-old girl, Tiffany Eunick. The trial gained national attention by identifying controversies in juvenile and criminal justice in the United States. The Florida state legislature had a year earlier allowed for **waivers** of violent juveniles to be tried in adult court instead of juvenile court. The aim of the move was to enable the court to impose longer prison and probation sentences to deter dangerous juveniles, yet others vehemently oppose the practice. The initial prosecution of the case also brought considerable media coverage due to the public's fascination with extraordinary murders. Tate was the youngest adolescent to be sentenced to life without parole in the United States.

Initially, Florida prosecutors sought to plea bargain with Tate's defense attorneys. In return for a guilty plea from Tate, the prosecution would recommend a three-year sentence, followed by ten years probation. Tate's legal team, in concert with his mother, Kathleen Grosett-Tate, rejected the plea bargain and young Tate pleaded not guilty to murder. Facing a trial by jury in the adult criminal court, Tate's legal team attempted to demonstrate Tate's immaturity.

The televised trial detailed the circumstances of the offense and was highlighted by the physical descriptions of the injuries to Tiffany Eunick. Eunick was killed when Tate claimed he mimicked wrestling moves he watched on televised matches involving World Wide Wrestling Federation (WWF) celebrities. Tiffany Eunick's injuries were extensive and severe, and the prosecution gave detailed listings of thirty-five traumas. They also emphasized that Tate was nearly 120 pounds heavier than Eunick. The defense described the violent incident as "playing gone bad" and reframed it as a tragic accidental death.

While the trial was underway, the print and television media expanded on numerous story lines concerning the case. One was the history of Tate's childhood, with descriptions of his misbehavior in school. He was characterized as a bully and was suspended from school numerous times for disruptive behavior.

The main defense used by Tate's attorney centered on his imitation of professional wrestlers (WWF). Their point was that Tate was naïve and believed that displaying the series of moves he did on Eunick would not injure her. They indicated Tate was immature and did not believe that the WWF wrestlers' moves and reactions were stage-managed. The defense even showed wrestling videos to the jury to emphasize that point. In contrast, the prosecution stressed Tate could understand Eunick's injury.

The wrestling defense was not convincing to the jury, given the extensiveness of the injuries. They handed down a first-degree murder conviction. It was the judge, however, who made the March 9, 2001, sentencing decision. Following the decision, the defense appealed the case to the Fourth District Court of Appeals.

After the trial, a nonprofit organization, the Parents Television Council (PTC) condemned the WWF (later changed to World Wrestling Entertainment [WWE]). Their claim was that televised wrestling activity is in reality teaching children to be violent and engage in violent actions toward others. The PTC made allegations that the WWF is responsible for being the model for the youth's murderous actions. In response to the allegations, the WWF won a 2002 suit that asserted the PTC's allegations could not be demonstrated, that televised wrestling matches are not generative of youth murder. They settled out of court for 3.5 million dollars. The PTC continues to raise objections to violent television programming and seeks to educate the public about the dangers of youth modeling violent behavior from television and movies.

Following the sentencing hearing, Tate was turned over to corrections officials for incarceration at a maximum security prison for juveniles. Further, Tate's attorneys filed a clemency application that was forwarded to Governor Jeb Bush. Bush refused consideration, given evidence by corrections officials that Tate engaged in serious misbehavior in prison. During his incarceration, Tate's mother continued to make the case that her son's sentence was excessive. Picked up by the major media, Barbara Walters of *ABC* television interviewed sixteen-year-old Tate, his mother, and the parent of Tiffany Eunick. A year later, Kathleen Tate was in the Vatican and met the pope, which served to maintain publicity about her son's case.

In December 2003, the Fourth District Court of Appeals made a decision to allow a new trial for Lionel Tate. They asserted that Tate should have had a mental competency evaluation prior to trial proceedings. During the trial, the appellate court ruled, Tate's lawyers discussed his immaturity, but the court did not take proper steps to document his mental level and ensure that Tate understood the consequences of the plea bargain if he turned it down. This enabled prosecutors to once again permit a plea bargain, which was accepted by Tate's attorneys. The deal required a sentence of three years in prison and ten years of probation. Having nearly served the three-year sentence, Tate was released from jail to live once again with his mother.

The rules of Tate's probation were to be in school or at a place of employment or church. In September, Tate was arrested for violation of his probation by being out past curfew and possession of a knife. The judge in the case added five years to Tate's probation.

On May 23, 2005, Tate was again arrested on charges of armed robbery and battery and of violating probation. Now aged eighteen, Tate is expected to plead guilty in exchange for a sentence of 10–30 years in prison. In May 2006, Tate received the maximum sentence.

The Florida case raised legal questions concerning proper procedures in the waiver of juveniles to adult court. Youth under the age of fifteen in particular need to be assessed for incompetence due to developmental immaturity. The Supreme Court decision *Drope v. Missouri* has been the legal standard for competence to stand trial. Following the Tate decision, it appears that prosecutors may follow *Drope* closely and waive offenders who meet its standard.

Although Tate's record shows repeated crimes, research establishes that some chronic offenders cease after a single offense. The decision to waive violent juveniles to adult court will be revised as problems arise, as was the case with Lionel Tate.

See also Social Learning Theories; Television, Juvenile Violence and; Victims of Juvenile Violence, Very Young

FURTHER READING

Brink, D. (2004). Immaturity, normative competence, and juvenile transfer: How (not) to punish minors for major crimes. *Texas Law Review, 82*(6), 1555–1558.

Scott, E., & Grisso, T. (2004). *Developmental incompetence, due process and juvenile justice policy.* University of Virginia Law School Public Law and Legal Working Paper Series, Paper 11.

James Steinberg

TECHNIQUES OF NEUTRALIZATION. Referring to verbal statements used by youth to rationalize and initiate delinquent behavior, techniques of neutralization are also called verbalized motives. David Matza's 1964 book titled *Delinquency and Drift* set forth the theory, called either **drift theory** or neutralization theory. The key actors in this theory are minors or juveniles, usually seventeen years old and under. What is problematic for Matza is the interpersonal process involved when youth make the decision to engage in illegal behavior. He uses the concepts of drift and neutralization to explain youth's thinking and potential use of neutralizations.

Juveniles, according to Matza, both internalize law-abiding norms and are exposed to delinquency-provoking routine influences and circumstances that may present themselves. Drift involves juveniles temporarily loosening their grip on conformity and engaging in delinquency. Situational elements and emotional states may generate drift. After the commission of the delinquent act, juveniles revert to being a conforming individual and resist engaging in delinquency, unless a subsequent circumstance presents itself that steers the juvenile toward verbalizations and then delinquency once more. Delinquency is seen as episodic, an infrequent lapse of judgment. Youth elicit delinquency and then reverse back to conformity, thus their identity and behavior is not centered around persistent delinquency.

The process that causes the delinquent act involves a youth's decision to use excuses or rationalizations to justify acts before and after they are committed. Techniques of neutralization is a concept in which a youth verbally frees himself or herself from inner moral constraints. For youth, experiencing a sense of injustice or lack of fairness in a particular situation generates an emotional reaction of perceived hypocrisy. This loosens the usual restraining forces of one's moral code of avoiding law violation and associated feelings of guilt. Matza contends that delinquency generally involves more than one offender. The presence of other peers increases exposure to the member's mutual use of neutralizations.

Matza proposed five types of techniques of neutralizations that are used individually or in combinations. These refer to a verbal class of excuses that are used to justify delinquency, some prefaced with the concept "denial," the rejection of a particular social value.

Denial of responsibility occurs when a juvenile rationalizes his or her illegal action as not his or her fault because other factors are the actual reasons for the victim's fate. The identification of specific social factors responsible for the act are race, poverty, and family characteristics.

Denial of injury involves explaining away the infliction of fear and pain. It is used to infer that, with no injury, there is no crime. This technique minimizes or ignores actual injury, and in crimes without actual visible injuries, the act is dismissed. In violent crimes, the injury is reframed as minor or exaggerated by the victim.

Denial of a victim involves an explanation that the victim was in some way culpable and deserving of the illegal act, thus the act is not actually serious. Even as harm is inflicted, verbalizations that imply the victim is deviant, and thus deserving, dissipate the youth's illegal action as justifiable. Dehumanization is the result of some verbalizations. This type would be used in crimes of violence in which the delinquent injured a victim.

Condemnation of the condemners is a verbal style in which the juvenile accuses authority figures, such as teachers, police, and truant officers, of being involved in corruption or abuse of youth. Amplifying their hidden abuses may ostensibly cancel out any illegal actions or violence that the juvenile perpetrates.

Appeal to higher loyalties is an abstract vocalization in which youth justify their actions by claiming a higher moral cause is being accomplished. This gives the act a cachet of moral superiority and importance that redefines the delinquency as actually a noble act. Usually the cause is related to a particular group-based and defined value that is deemed more important than legal standards. This technique may also be used by gang youth, who assert that leaders made them commit an act of crime or violence.

Neutralization theory is seen as similar to assumptions of Sutherland's **differential association theory**. Both theories concentrate on particular circumstances that need to be taken into consideration. Thus, delinquent acts are situational and not an inflexible characteristic of the delinquent. A second assumption is that delinquents engage in both nondelinquent and delinquent behavior and vacillate between the two. Techniques of neutralizations in a particular situation foster delinquency in that they push juveniles toward the delinquent behavior. Finally, delinquency is viewed largely as a group phenomenon. Most delinquency involves the participation of others that collaborate in the attitudes conducive to delinquency.

Drift theory contrasts with Hirschi's **control theory**. According to Hirschi's model, attachments are more permanent, so delinquents are viewed as more established in their actions and identity. For Matza, youth have more tenuous ties to a permanent delinquent identity and move back and forth as inducements in delinquent groups lead them to occasionally use a verbalized motive to justify delinquency.

Middle-class delinquency theorists, a form of control theory, stress that most delinquents age out of delinquency. Through maturation, youth become more enmeshed in adult responsibilities, such as work and family roles. Both theories agree that youth are not committed to a career of delinquency.

Critics of neutralization theory contend that the theory does not consider sources of structural strain that may facilitate delinquency. In addition, the actual forces imbedded in the circumstances facilitating delinquency are unclear. There is no distinct process by which the juveniles makes the decision to use a verbalization and engage in action, nor is it clear whether whether each excuse inevitably leads to law violation. Because the theory is abstract and difficult to empirically verify, it has not been subject to extensive research in delinquency.

The theory has been expanded beyond delinquent groups. Consumers, medical professionals, pedophiles, sex offenders, and college students are additional samples that have been subject to an expanded application of the theory. Modifications of the theory focus on the rationalization of behavior through elaborate verbal and written reasoning, the mechanisms that redefine illegal behavior as normal or acceptable.

FURTHER READING

Agnew, R., & Peters, A. (1986). The techniques of neutralization: An analysis of predisposing and situational factors. *Criminal Justice and Behavior, 13*(1), 81–97.

Matza, D. (1964). *Delinquency and drift*. New York: John Wiley and Sons, Inc.

McCaghy, C. (1968). Drinking and deviance disavowal: The case of child molesters. *Social Problems, 16*(1), 43–49.

Shoemaker, D. (2005). *Theories of delinquency: An examination of explanations of delinquency behavior*, 5th ed. New York: Oxford University Press.

James Steinberg

TEEN COURTS. Teen courts, additionally referenced as youth courts, peer courts, student courts, and peer juries, provide an alternative means of addressing legal issues involving young people. The purpose of teen courts is twofold. On one level, the initiative aims to expose young people to the workings of the U.S. legal system by enabling them to assume key responsibilities associated with law proceedings. For instance, participants may serve as a lawyer, bailiff, clerk, or juror. On a second level, teen courts allow youths charged with legal violations to be held accountable for their actions by their peers. Proceedings parallel the structure of the juvenile justice system by requiring participants to be sworn in, creating space and time for students and their families to receive legal counsel, and so forth. Court activities themselves generally follow a trial or peer jury model.

Programs based on the trial model include two basic models as well as a variety of hybrid choices. The adult judge model, the most popular version, requires youth volunteers to serve in all major capacities except that of the judge. The youth judge model, in contrast, permits a minor to fulfill the responsibilities of the judge. In peer jury models, youths who serve as jurors as well as youth advocates are permitted to question defendants directly without the participation of court attorneys. In all cases, young people complete training appropriate to their roles to uphold the integrity of the judicial process. Examples include learning how to complete direct and cross-examinations of witnesses, identifying questions that allow for courtroom objections, and gaining skills in the preparation and delivery of opening and closing statements. Instruction in such areas is frequently provided by retired court officers or community volunteers who possess legal expertise. Guidelines set by the National Youth Court Center (NYCC) recommend an average of sixteen to twenty hours of youth training. Moreover, the organization encourages all teen court programs to provide educational insights into the following areas: (1) program planning and community mobilization; (2) program staffing and funding; (3) legal issues; (4) identified respondent population and referral processes; (5) program services and sentencing options; (6) volunteer recruitment and management; (7) volunteer training; (8) youth court operations and case management; and (9) program evaluation. States that host teen court programs generally set regulations and mandates specific to their needs.

Examinations of teen court programs suggest that most defendants are first-time offenders between the ages of seven and nineteen who are charged with misdemeanor criminal activity such as vandalism. Program advocates argue that teen courts fulfill a critical role by attending to criminal behavior that is unlikely to receive serious attention from the traditional justice system. In many conventional cases, supporters argue, offenders may receive a mild sanction that fails to resonate with young people. Experiences in teen courts, in contrast, appear to reduce the likelihood of future offenses by connecting with students from an educational standpoint and demonstrating the ways in which breaking the law invites consequences. For example, defendants who are found guilty of a given crime may be required to write letters of apology to victims and parents or write essays, complete tours of jails or **boot camps**, or complete reparations for their actions. Yet, because teen courts operate on a voluntary basis, defendants may reject decisions reached by these bodies and elect to resolve their cases in the traditional juvenile court system.

Researchers largely trace the conceptualization and implementation of modern teen courts to the 1970s. However, such programs primarily gained national popularity during the 1990s as a result of increased financial assistance, particularly from the Justice Department's **Office of Juvenile Justice and Delinquency Prevention (OJJDP)**. Other sponsors include a variety of agencies, such as juvenile courts, schools, probation departments, and community organizations. Currently, more than three hundred teen court programs operate in over half of the nation. In their totality, the efforts aim to redress youth crime while simultaneously engaging young people in the civic process, promoting responsible behavior, educating youths about judicial processes, and seeding life skills and job opportunities. Program advocates argue that teen courts have been successful based on the courts' cost-effectiveness, low rates of recidivism, and high degree of satisfaction among youths and their families with court outcomes—even when defendants are found guilty and penalties are assigned. Critics, however, contend that empirical research is limited and that commonly cited benefits appear to be grounded in anecdotal evidence derived from "cream of the crop" offenders.

See also Specialized Courts

FURTHER READING

Godwin, T. (1996, Winter). Teen courts: Empowering youth in community prevention and intervention efforts. *American Parole and Probation Association Perspectives*, 20–24.

Mullins, T. (2004). *Selected topics on youth courts: A monograph.* Washington, DC: National Criminal Justice Reference Service.

Pearson, S. (2004). *Policymakers support youth court growth: Voices and recommendations from the field.* Lexington, KY: National Youth Court Center.

Williamson, D., & Wells, J. (2004). *Making youth court as effective as possible.* Chicago: American Bar Association.

Carla R. Monroe

TELEVISION, JUVENILE VIOLENCE AND. For decades, violence on television has been a controversial subject among researchers, parents, and policymakers. Research on the effect of televisual violence on juveniles has been of special concern given the easy access to televisions, especially in comparison to other media. However, although over 60 percent of all television programs contain some violence, a recent study found that the amount of serious violence on television decreased by 17 percent from 1999 to 2001. Limited research suggests television characters under age eighteen commit fewer acts of violence than do young adult and adult characters. Nonetheless, a child who watches three hours of American television per day will see at least two incidents of violence perpetrated by a character under the age of eighteen during that time. Children and teens in poverty watch more television than do their more affluent peers, and African-American children and teens watch more television than do Caucasian children and teens. Consequently, these groups are exposed to more violent imagery.

Various studies have shown that televisual violence can influence future aggressive behavior on the part of child and adolescent viewers. The National Television Violence Study, a longitudinal examination of violence on American television, lists three main effects of televised violence: viewers can learn aggressive attitudes and behaviors; viewers can become desensitized to violence; and viewers can experience an increased fear of victimization. Such authorities as the American Psychological Association, the American Medical Association, the National Academy of Sciences, the National Institute of Mental Health, and the U.S. Surgeon General have all agreed that television violence can have various adverse effects on children and adolescents. In all, more than 3,000 studies have found a connection between television violence and actual violence. A longitudinal study from the 1960s and 1970s found the heaviest viewers were the most likely to have been in trouble, including greater numbers of arrests as well as aggression at home. As early as 1972, the Surgeon General declared a causal relationship between viewing television violence and aggressive behavior.

Not all viewers are affected in the same way by televised violence, however. Children age seven and below are the most vulnerable because of their inability to distinguish fantasy from reality. Children in this age group also have trouble connecting events that occur in different scenes, so that if punishment occurs several scenes after the violent act is perpetrated, children may not acknowledge it or associate it with the violence. The National Television Violence Study found that cartoons are most likely to showcase high-risk portrayals of violence that teach aggression to children seven years of age and younger. Cartoons are also the most likely television shows to feature heroes participating in justified violence that goes unpunished and results in a minimum amount of harm to the victim.

Furthermore, not all televisual violence is equal; certain characteristics make violence seem more acceptable to viewers. Television characters portrayed as good or heroic are attractive to juvenile viewers, and characters (good or bad) that show little or no remorse and that experience no negative repercussions help make violent behavior seem appropriate. Also, violence appears acceptable when no physical pain or harm is done to victims and the short- and long-term consequences are not addressed. Finally, the use of humor trivializes violence. Given that humor is a mainstay of children's cartoons, this is tremendously important.

One recent study of child and adolescent television perpetrators found that such younger violent characters are often portrayed as attractive to viewers, are less likely to be punished than adult perpetrators, and their victims experience fewer negative consequences than those of violent adult characters. Research suggests that juvenile television viewers are more likely to emulate characters portrayed as attractive and characters with whom they can relate or who they perceive to be similar to themselves, especially with respect to age, race, and gender. The vast majority of young television perpetrators are male. Televisual juvenile violence tends to target victims of similar age, and juvenile television perpetrators are more likely than adults to use physical means of violence and less likely to use guns. While one in three juvenile television perpetrators engage in lethal violence, both the prevalence and the rate of younger characters engaging in violence on television are lower than those of adult characters.

Music television, first introduced twenty-five years ago, continues to be most popular among youth. When violence occurs in music videos, it is both gendered and raced. Males are usually portrayed as the aggressors, black males disproportionately so. White females are usually portrayed as victims.

There are two theories that best explain the role televised violence may play in regard to actual violence. **Social learning theory**, based on Bandura's classic Bobo doll experiment, asserts people learn violence from their environment. **Differential identification**, which built on **differential association**, maintains that we learn violence not just from those with whom we are intimately and frequently associated, but also those with whom we identify. Thus a violent television character might serve as a behavioral model for children and teens.

See also Film, Juvenile Violence and; Music, Juvenile Violence and; News, Juvenile Violence and; Victims in the Media

FURTHER READING

Carter, C., & Weaver, C. (2003). *Violence and the media*. Philadelphia, PA: Open University Press.

Federman, J. (Ed.). (1998). *National television violence study*. Santa Barbara, CA: University of California, Santa Barbara. Available from: http://www.ccsp.ucsb.edu/ntvs.htm.

Wilson, B., Colvin, C., & Smith, S. (2002). Engaging in violence on American television: A comparison of child, teen, and adult perpetrators. *Journal of Communication, 52*(1), 36–60.

Allison Wright Munro

TRAIT THEORIES. Trait theory is a model of personality that seeks to identify the basic traits necessary to describe personality. The term "traits" refers to the enduring dimensions of personal characteristics along which people differ. While people may share the same traits, individuals may vary in the degree they express those traits. For instance, while everyone may share the trait of agreeableness, people vary from each other on the degree to which they are agreeable (on a continuum from very agreeable to very disagreeable).

The list of traits considered important for measurement has constantly evolved for trait theorists. In 1936, one of the earliest trait theorists, Dr. Gordon Allport (1897–1967), developed a list of 18,000 trait names by recording all of the separate terms used to describe personality in an unabridged dictionary. Even after eliminating words with the same meaning, he was left with 4,500 descriptors. Allport later suggested the existence of central traits, which make up the major characteristics of an individual, and secondary traits, which affect behavior in fewer situations and are less influential than central traits. In 1965, Dr. Raymond Cattell (1905–1998) developed the Sixteen Personality Factor Questionnaire (16PF) to provide scores for each of the sixteen source traits that his research suggested represented the basic dimensions of personality. Currently, the "Big Five" trait approach is the most influential description of personality. The Big Five are five broad trait factors, consisting of openness to experience (imagination, independence), conscientiousness (responsibility, self-control, persistence), extraversion (sociability, assertiveness), agreeableness (cooperativeness, friendliness), and neuroticism (emotional stability). Scientifically, there is no trait theory that has the "right" number or division of personality characteristics. Any trait theory that is plausible and addresses the needs of the particular situation is acceptable for use.

Studies that examine violent behavior through trait theory approaches typically either examine differences in traits between violent and nonviolent individuals or the similarities in traits among violent individuals. By determining which scores on which traits separate violent and nonviolent individuals from each other, the likelihood of predicting violence-prone individuals is increased.

An individual's score for a particular trait can usually be measured easily. Testing is typically done through self-report measures of personality, such as the 16PF, or through projective methods of personality, such as the Thematic Apperception Test (TAT). In a self-report measure, people report about their own behavior through a series of questions. The projective method has people describe or tell stories about ambiguous pictures, with those responses interpreted by trained interpreters. In both types of testing, individuals receive numerical scores on the traits that are being measured. This allows easy comparisons to be made.

In addition to the previously mentioned advantages to trait theory, there are numerous disadvantages as well. It is often difficult to determine which particular traits might be important and should be measured. Only the traits that have been measured can be used in such a comparison. In addition, even when a comparison is made, the results may not be applicable to anyone other than those that were tested in the first place. For example, low agreeableness scores may be an indicator of susceptibility to violent behavior in one culture, but not in another. Another disadvantage is that the measurement of a trait occurs at a single point in time, while human behavior changes across time. While traits are enduring dimensions of personal characteristics, there may be secondary traits that only influence behavior under certain circumstances. As an example, we may record the level of physical agitation that a violent offender exhibits. This is a trait that may change over the course of time and may vary depending on the behavior the offender is committing at that time. Unless we measure the level of physical agitation before, during, and after a violent act, we might not have an accurate snapshot of the relationship that particular trait has with violent behavior.

Finally, even if consistent differences between violent and nonviolent groups of people are found to exist, there exists yet another problem. Trait theories can only describe a correlational relationship between traits and behavior. They cannot, by themselves, explain the cause of the measured traits or how the measured traits caused the violent behavior. In fact, there can be no certainty that the traits caused the violent behavior at all. For instance, we could measure the levels of violence and the levels of agreeableness in several neighborhoods. We might then compare the levels of agreeableness for the violent neighborhoods with those of nonviolent neighborhoods and find that the more violent the neighborhood, the less agreeable the residents are. The decreased level of agreeableness among the residents may be the cause of the increased violence. However, the increased violence could be the cause of the decreased agreeableness, with scared residents being less friendly than nonscared residents. A third alternative is the possibility of a third variable in this equation. Perhaps the presence of illicit drug use has caused both the violence levels to increase and the agreeableness levels to decrease.

Because of these disadvantages in trait theory, it is typically not used to explain violent behavior by itself. Instead, it is used in conjunction with other theories, where trait measurement is a valuable tool for describing potential susceptibilities to violence.

See also General Theory of Crime; Problem Behavior Syndrome (PBS)

FURTHER READING

Allport, G. (1961). *Pattern and growth in personality*. New York: Holt, Rinehart and Winston.

Cattell, R. (1965). *The scientific analysis of personality*. Chicago: Aldine.

Dorfman, W., & Hersen, M. (2001). *Understanding psychological assessment*. Dordrecht, Netherlands: Kluwer Academic Publishers.

Zucker, R., Aronoff, J., & Rabin, A. (1984). *Personality and the prediction of behavior*. Orlando, FL: Academic Press.

Dave D. Hochstein

UNIFORM CRIME REPORTS (UCR). Overseen by the FBI since 1930, the Uniform Crime Reporting Program was created in 1929 by the International Association of Chiefs of Police. The program was based on a need to provide uniform, reliable crime statistics for the United States on an annual and ongoing basis. The FBI collects, publishes, and archives all data obtained through the program. Annually, the FBI produces and distributes several nationwide statistical publications, such as *Crime in the United States*, *Hate Crime Statistics*, and *Law Enforcement Officers Killed and Assaulted*. These publications provide information including volume and rates of crime on national, state, and local levels, incident information, victim information, bias involved in specific (hate) crimes, weapons used in crimes, accidental and intentional deaths of law enforcement officers, and circumstances surrounding crimes. The uniform format in which crimes are documented under the Uniform Crime Reporting Program is set forth in the *UCR Handbook*, also a publication of the FBI.

In 1982, the Bureau of Justice Statistics and the FBI made a collaborative effort to study and revise the existing Uniform Crime Reporting Program. The National Incident Based Reporting System (NIBRS) was born as the result of a five-year revision effort to produce more detailed and comprehensive crime statistics. The current UCR program is still in the process of being converted to NIBRS. Under the current summary system, agencies report the number of crimes by type monthly to the FBI. Under NIBRS, each crime reported will come with an individual record providing specific details about the incident. At present, about half of the states in the United States are certified by the FBI and submit monthly reports under the NIBRS format. In an effort to increase participation in NIBRS, the Bureau of Justice Statistics sponsored a project through the Police Executive Research Forum (PERF) in 2001. PERF designed an information resource manual to assist law enforcement agencies with implementing NIBRS-compatible reporting systems and has since held two annual conferences aimed at the progressive implementation of NIBRS in the United States.

The implementation of NIBRS hopes to provide more incident-specific information about victims and crimes, leading to a more comprehensive understanding of juvenile violence. More information will exist as a resource for teachers, parents, counselors, law enforcement, and school administrators. Still, the UCR system is limited in its informational capabilities. When compared with data gathered by the **National Crime Victimization Survey**, the UCR system reflects that only about 35 percent of all crimes are reported to the police. In addition, the UCR system is under police discretion, meaning some crimes, while they occurred, may not be documented. For these reasons, other governmental studies have been implemented to better study and prevent crime and more accurately reflect statistics.

FURTHER READING

Uniform Crime Reports. (n.d). *The Federal Bureau of Investigation Website.* Available at: http://www
.fbi.gov/ucr/ucr.htm.

About the National Incident-Based Reporting System. (n.d.). *Bureau of Justice Statistics. U.S.
Department of Justice.* Available at: http://www.ojp.usdoj.gov/bjs/nibrs.htm.

Adam Doran

UNITED STATES DEPARTMENT OF JUSTICE (USDOJ). In the years immediately following the Civil War, there was a dramatic increase in the number of cases involving litigation against the U.S. government. As a result, a large number of private sector attorneys were retained to handle the increasing workload at an extremely high cost to the U.S. government and its taxpayers. In response, Congress passed an act in 1870 that officially established the Department of Justice (DOJ) as a governmental agency, with the U.S. attorney general as its leader. The newly created DOJ was to handle the primary legal business of the United States, including all criminal prosecutions and civil matters. Furthermore, the 1870 act gave the DOJ control over all divisions and agencies of federal law enforcement.

Over the last century, the internal structure of the Department of Justice has changed dramatically, especially with regard to the establishment of the various agencies falling under the purview of the DOJ, including the Office of Juvenile Justice and Delinquency Prevention (OJJDP).

In 1974, Congress enacted the Juvenile Justice and Delinquency Prevention Act, establishing the Office of Juvenile Justice and Delinquency Prevention as part of the Department of Justice. The mission of the OJJDP is to provide a national base of leadership and centralized resources to assist local and state governments with issues of juvenile delinquency and victimization and to facilitate improvements in prevention, community involvement, and the treatment of juveniles.

FURTHER READING

Kelley, B. T., Thornberry, T. P., & Smith, C. A. (1997). *In the wake of childhood maltreatment.*
Washington, DC: U.S. Department of Justice, Office of Juvenile Justice and Delinquency
Prevention.

Mission Statement and History. (2005, November). U.S. Department of Justice. Available at: http://www
.usdoj.gov/02organizations/index.html.

Jeffrey A. Walsh

URBAN JUVENILE VIOLENCE. During the late nineteenth and early twentieth centuries, women activists organized settlement homes and charitable organizations to address the problems associated with urban juvenile delinquency and violence. Notwithstanding these efforts, most of the concerns about juvenile violence relied upon controversial interpretations about its origins and causes.

The dominant viewpoint among criminologists during this period was that a select number of juveniles inherited biological traits that made them prone to commit violence. This **socio-biological** approach, influenced by social Darwinists and the work of Cesare Lombroso, insisted that violent juveniles had a certain genetic makeup that predisposed them to violence. This approach was reinforced by the negative stereotypes of central city inhabitants, who were seen as unruly, unsocialized, and in direct conflict with the provincial character of rural and small-town life at the turn of the twentieth century. Not surprisingly, many central city dwellers and urban youth who committed violence were poor European immigrants who faced the brunt of discriminatory policies and practices.

The early frameworks of juvenile violence also failed to account for state-sponsored forms of violence against youth. Although urban youth were viewed as the perpetuators of violence, the state—the collective power of government, political institutions, and law enforcement agencies—was considered an innocent bystander. Yet in the nineteenth century, many groups of youth and juveniles were targets of state-sanctioned violence: black slave youth in northern urban localities, white and black youth who were indentured servants, and immigrant children who were brutalized by unfair (and violent) labor practices.

By the turn of the century, there was a subtle shift in some of the thinking about juvenile delinquency and violence. The state of Illinois created the nation's first juvenile court in 1899, which signaled a move toward the rehabilitation, rather than punishment, of violent youth offenders. Additional attention was given to the unique problems facing juveniles, exemplified by the passage of protective labor laws for children, the expansion of public education to at-risk youth, and the emergence of academic research countering social Darwinist interpretations of juvenile violence.

Urbanization, industrialization, and the continued influx of immigrant groups brought attention to the challenges confronting urban youth in the 1930s and 1940s. Chicago became a laboratory for studying juvenile delinquency and violence during this period. Clifford Shaw of the Institute of Juvenile Research organized the **Chicago Area Project** (CAP), which studied the causes of and remedies for youth violence and crime. He believed youth violence was not biological or hereditary, but was mostly attributed to poverty, discrimination, and other structural factors. Over a decade later, Shaw's sentiments were echoed by *Life* magazine photojournalist, Gordon Parks. Yet, whereas Shaw's research studied white immigrant youth, Parks documented the activities of a black street gang called the Midtowners in Harlem, New York.

In the 1960s and early 1970s, juvenile delinquency garnered the attention of national-level politicians who implemented a series of measures to address this problem. Presidents Lyndon B. Johnson and Richard Nixon created the President's Commission on Law Enforcement (1967), the National Commission on the Causes and Prevention of Violence (1969), and the National Commission on Criminal Justice Standards and Goals (1973). Congress also passed two pieces of legislation called the Juvenile Delinquency Prevention and Control Act of 1968 and the **Juvenile Justice and Delinquency Prevention Act of 1974**. The renewed attention to juvenile violence was partially due to the wave of civil disturbances and riots. These disturbances, which occurred in almost every major American city in the 1960s, usually involved confrontations between ghetto youth and the police.

The federal judiciary further debated remedies for juvenile delinquency and violence in the 1960s and 1970s. The locus of the debate centered on civil liberties for juvenile offenders. For youth who committed the most violent offenses, the judiciary debated whether they should be **transferred to adult courts** and subsequently to adult prisons. This debate also spilled into the state legislatures. New York, for example, was one of the first states since the early twentieth century to implement harsh penalties for juvenile violent offenders. It allowed thirteen-year-olds convicted of murder and fourteen-year-olds who committed other serious violent offenses to be prosecuted as adults. Civil rights activists believed this adversely affected urban youth from the state's poorest communities.

By the 1980s and 1990s, **zero tolerance policies** had become the central theme of public discourse and policies on juvenile justice. Some attributed this to the soaring rates of violent crimes in urban communities. Others believed lawmakers used juvenile violence as political cannon fodder—that is, to mobilize their constituents to support prison expansion and the downsizing of social programs and civil liberties. Regardless, urban juveniles during this period were often viewed as "super-predators," or as lawless, uncontrollable, and absent of any redeemable virtues.

The shift toward zero tolerance policies underscores a larger policy debate about how best to address urban juvenile violence. Those favoring punitive measures argue that juvenile violence is a consequence of dysfunctional families, pathological behavior among urban youth, and the overdependence of poor families on social welfare programs, which undermined their individual initiative and personal responsibility. Their opponents believe juvenile violence is the result of poor gun control policy, the loss of jobs in urban communities as a result of deindustrialization and suburbanization, the elimination of social welfare and antipoverty programs, and the unequal treatment of poor youth by law enforcement officials.

Notwithstanding these disagreements, juvenile justice and child advocates contend that remedies and policies that address the persistent problem of juvenile violence must take into account several interrelated phenomena. First, the more exposure youth have to violence—either as the victims, witnesses, or through the media—the more likely they are to commit violence. Second, children who have been victimized by or witnessed abuses and violence in the home may be more inclined to commit violent acts. Third, incarceration encourages violence instead of curbing it. Youth confined for violent and nonviolent offenses, the latter of which consists of most urban youth, are more likely to commit violent acts during their adolescent years. All of this suggests that for urban youth, violence, either as victims of or witnesses to it, only begets violence.

See also Abused/Battered Children; Illinois Juvenile Court; Juvenile Violence 1920–1929; Juvenile Violence 1930–1939; Juvenile Violence 1940–1949; Juvenile Violence 1950–1959; Juvenile Violence 1960–1969; Juvenile Violence 1970–1979; Juvenile Violence 1980–1989; News, Juvenile Violence and

FURTHER READING

Dilulio, J. (1995, November 27). The coming of the super-predators. New York *Weekly Standard*, 23–28.

Feld, B. (1999). *Bad kids: Race and the transformation of the juvenile court.* New York: Oxford University Press.

Finkelhor, D., & Ormrod, R. (2001, October). Homicides of children and youth. *Juvenile Justice Bulletin.* Washington, DC: Office of Juvenile Justice and Delinquency Programs, 1–12.

Howell, J. (1997). *Juvenile justice and youth violence.* Thousand Oaks, CA: Sage.

Loeber, R., & Farrington, D. (Eds.). (1998). *Serious and violent juvenile offenders: Risk factors and successful interventions.* Thousand Oaks, CA: Sage.

Magnani, L., & Wray, H. (2006). *A new interfaith paradigm for our failed prison system.* Minneapolis, MN: Fortress Press.

Parry, D. (2005). *Essential readings in juvenile justice.* Upper Saddle River, NJ: Pearson Education, Inc.

Tanehaus, D. (2004). *Juvenile justice in the making.* Oxford, England: Oxford University Press.

Sekou Franklin

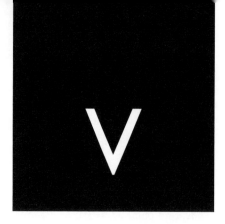

VICTIMS IN THE MEDIA. The role of the media is essentially to report the news, which oftentimes is focused predominately on crime and crime victims. As such, the traumatic nature of victimization dictates that a precarious relationship exists between the media and victims. The media, on the one hand, has to report the news, which at times can be demoralizing for the victim. On the other hand, the victim has a certain expectation of the right to privacy, which requires that the media demonstrate compassion and respect for victims. When reporting stories involving victims, the media should remain objective while deciding whether the potential harm to the victim outweighs society's right to know about crimes in their localities, as well as the media's right to freedom of speech.

The media functions under the provisions of the First Amendment, which prohibits the government from restricting free speech or a free press. Under the First Amendment, the media has the right to publish any relevant information about a story, which includes any public information found in police and/or court records. This information includes the names and addresses of victims of crimes, information regarding the offender, and the circumstances surrounding the alleged incident.

Most media outlets also function under professional codes of ethics designed to establish criteria for journalists to consider when reporting news stories. One example, the Code of Ethics established by the Society of Professional Journalists (2005), contends that only an overriding public need can justify intrusion into anyone's privacy. This code further recommends that journalists should be cautious about identifying juvenile suspects or victims of sex crimes and suggests that ethical journalists treat sources, subjects, and colleagues with respect.

While most media outlets are governed by and subscribe to professional codes of ethics that address to some extent the individual rights of citizens, these codes do not necessarily preclude journalists from reporting the names and addresses of victims. However, the code does recommend that the media treat victims and children with sensitivity and compassion and that they balance the rights of the victim with the right of freedom of the press and the public's right to know and make a decision based on fairness and equity.

There is a dearth of research regarding the media and victims of crime. The majority of research that is available has focused on satisfaction/dissatisfaction with interview techniques, reporting by race and gender, and reporting and naming of rape/sexual assault victims. Most research indicates that victims often receive less attention than perpetrators in the media because the media predominately focuses on stories that are designed to capture the public's attention. Further, when addressing the media's response to victims, research suggests that victims are concerned about the news media practices of interviewing victims/survivors at inappropriate times, which can further traumatize victims. Additionally, there is a concern that journalists will take inappropriate videos and/or pictures, focus on the negative aspects of victims' lives, and print or broadcast the name and address of the victim. Consequently, journalists may have an ethical responsibility to weigh the benefits and harm when reporting incidents of victimization that is consistent with protecting the rights of victims.

Furthermore, the media tends to focus its reporting efforts on the victimization of men rather than women. Research indicates that the media personalized reporting of male victimization more than female victims and that the media also provided more personal information about male victims than females. The names of the male victims were also more likely to be reported than females, thereby minimizing the impact of victimization on females.

A particular victimization that is noteworthy is the crime of rape. Currently, most media outlets will not report the names of rape victims unless there is a compelling reason to do so. However, the hesitancy of the media to report the names of rape victims may be more of a response to public opinion than out of respect for the victim. Research indicates that the public strongly supports protecting the rights of rape victims, with a majority of women (75 percent), rape victims (78 percent), and rape service agencies (91 percent) supporting legislation that would prohibit the media from disclosing the names of rape victims.

The National Victims Assistance Academy (NVAA) provides several recommendations for the media when dealing with victims. NVAA suggests that the media engage in sensitivity to reduce the amount of trauma to victims, indicating that the coverage sometimes provided by the media is viewed as insensitive, voyeuristic, and uncaring and can compound victims' emotional and psychological suffering. The public also supports this view, with research indicating that 82 percent of respondents think that reporters are insensitive to people's pain when covering disasters and accidents.

There have also been some positive impacts of the media's involvement with victims. Reporting by the media on the plight of some victims has facilitated significant changes in laws relative to victim rights and victim notification pending offender release, among other laws. Additionally, victims use the media to promote their agendas in an effort to improve programs and services. Each of these initiatives has promoted the influx of additional resources to assist victims in the recovery process and has facilitated increased coverage of victims' issues in the media.

See also Film, Juvenile Violence and; Music, Juvenile Violence and; News, Juvenile Violence and; Television, Juvenile Violence and

FURTHER READING

Anastasio, P., & Costa, S. (2004). Twice hurt: How newspaper coverage may reduce empathy and engender blame for female victims of crime. *Sex Roles, 51*, 535–542.

Code of ethics. (n.d.). *Society of Professional Journalists.* Available at: http://www.spj.org/ethics_code.asp.

Hackney, S. (n.d.). Covering crime and victims. *Criminal Justice Journalists.* Available at: http://www.justicejournalism.org/crimeguide/chapter05/chapter05_pg02.html.

Kawamoto, K. (n.d.). Best practices in trauma reporting. *Dart Center for Journalism and Trauma.* Available at: http://www.dartcenter.org/media/da_best_practices.pdf.

Sacco, V. (2000). News that counts: Newspaper images of crime and victimization statistics. *Criminologie.* Retrieved August 5, 2005, from: http://www.erudit.org/revue/crimino/2000/v33/n1/ 004744ar.html.

Seymour, A. (2000). Chapter 18: The news media's coverage of crime and victimization. *National Victims Assistance Academy.* Retrieved August 5, 2005, from: http://www.ojp.gov/ovc/assist/ nvaa2000/academy/chapter18.htm.

U.S. Department of Justice. (n.d.). *Office of Victims of Crime Bulletin*. Available at: http://www.ojp .usdoj.gov/ovc/new/directions/pdftxt/bulletins/bltn14.pdf.

Patricia Hylton Grant

VICTIMS OF JUVENILE VIOLENCE, ADULTS AS. While young people are more likely to be violently victimized by adults, in some cases children and teens commit violent crimes against adults. In the most serious cases, juveniles kill. Perhaps the most common and most disturbing example of teens victimizing adults is parricide, when young people kill their own parents. In each of the years between 1977 and 1986, more than three hundred parents were killed by their own offspring. In 1995, several cases made national news, all occurring within the months of February and March. A sixteen- and seventeen-year-old, both skinheads, killed their parents and younger brother in Pennsylvania, and only a few miles away and a few days later, a sixteen-year-old killed his parents. Girls are more likely to murder family members than are boys. Girls are also more likely to perform secondary roles in attacks on adults, especially in regard to gang-related assaults.

Parricide happens for a number of reasons. The explanation used most frequently is that young people kill parents who have been abusive. One psychologist estimates that young people who have been severely abused commit 90 percent of all parricides. These young people were generally not violent prior to the killing and typically have no criminal record. Most of these young people consider running away, but perceive that they have nowhere to go. Most sought help, often repeatedly, only to have teachers, relatives, and other adults turn them away or fail to provide any real assistance. In addition to being physically, sexually, and/or emotionally abusive, parents who are killed by their children are frequently substance abusers. The actual murder typically takes place after some escalating event, such as a caring family member moving out. The young person then sees no hope left and no way out of the abusive situation. After the killing, most of these teens feel a great deal of remorse. Oftentimes, they do not remember killing their parents, although they do not deny they did it.

Sometimes, young people perceive abuse, although what is happening might not meet the legal definition. For instance, a fourteen-year-old in China stabbed his father, mother, and grandmother because he felt he was inadequately cared for, even though his evidence was that his mother told him to go back to bed, rather than see a doctor, when he complained of being ill. The most infamous case of parricide involving a claim of abuse was the killing by Erik and Lyle Menendez of their parents, Kitty and Jose. Teenagers at the time of the murders, the brothers claimed they killed Jose because he had been sexually abusive throughout their childhoods. They asserted that the killing was really a form of self-defense, as they knew more abuse would come. They killed Kitty because she did nothing about the abuse. Psychiatrists testifying for the defense said that the brothers suffered from post-traumatic stress disorder (PTSD), as do many victims of abuse. In 1996, jurors rejected the claim of self-defense, and both the Menendezes were convicted of first-degree murder and sentenced to two consecutive life terms without the possibility of parole. The brothers are now in their 30s.

Other kids who commit parricide are seriously mentally ill, although this is fairly rare. The most well-known cases involve young people who are dangerously antisocial, not because these are more common but because they attract the most media attention. Some argue the Menendez brothers were not abused but were in fact sociopaths. The most common form of mental illness associated with teen killings is conduct disorders, such as oppositional defiance disorder, disruptive behavior disorder, adjustment disorder, and antisocial disorder. Many of these disorders occur in conjunction with **ADHD**. Youth violence experts maintain that the number of young people in need of professional mental health services has more than doubled in the last quarter century. At the same time, there are fewer child psychiatrists than ever. Further, many schools do not provide adequate counseling for juveniles with mental health issues.

Young people also victimize adults that are not relatives. Teens commit **hate crimes** against both adults and fellow juveniles. Sometimes, teens who commit violent hate crimes against adults are members of hate groups, as in some of the parricide cases mentioned earlier. More frequently they are not actual members. In recent years, much media attention has been given to examples of teenagers beating and even killing homeless adults. These attacks tend to be especially brutal. In Wisconsin, three teenagers murdered a homeless man when they came across his forest campsite. They beat the man with rocks, a flashlight, and a pipe, then smeared him with feces. In New York City, two teenagers kicked, punched, and bludgeoned a homeless man in a churchyard. In Fort Lauderdale, Florida, two teenagers killed one homeless man and beat at least one other on a single night. These teens were caught on a surveillance camera, and nationwide coverage ensured public outrage. Gangs also victimize adults, although rival gang members are typically the primary target for violence, and they are generally of similar age as the offender(s).

Yet another form of teen violence in which adults are victimized is attacks on teachers. **Barry Loukaitis**, fourteen at the time, killed his teacher and two classmates in 1996. **Andrew Wurst** killed one teacher, injured another, and injured two students in his 1998 school shooting in Edinboro, Pennsylvania. **Eric Harris and Dylan Klebold** killed one teacher and twelve classmates before killing themselves at Columbine High School in 1999. It does not seem, however, that the adults are the primary targets of this form of violence. In other examples, it is clear a teacher was the intended target. For instance, in 1995, a nine-year-old boy repeatedly punched a substitute teacher in the chest because he did not like the assignment the class was given. The substitute died later.

One explanation for teen violence against adults has focused on violent media. A widely documented 1999 study found that, by age eighteen, the average American youth will have seen 200,000 dramatized acts of violence and 40,000 dramatized murders. It was widely documented that the Fort Lauderdale teens had viewed a video series called *Bumfights*, which celebrate the beating of "bums." In 2006, two brothers, ages twenty and fourteen, were inspired to kill their mother after watching the murder and dismemberment of a New Jersey gangster on HBO's *The Sopranos*. In another macabre case, two teenaged boys stabbed one of their mothers forty-five times, saying they were inspired by the slasher/comedy *Scream*. Barry Loukaitis was a fan of the violent film *Natural Born Killers* and identified with the bullied student who seeks revenge in the Pearl Jam video *Jeremy*. Eric Harris and Dylan Klebold loved to play the violent video game *Doom*. Andrew Wurst enjoyed the horror stories of Stephen King, as did Barry Loukaitis.

When teens victimize adults, especially in cases where the attacks are brutal and lethal, many call for them to be **tried as adults**. To date, jurors seem to be not terribly receptive to arguments that their youth is a mitigating factor.

See also Abused/Battered Children; Film and Juvenile Violence; Gang-on-Gang Violence; Gang Violence, Against Bystanders; Music, Juvenile Violence and; News, Juvenile Violence and; Television, Juvenile Violence and

FURTHER READING

Davis, C. (2003). *Children who kill: Profiles of pre-teen and teenage killers.* London: Allison and Busby.

Flowers, R. (2002). *Kids who commit adult crimes: Serious criminality by juvenile offenders.* Binghamton, NY: Haworth.

Garbarino. J. (2000). *Lost boys: Why our sons turn violent and how we can save them.* New York: Anchor.

Heide, K. (1992, September). Why kids kill their parents. *Psychology Today.* Available at: www.psychologytoday.com/article/pto_19920901-000027.html.

Heide, K. (1999). *Young killers: The challenge of juvenile homicide.* Thousand Oaks, CA: Sage.

Kellerman, J. (1999). *Savage spawn: Reflections on our violent children.* New York: Ballantine.

Males, M. (1999). *Framing youth: Ten myths about the next generation.* Monroe, Maine: Common Courage Press.

Ramsland, K. (2005). The unthinkable: Children who kill. *Court TV's Crime Library.* Available at: www.crimelibrary.com.serial-killers/weird/kids2/index_1.html.

Laura L. Finley

VICTIMS OF JUVENILE VIOLENCE, JUVENILES AS. Historical trends regarding who is most likely to be the victim of violent crime continued in both 2003 and 2004, according to FBI reports. They are males and youths. Males were victims of overall violent crime, robbery, total assault, simple assault, and aggravated assault at rates higher than females. However, females were more likely to be victims of rape or sexual assault. In the years 2003 and 2004, there was a general pattern of decreasing crime rates for people in the older categories. Juveniles between twelve and nineteen years of age experienced overall violence at rates higher than rates for age twenty-five or older. Important to consider, however, is that violent crimes against females are more likely to be reported to police than those against males.

In the United States, one of the leading causes of death for juveniles is homicide. In 2004, the **Uniform Crime Report** (UCR) figures indicate that 12.1 percent of violent crime clearances nationwide involved juveniles. A comparison of UCR data for 2004 and 2003 indicated that there was a 0.8 percent decline for juveniles arrested for violent crimes, 1.6 percent decline for juveniles arrested for aggravated assault, 0.4 percent decrease for rape. The number of juveniles arrested for murder increased 21.6 percent and robbery rose by 0.3 percent. The **National Crime Victimization Survey** (NCVS) shows that the average annual rate of violent crime continues to be highest among youth between the ages of sixteen and nineteen who were victimized at a rate of 55.6 per 1,000 persons in the 2002–2003 time period.

Homicide data compiled in the UCR for 2004 indicates that 9.8 percent of the total number of victims were juveniles. The 2004 data indicates that 49.8 percent of the victims were white and 47.6 percent black. The 2004 UCR statistics show that for murders for which the offenders were known, 91.7 percent of offenders were adults and 8.3 percent were juveniles. For incidents in which the relationships were known, 76.8 percent of the victims knew their killers, 29.8 percent were killed by family members, and 70.2 percent were killed by acquaintances. The victim offender relationship was unknown for 44.1 percent of the victims; 23.2 percent were murdered by strangers.

Nearly 38,000 juveniles were murdered between 1980 and 1997. A juvenile offender was involved in 26 percent of these crimes when an offender was identified. In murders of juveniles by juveniles, about 1 of every 6 also involved an adult offender. Between 1980 and 1997, the victim and the offender were the same race in 97 percent of murders of juveniles by juveniles.

Data from the Bureau of Justice Statistics in 2004 indicated that more than 4 million youths participated in a serious fight in school or elsewhere. About two-thirds of the victims of nonfatal violent crime by juveniles were other juveniles between 9 and 16 years old; 54 percent of reported juvenile sexual assaults in the same period were committed against juveniles younger than twelve years of age; 36 percent of the victims of sexual assaults were younger than six years of age, 84 percent were younger than twelve. Furthermore, the proportion of juvenile murders that involved a juvenile offender increased from 21 percent in 1980 to 33 percent in 1994—the peak year for all murders by juveniles. In 1980, an estimated four hundred juveniles were killed by other juveniles, growing to nearly 900 in 1994. By 1997, this figure had fallen to about five hundred, or about 1 of every 4 juvenile murders that year. Of the juveniles killed by other juveniles between 1980 and 1997, 13 percent were under age six. Of juveniles killed by other juveniles since then, 63 percent are age fifteen or older.

Bureau of Justice Statistics data indicate that in 1993, there were 63,500 cases of violence by juveniles against other juveniles, 30,400 cases of violence by juveniles against adults, and 31,300 cases of adult violence against juveniles. Nearly 9 of 10 violent crimes committed by juveniles and 7 of 10 violent crimes committed against juveniles involved rape or assault. Of the 1,367,009 estimated violent crimes committed in the United States in 2004, juveniles were 25 percent of both perpetrators and victims.

Victim age is related to differences in medical care costs, especially for rape victims, because of higher average mental health treatment costs for the juvenile victims. Estimated total victim costs of all violent crime in the United States in 2003 exceeded $15.7 billion. Of this total, juvenile violence accounted for $6.4 billion of victim costs (47 percent). Quality of life losses accounted for 83 percent of total victim costs, and future earnings losses accounted for 11 percent. Including Medicare and Medicaid costs, public programs targeted toward the victims of juvenile violence cost an estimated $42 million. The victim costs of violence against juveniles ($4.5 billion) greatly exceeded the victim costs of violence by juveniles ($2.6 billion). Most juvenile violence occurred in the urban counties of the state, which together accounted for 72 percent and nearly 71 percent of the total violent crimes committed by juveniles and against juveniles, respectively.

As with the incidence of violent crime, victim costs were higher in urban counties than in rural ones ($4.0 billion vs. $1.4 billion), accounting for nearly 7 percent of total victim costs. In both urban and rural counties, the largest share of victim costs of juvenile violence was for crimes by adults against juveniles; the smallest share was for violent crimes by juveniles against adults. Several violent crimes—rape, assault, and robbery—were more likely to result in physical injury when committed in rural areas.

The estimated total criminal justice costs for perpetrators of juvenile violence in the United States exceeded $46 million in 1993 and nearly doubled in 2004 ($82 million). Juvenile treatment program costs accounted for 55 percent of total perpetrator costs, and probation costs and detention costs 20 percent each. Incarceration costs, although large per unit, accounted for only 6 percent of total costs. Total public spending on victims and perpetrators of juvenile violence was approximately equal. On a per capita basis, however, spending per known perpetrator was nearly five times greater than spending per known victim. Contrary to recent concerns over rates of violence among juveniles, the results of this study suggest that violence against children and adolescents is a much larger problem than is violence committed by youth. Although incidence data suggest that juveniles are 25 percent of victims and perpetrators, our cost estimates show that because of differences in the distributions of youth and adult victims across crimes and the impact on victims, greater losses are associated with violence against youth than with violence by youth. The finding that total public spending on victims of juvenile violence roughly equals total spending on juvenile perpetrators of violence lacks both theoretical and methodological evidence. Public debate is needed about whether equity in expenditures on victims versus perpetrators is appropriate, as well as the extent to which resources should be directed toward prevention programs.

FURTHER READING

Elikann, P. (2002). *Superpredators: The demonization of our children by the law*. New York: De Capo Press.

Moser, R., & Frantz, C. (Eds.). *Shocking violence: Youth perpetrators and victims—a multidisciplinary perspective*. New York: Charles C. Thomas.

Polakow, V. (2000). *The public assault on America's children: Poverty, violence, and juvenile injustice*. New York: Teachers College Press.

Sickmund, M., & Snyder, H. (1995). *Juvenile offenders and victims: A national report*. Washington, DC: Office of Juvenile Justice and Delinquency Prevention.

Uniform Crime Report. Available from: www.fbi.gov/ucr.

Evaristus Obinyan

VICTIMS OF JUVENILE VIOLENCE, TREATMENT OF. Historically, the treatment of victims in the United States has centered on victims' interaction with law enforcement and prosecutors' contact with victims regarding the prosecution of criminal offenses. While numerous public and private organizations exist throughout the United States that serve victims' needs, only recently have the treatment and rights of victims of juvenile crime gained visibility within federal, state, and local justice agencies.

Literature regarding the treatment of victims of juvenile crime suggests that victims have been traditionally excluded from, even further victimized by, the juvenile justice system. A 1997 study by the Office for Victims of Crime found that virtually all victims that participated in the study reported negative experiences regarding their treatment and participation in court processes. Most often, the exclusion of victims of juvenile crime takes the following forms: exclusion of victims from participation in and input into prosecution; exclusion from sentencing recommendations; failure of notification regarding disposition and sentencing; failure to inform victims of dropped court dates; failure of notification for release of offenders; lack of victims' support regarding restitution, trauma, and other victim needs; lack of attention to victims' personal safety; and lack of empathy regarding victimization. Moreover, many victims, particularly victims of violent and sexual crimes, are further victimized by law enforcement and prosecutors, who see victims as necessary for prosecution, but fail to take steps to address harms that arise in the collection of evidence, victims' testimony, and plea agreements.

In the late 1960s and early 1970s, victims' rights advocates began to address the problems and treatment of victims in the United States. At this point, significant effort was being placed on the rehabilitation of offenders. Victims' rights groups argued that funding and services should be equally extended to the victims of these offenders. Also, beginning in the late 1970s and 1980s, significant media attention was given to several cases (most notably that of

Willie Horton) where convicted violent criminals were released on parole or furlough and committed further violent crimes, either against their previous victims or new ones. As a consequence, significant victims' rights legislation was passed on both state and federal levels. By 1970, five states had developed victim compensation programs under the growing recognition that victims very often did not receive **restitution** and that the costs of crime to victims often far exceeds restitution. Victim impact statements, now commonly used in every state, were first introduced in Fresno, California in 1976. These statements provide a crucial "voice" for victims by allowing them to introduce the impact and effect of their victimization to judges and prosecutors in their decisions on sentencing and plea agreements. Wisconsin passed the first state "Crime Victims' Bill of Rights" legislation in 1980, which provided several statutory rights for victims of crime.

On the federal level, the 1982 Presidential Task Force on Victims of Crime issued recommendations for legislation and initiatives regarding crime victims. Also in 1982, the Victim and Witness Protection Act legislated standards of treatment for victims of federal crimes, the inclusion of victim impact statements, criminal penalties for victim and witness intimidation and harassment, and victim restitution. The 1984 Victims of Crime Act (VOCA) mandated the Office for Victims of Crime (OVC), part of the U.S. Department of Justice, to assist victims of crime with restitution and other needs and provide education for law enforcement, prosecutors, and other agencies to improve the treatment and services available to victims. Finally, the 1990 Crime Control Act included a provision that further codified victims' rights for federal crimes.

Throughout the 1980s and 1990s, virtually every state adopted some form of victims' rights legislation. However, the majority of these states did not include provisions for victims of juvenile crimes, so that by 1988, only thirteen of the forty-five states that had passed some form of victims' rights legislation did so to include victims of juvenile crimes. Coupled with the rise of violent juvenile crime in the late 1980s and early 1990s, this exclusion became strikingly transparent; yet to date only about half of the states have adopted legislation regarding victims' rights to be notified of disposition and adjudication hearings and decisions, to be present at these decisions, and to submit victim impact statements. Even fewer states require victim notification or input regarding plea agreements and bail hearings. A majority of states do allow for restitution as part of disposition and adjudication.

Moreover, as the Department of Justice notes, while over 30,000 statutes have been passed regarding victims' rights, only a small number of these include or address victims of juvenile crime. This is important, as the juvenile justice system varies in significant ways from adult courts, as well for the reason that victims of juvenile crime suffer unique hardships. Juvenile offenders are often granted rights not afforded to adult offenders, such as confidentiality, closed hearings, and mandated **diversion**. Consequently, victims of juvenile crime often have less participatory rights than victims of adult offenders. They may not be able to attend disposition and sentencing hearings or submit victim impact statements and are not generally informed of outcomes. In terms of the effects of juvenile crime on victims, juvenile offenders very often cannot pay full restitution due to their age and income. Also, court programs for victims are usually designed around adult offenders and may be of little help to victims of juvenile crime in terms of navigating and understanding local and state provisions regarding juvenile court processes and the rights of juvenile offenders. Finally, few victim services programs are able to address the specific trauma that may accompany victimization by a child or young offender.

Finally, for victims of juvenile crimes, implementation of victim rights' legislation varies widely between states. Many states that do have laws for victims of juvenile crime enforce them sporadically at best, according to a 1996 study by the National Victim Center. Many states that do have laws have provided little or no funding for the development of programs mandated by legislation. **Restorative justice** is one alternative that provides greater involvement of victims in the juvenile justice process.

See also Restitution; United States Department of Justice (USDOJ); Victims in the Media; Victims of Juvenile Violence, Adults as; Victims of Juvenile Violence, Juveniles as

FURTHER READING

Crawford, A., & Burden, J. (2005). *Integrating victims in restorative youth justice*. Bristol: Policy Press.

Feld, B. (1999). *Bad kids: Race and the transformation of the juvenile court*. New York: Oxford University Press.

Humes, E. (1997). *No matter how loud I shout: A year in the life of juvenile court*. New York: Touchstone Books.

Moriarty, L., & Jerin, R. (Eds.). *Current issues in victimology research*. Durham, NC: Carolina Academic Press.

Sickmund, M. (2003). *Juveniles in court*. Washington, DC: Office of Juvenile Justice and Delinquency Prevention.

Wolcott, F., Davies, C., & Bull, R. (2002). *Children's testimony [electronic reference]: A handbook of psychiatric research and forensic practice*. New York: J. Wiley.

Zehr, H., & Toews, B. (Eds.). (2004). *Critical issues in restorative justice*. Monsey, NY: Criminal Justice Press.

William R. Wood

VICTIMS OF JUVENILE VIOLENCE, VERY YOUNG

Introduction

Cases in which very young juveniles fall victim to older juveniles have occurred worldwide. Spectacular cases like that of Jon Venable and Robert Thompson in England alarmed the public and led to scientific and less-scientific discussions in respect to the causes of this problem and promising ways to address it. Although the discussion is in full swing and producing lots of results, there is no final answer so far.

A Case Study

In February 1992 two ten-year-olds lured two-year-old James Bulger away from his mother in a shopping mall near Liverpool to the nearby railroad tracks. They sprayed paint in his eye and beat him with bricks. Thinking that he was dead, the boys placed his badly injured body on the railroad tracks. James Bulger died shortly thereafter. His small body lay on the railroad track having been butchered by a train.

Violence in Schools

Due to the outstanding cruelty of the crime, it gained a lot of attention by scientists, politicians, the press, and the public. However, there are lots of cases of nonlethal violence against very young children, especially in school, which hardly become known to the public. School violence includes extortion and bullying and very often takes place outside school grounds, in subways, sporting grounds, and on the way home from school. This violence tends to involve gangs of children rather than lone bullies. For instance, police were called to an elementary school in Laval, Canada in 1997 to stop a group of ten-year-olds who were running a protection racket against younger pupils, charging them $1 a week. Increasingly, girls are getting into the act. Most of these cases do not get reported, however, because the victims are afraid of retaliation from the culprits. Victims are often frightened into silence by gang members brandishing a knife or gun or are told that their homes will be burned down, their parents will be killed, and so forth. Moreover, the victims often don't trust that the adults can solve their problem. It also seems that there is little peer pressure to stop violence against young and very young victims. Teachers and other children only infrequently intervene to help them.

Explanations for Violence against the Very Young

Researchers point out that juvenile violence against very young victims may have multiple causes. In the case of the Bulger murder, the distorted family background of the two culprits was identified as one possible starting point for an explanation. Robert Thompson was one of the youngest of seven boys. His mother, a single parent, was an alcoholic. His father, who left home when Robert was five, was also a notorious drinker who beat and sexually abused his wife and children. At home it was normal practice for the older children to violently attack the younger ones, and Robert, as one of the weakest, was invariably on the receiving end. Jon Venable's parents were also separated. His brother and sister had educational problems and attended special needs schools, while his mother suffered psychiatric problems. Following his parents' separation, Venable became isolated and was constantly seeking attention. At school he would regularly bang his head on walls or slash himself with scissors. No effort was made to find the cause of his obvious distress. Apart from the family situation, their social environment also may have played a role: The boys and their families lived in the Liverpool area, one of the most deprived areas of the United Kingdom. One of the aspects of the case that gained much media attention was whether Venable and Thompson had been watching violent films in the days prior to the killing and whether or not those movies had contributed to making the two boys act in the way they did. One of the fathers possessed a large collection of violent videos, and the two probably had access to them. Suspicion was fed by the fact that Bulger's death was similar to the death in a film. However, as of yet, research cannot conclusively prove whether video violence causes crime. The case does highlight the importance of family background and the offender's own personality and thoughts in determining the effects of film violence. The research points to a pathway from having a violent home background to being an offender, to being more likely to prefer violent films and violent actors. Distorted perceptions about violent behavior, underdeveloped empathy for others, and low moral development all enhance the adoption of violent behavior and violent film preferences.

School violence against young and very young victims is thought to originate from five basic reasons. First, individual reasons, such as failure at school and distortions in the development of personal identity can cause school violence. Second are parental factors. Unstable and distorted family life, neglected education due to sheer laziness of the parents, and the fact that the culprit has been a victim earlier in his life are primary parent-related factors. Third, school-related factors include large classes, dilapidated school buildings, and lack of social ties between teacher and student. The fourth reason is the media. Violence in the media may model a strategy for the solution of problems. Fifth, classmates/other pupils are often a factor. A multiplicity of effects combined with children's sometimes less-developed understanding of the consequences of actions can all contribute, but none has been proven to date.

Impact on Very Young Victims

The impact of violence on very young victims may be dramatic. Behavior in everyday life may change; a child may become afraid to go anywhere, or he/she may display eating and sleeping disorders and learning difficulties. The Mental Health Association in New York State maintains that clinically, children involved with frequent violence have altered brain development. An infant is born with brain functions that control involuntary life-sustaining functions, but the rest of the brain is not yet organized. Events in a child's life prompt connections between brain cells, forming circuits literally shaped by experience. The circuits get stronger the more often an experience is repeated. Constant violence creates a fear circuit that comes to dominate the brain of very young victims, changing their baseline resting state from calm to fear.

See also Biochemical Theories; Biosocial Theories; Bullying; Film, Juvenile Violence and

FURTHER READING

Guarino, S. (1985). Delinquent youth and family violence: A study of abuse and neglect in the homes of serious juvenile offenders. Commonwealth of Massachusetts, Department of Youth Services.

James, O. (1995). *Juvenile violence in a winner-loser culture: Socio-economic and familial origins of the rise of violence against the person.* New York: Free Association Books.

James Bulger. (n.d.). *Wikipedia: The online encyclopedia.* Available at: http://de.wikipedia.org/wiki/James.Bulger.

The Mental Health Association in New York State. Available at: http://www.mhanys.org/cc/cc2003f-fewthoughts.htm.

Ruth Erken

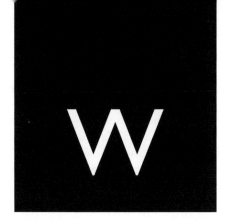

WAIVERS TO ADULT COURT. When a juvenile is arrested and begins the intake process, criminal justice professionals make a determination if the charges and characteristics of the offense warrant transferring the youth so that he or she can be tried or prosecuted in an adult criminal court. This transfer is referred to as waiver. A waiver hearing may be held to determine the adequacy of the case in meeting legal criterion, or in some states specific offenses are automatically transferred to criminal court. Waiver of a juvenile is based on requirements and procedures specified in state law, and these vary from state to state. One important characteristic of juveniles in potential waiver decisions is what is known as person offense cases. These cases are considered the most violent offenses and may involve serious injury to a victim.

There are four major types of waivers, each with varying amounts of discretion allowed in the waiver decision. The types of waivers are: judicial waivers, legislative exclusion, concurrent jurisdiction provisions, and blended sentencing. Thus, while all states use waivers, their particular mechanisms depend on legislative decisions in the use of different combinations of waivers.

The oldest and most common type of waiver is referred to as the judicial waiver. There are three types of judicial waivers. It provides for the juvenile judge to make the waiver decision. This decision is based on a motion filed by the prosecutor. Referred to as a discretionary waiver, it allows judges and prosecutors to make the waiver decisions based on their own assessment of the gravity of the offense characteristics and background of the juvenile. The second version of judicial waiver is a mandatory waiver in which the judge makes a determination of probable cause and verifies that the presumed offense is specified as a mandatory waiver. In a third version, the presumptive waiver case, the judge is required by statute to waive the offender to criminal court unless the juvenile can document that they are capable of rehabilitation. These forms of waiver are more commonly referred to as various forms of transfer, since waiver resides with judges.

The second type of waiver is the legislative exclusion, sometimes referred to as statutory exclusion, in which state governments specify provisions that delineate which juveniles should be waived to adult court. These provisions use very specific criteria, such as particular ages that are automatically waived, hence they are often referred to as mandatory transfer. This results in making a judicial waiver presumptive as it is based on specified juvenile offenses and other legal criterion. Generally, older youth and those involved in serious offenses are subject to statutory exclusion. These are usually person offenses, which include homicide, forcible rape, robbery, aggravated assault, simple assault, other violent sex offenses, and other person offenses. However, in some states younger and less violent offenders have been added to mandatory waiver due to an increasingly strict legislative philosophy on punishment. Thus, if the juvenile meets the provisions they are automatically waived to adult court. Twenty-eight states have enacted statutory exclusion provisions.

A third type of waiver is the concurrent jurisdiction provision, or prosecutorial waiver. In this form, the prosecutor has the discretion to move a juvenile case directly to the adult court or retain the case in juvenile court. The prosecutor bases their decision to file on the provisions determined by state laws that specify the juvenile's age and particular offense characteristics. This waiver was used by approximately fifteen states by 1997.

The fourth type of waiver is blended sentencing, which permits the juvenile or criminal court the power to render a juvenile and adult sentence at the same time. There are many variations on blended waivers by state. In juvenile court, common variations are giving either juvenile or a criminal sentence, imposing both sentences, or allowing for the contingency of imposing criminal sentence at a later date. For criminal courts, the two options are imposing either sentence or imposing both. In cases where both sentences are imposed, the criminal sentence is tabled and used only if the juvenile violates requirements of their sentence. This gives juvenile judges and criminal judges the ability to sentence beyond the limit of usual juvenile court jurisdiction.

Two provisions related to waiver are reverse waiver and "once an adult, always an adult." The reverse waiver permits the criminal court to send the youth back to the juvenile court in the event of additional offenses. The "once an adult, always an adult" posits that once a juvenile is transferred to adult court, all later offenses he or she may perpetrate will be handled by the criminal court. As such, blended sentencing and provisions has its critics that argue that the array of blended schemes creates confusion and brings more nonserious offenders into the adult system.

Since the early 1990s, many state legislatures have established exclusion laws (legislative, prosecutorial, and blended transfers) that circumvent the authority of the juvenile court. Only discretionary and mandatory judicial waivers involve the juvenile court prior to adjudication. Thus, juvenile court statistics used alone do not provide a complete picture of the total number of juveniles transferred to adult court. Juvenile court waivers, however, reveal certain trends.

Judicial waivers to criminal court fluctuated from 6,000 to 12,000 cases, peaking in 1994 and gradually declining to 6,000 cases in 2000. Since the late 1990s, with the advent of exclusionary laws that omitted serious offenders from the juvenile court, the actual number of cases is greater than 6,000 annually. The juvenile court tends to waive juveniles who are older (age sixteen or seventeen) and were arrested for serious offenses that involved the use of weapons, injured their victim, and had a longer history with the court. Youth who were on probation or served in a residential facility were more likely to be waived. Violent offenses are not the predominant reasons for waiver; in practice, property offenses were similar to violent offenses in percent waived, as were drug offenses.

Exclusionary provisions result in transfers of younger youth that are charged with a violent crime and used a deadly weapon or were adjudicated prior to the arrest. While the laws' intentions are to incarcerate juveniles for longer periods, preliminary research shows similarity in sentence length with juvenile court decisions.

See also Differences between Juvenile Justice and Criminal Justice: Juveniles in Adult Prisons; Zero Tolerance Laws

FURTHER READING

Howell, J. (2003). *Preventing & reducing juvenile delinquency: A comprehensive approach.* Thousand Oaks, CA: Sage.

National Council of Juvenile and Family Court Judges. (2005). *Juvenile delinquency: Improving court practice in juvenile delinquency cases.* Reno, NV: National Council of Juvenile and Family Court Judges.

Snyder, H., Sickmund, M., & Poe-Yamagata, E. (2000). *Juvenile transfers to criminal court in the 1990s*. Washington, DC: U.S. Department of Justice, Office of Juvenile Justice and Delinquency Prevention.

James Steinberg

WEISE, JEFF. On March 21, 2005, Jeff Weise, a high school student at Red Lake High School in Red Lake, Minnesota, went on a shooting spree, first killing his grandparents at their home and then six people at school. Weise's victims included students as well as a teacher and a security guard. After killing the others and wounding fourteen, Weise shot himself. The shooting was the nation's worst since the 1999 Columbine shooting by Eric Harris and Dylan Klebold and was the second fatal shooting incident in a Minnesota school in recent years. In September 2003, John Jason McLaughlin, a fifteen-year-old, killed two students at Rocori High School in Cold Spring.

Weise used his grandfather's guns to perpetrate the crime. After shooting Daryl Lussier and his girlfriend, Michelle Sigana, Jeff stole the man's police-issued weapons, bulletproof vest, and squad car, which he drove to Red Lake High School. Lussier had been a longtime officer with the Red Lake tribal police. Red Lake High School is on the Red Lake Indian Reservation. The reservation is home to the Red Lake Chippewa tribe, one of the poorest in the state.

Red Lake High School did have an emergency response plan that called for a warning to be broadcast over the school's intercom. The warning never came, as Weise entered the building, first shooting unarmed security officer Derrick Brun twice, killing him. He allegedly tried to open several classroom doors before finally breaking into the classroom where he shot five students and a teacher. According to students in the school at the time of the shooting, Weise was grinning as he shot. He was wounded three times by a police officer before he killed himself.

It was initially thought that Weise acted alone, but late in March tribal police arrested Louis Jordain, son of the chairman of the Red Lake band of Chippewa, for his involvement in the shooting. Authorities were lead to arrest Jordain after examining Weise's computer, including e-mails he exchanged with Jordain. Jordain allegedly helped plan the attack and had been prepared to assist in executing the plan. At least twelve other students were said to have heard of the attack prior to it.

There is much speculation about what might have motivated Weise to commit this crime. Family members expressed shock, claiming not to have seen any warning signs. Yet they do remember he preferred to play alone as a child and that even as a young child he wore dark clothes. Weise did have a hard childhood. His father committed suicide in 1997 after a standoff with police, and his mother suffered brain damage after a drunk-driving car accident. She had to live in a nursing home in Minneapolis, where she, Jeff, and an aunt had been living, so Jeff moved back to Red Lake to live with his grandfather. He expressed frustration with the move.

Some suggest that Weise, like **Harris and Klebold**, was obsessed with nazism. He had allegedly posted a number of comments on a neo-Nazi website. Weise posted his comments under the names "NativeNazi" and "Todensengel," which means "angel of death" in German. He was also a regular contributor to fiction sites. On one, he wrote a story about a school massacre involving zombies. He also created flash animations and posted them on the Internet, including one depicting a shooting with an assault rifle. The Southern Poverty Law Center claims it is not unusual for a member of a racial minority to join a hate group or to advocate a similar message.

There is some suggestion that Weise was bullied in school, as were many of the other school shooters. Students classified him as a "goth," meaning he wore black clothes, combat boots, and liked dark music. He was also said to have affected the sullen mood of the gothic culture. Weise drew strange pictures of skeletons, and others of people with bullets going through their heads. According to some former classmates, he talked about death frequently. In addition to his dress and behavior, Weise stood out for his size. He was six feet tall and weighed 250 pounds. He had been held back in school several times. Students who had classes with Weise say he was "terrorized" by other students who thought he was weird, although sources say he rarely responded to the taunts.

Others speculate that, rather than overt bullying, it was social isolation that triggered Weise's rage. Former classmates called him a loner with no friends, and adults in the Red Lake community claim he was not well known—unusual on a sparsely populated reservation where everyone seems to know one another. A social worker familiar with Weise called him "a mixed-up kid who seemed lost in life." A few of Weise's closer acquaintances said he was suicidal and that he once said "that would be cool if I shot up the school." One schoolmate claims he attempted suicide in early 2005.

Weise had been in trouble before, although accounts vary regarding his actual responsibility for some of the incidents. Not long before the shooting, Weise was blamed for a bomb threat at the school. He was also involved in numerous fistfights. He left school the year before due to unspecified medical reasons and was receiving tutoring at home.

Some have suggested that a common link among many of the school shooters is the use of **prescription drugs**. Weise had been taking Prozac for some time, and his dosage was increased a week prior to the shooting. According to an aunt, he was taking three twenty-milligram pills per day. Friends noted he got quieter after the dosage was upped. Recent studies have shown an increased suicide rate among teens taking Prozac. Other possible side effects include apathy, euphoria, hallucinations, neurosis, paranoid reaction, personality disorder, psychosis, antisocial reaction, delusions, confusion, and violent behaviors. **Kip Kinkel**, who killed two and injured twenty-two at his Paducah, Kentucky high school had been taking Prozac, while **Eric Harris** was taking Luvox, a similar antidepressant.

FURTHER READING

Bakken, R. (2005, March 27). Teen "seemed lost in life." *Seattle Times* [Online version].

Bystrianyk, R. (2005, March 27). Prozac—ingredient in a deadly rampage? *Health Sentinel* [Online edition]. Available at http://www.healthsentinel.com.

Haga, C., Padilla, H., & Meryhew, R. (2005, March 23). Jeff Weise: A mystery in a life full of hardship. *Minneapolis Star-Tribune* [Online version].

Laura L. Finley

WILKINS, HEATH. Heath Wilkins was the youngest person to be sentenced to death in the state of Missouri. Although his sentence was initially upheld by the Supreme Court in *Stanford v. Kentucky* (1989), the Court later ruled in *Roper v. Simmons* (2005) that state laws that authorized capital punishment for sixteen- and seventeen-year-olds violated the Eighth Amendment of the U.S. Constitution.

On the night of July 27, 1985, Wilkins and his accomplices Patrick Kelly Stevens, Ray Thompson, Jr., and Marjorie Filipiak, conceived a plan to rob Linda's Liquors, a convenience store located in Avondale, Missouri, and murder the store clerk so as not to leave any witnesses. Wilkins and Stevens entered the store shortly before 11 p.m., whereupon Wilkins distracted the clerk, Nancy Allen, a twenty-six-year-old mother of two, while Stevens hid in the bathroom. When Allen turned her back, Stevens emerged from hiding, and Wilkins brandished the knife he had kept concealed. As Stevens held her, Wilkins stabbed Allen a total of seven times, penetrating both her heart and carotid artery. Before they fled the scene and left Allen to die, Wilkins and Stevens helped themselves to liquor, cigarettes, rolling papers, and approximately $450 in cash and checks.

At the time of his crime, Wilkins was sixteen years and six months of age, just short of the age of majority for purposes of criminal prosecution in Missouri. Because he could not be tried automatically as an adult, the juvenile court had to terminate its jurisdiction and certify Wilkins for trial as an adult. The court did so based on the viciousness of the crime, Wilkins' maturity, and the apparent failure of the juvenile court system to rehabilitate him after previous delinquent acts. Wilkins was charged with first-degree murder, armed criminal action, and carrying a concealed weapon. After being found competent by the court, he plead guilty to all charges and was sentenced to death on June 27, 1986. Upon mandatory review, the Supreme Court of Missouri affirmed Wilkins' sentence, rejecting the argument that the punishment violated the Eighth Amendment.

Wilkins, who had urged the imposition of the death penalty at his punishment hearing, later signed on to the state public defender's Supreme Court appeal of his sentence. His case was consolidated with that of Kevin Stanford, a seventeen-year-old sentenced to death for first-degree murder, first-degree sodomy, first-degree robbery, and receiving stolen goods. Both petitioners argued that the imposition of the death penalty on those who were juveniles when they committed their crimes violated the Eighth Amendment prohibition against cruel and unusual punishment.

Stanford v. Kentucky (1989) fell on the heels of *Thompson v. Oklahoma* (1988), in which the Supreme Court ruled that it was unconstitutional to execute a juvenile who had committed a capital offense prior to age sixteen, unless the state had a minimum age limit in its death penalty statute. In its decision, the Court applied the three-part criteria established by *Furman v. Georgia* (1972) for determining Eighth Amendment cases. A punishment is cruel and unusual if: (1) the punishment was considered cruel and unusual by the framers of the Constitution; (2) societal consensus holds that the punishment offends civilized standards of human decency; and (3) the punishment is disproportionate to the severity of the crime or makes no discernable contribution to either rehabilitation or deterrence. These criteria supplemented those established in *Kent v. United States* (1966), the first juvenile case heard by the Supreme Court. Kent limited the discretion of juvenile courts to waive cases to criminal court and provided for a number of factors the juvenile court judge had to consider when making waiver decisions: the seriousness and type of offense, the sophistication and maturity of the juvenile, the juvenile's record and history, and the prospects for public safety and the rehabilitation of the juvenile in question. Although this decision guaranteed juveniles certain rights, they still faced potential prosecution and punishment as adults.

It was not until 1982 that the Supreme Court agreed to hear its first challenge to the Eighth Amendment based on the defendant's age. In *Eddings v. Oklahoma*, the Court, without considering the constitutionality of the death penalty per se, held that chronological age was a relevant mitigating factor in sentencing. That decision was informed by the Courts determination that youth are generally less mature and responsible than adults.

Like *Eddings*, the *Thompson* decision refined, rather than challenged, the application of the death penalty for juveniles. Although the Court had applied the three-part criteria in *Thompson*, they rejected the third part in *Stanford v. Kentucky* and based their decision instead on the evolving standards of decency as reflected in the legislative authorization of the death penalty. The Court determined that neither a historical or societal consensus existed that forbade the imposition of the death penalty on juveniles who committed capital offenses at sixteen or seventeen years of age. The death sentences of both Stanford and Wilkins were affirmed.

Although the sentences of Stanford and Wilkins were later commuted, the Supreme Court reversed itself in 2005 and ruled that state laws authorizing capital punishment for sixteen- and seventeen-year-olds violated the Eighth Amendment prohibition against cruel and unusual punishment. *Roper v. Simmons* held that a national consensus had emerged in opposition to the execution of juveniles. Furthermore, the Court determined that youth, like a mental disability, could so reduce a criminal's culpability as to require a constitutional ban. As a result of this decision, seventy-two death sentences were commuted. Wilkins is currently serving a life sentence without the possibility of parole.

See also Death Penalty

FURTHER READING

American Bar Association Juvenile Justice Committee. (1991). *Juvenile death penalty.* Available at: http://www.abanet.org/crimjust/juvjus/juvdp.html.

Amnesty International. (1991). *USA: The death penalty and juvenile offenders.* New York: Amnesty International USA Publications.

Cothern, L. (2000, November). Juveniles and the death penalty. *Coordinating Council on Juvenile Justice and Delinquency Prevention Bulletin, 1–15.*

Horowitz, M. (2000). Kids who kill: A critique of how the American legal system deals with juveniles who commit homicide. *Law and Contemporary Problems, 63,* 133–177.

Rosenbaum, R. (1989, March 12). Too young to die? *New York Times,* 32.

Streib, V. (1987). *Death penalty for juveniles.* Bloomington: Indiana University Press.

Angela Winkler Thomas

WILLIAMS, ANDY. Violence has been occurring in inner-city schools for years with little media attention. In 1996, however, the violence that was occurring in urban American schools arrived in suburban neighborhoods. As a result of the events of Pearl, Springfield, Jonesboro, and Littleton, school violence, specifically school shootings, has been brought into everyone's focus, including the residents of Santee, California.

An Ohio University poll found that one-third of the nation's adults believe that children are safer in shopping malls and walking the streets than they are in school, while 81 percent of the adults surveyed admitted to feeling that children are safer at home than they are in school. These beliefs are in contrast to reality, where schools are still the safest places for youth and the home is the least safe. Many will argue these and other survey findings are a result of the media sensationalism of past school shootings. However, sensationalism and media grandstanding is not what the residents of Santee California felt in early March of 2001.

On March 5, 2001, the members of the Santee, California community had their lives forever changed when the local police department responded to a call of shots fired at the local high school. Police officers entered Santana High School with concern and hesitation, the school shooting of Littleton not far from their minds. The officers' hesitation that day was well warranted. When they entered the high school on that Monday morning they found a hunch-framed fifteen-year-old named Charles Andrew "Andy" Williams slumped to the floor in the boys' restroom. Williams was sitting next to the dead body of one of his classmates and the wounded body of another. This young man was not another victim of the shooter in the school, but the perpetrator of this tragedy.

To the shock of the Santee Police Department, Andy Williams was not hidden behind a makeshift bunker waiting to fire upon them, like many of the school shooters that came before him had done. Instead, Andy sat patiently awaiting their arrival with his gun dropped by his side. Andy acted alone on that sunny day in early March when he killed two of his classmates—seventeen-year-old Randy Gordon and fourteen-year-old Bryan Zuckor. Williams' attack injured thirteen others.

On August 15, 2002, more than a year after gunfire shattered the Santee community, Supreme Court Judge Herbert Exarhos sentenced Charles Andrew Williams, who had been charged as an adult for his crimes, to fifty years to life in prison.

Some in the Santee community were outraged with what they felt was too lenient of a sentence. The prosecutor, Kris Anton, had asked for the maximum sentence of 425 years to life for Williams and was as disappointed with the judge's sentence as were those seventeen family members, friends, and victims that testified during the sentencing phase of the trial.

As Andy Williams serves his half-century sentence in a California state prison, one must ask, why? Why would a young man slip into the stall of the restroom with a loaded .22 caliber handgun and over a six-minute period cause such a tremendous tragedy? Was it jilted love or a vendetta against a teacher or a member of the administrative staff?

According to the over five hundred pages of court documents that Williams' trial attorneys', Randy Mize and Ronald Bobo, filed during the sentencing phase of the trial, the acts on that Monday morning in March were a result of a "depressed, alienated boy who could no longer handle the taunting and bullying by a group of neighborhood youths he had befriended" (Moran, October 11, 2002: p. 19). According to the court reports, the depression that Andy was suffering was exacerbated by the death of a friend, a desire to live with his mother (Andy's mother and father divorced when he was three years old), and a wish to return to rural Maryland.

According to a psychiatric report prepared by the defense expert, Dr. Charles Scott, Williams had been suffering from depression throughout his life and it intensified when he and his father left Brunswick, Maryland in June of 2000. According to Scott, Williams had developed a support network of family and friends while in Maryland to help him cope with his parents' divorce and his mother living in South Carolina. When Andy and his father moved to Santee, Andy became isolated and withdrawn. Shortly after a trip to South Carolina to visit his mother in December of 2000, Andy began to have thoughts of suicide, running away to Mexico, and ultimately carrying a gun to school as a way to get his neighborhood friends to stop taunting him.

Williams stated he began thinking more and more about carrying a gun to school on Friday, March 2, 2001, when he was reprimanded by one of his favorite teachers. These thoughts intensified when he hung out with his friends, Josh Stevens and A. J. Gilbert, and he talked about "shooting up the school on Monday" (Moran, August 18, 2002: p. 16). According to his reports, Andy stated he felt obligated to carry out the attack he and his friends had talked about the night before. According to the court report, Andy believed that if he did not carry out their plan he would be "bullied and taunted by others and face humiliating consequences for not following through" (Moran, August 18, 2002: p. 16).

The rationale behind the actions of Charles Andrew Williams sound similar to many of the school shooters that came before and others that have followed. **Bullying**, isolation, and taunting seem to resonate so loudly in the minds of other teenagers in a suburban school that he lashed out in a way that has left another community forever scarred.

See also Harris, Eric (and Dylan Klebold)

FURTHER READING

Cox, S., Bynum, T., & Davidson, W. (2004). Understanding the relationship between carrying weapons to school and fighting. In S. Holmes & S. Holmes (Eds.), *Violence: A contemporary reader*. Upper Saddle River, NJ: Prentice Hall.

Makward, M. (2004). Does a sociological perspective contribute to understanding school shootings? *PsycCritiques, 49*, 8, 112–115.

Moran, G. (2002, August 16). Teen's explanation given in interviews with psychiatrist. *Urban-Tribune*. Available at: www.signonsandiego.com/news/metro/santana.

Moran, G. (2002, August 18). Williams reluctant to discuss past, future. *Urban-Tribune*. Available at: www.signonsandiego.com/news/metro/santana.

Moran, G. (2002, October 11).Williams: 5,000 bullies in one place. *Urban-Tribune*. Available at: www.signonsandiego.com/news/metro/santana.

Rabrenovic, G., Kaufman, C. & Levin, J. (2004). School violence: Causes, consequences, and interventions. In S. Holmes & S. Holmes (Eds.), *Violence: A contemporary reader*. Upper Saddle River, NJ: Prentice Hall.

Website on Andy Williams: www.signonsandiego.com/news/metro/santana.

Robyn Diehl Lacks

WOODHAM, LUKE. Luke Woodham is currently serving three life sentences and seven twenty-year sentences for the shooting deaths of Mary Woodham, 50, Christina Menefee, 16, and Lydia Drew, 17, as well as the aggravated assault of seven others. With the exception of Mary Woodham, his mother, the victims were fellow classmates at Pearl High School, located in Pearl, Mississippi. Woodham's killing spree marked the first in a series of school-related attacks across the United States during the late 1990s.

Woodham, born in 1981, was raised by his mother following his parents' divorce when he was seven years old. At trial, he would claim that his father abused him emotionally and his mother physically. Although no charges were ever filed, Woodham believed that his mother neglected him and never loved him. A self-described loner and average student, Woodham was frequently bullied, and until his association with Grant Boyette, 19, the leader of a cult-like group called "The Kroth," he had few friends.

On the morning of October 1, 1997, Woodham, then sixteen years old, beat his mother with a baseball bat and stabbed her to death with a butcher knife while she was sleeping. Three hours later, Woodham, armed with a rifle that he concealed under his trench coat, drove to Pearl High School intent on killing Menefee, who had ended their short-lived relationship a year earlier. When he arrived, Woodham entered the school's large indoor courtyard, spotted Menefee and her best friend Lydia, and opened fire. Before the shooting spree ended, seven students were wounded and both Menefee and Drew lay dead. As he attempted to flee the scene, Assistant Principal Joel Myrick apprehended Woodham, who was armed with a pistol he had retrieved from his car during the melee. Less than an hour after the shootings, Woodham was in police custody.

In his videotaped confession, Woodham stated that the school shootings were motivated by a desire to exact revenge on Menefee, but after she was dead, he "snapped" and began shooting at random. He further claimed that he could not remember the attack on his mother and insisted that his actions were those of a sane individual. His defense team would later attempt to quash his confession, which they argued was inadmissible because Woodham had no guardian or attorney present to advise him when he waived his rights.

Days after his arrest, six other teens, including Boyette, the alleged mastermind behind the attack at Pearl High School, were arrested as co-conspirators. During his subsequent trials, Woodham testified that Boyette had befriended him shortly after his relationship with Menefee ended. Woodham claimed that he had always been an outcast at school and was devastated over the breakup. Boyette offered his friendship and promised to help Woodham take revenge on Menefee through the occult. The boys often met at Woodham's house to discuss the occult, Hitler, and death. It is also where they tortured and killed Woodham's dog. According to the district attorney, the attack at Pearl High School was part of a larger conspiracy to kill others in the Pearl community, including a local firefighter. Their plan also included an escape to Louisiana, then Mexico, and a boat trip to their final destination, Cuba. Although their plan never fully materialized, in February 2000, Boyette pleaded guilty to a reduced charge of conspiracy; he was ordered to serve in a military-style prison program and was placed on five years of supervised probation.

In June 1998, Woodham was found guilty and sentenced to life imprisonment for the murder of his mother. Just a week later, he stood trial for the Pearl shootings, during which the defense painted him as a pathetic loner who ached for acceptance by his peers. Informed by Woodham's obsession with demons and the occult, as well as psychiatric testimony that claimed he suffered from psychotic processing and borderline personality disorder, Woodham's defense team argued that he was insane under Mississippi law because he could not fathom the consequences of his actions. After three days of testimony and five hours of deliberation, a jury found Woodham guilty of two counts of murder and seven counts of aggravated assault. Circuit Court Judge Samac Richardson expressed regret that he could not sentence Woodham to death; he ordered two life sentences and a twenty-year sentence for each of the seven counts of aggravated assault. Further, he ordered Woodham to pay the victims or their survivors $10,000 each, as well as restitution to the victims for their burial costs, to the city for the damage to Pearl High School, to the county for his prosecution, and to the state for all future costs of his incarceration.

FURTHER READING

Davis, C. (2003). *Children who kill: Profiles of pre-teen and teenage killers*. London: Allison & Busby.

Espelage, D. (Ed.). (2004). *Bullying in American schools: A socio-ecological perspective on prevention and intervention*. Mahwah, NJ: Lawrence Erlbaum Associates, Inc.

Kimmel, M., & Mahler, M. (2003). Adolescent masculinity, homophobia, and violence: Random school shootings, 1982–2001. *American Behavioral Scientist, 46*, 1439–1458.

Messerschmidt, J. (2000). *Nine lives: Adolescent masculinities, the body, and violence*. Boulder, CO: Westview Press.

Popyk, L. (1998, November 9). Luke's tormented world. *Cincinnati Post*, 1.

Angela Winkler Thomas

WURST, ANDY. At approximately 9:40 p.m. on Friday, April 24, 1998, Andrew Jerome Wurst, then fourteen, carried out a school-related shooting in Edinboro, Pennsylvania. Using his father's .25 caliber semiautomatic handgun, Wurst fatally injured one teacher, John Gillette, and injured another teacher and two students. The attack occurred just north of Edinboro at "Nick's Place," a restaurant where Parker Middle School was hosting an eighth grade dance. After psychological evaluation, Wurst was determined to be mentally competent and was adjudicated in adult court. He received a sentence of thirty to sixty years with eligibility for parole in thirty years.

On the day of the shooting, Andrew Wurst attended his eighth grade classes, after which he took the school bus home. At approximately 5:00 p.m., Wurst dressed for his eighth grade dinner dance, at which time he placed his father's handgun in a holster under his shirt. Before leaving for the dance, he left a suicide note on his pillow. At 5:30 Wurst's parents dropped him off at Nick's Place, and the dinner dance began at 6:00.

Around 9:25 p.m., Wurst went into the bathroom where he removed the gun from its holster and placed it in his pocket. At approximately 9:40 p.m., Wurst was outside on the back patio when teacher John Gillette, age forty-eight, went onto the patio to ask a group of students to come inside. As students began to walk back into the restaurant, Wurst pulled out the semiautomatic handgun and fatally shot Gillette in the face and back.

Wurst then went inside the building and began shouting for a fellow student, Eric Wozniak. Students scrambled to get out of the way, sometimes pleading with Wurst not to shoot them and asking him why he was doing this. As an explanation for his actions, Wurst replied that he was crazy. Wurst fired the gun two more times, grazing another teacher, Edrye May Boraten, age fifty-one, and wounding one student, Jacob Tury. At that time, Justin Fletcher, another student, challenged Wurst to shoot him rather than anyone else. Wurst discharged the gun, grazing Fletcher's shirt, and hitting another student, Robert Zemcik, in the foot.

Andrew Wurst then left the reception hall and went into a grassy area behind the building. Having heard gunshots, James Strand, the owner of Nick's Place who lived next door, grabbed his shotgun and ran toward the restaurant. At approximately 9:50 p.m., Strand confronted Wurst behind the building. After pointing his gun at Strand, Wurst dropped his weapon and got on the ground, saying that he was already dead and that none of this was real. Strand and two teachers then walked Wurst back to the building to wait for the police to arrive. The dance was scheduled to end at 10:00 p.m., and parents arrived alongside ambulances and other emergency vehicles. Catherine Wurst, the shooter's mother, arrived to pick up her son, but discovered instead that he was in police custody.

Andrew Wurst was arraigned the following day on charges of criminal homicide. Given the severity of the offense and since juvenile offenders are automatically released at age twenty-one, the county district attorney sought to have Wurst tried as an adult. While criminal homicide might have been punishable by death, at the time the minimum age for execution was sixteen. Therefore, the strictest punishment Wurst could receive would be life imprisonment without parole. However, before trial could proceed, the court requested a psychological evaluation of Wurst's mental state.

Experts disagreed regarding Andrew Wurst's mental health and competency to stand trial. A forensic psychologist and expert witness determined that Wurst had a mental illness characterized by psychosis, delusional ideation, and paranoia, ultimately concluding that Wurst needed significant treatment and hospitalization for his mental condition. The essence of this determination lay in Wurst's apparent feelings that nothing in the world was real, including other people. While Wurst was too young to be diagnosed with schizophrenia, he nonetheless was considered mentally ill and at risk for schizophrenia and serious depression. In contrast, the psychological evaluation conducted for the prosecution concluded that Wurst did not suffer from any significant mental illness. In the prosecution's view, Wurst was not delusional, and while he did have a history of emotional upset, he was nonetheless competent to stand trial.

Meanwhile, police and the media sought to unravel the context in which Andrew Wurst executed his school-related shooting. Despite rumors that Wurst had as many as two coconspirators, police were unable to reveal any evidence to support these rumors. Therefore, police investigators have concluded that, while Wurst may have mentioned his plans to others, he acted alone in planning and carrying out the shooting. While the media reported that Wurst was a social outsider, interviews with friends have revealed that this is inaccurate. Wurst had a small group of friends, but recently had changed peer groups to associate with a rougher group. Peers noted Wurst experienced a change of demeanor shortly before the shootings. In addition, Wurst had recently been rejected by at least one girl.

In their investigation, the police and the media also discovered evidence that Andrew Wurst had a slightly troubled childhood. At the time of the shooting, Wurst was about average size and weight for his age. While Wurst did like to read Stephen King novels, his grades slipped over his middle school years so that he was earning D's and F's at the time of the shooting. He also enjoyed heavy metal music, including Marilyn Manson. While there are reports of Wurst having used alcohol and marijuana, lab analysis following the shootings did not reveal any trace of the drugs in his system. Andrew Wurst evidently experienced nightmares and slept poorly. As a child he had often wet his bed, and he claims to have begun having suicidal thoughts at age ten. Investigation did not reveal any abuse at home, although the marriage of Andrew Wurst's parents may have been in trouble.

Despite the official disagreement about Andrew Wurst's mental illness and competency to stand trial, the court determined that Wurst would be competent to stand trial. Instead of going to trial and risking a life sentence without parole, Wurst accepted a plea bargain in which he pled guilty to third-degree murder.

See also Differential Identification Theory; Music, Juvenile Violence and

FURTHER READING

DeJong, W., Epstein, J., & Hart, T. (2003). Bad things happen in good communities: The rampage shooting in Edinboro, Pennsylvania, and its aftermath. In Mark H. Moore, Carol V. Petrie, Anthony Braga, and Brenda L. McLaughlin (Eds.), *Deadly lessons: Understanding lethal school violence* (pp. 70–100). Washington, DC: National Academies Press.

Popyk, L. (1998, November 9). Violence is seductive to new breed of killers. *Cincinnati Post*. Available from: www.cincypost.com/news/1998/2kill/110998.html.

Ramsland, K. (2005). The list. *Court TV Crime Library*. Available at: www.crimelibrary.com/serial_killers/weird/kids1/index_1.html.

Glenn W. Muschert

YOUTH VIOLENCE STRIKE FORCE. A section of the Boston Police Department's Special Operations Division, the Youth Violence Strike Force, is a task force consisting of forty-five officers from Boston and fifteen officers from police agencies beyond the city, including the Bureau of Alcohol, Tobacco, and Firearms, the Massachusetts State Police, and the Massachusetts Department of Youth Services. The Strike Force is tasked with responding decisively to violent incidents in gang-dominated areas of the city (Operation Cease Fire), with facilitating prosecution of gang members who have committed crimes with guns and monitoring the activities of those who have been paroled (Operation Night Light), and with interdicting the illicit trade in guns (the Boston Gun Project).

In the 1980s, Boston's murder rate had increased sharply from year to year, with the increases largely traceable to increased use of firearms by youths and, in particular, by gang members. The Youth Violence Strike Force was established in 1990 as a dramatic response to an escalating problem that many observers believed had already grown beyond remediation. Funded by a Department of Justice grant, researchers from the Kennedy School of Government at Harvard University provided a rationale for the Task Force's activities by statistically mapping the effects of youth violence in Boston. They also provided a tool for interdiction by mapping gang territories, by tracing relationships among the gangs, and by identifying many of the gang members.

Although the Strike Force is not a program *per se*, officers on the task force have initiated a complementary program to counter the glorification of gun use among gang members. Working with local clergymen, the officers, while off-duty, visit the homes of high-risk adolescents and attempt to define alternatives to the gang culture that seeks to legitimize gun violence as a response to a broadening spectrum of situations. Other similar outreach programs have included the Summer of Opportunity, through which at-risk youth are placed in vocational programs and even with companies to demonstrate the real opportunities for realizing personal ambitions outside of the gang milieu. Likewise, the Department of Health and Human Services has administered programs in community schools to provide a refuge for young people who might be victimized by gangs or coerced into involvement in gang activities.

In 1999, the success of the Youth Violence Strike Force in reducing gang violence was recognized when the International Association of Chiefs of Police selected the Strike Force to receive the Webber Seavey Award. Although the Strike Force's success extends beyond simple measures such as homicide rates, homicides committed by Boston youths did decline from sixty-two in 1990 to fifteen in 1997.

See also Gang Units, Police; Gang Violence, against Bystanders; Gang-On-Gang Violence; Gun-Related Violence, Rates of; Gun-Related Violence, Types of

FURTHER READING

Bello, M. (1997, February 17). Clinton visit a nod to the hub—Officials cite success in fighting youth crime. *Boston Herald*, 7.

Holmstrom, D. (1996, May 15). "Operation Night Light" keeps offenders in for the evening. *Christian Science Monitor*, 1.

McPhee, M. (2005, April 21). Narc officers to pump up youth force. *Boston Herald*, 4.

Strangled. (1997, April 19). *The Economist*.

Talbot, D. (1997, February 9). Youth force strikes at crime. *Boston Herald*, 4.

Martin Kich

YOUTHFUL OFFENDER SYSTEM (YOS). Authorized by the state legislature in a 1993 special session, YOS was created in response to a spike in gang-related violence in and around Denver. YOS is intended to be a middle tier between youth corrections and the Department of Corrections for youth convicted of violent felonies. The 231 line staff and ten other staff members emphasize firm discipline, academics, work and prevocational skills, interpersonal relations, and a positive peer culture.

To be sentenced to YOS, youth ages fourteen to eighteen must be convicted of a violent, weapons-related Class 2-6 felony or be chronic offenders who were direct filed (**waived**) to be tried as an adult. In the case of a direct file, the court can suspend the adult sentence if the youth completes a YOS sentence. All YOS sentences are indeterminate in length, generally between two and seven years. The sentence includes a mandatory intensely supervised community release of six to twelve months.

There are four phases involved in a YOS sentence. Intake, diagnostic, and orientation (IDO) occurs in the first thirty to forty-five days. Here, a youth is introduced to the system of group discipline and incentives. Following a physical assessment, youth get started on the intense physical regimen as well. In Phase I, the youth begins his or her intense residential program, which might last between eight months and six years. Each youth must take a core program of education, as well as cognitive restructuring and supplemental programs, such as substance abuse counseling, if needed. Phase II is the prerelease time, which is three months long. This phase involves individualized, community-based support programs designed to ready the youth for community reintegration. IDO, Phase I, and Phase II all occur at the YOS facility in Pueblo, Colorado. Phase III involves supervised community release, which might take place anywhere in the state. In Phase III, a youth must check in, at minimum, with the assigned community parole officer twice per week. In addition, youth wear **electronic monitoring devices** through most of the phase, as well as an electronic paging program (EPP), an alphanumeric pager to monitor the youth's location, movement, and activities both day and night. Youth in Phase III are also subject to weekly urinalysis, and community parole officers must enforce curfew compliance. Community parole officers, in addition to their supervision duties, serve as liaisons with local law enforcement, in particular with **police antigang units**. It is recommended they have caseloads no larger than ten youth.

Under an agreement between YOS/Century High School and Pueblo School District No. 60, high school diplomas are awarded to offenders meeting District 60 graduation requirements. Unless the youth had previously obtained a diploma or Graduate Equivalency Degree (GED), he or she is required to be enrolled in core courses.

If a youth is to return to live with family or guardians after completing his or her sentence, YOS requires counseling as well as visits by the community parole officer for three months to assess its appropriateness. If the youth is not returning home, he or she is involved in the Emancipation Program. In the three to six months prior to release, the community parole officer assesses a number of supervised group homes or apartments for their appropriateness. Youth who will be living independently receive help from YOS staff in acquiring an appropriate living place and needed furniture and daily living items. Youth who live independently after their sentence are subject to greater supervision.

During Phase III, the youth must get at least part-time employment in order to build a work ethic, self-confidence, and work toward becoming independent and self-sufficient. In addition, YOS juveniles must complete one hundred hours of meaningful community service. Youth who do not, or who violate any of the YOS rules and regulations, face sanctions. The most typical sanction involves removal of privileges.

The 2004 evaluation of the YOS program found the program to be successful on a number of measures. While only 10.3 percent of youth entered the program with a high school diploma or GED, 59.1 percent received one of these while in the program. Attaining secondary education was shown to increase the chance of success upon release from the program and decrease the likelihood of re-offense. For instance, those who did not receive a diploma or GED were 3.8 times more likely to be revoked from YOS to prison, 1.6 times more likely to have a felony filing within two years after release, and 2.7 times more likely to be sent to prison for a new charge. Recidivism rates for YOS youth were lower than for comparable Department of Corrections inmates. The evaluation did, however, express some concerns. Reduction of staff members and services had jeopardized the program's ability to provide needed individualized treatment for youth. Further, many staff members and detained youth expressed in focus groups that there was tension and a lack of cohesiveness with the program's philosophy, as in some ways it was a rehabilitative program and in others ways it was a punitive setting.

While proponents maintain YOS is an innovative approach to dealing with the most seriously violent youth without subjecting them to adult court, YOS has faced criticism. In 1997, Human Rights Watch said conditions for youth in many Colorado facilities, including the YOS Pueblo facility, did not meet international standards. They pointed to overcrowded and unsafe conditions, with some facilities at two and a half times their capacity. In addition, Human Rights Watch expressed concern about the overrepresentation of minorities in Colorado youth facilities, as well as complaints by detained youth of chronic hunger and verbal and physical abuse.

FURTHER READING

Colorado Youthful Offender System (YOS). Available at: www.doc.state.co.us/Facilities/ YOS/yosasp.

Department of Corrections—Division of Adult Parole, Community Corrections, and YOS. Available at: www.doc.state.co.us/comcorr/yos_programs.

Human Rights Watch. (1997, September 11). Conditions of confinement in Colorado fail to meet international standards. *HRW News*. Available at: www.hrw.org/english/docs/1997/09/11/usdom 1531.html.

Ploughe, P. (2002, October). *Corrections Today*. YOS: Colorado Department of Corrections.

Rosky, J., Pasini-Hill, D., Lowden, K., Harrison, L., & English, K. (2004, November 1). Evaluation of the youthful offender system (YOS) in Colorado. Available at: www.dcj.stateco.us/ors/pdf/docs/YOS_REPORT_2004.pdf.

Youthful Offender System (YOS) annual report. (2003). National Institute of Corrections. Available at: http://www.nicic.org/library/018803.

Laura L. Finley

ZERO TOLERANCE LAWS. The law and order agenda that emerged at the turn of the century represents one of the major political shifts in state power that occurred in western societies, and more specifically, in the United States. Opposing the welfare state progressive policies, this coercive social control system was first voiced by the new right and progressively endorsed in varying degrees by policymakers across the national political spectrum. Zero tolerance doctrine conveys fully this ideological crusade. If this expression is borrowed from the U.S. Department of Justice's Asset Forfeiture Program designed to fight crime, its inspiration stems from the "Broken Windows" thesis that was formulated in the 1980s by George Kelling and James Wilson through various articles, books, and consultancies. According to these two authors, low-level incivilities force law-abiding citizens to withdraw from public spaces, providing an occasion for more serious offenders to perpetrate significant crimes. Building on this assumption, proactive law enforcement of minor misdemeanors could help to prevent crime. Even if the scientific accuracy of this theory has never been established, policymakers drew on it to justify major changes, not only in the management of cities such as Baltimore, San Francisco, and New York City, but also in the organization of state schools.

The American educational system was permeated by the zero tolerance doctrine in order to improve school safety. The first zero tolerance laws were enacted with the passing of the Gun-Free School Zones Act, part of the Crime Control Act of 1990, which demanded expulsion for no less than one year of any student knowingly bringing a firearm in a school zone. The Gun-Free Schools Act of 1994 was passed under the Clinton administration and reauthorized in the No Child Left Behind Act of 2001 by the Bush administration. This firearm regulation provided Elementary and Secondary Education Act funds for the enactment of zero tolerance laws and mandatory minimum sentences. This act has been endorsed in all fifty states. As a result, the vast majority of school districts have adopted their own disciplinary policies, even if their effectiveness on violence deterrence has not yet been demonstrated. These punitive policies appear to have, on the contrary, depressing and critical effects on the children's personal development and educational achievement.

Extensive interpretations of the Gun-Free Schools Act have enabled state legislatures and school authorities to justify the overuse of disciplinary sanctions, which, according to the U.S. Department of Education, resulted in more than three million children suspended and 85,000 expelled during the 1997–1998 school year. State laws and student disciplinary codes came to encompass a range of misbehaviors that extends far beyond the weapon possession violations provisioned by the federal legislation. Suspensions or expulsions can be grounded on offenses such as continued defiance of authority, consumption of alcoholic beverages, physical aggression among students, and the use of profane language directed at school employees or pupils. Disruptive adolescents, whose trivial misconducts were once treated by social workers or guidance counselors, are increasingly deferred to law enforcement agencies. These deferrals do not necessarily take into account the children's personal history or academic records, nor do they provide, in most cases, alternative educational programs for the neediest students. In the wake of widely publicized school shootings, like the Columbine massacre in April 1999, many schools introduced new stringent security policies against firearms and threatening behaviors.

Low-income or minority children and, more specifically, African-American juveniles, appear to bear the brunt of this sanctioning process. According to the U.S. Department of Education, African-American children represented 33 percent of the out-of school suspensions in 2000, yet they only constituted 17 percent of the national public school enrollment. The Children's Defense Fund had established in the mid-1970s that black students were punished more frequently by school authorities than white students. Further statistical surveys carried out in the late 1990s seem to indicate the persisting minority overrepresentation in school expulsions and suspensions. Different interpretations of this disparity have been advanced, such as the lower socioeconomic status of the black children and school authorities' racial stereotypes in the management of African-American children's misbehaviors. Zero tolerance laws' impact on minorities has been particularly highlighted in the "Decatur Seven" case. The two-year expulsion of seven black students for a fistfight at a school football game in 1999 began a national controversy over civil rights violations. The Reverend Jesse Jackson launched a widely reported protest march in this Illinois city to denounce racial inequalities in zero tolerance policies that had been set by a Decatur school board decision.

Zero tolerance policies appear to be counterproductive, both in terms of educational opportunities and violence prevention. They contribute to the erosion of students' confidence in the educational system and alienate them from teachers and educators. Children who have suffered suspensions and expulsions are more likely to have lower academic achievement and to drop out of school. Without proper alternative schooling programs, juveniles are being deprived of appropriate education but also disadvantaged in terms of the socialization process. Harsh school sanctioning is an important predictive factor for further exposure to street violence and for premature adolescence role exit. Criminologists and psychologists have pointed out that the increasing penal treatment of juveniles arrested for low-level offenses seem to put them at greater risk of delinquency.

If the legal status of the adolescent has been progressively institutionalized in the early twentieth century, zero tolerance laws have undermined these social conquests and have significantly corroded the educational system.

See also Educational Opportunity and Juvenile Violence; Systemic Violence in Schools

FURTHER READING

Advancement Project and the Civil Rights Project. (2000). *Opportunities suspended: The devastating consequences of zero tolerance and school discipline policies.* Cambridge, MA: Harvard University Press.

Casella, R. (2001). *At zero tolerance: Punishment, prevention and school violence.* New York: Peter Lang.

Noguera, P. (1995). Preventing and producing violence: A critical analysis of responses to school violence. *Harvard Educational Review, 65*(2), 189–212.

Skiba, R., Michael, R., Nardo, A., & Peterson, R. (2000). *The color of discipline: Sources of racial and gender disproportionality in school punishment.* Bloomington: Indiana Education Policy Center.

Jean-Philippe Dedieu

USEFUL WEB SITES AND RECOMMENDED READING

WEB SITES

Children and Adolescents' Health and Welfare

Children's Defense Fund: www.childrensdefense.org
Kids Count: www.aecf.org/kidscount.html
Parenting Project: www.parentingproject.org

Drugs

Drug Free Schools: www.drugfreeschools.com
Monitoring the Future: www.monitoringthefuture.org
NIDA for teens: www.teendrugabuse.gov
Safe Youth: www.safeyouth.org

Gangs

Gangs and At-Risk Kids: www.gangsandkids.com
National Youth Gang Center: www.iir.com/nygc
Street Gangs Resource Center: www.streetgangs.com

Juvenile Detention/Alternatives

American Bar Association: www.abanet.org/child/capita/html
Annie E. Casey Foundation: www.aecf.org/initiatives/jdai.html
Boot Camps for Teens: www.bootcampsforteens.com
Center for Court Innovation: www.problem-solvingcourts.org
Death Penalty Information Center: www.deathpenaltyinfo.org
The Sentencing Project: www.sentencingproject.org
Youth Law Center: www.youthlawcenter.org

Juvenile Violence and Juvenile Justice

Center for Disease Control: www.cdc.gov
Center for the Study and Prevention of Violence: www.colorado.edu/cspv.index.html
Center on Juvenile and Criminal Justice: www.cjcj.org
Child Welfare League of America: www.cwla.org/programs/juvenilejustice/jjpublicpolicy.html
Children's Rights Council: www.gogrc.com
Citizens for Juvenile Justice: www.cfjj.org

Coalition for Juvenile Justice: www.juvjustice.org/about/index_about.html

Florida State University—School of Criminology and Criminal Justice: www.criminology .fsu.edu/cjlinks/

Human Rights Watch: www.hrw.org

Justice Policy Institute: www.justicepolicy.org

Juvenile Law Center: www.jlc.org/home/juvenilejustice/

National Bureau of Justice Statistics: www.ojjdp.org/staeprofiles/

National Council on Crime and Delinquency—Children's Research Center: www.nccd-crc.org

National Criminal Justice Reference Center: www.ncjrs.org

National Youth Violence Prevention Resource Center-Safe Youth: www.safeyouth.org/ scripts/about/doj.asp

Stopviolence.org: www.stopviolence.org

Violentkids.com: www.violentkids.com

Media

Accuracy in Media: www.aim.org

Center for Media Literacy: www.medialit.org

National Coalition of Television Violence: www.nctvv.org

Minorities and Juvenile Justice

Material on Disproportionate Minority Contact (DMC): www.ojjdp.ncjrs.org/dmc.html

National Center on Education, Disability, and Juvenile Justice: www.edjj.org

Tribal Institute (Native Americans): www.tribal-institute.org/lists/juvenile

School Violence

Center for the Prevention of School Violence: www.ccdjjdp.org/cpsv/

Information About Corporal Punishment: www.stophitting.com

Keep Schools Safe: www.keepschoolssafe.org

National Association of School Resource Officers: www.nasro.org

School Violence Resource Center: www.svrc.net

Victims

Crime Victims United: www.crimevictimsunited.org

National Center for Children Exposed to Violence: www.nccev.org/index.html

National Center for Victims of Crime: www.ncvc.org

Office for Victims of Crime: www.ovc.gov

RECOMMENDED BOOKS

Drugs

Butts, J., & Roman, J. (Eds.). (2004). *Juvenile drug courts and teen substance abuse*. New York: Urban Institute Press.

Dudley, W. (Ed.). (2001). *Drugs*. New Haven, CT: Greenhaven.

Ksir, C., Hart, C., & Ray, O. (2006). *Drugs, society, and human behavior*. Boston: McGraw Hill.

Gangs

Anderson, E. (2000). *Code of the streets: Decency, violence, and the moral life of the inner city*. New York: W.W. Norton & Co.

Decker, S. (Ed.). (2003). *Policing gangs and youth violence*. Belmont, CA: Wadsworth.

Klein, M. (2006). *Street gang patterns and policies*. New York: Oxford.

Shakur, S. (1993). *Monster: The autobiography of an L.A. gang member*. New York: Penguin.

Shelden, R., Tracy, S., & Brown, W. (2003). *Youth gangs in American society*. Belmont, CA: Wadsworth.

Sikes, G. (1997). *8-ball chick: A year in the violent world of girl gangsters*. New York: Anchor.

Gender

Chesney-Lind, M., & Hagedorn, J. (Eds.). (1999). *Female gangs in America: Essays on girls, gangs, and gender*. Chicago, IL: Lake View Press.

Chesney-Lind, M., & Pasko, L. (2003). *The female offender: Girls, women, and crime*, 2nd ed. Thousand Oaks, CA: Sage.

Chesney-Lind, M., & Shelden, R. (2003). *Girls, delinquency, and juvenile justice*. Belmont, CA: Wadsworth.

Messerschmidt, J. W. (1993). *Masculinities and crime*. Lanham, MA: Rowman & Littlefield.

Simmons, Rachel. (2002). *Odd girl out: The hidden culture of aggression in girls*. New York: Harcourt.

General Discussion of Youth Violence

Barbour, S. (1998). *Teen violence: Opposing viewpoints*. Farmington Hills, MI: Greenhaven.

Calhoun, C., & Chapple, C. (Eds.). *Readings in juvenile delinquency and juvenile justice*. Upper Saddle River, NJ: Prentice Hall.

Canada, G. (1998). *Things get hectic: Teens write about the violence that surrounds them*. Carmichael, CA: Touchstone.

Crews, G., & Montgomery, R. (2000). *Chasing shadows: Confronting juvenile violence in America*. Upper Saddle River, NJ: Prentice Hall.

Elikann, P. (1999). *Superpredators: The demonization of our children by the law*. New York: Insight.

Fearnley, F. (Ed.). (2004). *I wrote on all four walls: Teens speak out on violence*. Toronto, Canada: Annick.

Hoffman, A., & Summers, R. (Eds.). *Teen violence: A global view*. New Haven, CT: Greenwood.

Holmes, S., & Holmes, R. (Eds.). (2004). *Violence: A contemporary reader*. Upper Saddle River, NJ: Prentice Hall.

Iadicola, P., & Shupe, A. (1998). *Violence, inequality and human freedom*. Dix Hills, NY: General Hall, Inc.

Kappeler, V., Blumberg, M., & Potter, G. (2000). *The mythology of crime and criminal justice*. Prospect Heights, IL: Waveland Press.

Kipnis, A. (1999). *Angry young men*. San Francisco; Jossey-Bass.

Males, Mike. (1999). *Framing youth: Ten myths about the next generation*. Monroe, ME: Common Courage Press.

Moffatt, G. (2003). *Wounded innocents and fallen angels*. Westport, CT: Praeger.

Stevenson, L. (2003). *From the inside out! A look into teen violence and rebellion*. Authorhouse.

Weill, S. (2002). *We're not monsters: Teens speak out about teens in trouble*. New York: HarperTempest.

Zimring, F. (2005). *American juvenile justice*. New York: Oxford.

Juvenile Justice and Alternatives

Ahranjani, M., Ferguson, A., & Raskin, J. (2005). *Youth justice in America*. Washington, DC: CQ Press.

Anderson, J. (1999). *Boot camps*. Lanham, MD: University Press of America.

Bazemore, G., & Schiff, M. (2005). *Juvenile justice reform and restorative justice: Building theory and policy from practice*. Portland, OR: Willan.

Bedau, H., & Cassell, P. (2005). *Debating the death penalty*. New York: Oxford.

Bellesiles, M. (2005). *Documenting American violence*. New York: Oxford.

Braithwaite, J., & Strang, H. (Eds.). *Restorative justice and family violence*. Cambridge: Cambridge University Press.

Champion, D. (2001). *Probation, parole, and community corrections,* 4th ed. Upper Saddle River, NJ: Prentice Hall.

Feld, B. (1999). *Bad kids: Race and the transformation of the juvenile court*. New York: Oxford University Press.

Humes, E. (1997). *No matter how loud I shout: A year in the life of juvenile court*. New York: Touchstone Books.

Krisberg, B., & Austin, J. (1993). *Reinventing juvenile justice*. Newbury Park, CA: Sage.

Maggy, L. (1998). *Youth, crime, and police work*. New York: St. Martins.

Myers, D. (2005). *Boys among men*. Westport, CT: Greenwood.

Platt, A. (1977). *The child savers: The invention of delinquency,* 2nd ed. Chicago: University of Chicago Press.

Prothrow-Stith, D. (1991). *Deadly consequences*. New York: Harper Collins.

Schlossman, S. (1977). *Love and the American delinquent*. Chicago: University of Chicago Press.

Sharp, P., & Hancock, B. (Eds.). *Juvenile delinquency: Historical, theoretical, and societal reactions to youth,* 2nd ed. Upper Saddle River, NJ: Prentice Hall.

Sullivan, D., & Tifft, L. (2005). *Restorative justice: Healing the foundations of our everyday lives,* 2nd ed. Monsey, NY: Criminal Justice Press.

Tanenhaus, D. (2005). *Juvenile justice in the making*. New York: Oxford.

Watkins, J. (1998). *The juvenile justice century*. Durham, NC: Carolina Academic Press.

Weitzer, R. (Ed.). (2003). *Current controversies in criminology*. Upper Saddle River, NJ: Prentice Hall.

Zehr, H., & Toews, B. (Eds.). (2004). *Critical issues in restorative justice*. Monsey, NY: Criminal Justice Press.

Media

Bok, S. (1999). *Mayhem: Violence as public entertainment*. New York: Perseus.

Jones, G. (2003). *Killing monsters: Why children need fantasy, super heroes, and make-believe violence*. New York: Basic.

Potter, W. (2002). *The 11 myths of media violence*. Thousand Oaks, CA: Sage.

Rafter, N. (2000). *Shots in the mirror*. New York: Oxford University Press.

Ravitch, D., & Vileritte, J. (2003). *Kid stuff: Marketing sex and violence to America's children*. Baltimore, MD: Johns Hopkins University Press.

Schechter, H. (2005). *Savage pastimes: A cultural history of violent entertainment*. New York: St. Martin's Press.

Singer, D., & Singer, J. (Eds.). (2002). *Handbook of children and the media*. Thousand Oaks, CA: Sage.

Strasburger, V. (2002). *Children, adolescents, and the media*. Thousand Oaks, CA: Sage.

Surette, R. (1992). *Media, crime, and criminal justice*. Pacific Grove, CA: Brooks/Cole.

Minorities

Cole, D. (1999). *No equal justice*. New York: New Press.

Males, M., & Macallair, D. (2000). *The color of justice: An analysis of juvenile adult court transfers in California*. Washington, DC: Building Blocks for Youth.

Markowitz, M., & Jones-Brown, D. (Eds.). *The system in black and white: Exploring the connections between race, crime, and justice*. Westport, CT: Praeger.

Smith, A. (2005). *Conquest: Sexual violence and American Indian genocide*. Boston: South End.

Wilkinson, D. (2003). *Guns, violence, and identity among African American and Latino youth*. Boulder, CO: LFB Scholarly Publishing.

Poverty

Hagan, J. (1998). *Mean streets: Youth crime and homelessness*. New York: Cambridge University Press.

Polakow, V. (2000). *The public assault on America's children: Poverty, violence, and juvenile injustice*. New York: Teachers College Press.

School Violence

Aronson, E. (2000). *Nobody left to hate: Teaching compassion after Columbine*. New York: W.H. Freeman & Co.

Casella, R. (2001a). *At zero tolerance: Punishment, prevention, and school violence*. New York: Peter Lang.

Casella, R. (2001b). *"Being down": Challenging violence in urban schools*. New York: Teachers College.

DiGuilio, R. (2001). *Educate, medicate, or litigate? What teachers, parents and administrators must do about student behavior*. New York: Corwin Books.

Eisler, R., & Miller, R. (Eds.). (2004). *Educating for a culture of peace*. Portsmouth, NH: Heinemann.

Finley, L., & Finley, P. (2005). *Piss off! How drug testing and other privacy violations are alienating America's youth*. Monroe, ME: Common Courage.

Hyman, I., & Snook, P. (1999). *Dangerous Schools*. San Francisco: Jossey Bass.

Lawrence, R. (2006). *School crime and juvenile justice,* 2nd ed. New York: Oxford.

Newman, K. (2004). *Rampage*. New York: Basic Books.

Nuwer, H. (1990). *Broken pledges*. Atlanta, GA: Longstreet.

Nuwer, H. (2000). *High school hazing: When rites become wrongs*. New York: Franklin Watts.

Webber, J. (Ed.). (2001). *Failure to hold: The politics of school violence*. Lanham, MD: Rowman & Littlefield.

Specific Cases

Lefkowitz, B. (1997). *Our guys*. New York: Vintage.

Sullivan, T. (1992). *Unequal verdicts: The Central Park jogger trials*. New York: Simon & Schuster.

Theory

Cullen, F., & Agnew, R. (Eds.). (1999). *Criminological theory: Past to present*. Los Angeles: Roxbury.

Garbarino, James. (2000). *Lost boys: Why our sons turn violent and how we can save them*. New York: Anchor Books.

Karr-Morse, Robin, Wiley, Meredith, & Brazelton, Terry. (1999). *Ghosts from the nursery: Tracing the roots of violence*. Atlanta: Atlantic Monthly Press.

Katz, J. (1988). *Seductions of crime*. New York: Basic.

Oliver, J. (1995). *Juvenile violence in a winner-loser culture: Socioeconomic and familial origins of the rise of violence against the person*. London: Free Association Books.

Pepinsky, H., & Quinney, R. (Eds.). (1991). *Criminology as peacemaking*. Bloomington: Indiana University Press.

Shoemaker, D. (2004). *Theories of delinquency*. New York: Oxford.

Vold, G., Bernard, T., & Snipes, J. (1998). *Theoretical criminology,* 4th ed. New York: Oxford.

Types of Crime

Cook, P., & Ludwig, J. (2002). *Gun violence: The real costs*. New York: Oxford.

Cox, V. (1997). *Guns, violence and teens*. Berkeley Heights, CA: Enslow.

Davis, C. (2003). *Children who kill: Profiles of pre-teen and teenage killers*. Allison and Busby.

Flowers, R. (2002). *Kids who commit adult crimes: Serious criminality by juvenile offenders*. Binghamton, NY: Haworth.

Graupner, H. (Ed.). (2005). *Adolescence, sexuality, and the criminal law*. Binghamton, NY: Haworth.

Harcourt, B. (2006). *Language of the gun: Youth, crime, and public policy*. Chicago: University of Chicago Press.

Heide, K. (2006). *Kids who kill their parents*. New York: Oxford.

Kohn, A. (2005). *Shooters: Myths and realities of America's gun cultures*. New York: Oxford University Press.

Levin, J., & McDevitt, J. (2002). *Hate crimes revisited: America's war on those who are different*. Boulder, CO: Westview.

Mitchell, H. (2000). *Teen suicide*. Farmington Hills, MI: Lucent.

Moser, R., & Frantz, C. (Eds.). (2002). *Shocking violence: Youth perpetrators and victims—a multi-disciplinary approach*. Springfield, IL: Charles C. Thomas.

Slaughter, R. (2004). *Teen rape*. Farmington Hills, MI: Lucent.

Victims

Coston, C. (Ed.). (2004). *Victimizing vulnerable groups*. Westport, CT: Praeger.

Elias, R. (1986). *The Politics of Victimization: Victims, Victimology and Human Rights*. New York: Oxford University Press.

Elias, R. (1993). *Victims still: The political manipulation of crime victims*. Newbury Park, CA: Sage.

Mullings, J., & Hartley, D. (Eds.). *The victimization of children: Emerging issues*. Binghamton, NY: Haworth.

Vieth, V., Bottoms, B., & Perona, A. (Eds.). (2005). *Ending child abuse*. Binghamton, NY: Haworth.

RECOMMENDED JOURNALS

Contemporary Justice Review
Corrections Today
Criminal Justice Policy Review
Criminal Justice Studies: A Critical Journal of Crime, Law and Society
Criminology
Criminology and Public Policy
Critical Criminology
Homicide: An Interdisciplinary and International Journal

Journal for Juvenile Justice and Detention Services
Journal of Abnormal Psychology
Journal of Contemporary Criminal Justice
Journal of Criminal Justice and Popular Culture
Journal of Criminal Law and Criminology
Journal of Drug Issues
Journal of Ethnicity in Criminal Justice
Journal of Gang Research
Journal of Research in Crime and Delinquency
Journal of School Violence
Journal of Youth and Adolescence
Justice Quarterly
Juvenile Justice Journal
Social Problems
Violence and Victims
Women and Criminal Justice
Youth and Society

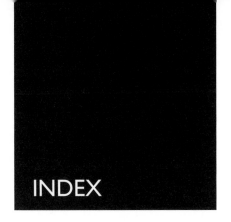

INDEX

ABOUT THE EDITOR AND CONTRIBUTORS

Celene Andreano is a student at Florida Atlantic University seeking a bachelor's degree in sociology. She is a graduate of Broward Community College and currently resides in Broward County, Florida. Her work experience includes fine arts teacher, environmental engineering assistant, and legal assistant.

Joanne Ardovini is an associate professor in the College of Human Services at Metropolitan College of New York. She has written on issues such as juvenile boot camps, media portrayal of rape, feminist methods, and violence against women. Her book, *It's Cold and Lonely Here at the Middle: Discrimination against Female Graduate Teaching Assistants* (2003), explores issues of classroom climate and discrimination. In 2004, Dr. Ardovini won the United Who's Who of Executives and Professionals.

Sarah Boslaugh is a senior statistical data analyst at the Washington University School of Medicine. Her research interests focus on contextual influences on human behavior. In 2005 she published *An Intermediate Guide to SPSS Programming: Using Syntax for Data Management* (Sage Publications) and is currently writing *Secondary Data Sources for Public Health: A Practical Guide* for Cambridge University Press and editing the *Encyclopedia of Epidemiology* for Sage Publications.

Mindy S. Bradley is an assistant professor in the Department of Sociology and Criminal Justice at the University of Arkansas and a 2004 Ph.D. graduate of Pennsylvania State University. Her research focuses on the organization and experiences of stigmatized groups; she is currently involved in studies of victimization and deviant behavior among sexual minorities.

Dale J. Brooker is assistant professor of criminal justice at Saint Joseph's College of Maine. His research interests include the reentry process for inmates and the effect of the incarceration process on families and children. He has recent publications dealing with women in the reentry process and correctional education.

Ben Brown is associate professor of criminal justice at the University of Texas at Brownsville, where he teaches courses on criminological theory, research methodology, and policing. His research has been published in a number of journals, including *Crime and Delinquency, Criminal Justice Policy Review, Policing: An International Journal of Police Strategies and Management,* and *Youth Violence and Juvenile Justice.*

Bill Bush is a visiting assistant professor in the Department of History, University of Nevada-Las Vegas.

Kelly Cheeseman is a Ph.D. student at Sam Houston State University and is employed by the Texas Department of Criminal Justice—Correctional Institutions Division as the unit culture profile coordinator. She is a coauthor for the book *The Death Penalty: Constitutional Issues and Case Briefs* and has also published in other criminal justice journals.

Jean-Philippe Dedieu is a Ph.D. candidate in sociology at Ecole des Hautes Etudes en Sciences Sociales (France). In 2004, he was awarded a Fulbright Fellowship at the University of California at Berkeley. Apart from his contribution to the *Encyclopedia of Twentieth-Century African History,* edited by par Dickson Eyoh et Paul Zeleza (London & New York: Routledge, 2002), he has published "L'intégration des avocats africains dans les barreaux français," *Droit et Société. Revue Internationale de Théorie du Droit et de Sociologie Juridique*, 56/57, 2004, pp. 209–230.

Adam Doran has been a police officer in Kansas for four years. He is currently completing a B.A. in sociology from Fort Hays State University. He specializes in creative, narrative, and research writing.

Kristin Emanuel describes herself as a late-blooming, newly graduated English major with ten compositions that will someday be published.

Ruth Erken received her M.A. from the University of Cologne in Germany, where she studied education, sociology, and psychology. Her work focuses largely on human rights, comparisons of international education, intracultural studies, and multi-problem families. She is a Ph.D. candidate at the University of Ulm in Germany working on a dissertation comparing Tibetan and Bhutanese torture victims in India and Nepal.

Laura L. Finley, editor and contributor, earned her Ph.D. in Sociology from Western Michigan University in 2002. She currently teaches sociology courses at Florida Atlantic University, and does training for a domestic violence agency in Broward County, Florida. She has co-authored two books, is under contract to write two others, and has written numerous journal articles, encyclopedia entries, and book chapters.

Peter S. Finley is professor of sport administration in the H. Wayne Huizenga School of Business and Entrepreneurship at Nova Southeastern University. He has coauthored a book on student privacy rights and has another coauthored book due to be published in the fall of 2006.

Sekou Franklin is an assistant professor in the Department of Political Science at Middle Tennessee State University. His research focuses on social movements, civil rights policy, and intergenerational politics. He has also researched statewide and locally based movements seeking to reform juvenile justice systems throughout the country. His research on juvenile justice was supported by a grant from the W.T. Grant Foundation.

Erika Gebo is an assistant professor of sociology at Suffolk University in Boston. Her research interests and publications are in the areas of juvenile justice, family violence, and juvenile and family policy and evaluation.

Patricia Hylton Grant is assistant professor and coordinator of the criminal justice program at Virginia Commonwealth University's Wilder School of Government and Public Affairs.

Georgen Guerrero is an assistant professor of criminal justice at Stephen F. Austin State University and a criminal justice doctoral candidate at Sam Houston State University, where his area of specialization is criminology. Through the years he has taught several courses in criminal justice, such as Juvenile Delinquency, Juvenile Justice, Criminology, Penology, Social Deviance, Community Based Corrections, the History of Criminal Justice, Correctional Procedural Law, Ethics and Morality, and many others. His primary research interests include incarcerated offenders, ethics in criminal justice, and criminal deviance. He is a member of several local and national criminal justice organizations, including the American Society of Criminology, the Southwestern Association of Criminal Justice, and the Texas Association of Criminal Justice Educators.

Dave D. Hochstein is an assistant professor of psychology at Wright State University Lake Campus, Celina. His research interests include memory for spatial location and the mnemonic characteristics of computerized augmentative and alternative communication systems.

Arthur Holst received his Ph.D. in political science from Temple University. He is a government affairs manager for the City of Philadelphia and teaches in the MPA Program at Widener University. He has written extensively on politics, public administration, history, and the environment.

Martin Kich is a professor of English at Wright State University—Lake Campus in Ohio.

Robyn Diehl Lacks is an assistant professor at the L. Douglas Wilder School of Government and Public Affairs, Virginia Commonwealth University.

Joanne McDaniel is a chief of staff of the North Carolina Department of Juvenile Justice and Delinquency Prevention (NCDJJDP). Prior to her current role, she served as the director of NCDJJDP's Center for the Prevention of School Violence. Her work in the arena of school safety included research about school resource officers, safe schools planning, and comprehensive safe school programming.

J. Mitchell Miller is an editor of the *Journal of Criminal Justice Education* and chair at the University of Texas, San Antonio.

Monir Hossain Moni is currently a doctoral student in the fellowship program at the Graduate School of Asia-Pacific Studies, Waseda University, Tokyo, Japan. He is on study leave from his position as assistant professor of social sciences at the University of Dhaka, Dhaka, Bangladesh. His area of specialization is Asia-Pacific studies, and, in line with his research interests, he contributed a number of research articles to international refereed journals. His book-length publication titled "Japan in the New Era: Some Salient Political and Social Aspects" has also been awarded generous support by the Japan Foundation.

Carla R. Monroe is a codirector of the Spencer Foundation-funded study *African-American Adolescents in a Black Suburb in the U.S. South: A Social Study of Schooling, Identity, and*

Achievement based at the University of Georgia. Dr. Jerome Morris serves as the study's principal investigator. Her work is published in the *Journal of Teacher Education*, *Educational Horizons*, and the *Journal of Moral Education*.

David R. Montague is an assistant professor in the Department of Criminal Justice at the University of Arkansas at Little Rock. He holds a B.A. from Morehouse College, an M.A. from George Washington University, and earned his Ph.D. from Howard University. His research and teaching interests include drugs, public policy, national security, and social justice.

Melanie Moore is a professor of sociology at the University of Northern Colorado. Her research publications are varied, including articles about juvenile delinquency, value change, gender prejudice, and family. In 1998, she received the College of Arts and Sciences Teaching Excellence Award.

Allison Wright Munro is a Ph.D. student in American studies at the University of Texas at Austin. Her research interests include youth culture, crime and punishment, girls' culture, and sports culture. Her M.A. thesis included an ethnographic study of girls' cheerleading and an examination of the history of cheerleading and its impact on American culture.

Glenn W. Muschert is an assistant professor of sociology and the criminology program coordinator at Miami University. His research interests include school shootings, child abductions, and mass media coverage of high-profile crimes. In 2002, he earned his doctorate in sociology at the University of Colorado at Boulder, after he served an appointment in the Law and Society Department at Purdue University, West Lafayette, Indiana.

Caryn Neumann earned a B.A. and an M.A. from Florida Atlantic University. She is currently a lecturer in the Department of History at Ohio State University.

Evaristus Obinyan earned his Ph.D. from the University of South Florida in 2005. He is currently at Fort Valley State University in Georgia.

Mike Olivero received his Ph.D. from Southern Illinois University in 1990. He is currently a full professor in the Department of Law and Justice at Central Washington University and served as a consultant with EPIC Youth Services in Yakima, Washington, working with at-risk youth and their families.

Nicolle Parsons-Pollard is an assistant professor in the criminal justice program in the L. Douglas Wilder School of Government and Public Affairs at Virginia Commonwealth University.

Wendy Perkins is the violent crime resource specialist for the Indiana Coalition Against Sexual Assault and is a doctoral student in the Division of Criminal Justice at the University of Cincinnati. She is currently conducting a study on routine screening for violence by physicians. Her research interests include adult and juvenile violent victimization and police decision-making. She has been recognized locally and nationally for excellence in law enforcement and victim advocacy.

Edward L. Powers is an assistant professor of sociology at the University of Central Arkansas. His current research interests include peer influence, chronic offending, and deviant identity formation.

Dionne R. Pusey graduated from Florida State University with a Bachelor of Science in Clothing Textiles and Merchandising in the spring of 2001. In 2005, she went back to school to complete her minor in sociology from Florida Atlantic University in preparation for entering a Master's in Sociology program.

Monica L. P. Robbers is an associate professor of criminal justice and the chair of the criminal justice and forensic science programs at Marymount University in Arlington, VA. She has written numerous articles and chapters on delinquency, the death penalty, strain theory, and school violence.

Brion Sever is a professor of criminal justice at Monmouth University.

Paula Smith is an assistant professor of human development at the University of Utah's Department of Family & Consumer Studies.

James Steinberg is an associate professor of sociology at Wright State University–Lake Campus in Ohio. His writing ranges from topics in delinquency, science, and modern Chinese history.

Leonard Steverson is an assistant professor of criminal justice at Valdosta State University.

Sharon Thiel is a graduate student of sociology and a teaching assistant at Florida Atlantic University, Boca Raton. Her research interests include power struggles and inequality within society.

Angela Winkler Thomas has currently completed all the requirements for a Ph.D. in history at the University of Iowa except the dissertation. She serves on the editorial board of *Cognitio: A Graduate Humanities Journal*. Her dissertation, "Can German Youth Be Saved?: Juvenile Delinquency and Re-education in British Occupied Germany," explores the intersection of crime, education, and reconstruction in postwar Germany.

Emily I. Troshynski has her Master's in Sociology from the London School of Economics and is currently a graduate student within the Criminology, Law and Society Department at the University of California, Irvine. She is interested in transnational crime, critical criminology, and feminist theory.

Aviva Twersky-Glasner has an M.A. and an M.Phil. She is also a doctoral candidate in criminal justice at the graduate center of the City University of New York.

Michael G. Vaughn is an assistant professor in the School of Social Work at the University of Pittsburgh. Publications have focused on adolescent substance abuse, juvenile offenders, and theories of antisocial behavior.

Lorenn Walker is a Hawai'i-based public health educator. Since 1996 she has been designing, implementing, and evaluating restorative justice (RJ) practices for adults and juveniles through prisons, courts, police, schools, and public housing communities. Currently, she is working with homeless youth and prison inmates, applying new RJ practices that she designed.

Jeffrey A. Walsh is an assistant professor of criminal justice at Illinois State University. He teaches courses in Juvenile Justice and studies predatory crimes and community structural correlates of crime.

Kelly Welch is an assistant professor of sociology at Villanova University where she teaches in the criminal justice program. Her research interests include criminological theory, race and crime, social justice, and the sociology of punishment.

LaVerne McQuiller Williams obtained her J.D. from Albany Law School and her M.S. in Criminal Justice from Buffalo State College. She is an assistant professor of criminal justice at the Rochester Institute of Technology. Her research interests include therapeutic justice and intimate partner victimization. Prior to joining the RIT faculty, she was an assistant district attorney specializing in sexual assault and domestic violence cases.

April C. Wilson contributed five entries for this volume. No biographical information is available.

William R. Wood is completing a Ph.D. in sociology at Boston College. His current research focuses on restorative juvenile justice. He also studied at the Union Theological Seminary in New York City, where he completed an M.Div in Religious History and Ethics.

Robert Worley is an assistant professor at the University of Texas, Permian Basin and a former prison guard with the Texas prison system. His research interests include white-collar crime, qualitative methods, and capital punishment.

Emily Wright is a graduate student in the Department of Criminal Justice at the University of Cincinatti. Her interests are in juvenile psychopathy and the implications for sentencing and assessment, as well as juvenile waivers.

Douglas L. Yearwood is director of the North Carolina Criminal Justice Analysis Center. In addition to government reports, he has published articles and book reviews in *Justice Research and Policy, Criminal Justice Policy Review, Journal of Family Violence, American Journal of Police, African American Male Research, Journal of Gang Research, FBI Law Enforcement Bulletin, The Criminologist, Federal Probation, Police Chief,* and *American Jails.* He is a coauthor, with James Klopone and Michael Vasu, of *Effective program practices for at-risk youth: A continuum of community-based programs* published by the Civic Research Institute. He also serves as the current president of the Justice Research and Statistics Association.